Russian Empire

T0385561

Indiana-Michigan Series in Russian and East European Studies

Alexander Rabinowitch and William G. Rosenberg, editors

EDITED BY
JANE BURBANK, MARK VON HAGEN,
AND ANATOLYI REMNEV

Russian Empire

Space, People, Power, 1700–1930

INDIANA UNIVERSITY PRESS

Bloomington and Indianapolis

This book is a publication of

Indiana University Press
601 North Morton Street
Bloomington, IN 47404-3797 USA

http://iupress.indiana.edu

Telephone orders   800-842-6796
Fax orders   812-855-7931
Orders by e-mail   iuporder@indiana.edu

The maps in chapter 5 were reprinted from *Empire of Nations: Ethnographic Knowledge and the Making of the Soviet,* by Francine Hirsch, copyright © 2005 by Cornell University by permission of the publisher, Cornell University Press.

Chapter 6 is adapted from *At the Margins of Orthodoxy: Mission, Governance, and Confessional Politics in Russia's Volga-Kama Region, 1827–1905,* by Paul Werth, copyright © 2002 by Cornell University by permission of the publisher, Cornell University Press.

Material in this work was presented to the University Seminar on Slavic History and Culture at Columbia University.

Library of Congress Cataloging-in-Publication Data

Russian empire : space, people, power, 1700–1930 / edited by Jane Burbank, Mark von Hagen, and Anatolyi Remnev.
     p.   cm. — (Indiana-Michigan series in Russian and East European studies)
  Includes bibliographical references and index.
  ISBN-13: 978-0-253-34901-9 (cloth : alk. paper)
  ISBN-13: 978-0-253-21911-4 (pbk. : alk. paper) 1. Russia—Politics and government—1801–1917. 2. Soviet Union—Politics and government. 3. Russia—Ethnic relations. 4. Soviet Union—Ethnic relations. I. Burbank, Jane. II. Von Hagen, Mark. III. Remnev, A. V.
  DK189.R873 2007
  947—dc22
                                                                              2006037050

1 2 3 4 5   12 11 10 09 08 07

To Boris Vasil'evich Anan'ich

Contents

Preface and Acknowledgments

This project was conceived at Sobinka, a holiday camp on the outskirts of Vladimir in 1996. It spent a second summer idyll near Iaroslavl', took a winter break at Sestroretsk and another in New York, attained adolescence in Siberia (Omsk), and came to maturity in Samara. The project had generous parents—the Moscow Social Science Foundation, the Ford Foundation, and the Harriman Institute—and wonderful institutional hosts. Above all, we thank Petr Savel'ev, rector of the Samara Municipal Institute of Administration, historian, one of the founding members of our collective, and organizer of our final meeting on the Volga. Two other scholars guided us along our way: Steven Smith of Essex University and Mary McAuley, then director of the Ford Foundation office in Moscow. Throughout, we had a wonderful *nauchnyi rukovoditel'*—Boris Vasil'evich Anan'ich—to whom this book is dedicated. Later, Ronald Meyer helped us transform individual manuscripts into a collective volume, much improved by his superb editing and translating skills. Dominic Lieven, in turn, read the manuscript, generously shared with us his vast knowledge of empires, and offered just the right balance of enthusiasm and caution. We profoundly thank our editor, Janet Rabinowitch, historian and director of Indiana University Press, for seeing this multi-year, transcontinental project to completion. Finally, we are deeply grateful to Robert Belknap, leader of the Columbia University Faculty Seminars, and Richard Foley, Dean of the Faculty of Arts and Sciences at New York University, for their material and intellectual support when we most needed it.

Our transient seminar brought together scholars from Russia, the United States, and the United Kingdom, three polities with experience of empire. Russian participants come from Taganrog, Samara, Omsk, Kazan, Petrozavodsk, and Arkhangel'sk as well as the two capitals. American and British contributors also live and work in cities, towns, and villages widely dispersed over their continent and island. Our disciplines are history—the majority of us—as well as anthropology and political science. What unites us is our effort to escape from the nationalizing assumptions of most studies of the Russian empire. We began our collective work by using "region" as a provisional category, an approach that permitted us to recast traditional questions of ethnicity, social history, and high politics. This book makes use of the extensive and growing literatures in these areas, but its major focus is on the geographies of rule in Russia.

Core members of our group published a volume of essays on the regional problematic: *Imperskii stroi Rossii v regional'nom izmerenii (XIX–nachalo XX veka)* appeared in Russian in 1997. Our seminar expanded upon this earlier project, drew in new people, and worked over several years to develop new perspectives on the empire, with the goal of producing a larger study in English. Our workshops were conducted in Russian. Russian-language articles were translated by members of the seminar, a process that pushed forward our knowledge and interpretation. Our project does not set region and metropole in opposition to each other. Instead we profited from the creative intersection of people of different backgrounds and from our chance to experience new territories ourselves. An openness to uncertain outcomes and a willingness to let diversity take its own form—these attitudes shaped our times together and this book.

The Editors

Russian Empire

Russian Empire in 1700

ARCTIC OCEAN

Bering Sea

Sea of Okhotsk

Sea of Japan

CHUKCHI TERRITORY

Siberian Sea

Kolyma

Laptev Sea

Amur

S I B E R I A

Lena

Kiakhta

Lake Baikal

Q I N G   E M P I R E

Irkutsk

R U S S I A

Enisei

Tomsk

Ob

Barents Sea

Irtysh

Arkhangelsk

Dvina

Ob

U R A L   M O U N T A I N S

Tobolsk

Aral Sea

KAZAKH HORDES

SWEDEN

Kama

Kazan

Ufa

Moscow

Oka

Samara

Volga

Ural

Smolensk

Voronezh

Astrakhan

North Sea

Baltic Sea

POLISH-LITHUANIAN COMMONWEALTH

Don

Azov

Caspian Sea

Kiev

CRIMEAN KHANATE

Black Sea

OTTOMAN EMPIRE

Russian Empire in 1700

500 Miles

0

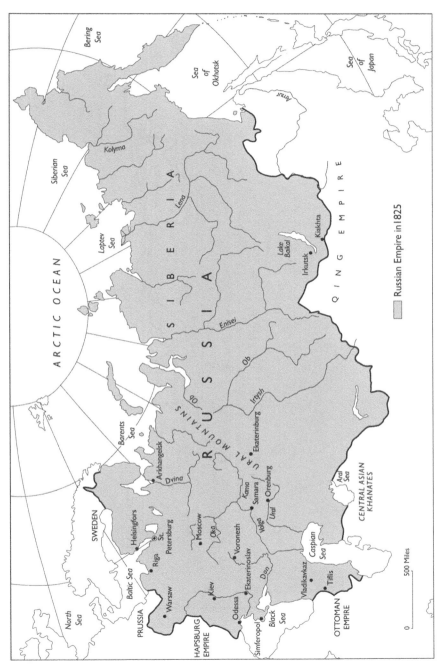

Russian Empire in 1825

Russian Empire in 1825

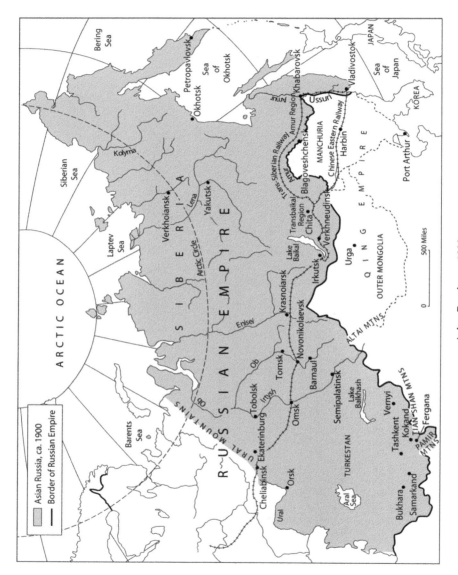

Asian Russia, ca. 1900

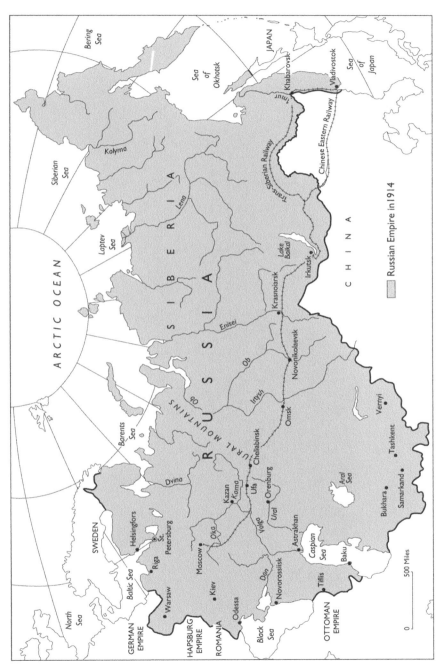

Russian Empire in 1914

U.S.S.R. in 1930

Coming into the Territory: Uncertainty and Empire

Jane Burbank and Mark von Hagen

Following in the often unacknowledged footsteps of nineteenth-century Romantic nationalists, scholars and publicists of the last fifty years generally have condemned empires to the dustbin of history. In their analyses of past, present, and future political transformations, social scientists, and even more critically, policymakers, describe a historical trajectory from empires to nation-states. This asserted hegemony of the nation-state bears the normative imprints of anti-colonial struggles and liberation movements of the twentieth century as well as the more recent fulminations of post-colonial studies. In polemical discourses and from opposing sides, "empire" has become an epithet. For anti-globalists, empire is the name for worldwide, capitalist, supra-statist, and exploitative power; for some American presidents, it has been the realm of evil.

The implication that imperial power has something inhuman about it is shared across a wide spectrum of opinion. But this present-day revulsion against empire would have been inconceivable only a century and a half ago, when entrepreneurs and architects, not to speak of claimants to political authority, sought the symbolism of imperial power. The Empire State and the Empire State Building are reminders of the domestic appeal of imperial imagery in the United States in a not so distant past. Earlier, empire had shaped the new polities created during eighteenth-century revolutions against old regimes in France and the Americas. The United States was imagined as an "empire of liberty"; Napoleon reconstructed Europe on imperial lines, made himself an emperor, and revitalized French empire for his successors. In the nineteenth century, empire was the ordinary kind of state: the continental polities of Central Europe, Eurasia, and Asia, the extended colonial powers of Western Europe, the democracies of the Americas all were built on or out of empire.

Attention to the structure of states and to the nature of their populations reveals the preeminence of empire as a state form well into the twentieth century. The nation-state—if we take its premise at face value—is a historical rarity, if not an impossibility. Even the new states formed in an era of national liberation after the First World War included people who did not all share a nationality. The model nation-states themselves—France and Great Britain—were self-declared empires until the mid-twentieth century, and their long-term nation-building efforts have still not produced homogeneously nationalized populations. Indeed, we might imagine that a historian writing a hundred years from now might see the nation-state not as an enacted structure, but as a powerfully disruptive, unrealizable ideal that set people at each other's throats for over a century and did not provide them with a sustainable political form.

Some may take issue with this literal understanding of nation-state, defined by national homogeneity of citizens. But the most basic appeal of efforts to form nation-states has been to uniform nationality, based on shared ethnicity and culture, however constructed, of a population. Modifying the definition of nation-state to include a multiplicity of ethnic or confessional groups within the citizenry moves us away from the empowering and disruptive ideal that brought us romantic nationalism in the first place. Why not instead retain the distinctions that the ideal types of nation-state and empire pose to political theory and scholarship, without placing them in historical trajectories or normative frames? An unabashed address to empire as a state form allows us to study polities based on difference, not likeness, of their subjects and to begin an assessment of the limitations and possibilities of particular historical imperial projects.

Turning to the study of empires does not necessarily mean turning back the clock. Empires as state forms have outlived some polities that named themselves empires, and even survived in structures of states that claimed to be anti-imperial. The Russian empire, the subject of this volume, is a case in point. Empire as a state form did not perish with "imperial Russia" in 1917. As several of the essays in this volume demonstrate, assumptions about the nature of the populations on Soviet territory and how they should be governed were carried across the revolution by experts and officials. Scholars outside Russia's borders have repeatedly drawn attention to nationality and its role in Soviet projects, testifying to the imperial dimension of Soviet power exercised over three-quarters of a century.

The habit of imperial governance was a critical ingredient in determining both how the Soviet Union came apart and how new polities took shape in its wake. In 1991 a great composite state was dismembered and reconfigured by its elites for the most part without bloodshed. A critical part of the explanation of this collapse and reconstruction is the long-term experience of the imperial state-form shared by all major actors. The usefulness, manipulability, and power of imperial structures and imperial political culture can be seen in the relatively peaceful way the USSR was reconfigured into fifteen separate states. The glaring tragedy of the Russian/Chechen wars is part of the heritage of the Russian empire, but this disaster should not blind us to empire's other effects. Empire as a principle of state organization on "Russian" and other post-Soviet space has survived well beyond 1991. The Russian Federation, with its multiple territorialized and subordinated components, is in form an empire-state.

If we allow ourselves to focus on the structure of states, rather than their names, Russia presents itself as a particularly enduring imperial structure. Unlike its rivals in the early twentieth century—the Ottoman, Habsburg, British, German, and French empires—Russia to this day is not only an imperial polity but one that has retained the most extensive and valuable of its territories. Siberia, the jewel in Russia's crown, was not lost to empire, but remains with its vast resources a part of Russian political space.[1] By shifting the level of our inquiry from ideologies (whether of scholars or of states) to political forms, we can both illuminate weaknesses of Romanov and Bolshevik endeavors and investigate the organizing capacity of the empire state form, preserved for several centuries and operative even in moments of apparent political collapse.

The studies in this volume address several critical moments in the Russian imperial project and an array of questions about the ways that living in an empire shaped the understandings and aspirations of individuals and groups. Our time frame is 1700 to 1930, and our focus is upon the conceptual and institutional significance of imperial governance. Our work builds upon a bounteous heritage of scholarship on the imperial dimension of Imperial Russia. We draw upon—as sources and inspiration—the engaged research of Russia's state-juridical scholars as well as studies produced by regionalist and federalist historians, publicists, geographers, and ethnographers at work in the nineteenth and twentieth centuries on "Russian" and Soviet territories.[2] Many of these scholars themselves served as intermediaries between local populations and metropolitan centers, or participated at critical moments in the formation of state policy. Baron B. E. Nol'de, for example, was in 1917 a member of the Provisional Government's Juridical Council, a body that undertook to reconfigure the successor state after the fall of the Romanovs. Nol'de's later efforts in emigration to write a history of Russia's imperial formation and the seminal studies of Marc Raeff and Richard Pipes set in motion a series of inquiries into imperial and national questions.[3] In addition to these foundational texts, we are indebted to the current outburst of superb works on imperial Russia.[4] This new wave of scholarship is transnational and collaborative. Our volume, like several other recent projects, unites scholars from across oceans and continents with a shared interest in the history of imperial Russia.[5]

This study takes as a starting premise the importance of differentiated space to imperial institutions and imaginations. Our project began with the idea of putting region—not ethnicity or religion—first, as a way to study imperial Russia and with the goal of addressing the empire's territory as a whole space, rather than proceeding from the center outward.[6] For two centuries the historiography of Russia and the Soviet Union has been dominated by perspectives, institutions, and records produced or gathered in the two capitals, Moscow and St. Petersburg. An outlook from the two metropoles reinforced the center's preferred image of orderly control and prioritized narratives of domination and resistance. The essays in this volume challenge this dichotomous and unidirectional casting of center-periphery relations, call into question the certitude of central authorities, and expand the agency of many actors situated in a variety of territorial situations. The opening of archives throughout the former Soviet Union, the substantial devolution of power from the capitals to new states and newly empowered regions, and the bold efforts of scholars themselves have redressed long-standing asymmetries in access to scholarly resources and contacts between capitals and provinces or peripheries.[7] Our project, whose key moments were workshops held in Omsk and Samara, embodies a commitment to the integration of various perspectives into a single—but not monolithic—imperial history and a willingness to let research projects lead us onto new intellectual terrain.

Taken together, the articles in this volume suggest several hypotheses about principles of sovereignty that grew from the imperial context of Russian state formation, about the fragilities and strengths of Russian ways of rule, and about how the imperial state form inflected historical transformations, both gradual and rapid. This introductory essay will introduce the main lines of argument of each of our authors, propose principles that could be applied to the study of Russian society and governance, and sketch out a conceptual framework for further work on Russia and other empires. Finally, we suggest ways that our work on Russia might be used to highlight differences and similarities among imperial projects and to better understand the costs and possibilities of empire as a form of state.

Space, People, Institutions, and Designs

This volume stresses the importance of territory to understandings of the polity. Our first section focuses on concrete and imagined organizations of the empire's space from the eighteenth through the twentieth centuries. The authors emphasize the role of imaginary geographies as well as the making of real maps in efforts to define state frontiers and intra-imperial boundaries. Representations of centers, borderlands, and areas in between were shifting, contingent, and never securely fixed. These essays, like other recent scholarship on Russia, display the intersecting roles of cultural assumptions, geographical knowledge, economic goals, and administrative practices in the extensions and attempted extensions of Russian state power over its enormous realm.[8]

Willard Sunderland argues that the eighteenth century was a time when territory became not just a goal, but a principle of governance. The importation of European notions of mapping, a series of expeditions to study the empire, and a concern for detailed knowledge of imperial space were characteristic of Peter's reign. Catherine II's era was one of "high territoriality" as the administration tried to rationalize units of territory, draw boundaries, and define its domain. Interest in geographic knowledge entered into public consciousness as well and helped to establish the influential myth of Russian state power as derivative from territory. Sunderland's discussion of the evolution of Russian thinking about territoriality introduces one of the basic and elusive aims of the empire's rulers: the rational pairing of population to territorially defined resources.

How and when did central Russia come to be regarded as an imperial core? Leonid Gorizontov takes the problem of defining boundaries, usually addressed to frontier, colonial, or peripheral regions, to the center of the empire. Gorizontov shows that the evocative and powerful terms "interior Russia" (*vnutrenniaia Rossiia*), "native Russia" (*korennaia Rossiia*), and "central Russia" (*tsentral'naia Rossiia*) emerged as cultural constructs in the first half of the nineteenth century. In the wake of the victory against Napoleon, Russian scholars, literati, and administrators traveled through central Russian territories, the better to know "their" Russia. Gradually a series of rough boundaries around "internal" Russia emerged: the steppe zone to the south; a religious, ethnic, river border along the Volga; to the north, a sense of historic difference; and to the west, the Polish lands. No single criterion of difference—historical, ethnic/linguistic, natural/geographical—was used uniquely or consistently. "Internal Russia" was never definitively identified; nor were scholars, artists, and officials sure of where the "Russian heartland" ended in any direction. The indeterminancy of Russia's "core" was expressed in the question of whether the capital, St. Petersburg, was really part of the heartland as well as in the uneasy sense that people of the surrounding areas (however these were defined) lived better than those in the impoverished center.

Charles Steinwedel provides an example of how "European Russia"—a transnational category laden with great significance in Russian imperial discourse—came to include a region—Bashkiria—where most inhabitants did not speak Russian as a first language, were not Christian, and engaged in what people at the center thought of as "backward" economic practices. Clearly, a straightforward civilizational model of imperial boundary drawing is not relevant here. Steinwedel argues that it was the gradual extension of institutions of governance consistent with those of the central regions that made Bashkiria, with its Turkic-speaking population, part of "European Russia" in the minds of imperial officials and on their maps. During the eighteenth century, Catherine II's 1773 Edict of Toleration, the formation of officially sanctioned and controlled Muslim institutions, and the introduction of local, territorially defined units of self-governance allowed the formation of a Muslim elite loyal to the center on Bashkir territories—a process typical of what we might call the "classical" period of imperial absolutism. The great reforms of the nineteenth century granted Bashkirs the same rights as those of Russian peasants, and introduced zemstvo institutions to the region. New legal possibilities eventually led to an excessive land grab on the part of local nobles, resulting in intervention by the central government. The military governor-generalship was eliminated; with the introduction of a civilian governor, Bashkiria attained the status of an administrative institution of European Russia in the late nineteenth century. Local initiatives, public scandals, demands for imperial intervention, and notions of appropriate governance drove the transformation of Bashkiria's institutions; clearly, ruling at a distance could have unpredictable and unintended consequences.

Nailya Tagirova's article turns back to planning—always easier for officials than managing. Tagirova describes several efforts from the eighteenth to the twentieth century to carve up the empire into effective economic regions using "scientific" principles; she stresses the engagement of scholars in the state's attempts to rationalize exploitation of territory, resources, and people. Before the reforms of the 1860s, *raionirovanie* (regionalization) was primarily based on "natural-geographic" criteria, but in the late nineteenth century a number of schemes driven by economic characteristics emerged to compete with earlier categories. Market location, climate, population, and economic activity were all identified as factors creating a distinct region. The numbers of regions proposed by scholars in the late nineteenth and early twentieth centuries varied widely (from sixteen to thirty-four), demonstrating the difficulty of containing the empire in these rationalizing designs.

Francine Hirsch's article shows how early Soviet authorities continued this effort to divide and govern the polity along scientific principles. After the revolution, social scientists trained before 1917 attempted to formulate appropriate categories and policies for regions and communities on the regained territory of the former Russian empire. Ethnographers generally favored structuring the new state by nationality. While the old imperial authorities had feared national irredentism, the ideology of the new Soviet state appeared to privilege nationality rights and to suggest some kind of federative structure along national lines. But a rival paradigm for socialist organization was regionalism defined by economic specialization and/or development. Regionalization by "economic principle" would mean that each geographic area of the new state would have an economic specialization; all large industry and all coordinating administrative organs would be located in the center. In 1924, the clash between these two models was reflected in the structure of the officially constituted Soviet Union, based on territorial units defined by nationality—regions, districts, and republics—as well as on economic regionalization of administration and development planning.

As the essays in this first section suggest, the space of the empire profoundly affected the ways that rulers tried to govern the polity. The problem was not just size and distance, but the variability of the territory in multiple registers. The heterogeneity of imperial space became a habit of thought and an imperative for governors. The people of the empire were part of this landscape, and their differentiated ways of being had to be understood in order to be addressed and utilized. Part 2 of our volume highlights the diverse, evolving, frequently contradictory, and yet powerful nature of the categories used by both administrators and subjects in defining their relations to each other.[9]

The human heterogeneity of the polity was a given for Russian leaders, but just what constituted grounds for classification and division and what was thought to be gained from differentiated governance shifted over time. Metropolitan categories had to be adapted and fine-tuned to populations with an enormous array of practices and possibilities. The often competing institutional interests and aims of different ministries or levels of government contributed to the ambiguity, conditionality, and porousness of borders that were meant to demarcate populations across the empire. At the same time, the existence of different kinds of ascribed boundaries allowed the empire's subjects to develop local, cultural, or confessional affiliations and to utilize these linkages for their various interests. Imperial categories not only set limits but also offered possibilities for groups and individuals.

Paul Werth investigates these questions by tracing a terminological and conceptual shift from reliance on "traditional" confessional affiliations to more "modern" ethnic and national ones. Focusing on the ways in which Russian administrators and churchmen defined their subject populations in the Volga-Kama region, Werth argues that principles of imperial administration typical of the eighteenth century were gradually replaced by a new kind of thinking about religion. Religion became less a formal attribute of a person or a group and more an internal commitment subject to influence and will. This shift in conceptualization was reflected in a change in the category used to describe non-Orthodox people. These were transformed from *inovertsy* to *inorodtsy*—from "those of other belief" to "those of other origin"—in a shift that exemplifies the ethnicizing of alterity in the empire. During the period of reforms, the notion of *obrusenie*—Russification—became more salient as a way forward toward a new, culturally unified empire. By emphasizing their genetically alien—rather than their religious and thus presumably mutable—qualities, non-Russians were put at a distance from the homogeneous "Russia" of the future.

Jane Burbank focuses on a different kind of division in the empire: the use of legal estates as a basic principle of governance. Not just non-Russians, but all people of the empire were ruled and received rights by virtue of belonging to legally established groups. Based on an exploration of the lowest level courts, where peasant judges interpreted imperial law, Burbank argues that estate-based legalism had empowering effects upon local populations. The long-term practice of legalizing self-administration and a large degree of judicial autonomy included subaltern populations in the process of governance. The history of the township courts displays the inclusionary possibilities of heterogeneous and diffuse administration as well as the obstacles that group-based thinking presented to the attempted introduction of a uniform judicial system by liberals in 1917. Even in the heartland of the empire, the polity was ruled through groups and group-ness, not as a unified citizenry with equal rights. Contrary to liberal idealizations of formal equality, diversity as a principle of rule enabled inclusivity and self-governance well beyond the capacity of states based on a single, homogeneous "nation" of citizens.

Social difference is the topic of Shane O'Rourke's article on the Don Cossacks' shifting aspirations during the late imperial and early revolutionary periods. O'Rourke argues that it was not state institutions but a group's own preservation of particular practices and ideologies that created a distinctive Cossack community. The Don Cossacks sustained the tradition of a warrior brotherhood—based on democratic governance, Orthodoxy, Russian language, and steppe culture—from the Muscovite period into the twentieth century. Responding to the political opportunities offered by the revolutions of 1917, Cossacks rapidly instantiated their traditions in a new Krug and Ataman and, at first, in a demand for autonomy, not nationhood. During the course of the Civil War, Cossacks were pushed to fight for independence by the Bolsheviks' terror against them. This article highlights the way that violence, directed by the state against particular groups, could transform their political goals. Cossacks were not merely a creation of the Russian state, not merely its agents, and not, until assaulted, its opponents. Cossack institutions of self-rule had been developed and protected under imperial auspices, but this legalized autonomy was also a weapon that could be wielded against a too intrusive government.

Vladimir Bobrovnikov's study of the politically laden category *abrechestvo* —professional banditry—also shows how state violence can shape aspirations, myths, and self-representations of groups inside the empire. Bobrovnikov argues that the idea of tribal propensity to banditry is a product of the Russian conquest and governance of the Caucasus. The roots of *abrechestvo* as a social institution can be found in the self-regulatory practices of mountain people before Russian expansion into the region, particularly in the accepted prerogative of outlawed princes to declare war, lead a band of warriors, and carry out raids. In the nineteenth century, Russian authorities took away the right of princes to raise troops, outlawed blood vengeance, and attempted to resettle the dependents of outlawed princes out of the mountains. The result of these assaults on elite practices was that many leaders of mountain society became "professional *razboiniki-abreki*"; some of them provided models for widely circulating and long-lasting images of mountain bandits. At the same time, Russian settlement policy produced new support groups for these rebels among the resettled populations of the area. Russian expansion into the Caucasus and Russian policy created the conditions for *abrechestvo* as a phenomenon, as well as for both heroic and demonic myths of bandit outlaws.

Bobrovnikov's work describes the powerful complicity of Russian elites in the emergence of a culture of violence in the north Caucasus. Similarly, Nikolai Ssorin-Chaikov illustrates how ethnographers after 1917 helped create categories of Soviet people in Siberia and simultaneously asserted their own scholarly legitimacy in the new regime's intellectual capitals. The practice of participant-observation provided ethnographers with an ideal terrain for promoting the concept of "authentic" native traditions. In the 1920s, Soviet ethnographers interpreted the culture of native Siberians as examples of "natural" and thus "authentic" clan-based socialism. Ssorin-Chaikov emphasizes that ethnographers participated in ceremonies that provided evidence for the existence of "organic," "pre-capitalist" social organization and then erased the evidence of their intrusion, thus creating ethnographically correct—but in fact highly manipulated—images of solidaristic native cultures.

These studies of imperial people do not assign a primary role to rulers or the ruled, nor do we accept the stark dichotomy of this classification. Our emphasis instead is on a different, more muted and interactive kind of agency. What is imperial about all the actors studied—officials, military men, churchmen, peasants, Cossacks, even *abreki*—is that their histories were shaped by their participation in a particular kind of polity where difference among groups was accepted by all as the normal way of being. Alterity was not in itself regarded as a problem by most of the empire's subjects; what was important to them were the kinds of possibilities both individuals and groups could gain from their different subject positions, in the most literal sense of the term. Our authors also show how elites connected to, but not necessarily part of, the state could influence or try to influence the differentiated possibilities of various people in the empires, both imperial and Soviet. In a polity where knowledge of resources—both territorial and human—was highly valued, the labeling of one's group as "of another origin," "given to banditry," "backward," or even "authentic" could make a difference. A differentiated rights regime was a two-edged sword. Subjects could seize established rights or claim new ones on the basis of their separate status, but if rulers went too far in their own projects, group identification provided a framework for ignoring, rejecting, or rebelling against the state's initiatives.

Rebellion was exactly what rulers feared, and a politics of caution, uncertainty, and hesitation is visible in the actions and proposals of imperial governors, particularly when looked at over a long time. Part 3 on institutions considers policies, approaches, reforms, and reactions of imperial administrations. This section illustrates asymmetries of imperial power over space and time, as well as adaptations and evolutions of central and local officialdom. Read together, these articles describe the growth of national and confessional awareness in the nineteenth century, a rise in political activity among various sub-imperial communities, and the challenges posed by these emergent movements to imperial control.

We begin with Ekaterina Pravilova's pioneering study on a most basic institution of the empire: money. The long-term survival of a separate Polish currency, the zloty, despite the efforts of nineteenth-century policymakers to better integrate the imperial economy, is a testament to the tension between diversity and standardization in the management of the empire. The history of protracted efforts to make the ruble the standard currency in the Polish territories returns us to an earlier observation: the Russian center was poorer than some of its imperial borderlands. Imperial leaders were unable to make a single Russian currency work in Poland for many years because the material backing for such an endeavor was not available. For a time in the 1830s, coins with dual denominations, in rubles and zlotys, were coined and circulated—an effort that renders visible the legitimizing strategies of imperial administration. For several decades, multiple currencies—foreign money, Polish zlotys, and small Polish tender, as well as Russian rubles—circulated in Poland, until the Polish and Russian budgets were consolidated in the 1860s in the aftermath of the Polish rebellion.

The reforms of the 1860s and the Polish rebellion of 1863 were critical to rethinking many principles of imperial rule. Elena Campbell's article on the "Muslim question" points out that Islam became a question only in the second half of the nineteenth question, when some Russian elites began their search for state unity on new terms. Campbell notes that administrators and advisors put forward different and contradictory proposals on the Muslim issue, as well as on other questions of imperial policy. Leaders of the Orthodox Church, always worried about Islam, wanted strong policies to deal with what they perceived as a threat to the very essence of

Russian statehood, while officials of the Ministry of Internal Affairs and other state institutions put a lower priority on what they considered primarily a religious issue. Concerns about Muslim fanaticism, Pan-Turkism, and Islamic expansion were raised in the early twentieth century, but many imperial leaders persisted in regarding Muslims as loyal subjects. Campbell's article illustrates once again the tensions within the late empire between the customary recognition of religious difference and the new notion that diversity was a threat to state well-being. In addition, her study suggests the relatively weak impact upon state policy of Orthodox leaders, for whom Islam was indeed a powerful challenge. The administration did not take this "question" as seriously as the Polish or Jewish "questions," and it had no consistent Muslim policy in its last years.

Aleksei Volvenko describes how a new institution designed to effect reform—the famous zemstvo—was engaged, interpreted, and resisted by the Don Cossack Host in the last half of the nineteenth century. In this study of a typically imperial impasse, Volvenko reveals the fundamental conflict between unitarian ideas promoted by the central administration in the 1860s and 1870s and Cossacks' estate-based conceptions of their rights and duties. The zemstvo reform proved unpopular with most Cossacks in the Don area. The equalization of tax-paying obligations and the inclusion of non-Cossacks in local governance were at odds with entrenched notions of an array of privileges and duties accorded to Cossacks as members of various service groups. Zemstvo regulations privileged hereditary Cossack nobles over other landholders; other central decrees abolished the electoral principle for selecting administrators of the Cossack territories. Ultimately, after much resistance from the Don and much discussion at the center, the zemstvo introduced in Cossack areas in 1876 was closed in 1882.

The gradual, uphill struggle for the ruble-based economy in Poland was, in the long run, a success; the many discussions of the Muslim question resulted in no new institutions; the introduction of the zemstvo in Cossack areas was a failure. Each of these initiatives, with their different results, was directed toward standardization of governance, a goal that seemed more important in the late nineteenth century than before. The most fundamental political restructuring of the empire's history was the introduction of an elected parliament, the State Duma, in the aftermath of the 1905–1906 revolution. Rustem Tsiunchuk examines national elites and electoral politics in this radically new institution from an imperial perspective.

If the Muslim question provoked state officials to worried inaction, the central administration actively manipulated the franchise for elections to the Duma in favor of Russian and Orthodox deputies. Russia's first parliament was engineered to reduce the representation of national regions and to counter the presumed threat of separatism on the part of non-Russians. By the time of the Fourth Duma, Russians and Orthodox were distinctly over-represented in relation to their proportion of the population. Tsiunchuk's article underlines the uncertain relationship between democracy and empire in Russia. The State Duma could possibly have become a forum for a new kind of multi-national and federal politics, but the central authorities undercut this potential with their preemptive privileging of Russian and conservative delegates. At the same time, the electoral rules shaped representation along national lines, opening the way for delegates elected by non-Russian people to enter political life with ethnicized and confessional mandates. As Tsiunchuk shows, the State Duma was a formative political experience for many future leaders of national movements.

Tensions over how parliamentary democracy and empire could intersect broke into the open with the 1917 revolution. Irina Novikova's article addresses the dilemmas of empire in the revolutionary year, when the Provisional Government and Finnish political elites found themselves locked into an escalating series of requests, demands, and conflicts concerning new political configurations. Finnish leaders, including leftists, made only moderate demands upon the new leadership, but the liberals and socialists in the Provisional Government, like their autocratic predecessors, could not bring themselves to modify Russian sovereignty over the region in a significant way. Novikova compares the situation in 1917 to 1989, when once again democratization led to an outburst of nationalist activity and once again Russian reformers were unable to work out a satisfactory compromise with national elites.

As Novikova's article emphasizes, the ultimate institution in the empire was the emperor himself. However, once the monarch was dispatched, Russian elites who claimed his place were still bearers of imperial consciousness. The habit of imperial thinking and, in particular, the incapacity of Russia's liberals and moderate socialists to cede significant autonomy to constituent parts of the polity outlasted the autocracy. The actions and inactions of Russian state leaders in 1917 illustrate the critical legacy of imperial rule and ideology. But the message from the past was not easy to interpret; over the preceding centuries Russian leaders and elites had worked with several different notions of how empires should be ruled. Our final section, *Visions,* addresses different models of imperial governance developed in conjunction with the shifting expectations of Russian administrators and theorists.

Anatolyi Remnev provides us with a way to conceptualize the articulation of space and governing practices. The Russian empire can be understood through its particular "geography of power." For a long period, the empire steadily expanded, incorporating new people, new resources, new practices, and new territories into the polity, thereby transforming it. This dynamic was not only a consequence of imperial ambitions; it shaped the very notion of what the state aspired to be. Over time new spaces became objects of consciousness and conscious policymaking. A profoundly geographic vision of power gave regions a significant presence in the imagination of both officials and people living in them. At the same time, as Remnev shows in the case of Siberia and the Far East, regions could be and were fundamentally transformed and redefined by administrative structures, settlement policies, military concerns, and the aspirations of both their occupants and central authorities.

Sviatoslav Kaspe's article provides a different conceptual framework for understanding imperial politics in the nineteenth century. He argues that the entire period can be described by a tension between two conflicting state principles—the empire and the nation-state—and by policies that tilted in one direction or another. After the Crimean War, a Westernized elite sought to modernize the country along European lines. In Kaspe's view, the Polish uprising put an end to this first stage of liberalization and set a new agenda linking nationalism with democratic reform in a move toward a unified state. Assimilationist and Russifying politics in many areas replaced the older imperial model based on collaboration with local elites. In the context of imperial society and in the absence of democratic institutions, Russia's "segmented modernization" nationalized local populations, rather than integrating them. The failure of the nation-state project of Russian reformers before 1917 was a factor in the reemergence of an imperial form of state in the Soviet period.

Did Russian rulers and subjects have to choose between empire and nations? Was democratic reform inextricably linked to the emergence of separate nationalized states? Mark von Hagen's article presents a little-known aspect of Russian, Siberian, and Ukrainian intellectual history— the existence of federal and regional autonomist programs that opened up different possibilities for political organization. From the late eighteenth century, many proponents of political reform included federal elements in critiques of the autocracy and in proposals for a different state form. Von Hagen's analysis of reformers' work recovers the normalcy of transnational and regional political thought for Russia's intellectuals, who found models in the Russian north, in Siberia, in the United States, in Switzerland. This new history of federalist thought reveals alternatives to autocracy that were different from the centralist designs hitherto regarded as characteristic of the Russian intelligentsia. What could be more logical for intellectuals situated in an imperial context than to espouse ideas reflecting both their situation in a multi-national polity and the tensions over uniformity and diversity that beset their rulers?

To accept this logic is to enter the world of political imagining and political action of people accustomed to, if not content with, diversified governance of a diversified population. One could aspire to replace or reform the government, without having to reject all the qualities of an imperial state. One problem with the conceptual and practical dichotomy of empire and nation-state is the habitual connection of empire to autocracy, to the "old regime," and to absolutist rule. Even in France, the homeland of the modern republic, what was overthrown in 1789 was monarchy, not empire. (In short order, Napoleon gave the French Empire new energy and range.) In Russia's revolutionary age, critics of the autocracy proposed a variety of reformist projects, only some of which set republicanism and social uniformity as ideals.

Indeed, the zealous pursuit of homogeneity by Russian officials with their designs for uniform governance, by Russian liberals with their pursuit of idealized equality, or by an early Russian republican like Pestel' can be seen as one of the less creative responses to the everyday provocation of uncontrollable difference in Russian imperial life. The empire was a muddle, as the articles in this book demonstrate—incapable of being divided according to a single kind of line, without fixed internal or external borders for much of its history. However, the "problem" of empire, or even its tensions, may be an intellectual's rather than a subject's dilemma, for the contradictions of imperial existence are not necessarily an evil. One possible explanation for the long-lasting imperial structure of polities on the territory of imperial Russia and the Soviet Union may be the ability of flexible, non-uniform, and inconsistent governance to accommodate the coexistence of a multiplicity of social arrangements within a single state.

A Russian Way of Ruling

We turn now to what we propose as operational characteristics of Russian imperial governance. From different vantage points, our authors all address "geographies of power" that infused Russian imperial construction, maintenance, and crises. What general principles or hypotheses do these studies suggest for understanding how the Russian empire worked, as well as its vulnerabilities and periods of dysfunction?

First, the empire was a moving target, not just in the sense of its constructedness, but in the variety of ways that power could be used at a multiplicity of levels, over an ill-defined space, and in different economic, technological, and international contexts. Self-understanding of the polity took shape and later took on other shapes through long-term territorial expansion and the incorporation of new people and new resources. The empire was always, as Francine Hirsch suggests, a "work-in-progress,"[10] but more to the point, the ongoing outward growth of territory kept changing the fundamental parameters of statehood.

Second, a history of indeterminate expansionism left its mark on Russian notions of a state worthy of the name. As for other empires, size mattered. In the Russian case, extensive territory was a source of state pride and self-definition. In addition, diversity—of territory, people, culture—was not only taken in stride, but for the most part celebrated. A great state was composed of a great number of peoples, with different ways of being. Another dimension of strong statehood concerned wealth and productivity, again in a differentiated mode. A large and variegated territory, a multitude of different peoples, a rich array of economic activities—these were essential to well-being and confidence in the empire.

Third, these conditions for powerful statehood made knowledge a priority for governors, a goal for elites, and a tool for every imperial subject. Space, people, and resources were all mental objects, and rulers strove to know, understand, and align them rationally. The search for secure knowledge of territories old and new, for useful mental maps, for correct pairings of population and land was fundamental to governance from the eighteenth century through the twentieth.[11] "Conceptual conquest"—in Francine Hirsch's term—was a goal of both officials and elites more generally. A long-term positivist imperative is visible in this dependence on imperial knowledge. Measuring, counting, mapping, describing were tasks assumed to be critical for efficient and productive administration.

But which measures would provide the key to good governance? As many of our articles suggest, no single scale worked to describe, or rule, the empire. Different areas offered different possibilities and demanded different strategies. The never-ending adaptation of governance to local conditions *created* imperial technologies of rule, and these were in their essence inconsistent with each other. Policies could be framed with ethnicity, confession, territory, economic "stage," resources, loyalty, degree of "civilization," or status at their core, depending on changing visions of just what was at stake and where and when and for whom. Our authors use a number of terms to refer to the lack of a single systemic principle of Russian imperial rule. *Mnogovariantnost', mnogosostavnost', mnogouslovnost', raznoobraznost'*—the qualities of being "multiply variable," "multiply composed," "multiply conditioned," and "of unlike forms"—these descriptors for Russian imperial practice are not accidentally difficult to translate. In a less evocative English mode, then, we suggest a fourth, and critical, dimension of Russian governance—its multiple frames of reference. A technology of ruling Russia was the simultaneous use of different registers for ruling different regions and different people.

Is a political project based on different strokes for different folks sustainable? Nothing could have been more normal for eighteenth-century imperial absolutists than coming to satisfactory arrangements with local elites, incorporating various nobles, bureaucrats, and officials into imperial governance, permitting and exploiting self-administration of the lower orders, and making some efforts at standardization—the Table of Ranks, provincial boundary drawing, establishing a network of administrative towns—but always proceeding with the project of absorbing vastly unlike territories and applying the principle of multiple-variantness (*mnogovariantnost'*) in dealing with the whole. Still, notions of the normal state, as well as aspirations and practices, changed in Russia as elsewhere in the long age of European revolutions, inter-empire wars, and colonial expansion overseas. Competition—and war—with European empires for territories and influence in Eurasia as well as exposure to Western Europeans' exclusionary colonial practices enlarged—or narrowed, depending on your point of view—Russian notions of what their empire could be. The articles in this volume suggest that while some tension between desires for uniformity and the reality of multiplicity was always present in imperial governance, from the mid-nineteenth century some elites (but not all) began to tilt in the direction of uniformity as a new principle of state. The great reforms of the 1860s have been interpreted as a move toward direct and nationalized citizenship, but, in accord with the strong habits of imperial rule, the reform policies themselves were not introduced everywhere or equally across the empire. The Polish rebellion of 1863 is identified by several of our authors as a more critical turning point. After this time and for the rest of the imperial period formally defined, nationalized notions of the polity, or more precisely of the future polity, were more visible on the horizon for imperial elites.

The horizon, however, remained the appropriate metaphorical location of nationalist aspirations. Perhaps characteristically of their imperial reflex, Russia's rulers weathered the tension between national-standardized and imperial-differential principles, and did not move decisively toward a "Russian," nationalized, or republican kind of sovereignty in the early twentieth century. But neither did they shift the empire's politics in the direction of accommodating nationalist sentiments among the non-Russian peoples. Although ideas of constitutional government and parliamentary democracy became more popular in the early twentieth century, the concepts of national autonomy and federalism were not accepted by the empire's rulers.

The first revolution of 1917 brought to power liberals and moderate socialists who, after the overthrow of the monarchy, tried to organize representative democracy as the form of sovereignty and to abolish legal estates—one major kind of difference in citizens' status. But as Irina Novikova shows, the habit of imperial thinking persisted in the unwillingness of Russia's liberals and moderate socialists to cede significant autonomy to constituent parts of the polity. Imperial principles of governance outlasted the autocracy and spilled over into the extended reconfiguration of the polity by Soviet authorities. Both the ethnographic projects of the People's Commissariat of Nationalities and the economic regionalization schemes of Gosplan were informed by cartographic, ethnographic, and economic specialists who began their work under the old regime. The replication in Soviet times of earlier struggles over ways to organize territories and people resulted in compromises between economic-rationalist and ethnic-confessional principles. Once again, full nationalization—in the sense of homogeneous citizenship—did not occur.

The carry-over of certain imperial kinds of thinking from the tsarist period did not mean that the Soviet Union was the same empire as that of the tsars, but it does display another characteristic property of Russian administrative practice. A fifth observation about Russian imperial governance is that tensions between uniform and differentiated governance were not resolved but were sustained over three centuries. One might argue that a choice between nation-state or empire was a false proposition in the first place. Paul Werth puts this somewhat differently by noting that Russia became a "strange hybrid" in relationship to three available state models—dynastic composite, national, and modern colonial empire. But all of our authors' work is consistent with the proposition that no clear choice for nation over empire emerged from the various movements to standardize relationships of subjects to the polity.

As a wise university administrator once observed: "A decision postponed is a decision." The putting off of ultimate choices until a future time was one way that Russian officials and elites dealt with apparent inconsistencies in their state project. It took a long time to make the ruble the currency of Poland, but just as this reform was finally carried off, a separate Finnish currency was introduced. The polity was always taking on new dimensions, as geographical, economic, linguistic, and confessional developments—intersecting with each other—shifted the priorities and possibilities for both subjects and rulers. The configurations of the State Duma make the choices of political boundary-drawers visible, but even as imperial authorities altered the franchise to reduce or enhance the representation of certain regional, ethnic, and religious groups, they still kept an array of constituencies in play. The Duma was manipulated to produce the ideal imperial assembly—ideal for the shortsighted autocracy anyway—using multiple registers of imperial imagination. The playing field was tilted toward ethnic Russians and the Orthodox, but no single opposition defined the game of state. This refusal to fully privilege an ethnically Russian state or to accept a pure politics of numbers applied equally to all parts of the empire was a typically indecisive, and pragmatic, choice for imperial authorities.

The "uncertainty principle" of Russian empire is expressed in not really choosing for or against nationalized sovereignty, as well as in the multiple and inconsistent maps flung over territory and population. Russian rulers strove for control and order, but no single universal scheme would adequately organize the unwieldy polity. Uncertainty was expressed in the multiple classifications of the people of the empire: ethnicity, belief, language, culture, physical type were all deployed at various times, but what was Russian, what was European, what was Siberia, what was the heartland remained questions throughout the long period we have covered. Perhaps this uncertainty about conceptualization was connected to worries about control. As several of our authors note, official fears of separation occurred before separatist movements formed.

The uncertainty of Russian imperial governance meant particular kinds of strengths and weaknesses. On the one hand, refusals to make a choice for nationalized homogeneity or to decide definitively upon a single organizational principle kept the polity flexible and open to a vast array of practices of self-regulation, education, and production. Not deciding whose civil law was right or on what basis to create a universally applicable code can be read as a success of Russian empire rather than a failure, as liberals would have it. Spreading a network of lower-level courts across the countryside and allowing local authorities to produce legal judgments empowered subaltern people and automatically adjusted government to social realities. This kind of ad hoc administration can be seen as strengthening the polity, if not the central government, over the long term. On the other hand, officials' inability to find a framework for legalizing significant autonomy in restive and ambitious regions of the empire, or for devolving power to reform the state to equally elected representatives of the whole population, created forums for national independence movements and made the government more vulnerable to mobilized discontent during the world wars. And again in 1989–1991.

The phenomenon of uncertain empire brings us back to the question of democracy and its different meanings and potentials. Could more inclusive political institutions and cultural heterogeneity be accommodated within the framework of empire? Or could the empire have transformed itself into a multi-ethnic, multi-confessional federation based on electoral democracy? Russian liberals in the Provisional Government struggled with the problem of how to organize elections to what turned out to be an aborted Constituent Assembly. But their dilemmas, like those of the Bolsheviks after them, were inflected by the imperial past. At a critical moment in the revolutionary year, liberals drew back from granting Finland the significant autonomy that might have kept it in the polity. When Communists put the empire back together, they reenacted a basic tension of imperial rule—between horizontal, heterogeneous, inclusive principles and vertical "civilizational" standards that arranged peoples in cultural hierarchies. As in the past, state violence created its own enemies and outlaws—Cossacks and *abreki* are examples treated in this volume—and ethnographers found human evidence to support the state's mandate for development. The Soviet state, like the tsarist one, proved unwilling to follow out the nationalist agenda, but it also held back from what might be seen as a thorough-going commitment to federalism. Once again, ultimate power over resources, people, and goals was retained by a highly centralized command, without institutions that could provide a democratic means for making choices about leaders, structures, and policies. The knowledge imperative worked as in tsarist times to draw elites into the Soviet centers of rule, where decisions and non-decisions about the direction of the new imperial state would be made. The flexibility of multiple registers was preserved, but an experiment in federalized democracy was not tried.

Russia's Word to Other Empires

Scholars of Russian history cannot testify to the plausibility or possibilities of imperial democracy, but we can provide conceptual provocations to studies of other imperial polities. Boris Nol'de, who knew Russia as historian, jurist, and official, claimed that the Russian empire was a "unique edifice" and one of the "most interesting political phenomena . . . in the world."[12] Is it possible that in the matter of empire, Russia has its word to speak to scholarship? As with many other areas of academic investigation, the study of empires has primarily been based on both political and knowledge regimes of the so-called West. Our authors gratefully acknowledge the profound impact of earlier scholarship on empires, nationalism, and colonialism upon their work, as well as the methodological and theoretical insights provided by an array of scholars who focus on both Europe and other world regions.[13] With few exceptions, however, much contemporary study of empire still focuses on what once were called the first and second worlds—on Western European colonialism and on modern capitalism. We see ourselves as participants in a new wave of scholarship that reaches out to other times and places for both comparison and understanding.[14] What kinds of propositions can research on a Eurasian, never fully capitalist or bourgeois polity provide to further studies of empires as social and political formations?

One message of our Russian case is the fruitfulness of beginning with territory, rather than with people and their presumed kinds of allegiances. Most empires present complex and incongruent overlays of ethnicity and religion upon territory. Starting out a study of empire with categories of ethnicity, or religion, or nationality shapes the description of people and their aspirations in ways they may not themselves have chosen. The national should not be set as scholarship's problem where it might not yet—or ever—have been an issue for the people under study. A regional-territorial approach provides a more open vision of a polity and its future and permits an understanding of when and where and if national or religious difference became an issue.

Starting with territory should not entail a return to the dichotomy of center and periphery. Instead, study of Russia suggests that imperial space can be regarded in more open-ended, variegated ways. Muscovy was a spreading center, not a fixed one. State power overflowed into adjacent lands, drawing some into the heartland, but leaving the boundary between "Russian" and other areas unclear. The Russian imperial polity had at least two metropoles, St. Petersburg and Moscow, with different claims to superiority based on different measures of the cities' worth. Europeanness could be a mark of alien culture or a source of pride. If even the capital moved around over two centuries, it is not surprising that the understanding of where Russia ended and borderlands began was vague and relied on different criteria, such as travelers' comfort, psychic familiarity, and economic activity. Instead of assuming that every empire has a center and a periphery, we should address the more thorough-going openness of imperial projects. In Russia's case, political, geographical, economic, linguistic, cultural strategies and actions changed dynamically and interactively, transforming the maps and the understandings of the empire over time.

This historical dynamism suggests caution about the boundary-drawing issues that have become conventional in recent scholarship.[15] A fascination with borders, linked to notions of social inclusion and exclusion, is prominent in many studies of modern states and societies. But the Russian case prompts us to suggest that in some imperial settings even elites who wanted to draw definitive boundaries were unable to do so. As for people living on the territories of empires, absolute boundaries between groups defined by ethnicity, nationality, or religion were not always clear or of immediate importance. Even a polity that assigned rights and duties according to legal estate did not always prioritize this boundary in making policies. Nobles in Poland could be penalized when the autocrat gave more rights to their former dependents than to former serfs in Russian areas. Imperial officials used a number of different kinds of categories in their address to populations, but no single boundary—territorial, estate, religious, ethnic—defined people in or out of the polity or defined privilege and disadvantage in a fixed way. Muslims, for example, could be provided with schools and translations of scripture in areas where Russian peasants had no such opportunity. The existence of a number of ways of categorizing the population meant that there was no fixed policy of divide and rule, and no absolute ladder of ranks, and no definitive we/they divide.

Related to the conditionality of boundaries in the empire was the indeterminacy of the categories that boundaries supposedly marked off. As Vladimir Bobrovnikov shows, even an "outlaw" category, such as *abrek* (bandit) changed meanings over time for Russian elites and for people who lived in areas of *abrechestvo*. For Russian authorities, *abreki* could mean "non-pacified highland people from the Caucasus" or "Islamic terrorists" or "noble and religious renegades." To people living in the Caucasus, *abreki* could be bandits, predators, Robin Hoods, and model warriors. The point is not just that social categories were constructed, but that this construction was ongoing and open-ended. The creation of a range of categories and a range of possible meanings for them provided imperial people with a multiplicity of ways to identify and relate to others in the polity.

The point we make here is not that the official boundaries of the empire or the dichotomous categories of scholarship were "transgressable." Mixing of people of different groups was of course a social fact and even in some cases imperial policy. What the Russian empire introduces as a challenge to ways that histories of empire are being written is the observation that people did not orient their ideas of normativity or transgression around these boundary crossings. Imperial people took for granted that they were part of various groups defined legally and socially—peasants, Cossacks, tribes, etc.—and individuals might put a great deal of effort into moving into another group. Leaving the peasantry to become a merchant was a possible if costly goal, but defining or defying boundaries themselves would not have been of particular interest. Everyone in the empire, from nobles to serfs, belonged to marked categories, and there could be no aspiration to enter the realm of the unmarked. The normalcy of multiple and legal categories may present a different field of social play than racial or class differences in polities where citizens are legally equal, but socially stratified.

Critical to daily life in the Russian empire was what people could accomplish with their group-assigned rights. This point is visible in peasant responses to attempts to eliminate estate distinctions in courts and administration in the countryside. Peasants saw the abolition of estate-based administration as a threat to their self-governance. "Better separate than equal" made sense for peasants in a world where homogenization of status would advantage social (rather than legal) superiors. This context was a specific one—an empire in which both oppositional elites and officials shared an autocratic notion of their right to rule, all rights were collectively assigned, and the absence of universal education created enormous disparities in political power within localities.

If peasants and Cossacks were "thinking imperially" during the struggle to reset the rules in the early twentieth century, other people in the empire worked in different settings according to different scenarios. Peasant settlers in distant regions could be bearers of "Russian civilization"—at least in the minds of imperial officials—when they set up homesteads on the steppe or took up farming as Siberian exiles. Empire-builders were of many kinds—settlers, missionaries, petty and powerful officials, prisoners and military men, as well as governors-general and generals. As Anatolyi Remnev notes, the "Russian bureaucrat" in Siberia was often a German, a Pole, or a Tatar. High-ranking officials were moved from one region to another, in careers that brought them later advancement in the tiers of administration and policymaking in the capitals. Even the personnel of empire cannot be fit into neat dichotomies of ruler and ruled, or aligned by nationality or rank or confession. Across this huge empire, and across many others, people's lives were not oriented for or against the empire, but rather shaped by multiple, cross-cutting opportunities made available by imperial settings.

The history of imperial Russia in the early twentieth century and, in particular, the ways that authorities and subjects thought and acted when the rules of the polity were up for reconsideration, highlight differences between "bourgeois" and absolutist empires. While people in the colonies and metropoles of French and British empires struggled with the implications of "universal reason, . . . market economics, and . . . citizenship," subjects and rulers of the Russian empire were not drawn fully into this imperial tension.[16] Some elites, as Sviatoslav Kaspe informs us, were explicitly concerned with economic modernization; others, such as the liberals in the Provisional Government, aimed at extending citizenship in the polity. But while imperial authorities understood both property and education as critical to subjects' loyalty, the administration never put its resources wholeheartedly behind "bourgeois" property rights or universal education. The notion that in essence each subject was a source of labor for the state carried over into the Soviet period, as Francine Hirsch's Soviet planners show us. Even as Russian authorities copied tactics from "modern colonial empires," their view of what power should achieve and how it could operate was part of a profoundly different human landscape. This difference in political vision and economic structure, rather than the often cited physical quality of contiguity, should be emphasized as a critical difference between Russian and other non-bourgeois empires and Western colonial powers in the late nineteenth and early twentieth centuries.

These observations put on the table a number of questions concerning empire itself as a category. If we are to advocate the understanding of empire as a more useful scholarly endeavor than recovering nationalized communities where they might not have been imagined, we need to work with frameworks that reveal differences among imperial structures and to explore the implications of these differences for political and social transformations. We noted at the beginning of this essay that the imperial structure of the Russian empire outlived two states technically and ideologically defined: empire survived 1917 and 1991. Is there something about the particularities of Russian ways of empire that made this possible? The modern colonial empires of Western Europe were short-lived ventures compared to the Romanov or Ottoman empires. What kinds of structural, cultural, or economic factors could allow some empires and not others to outlast the turbulent twentieth century?

Part of the answer is that empire is compatible with a wide array of political institutions and ideologies. We want to distinguish between empire as a state form—a polity based on differentiated governance of differentiated populations—from the political arrangements by which imperial authorities claim their legitimacy. Empire and monarchy are not coterminous; neither are empire and autocracy. The French Revolution overthrew monarchical absolutism and the estate system, but Napoleon reinvigorated the empire on different, and mixed, principles.[17] In other words, monarchy as the politics of rule was overturned, more or less permanently for France, but empire as a form of state remained. Many Russian elites at the beginning of the twentieth century rejected the legitimacy of autocracy, but empire as a state form prevailed even after the autocracy was limited in 1905 and defeated in 1917.

The question of whether empire as a state form is compatible with institutional and ideological democracy is an open one.[18] Even the demise of bourgeois colonial empires in the mid-twentieth century, conditioned by the spread of democratic and universalistic ideologies and the unwillingness of metropolitan governments to pay the costs of social equality,[19] does not mean that the final word has been spoken on what we might call the problem of democratic empire. Could inclusive and representative institutions, cultural heterogeneity, and economic well-being be accommodated within the framework of empire?

Mark von Hagen's essay reminds us that Russian theorists and activists proposed a variety of federalist projects in the nineteenth and early twentieth centuries. Since then, the potential for post-Soviet people to produce new kinds of differentiated governance has been enormously enhanced by the structural and ideological federalism sustained for over seventy years of Soviet rule. In addition, the possibilities for democracy in this region have been expanded in significant respects by some of the totalizing strategies of Soviet administrators. The liberal argument for representative democracy based on equal citizenship would have disempowered peasants and other subalterns in their own neighborhoods and in state politics in 1917, but two fundamental accomplishments of Soviet policy—the achievement of universal education and the production of a common language of governance—have opened up the ways that collectivities and individuals on the territories of the former USSR can relate to each other in the early twenty-first century.

The constitution of the Russian Federation, adopted in 1993, addresses issues of democratic citizenship in an empire. It omits the idea of political organization based on ethnicity and defines its constituent republics only by the legality of the process by which they are founded or dissolved. At the same time, the constitution offers all republics the right to establish their own state languages, while Russian is the "state language of the Russian Federation as a whole." All citizens have the right to "preserve their native language" and to create "conditions for its study and development." The rights of "national minorities" are guaranteed in accord with international principles of human rights.[20] This less than rigorous hodgepodge of rights and powers could be viewed by cynics as a ritual stamp over the multiple disagreements of its framers. But as much of the scholarship in this volume has suggested, the incorporation of inconsistent and various social formations—rather than the overcoming of "contradictions" as defined by intellectuals—characterized durable empires in the past. Over the long run, an amalgam of citizenship based on equal rights and equal access to the state, combined with recognition and legitimation of multiple languages, could produce a new resilient and democratic technology of Eurasian federalism.

Notes

1. Dominic Lieven makes this point in his inspiring comparative study, *Empire: The Russian Empire and its Rivals* (New Haven: Yale University Press, 2000), 224. See also Anatolyi Remnev's comments in his article in this collection.

2. On the state school, see Gary Hamburg, "Inventing the 'State School' of Historians, 1840–1995," in Thomas Sanders, ed., *Historiography of Imperial Russia: The Profession and Writing of History in a Multinational State* (Armonk, N.Y.: M.E. Sharpe, 1999), 98–117.

3. Boris Nol'de, *La formation de l'empire russe: Etudes, notes et documents* (Paris: Institut d'études slaves, 1952); Richard Pipes, *The Formation of the Soviet Union: Communism and Nationalism, 1917–1923* (Cambridge, Mass.: Harvard University Press, 1954); Marc Raeff, *Siberia and the Reforms of 1822* (Seattle: University of Washington Press, 1956); Marc Raeff, *Michael Speransky: Statesman of Imperial Russia, 1722–1839* (The Hague: Martinus Nijhoff, 1957).

4. From an enormous literature, see Ronald Grigor Suny, *The Revenge of the Past: Nationalism, Revolution, and the Collapse of the Soviet Union* (Stanford, Calif.: Stanford University Press, 1993); Yuri Slezkine, *Arctic Mirrors: Russian and the Small Peoples of the North* (Ithaca, N.Y.: Cornell University Press, 1994); A. V. Remnev, *Samoderzhavie i Sibir': Administrativnaia politika v pervoi polovine XIX v.* (Omsk: Izdatel'stvo Omskogo universiteta, 1995) and *Samoderzhavie i Sibir': Administrativnaia politika vtoroi poloviny XIX–nachala XX vekov* (Omsk: Omskii gosudarstvennyi universitet, 1997); Bruce Grant, *In the Soviet House of Culture: A Century of Perestroikas* (Berkeley: University of California Press, 1995); Theodore R. Weeks, *Nation and State in Late Imperial Russia: Nationalism and Russification on the Western Frontier, 1863–1914* (Dekalb: Northern Illinois University Press, 1996); John LeDonne, *The Russian Empire and the World, 1700–1917: The Geopolitics of Expansion and Containment* (New York: Oxford University Press, 1997); Thomas M. Barrett, *At the Edge of Empire: The Terek Cossacks and the North Caucasus Frontier, 1700–1860* (Boulder, Colo.: Westview Press, 1999); L. E. Gorizontov, *Paradoksy imperskoi politiki: Poliaki v Rossii i russkie v Pol'she* (Moscow: Indrik, 1999); A. I. Miller, *"Ukrainskii vopros" v politike vlastei i russkom obshchestvennom mnenii (vtoraia polovina XIX v.)* (St. Petersburg: Aleteiia, 2000); Shane O'Rourke, *Warriors and Peasants: The Don Cossacks in Late Imperial Russia* (New York: St. Martin's Press, 2000); Robert Geraci, *Window on the East* (Ithaca, N.Y.: Cornell University Press, 2001); Andreas Kappeler, *The Russian Empire: A Multiethnic History,* trans. Alfred Clayton (Harlow, England: Longman, 2001); S. I. Kaspe, *Imperiia i modernizatsiia: obshchaia model' i rossiiskaia spetsifika* (Moscow: ROSSPEN, 2001); Terry Martin, *The Affirmative Action Empire: Nations and Nationalism, 1923–1939* (Ithaca, N.Y.: Cornell University Press, 2001); V. O. Bobrovnikov, *Musul'mane severnogo Kavkaza: Obychai pravo nasilie* (Moscow: Vostochnaia literatura, 2002); Austin Jersild, *Orientalism and Empire: North Caucasus Mountain Peoples and the Georgian Frontier, 1845–1917* (Montreal: McGill-Queen's University Press, 2002); Paul Werth, *At the Margins of Orthodoxy: Mission, Governance, and Confessional Politics in Russia's Volga-*

Kama Region, 1827–1905 (Ithaca, N.Y.: Cornell University Press, 2002); Willard Sunderland, *Taming the Wild Field: Colonization and Empire on the Russian Steppe* (Ithaca, N.Y.: Cornell University Press, 2004); Francine Hirsch, *Empire of Nations: Ethnographic Knowledge and the Making of the Soviet Union* (Ithaca, N.Y.: Cornell University Press, 2005).

5. Among publications resulting from collaborative projects, see Daniel R. Brower and Edward J. Lazzerini, eds., *Russia's Orient: Imperial Borderlands and Peoples, 1700–1917* (Bloomington: Indiana University Press: 1997); Jane Burbank and David L. Ransel, eds., *Imperial Russia: New Histories for the Empire* (Bloomington: Indiana University Press: 1998); Catherine Evtukhov et al., eds., *Kazan, Moscow, St. Petersburg: Multiple Faces of the Russian Empire* (Moscow: O.G.I., 1997); Robert P. Geraci and Michael Khodarkovsky, eds., *Of Religion and Empire: Missions, Conversion, and Tolerance in Tsarist Russia* (Ithaca, N.Y.: Cornell University Press, 2001). The new journals *Kritika* and *Ab Imperium* both focus on imperial topics.

6. A forerunner of the present volume appeared in Russian in 1997, based on the work of a seminar sponsored by the Ford Foundation and the Moscow Social Science Foundation: *Imperskii stroi Rossii v regional'nom izmerenii (XIX–nachalo XX veka).* (Moscow: Moskovskii obshchestvennyi nauchnyi fond, 1997).

7. Regional initiatives were encouraged in the funding priorities of the Ford Foundation (the sponsor of the current project), MacArthur, Carnegie, Soros, and governmental (U.S. and European) funding agencies.

8. See the influential work of Marc Bassin, especially his *Imperial Visions: Nationalist Imagination and Geographical Expansion in the Russian Far East, 1840–1865* (Cambridge and New York: Cambridge University Press, 1999) and Larry Wolff's *Inventing Eastern Europe: The Map of Civilization on the Mind of the Enlightenment* (Stanford: Stanford University Press, 1994).

9. Anthropologists as well as historians have been among the important influences on this section's themes. See in particular Grant, *In the Soviet House of Culture;* Caroline Humphrey, *Marx Went and Karl Stayed Behind* (Ann Arbor: University of Michigan Press, 1998); Kappeler, *The Russian Empire;* Slezkine, *Arctic Mirrors.*

10. Hirsch, "The Soviet Union as a Work-in-Progress: Ethnographers and the Category *Nationality* in the 1926, 1937, and 1939 Censuses," *Slavic Review* 56, no. 2 (Summer 1997): 251–278.

11. See Yuri Slezkine's article, "Naturalists versus Nations: Eighteenth-Century Scholars Confront Ethnic Diversity," *Representations* 47 (Summer 1994): 170–195, on the emergence of uncertainty and attempts to overcome it.

12. Boris Nol'de, *La Formation de l'empire russe,* vol. 1 (Paris: Institut d'études slaves, 1952), xi–xii.

13. Among this huge scholarship, see in particular Frederick Cooper and Ann Laura Stoler, eds., *Tensions of Empire: Colonial Cultures in a Bourgeois World* (Berkeley: University of California Press, 1997); Edward W. Said, *Orientalism* (New York: Vintage Books, 1994); Ernest Gellner, *Nations and Nationalism* (London: Basil Blackwell, 1981); and Benedict Anderson, *Imagined Communities* (London: Verso, 1983).

14. For comparisons of Russia, the Ottoman empire, and Austria-Hungary, see Karen Barkey and Mark von Hagen, *After Empire: Multiethnic Societies and Nationbuilding: The Soviet Union and the Russian, Ottoman, and Habsburg Empires* (Boulder,

Colo.: Westview Press, 1997). Dominic Lieven's ambitious study *Empire* compares Russia with the British and Chinese empires.

15. See Michèle Lamont and Virág Molnár, "The Study of Boundaries in the Social Sciences," *Annual Review of Sociology* 28 (2002): 167–195.

16. Cooper and Stoler, *Tensions of Empire*, 3.

17. On Napoleonic empire, see Stuart Woolf, *Napoleon's Integration of Europe* (London: Routledge, 1991).

18. For a different view, see Charles Tilly, "How Empires End," in Barkey and von Hagen, *After Empire*, 7.

19. On this process in Africa, see Frederick Cooper, *Decolonization and African Society: The Labor Question in French and British Africa* (Cambridge: Cambridge University Press, 1996).

20. *Konstitutsiia Rossiiskoi federatsii. Priniata vsenarodnym golosovaniem 12 dekabria 1993 g.* (Moscow: Iuridicheskaia literatura, 1993), sts. 3, 5, 68, 69.

Part One   *Space*

1   Imperial Space: Territorial Thought and Practice in the Eighteenth Century

Willard Sunderland

In 1647, Tsar Aleksei learned from his officials in northeastern Siberia that a large island called New Land (*Novaia Zemlia*) had been discovered in the Arctic Ocean near the mouth of the Kolyma river. The tsar promptly ordered his servitors to determine whether the island contained any walrus-hunting peoples and, if it did, they were to be brought "under the tsar's high hand" and forced to submit hostages and tribute. Beyond that, Aleksei showed no interest in the new territory.[1] He said nothing about laying claim to the island à la Columbus ("by proclamation and with the royal standard unfurled"[2]) nor did he issue any instructions to rename, survey, map, or describe it. By 1724, however, the world had changed—or at least the way in which the world was perceived. In that year, Aleksei's son, Peter the Great, ordered Vitus Bering to the Arctic with the express purpose of charting a sea passage to North America. A second "Great Northern Expedition" was then dispatched in the mid-1730s, followed in turn by a series of state-sponsored voyages over the rest of the century, and in all of these voyages matters of territory were a central, if not *the* central, concern. New walrus-hunters, wherever possible, still needed to be found and turned into subjects, but now the lands of the walrus-hunters were themselves to be possessed, mapped, and described.[3] In fact, by the early 1700s even lands without people or walruses seemed important enough to require the fullest sort of claiming and accounting.

The difference between Tsar Aleksei's concerns and those of the eighteenth-century rulers who followed him was a difference in degrees of territoriality. Muscovite tsars ruled over territory and cared about it enough to try to keep track of it, but they did not view acquiring territorial knowledge as an intrinsically valuable pursuit, nor did they have the means or the ambition to manage territory in anything close to total fashion. By contrast, Peter and his successors saw the world differently and their inclination and expectation for knowing and shaping territory were much more pronounced. This heightened territorial consciousness was reflected in a range of ideas and practices, which in turn both influenced and were influenced by far-reaching changes in Russian techniques of governance and in the national and imperial imaginings of the Russian elite. In the course of Russia's Westernizing century, geography became a scientific discipline; external borders became increasingly defined; internal lands and resources became increasingly surveyed, catalogued, and managed; and members of the Russian establishment became increasingly likely to think of their country in territorial terms. There were continuities with older ways, but there was also great innovation, foreign borrowing, and native adaptation, and the net result was the creation of a new territorial order that underscored as much as anything else the palpable differences between "medieval Muscovy" and "modern Russia."[4] Of course, new orders always come with ironies and complexities, and the making of the new territoriality of eighteenth-century Russia was no exception. The present chapter charts the unfolding of this process, emphasizing the ways in which new ideas and practices of territory influenced both the nature and the aspirations of state power and the national/imperial belonging of state elites, from late Muscovy to the age of Catherine the Great.

Late Muscovy and the Petrine Transition

By comparison with the Petrine state that replaced it, the Muscovite state was markedly less territorial, though this was not for lack of territory. In the late 1600s, Muscovy was by far the largest contiguous state in the world, with lands extending from the "Frozen Sea" in the north to the edges of "the wild field" in the south and from Poland in the west to China in the east.[5] But while the Muscovites claimed to rule an immense area, they lacked coherent territorial organization or even a clear idea of the shape and resources of their realm. Moscow's domain was organized into an uncoordinated patchwork of over 200 districts (uezds) that coexisted alongside a smaller number of larger units, such as regional groupings of towns (*Novgorodskie goroda, Ponizovye goroda,* etc.), frontier military districts (*razriady*), and other regional entities (*Zamoskovnyi krai, Pomor'e, Belaia Rossiia,* etc.), some of which had their own chancelleries (viz. the Siberian *prikaz,* the Kazan *prikaz,* etc.) but most of which did not.[6] As for territorial knowledge, the Muscovite royal establishment had some, but not much. Despite the fact that the late 1600s saw an increase in official map-making and the production of other forms of territorial information, the quality of most Muscovite maps was low, cartographic literacy was extremely limited, and the state's territorial information largely amounted to inventories of land holdings or descriptions listing the whereabouts of rivers, roads, towns, frontier outposts, and various economic sites, such as mines and mills.[7] The most complete territorial materials were probably the maps (*chertezhi*) and geographic descriptions (*opisaniia*) of Siberia composed by Semen Remezov beginning in the 1680s, but even these materials were sketchy and unsystematic.[8]

Muscovite territory was not particularly well defined or organized in the late seventeenth century because late Muscovite Russia was not, strictly speaking, a territorial state. While the Muscovites had territory-based institutions and recognized territorial resources, such as land, precious metals, and furs, as sources of profit (*pribyl'*), they did not have a coherent state ideology that valued territory as an intrinsic good, and their sense of territorial sovereignty was at best incomplete. With the exception of the proto-mercantilist views of scholars such as Iurii Krizhanich or officials such as Vasilii Golitsyn, the late seventeenth-century Muscovite establishment had no abiding ideological justification for paying attention to territory.[9] Territory was something to acquire and rule over, but not to manage or think about, except insofar as it had a direct impact on matters of tax collecting, foreign relations, foreign trade, and state defense.[10] Muscovite notions of the state as something defined by an integral territorial space were likewise somewhat undeveloped. The tsar laid claim to a list of territories in his official title, but these territories were only beginning to be united under a single territorial definition, and the state's international borders varied in terms of how well they were defined.[11] In the west, where Muscovy ran up against organized territorial states such as Sweden and Poland-Lithuania, borders (*granitsy* or *rubezhy* in official parlance) were relatively well described, but in the Far East, where the Muscovites ran into the Chinese, there was much less concern with a detailed definition of the border. Across parts of the southern steppe the state built forts and defensive lines, but since these lines were understood as the edges of a frontier zone rather than as the boundaries of the state, borders were not delineated.[12]

Thus the Muscovite state in the late 1600s possessed territorial administration, some sense of territorial sovereignty, increasing territorial knowledge, and a great deal of territory itself; but its overall "political culture of territoriality" was still somewhat unpronounced.[13] This situation started to change with the beginning of Peter I's independent rule in 1696, and what followed was a transition toward a new degree of territoriality. This transition was affected by three changes of the Petrine epoch. First, a shift took place in thinking about the nature of the state and the purpose of government. Under Peter, the embrace of cameralist political theory turned the state into the rational master of an under-exploited universe whose resources had to be better known, better managed, and more fully maximized in order to achieve "happiness" (*blago*) and "utility" (*pol'za*).[14] The fact that the Petrine establishment placed a new cachet on practical science was also key. Practical science, as Leibniz put it, increased "the welfare and commodities of men" and led to "new and useful discoveries."[15] It was thus Man's God-given tool to unlocking the under-exploited universe that he inhabited, and was therefore to be encouraged whenever possible. Finally, new concerns with territory were clearly influenced by the Petrine government's new political concerns. Peter's regime was preoccupied with war. War led to eventual losses of territory (for example, with the Turks), but it also produced territorial gains (vis-à-vis the Swedes and Persians most importantly) and these acquisitions provided Russians with a new and compelling justification for thinking of their state as an international power.[16] It was not by coincidence that after defeating the Swedes, Peter's official title changed from tsar to emperor (*imperator*) and Russia itself became an empire (*imperiia*).[17] The essential meaning of these changes was clear: Russia was a great state whose new great name underscored the state's place in European politics and its common ground with European civilization.[18]

All of these developments—the Petrine state's faith in the new religion of state utility, its promotion of practical science, and its drive to acquire full status as a European power—combined to produce a profound change in the nature of Russian territoriality. Not all of what went into this new territoriality was new to the Petrine era, but it was packaged in a new idiom and applied with a new zeal that made it ultimately quite different from the Muscovite variant that had preceded it. The Petrine establishment now explicitly regarded territorial space as (1) a resource to be studied, managed, and exploited; (2) a terrain to be shaped and molded as the physical expression of state power; and (3) a symbol of national pride and a basis for national identity. As one of the ideologues of the new Petrine world-view put it, giving voice to all of these ideas, "our Russian land (*zemlia nasha rossiiskaia*) is certainly no less extensive than the lands of the Germans and it has within it places that are warm and cold and mountainous, and it has various seas and a length of coastline that is so enormous that it can hardly be measured." Yet at the same time "the tsar's interest" goes under-fulfilled because the land in many places is unused or empty, and "emptiness produces no profit" (*s pusta nikakova dokhodu ne byvaet*).[19] This cluster of national-cameralist attitudes toward territory led Peter and his servitors to place greater emphasis on developing ways to enhance both their knowledge of territory and their ability to act on it, with the two usually going hand in hand. The result was a change in the morphology of the state's territory as well as in ideas of state sovereignty and national identity.

One of the most fundamental territory-related changes to occur under the Petrine order was a change in thinking about geography and geographical practice. While late Muscovite culture produced a base of geographical information about Russia and (to a lesser extent) other countries, and while this information was assembled according to a certain logic, Muscovite geographic data was not systematized, and the people who produced it did not look on what they were doing as a matter of science. By contrast, the geographic practitioners of the Petrine and post-Petrine eras saw themselves as scientists and defined their activities accordingly. As Vasilii Tatishchev pointed out, geography was a science that "described the earth" and consisted of various subfields, some of which, such as "historical geography" or "physical geography," described the earth in terms of different subjects, and others, such as "general geography" and "particular geography," described it on different scales. As such, geography was broadly conceived (it included studying everything from soils to climates to customs) and "useful," since it contributed both to the practical needs of states as well as to the scientific interests of patriotic subjects who wished to be informed about their "fatherland" and the world. Not surprisingly, as Tatishchev suggested, the geographer who engaged in this "useful science" was expected to have many talents, including a knowledge of "astronomy, geodesy, and history" and the ability to "describe all things completely" and to "compose accurate maps" (*chertezhi*).[20]

The redefinition of geography as a science validated and accelerated the Russian state's growing interest in applying geography as a tool of statecraft. The clearest expression of this tendency appeared in the state's drive to acquire new maps. Peter I had a personal fascination for maps and globes and was a devoté of European cartography, which he saw as a shining symbol of scientific accuracy and utility.[21] Not surprisingly, this combination of cartographic passion and European bias led to the tsar's ardent promotion of European-style mapping in Russia in the first decades of the 1700s. The result was the eclipse of the old Muscovite *chertezh*, with its lack of scientific proportion and positioning, and the emergence of the new and freshly "scientized" European-style *karta/landkarta*, which was calculated on the basis of scientific instruments and drawn according to a geometric grid of longitudes and latitudes.[22] The earliest of these new maps were composed with military applications in mind (for example, the maps of the lower Don that Peter commissioned while on his "Great Embassy" in Amsterdam in 1696–1697), but the new maps quickly entered the domain of civilian government as well, which was only to be expected since scientific maps were increasingly regarded as the necessary tools of a scientific administration. Consequently, over the first two decades of the eighteenth century, the government opened schools to train surveyors and navigators "according to the new methods"; established printing houses for producing civilian maps; commissioned maps on everything from road projects to mining projects; launched a general geodesic survey of the empire in 1715; and required as of 1720 that "general and particular maps of all the empire's provinces" be kept in each of its newly founded colleges so that government officials would be fully informed of "the condition of the state."[23]

The recognition that maps were important to government practice was not new to the Petrine era. The Muscovites had used maps for governing purposes since at least the sixteenth century, but the goal now was to produce new maps that reflected the state's new and improved condition. The compilation of a new general map of the state was particularly important. The Petrine rulership needed a map whose accuracy would (1) communicate the state's new ideal of scientific progress and (2) underscore Russia's new identification with Europe, while at the same time making it clear that Russia had both a geographical science and a physical extent that were just as impressive as (if not more impressive than) anyone else's. The gathering of the readings and data for a state map began with the geodesic survey (initiated in 1715) and the process then continued over next three decades, culminating in two early state atlases, the first produced in 1734 by Ivan Kirilov and the second by the Academy of Sciences in 1745. The atlases each came with one "general map" of the empire as a whole and numerous "particular maps" of individual provinces, regions, or parts of regions, all of which included standardized markings for physical and man-made features (steppes, mountains, villages, forts, roads, etc.); allegorical cartouches that celebrated Russia's natural abundance, military victories, and/ or providential wisdom; tables indicating the coordinates of the empire's important places; and titles that explicitly stressed both the scientific basis of the atlases and the vastness of the empire.[24]

Like all state atlases, the two Russian works implicitly reinforced a vision of the state as a cohesive, unified territory, and the general maps in each atlas underscored this idea more directly.[25] As Kirilov's announcement to his atlas suggested, his general map revealed "the expanse of . . . a great empire," and the map itself made it plain that areas as far removed from one another as Smolensk Province (*Smolensce gub.*), the "Kingdom of Astrakhan" (*Astrakhan regnum*), and the area in northeastern Siberia marked with the name of "the Yukagir people" (*Iukagiri populus*) all belonged to the same state.[26] The Academicians made a similar point in their atlas, noting that the most valuable thing about general maps (theirs included) was the fact that they provided their viewers with the chance to observe a picture of "lands collected together" (*soedinenie zemel'*).[27] In presenting the state in these terms, the atlases symbolized the new cartographic imagination that took hold of the Russian elite over the course of the Petrine and immediate post-Petrine periods and confirmed the fact that the representation of the state in the form of a "graphic picture" was increasingly recognized as an "accepted method of apprehending territory" and even as the very definition of territory itself.[28] In fact, the idea of knowing the state's territory *without* recourse to a map was rapidly becoming an impossible proposition. As the geographer-statesman Tatishchev remarked in 1739, "the fullest apprehension of geography" required "a map of the state" indicating the "divisions between provinces, counties, and districts" without which "the location of places, the distance between towns, the course of rivers, the situation of mountains, swamps, lakes, and so forth . . . cannot be fully understood" (*vniatno razumet' ne mozhno*).[29]

The new European-style maps epitomized by these atlases were a vivid expression of the early eighteenth-century establishment's new interest in territory, but this interest took other forms as well. In addition to maps, scholars and statesmen of the Petrine and early post-Petrine periods made use of textual and statistical methods designed to document the territory, such as registers on towns and their inhabitants, tallies of the tax-paying population, parish registers recording births and marriages, reports on mineral and timber resources, and questionnaires and instructions sent out by inquiring minds such as Tatishchev, who assembled a list of 198 questions in 1737 designed to elicit information about the empire; and Gerhard Friedrich Müller, who outdid Tatishchev in 1739 by coming up with over 1,200 points of inquiry about Siberia.[30] The fact that Müller came up with more concerns than Tatishchev was not surprising, since territory-related data had a tendency toward natural increase. The double pursuit of ever-increasing accuracy and ever-increasing utility gave rise to an information culture in which even the most detailed territorial compendia and descriptions always seemed to require updating and improvement.[31] The same logic applied to maps.[32] The result, not surprisingly, was a situation in which the production of one piece of territory-related data generally led to the production of another.

The interest in assembling ever-increasing amounts of territorial information was a clear motivating factor behind the Russian state's new and zealous sponsorship of geographic exploration in the early 1700s. Ad hoc exploration à la Muscovy was out; organized exploration for the explicit purpose of uncovering, mapping, and recording unknown lands and coastlines was in, with the latter emerging as a regular state practice by the 1710s (viz. explorations in Central Asia [1714], the Volga and the Caucasus [1717], the Kurile Islands [1718], the Upper Irtysh [1718], the Caspian [1719], etc.) and becoming all the more entrenched with the founding of the Academy of Sciences in 1724.[33] The preferred mode of exploration of the day—one which the Academy took on with gusto—was the military-scientific "expedition" (*ekspeditsiia*), defined by Tatishchev as "an extraordinary enterprise, usually involving troops, carried out by sea or across land, and placed under the command of a talented officer."[34] In practice, this meant that expeditions almost always conducted both scientific and political activities and, in their broadest form, could involve everything from describing new plants and peoples to claiming new lands, mapping new harbors, promoting commerce, and organizing colonization. The explicitly territorial goals of expeditioning became more pronounced as the 1700s proceeded. "Instructions" to expeditionaries under Peter tended to be brief and/or vague, but by the 1730s and 1740s they were much more detailed, reflecting the government's rising territorial culture.[35]

The Petrine take-off in organized geographical exploration made a direct contribution to the government's accumulation of territorial knowledge. In addition to the maps that they were invariably required to produce, explorers also kept journals and logs, submitted reports, and composed more protracted territorial descriptions (*opisaniia*). The latter were especially noteworthy. The practice of describing territories had existed in

Muscovite times, but the eighteenth-century descriptions were different in that, like the foreign writings of scientific travel on which they were based (the French *déscription* and the German *Beschreibung*), they were intensely empirical and given to providing the fullest possible territorial picture.[36] As the explorer-scholar Müller suggested in his introduction to another explorer-scholar's *opisanie* of Kamchatka, a good description should relate

> . . . the natural condition of any area of land; its fertility and other qualities, its positive and negative attributes; it is likewise necessary to determine where the land is mountainous and where it is flat, where there are rivers, lakes, and forests, where profitable metals can be found, where there are areas suitable for farming and herding, and where there are infertile plains (*stepi*); what rivers are used by ships and whether other rivers can be opened to shipping . . . ; what animals, birds, and fish live in what places and where what grasses, bushes, and trees can be found and whether any of them can be used for medicines or paints or some other economic purpose; where the land is inhabited and uninhabited; the names and locations of its important towns, forts, churches, monasteries, ports, commercial places, mines, and forges . . . ; the distances between places; the state of roads; what people live in each place or district, their number, and their language, appearance, habits, morals, occupations, law, and so forth; . . . the location of ruins; the history of how the country was conquered and populated; the lie of its borders, its neighbors, and their mutual relations.[37]

Thus defined, the "description" represented a new genre that perfectly expressed the territorial impetus behind the new exploration and also provided a perfect accompaniment to the new map. Indeed, the new description and the new map were expected to complement one another. As the French cartographer Joseph-Nicolas de L'Isle recommended in a memorandum to the Academy of Sciences in 1728, "geographic and historical descriptions of the country, replete with notes of interest [*remarques curieuses*] on the unique attributes of each province and the special customs of its inhabitants," should accompany the empire's new maps, because "without such descriptions, Geography is too dry and has limited appeal [*n'est du goût que de peu de personnes*]."[38] The principal idea behind all these methodologies of territorial knowledge was to define the territorial space of the state and its natural, man-made, and human resources. But as Russian scholars and statesmen of the early eighteenth century went about defining the territory of the state, they also unavoidably engaged in defining the nation, and as a result the two projects of representing the territory of the state and the state of the nation were often intertwined. Almost from its inception the new geography of the Petrine era was highly nationally conscious, and geographer-cartographers like Kirilov and Tatishchev routinely noted that their efforts were designed to correct the misinformation provided about Russia in "foreign" (i.e., European) maps and to produce a domestic geographical science that would be a truly Russian endeavor.[39] Consequently, native knowledge of the territory was increasingly praised and the foreign geographer and the foreign map were increasingly stigmatized, all at the very same time (ironically) that foreign methods were radically changing Russian geography and making it more foreign. This dynamic of national *ressentiment* went hand in hand with the equally novel and popular idea that the duty of every true "son of the fatherland" was to know his geography, which, since geography was so broadly defined, meant knowing not only the physical extent and characteristics of the state but also its history and the "morals and customs" (*nravy i obyknoveniia*) of its inhabitants. Geography thus emerged as a repository for the patriotic feelings of the Petrine establishment, and knowledge of the territory and exposure to maps became prerequisites for good subject-hood.[40]

In the same way that territorial knowledge became a vehicle for the expression of Russian state patriotism, it also became a basis for identifying (or at least trying to identify) the Russian nation. In the view of Petrine and post-Petrine scholars, the Russians, like every one else, lived on a given piece of territory (*obitanie*) and this territory was one of the elements—along with religion, language, "morals and customs," and "History"—that helped to define them as a people.[41] Determining the Russians' territory was thus a basic part of determining the Russians' nationality and, consequently, nationally conscious Russian scholars—beginning with Tatishchev —made repeated efforts to define the Russians' national habitat, both past and present.[42] In each case, a clear link was suggested between the nation's territory and the territory of the state. The logic was fairly straightforward: the Russians were a nation; the first members of the Russian nation (the "ancient Russians") lived on the territory of Ancient Rus; the territory of Ancient Rus over time expanded into the territory of the Russian empire; and the descendants of the "ancient Russians" ultimately ended up living all over the empire's territory (*drevnie i prirodnyia rossiiane . . . koi po vsei imperii rasprastraniaiutsia*). The space of the Russian nation and the space of the Russian state were thus largely equivalent.[43] This seemingly straightforward scenario was complicated, however, by two points that Russian scholars also readily recognized. First of all, the Russians were not the only people living within the state's space (Tatishchev himself listed forty-two peoples as current or ancient "inhabitants"); and second, some Russians within the state (the "Little Russians," for example) had lived for so long in other peoples' states that they had a different history, spoke a different language, and thought of themselves as a "distinct people."[44] In other words, Russians lived all across the Russian state, but this state was also home to many people who were clearly not Russian as well as some Russians who had apparently forgotten about their Russianness.

Such complexities in the relationship between Russian nationality and state territory were not resolved in the early eighteenth century (or later, for that matter), but Russian scholars nonetheless did what they could to make sure that the state's territory made the Russians look as good as possible. Given the new preoccupations with Russia's European identity and its new status as a European-style empire, underscoring the European and imperial attributes of the state's territory was particularly key. Thus, beginning in the 1730s, Russian scholars (in a move pioneered by Tatishchev) shifted the boundary between Europe and Asia from its traditionally accepted location on the Don River farther east to the Ural mountains, which were much deeper in Russian territory and therefore provided the Russians with a much more sizeable claim to geographic Europeanness.[45] This new conceptualization then led to the new practice of using the Urals to divide the Russian state into two halves, a western half called "European Russia" and an eastern one called "Asiatic Russia." This division obviously did not make Russia wholly geographically European (the larger half of the state was still in Asia), but it did reinforce the impression that the more populous and, of course, more "European" European side was a kind of metropole, while the Asian side was a kind of colony.[46] Similar to the new distinction between the two halves of the state, other new notions gave the state a more expressly imperial morphology. Beginning again with Tatishchev, Russian scholars reinforced the idea that the state's territory consisted of a historically Russian core and a historically non-Russian periphery. The core, which occupied much of "European Russia" at the time, amounted to "the regions of ancient Russia" or "Russia proper" (*Rossiia sama soboiu*), while the periphery, located to the west (the Baltic) and to the east (the Urals, Siberia), was made up of formerly independent kingdoms, tsardoms, and "newly discovered places" that were grafted onto the empire as "conglomerated" or "conquered provinces" (*prisovokuplennye [t.e.*

zavoevannye] oblasti).[47] All of these scholarly concerns about the boundaries of Russian space make it plain that the Russian academic establishment's rising national consciousness and rising territorial culture were deeply intertwined. At the same time, scholars were not the only ones concerned with boundaries. In the Petrine and early post-Petrine periods, efficient government was increasingly perceived as requiring efficient spatial management, and consequently the state's political leaders (some of whom were also scholars) were also preoccupied with boundary-making. In a series of measures between 1708 and 1727, the Russian government retailored the Muscovites' hodgepodge territorial system and created a three-tier framework of territorial administration consisting of provinces (*gubernii*) that were then subdivided into counties (*provintsii*) and districts (*uezdy*).[48] This territorial reform was not utterly revolutionary (prior movement in this direction had taken place in the late 1600s) and it did not eliminate all the inconsistencies of Muscovite administration, but it was nonetheless a step toward rationalizing and homogenizing the state's space by dividing it into more standardized units.[49] Similar concerns were shown toward defining or redefining the state's external borders, particularly in the west and the south where near-constant warring produced territorial changes that Russian statesmen needed to keep track of, but also on "quieter" frontiers, such as the Russo-Chinese border, where there were no significant land changes in the early 1700s, but where diplomatic treaties nonetheless came with detailed textual descriptions of the border, required the drawing of border maps, and stipulated the placing of markers, frontier signposts, and guard stations along the border itself to make it clearly delineated.[50] The trend toward a fuller definition of external borders naturally complemented the internal territorial reform. New internal boundaries created a new domestic space for the operations of state governance, while more precisely defined foreign borders unified this space and enclosed it by setting it off from other surrounding spaces. Not surprisingly, all of this spatial redefinition and reorganization helped to create an operational terrain in which the cameralist state could seek to do what it was supposed to do best: maximize the exploitation of its territory. In order to make their territory as productive as possible, the Russian governments of the early 1700s attacked the problem of territorial underproduction by embarking on a concerted (if somewhat disorganized) campaign to conquer territorial distance by building roads and canals, overcome territorial negligence by fining derelict landowners, and defeat territorial inefficiency by creating institutions whose *raison d'être* was systematic territorial extraction (for example, the Berg-Kollegiia and the Kamer-Kollegiia). St. Petersburg also sponsored the exploration of its lesser-known regions so that their riches could be counted up, carted out, and/or funneled into foreign exchange, just as it promoted the settlement of "empty places" because "empty places" were increasingly seen as woefully underutilized and therefore unprofitable. What came of all of this was a qualitatively new brand of territorial economics that was still glaringly incomplete and far from fully systematized, but nevertheless different from the system that came before it.[51]

High Territoriality

If Russia's new territorial order was well established by the early-to-mid-1700s, it became even more so over the rest of the century. By the close of the eighteenth century, the territory-related ideas and practices discussed to this point had become so entrenched within the political and cultural worldview of Russian elites that the novelty of the Petrine territorial order had worn off and the order itself was completely naturalized. The high-water mark in this process was reached between the 1760s and the end of the century, which roughly coincides with the reign of Catherine the Great (1762–1796), and represents what could be called a period of high territoriality. This shift to a higher territorial gear was facilitated by the enshrinement of rationality and *esprit géometrique* as the golden rules of Russian territorial science, the consolidation of political economy as a way of thinking about Russian statecraft, the dynamism of a Russian public (*publika, obshchestvo*) that was interested in proving its patriotic and scientific credentials in the public sphere, and a protracted period of imperial conquest and "discovery" that resulted in the dramatic territorial expansion of the Russian state. Together and separately, these developments created a context in which Russia ultimately ended up both physically and conceptually more territorial than before.

The intensification of the new territoriality of the late eighteenth century is particularly visible in the pronounced territorial preoccupations of the Catherinian elite. The empress and her contemporaries, much like their counterparts in Europe, were fascinated with writings on geography and territory-related subjects, and Russia's imperial successes only made territory topics all the more popular. The unsurprising result was a deluge (by the standards of the time) of published territory-oriented materials. Beginning in the 1750s and increasing substantially after the 1770s, Russian printers pumped out (among other things) serials devoted to topics on Russian commerce, agriculture, history, ethnography, and geography; geographical textbooks; geographical "descriptions"; travel accounts of foreign and Russian travelers; various kinds of handbooks on the empire (which always included healthy attention to the empire's territorial dimensions and attributes); printed maps and atlases; and primers on how to read these maps and atlases ("First set the map on a large table . . . ").[52] Through these materials, the Russian public defined itself as a body of patriotic subjects who "knew the fatherland" and whose fatherland knowledge was precisely one of the things that (a) distinguished them from the non-public (i.e., the *chern'*, *narod*); and (b) underscored their identification with and importance to the state.

In their territory-related writings, Catherinian scholars, officials, and other contributors to the public sphere of print tended to confirm the tenets of territorial thinking that had emerged earlier in the century. It was now widely accepted that the Russian empire was a European country with an Asian extension, that it consisted of a core of historically Russian territories surrounded by a historically non-Russian periphery, and that the territorial habitat of the Russian nation overlapped with the territory of the state, making the two forms of territory seemingly interchangeable.[53] Through the acceptance of these postulates, Russian territorial and national consciousness became ever more intertwined, with the result that the state's territory became an increasingly resonant repository for Russian national sentiment. Nowhere was this more visible than in the intense adulation of the size of the Russian state that emerged as a staple in writings of the period. Territorial immensity had been lauded by Russian writers since at least the Petrine era, but in the late 1700s it became a point of obsession that clearly reflected the elite's heightened national sentiment.[54] Thus Catherinian writers claimed, often with exclamation points or in bold type and by citing scientific measurements and geographical coordinates, that the Russian state was larger than all states of the past and the present ("even ancient Rome"), was twice the size of Europe, and occupied (depending on the empire's changing size) some invariably large share of the world's surface.[55] The obvious implication behind these assertions was that territorial greatness reflected the greatness of the nation.

In addition to their increasing preoccupations with national territorial identity in the Catherinian period, Russian elites also expressed a growing interest in regions. At the center of this growing regional consciousness was the province, or rather the newly refashioned province (*guberniia*) that emerged as the final product of the Catherinian territorial reform that was begun in 1775. Elite identification with the province was expressed particularly clearly in two new territorial instruments: the provincial "topographic description" (*istoriko-topograficheskoe opisanie, topograficheskoe opisanie*) and the provincial atlas, both of which were related to the general processes of the provincial reform and the land survey. The topographic descriptions, most of which were compiled between the late 1770s and the early 1790s, were territorial compendia written by local nobles/officials that invariably began with a description of the province's geographic location (measured in terms of coordinates), surface area, boundaries, natural environment, and administrative subdivisions, all of which then served as the essential territorial frame for subsequent points/chapters on history, the local economy, and the local population that contained everything from statistical data on local markets to lists of local monasteries and "curious facts" about local insects and local customs.[56] Given their structure and content, the descriptions vividly expressed the local elite's provincial patriotism as well as their commitment to the prevailing values of scientific accuracy, exhaustive empiricism, and state utility, all of which only tended to reinforce the virtue of provincial pride. As Petr Rychkov noted in his early topography of Orenburg Province in 1762, his "modest description" was designed to bring "undescribed" (*neopisannyi*) Orenburg into the domain of scientific knowledge so that the region's many attributes and "great importance to the state" could be fully appreciated.[57]

The same three-way love of province, accuracy, and utility was on display in the provincial atlases that were ordered by decree in 1783 and reflected cartographic knowledge drawn from the cadastral survey. These atlases were hand-drawn and consisted of either oversize or book-size sheets that included one general map of the province, usually set out on its own on a blank page and marked with the provincial herald, as well as various district maps, also set out on their own and replete with lines delineating noble estates, lists of district landowners, and lists of villages and "empty areas" (*pustoshi*).[58] The atlases expressed the social power of the nobility by underscoring the principle of territorial ownership, while at the same time expressing the importance of the province by highlighting it as a distinct space cut out from the space of the state.[59] The same tendency to bring out the distinctiveness of the province appeared in other provincial maps (both before and after the provincial atlases), which displayed individual provinces set out in bold colors against a background of blank space.[60] Even atlases that did not represent individual provinces cut out from the space surrounding them still underscored their distinctiveness through elaborate cartouches depicting provincial heralds or images of local resources, landscapes, or peoples.[61]

These provincial maps and topographical descriptions not only underscored and reflected provincial identities, but they also represented tools of territorial knowledge and thus reflected the state and society's broader interest in knowing territory. It was simply assumed by now that comprehensive territorial knowledge provided an essential foundation for effective governance and true patriotism. Consequently, both the public and the government had good reasons to acquire as much of it as possible. The various tools and methods used for collecting and representing territorial information in the Catherinian age (maps, registers, questionnaires) were not new, but their use in government became more routinized, and they were eagerly embraced by newly created public organizations with their own interests in collecting and deploying territorial information. During the last decades of the 1700s the Academy of Sciences, the Free Economic Society, and the School of Cadets (*Kadetskii korpus*) sent out detailed questionnaires to obtain information on agriculture, population, natural resources, and other territory-related phenomena;[62] the Academy dispatched a wave of organized "physical expeditions" (*fizicheskie ekspeditsii*) to scour the empire's regions for similar data;[63] the General Staff (created in 1763) commissioned military-topographical maps of the empire;[64] and newly appointed governors were instructed to map and catalogue their provinces in "all [their] conditions and environs."[65] The conviction behind all these efforts was that useful territorial information had to be current, detailed, and accurate, and that the only way to obtain this sort of information was through meticulous empirical inquiry and constant updating.[66]

Of course, in addition to knowing about territory, the Catherinian establishment was also interested in transforming it and rendering it as rational and productive as possible. This cameralist impulse was especially clear in two massive state initiatives that extended across much of Catherine's reign: the cadastral survey launched in 1765 and the territorial reform begun ten years later. The former was designed to clarify land ownership in the countryside by drawing property lines and cataloguing the rural economic landscape through the compilation of tables and "economic notes";[67] while the latter aimed to clarify the administrative space of the state by (a) creating a new territorial division based on a new structure of provinces and districts (initially the *namestnichestvo*, then the modern guberniia and uezd) that were smaller and had roughly uniform populations; and (b) extending this new structure into borderland areas that had previously been subdivided and administered according to local historical practice.[68] Given official zeal for the *esprit géometrique,* both the survey and the provincial reform were infused with a "rhetoric of accuracy" and a vision of the state's space as an abstract plain that could be plotted in terms of geometric points and inventoried in terms of its economic contents (villages, fields, ponds, etc.), the premise being that territory known in this way would be better managed and therefore more productive.[69] As such, the two initiatives represent the apex of the eighteenth-century state's already well-established practice of reducing the complexities of territory by attempting to reify and rationalize them.[70] Reifying and rationalizing territory was not the government's only concern, however. Territorial transformation was also linked to another key preoccupation of Catherinian governance: the increase and improvement of population (i.e., populationism). Managing the relationship between population and territory emerged as a special vector of government in Europe in the seventeenth century, when "police scientists" first began to see the state as a political economy that rested on "continuous and multiple relations between population, territory, and wealth."[71] Peter the Great and his followers (preceded slightly earlier by thinkers such as Krizhanich) introduced this worldview into Russian governance in the early 1700s, and by the latter part of the century Russia's ruling elite had no doubts about the fact that population and territory were fundamental state resources, that they were inherently related, and that the optimization of their interrelationship was necessary for the increase of state utility and public welfare. As one of the court's foreign specialists, A. L. Schlözer, suggested in 1768, "The essence of the state lies in its land and its people. The wealth, power, and happiness of the state stem from these sources and the two are mutually connected."[72] What flowed from this view was a vigorous commitment on the part of the Catherinian establishment to find out about the configuration of population and territory within the empire (which it did through surveys and questionnaires) and to harmonize that configuration wherever possible in order to make both population and territory more productive.[73]

The goal of aligning population and territory was clear in the 1775 territorial reform, which used population as a basis for inventing new provinces and districts, and it was also apparent in the Catherinian government's ardent promotion of organized borderland colonization. Long valued for purposes of defense and minimal economic exploitation, colonization now began a new career as an instrument for increasing and redistributing the empire's population. As Catherine and her pro-population leadership saw it, the empire suffered from a basic territory-population imbalance. In most areas, it possessed too much land and not enough people (this was the case throughout the southern and eastern borderlands, for example), while in other areas it had too many people and not enough land (viz. the agricultural center, where natural demographic increase, traditional forms of agriculture, and noble land encroachment led to complaints of "insufficient land" (*malozemel'e*) as of the 1770s). Not surprisingly, given the rationalizing impulses of the day, St. Petersburg's instinctive response to this situation was to try to readjust it through state-sponsored colonization and resettlement. Thus, over the second half of the 1700s, the court and the colleges encouraged a wide range of rural people (everyone from foreign colonists to Old Believer refugees) to colonize "open" areas in the borderlands, while making sure (especially as of the 1770s–1780s) that a large portion of these settlers (both state peasants and serfs) were resettled from crowded areas in the interior.[74]

Plans for the settlement of the southern steppe revealed this line of thinking especially clearly. In the late eighteenth century, a steppe was defined as a vast, unpopulated place—the ultimate *tabula rasa* for engineering the mutual potential of land and people.[75] Of all the empire's steppes, the most attractive in this respect were those of the northern Black Sea region and the Northern Caucasus: they were (1) newly conquered from the Ottoman Turks and Crimean Tatars; (2) strategically important; (3) relatively close to the Russian interior; (4) highly suitable for farming and/or stock-raising; and, last but not least, (5) largely devoid of people, except for small groups of steppe nomads, who were considered backward, irrelevant, and all but predestined for sedentarization. ("Free" Cossacks, like the Zaporozhians, were not considered to be much better.) The southern steppe thus quickly emerged as the government's premier venue for colonization-related planning.[76] Beginning in 1751, with the founding of New Serbia, and then accelerating in 1764 with the creation of New Russia, the government styled the southern steppe as a rationally constructed colonization zone that was to be divided into standardized settlement districts (*okrugi*) that would then be subdivided into standardized land allotments (*uchastki*) and settled with a proportionate number of mostly military settlers.[77] As Russia's position in the south became more assured, the emphasis on military settlement declined, but the stress on organized territorial transformation remained constant. The result was an enduring vision of the southern steppe as a "desert" that needed to be turned into a busy but rationally designed terrain of "civilization," replete with ordered settlement districts, villages spaced evenly along postal roads, colonists directed to settle where their economic skills were most applicable, and particular trees and crops planted exactly where they were most likely to thrive.[78]

The enthusiasm for transforming the steppe was directly related to state and society's larger interest in new or unknown regions, which in turn produced a new interest in geographic exploration. As mentioned earlier, the Academy of Sciences organized a series of major scientific expeditions (five in all) between 1768 and 1774 that were dispatched (not surprisingly) to the south and southeastern steppes, parts of which (like New Russia) had only recently been acquired by the empire. Visiting and studying such new regions was a key part of the Academy's plan: As the expeditionary Vasilii Zuev suggested, "the fortunate reign of Catherine the Great" led to the acquisition of new territory, and new territory "provided the rationale for new travels."[79] While the academic expeditions of the 1760s and 1770s were relatively small in terms of their staff and did not have the explicit political-military objectives of the earlier Kamchatka or Orenburg expeditions, they were nonetheless highly organized, were headed by prominent "men of Science" with strong ties both to the Russian establishment and the European "Republic of Letters," resulted in encyclopedic territorial writings that described "everything worthy of note" (*vse . . . chto tol'ko dostoino primechaniia*) (i.e., fauna, flora, local peoples, local products, etc.), and attracted large public and official interest.[80] These expeditions were not "voyages of discovery" per se, since they did not uncover wholly unknown territories, but they did serve to claim symbolically territory already in the state's possession, clearly reinforcing a vision of the empire as an enterprise defined by Russian knowledge.[81]

In addition to explorations in the southern and southeastern steppes, the other great arena of Russian exploration in the second half of the eighteenth century was the Bering Sea and far northern North America. Like the steppe-oriented expeditions, Russian voyages in the "Northern Ocean" led to detailed "scientific" descriptions of territories and their contents, but their principal objectives were economic (they were pursuing the valuable pelts of the sea otter) and expressly political (they were also aiming to "extend the borders of the Russian empire" [*razshireniia vserossiiskoi imperii granits obyskivat'*]).[82] With these goals lighting their way, Russian explorers looked for otters throughout the Bering Sea and up and down the Alaskan coast, all the while bringing new peoples "under the scepter of the Russian monarch," uncovering "heretofore unknown lands," and planting Russian standards and plaques of ownership inscribed with the notice "This Land Belongs to Russia" (*Zemlia Rossiiskogo Vladeniia*) on virtually every attractive cove they came across.[83] Not surprisingly, these activities generated enormous excitement among patriotic observers, who rarely failed to compare Russia's exploits to the great discoveries of other European powers and who drew a direct link between territorial discovery and national achievement.[84] This linkage was underscored in pictorial terms by maps of the north that displayed Russia's new possessions and the routes taken by Russian explorers; and by maps of the empire as a whole, which often included textual commentaries on Russian discoveries on the northern coastlines.[85] Maps of the new territories further affirmed the power of Russian discovery by routinely representing the North American interior as a huge blank space that seemed to call out for future exploration and expansion.[86]

The excitement that surrounded the Russian advance in new regions like North America and the steppe went hand in hand with a last point of note about the high territoriality of the late eighteenth century: the intense interest at the time in defining and describing the state's borders. Even more than their Petrine predecessors, the ruling and cultural elites of the Catherinian era were preoccupied with borders, which was understandable since the last decades of the 1700s marked a new high point in terms of the century's imperial expansion, most dramatically to the south and west. As a result of wars and annexations, Russia's borders with Poland, the Ottoman Empire, and the Crimean Khanate changed a total of six times between 1772 and 1795, redefined in almost every case by peace treaties and international conventions providing detailed "descriptions" of the run of the new borders, which were followed by other inventory-like "descriptions" (*kameral'nye opisaniia*) of the empire's new acquisitions.[87] The importance attached to knowing about borders prompted the publication of additional materials, such as pocket-sized "geographical descriptions" and maps of Russian campaigns against the Turks, designed to provide readers with "a convenient way" of following the "glorious progress of Russian arms"; maps of border regions, like Poland-Ukraine or the New Russian steppe, replete with lines that indicated the past and present limits of the Russian state; and a general map of the empire printed by the Academy of Sciences in 1783 that depicted the empire in its then current boundaries, surrounded by a text describing all the border changes that had occurred since the reign of Peter the Great (the border changes were conveniently highlighted in different colors on the map).[88] The message implied by these historical-geographical materials was simple yet profound in its nationalistic implications: the Russian state was defined by its borders, and these borders had expanded.

Conclusion

I have argued that a profound transformation occurred in the way that the Russian state and the Russian elite understood and acted on territory in the eighteenth century, and that this transformation can be broken down into two rough stages: First, a period of transition to a new territorial order during the Petrine and early post-Petrine eras; and second, a period of high territoriality during the late 1700s when the assumptions and practices of this new order were further enhanced and assimilated. The end result, by the time this second phase concluded, was the consolidation of a highly territorial state presided over by a highly space-conscious elite, whose ways of seeing and ambitions for shaping territory were distinctly different from those that had prevailed a century earlier and whose territorial values set the terms for a modern Russian territoriality.

While this transformation in territoriality led to a range of consequences, its impact was arguably most profound in terms of how it influenced the shape of Russian governance and Russian national consciousness. The rulers of late seventeenth-century Muscovy inventoried and managed their territorial resources for fiscal and military purposes, but they did not have a ruling ideology that predisposed them to view territory —knowing it and acting on it—as an inherent goal of government. Beginning with the European-inspired reforms of the Petrine period, this situation changed dramatically. The Russian ruling establishment now acquired a more essentially spatial view of government and gradually developed a diverse range of tools and practices that allowed it to deepen its conceptual and physical grip on the territory of the state. Of course, at the same time that Russian political and cultural elites were trying to categorize, delimit, and govern territory, they were also engaged in trying to define the nation, and this, in turn, led to a situation in which Russian territorial consciousness and Russian national consciousness became deeply intertwined. Thus eighteenth-century values stressed the size and expansion of Russia's territory as national achievements and the acquisition and display of Russian territorial knowledge as acts of patriotism. And through all of this, despite the fact that the Russian state came to be typed as a European-style empire consisting of a national core ("Russia proper") and a colonial periphery, members of the Russian establishment—like good imperialists—tended to identify all of the empire as Russian space. They developed this identification not just because the space was ruled by Russians, but also because they saw its vast extent as the natural outgrowth of historically Russian territory and the Russians themselves as the only people who seemed to live all over it.

In terms of Russian political culture, the long-term consequences of these territory-related developments were profound, leading to the deepening in Russia of what Michael Biggs has called the "territorialization of rule"—the process by which political authority becomes "symbolically fused" with geographical area.[89] As Richard Wortman has noted, monarchical image-makers in the 1700s increasingly stressed a representation of the Russian tsar as "ruler of empire" and tied the legitimacy of the autocrat to the claim of imperial territorial sovereignty.[90] But court display and ritual were only one expression of a more comprehensive politico-cultural logic that cemented this link between autocratic power and territory. The tenets of this logic worked roughly as follows: The Russian autocrat (beginning with Peter) was styled as the "first servant of the state"; the Russian state was styled as an empire; the empire was increasingly defined and conceived of in territorial terms; and the art of governing it was increasingly understood as a science of territorial management. The effect of these interlocking postulates was to give the principle of imperial territorial power *through* autocracy a new resonance in the modern period. Right up to the end of the tsarist regime, Russian autocrats continued to make much of the fact that they ruled over both a diverse universe of subjects and a huge swath of territory; and because of the particular quality of the new territorial sensibilities of the eighteenth century, the possession—naming, mapping, tabulating, exploiting, expansion, and physical transformation—of this territory became an element as central to the practical definition of empire and autocracy as anything else.

In terms of understandings of Russian nationality, the long-range consequences of the new territoriality were just as important but ultimately more complicated. The eighteenth-century elite's preoccupation with defining the Russian nation produced a related impulse to define both the national territory and the territory of the empire. Eighteenth-century scholars did indeed draw some distinctions between national and imperial space—one can see this, for example, in the new role that Tatishchev proposed for the Urals, or in the new semantic juxtaposition of *Rus'/Rossiia* and *russkii/rossiiskii*—but, at the same time, these very scholars also had a variety of reasons for conflating the two spaces. The result was that Russian ideas of national and imperial territory tended to merge, and this conceptual overlapping, in turn, became one of the abiding elements of Russian national consciousness. Eighteenth-century territorial investigators, in effect, dissolved the nation into the empire and the empire into the nation, with the result that—territorially speaking—one could not really have one without the other. By the mid-nineteenth century, in a world defined by a different kind of Russian nationalism, some Russian scholars and statesmen began to argue that it was unfortunate that Russia's national territory had such a "symbiotic relationship" with the empire; but in the eighteenth century, when this "symbiotic relationship" was first conceptually assembled, it seemed altogether more natural than unfortunate, and no one saw it as much of a problem.[91]

Notes

1. A. V. Efimov and N. S. Orlova, eds., *Otkrytiia russkikh zemleprokhodtsev i poliarnykh morekhodov XVII veka na severo-vostoke Azii: sbornik dokumentov* (Moscow, 1951), 238–239.

2. Quoted from "The Letter of Columbus (1493)," in Peter Hulme and Neil L. Whitehead, eds., *Wild Majesty: Encounters with Caribs from Columbus to the Present Day* (Oxford, 1992), 10.

3. For examples of attention to territory during the Russian northern expeditions, see A. I. Andreev, ed., *Russkie otkrytiia v Tikhom okeane i severnoi Amerike v XVIII–XIX vekakh* (Moscow and Leningrad, 1944), 90, 102, 115–117; A. Pokrovskii, ed., *Ekspeditsiia Beringa: sbornik dokumentov* (Moscow and Leningrad, 1941), 151–173; and Anatole Senkevitch, Jr., "The Early Architecture and Settlements of Russian America," in S. Frederick Starr, ed., *Russia's America Colony* (Durham, N.C., 1987), 166–167.

4. These terms are drawn from James Cracraft, *The Petrine Revolution in Russian Imagery* (Chicago, 1997), xxiii, 272–278.

5. For descriptions of the general territorial limits of the Muscovite state in this period, see M. A. Chepelkin and N. A. D'iakova, *Istoricheskii ocherk formirovaniia gosudarstvennykh granits rossiiskoi imperii (2-aia polovina XVII–nachalo XX v.)* (Moscow, 1992).

6. Pavel Miliukov, *Gosudarstvennoe khoziaistvo Rossii v pervoi chetverti XVIII stoletiia i reforma Petra Velikogo* (St. Petersburg, 1905), 221–222, 227–228, 251; V. S. Kusov, *Chertezhi zemli russkoi XVI–XVII vv.* (Moscow, 1993), 28; Michael Rywkin,

"Russian Central Colonial Administration: From the Prikaz of Kazan to the XIX Century; A Survey," in idem, ed., *Russian Colonial Expansion to 1917* (New York, 1988), 8–22; Andreas Kappeler, "Das Moskauer Reich des 17. Jahrhunderts und seine nicht-russischen Untertanen," *Forschungen zur Osteuropäischen Geschichte*, 50 (1995): 195; E. V. Anisimov, *Gosudarstvennye preobrazovaniia i samoderzhavie Petra Velikogo v pervoi chetverti XVIII veka* (St. Petersburg, 1997), 52–53.

7. For a few descriptions of the various Muscovite materials that included territory-related information, see D. M. Lebedev and V. A. Esakov, *Russkie geograficheskie otkrytiia i issledovaniia s drevnikh vremen do 1917 goda* (Moscow, 1971), 102; B. A. Rybakov, "Geograficheskie znacheniia," *Ocherki russkoi kul'tury XVI v.* (Moscow, 1977), 209–227; V. S. Kusov, *Kartograficheskoe isskustvo russkogo gosudarstva* (Moscow, 1989); Kusov, *Chertezhi zemli russkoi XVI–XVII vv.*, 1–54; A. V. Postnikov, *Razvitie krupnomashtabnoi kartografii v Rossii*, 10–33. For a seventeenth-century textual sketch of the course of rivers, frontier lines, roads, and miscellaneous politico-economic objects (forts, mines, etc.) within the Muscovite state, see K. N. Serbina, ed., *Kniga bol'shomu chertezhu* (Moscow and Leningrad, 1950).

8. L. A. Gol'denberg, "Semen Ul'ianovich Remezov, 1642–posle 1720," in V. A. Esakov, ed., *Tvortsy otechestvennoi nauki: geografy* (Moscow, 1996), 5–20; Leo Bagrow, *A History of Russian Cartography up to 1800* (Cambridge, Mass., 1966), 38–44. For accessible reproductions of Remezov's maps, see Leo Bagrow, ed. and comp., *The Atlas of Siberia by Semyon U. Remezov* (Gravenhage, 1958); and A. V. Postnikov, *Karty zemel' rossiiskikh: ocherk istorii geograficheskogo izucheniia i kartogravirovaniia nashego otechestva* (Moscow, 1996).

9. Iu. F. Krizhanich, *Politika* (Moscow, 1965). For the mercantilist views of Golitsyn and other members of Muscovy's ruling elite, see Mark Bassin, "Expansion and Colonialism on the Eastern Frontier: Views of Siberia and the Far East in Pre-Petrine Russia," *Journal of Historical Geography* 14, no. 1 (1988): 3–21.

10. One suggestive reflection of territory's relative lack of prominence in Muscovite political thought can be found in Grigorii Kotoshikhin's famous overview of the Russian state in the seventeenth century. Kotoshikhin's manual includes only one brief chapter describing the "kingdoms, states, lands, and towns that are under the possession of Muscovy," but this chapter does not provide a territorial description of the realm so much as information on provincial officials (*voevody*), the proper way for these officials to address the tsar, and some description of frontier towns. See Grigorii Kotoshikhin, *O Rossii v tsarstvovanie Alekseia Mikhailovicha*, 4th ed. (Moscow, 1906), 124–129.

11. As of the late seventeenth century, the terms *Rossiiskoe tsarstvo, Rossiiskoe gosudarstvo*, or *Velikorossiiskoe tsarstvo* began to be used increasingly as the title of the Russian state and were either used interchangeably with or simply replaced the older term *Moskovskoe tsarstvo/gosudarstvo*. While both old and new terms were used to represent the state in seventeenth-century diplomacy, the title *Rossiiskoe gosudarstvo* appears to have had a more comprehensive territorial-imperial meaning than *Moskovskoe gosudarstvo*, since *Rossiiskoe gosudarstvo* referred to "the three khanates of Kazan, Astrakhan, and Siberia . . . and Great, Little, and White Russias," while *Moskovskoe gosudarstvo* (at least in some uses) seemed to refer only to Great Russia (*Velikaia Rossiia*). On the uses and meanings of these terms, see Joel Raba, "Von *Russkaja Zemlja* zu

Rossiiskoje gosudarstvo: Wandlungen des Begriffs in der altrussischen Reiseliteratur," in Uwe Halbach et al., eds., *Geschichte Altrusslands in der Begriffswelt ihrer Quellen: Festschrift zum 70. Geburtstag von Günther Stökl* (Stuttgart, 1986), 111–112; and Kappeler, "Das Moskauer Reich des 17. Jahrhunderts und seine nichtrussischen Untertanen," 195. See also Kotoshikhin, *O Rossii v tsarstvovanie Alekseia Mikhailovicha,* 126, and Iurii Krizhanich's *Povestvovanie o Sibiri: latinskaia rukopis' XVII stoletiia* (St. Petersburg, 1822), 1, where the term *Moskovskoe gosudarstvo* is clearly used to refer to Great Russia and not to the entire Muscovite realm.

12. For example, a Muscovite-Swedish treaty of 1649 included a detailed 23-page textual description of the border between the two states; by comparison, the Treaty of Nerchinsk, signed between Muscovy and China in 1689, described the Russo-Chinese border in only the sketchiest terms and left a full drawing of its contours until a future date. The steppe frontier, in contrast to both of the above, was not codified as an international border at all. See Kusov, *Kartograficheskoe iskusstvo russkogo gosudarstva,* 73; *Sbornik dogovorov Rossii s Kitaem 1689–1881 gg.* (St. Petersburg, 1889), 1–6; and Michael Khodarkovsky, "From Frontier to Empire: The Concept of the Frontier in Russia, Sixteenth-Eighteenth Centuries," *Russian History/Histoire Russe* 19, no. 1/4 (1992): 115–116.

13. The quoted phrase is borrowed from Chandra Mukerji, *Territorial Ambitions and the Gardens of Versailles* (New York, 1997), 3.

14. For definitions of the Petrine state as Peter and his followers understood it, see Lindsey Hughes, *Russia in the Age of Peter the Great* (New Haven, Conn.,1998), 378–389. For discussions of cameralism and the "well-regulated state" more generally, see Marc Raeff, *The Well-Ordered Police State: Social and Institutional Change through Law in the Germanies and Russia 1600–1800* (New Haven, Conn., 1983).

15. V. Ger'e, ed., *Sbornik pisem i memorialov Leibnitsa otnosiashchikhsia k Rossii i Petru Velikomu* (St. Petersburg, 1873), 219.

16. For territorial changes under Peter, see Chepelkin and D'iakova, *Istoricheskii ocherk formirovaniia gosudarstvennykh granits rossiiskoi imperii,* 12–13, 31–32, 40–41.

17. The petition submitted by Peter's senators proposing these name changes and linking them to the Russian victory over the Swedes appears in N. A. Voskresenskii, *Zakonodatel'nye akty Petra I: redaktsii i proekty zakonov, zametki, doklady, donosheniia, chelobit'ia i inostrannye istochniki* (Moscow and Leningrad, 1945), 155.

18. Liah Greenfeld, *Nationalism: Five Roads to Modernity* (Cambridge, Mass., 1992), 195. For a contrasting assessment of the implication of these new names, see Isabel de Madariaga, "Tsar into Emperor: The Title of Peter the Great," in Robert Oresko, ed., *Royal and Republican Sovereignty in Early Modern Europe* (New York, 1997), 351–381.

19. I. M. Pososhkov, *Kniga o skudosti i bogatstve* (1724; Moscow, 1937), 226, 260.

20. V. N. Tatishchev, *Leksikon rossiiskii, istoricheskii, geograficheskii, politicheskii i grazhdanskii* (composed pre-1745; published: St. Petersburg, 1793), 38–40. See also V. N. Tatishchev, "Razgovor dvukh priiatelei o pol'ze nauki i uchilishchakh," in his *Sobranie sochinenii,* vol. 8 (Moscow, 1996), 91–92; and the definition of "geographer" provided by Guillaume de L'Isle for the Russian Academy of Sciences in 1727 in V. F. Gnucheva, ed., *Geograficheskii departament Akademii Nauk xviii veka* (Moscow and Leningrad, 1946), 121.

21. Hughes, *Russia in the Age of Peter the Great,* 311–312, 367; Belov, "Rol' Petra I v

rasprostranenii geograficheskikh znanii v Rossii," 4–5; Denis J. B. Shaw, "Geographical Practice and Its Significance in Peter the Great's Russia," *Journal of Historical Geography* 22, no. 2 (1996): 168.

22. For a discussion of the importance of the semantic shift from *chertezh* to *karta*, see Cracraft, *The Petrine Revolution in Russian Imagery,* 273–275.

23. For early decrees related to the survey, see *Polnoe sobranie zakonov rossiiskoi imperii,* series 1, vol. 6, no. 3682 (1720): 266; vol. 6, no. 3695 (1720): 277; vol. 8, no. 5320 (1728): 70–72. On the "General Regulation" specifications of 1720, see Voskresenskii, *Zakonodatel'nye akty Petra I,* 506–507. For a general overview of these and other map-related developments, see also L. A. Goldenberg and A. V. Postnikov, "Development of Mapping Methods in Russia in the Eighteenth Century," *Imago Mundi,* 37 (1985): 63–80.

24. The two full titles of the atlases are *Atlas vserossiiskii imperii v kotorom vse eia tsarstva, gubernii, provintsii, uezdy i granitsy skol'ko vozmogli rossiiskiia geodezisty opisat' onyia i v landkarty polozhit' po dline i shirote tochno iz"iavliaiutsia i gorody, prigorody, monastyri, slobody, sela, derevni, zavody, mel'nitsy, reki, moria, ozera, znatnye gory, lesa, bolota, bol'shie dorogi i protchaia so vsiakim prelezhaniem izsledovannye rossiiskimi i latinskimi imenami podpisany imeiutsia trudom i tshchaniem Ivana Kirilova. Ves sei atlas razdelen budet v tri toma i budet soderzhat' v sebe vsekh na vse 360 kart, ezheli vremia i sluchai vse onyia sobrat' i grydorom napechatat' dopustit'. Dliny zachalo svoe priemliut ot pervogo meridiana chrez ostrova Dagdan i Ezel' provedennogo, konchaiutsia zhe v zemle Kamchatke, tak chto imperiia rossiiskaia bolee 130 gradusov prostiraetsia kotorykh ves zemnyi globus 360 v sebe soderzhit* (St. Petersburg, 1734); and *Atlas rossiiskoi, sostoiashchei iz deviatnadtsati spetsial'nykh kart predstavliaiushchikh rossiiskuiu imperiiu s pogrannychnymi zemliami, sochinennoi po pravilam geograficheskim i noveishim observatsiiam s prilozhennoiu pri tom general'noiu kartoiu velikoi seia imperii, staraniem i trudami Imperatorskoiu Akademii Nauk* (St. Petersburg, 1745).

25. See the discussions in John Brian Hartley, "Power and Legitimation in the English Geographical Atlases of the Eighteenth Century," and Mark Monmonier, "The Rise of the National Atlas," in John A. Wolter and Ronald E. Grim, eds., *Images of the World: The Atlas Through History* (Washington, D.C., 1997), 161–204 and 369–400 respectively.

26. Karl Svenske, ed., *Materialy dlia istorii sostavleniia atlasa rossiiskoi imperii izdannogo imperatorskoiu Akademieiu Nauk v 1745 godu* (St. Petersburg, 1845), 23. For a full-color reproduction of Kirilov's general map, see Postnikov, *Russia in Maps,* fig. 20, pp. 44–45. For a lower-quality reproduction of the general map and the atlas as a whole, see *Atlas vserossiiskoi imperii* (Leningrad, 1959).

27. *Atlas rossiiskoi,* 6.

28. Jacques Revel, "Knowledge of the Territory," *Science in Context* 4 (1991): 148. On the centrality of modern cartography to the definition of territorial space in post-Renaissance France and England, see Michael Biggs, "Putting the State on the Map: Cartography, Territory, and European State Formation," *Comparative Studies in Society and History* 4, no. 2 (1999): 374–405.

29. V. N. Tatishchev, *Izbrannye trudy po geografii Rossii* (Moscow, 1950), 99.

30. For an overview of these activities, see M. V. Ptukha, *Ocherki po istorii statistiki v SSSR,* vol. 1 (Moscow, 1955): 296–308; Shaw, "Geographical Practice and Its Signifi-

cance in Peter the Great's Russia," 166. For the questions and instructions, see V. N. Tatishchev, "Predlozhenie o sochinenii istorii i geografii rossiiskoi," in N. Popov, *V. N. Tatishchev i ego vremia* (Moscow, 1861), 663–696; and G. F. Müller, "Instruktion G. F. Müller's für den Akademiker-Adjuncten J. E. Fischer. Unterricht, was bey Beschreibung der Völker, absonderlich der Sibirischen in acht zu nehmen," *Sbornik Muzeia po antropologii i etnografii,* 1 (1900): 37–99.

31. See, for example, Tatishchev's own comments in 1749 about geographical materials prepared by the historian-geographer Petr Rychkov in P. Pekarskii, ed., *Zhizn' i literatura perepiski Petra Ivanovicha Rychkova* (St. Petersburg, 1867), 161–166.

32. See the remarks of Tatishchev, Kirilov, Joseph de L'Isle and other contemporary scholars in Svenske, ed., *Materialy dlia istorii sostavleniia atlasa rossiiskoi imperii izdannogo imperatorskoiu Akademeiu Nauk v 1745 godu,* 113–14, 144, 151–52, 181, 185; and Rossiiskii gosudarstvennyi arkhiv drevnikh aktov (hereafter RGADA), f.248, kn.772, ll.341(b)-342.

33. For overviews of Russian expeditions up to the 1750s, see V. F. Gnucheva, *Materialy dlia istorii ekspeditsii akademii nauk v XVIII i XIX vekakh* (Moscow and Leningrad, 1940), 23–86; Shaw, "Geographical Practice and Its Significance in Peter the Great's Russia"; Aleksandrovskaia, *Stanovlenie geograficheskoi nauki v Rossii v XVIII veke,* 40–42.

34. Tatishchev, "Leksikon rossiiskoi, istoricheskoi, geograficheskoi, politicheskoi i grazhdanskoi," in his *Sobranie sochinenii,* vol. 8, 273.

35. The two Kamchatka expeditions under Vitus Bering provide the clearest evidence of this evolution. Peter's instructions in 1724 for what became the first Kamchatka expedition were extremely brief. By contrast, in 1733, when Bering was dispatched a second time, his instructions had grown into a long, detailed document. See Pokrovskii, ed., *Ekspeditsiia Beringa,* 59, 151–173 *passim.* For other lengthy instructions from the 1730s, see RGADA, f.248, kn.750, ll.37–46 (the Orenburg expedition); and Andreev, ed., *Russkie otkrytiia v Tikhom okeane i severnoi Amerike v XVIII veke,* 97–101 (excerpt from the expedition to Japan and the Kurile Islands commanded by M. P. Shpanberg).

36. Revel, "Knowledge of the Territory," 139. See also Hans Erich Bödeker, "Reisebeschreibungen im historischen Diskurs der Aufklärung," in idem et al., eds., *Aufklärung und Geschichte: Studien zur deutschen Geschichtswissenschaft im 18. Jahrhundert* (Göttingen, 1986), 281–283; and David N. Livingstone, *The Geographical Tradition: Episodes in the History of a Contested Enterprise* (Cambridge, Mass., 1992), 126–130. On the rise of eighteenth-century scientific travel in the Russian context, see Yuri Slezkine, "Naturalists versus Nations: Eighteenth-Century Russian Scholars Confront Ethnic Diversity," *Representations,* no. 47 (1994): 170–195.

37. Stepan Krashenennikov, *Opisanie zemli Kamchatki,* vol. 1 (St. Petersburg, 1755), foreword (no page number indicated). Krashenennikov's description was based on observations completed between 1737 and 1741; the work was only published after his death. Müller is not indicated as the author of the foreword, but his authorship is known from other sources.

38. Gnucheva, ed., *Geograficheskii departament akademii nauk XVIII veka,* 129. Tatishchev also noted the need to link maps and descriptions in his commentaries on geography. See his *Izbrannye trudy po geografii Rossii,* 214.

39. Tatishchev, *Izbrannye trudy po geografii Rossii*, 98, 212; Svenske, ed., *Materialy dlia istorii sostavleniia atlasa rossiiskoi imperii izdannogo imperatorskoiu Akademeiu Nauk v 1745 godu*, 23.

40. Tatishchev particularly stressed this point, though recognition of the importance of geographical education for the elite is also clear from Peter's introduction of geography as a subject matter in newly founded schools, official sponsorship for the translation of foreign geographical textbooks, and then the compilation of the first bona fide Russian geographical schoolbook in 1742. See Tatishchev, *Izbrannye trudy po geografii Rossii*, 77–78, 98 (on the "utility" and "necessity" of the Russian nobility acquiring sound geographical knowledge); L. Vesin, comp., *Istoricheskii obzor uchebnikov obshchei i russkoi geografii izdannykh so vremen Petra Velikogo po 1876 god (1710–1876 g.)* (St. Petersburg, 1877), 23–25 (on the first Russian textbook); and Shaw, "Geographical Practice and Its Significance in Peter the Great's Russia," 165–166 (on geographic instruction and publishing).

41. Slezkine, "Naturalists versus Nations," 174.

42. Attention to historical borders and the ancient lands of the Russian state was pronounced in the works of Tatishchev and later Müller, Mikhail Lomonosov, and other scholars of the first half of the 1700s whose studies touched on the inflammatory question of Russia's ethnic origins and the beginnings of Russian statehood. On these scholars and their historical works, see Hans Rogger, *National Consciousness in Eighteenth-Century Russia* (Cambridge, Mass., 1960), 194–218. In addition to the well-recognized need to describe historical borders, scholars also advised compiling historical maps. Kirilov planned to add such maps to his Russian atlas but died before the work was done. Joseph-Nicolas de L'Isle, in the employ of the Russian Academy of Sciences, also proposed historical maps of the state's borders in 1728, noting that "maps are quite useful for the study of a country's history." See Gnucheva, ed., *Geograficheskii departament Akademii Nauk XVIII veka*, 128.

43. For the threads of this logic, see the remarks in Tatishchev, *Izbrannye trudy po geografii Rossii*, 108–112, 146–147, 171. The quoted excerpt appears on page 171.

44. Tatishchev, *Izbrannye trudy po geografii Rossii*, 173, 171.

45. Mark Bassin, "Russia between Europe and Asia: The Ideological Construction of Geographical Space," *Slavic Review* 50, no. 1 (1991): 6–8.

46. Tatishchev, *Izbrannye trudy po geografii Rossii*, 112, 114–115, 129; and Bassin, "Russia Between Europe and Asia," 5. The notion that European Russia represented something akin to a metropole while Asian Russia represented a colony is also hinted at by Russian maps of the early 1700s (like the general maps in the Kirilov and Academy atlases) in which the European side of the state is covered with place names and other markers of cartographic knowledge and the Asian side (by comparison) appears much emptier and open for inscription. A full citation for these atlases is provided in note 33. For a discussion of the eighteenth-century European gloss on the importance of mountain chains (such as the Urals) as "natural frontiers," see Peter Sahlins, "Natural Frontiers Revisited: France's Boundaries since the Seventeenth Century," *American Historical Review* 95, no. 5 (1990): 1423–1451.

47. Tatishchev, *Izbrannye trudy po geografii Rossii*, 147; and Philipp Johann von Strahlenberg, *Zapiski kapitana Filippa Ioganna Stralenberga ob istorii i geografii Ros-*

siiskoi imperii Petra Velikogo: severnaia i vostochnaia chast' Evropy i Azii vol. 1 (Moscow, 1985), 37–38.

48. For the background and details of these early eighteenth-century reforms, see Miliukov, *Gosudarstvennoe khoziaistvo Rossii,* 255–382; Hughes, *Russia in the Age of Peter the Great,* 115–116; John P. LeDonne, *Absolutism and Ruling Class: The Formation of the Russian Political Order, 1700–1825* (New York, 1991), 70–93.

49. For the confusing consequences of the Petrine and 1727 territorial reforms, which were only fully resolved with the provincial reforms of the 1770s, see John P. LeDonne, "The Territorial Reform of the Russian Empire, 1775–1796; Part I: Central Russia, 1775–1784," *Cahiers du monde russe et soviétique* 23, no. 2 (1982): 148.

50. See the provisions of the treaties of Bura and Kiakhta in 1727 reprinted in *Sbornik dogovorov Rossii s Kitaem 1689–1881 gg.,* 11–14, 30–32, 50–60.

51. For references to various well-known state attempts to use territory in the early-to-mid 1700s, see Miliukov, *Gosudarstvennoe khoziaistvo Rossii v pervoi chetverty xviii stoletiia i reforma Petra Velikogo;* and Hughes, *Russia in the Age of Peter the Great.*

52. Titles to a selection of these materials appear in the footnotes below. The quote from the map-reading primer appears in I. N. (Nekhachin), *Sposob nauchit'sia samim soboiu geografiiu* (Moscow, 1798), 39.

53. These views were expressed in a variety of both official and unofficial publications and pronouncements, ranging from Catherine's definition of Russia as a "European state" (*evropeiskaia derzhava*) in her *Nakaz* (1767) to reiterations of Russia's Europeanness in imperial textbooks and references to the state-wide habitat of the Russians in manuals on the empire and its peoples. For a few such references, see N. D. Chechulin, ed., *Nakaz imperatritsy Ekateriny II, dannyi komissii o sochinenii proekta novogo ulozheniia* (St. Petersburg, 1907), 2–3; F. G. Diltei, *Opyt rossiiskoi geografii s tolkovaniem gerbov i rodosloviem tsarstvuiushchego doma, sobrannyi iz raznykh avtorov i manuskriptov* (Moscow, 1771), 6, 8, 26; Mikhailo Chul'kov, *Istoricheskoe opisanie rossiiskoi kommertsii pri vsekh portakh i granitsakh ot drevnikh vremen do nyne nastoiashchego i vsekh preimushchestvennykh uzakonenii po onoi gosudaria Petra Velikogo i nyne blagopoluchno tsarstvuiushchei gosudaryni imperatritsy Ekateriny Velikoi,* vol.1 (St. Petersburg, 1781), 1; *Kratkoe rukovodstvo k obozreniiu rossiiskoi imperii sochineno v pol'zu iunoshestva* (Moscow, 1788), 4; *Noveishee povestvovatel'noe zemleopisanie vsekh chetyrekh chastei sveta, s prisovokupleniem samogo drevnego izucheniia o sfere, tak zhe i nachal'nogo dlia maloletnykh detei ucheniia o zemleopisanii* (St. Petersburg, 1795), 3, 5; and I. G. Georgi, *Opisanie vsekh obitaiushchikh v rossiskom gosudarstve narodov,* vol. 4 (2nd ed.; St. Petersburg, 1799), 83.

54. For a few references to the immense size of the Russian state, see Catherine's charter to the nobility reprinted in *Polnoe sobranie zakonov* (hereafter *PSZ*), ser. 1, vol. 22, no. 16187 (1785), 344; and her *Nakaz* in Chechulin (ed.), *Nakaz imperatritsy Ekateriny II,* 2–3; Diltei, *Opyt rossiiskoi geografii,* 34; Kn. Chebotarev, *Geograficheskoe metodicheskoe opisanie Rossiiskoi imperii s nadlezhashchim vvedeniem k osnovatel'nomu poznaniiu zemnogo shara i Evropy voobshche, dlia nastavleniia obuchaiushchego pri Moskovskom universitete iunoshestva* (Moscow, 1776), 91; Chul'kov, *Istoricheskoe opisanie rossiiskoi kommertsii pri vsekh portakh i granitsakh,* 2; *Prostrannoe zemleopisanie rossiiskogo gosudarstva izdannoe v pol'zu uchashchikhsia* (St. Petersburg, 1787), 3; Irinarkh

Zavalishin, *Sokrashchennoe zemleopisanie rossiiskogo gosudarstva sochinennoe v stikhakh dlia pol'zy iunoshestva* (St. Petersburg, 1792), 17 passim. Stress on the immensity of the state was also taken up by foreign observers, some of whom were contracted by the Russian Academy of Sciences. See, for example, Anton Friedrich Büsching, *Neue Beschreibung des russischen Reiches nach allen seinen Staaten und Ländern* (Hamburg, 1763), 602; A. L. Schlözer, *Von der Unschädlichkeit der Pocken in Russland und von der Russlands Bevölkerrung überhaupt* (Göttingen and Gotha, 1768), 117–118; and M. Krafft, "Sur la surface géometrique de la Russie selon la nouvelle carte de cet empire publiée par l'académie (presenté le 21 septembre 1786)," *Nova acta academiae scientiarum imperialis petropolitanae*, vol. 1 (1787): 399 passim.

55. As S. I. Pleshcheev noted in his description of the empire in 1793, "Russia occupies over a seventh of the world's terrestrial surface, or one twenty-sixth of the total surface of the globe . . . and from this it is clear that it has no rival among states, either in the present or in ancient times." S. I. Pleshcheev, *Obozrenie rossiiskoi imperii v nyneshnem eia novoustroennom sostoianii s pokazaniem novoprisoedinennykh k Rossii ot Porty Ottomanskoi i ot Rechi Pospolitoi Pol'skoi oblastei* (St. Petersburg, 1793), 1–3.

56. Some topographical descriptions were published at the time or subsequently, but others were produced only in manuscript form. For some of the published materials, see Larionov, *Opisanie Kurskogo namestnichestva* (Moscow, 1786); *Istoricheskoe i topograficheskoe opisanie gorodov Moskovskoi gubernii s ikh uezdami* (Moscow, 1787); *General'noe soobrazhenie po Tverskoi gubernii, izvlechennoe iz podrobnogo topograficheskogo i kameral'nogo po gorodam i uezdam opisaniia 1783–1784* (Tver', 1875); A. Hupel, *Topographische Nachrichten von Lief- und Ehstland* (Riga, 1774–1782) 3 vols.; Ivan Afanas'evich Pereverzev, *Topograficheskoe opisanie Khar'kovskogo namestnichestva s istoricheskim preduvedomleniem o byvshikh v sei strane s drevnikh vremen peremenakh* (Moscow, 1788); Afanasii Shafonskii, *Chernigovskogo namestnichestva topograficheskoe opisanie s kratkim geograficheskim i istoricheskim opisaniem Maloi Rossii iz chastei koi onoe namestnichestvo sostavleno, sochinennoe . . . v Chernigove, 1786 goda* (Kiev, 1851); Dimitrii Zinov'ev, *Topograficheskoe opisanie goroda Kazani i ego uezda* (Moscow, 1788); G. A. Riazhskii, ed., *Topograficheskoe opisanie Vladimirskoi gubernii sostavlennoe v 1784 godu* (Vladimir, 1906); "Kratkoe izvestie o Simbirskom namestnichestve," *Sobranie sochinenii vybrannykh iz mesiatsoslovov na raznye gody*, vol. 6 (St. Petersburg, 1790), 262–276; "Kratkoe opisanie Tobol'skogo namestnichestva," *Sobranie sochinenii vybrannykh iz mesiatsoslovov na raznye gody*, vol. 6 (St. Petersburg, 1790), 148–218; and Ivan Markovich, *Zapiski o Malorossii, eia zhiteliakh i proizvedeniiakh* (St. Petersburg, 1798). For a review of the topographical descriptions as a "genre of economic geography" and a history of how they were produced, see N. L. Rubinshtein, "Topograficheskie opisaniia namestnichestv i gubernii xviii v."

57. P. Rychkov, *Topografiia Orenburgskaia, to est' obstoiatel'noe opisanie Orenburgskoi gubernii* (St. Petersburg, 1762), vol. 2, 5, 7–8.

58. For provincial atlases composed as a result of the 1783 decree, see the holdings of the Military-Academic Archive (Voenno-Uchennyi Arkhiv, hereafter VUA) in the Rossiiskii Gosudarstvennyi Voenno-Istoricheskii Arkhiv (hereafter RGVIA). For example, RGVIA, f.VUA, n.18724 (Ekaterinoslav), n. 18336 (New Russia), n. 20256 (pocket atlas of Tobol'sk *namestnichestvo*).

59. On the social values of land ownership expressed in atlases, see the discussion in John Brian Harley, "Power and Legitimation in the English Geographical Atlases of the Eighteenth Century," in John Amadeus Wolter, *Images of the World: The Atlas through History* (Washington, D.C., 1997), 176–181.

60. See, for example, the reproduction of a map of Novgorod province published in Postnikov, *Karty zemel' rossiiskikh;* and *Atlas général et élementaire de l'empire de toutes les Russies divisé en quarante-deux gouvernements avec deux suppléments, et une province, la Tauride, ouvrage fait d'après les observations de l'académie de St. Petersbourg* (St. Petersburg, 1795).

61. This was the case, for example, with the Mining Institute atlas of 1792. See *Rossiiskii atlas iz soroka chetyrekh kart sostoiashchii i na sorok na dva namestnichestva imperiiu razdeliaiushchii* (n.p., 1792).

62. For decrees supporting the Academy and Corps of Cadets' questionnaires, see *PSZ*, series.1, vol. 15, no. 11029 (1760): 420–421 and vol. 15, no. 11165 (1760): 582. On the Free Economic Society questionnaire, see "Ekonomicheskie voprosy kasaiushchiesia do zemledeliia po raznosti provintsii," *Trudy vol'nogo ekonomicheskogo obshchestva,* 1765, vol. 1, 180–193.

63. For a reprint of the instructions provided to the expeditions beginning in 1768, see N. G. Fradkin, "Instruktsiia dlia akademicheskikh ekspeditsii 1768-1774 gg.," *Voprosy geografii,* vol. 17 (1950): 213–218.

64. Lloyd A. Brown, *The Story of Maps* (New York, 1977), 270.

65. See, for example, "Nastavlenie, dannoe grafu Petru Rumiantsevu, pri naznachenii ego malorossiiskim general-gubernatorom, so sobstvennoruchnymi pribavkami Ekateriny II (noiabria 1764 goda)," *Sbornik imperatorskogo russkogo istoricheskogo obshchestva,* 1871, vol. 7, 377.

66. The publishers and compilers of late eighteenth-century geographies and regional descriptions often directly requested their readers to send in information in order to correct mistakes and improve "the knowledge of the Fatherland." See, for example, the Müller's foreword in F. Polunin, *Geograficheskii leksikon rossiiskogo gosudarstva, ili slovar' opisaiushchii po azbuchnomu poriadku reki, ozera, moria, gory, goroda, kreposti, znatnye monastyri, ostrogi, iasychnye zimoviia, rudnye zavody i prochiia dostapamiatnye mesta obshirnoi rossiiskoi imperii* (Moscow, 1773) page numbers not indicated; and Diltei, *Opyt rossiiskoi geografii,* foreword, no page number.

67. The fullest study of the land survey initiated in 1765 is I. E. German, *Istoriia russkogo mezhevaniia* (Moscow, 1910). On the "economic notes" prepared to accompany maps generated by the survey, see L. V. Milov, *Issledovanie ob "ekonomicheskikh primechaniiakh" k general'nomu mezhevaniiu: k istorii russkogo krest'ianstva i sel'skogo khoziaistva vtoroi poloviny xviii v.* (Moscow, 1965). For the background to the survey and important immediate antecedents in the Elizabethan period, see I. E. German, *Istoriia mezhevogo zakonodatel'stva ot Ulozheniia do general'nogo mezhevaniia* (1649-1765) (Moscow, 1893).

68. LeDonne, "The Territorial Reform of the Russian Empire, 1775–1796; Part I," 147–185; and idem, "The Territorial Reform of the Russian Empire, 1775–1796; Part II: The Borderlands, 1777–1796," in ibid., 24, no. 4 (1983): 411–457.

69. The term "rhetoric of accuracy" is borrowed from Sven Widmalm, "Accuracy,

Rhetoric, and Technology: The Paris-Greenwich Triangulation, 1784–88," in Töre Frängsmyr (ed.), *The Quantifying Spirit in the Eighteenth Century* (Berkeley and Los Angeles, 1990), 195–198.

70. See James C. Scott, *Seeing Like a State: How Certain Schemes to Improve the Human Condition Have Failed* (New Haven, Conn., 1998), 11–52.

71. Michel Foucault, "Governmentality," in Graham Burchell et al. (eds.), *The Foucault Effect: Studies in Governmentality* (Chicago, 1991), 101.

72. Schlözer, *Von den Unschädlichkeit der Pocken in Russland und von Russlands Bevölkerrung überhaupt*, 115.

73. For questionnaires and instructions that express concern with determining the relationship between population and territory, see, for example, Fradkin, "Instruktsiia dlia akademicheskikh ekspeditsii 1768–1774 gg.," 216; and "Ekonomicheskie voprosy kasaiushchiesia do zemledeliia po raznosti provintsii," *Trudy Vol'nogo Ekonomicheskogo Obshchestva*, 1 (1765): 184.

74. For an example of statements on territorial-demographic imbalance and on the promise of colonization as a solution, see *PSZ*, ser. 1, vol. 22, no. 16559 (1787): 877; *PSZ*, ser. 1, v. 21, n. 15177 (1781): 186–187; and P. Rychkov, "O sposobakh k umnozheniiu zemledeliia v Orenburgskoi gubernii," *Trudy vol'nogo ekonomicheskogo obshchestva*, 7 (1767): 22.

75. *Slovar' akademicheskoi rossiiskoi*, vol. 5 (St. Petersburg, 1794), 730; and Chebotarev, *Geograficheskoe metodicheskoe opisanie rossiiskoi imperii*, 16.

76. Though Catherine and key court figures like Grigorii Potemkin were enthusiastic about colonizing the southern steppes, it is worth pointing out that other members of the Russian elite were much less impressed. See the remarks in Robert E. Jones, "Opposition to War and Expansion in Late Eighteenth Century Russia," *Jahrbücher für Geschichte Osteuropas* 32, no. 1 (1984): 41, 46–48.

77. On colonization plans for New Serbia and New Russia, see *PSZ*, ser. 1, vol. 13, no. 9919 (1751): 552–558; ser. 1, vol. 16, no. 11861 (1763): 297–299; ser. 1, vol. 16, no.12099 (1764): 657–667; and RGADA, f.13, op.1, d.66, ll.2–7.

78. For a few of the diverse materials that reflect these steppe-related visions, see RGADA, f.16, op.1, d.699, ch.2, ll.445; f.16, op.1, d.189, ll.142–143; *PSZ*, ser. 1, vol. 19, no. 14052 (1773): 847–849; ser. 1, vol. 22, no. 16194 (1785): 388–392; "Sobstvennoruchnye bumagi kn. Potemkina-Tavricheskogo," *Russkii arkhiv*, 3 (1865): 394–395; P. Sumarokov, *Puteshestvie po vsemu Krymu i Bessarabii v 1799 godu s istoricheskim i topograficheskim opisaniem vsekh tekh mest* (Moscow, 1800), 211–212. See also Catherine's elaborate plan to recreate the New Russian landscape in Moscow as part of the celebration of the Russian victory over the Ottomans in 1775: "Pis'ma Ekateriny Vtoroi k Baronu Grimmu," *Russkii arkhiv* 16, no. 9 (1878): 17.

79. Vasilii Zuev, *Puteshestvennye zapiski Vasiliia Zueva ot S. Peterburga do Khersona v 1781 i 1782 godu* (St. Petersburg, 1787) foreword, no page number.

80. For a few of the published works resulting from these expeditions, see: "Zapiski puteshestviia akademika Lepekhina," *Polnoe sobranie uchennykh puteshestvii po Rossii* vol. 3 (St. Petersburg, 1821); "Zapiski puteshestviia akademika Fal'ka," *Polnoe sobranie uchennykh puteshestvii po Rossii*, vol. 6 (St. Petersburg, 1824); "Dnevnik puteshestviia v iuzhnuiu Rossiiu akademika Sankt-Peterburgskoi akademii nauk Gil'denshtedta v 1773–1774 g.," *Zapiski odesskogo obshchestva istorii i drevnostei*, vol. 11 (1879): 180–228;

P. S. Pallas, *Voyages de M. P.S. Pallas, en differentes provinces de l'empire de Russie et dans l'Asie septentrionale,* 5 vols. (Paris, 1788–1793); Samuil Georg Gmelin, *Puteshestvie po Rossii dlia issledovaniia trekh tsarstv estestva,* 2 vols (St. Petersburg, 1771–1777). The quoted phrase appears in Gmelin's preface to volume one, page number not indicated.

81. In this respect, the academic expeditions were similar in their impact to the operations of eighteenth-century European science in other colonial contexts. For comparative purposes, see Matthew H. Edney, *Mapping an Empire: The Geographical Construction of British India, 1765–1843* (Chicago, 1997) and John Gascoigne, *Science in the Service of Empire: Joseph Banks, the British State, and the Uses of Science in the Age of Revolution* (New York, 1998).

82. This quote is drawn from a petition sent to Catherine from the "Russian Columbus," Grigorii Shelikhov in 1785. See Andreev, ed., *Russkie otkrytiia v Tikhom okeane i severnoi Amerike v XVIII–XIX vekakh,* 42. For one example of such a "scientific" territorial description, see a description of the Aleutian islands composed in the 1760s and broken down into points (*punkty*) addressing the islands' locations, environments, inhabitants, and resources: RGADA, f.24, op.1, d.34.

83. For references to these activities, see Andreev, ed., *Russkie otkrytiia v Tikhom okeane i severnoi Amerike v XVIII–XIX vekakh,* 25, 30, 85–86, 90, 102, passim.

84. For a few writings of this sort, see M. V. Lomonosov, "Kratkoe opisanie raznykh puteshestvii po severnym moriam i pokazanie vozmozhnogo prikhodu Sibirskim okeanom v vostochnuiu Indiiu" (1763), in his *Polnoe sobranie sochinenii* vol. 6 (Moscow-Leningrad, 1952), 418–498; "Kratkoe izvestie o novoizobretennom severnom arkhipelage," *Sobranie sochinenii vybrannykh iz mesiatsoslovov na raznye gody,* vol. 3 (St. Petersburg, 1789), 335–362; P. Pallas, "O rossiiskikh otkrytiiakh na moriakh mezhdu Azeiu i Amerikoiu," *Sobranie sochinenii vybrannykh iz mesiatsoslovov na raznye gody,* vol. 4 (St. Petersburg, 1790), 263–392; and G. F. Miller, "Opisanie morskikh puteshestvii po Ledovitomu i po Vostochnomu moriu, s rossiiskoi storony uchinennykh," in his *Sochineniia po istorii Rossii: izbrannoe* (Moscow, 1996), 126.

85. For an example of these inscriptions highlighting Russian discoveries, see maps of the far northeastern coasts of Siberia in the *Rossiiskii atlas iz soroka chetyrekh kart sostoiashchii* (1792) (RGVIA, f.VUA, d.19862) and the *Novaia karta rossiiskoi imperii razdelennaia na namestnichestva, sochinennaia 1786 g.* in RGVIA, f.VUA, d.19855. For "new discoveries" in the "Northern Ocean," see maps in RGVIA, f.VUA, n.23756 (1781); and f.VUA, n.23784 (1802).

86. See, for example, the maps reproduced in Postnikov, *Karty zemel' rossiiskikh,* pp. 72–75. On the power and symbolism of such blank spaces on eighteenth-century British maps of North America, see Harley, "Power and Legitimation in the English Geographical Atlases of the Eighteenth Century," 191. See also G. N. G. Clarke, "Taking Possession: The Cartouche as Cultural Text in Eighteenth-Century American Maps," *Word and Image* 4, no. 2 (1988): 456.

87. For a discussion of the various treaties and conventions that established Russian borders in the west and south between the 1770s and the 1790s, see John P. LeDonne, *The Russian Empire and the World, 1700–1917: The Geopolitics of Expansion and Containment* (New York, 1997), 43–62, 104–115. For an example of the inventory-like "descriptions" of newly acquired lands, see "Topograficheskoe opisanie dostavshimsia po

mirnomu traktatu ot Ottomanskoi Porty vo vladenie rossiiskoi imperii zemliam 1774 goda," *Zapiski odesskogo obshchestva istorii i drevnostei,* 7 (1868): 166–198.

88. See "Kratkoe geograficheskoe opisanie kniazhestva Moldavskogo i lezhash-chikh mezhdu Chernym i Kaspiiskim moriami zemel' i narodov, s landkartoiu sikh zemel'," *Sobranie sochinenii vybrannykh iz mesiatsoslovov na raznye gody,* vol. 3 (St. Petersburg, 1789) 91–106 (first published in 1770); "Geograficheskie i istoricheskie izvestiia o novoi pogranichnoi linii Rossiiskoi imperii, provedennoi mezhdu rekami Terekom i Azovskim morem," *Mesiatsoslov istoricheskii i geograficheskii na 1779 god* (St. Petersburg, 1778), 127–177; "Pogranichnaia karta rossiiskoi imperii s Turtseiu, Prusseiu i Avstreiu" (1798) in RGVIA, f.VUA, n.19871; and "General'naia karta rossiiskoi imperii" (1783), reprinted in *Ekaterina Velikaia: russkaia kul'tura vtoroi poloviny XVIII veka; katalog vystavki* (St. Petersburg, 1993), 93.

89. Biggs, "Putting the State on the Map," 390–391.

90. Richard Wortman, "Ceremony and Empire in the Evolution of Russian Monarchy," in Catherine Evtukhov et al., eds., *Kazan, Moscow, St. Petersburg: Multiple Faces of the Russian Empire/Kazan', Moskva, Peterburg: rossiiskaia imperiia vzgliadom raznykh uglov* (Moscow, 1997), 29, 31–32.

91. On the question of disentangling national and imperial space in the mid-nineteenth century, see Mark Bassin, *Imperial Visions: Nationalist Imagination and Geographical Expansion in the Russian Far East, 1840–1865* (New York, 1999). The quoted phrase appears on page 15.

2 The "Great Circle" of Interior Russia: Representations of the Imperial Center in the Nineteenth and Early Twentieth Centuries

Leonid Gorizontov

For scholars interested in the regional structure and symbolic geography of the old tsarist empire, the question of what constituted the imperial core—the territory that represented the empire's center of gravity—is obviously of great significance.[1] One hundred to two hundred years ago Russians referred to this region as "interior Russia" (*vnutrenniaia Rossiia*), "native Russia" (*korennaia Rossiia*), or "central Russia" (*tsentral'naia Rossiia*). "Interior Russia" became entrenched in the vocabulary of the Russian public and the tsarist government in the nineteenth century, and it remains very much in use today in Russian historical writing, though with little attention to or concern with defining its exact meaning. In this literature, as a rule, the prevailing approach to defining the Russian interior (as well as the other regions of the empire) has been to rely solely on economic factors,[2] but this method has some obvious shortcomings. It is clear that regions amount to much more than aggregates of supposedly objective realities; they are rather the product of mentalities and perceptions. Of course, objective realities invariably influence how regions are perceived, but these realities can never be reduced to economic factors alone. Indeed, this fact was already quite obvious in the nineteenth century.

Definitions of the core area of the Russian empire have a long history and naturally tended to shift over time with the expansion of the state. The outlines of what would later be called "interior Russia" are already apparent in an official term of the Muscovite period, *Zamoskovnyi krai*, which was identified with the region surrounding Moscow and more specifically with the towns of the area.[3] One can also find references to the term "interior provinces" and to these provinces' various defining characteristics in Catherine the Great's correspondence with her consort and viceroy Grigorii Potemkin in the 1780s.[4] Yet it was in the nineteenth century, in particular the first half of the nineteenth century, that questions about "interior Russia" became especially important to the Russian public. Dramatic territorial growth in European Russia in the late 1700s, followed by still more expansion in the early 1800s, made the pressures of territorial aggrandizement more palpable than before, which in turn led to greater attention to the core area of the state.[5] Some Russians, like the Decembrist Pavel Pestel, for example, warned that governmental experimentation with federalist projects was dangerous because it could result in the empire's "diverse regions quickly slipping away from the Russian heartland" (*korennaia Rossiia*).[6]

The War of 1812 marked an important turning point in public and government attention to the interior. Nothing, it seems, is quite as effective at increasing one's awareness of one's own country as a war fought to defend it against outside invaders. Towns, natural barriers, roads all acquire a special, almost symbolic significance. News from the provinces often becomes more important than news from the capital. Legends of the past come alive. Is it any wonder that the Russians after 1812 filled their geography with symbolic content when their enemies did the same thing? "If I take Kiev," Napoleon famously remarked, "I will force Russia to her knees; if I take Petersburg, I will have her head; and taking Moscow, I will have her heart."[7] "Moscow," F. F. Vigel recalled, "had a strong influence on the interior provinces at that time . . . the entire state was affected by her example." S. D. Sheremet'ev concurred: "The Patriotic War expressed to the world the importance of Moscow."[8] Yet at the same time the lesson taught by Kutuzov was that Moscow was *not* in fact the same thing as Russia as a whole.

It is no accident that one of the most interesting images of the Russian center was produced by F. N. Glinka, the author of "Letters of a Russian Officer." In 1847, assuming the pedantic air of a geometry teacher, Glinka offered the following suggestions for delineating the scope of "interior Russia":

> On the basis of ancient maps (*chertezhi*) and taking Moscow as the center, trace six, even seven, nearly perfect circles around the city. Along each of these circles you will then find large suburbs, trading villages and then towns—some no longer in existence, others still to be seen

today—all arrayed at intervals of 30, 60, and 90 versts, and then at two, three, and four [units of] 90 versts beyond that. The [circles] located at the far outer edge were known in the past as the frontiers (*poslednie nazyvalis' ukrainami*).

Glinka drew this system of measurement from the traditional practices of Russian coachmen. The towns of Klin, Serpukhov, and Kolomna were located at the first of the "nineties." Tver and Tula, plus Kaluga, Vladimir, and Riazan, then fell at the second; Orel and Tambov at the fourth and fifth. As for Glinka's so-called "frontiers" (*ukrainy*), they were to be found along the whole extent of the state's former perimeter, not just in the south even though it was there that the term *ukraina* ultimately took root.

"This harmonious, family-like configuration (*stroinoe semeinnoe raspolozhenie*) of [the country's] major places and towns," Glinka continued, "inevitably invites comparison with the solar system. Moscow thus appears as the central sun, while the other towns appear like planets around it." Glinka greatly appreciated the position of the Muscovite capital, not only because of its general economic significance but also because of its crucial place within the country's road network, a fact that was again strikingly underscored by the experience of 1812.[9] Indeed, Glinka had expressed his view of Moscow's shining centrality in lines from an earlier poem:

> City of the center, city of the heart,
> City of native Russia! (*Korennoi Rossii grad!*)[10]

The sentiments and structure of this couplet also seem to offer a pointed echo to Pushkin's famous 1828 description of St. Petersburg as a "city of luxury, city of want" (*gorod pyshnyi, gorod bednyi*).

But Russia's heart was not just understood as the city of Moscow. Much like the concept of the center, it too was identified with a broader region. As Nicholas I wrote to his son Alexander in 1837 after learning that the latter had arrived in Tver on a trip from Petersburg, "Only now have you entered Russia's heart (*v serdtse Rossii*)." As Alexander reached Kostroma, Nicholas noted that the tsarevich "had learned something about a part of the Russian heart" and would now be able "to appreciate the true value of that blessed region."[11] Nicholas' highly emotional interpretation of the center appears to stem from the fact that it was precisely in the center—in the "heart"—that one found the root of the supposedly organic unity that bound the imperial family to the Russian people. Of course, what Nicholas' understanding of "Russia's heart" also underscored was that the imperial family—given its permanent residence in the capital of St. Petersburg—actually lived *outside* of the "heart," only visiting it periodically and usually for purely symbolic purposes. The image of the center as a metaphorical place, a place symbolic of the essence of the state, thus had an appeal that extended well beyond the world of a few Romantically inclined writers.

Glinka's interest in geometrical designs and popular ways of measuring distance was not unique. The writer S. V. Maksimov, a prolific ethnographer of the second half of the nineteenth century, had similar inclinations, and his investigation into the historico-geographical meanings of the word "ninety" produced a still more detailed description of Moscow's "solar system." As Maksimov saw it, Moscow lay "at the very center of Rus," its unique position determined through "mathematical precision." Moscow's centrality was thus "no accident" but rather entirely "understandable." To demonstrate his point, Maksimov first noted the different feel of distance in past times. In old Russia, he explained, a journey of one-sixth of a "ninety" (fifteen versts) was considered long enough that travelers were normally required to rest upon arrival, while trips covering two-thirds of a "ninety" (that is, sixty versts—the distance, for example, from Moscow to Troitsy-Sergievaia lavra) were seen as a veritable exploit. Thus, Maksimov continued,

> to travel an entire "ninety," one had to travel by horse. As a result, the rate of movement by horseback became the unit for measuring distances and ultimately determined the distribution of settlements . . . After 30 versts the horse would tire and required food and rest. And it was precisely there, at the 30-verst point from the center, like points along the radii of a circle, that trading settlements would form. In the old days, in a practice whose consequences are still evident today, the center around which these settlements formed would be recognized as a "town" and often as the "head town" (*stol'nyi gorod*).

At one "ninety" from Moscow, one found appanage or "intermediary towns" such as Kolomna, Klin, Serpukhov, Ruza, Mozhaisk, and Pereiaslavl-Zalesskii. "At the next 'ninety' from these towns," as Maksimov put it, "one then found capital towns, towns associated with princely or ruling seats," including Vladimir, Tver, and Riazan. Later on they became known as provincial capitals (*gubernskie goroda*). Maksimov then concluded: "Regardless of how the process unfolded in every instance, what we have described here generally took place all across Suzdalian and Riazanian Rus. To see that this is so, all you have to do is travel with a compass around Moscow—

from Vladimir to Murom, to Iaroslavl and beyond Kostroma to the water-sheds (*vodorazdely*), in any direction you please."[12]

While Maksimov, unlike Glinka, did not explicitly discuss the larger 90-verst rings extending beyond Moscow, he did provide the names of a number of towns located on these more distant circumferences. Citing the folk proverb "the morning bells ring in Moscow and are heard in Vologda" (*V Moskve k zautrene zvoniat, a na Vologde tot zvon slyshen*), he ultimately provided a picture of a region that very much resembled the one described by Glinka.

Thus "interior Russia" in the nineteenth century was imagined as an almost perfect circle extending from Moscow along a radius of more than 450 kilometers. After this perimeter one then found the historical frontiers (*ukrainy*) whose importance in the distant past was symbolized by the defensive earthworks and whose remains, as Glinka noted, "can still be seen today in the provinces of Riazan, Orel, Kursk, and Tambov."[13] In general, however, with the exception of these ruins, the edge of the interior was utterly invisible. Of course, even though the interior thus defined appeared somewhat modest when compared to the empire as a whole—even compared to just the empire's European half—it was still approximately twenty-two times the size of modern-day France.

If Glinka and Maksimov emphasized the Moscow region's centrality in defining the Russian interior, the writer V. V. Passek saw Moscow as just one of several important "nodes of nationality" (*uzly narodnosti*).[14] As he observed in his *Travel Notes,* Russia "possesses a series of centers or points of concentration that operate as the very source of its life, the hearts of its circulatory system . . . And each of these centers grew out of a particular locality, reflecting the imprint of a distinct tribe and then imparting this local distinction to the broader life of the entire state." In Passek's view, there were three such centers—Moscow, Novgorod, and Kiev—each of which deserved to be recognized for its unique contribution to "the current shape and integrity of the state." Passek's Moscow node—that is, the "non-Novgorodian north"—fell within the same general confines as Glinka's and consisted of ten provinces (Moscow, Vladimir, Tver, Kostroma, Iaroslavl, Riazan, Tula, Kaluga, Orel, and "even" Kursk). In general, Passek described this "node" with little commentary. He had more to say about the other two, Novgorod and Kiev.

According to the prolific geographical and statistical writer K. I. Arsen'ev, the "interior of European Russia . . . consists of all the lands lying between the middle course of the Volga and the headwaters of the Khoper,

Donets, Oka and Desna rivers. As such, the area includes the following provinces: Iaroslavl, Kostroma, Nizhnii Novgorod, Penza, Tambov, Voronezh, Kursk, Orel, Kaluga, Tula, Moscow, Vladimir, and Riazan. (Tver and Smolensk do not appear in this list because Arsen'ev includes them in other regional groupings.) As such, the interior appeared to Arsen'ev as "the very best of Russia's regions, especially in political, economic, and administrative terms." While Arsen'ev admitted that the low-lying topography of the region presented "the observer [with a view of] exhausting uniformity," the area possessed obviously positive features, including a number of navigable rivers, a moderate climate, and soils that were well suited for agriculture and had long supported a large population. Although relatively uniform in physical terms, Arsen'ev found enough variety to subdivide the region into four general zones, which themselves could then be further broken down into a number of smaller regional subunits. In fact, in his early work, Arsen'ev had gone even further in accentuating the variety of the territory and appeared to discount the very existence of a coherent "interior," dividing the region into four independent "areas" (*prostranstva*) (the Oka area, the Alauna area [*Alaunskoe*], the Volga area, and the Steppe area). Yet even acknowledging a certain ambivalence in his demarcations, Arsen'ev's overall appreciation of the interior was clear. As he wrote in 1848, the empire's "central or interior area" represents "the true foundation of her power, the genuine fatherland of the Russian people, and the center of all of European Russia. It is home to all the wealth [she has] achieved through the accomplishments of education, industry, and domestic trade." "The Russian lands," he continued,

> are bound by common traditions, uniform civil statutes, a single language, a single religion, and a broadly shared course of historical development that affected all of their inhabitants. As such, this territory represents the true keystone of the Russian state. It is the great circle to which all the remaining parts of the empire are joined like radii running in different directions, some near, some far, but all of them helping to varying degrees to ensure the state's essential indivisibility.[15]

Writing toward the end of the nineteenth century, M. O. Koialovich noted that "interior Russia," with "its population of pure Russian people [*naselennaia tsel'nym russkim narodom*], represents the kernel of Russia in historical, ethnographic, and even . . . economic terms . . . In order to understand any of Russia's peripheral regions, one thus has to start by understanding this seed that gave rise to the Russian strength and vitality that then spread outward to the borderlands." Extending his characterization of the interior, Koialovich defined the region as "that most Russian part of Russia," the "Russian center point," the "center of gravity in Russia's past and present life": "Interior Russia," he wrote, represents the country's "historical center."[16] According to V. O. Kliuchevskii, the core of Great Russia ran from the headwaters of the Volga to the southern edge of the forest zone.[17]

The inclination to compare Russian space to a circle did not apply only to "interior Russia." Minister of the Interior P. A. Valuev, for example, used the circle analogy to describe the state as a whole: "Fully half of the [Russian] state finds itself under extraordinary rule. Punitive measures predominate. In order to keep this circular periphery (*okruzhnost'*) bound to the center, we make use of force and this force naturally provokes centrifugal tendencies." The monarch today, Valuev continued, must act as "the moral gatherer of the Russian land in the same way that Ivan III served as its physical gatherer."[18] The Siberian regionalist G. N. Potanin likewise suggested that all of European Russia represented "a compact, symmetrically arranged sphere."[19]

The Boundaries of the Interior: The South and Southwest

But where exactly did "interior Russia" end and how were its boundaries determined? Let's start by looking at the borders of the region in the south and southwest.

On his way to Erzurum, Pushkin wrote the following:

> At last, I came upon the steppes of Voronezh and freely galloped across the green plains. One feels the shift from Europe to Asia with every passing hour: the forests disappear, the hills flatten, the grass grows thicker and richer; birds appear that are unknown in our woods; eagles rest on the posts that mark the great road as if they were on guard, proudly observing the traveler; while on the surrounding fertile pastures
>
> > Herds of indomitable steeds
> > Proudly graze
>
> Kalmyks hang about the roadside way stations.[20]

In the first half of the nineteenth century, a nobleman's visit to his estate in Tambov was considered a trip "to the steppe," and it was well known that agriculture had to be practiced differently in the province due to differences in soils and climate. Harvest time, for example, commenced two weeks earlier in Tambov than it did in the neighboring province of Riazan.[21]

V. V. Passek also described the steppe that cut across Poltava and parts of Voronezh, Khar'kov, Kursk, and Chernigov provinces as a border of sorts. "This band [of steppe]," he wrote, "marks the transition from Russia's interior provinces to those of the steppe proper." The provinces of the "steppe proper"—that is, the steppes of New Russia according to Passek— "are watered with rivers whose life originates in the heart of Russia." Here the interior, corresponding to Russia's heart, is clearly contrasted with the steppe. Indeed, it was precisely along the zone of transition between the woodlands and the steppe that one found the country's traditional southern frontiers (*ukrainy*). According to Passek, all of Kursk Province "was once the frontier of ancient Rus."[22] Little Russia began, as he saw it, "five degrees south of Moscow and almost ten south of Novgorod."[23]

The Kievan "node" (*uzel*) is one of the three that Passek identifies. And when one compares his description of the region with a look at the map, it is not hard to see that of the three "nodes," only Moscow's actually has an identifiable circular form. Passek admits as much in his *Travel Notes:* "The circle to be drawn from this central point is difficult to determine." Indeed, despite the fact that Passek suggests that "all the circles indicated here and every tribe within them have, in addition, their own secondary circles," he only provides a list of the latter in the case of Kiev, and it is hardly likely that this formulation would really apply to the more uniform Moscow region.[24]

Russia's regionalist pioneers were also drawn to questions of language. Vas'ianov, one of the authors whose work appeared in Passek's *Sketches of Russia* (*Ocherki Rossii*), noted that the "Kursk language" (*kurskoe narechie*) was spoken by "three million people [living in] the historic, long-settled, native Russian land"—that is, the provinces of Orel and Kursk as well as the southwestern parts of Kaluga and Tula. (Today linguists refer to the "Kursk language" as the Southern Russian dialect.) As Vas'ianov correctly noted, "the root of this language appear[ed] Great Russian in origin." He went on to add ethnographic evidence to prove his point: "The people who speak this language are quite distinct from Little Russians, in their physical appearance, their dress, and their way of life. They do not see themselves as mutually related in terms of blood."[25]

I. S. Aksakov was another traveler from the center who noted a striking difference as he crossed from Tambov into the territory of the Don Cossack Host or, in another case, to Khar'kov. "Between Kursk and Khar'kov I did not feel the dominant influence of the Little Russian character, but between Khar'kov and Poltava or between Poltava and Kremenchug—well now, that's the real land of the Ukes!" (*Khokhlandia*) According to Aksakov, in Little Russia "one finds little sympathy for Rus; despite Orthodoxy and the closest of ties, one simply doesn't feel at home there. Of course, this has a lot to do with us. The Russian is used to coming and going as he pleases, seeing himself as a man who is everywhere in his own home (*khoziainom*). As a result, he tends to be unusually indulgent when it comes to acknowledging the rights of other nations."[26] Here we see the invisible border of a region revealed by the sense that when one crosses over it one ceases to feel at home.

The governor of Vladimir Province, I. M. Dolgorukii, also felt a sense of dépaysement in places like Little Russia or Latvia (*Liflandiia*). While in Poltava, he noted, "Here I indeed feel myself in a foreign land, and the reason is perhaps petty, though for me it is sufficient: I simply cannot understand the language of the [common] people. I asked a local here a question, he answered, but he did not entirely understand me and I in turn had to ask for three out of every five words he said to be translated . . . Wherever we stop understanding the language of the people, we run up against the boundaries of our motherland and, in my view, even of the fatherland itself . . . The so-called common people (*chern'*)—they are the ones who determine the true gulfs between kingdoms that politics seem to unite. The Latvian (*Lifliandets*) will always be a foreigner to Russia even though he and I serve the same state."[27]

Aksakov's subsequent trips to Little Russia allowed him to be more precise when defining the border with Great Russia. "Kursk Province can be counted in general as one of the original parts of Great Rus. At the same time, one feels the imprint of a certain 'uke-ification' (*ottenok khokhlatskii*) among the peasants of the province, though this is really only in the border districts. There one finds a definite blending of language, accents, and dress." The reality of this blending then led Aksakov to be somewhat inconsistent in his categorizations. For example, in one instance he describes Ryl'sk as a Little Russian town and then later as "entirely Great Russian." From the perspective of Khar'kov, as Aksakov told it, Kursk Province seemed like "the North." Indeed, he continued, "here they refer to [Kursk] as Russia and call people from Kursk Russians, that is, Great Russians."[28] (Chernigov, in the same way, appeared "completely without a Little Russian physiognomy.") Aksakov in fact came to the conclusion that the true boundary of Little Russia was the Desna River, which marked a sharp transition in terms of soil type (this was the edge of the Ukrainian Black Earth) as well as in language, dress, and daily life. In conclusion, Aksakov advised, "we should consider the southern districts of Chernigov Province to be part of Little Russia; while the districts bordering on Orel are distinguished by Great Russian features and the rest are pure White Russian. Ancient Severiia is simply not Little Russia."[29]

The East and Southeast

According to one of Vadim Passek's writings, Nizhnii Novgorod and Kazan provinces and "the Lower Volga more generally" were not part of the Russian interior. Few of Passek's contemporaries agreed with this position, however. Passek's closest associates parted ways with him on this point and his widow even omitted a corresponding passage on the matter from a late synopsis of his *Travel Notes*.[30] Indeed, for many educated Russians in the nineteenth century Nizhnii Novgorod seemed an obvious part of "interior Russia," its inclusion justified by the region's long history as a part of the Muscovite state and by its role during the wars and invasions of the Time of Troubles.

There were more readily obvious justifications for this inclusion, however. The writer P. D. Boborykin, for example, remembered his first trip from his native Nizhnii Novgorod to Moscow in the middle of the nineteenth century in the following way: "I did not find anything special about Moscow as one of the *capitals* . . . I did not feel any particular discomfort as a visitor from the periphery." While in the city, Boborykin remembered "hearing the same accents and speech" and finding the same "level of culture" and similar sorts of "interests" among the Muscovites that he had found in other provincial centers.[31] Indeed, according to G. N. Potanin, resentment in Nizhnii Novgorod over the cultural hegemony of the capitals tended to be at most "limited," while in Kazan the feeling was "slightly stronger."[32]

According to Alexander Herzen, one of the authors who appeared in *Sketches of Russia*, one "first realized [one's] distance from Moscow" when one reached the Volga town of Cheboksary, the entry point into "another part of Russia." "Before reaching Kazan Province," Herzen wrote, "one does not really feel much of a difference between the ancient capital and the provincial towns. Vladimir and Nizhnii Novgorod remind one of the districts of Moscow, having all but blended with [Moscow] and shared her experience for several centuries. They look to Moscow as their center, the source of all things. The city of Kazan, however, is surrounded by a different region. This city . . . represents in effect its own kind of center for the provinces to the south and east."[33] In other words, Herzen appears to have been proposing Kazan as its own independent node (*uzel*) in the Passekian sense. Later in his account, he goes on to stress the city's important strategic position within the empire and its dual European-Asian character, though this last point, interestingly enough, did not keep him from concluding that "all of it [Kazan] is our Rus, our Holy Rus regardless!"[34]

Diomid Passek, Vadim's brother, agreed that Kazan was primarily Russian: "Asianness (*asiatstvo*) has had no bearing on [Kazan] society and has not given the city a European-Asian character."[35] Indeed, according to this Passek, Kazan was very much a center of Russian population and had sown "the seeds of European life" far to the south and east, to Orenburg, Astrakhan, and Kiakhta, where one found the real meeting points between Europe and Asia. In the "wedge" of land between the Volga and the Ural Mountains, as he saw it, one found Asianness of a special sort—an island Asian world cut off from the rest of Asia proper by regions that had been incorporated into Russian culture (the Urals, Siberia, the middle Volga). This in turn explained why the common Russian people loved Kazan "as the first city of Holy Rus."[36]

The nineteenth-century memoirist F. F. Vigel remembered that when he first went to Kazan, "I expected to see and indeed sought out the physiognomy of Asia, but everywhere I went I found instead the domes of churches topped with crosses, and only in the distance could I make out the shape of minarets. Indeed, Kazan has slavishly imitated as much as possible the ways of Moscow, her conqueror." Vigel went on to note that given the size of Kazan's population and its buildings, it should be ranked as "the third city of Russia [after St. Petersburg and Moscow] because Riga is in truth a German town, Vilna is Polish, and Odessa is Babylonian." It was only upon leaving Kazan for points east that one left Russia: "Here one indeed bids farewell to Mother Russia and moves toward the encounter with her immense daughter, Siberia."[37] Potanin, for his part, felt called to write about Kazan as "the primary outpost of Russian culture in the East," as a town that was "pointed to the East."[38] The town, after all, was a vital center of Orthodox missionary activity and for a long period home to the country's easternmost university.

But there was still enough hybridity for the region to appear confusing. I. S. Aksakov, for example, contemplating a trip to the Kazan region, openly doubted whether one could really say that it was "Russia": "What kind of Russia is this! Tetiushi, Mamadysh, Cheboksary and other [such strange names]!" But he then immediately contradicted himself by noting that for all its apparent un-Russianness the area nonetheless represented "one of the old parts of the Russian body" and "one of [its] national treasures."[39] Further east, Aksakov continued to jot down the contradictory quality of what he was seeing: "Everywhere places that have a crude Tatar sound to them. These places are no longer Russian, all the names are Tatar, even the [Russian] peasant beyond the Volga is different from his counterpart on the other bank . . . But despite all this, it's clear that these parts are alive with the Russian mind . . ."[40]

Even the place names that made such an impression on Aksakov did not always mean what one expected. For example, as A. N. Pypin noted, despite the fact that "Tatar village names are sprinkled throughout" Saratov Province, "it is only in the north that one finds any Tatars living in the villages; the overwhelming share of villages with Tatar names are in fact home to a pure Russian population."[41] The geographer and ethnographer V. Liadov defined the boundary of the interior somewhat further east of Cheboksary. "Upon crossing the Sura River," he noted, "you leave the land of the Slavs and step onto entirely foreign soil (vstupaesh' sovershenno na inoplemennuiu pochvu). It's true, that one finds Chuvash and Cheremisses (Mari) in Nizhnii Novgorod Province, but they are of the Russified sort; beyond the Sura, these little peoples (narodtsy) still live according to their original traditions and practice their original faith." Liadov paid particular attention to the degree of Russian assimilation that one found among these "foreign tribes," noting that it was especially pronounced among the Chud and the Mordvins, while the Bashkirs and Voguls (Komi) "remain as yet untouched by Russian civilization."[42] Minister Valuev also drew a distinction between "the interior provinces" and "the Volga region" (Privolzhskii krai), including Kazan.[43]

In Russian folk songs of the seventeenth and eighteenth centuries, the Volga figured as a special emotional touchstone of the country's history—this despite the fact that non-Russian peoples had themselves considered the Volga their "mother" long before the Russians did. (Indeed, the Russians knew this and do not appear to have minded much.)[44] At the same time, for all the national meaning associated with the Volga, by the close of the eighteenth century, observers like I. I. Dmitriev nonetheless remarked upon the dramatic changes that one could witness as one traveled south along the hilly right bank of the river from Syzran to Astrakhan. "After passing through a few Russian and Tatar villages," Dmitriev recalled, "you find yourself entering a series of European settlements founded principally by German colonists . . . Then as you draw closer to Astrakhan itself, you come across more and more nomadic Kalmyks . . . Sometimes you have the impression of being quite *outside of* Russia [my emphasis, L.G.] since you continuously run into different sorts of people, different customs, even different animals."[45] I. S. Aksakov had much the same thing to say in 1844: "As you approach Astrakhan along the Volga bank, you have a striking feeling of being far removed from Russia . . . There are no real woods anywhere, yet by almost every house you see Lombardy poplars . . . Only rarely will you see a Russian cart with a Russian peasant driving it, but everywhere you look there are two-wheeled carts with Kalmyks, Tatars, Kazakhs [*kirgizy*], Georgians, Armenians, and Persians . . . The weather around here in January is what we get back home in April." "And the Russians in these parts are not really like us. They themselves will tell you: 'In Russia, they do things in such-and-such a way, but we do it differently.'"[46]

This was the impression of the so-called Lower Country (*Nizovoi krai*) —that is, all of the southern and parts of the middle Volga regions. Indeed, it is quite indicative of the region's general psychological remove from Russia that there were plans in the early nineteenth century to unite Astrakhan Province with Caucasus Oblast and Georgia in a single vice-royalty that would have had its capital in Tiflis (Tbilisi).[47] As one contemporary scholar has noted, "the Lower Volga long persisted in being a foreign land for the Russians even as waves of incoming Slavic migrants regarded the river itself as their 'mother'" (*matushka*).[48]

But if the lower country of the Volga represented an alien place, to many Russians the familiar had already been left behind well before they got there. In Vigel's memoirs, for example, Penza Province is described in one reference as interior and in another as remote.[49] In these contradictory descriptions, one senses the influence of Penza's intermediary location. The provinces to the north clearly fell within Moscow's orbit and formed part of the interior, but the lands running to the south and east, like the lands of the middle and lower Volga, seemed to fall outside.

Two of the most important centers of the domestic economy were also located at points on the southern and eastern edges of the Moscow-centered region: the great fairs of Nizhnii Novgorod and Kursk (the Korennaia fair). Each of these commercial towns served as a link connecting central Russia with its interior peripheries (the middle Volga, Little Russia) on the one hand, and its more distant borderlands on the other. As P. A. Viazemskii noted in reference to the Nizhnii fair, the functioning of wholesale trade "required a central point from which it then could spread throughout Russia, and nature herself has dictated that this central point be Nizhnii Novgorod."[50] As for the Korennaia fair in Kursk, S. V. Maksimov aptly highlighted its significance as an economic meeting ground by noting that "both Russias—the northern industrial and the southern agricultural—[meet at Kursk] . . . where they exchange their products."[51]

The North and Northeast

The clearest limits of the center were in the north where the region butted up against the regions of Novgorod the Great and St. Petersburg, both towns that were either historical or contemporary antipodes and rivals of Moscow. Early nineteenth-century Romantics who celebrated the history of liberty (*vol'nost'*) in the Russian past often considered the *veche*-centered liberty of Novgorod on a par with the freedom-loving life of Cossack Ukraine, treating both the lands of Novgorod and those of Kiev as their own distinct civilizations.[52] Somewhat later A. K. Tolstoi saw things in similar fashion: "We should not look for Russia in Moscow, but rather in Kiev and Novgorod."[53]

Given these views, it is hardly surprising to find that Vadim Passek centered one of his three national nodes around Novgorod the Great, whose region he drew to include the provinces of St. Petersburg, Vologda, Olonets, Arkhangel'sk, Perm, Viatka, Novgorod, and Pskov. Passek was convinced that "neither the passage of time nor the course of events has managed to efface . . . those traditional characteristics that distinguished Novgorod," by which he meant the area's language and habits of daily life. Yet at the same time, Novgorod's role in the imperial period was clearly modest and had declined especially precipitously with the growth of St. Petersburg in the eighteenth century and the advent of the railroad in the mid-nineteenth. Indeed, the advent of the railroad led to the town being temporarily bypassed by the region's emerging transportation network.[54] For Russians of the mid-nineteenth century, it was hard not to see Novgorod the Great as little more than a provincial outpost. Even Novgorodians recognized that their town lay outside Russia's center. As one local zemstvo member noted in a letter to a Moscow colleague, "You're there in the central provinces, but we're up here in the North."[55]

The juxtaposition of Moscow and St. Petersburg was still more striking; indeed, by the mid-nineteenth century comparisons between the two cities—often referred to as the two capitals—had emerged as a classic theme of Russian culture. "We have two capitals: how then can you speak of one without comparing it to the other?"[56] Yet recognizing that the country had two capitals did not mean that they were equal, and of the two, Moscow appeared less prosperous. As Pushkin noted, comparing the Moscow of the 1830s to earlier times, "The decline of Moscow must be appreciated as an important development. [Its] impoverishment is proof of the impoverishment of the Russian nobility." As the poet saw it, great estates were disappearing "with terrible rapidity"; there was no money to maintain the great homes of Moscow; and the nobles who sold their homes for lack of funds then found themselves reduced to living in the country. For Pushkin, then, the robustness of Russian noble landownership was symbolic of the broader health of the national core: the crisis that appeared to be affecting "the nests of the gentlefolk" thus produced the decline of "the city of the center" (*sredinnyi grad*). Still, there were signs of hope: "Moscow has indeed lost its aristocratic shine but it is prospering today in other ways: industry . . . has come to life and has grown with uncommon strength. The merchants are growing rich and are moving into spacious homes abandoned by the nobility."[57]

V. G. Belinskii concurred, noting that given Moscow's industrial growth by the mid-1840s, "not even Petersburg can compete with her because her location close to the middle of Russia destines her to become an industrial center. And this will indeed come to pass when the railway links her to Petersburg and when great roads (*shosse*), like arteries extending from the human heart, will tie her to Iaroslavl, Kazan, Voronezh, Khar'kov, Kiev, Odessa . . . "[58] The fate of the old capital remained a matter of concern to Moscow-lovers throughout the imperial period. S. D. Sheremet'ev, a man quick to decry even the barest slippage in Moscow's prestige, noted in 1909, for example, that Moscow's significance was growing "as the center of popular and government life . . . as the center of the true Russia, old and new."[59]

Because Russia had two capitals, the provinces located in between were invariably pulled toward either the one or the other. Indeed, this fact was often noted by nineteenth-century observers. I. S. Aksakov wrote, for example, that "Life in Iaroslavl is almost entirely oriented toward Petersburg. That much one can say for certain. No one here ever has anything to say about Moscow." Aksakov explained this situation by noting that while Iaroslavl was geographically closer to Moscow, the road to Petersburg was much better.[60] Yet just a short time later, by the post-reform period, things had changed considerably and new observers saw the situation quite differently. As one observer noted, "In matters of commerce, the province of Iaroslavl is oriented entirely toward Moscow and the Nizhnii Novgorod Fair. Of Vologda Province, this is true only of the southern districts," while the northern parts of Tver Province "are primarily linked to Petersburg."[61]

St. Petersburg also found itself right next to regions with significant "alien" (that is, non-Russian) populations. In fact, one observer noted that one reached "the limit of the Russian settlements" just a little over one hundred versts to the west of the city itself and still well within the borders of Petersburg Province.[62] Nikolai Karamzin offered the following description of Narva and Ivangorod, two towns that faced one another on either side of the Narva River: "In the former everything is German, in the latter Russian. Here is clearly where our border once ran. O Peter, Peter!"[63] Peterburgers with country houses (*dachi*) northwest of the city found themselves in Finland, while to the northeast, "as soon as one gets past Olonets, one enters honest to goodness Karelia" (*nastoiashchaia Karelia*).[64] Petr Keppen expressed his surprise that despite the fact that non-Russian peoples lived "so to speak, right at the edge of the city line," citizens of the capital apparently knew "no more about them than they [did] about the Eskimoes."[65] In the mid-nineteenth century, Petersburg's surrounding Finnic peoples seemed alien but unthreatening. By the turn of the twentieth century, however, with the rise of national consciousness among the Finno-Ugric peoples of the region, local Russians increasingly feared that "the imperial capital may well soon find itself in the midst of a unified and nationally self-conscious alien population." Such views were expressed not only by isolated publicists on the far political right but also by military planners whose connections extended to the highest echelons of government.[66]

Given St. Petersburg's location, it is not surprising that its surrounding provinces related to it quite differently than did the provinces around Moscow. The natural landscape of the north and the density and pronounced ethnic diversity of the local population even influenced perceptions of distance. As Nikitenko observed in 1834, "Petrozavodsk is an ugly town, cast off in the depths of the forests and cut off from the educated world. One would think that it is close to St. Petersburg [indeed, no farther than Orel is from Moscow—L.G.], but O how far away it is!"[67]

The net result of the complicated relationships that one found between St. Petersburg and Moscow and between Petersburg and its own hinterland was the creation of a special and somewhat artificial region: the so-called Priozernyi krai (literally: the Lake Territory). Of course, the "Russian Great Lakes" that gave the region its name (Lakes Ladoga, Onega, Chud, Il'men, and others) in themselves hardly amounted to a coherent region. Ultimately, the decisive factor that made the region a "region" was the fact that it included St. Petersburg, Peter's "window to Europe."

To the north and northeast of the city was largely wilderness. Indeed, the far north and northeast contained five of the six provincial capitals of European Russia that were officially designated as "remote" in the early 1860s—Arkhangel'sk, Petrozavodsk, Vologda, Viatka, and Perm (the sixth was Astrakhan).[68] As Nikitenko wrote in his diary, "once you cross into Arkhangel'sk Province, all evidence of human settlement disappears."[69] Indeed, these provinces were remote enough to demand special salary supplements for state officials and to be used as a dumping ground for convicts. There was no need to maintain even a minimal military presence in the region. In *My Past and Thoughts*, Alexander Herzen plainly stated that Viatka was located beyond the confines of "interior Russia";[70] while F. F. Vigel for his part referred to the province of Perm as "the antechamber of Siberia."[71]

Only Vologda proved a partial exception to this general rule. As noted earlier, Vologda was occasionally represented as the outer edge of a broader region centered on Moscow, but as Liadov noted in the 1860s, the town and province nonetheless remained "quite unknown to the inhabitants of central Russia."[72] The fact that zemstvos were opened in just seven of Vologda's districts was proof of the province's perceived status as a periphery. When the question of extending zemstvo institutions to a broader range of territories resurfaced toward the close of the nineteenth century, the emphasis fell in particular on what to do in the case of four so-called "borderland" (*okrainnye*) provinces: Arkhangel'sk, Astrakhan, Orenburg, and Stavropol. All of these provinces were defined as "culturally backward" (*malokul'turnye*), though observers also noted that they differed little in this respect from Viatka, Olonetsk, and Perm, which already had zemstvo institutions.[73]

The West

There were two principal stages to the gathering of the Russian lands. The first occurred in northern Rus between the fourteenth and early sixteenth centuries; the second in western Rus from the sixteenth to the late eighteenth. As the Russian state expanded into these latter areas, it incorporated eastern Slavs who differed from the domestic Russian population. Prior to 1772, the traditional border with the Polish-Lithuanian Commonwealth lay just beyond Smolensk. In fact, the so-called "Lithuanian border" (*litovskii rubezh*) proved to be quite mobile, and Smolensk itself changed hands many times. The shifting quality of Smolensk as a border town was neatly captured in a Russian historical ballad in which Tsar Aleksei Mikhailovich gathers a council of his boyars to decide the fate of Smolensk. Some of the tsar's boyars insist that the town is "a Lithuanian stronghold, not a Muscovite one" and downplay its usefulness for Russia, while others argue the opposite—that the town is Muscovite rather than Lithuanian. Not surprisingly, the tsar in the ballad agrees with the latter view.[74]

Of course, even though Tsar Aleksei may have seen Smolensk as Russian, this did not keep Catherine the Great from committing herself to a long-term plan to Russify the province and integrate it—along with Little Russia, Lithuania (*Lifliandiia*) and Finland—more deeply within the empire.[75] These efforts were apparently successful. In 1812, the Smolensk region proved to be an important center of Russian resistance to Napoleon's Grande Armée, with the local population supporting the Russian side. "When we passed through formerly Polish places, the local inhabitants treated our troops with silent apathy . . . Things were quite different in Smolensk Province," one Russian remembered. To the east of Smolensk, Napoleon's army found empty villages, abandoned by the local populace as they fled the invader.[76] Yet for all this, not to mention the region's equally pivotal role during the Time of Troubles, neither Glinka, Passek, Arsen'ev, nor Maksimov included Smolensk in their definitions of "interior Russia." (This is somewhat ironic because a few of these authors actually had close ties to the area.) Maksimov, for example, refers to Smolensk as the capital of Belorussia.[77] In fact, seven of Smolensk Province's districts were officially deemed Belorussian, though as fears of Polish "expansion" increased, the region eventually came to be seen quite differently.

During the nineteenth century, Russians referred to the easternmost lands of the former Polish-Lithuanian Commonwealth as the "western provinces" (*zapadnye gubernii*) and the Polish element in these provinces remained predominant, both in socioeconomic as well as in cultural terms. Generally speaking, Polish influence tended to be weakest in eastern Belorussia (the provinces of Mogil'ev and Vitebsk).

Such were the boundaries of the Russian interior as perceived by Russian observers of the nineteenth century. The region as outlined here, with a few slight corrections and emendations, corresponds remarkably closely to the circumference of the seventh circle described by Glinka. As such, one thing that immediately leaps out about the region is its considerable remove from the international boundaries of the empire. "Interior Russia" was indeed interior. Even allowing for the humor of exaggeration, Gogol was not that far off when he described in his play *The Inspector General* a provincial town located more than a year's ride from the border of the state.

Within the immense and diverse Russian empire, "interior Russia" was widely perceived as a place apart, a homogenous and self-contained place whose defining characteristics appeared timeless and unchanging. Of course, the relative significance of the various historical, ethnic, environmental, and economic factors that defined the region changed over time. Thus, as the country modernized, economic considerations grew in importance. Concerns about ethnicity also began to figure more prominently. And the relative importance of the different factors could also vary considerably from one end of the region to another. The environmental divide between forest and steppe proved to be quite influential in shaping views of the interior's southern edges, for example. But in the west, where there was no such natural transition zone, the environmental factor tended to be less important in determining a boundary to the region. Regardless of how the edges of the interior were defined, however, the most palpable effect of leaving the interior remained the experience of contrast. The interior was a world of homogeneity, monotonality, uniformity. The regions beyond, by contrast, were lands of difference.

The complexities involved in defining the interior were reflected in the overlapping quality of some of the nomenclature used to describe the region. The terms "interior provinces" and "central provinces," for example, tended to mean the same thing and frequently ran together. Thus the Moscow governor-general P. A. Tuchkov, who declined an appointment to the prestigious post of viceroy of the Kingdom of Poland, wrote of a distinction between what he described as "our interior central provinces" and the "empire's border territories."[78] Understandings of these terms were closely related to the concrete realities of the country's territorial-administrative system.

It is possible that the concept of Inner Asia helped to inform the semantics of "interiorness" in nineteenth-century Russian thinking. In the 1800s, the term Inner Asia, which included Central Asia and Middle Asia, tended to apply to the landlocked central spaces of the Asian continent. The concept of "interior Russia" is also obviously tied to the region's most direct antitheses—the borderlands, the frontier (*ukraina*)—which invariably begin at that point where the interior ends.

According to the *Dictionary of the Russian Academy* published in the Catherinian period, the adjective "interior" (*vnutrennii*) owed its origin to the word for "core" (*nutro*)—that is, if something was "interior," that meant that it was "located inside the core (*vnutri nakhodiashchiisia*)."[79] This meaning was underscored by the semantic pairings "interior/of the heart" (*serdechnyi*) and "core/heart" that were common in Russian writing. As the lexicographer V. I. Dal noted in his *Tolkovyi slovar' zhivogo velikorusskogo iazyka*, "In relation to things, the word 'heart' sometimes acquires the meaning of core [*nutro*], nucleus [*nedro*], womb [*utroba*], center point [*sredotochiie*], [or] middle [*nutrovaia sredina*]; while in the realm of emotion, it is a symbol of love, will, passion, or moral and spiritual force, the opposite of intellect, reason, the brain."[80] In addition, the word "heart" can be taken to convey a still more powerful idea if one takes into account the organ's basic physiological function within the body—that is, the pumping of blood throughout the organism.

The adjective "native" (*korennoi*) was defined in the Academy's late eighteenth-century dictionary as "traditional, original, principal."[81] Dal's dictionary provided virtually the same meaning: initial, original, foundational, genuine. The term "native Russia" (*korennaia Rossiia*), or Russian heartland, thus evoked a historic entity, in particular, the entity formed by Moscow's gathering of the Russian lands. *Korennoi* literally comes from the Russian *koren'*, which means root. The root (or, as M. O. Koialovich put it, the seed) that is implied in the construction "native Russia" is thus very much the root of past times, of historical continuity, of ethnic purity. As one writer noted in the early twentieth century, "the Great Russian type of the Volga Region is somewhat different from the Great Russian types that one finds in the two neighboring, more historically Russian provinces (*bolee korennye velikorusskie oblasti*).[82]

The term "Great Russian provinces" appeared frequently in state decrees, indeed somewhat more frequently than the term "interior provinces," and it was the former that was noted in encyclopedia entries. Great Russia was not, however, the same thing as "interior Russia." Indeed, Great Russia was larger (twenty-eight to twenty-nine provinces) and itself encompassed the interior. At the same time, Great Russia was itself somewhat hard to determine. The ethnographer N. I. Nadezhdin attempted to pinpoint its location and found that it corresponded in geographical terms and its defining characteristics to "interior Russia" and more generally to a broad popular understanding of Russia itself. As he put it, "For ordinary people, the Great Russian provinces are simply 'Russia.' When people from there go to other provinces and regions within the empire, they see themselves as outside of Russia."[83]

V. S. Pecherin, for example, once wrote: "I have never lived in the real Russia (*v sobstvennoi Rossii*) but rather have spent my life moving between Latvia (*Lifliandiia*), Belorussia, Podol, Volynia, Bessarabia. Can one really call any of these places the fatherland?" (*Kakoe zhe tut otechestvo?*). Sergei Witte expressed a similar sentiment: "My knowledge of the Russian heartland was poor. I was born in the Caucasus and thereafter worked in the south and the west."[84] Both these statements, separated from one another by a considerable period of time, reflect the fact that much of the eastern Slavic lands, including Kiev (the "mother of Russian cities"), was perceived as lying outside the parameters of Russia proper.[85]

Holy Rus—as the presumed territorial core of Russian Orthodoxy—also appeared geographically larger than the Russian interior. Russia's spiritual heartland included Kazan, for example, the principal Orthodox missionary center in the east. The Russian North with its ancient monasteries also formed part of Holy Rus, as did the famous Monastery of the Caves located in Kiev.

Finally, the Russian interior was very much a part of European Russia. By the close of the nineteenth century, this vast territory encompassed fifty provinces.

While the geographical extent of the interior could vary from observer to observer, images of the region also changed over time. Toward the end of the nineteenth century, Russian statesmen recognized that the empire needed a better balance between its interior and its peripheries. One can therefore speak in retrospect of a dynamic of expansion on two levels: the expansion of the interior and the expansion of the territory of the state.

The increased integration of the middle Volga region in the late nineteenth century was also extremely important in shaping images of the center. This region, despite its highly ethnically diverse population, found itself increasingly incorporated within the orbit of "interior Russia." A similar process took place in regards to the Don Cossack Host region, which was also being drawn into understandings of the interior even as Russian observers recognized the distinctiveness of its political and cultural traditions and the presence of a Don Cossack regional identity.[86] On the interior's western edges, attempts as early as the 1830s and 1840s to claim that western areas—in particular the more Russianized areas of eastern Belorussia (Mogil'ev and Vitebsk provinces)—were part of the Russian interior met with greater difficulty, though it is also true that these attempts rarely faded from the political discussion. In the 1860s, for example, I. S. Aksakov proposed an elaborate plan to reorganize the state's administrative framework, subsuming part of the western provinces into the Russian interior and thus completing the overall western expansion of the Russian core. By the 1880s and 1890s, however, Russian public opinion was fixated on the opposite process—on the danger of "Polish expansion" to the east and, in particular, to the Smolensk region.[87]

In addition to shifts in the perception of the regions immediately surrounding it, images of "interior Russia" were also profoundly affected by the late nineteenth-century debate on the so-called "impoverishment of the center" (oskudeniie tsentra). The "impoverishment" in this phrase was initially used in conjunction with the "impoverishment of the nobility," which then shifted to refer to the difficult economic situation of the region where many nobles were concentrated. In 1889 and 1893 noble landlords from the center participated in the development of new railroad tariffs that were intended to protect them from the stiff competition that they had begun to face from agricultural producers in the south.[88] The debate on the "impoverishment of the center" then clearly came to be tied to the growing debate on the social and economic condition of the peasantry, the so-called "peasant question."

In the work of the Zvegintsov commission (1899–1901), named for its chairman, A. I. Zvegintsov of the Ministry of the Interior, one can clearly see that the study of "impoverishment" was focused on nine black-earth provinces (Voronezh, Kursk, Orel, Penza, Riazan, Saratov, Simbirsk, Tambov, and Tula), all of which appear to have been selected because of their overwhelmingly agricultural character. Obviously, the economic questions confronting the Commission led it to give the center a spatial configuration that differed from earlier interpretations. The northern non-black earth industrial area around Moscow was completely excluded, while the southern half of the traditional interior was broadened to include two Volga provinces that had previously fallen outside of it. As a result, the Zvegintsov Commission's center ended up looking less like a circle and more like a band or strip. The Commission emphasized the inequalities in revenues and expenditures that characterized the relationship between the center and the periphery. Much as in the case of the decision over the railroad tariffs, the region most to blame for the center's troubles was not the western periphery but rather the cheap grain-growing provinces of the trans-Volga and southeastern steppes.

In 1901 yet another state commission was convened, the so-called Kokovtsev Commission, which quickly became known to contemporaries as "the Commission on the Impoverishment of the Center" or simply "the Commission on the Center." This new commission had a center bigger than that of the Zveginstov Commission—it included an additional nine to the nine mentioned earlier (Nizhnii Novgorod, Samara, Orenburg, Ufa, Kazan, Khar'kov, Poltava, Chernigov, and the Don Cossack Host Territory). Furthermore, the Kokovtsev Commission also invited representatives from Kostroma, Viatka, Novgorod, and Smolensk provinces, and its geographic focus was now clearly defined as "Russia's central agricultural zone" (*polosa*). There were even calls for the Commission to extend its investigations to "the entire East and even parts of the South." In the end, however, the Commission resisted these temptations and limited its findings and policy directives to the eighteen "central" provinces that were originally specified. V. K. Plehve explained the Commission's reasoning in the following fashion: "Of all the inhabitants of the Russian empire, it is the peasantry of the central provinces that stands the firmest in terms of its allegiance to the state (*naibolee krepkimi s gosudarstvennoi tochki zreniia*). Therefore rumors of a supposed weakening of loyalty (*rasshatyvanie sredi nikh gosudarstvennykh osnov*) seem especially unjust in regard to this segment of the population and this part of the empire."[89]

In 1902, a Special Commission on the Needs of Agriculture was convened on the presumption that the country's agricultural troubles were general in nature rather than specific to a particular region. In the meetings of the Commission, however, individual members on the right insisted that the Commission's work be focused on "ancient Russian" (*iskonno russkie*) provinces. Minister of Interior Plehve remarked in 1903 that there was now "increasing proof of a decline in the well-being of the population of the interior provinces of European Russia." He went on to note that one of the solutions to this problem was to move peasants out of central areas afflicted by land shortages and resettle them in the empire's borderland regions.[90]

The members of state commissions were not alone in shaping new understandings of imperial space in the fin-de-siècle period. Reflecting the obvious regionalization of the imperial economy, late imperial economists also began suggesting a new framework for seeing the empire as a collection of economic regions. One result of this process was that "interior Russia" found itself conceptually swallowed by and divided between two newly defined economic areas, the Central Industrial Region and the Central Black Earth Region.

Still, the urge to define a center did not disappear. In the early twentieth century, the renowned chemist D. I. Mendeleev set out to pinpoint the exact location of the empire's center. As Mendeleev noted, "[w]hile there has been much talk about the center and the interests of the center have been considered by numerous commissions," no one had yet provided a strictly scientific determination of the center itself. In geographical terms, Mendeleev and his team concluded that the center point of the empire lay just south of Turukhansk in an inhospitable region close to the Arctic Circle. If one excluded the tundra zone from the calculation, the center then shifted to a gentler geographic location slightly north of Omsk. By contrast, the empire's "center in terms of population distribution," as based on the totals of the 1897 census, fell a good bit further west, in the northeastern corner of Tambov Province, between the towns of Kozlov and Morshansk. But Mendeleev predicted that this position was at most temporary. Given population growth and increased migration to Siberia and Central Asia, the center of population with time would inevitably shift "in a southeasterly direction."[91]

Of course, Mendeleev's research on these questions was wholly academic in character and had nothing to do with the various definitions of the center that were in the air at the time, but his interest in the theme is nonetheless revealing. Even though the formal grouping of "interior provinces" elaborated by the government in the first half of the nineteenth century did not change, the last years of the empire were marked by rising public commentary and government activity focused on making sense of "interior Russia" and determining the fate of the imperial center.

Translated by Willard Sunderland

Notes

1. J. P. LeDonne, *The Russian Empire and the World, 1700–1917: The Geopolitics of Expansion and Containment* (New York, 1997); A. S. Gerd et al., *Osnovaniia regionalistiki: formirovaniie i evoliutsiia istoriko-kul'turnykh zon Evropeiskoi Rossii* (St. Petersburg, 1999).

2. N. A. Ivanova, *Promyshlennyi tsentr Rossii 1907–1914 gg. Statistiko-ekonomicheskoe issledovanie* (Moscow, 1995).

3. M. K. Liubavskii, *Obzor istorii russkoi kolonizatsii s drevneishikh vremen i do xx veka* (Moscow, 1996), 253–254.

4. *Ekaterina II i G. A. Potemkin: lichnaia perepiska 1769–1791* (Moscow, 1997), 155, 239, 287.

5. J. Czubaty, *Rosja i świat: wyobraźnia polityczna elity władzy imperium rosyjskiego w początkach XIX wieku* (Warsaw, 1997), 79.

6. *Dekabristy: Izbrannye sochineniia v dvukh tomakh*, vol. 1 (Moscow, 1987), 46–48.

7. O. V. Orlik, *Groza dvenadtsatogo goda . . .* (Moscow, 1987), 26.

8. F. F. Vigel', *Zapiski* (Moscow, 2000), 299; S. D. Sheremet'ev, *Memuary* (Moscow, 2001), 301.

9. F. N. Glinka, *Pis'ma k drugu* (Moscow, 1990), 439–440.

10. Ibid., 438.

11. *Venchanie s Rossiei: perepiska velikogo kniazia Aleksandra Nikolaevicha s imperatorom Nikolaem I; 1837 god* (Moscow, 1999), 130, 132.

12. S. V. Maksimov, *Krylatye slova* (Nizhnii Novgorod, 1996), 75–77.

13. Glinka, *Pis'ma k drugu*, 440.

14. V. V. Passek, *Putevye zapiski* (Moscow, 1834).

15. K. Arsen'ev, *Statisticheskie ocherki Rossii* (St. Petersburg, 1848), 25–26, 164, 204–208, 214.

16. M. O. Koialovich, *Istoriia russkogo samosoznaniia po istoricheskim pamiatnikam i nauchnym sochineniiam* (Minsk, 1997), 480–481, 488.

17. A. S. Gerd et al., *Osnovaniia regionalistiki,* 341.

18. P. A. Valuev, *Dnevnik ministra vnutrennikh del,* vol. 2 (Moscow, 1961), 74–75.

19. Cited in N. Iu. Zamiatina, "Zona osvoeniia (frontir) i obraz v amerikanskoi i russkoi kul'turakh," *Obshchestvennye nauki i sovremennost'* 5 (1998): 80.

20. A. S. Pushkin, *Polnoe sobranie sochinenii v desiati tomakh,* vol. 6 (Leningrad, 1978), 435.

21. *Russkie memuary: Izbrannye stranitsy 1826–1856 gg.* (Moscow, 1990), 430, 484.

22. *Ocherki Rossii, izdavaemye Vadimom Passekom* (St. Petersburg, 1840), book 2, p. 90; book 3, pp. 157, 168.

23. Passek, *Putevye zapiski,* 116.

24. Ibid., 170, 172.

25. *Ocherki Rossii,* book 4, *smes',* p. 12.

26. I. S. Aksakov, *Pis'ma k rodnym 1844–1849* (Moscow, 1988), 13, 401, 403.

27. *Chteniia v obshchestve istorii i drevnostei rossiiskikh* 2 (1869): 64; V. Sichyns'kyi, *Chuzhyntsi pro Ukrainu* (Kiev, 1992), 182.

28. I. S. Aksakov, *Pis'ma k rodnym 1849–1856* (Moscow, 1994), 261, 270, 317.

29. Ibid., 306, 310.

30. T. P. Passek, *Iz dal'nikh let: vospominaniia*, vol. 2 (Moscow, 1963), 196.

31. P. D. Boborykin, *Vospominaniia*, vol. 2 (Moscow, 1965), 81–82.

32. G. N. Potanin, *Vospominaniia* (Novosibirsk, 1983), 303.

33. *Ocherki Rossii*, book 3, *smes'*, pp. 18–19.

34. Ibid., book 3, *smes'*, pp. 22–25.

35. *Ocherki Rossii* (St. Petersburg, 1838), book 1, p. 22.

36. Ibid., book. 3, *smes'*, pp. 18–25.

37. Vigel', *Zapiski*, 93, 171, 175, 480.

38. G. N. Potanin, *Pis'ma v chetyrekh tomakh*, vol. 1 (Irkutsk, 1977), 98.

39. Aksakov, *Pis'ma k rodnym 1844–1849*, 482.

40. Ibid., 377–378.

41. A. N. Pypin, *Moi zametki* (Saratov, 1996), 65.

42. V. Liadov, *Evropeiskaia Rossiia v fizicheskom i etnograficheskom otnosheniiakh* (St. Petersburg, 1861), 27, 62, 82–83.

43. Valuev, *Dnevnik ministra vnutrennikh del*, vol. 1, p. 216.

44. V. V. Trepavlov, "Volga v kul'turnoi traditsii narodov vostochnoi Evropy," *Etnograficheskoe obozrenie* 6 (1997).

45. I. I. Dmitriev, *Sochineniia* (Moscow, 1986), 311.

46. Aksakov, *Pis'ma k rodnym 1844–1849*, 23, 27.

47. S. V. Mironenko, *Samoderzhavie i reformy: politicheskaia bor'ba v Rossii v nachale XIX v.* (Moscow, 1989), 193.

48. Trepavlov, "Volga v kul'turnoi traditsii narodov vostochnoi Evropy," 107.

49. Vigel', *Zapiski*, 176, 302, 391.

50. P. Viazemskii, *Zapisnye knizhki* (Moscow, 1992), 49.

51. Maksimov, *Krylatye slova*, 58.

52. A. A. Formozov, *Klassiki russkoi literatury i istoricheskaia nauka* (Moscow, 1995), 85–91.

53. A. K. Tolstoi, *Sobranie sochinenii v chetyrekh tomakh*, vol. 4 (Moscow, 1980), 491.

54. A. F. Koni, *Izbrannoe* (Moscow, 1989), 239–240.

55. N. M. Pirumova, *Zemskoe liberal'noe dvizhenie: sotsial'nye korni i evoliutsiia do nachala XX veka* (Moscow, 1977), 136.

56. V. G. Belinskii, *Sobranie sochinenii v deviati tomakh*, vol. 7 (Moscow, 1981), 144.

57. A. S. Pushkin, *Polnoe sobranie sochinenii v desiati tomakh*, vol. 7 (Leningrad, 1978), 187–190, 439–440.

58. Cited in *Moskovskii letopisets*, vol. 1 (Moscow, 1988), 89.

59. Sheremet'ev, *Memuary*, 300.

60. Aksakov, *Pis'ma k rodnym 1849–1856*, 20, 41, 46, 251.

61. *Nizhegorodskii sbornik*, vol. 3 (Nizhnii Novgorod, 1870), 6.

62. Maksimov, *Krylatye slova*, 70.

63. N. M. Karamzin, *Pis'ma russkogo puteshestvennika* (Moscow, 1988), 39.

64. A. V. Nikitenko, *Dnevnik*, vol. 1 (Moscow, 1955), p. 149.

65. *Ob etnograficheskoi karte Petra Keppena, izdannoi Imperatorskim Russkim Geograficheskim Obshchestvom* (St. Petersburg, 1852), 23.

66. E. Iu. Sergeev, '*Inaia zemlia, inoe nebo . . .*': *zapad i voennaia elita Rossii (1900–1914 gg.)*. (Moscow, 2001), 191.

67. Nikitenko, *Dnevnik*, 1: 150–151.

68. D. A. Miliutin, *Vospominaniia 1860–1862*, ed. L. G. Zakharova (Moscow: Rossiiskii arkhiv, 1999), 252, 461.

69. Nikitenko, *Dnevnik*, 1: 149–151.

70. A. I. Gertsen, *Sobranie sochinenii v vos'mi tomakh*, vol. 5 (Moscow, 1975), 30.

71. Vigel', *Zapiski*, 176.

72. Liadov, *Evropeiskaia Rossiia v fizicheskom i etnograficheskom otnosheniiakh*, 61.

73. *Krizis samoderzhaviia v Rossii: 1895–1917* (Leningrad, 1984), 66.

74. *Russkaia istoricheskaia pesnia* (Leningrad, 1990), 156–157.

75. V. S. Ikonnikov, *Ekaterina II kak istorik* (Kiev, 1911), 11.

76. A. P. Butenev, "Vospominaniia russkogo diplomata," *Russkii arkhiv* 5 (1881): 70–72.

77. Maksimov, *Krylatye slova*, 65.

78. *Materialy, sobrannye dlia vysochaishe uchrezhdennoi Komissii o preobrazovanii gubernskikh i uezdnykh uchrezhdenii: otdel administrativnyi, chast' 1, Materialy istoricheskie i zakonodatel'nye* (St. Petersburg, 1870), section 6, p. 74.

79. *Slovar' akademicheskoi rossiiskoi*, vol. 1 (St. Petersburg, 1789), 791; vol. 4 (St. Petersburg, 1793), 570.

80. V. Dal', *Tolkovoi slovar' zhivogo velikorusskogo iazyka* (St. Petersburg-Moscow, 1882), 174.

81. *Slovar' akademicheskoi rossiiskoi*, vol. 3 (St. Petersburg, 1792), 816.

82. *Rossiia: polnoe geograficheskoe opisanie nashego otechestva*, vol. 6 (St. Petersburg, 1901), 157.

83. *Entsiklopedicheskii leksikon A. Pliushara*, vol. 9 (St. Petersburg, 1837), 261–265, 274.

84. V. S. Pecherin, "Zamogil'nye zapiski," *Russkoe obshchestvo 30-kh godov XIX v.: liudi i idei; memuary sovremennikov* (Moscow, 1989), 278; S. Iu. Vitte, *Vospominaniia*, vol. 2 (Moscow, 1960), 498.

85. L. E. Gorizontov, " 'Bol'shaia russkaia natsiia' v imperskoi i regional'noi strategii samoderzhaviia," in *Prostranstvo vlasti: imperskii opyt Rossii i vyzovy sovremennosti* (Moscow, 2001).

86. See the article by A. A. Volvenko in this volume.

87. L. E. Gorizontov, *Paradoksy imperskoi politiki: Poliaki v Rossii i russkie v Pol'she (XIX–nachalo XX vv.)* (Moscow, 1999), 61, 64.

88. Iu. B. Solov'ev, *Samoderzhavie i dvorianstvo v kontse XIX veka* (Leningrad, 1973), 232–233; A. P. Korelin, *Dvorianstvo v poreformennoi Rossii: sostav, chislennost', korporativnaia organizatsiia* (Moscow, 1979), 267.

89. M. S. Simonova, "Politika tsarizma v krest'ianskom voprose nakanune revoliutsii 1905–1907 gg.," *Istoricheskie zapiski*, 75 (Moscow, 1965): 214–215, 231; Idem, "Problema 'oskudeniia' tsentra i ee rol' v formirovanii agrarnoi politiki samoderzhaviia v 90-kh godakh XIX–nachale XX v.," *Problemy sotsial'no-ekonomicheskoi istorii Rossii* (Moscow, 1971).

90. *Krizis samoderzhaviia v Rossii*, 66.

91. D. I. Mendeleev, *K poznaniiu Rossii*, 7th ed. (St. Petersburg, 1912), 5, 125–127, 140–142.

3 How Bashkiria Became Part of European Russia, 1762–1881

Charles Steinwedel

The perception that the Ural mountains divided the Russian empire into European and Asian parts has a long history. As Mark Bassin's work has shown, the conception of the Urals as a continental boundary, first advocated by historian and geographer Vasilii N. Tatishchev in the 1730s, became widely accepted by the early nineteenth century.[1] Inspection of most historical works on the Russian empire amply confirms the continued acceptance and power of this division of the empire's space. Even today, most historians, to the extent that they are self-conscious about their focus on "European Russia," provide a map labeled as such or as "Provinces of European Russia" to help their readers imagine the space that they address.[2] On most such maps, the boundary of "European Russia" indeed follows Tatishchev's scheme. The Urals generally mark the border of European Russia, with Perm, Ufa, and occasionally Orenburg the easternmost provinces indicated.

The Europe-Asia divide may have begun as a cartographic convenience reflecting the vision of geographers in the empire's capital and a desire to mark off a European Russian core from broader claims of empire in Asia. The perception that Europe ended in the Urals region, however, soon entered the minds of those thinking about, writing about, and administering the area. One Orenburg-born official writing in 1851, for instance, described the diverse landscape and cultures of the Orenburg region in which " . . . Europe meets with Asia, the steamship meets the camel, [where] the dance hall of the Assembly of the Nobility, designed by [Konstantin] Ton, is twenty versts from the nomadic tent."[3] Although by the 1850s international boundaries had moved to the south and east, the Urals region remained a cultural borderland in which differences between Europe and Asia were marked out. The definitions of what constituted European Russia were never simple. Cartographic representations located Ufa Province, for instance, in European Russia by 1900. Yet by 1897, after more than a century of substantial migration from western Russia, less than half the province's population spoke Russian as its first language and practiced Orthodoxy. Contemporaries still considered the region poor and backward. Ufa fell short of Europeanness in three most commonly regarded dimensions—Russianness, Christianity, and economic development. Why, then, was Ufa located in the mental geography of European Russia? What did locating a province there involve?

In this chapter, I examine one essential aspect of a province's placement in European Russia. I will argue that the incorporation of a territory into European Russia required, above all, the replacement of military governors and a military style of governance with a civil administration rooted in a larger, more diverse local elite that identified with autocratic authority and with the administrative procedures and cultural values perceived to be European.[4] The introduction of administrative forms characteristic of the empire's European core indicated the center's confidence that a reliable elite was present in a region and was intended to have a catalytic effect, organizing the social and service elite already in place and drawing additional persons of status and education. The reproduction of the institutional arrangements of the European core in the borderlands enabled a geographer to map European Russia to particular provincial boundaries.

I examine how a region in the empire's east, known as Bashkiriia in Russian or Bashkortostan in Bashkir, gradually, haltingly, and never definitively became "European." Bashkiria took its name from the Turkic-speaking people who lived in the region, centering on Ufa and Orenburg provinces before 1917 and stretching west to Samara province, north into Perm province, and across the Urals into western Siberia. I examine the region's incorporation into European Russia in three overlapping stages, with a primary focus on the reigns of Catherine II (reigned 1762–1796) and Alexander II (1855–1881), two tsars who most strongly identified with Europe. The first stage, from the 1780s to the 1860s, involved attracting members of the political, service elite and nobles to the region and their organization in institutions. Despite Alexander I's and Nicholas I's many differences with Catherine II, the process of incorporation did not fundamentally change during their reigns. The next stage, that of the Great Reforms, involved the expansion of the institutional basis of the state in Bashkiria and the participation in the reformed institutions by a much broader range of the empire's population. In this regard, I address the creation of local units of self-administration, the zemstvos, as particularly important. Finally, I trace Bashkiria's incorporation into the post-reform arena of press and public activism, which became most visible toward the end of the 1870s. Revelations regarding the distribution of land to those close to the Orenburg governor-general helped speed the elimination of military governance of the region and the application of a civil administration more like that in central provinces. In doing so, however, activists called into question the Europeanness of imperial administration that had been assumed from Catherine's time forward.

Before 1735, the Russian empire had only a minimal presence in Bashkiria. The military conquest of Bashkiria and the building of a major garrison town in Orenburg, combined with the large-scale destruction of the local Bashkir population by military actions and hunger, greatly increased the tsar's position in the area.[5] Nonetheless, the Orenburg governor's overwhelming concern was the steppe frontier's security in the most immediate sense. As Orenburg Vice-Governor Volkov wrote to the Empress in 1763, "There is no one here other than military people."[6] The Pugachev uprising, which broke out in 1773, demonstrated the tenuousness of the tsarist regime's hold on Bashkiria. Rebels overthrew tsarist authority throughout the area, with the exception of the garrison towns of Ufa and Orenburg. By 1775, military action had restored order. But the long-term process of building a stable administration in the region had only begun.

The reforms in provincial administration under Catherine were applied to Bashkiria in the 1780s and transformed Bashkiria in two key respects. First, in 1782 the state demarcated the region in the manner of central Russia for the first time.[7] Second, the new territorial divisions greatly increased the number and status of personnel who governed in Bashkiria. Catherine's provincial reform elevated Bashkiria's leadership and injected new ideas and concepts of governance into the region.

Until 1781, Bashkiria's most important cities, Ufa and Orenburg, were under the authority of the Orenburg provincial governor located in that city. The Orenburg Territory was so sparsely populated that the province had not been subdivided into uezds (counties), as had most central parts of the empire.[8] The creation of the Ufa and Simbirsk *namestnichestvo* (a region ruled by a governor-general) with its headquarters in Ufa in 1782 was part of an empire-wide reform that combined the administration of two or more provinces under one governor-general. The reform elevated considerably the status of Bashkiria's administrators. The region's highest official had been a servitor of the seventh rank; now Bashkiria received a governor-general of the third rank. The first two men appointed to the post, General Iakobii (served 1782–1784) and Baron Osip Igel'strom (served 1784–1792 and 1796–1802), were two of the outstanding administrators of the Catherinian era.[9] Igel'strom was a protégé of Potemkin and a favorite of the Empress. Igel'strom made a great impression on those who served in his administration. One official described him as "a German with all the qualities of an ancient knight and of a latter-day *petit maître*."[10] Men such as Iakobii and Igel'strom, who could not write Russian, brought wide experience and cosmopolitan backgrounds to the eastern provinces. They also had solid connections in the capitals, improving the chances that their projects and plans would be approved. As many memoirists noted, the character and spending habits of a governor-general had a major impact on social and cultural life in a region well into the nineteenth century. The governor-general stood at the center of local society and, especially in sparsely populated regions far from the center, could dispose of substantial resources that greatly influenced the fortunes of those around him. Governor-generals often had entourages, bringing new men and women, nearly all from European Russia, into the region.[11] The presence of distinguished officials in Bashkiria increased the region's connections with Catherine's court and its European style and cultural norms.[12] At lower levels, ten new counties were created within the *namestnichestvo*. Each had seven positions in the table of ranks, substantially increasing the number of state officials in Bashkiria.[13] The administrative apparatus in Bashkiria remained small, but the changes substantially upgraded the local administration both qualitatively and quantitatively.

Perhaps most importantly, Catherine's provincial reforms stimulated the formation of a noble elite. Noble landownership was crucial to the tsarist state's search for support in Bashkiria. In a world of serfdom, political power rested primarily on the creation of a group of noble landowners who possessed land and people sufficient to support the autocracy's local military operations and to supplement the region's small core of state servitors. The tsar had given land grants to servitors in the region since the sixteenth century, but in the second half of the eighteenth century Bashkiria's large amounts of sparsely populated land increasingly drew to the area nobles who did not necessarily serve in the state administration. In his semi-autobiographical novel *The Family Chronicle*, Sergei Aksakov suggests motives and means by which nobles moved to Bashkiria. Aksakov's grandfather, a noble landowner in Simbirsk Province on the Volga, had seen his lands divided by marriages to the point that his holdings were, in essence, collectively run. He decided to move east in order to restore his independence. Nobles such as Aksakov's grandfather acquired large expanses of sparsely populated land from Bashkirs either through deception or by purchase at very low prices. The prominence of men such as Iakobii and Igel'strom and a greater number of state servitors increased the attractiveness of the region to men such as Aksakov's grandfather. The new positions created by reform improved chances for local nobles to improve their status by marrying off their daughters to rising servitors. The combination of land and opportunity drew approximately 150 noble families to Ufa province alone in the second half of the eighteenth century.[14]

Since eighteenth-century Bashkiria was overwhelmingly Muslim, the integration of Muslims into the elite was a crucial element in creating the local nobility. Until the middle of the seventeenth century, members of the Muslim noble elite frequently entered the Muscovite tsar's service.[15] In 1718, legislation stripped Muslim nobles of their privileges and equated with peasants those who did not convert to Orthodoxy.[16] Catherine II began to change this policy in 1773. In order to draw Muslims into the empire's political life and to pacify the restive local Bashkir population, in 1773 Catherine issued a decree entitled "On the toleration of all creeds":[17] "As the Most High God tolerates all faiths, languages, and creeds, so too Her Majesty, [proceeding] from the very same principles, corresponding to His Holy will, is pleased also to allow this, desiring only that love and harmony always reign among subjects of Her Majesty."[18] The secular state's assumption of authority in the religious affairs of the non-Orthodox population was a key element of toleration. As an extension of Catherine's policy of toleration, she decreed in 1784 that "princes and *murzas* [the Tatar word for prince] of Tatar origins" be allowed to regain the privileges of a Russian (*rossiiskii*) nobleman if they could provide written proof that their ancestors had been noble. According to her decree, all should enjoy the same privileges, no matter what their "clan or law."[19] As a result of this law, Ufa province, a primary place for resettlement of Muslim nobles from regions such as Simbirsk and Kazan, had a substantial concentration of Muslim nobles. In the second half of the eighteenth century, 14 of the 150 families newly registered in Ufa's Noble Assembly had Muslim surnames.[20] Some had lost most of their lands and lived little better than peasants. Nonetheless, the law made it possible for a small elite of Muslims to enjoy the privileges of nobility, including state service.

A Muslim religious leader captured this sense that Muslims could become privileged members of the empire's elite in a December 1789 speech.

Mufti Husein lavished thanks and praise upon Catherine, and asserted that those who cooperated with the tsarist regime could receive a high degree of acceptance: "The Russian [*rossiiskii*] son celebrates that Catherine reigns over him . . . But who is this lover, this devotee [*naperstnik*] of happiness? Is it really only he whom the Evangelist's spirit directs? Those who think so, do not think correctly. The sagacious mother does not consider [*vziraet*] various faiths, just loyalty of the heart [*predannost' serdtsem*]." Because of Catherine's tolerance of Islam and support of Muslim institutions, Husein called on Muslims to be loyal to Catherine.[21] Catherine's myth of empire was not a religious one but that of an enlightened monarch and administrative elite "bringing the benefits of law and improved material life" to the tsar's realm.[22] Elite Muslims could become "sons of the empire" regardless of their religious confession. The inclusion of Muslims in the nobility demonstrates the ability of the tsarist administration to integrate local elites into the privileged strata, and to draw nobles from other parts of Russia into new areas. These elites would then help spread the "enlightened" principles and values of the empire into newly conquered regions.[23]

The Orenburg Muslim Spiritual Assembly

The expansion of the nobility and inclusion of some Muslims in it did much to form an elite loyal to the Empress. But the Muslim nobility remained small. Few members of groups such as the Bashkirs were noble. The Orenburg Muslim Spiritual Assembly (OMSA) and the Bashkir cantons organized many more members of the Muslim elites in defense of the tsarist state's interest. The establishment of the OMSA in 1788 and the Cantonal Administration of the Bashkirs in 1798 highlight how the tsarist administration connected Bashkiria's non-Orthodox, non-Russian-speaking populations to the Europe-oriented culture at court. These two institutions helped create a loyal elite that spoke enough Russian to interact with the state administration but that retained sufficient ties to its communities to help bring about compliance with state policy.

In the early 1780s, Catherine's policy changed from one of toleration to active promotion of Islam as a means of achieving influence in the steppe.[24] Baron Osip Igel'strom provided the experience and determination necessary to bring coherence to the empire's policy toward Islam in Bashkiria. Igel'strom had been the "chief architect" of the Khanate of Crimea's integration into the Russian administration after its conquest in 1774.

Igel'strom viewed the cooperation of Muslim elites as essential to administration of the former Khanate.[25] When Igel'strom was assigned to Bashkiria in 1784, he sought cooperation with local Muslim leaders in Bashkiria just as he had in Crimea. In particular, Igel'strom sought to make use of Akhun Mukhametzhan Husein's contacts with the Kazakh hordes for diplomatic purposes.[26] The Ottoman declaration of war on the Russian empire in September 1787 made diplomacy with Muslim leaders more urgent.[27] In an effort to insure the loyalty of Muslims in Bashkiria, on May 31, 1788, Igel'strom convinced the State Council of the need to confirm Muslim teachers, imams, and *akhun*s (senior local legal experts) in their posts, and he proposed that their qualifications be certified by a commission established in Ufa.[28] To this end, Igel'strom sponsored legislation calling for the creation in Ufa of "a Spiritual Assembly of Muslim law." Akhun Husein was appointed to the position of mufti, head of the assembly, with a generous salary. Two or three salaried Kazan Tatar clerics were appointed to assist the mufti.[29] The assembly had jurisdiction over all Muslims of the eastern part of the empire. Catherine confirmed the decision of the Senate on April 20, 1789.[30]

Igel'strom and Catherine II established the Spiritual Assembly specifically to review the loyalty of the *ulema,* the Muslim learned elite; to raise the prestige of Akhun Husein, who had come to play an important role in diplomacy on the steppe; and to limit foreign influence on local religious elites in a frontier zone.[31] The examination of candidates was a top priority of Igel'strom's in the formation of the OMSA and remained one of its central functions throughout its existence.[32] In order to combat the influence of clerics from Central Asia or Ottoman lands, each candidate for the position of imam had to present to the OMSA a certificate from local police officials that he resided in the location in which he sought to be an imam and that he conducted himself properly.[33] If the judges of the OMSA determined that the candidate was competent, he returned to his village as an *ukaznyi* or official imam.[34] The Spiritual Assembly began to incorporate Muslims into the Russian empire by marking their elites off from the influence of other powers on the steppe. In doing so, Igel'strom initiated an unprecedented effort to incorporate certain Muslims into the tsarist administration itself.

As the empire's presence on the steppe frontier became more secure in the nineteenth century, the administration of Muslims became less a matter of steppe diplomacy and more a domestic concern. To reflect the OMSA's changing role, after the 1790s, the tsarist administration increased the OMSA's size, subordinated it to higher levels of the tsarist bureaucracy, and gave it greater responsibilities in primarily secular, domestic affairs.[35] At its founding, the OMSA was subordinate to the Ufa provincial administration. By 1832, the OMSA became subordinate to the Ministry of Internal Affairs in St. Petersburg.[36] By 1843, the institution's staff had increased to sixteen with a budget of over seven thousand rubles in addition to the mufti's and judges' salaries.[37] The OMSA had acquired a prominent position in the empire's increasingly bureaucratic, ministerial government.

In addition to the OMSA's supervision over Muslim clerics and the performance of religious services, the tsarist administration recognized numerous responsibilities of the OMSA and its clerics in the sphere of private law. In May 1811, Muslim marriages were officially recognized as within the jurisdiction of local clerics.[38] In 1835, Muslim clerics received official sanction to decide cases of disobedience (*nepovinovenii*) by children to their parents in a so-called "Conscience Court" (*sovestnyi sud*).[39] In 1836, the right of Muslim clergy to intervene in the division of estates was confirmed.[40] Another significant expansion of the imams' administrative duties came in 1828 with the introduction of metrical books and the collection of information on births, deaths, marriages, and divorces in all Muslim communities.[41] Imams acquired the responsibility of collecting this information, which was important to the application of criminal laws, the proper induction of draftees for military service, and other state functions that depended upon whether a person had reached the age of majority or whether a person was married or single.[42] Beyond these administrative responsibilities, the OMSA served the tsarist state by urging Muslims to respect the authority of the tsar and to pray for the tsar's well-being.[43] Mention of the tsar in Friday prayers became institutionalized at the time of Nicholas I's elevation to the throne. Mufti Abdrakhimov (served 1825–1840) called upon Muslims to give thanks to God for the tsar and to pray for him every morning, night, and every Friday in the mosque.[44]

The tsarist state did not give Muslim clerics the status and privilege of Orthodoxy clergy, and the responsibilities officially "granted" to Muslim clerics often amounted to the recognition of roles they had already assumed on the basis of traditional Muslim law. Yet by officially recognizing the authority of Muslim religious officials and organizing them under the jurisdiction of the OMSA, the tsarist administration helped to form a group of elite Muslims who would identify with autocratic authority. Moreover, the mufti and the OMSA's staff received privileges in exchange for loyal service. The tsars ennobled the muftis and granted them a number of honors and gifts.[45] The administrative reforms of 1822 reduced the power of the Kazakh elite, and the empire's southeastern border became more secure by the 1840s, thus lessening the need for the mufti's diplomatic work.[46] The tsar's recognition of the muftis declined as well.[47]

To a considerably lesser extent than the OMSA's mufti and judges (*kadis*), its clerics received privileges that varied over time in exchange for their service.[48] Laws of 1796 and 1801 freed clerics from conscription and from corporal punishment while they held their posts.[49] Muslim clerics enjoyed freedom from corporal punishment for only two decades, however, before they lost the privilege.[50] Late in Nicholas I's reign, however, Catherinian polices regarding the Muslim religious elite enjoyed a resurgence. In 1848, Count Kiselev, the Minister of State Domains and a person noted for his efforts to promote reform, proposed new policies toward the clerics. Noting the policy of religious toleration initiated by Catherine II, Kiselev pointed out that the regime did not grant privileges to the clergy of these religious groups. As the empire expanded to the south and east, and more and more Muslims came under Russian authority, Kiselev considered it necessary to tie Muslim clerics "more closely to the state." Subjecting all but the highest members of the Muslim clergy to corporal punishment and military recruitment had "inculcated a wholly disagreeable disposition" toward Russian authority.[51] In 1849, Kiselev sponsored laws reaffirming the mufti's authority over Muslim clerics and proposed that clerics should receive personal exemption from corporal punishment and conscription.[52] Some officials remained suspicious of Kiselev's plan, but the State Council ratified his proposal in 1850.[53] Such policies increased the tsarist administration's influence among Muslim elites.

The Cantonal Administration of the Bashkirs, 1798–1865

From the time the Bashkir tribes swore their loyalty to the tsar in the sixteenth century, the state had collected taxes and, upon occasion, mobilized recruits by district (*ulus* in Bashkir or *volost'* in Russian) under the leadership of an elder.[54] In the eighteenth century, this *volost'* structure began to break down into smaller units, called *tiub*s or commands (*kommandy* in Russian).[55] Such a system served the needs of the Bashkirs but did not provide the steady source of recruits and taxes that Governor-General Igel'strom required.[56] In an effort to mobilize Bashkir troops more systematically and to receive better men, Igel'strom established the cantonal system of administration. The first stage involved the enumeration of Bashkir and Meshcheriak households and the fixing of their locations into *iurts*, or tents.[57] Next, in 1798, Igel'strom established cantons as a new administrative position between the county or uezd and the smaller Bashkir *kommand*.[58] The creation of cantonal administration required a staff of more than four hundred men, including elders and their assistants. The reform thus opened new positions of authority to many Bashkirs. Cantonal administrators had behind them the power of the tsarist administration, which gave them considerable authority to control the movement of canton members and enabled the administration to begin to fix the nomadic or semi-nomadic Bashkir population in territorial units that corresponded to political divisions of European Russia.[59] Cantonal administration made Bashkirs and Meshcheriaks a military force much like the Cossacks. These groups provided and equipped soldiers in lieu of taxes.[60] The tsarist state thus created a new Bashkir service elite that dominated a military estate. The cantonal administration reported to the Orenburg governor-general, and remained distinct from the civil administration in the city of Ufa, which had jurisdiction over the non-Bashkir population.

The final stage in the reform made complete a shift from clan to territorial organization. The *iurts* had been drawn more or less on top of clan-based *kommands*, except when they spread across county lines. From the establishment of the cantons to the 1830s, *iurts* were subdivided still further. The new, smaller *iurt* bore little relation to the older Bashkir *volost'* and *kommand*. The clan-based organization existing before 1789, in which *volost'* and *tiub* elders had led people primarily of their own clans, broke down. Clan-based administrative forms survived in the ownership of land, but for administrative and conscription purposes the territorial principle triumphed. Leaders of the new cantons were more oriented to the state they served and depended less on their Bashkir constituency for authority. The breakdown of clan ties between the political elite and the Bashkirs made organized rebellion much less likely.[61]

The cantonal system of administration helped create a Bashkir elite that spoke Russian, had mastered at least some values of the empire's administration, and presided over cantons delineated geographically, as was European Russia, rather than by clan. The canton and *iurt* elders and their families received exemption from military service and freedom from corporal punishment.[62] Some cantonal elder positions became essentially hereditary, as son succeeded father.[63] Some Bashkirs were ennobled as a result of their service in cantons.[64] The formation of Bashkir cantons, along with

Catherine's provincial reform, the growth of the nobility, and the establishment of the OMSA, brought Bashkiria's inhabitants under greater control of a privileged, multi-confessional elite tied to the autocracy.

The European powers' defeat of the tsar's army in the Crimean War (1853–1856) demonstrated the limitations of Russia's existing administration and estate institutions to mobilize people and resources. The new tsar, Alexander II (reigned 1855–1881), and his key advisers no longer considered the development of a noble elite, as under Catherine, and of the state bureaucracy, as under Nicholas I, sufficient to insure Russia's power, prosperity, and stability. In the Great Reforms the autocracy began to supplement enlightened culture and ministerial government with liberal ideals of government then considered more European.[65] Most importantly for our purposes, through reforms Alexander and his officials sought to extend rudimentary civil status to all the tsar's subjects who seemed ready for it. The abolition of serfdom was the most obvious manifestation of this. Reformers sought to increase participation in public life and to create new institutions, such as zemstvos and city dumas, that would include non-noble representatives. Nobles maintained their leading role in political and civic life, but their power would come through participation in institutions rather than personal authority. The new institutions were also intended to be more than mere appendages of the bureaucracy. Participation in local self-administration, juries, and universal military service obligations was supposed to increase social responsibility and economic initiative.

Along with increased opportunities for participation, the Great Reforms brought greater demands upon those who would participate in civic life. The Great Reforms were not extended everywhere, but only to those areas that, in the opinion of state officials, had sufficient quantities of educated, loyal men who could be counted on to make them work. Areas with such populations received the European-inspired institutions of the core of the empire; those without did not. Most of the Great Reforms, including the emancipation of the peasants, judicial reforms, and military reforms, were applied to both of Bashkiria's core provinces, Ufa and Orenburg, which marked the second stage in the inclusion of Bashkiria into European Russia. The Great Reforms influenced the organization of power to an even larger extent in Bashkiria than they did elsewhere, however. The elimination of the Bashkir cantons in 1865 represents a "Great Reform" of Bashkir administration, one closely connected to those reforms applied elsewhere in European Russia.

Strategic factors played a major role in the change of Bashkiria's administrative structure after 1861. In 1861, Bashkiria's organization remained an anomaly in the empire, reflecting the region's uncertain status as a frontier zone. The provinces of central Russia by this time featured civilian governors who were the highest authorities in their province, while the border regions were led by military governor-generals.[66] Bashkiria's administration represented a compromise between civilian and military governance. The Orenburg governor-general still possessed the greatest authority in the region, but he shared his rather large jurisdiction with Ufa's civilian governor. The bifurcation of authority was reflected in the organization of the population as well. Those of the Bashkir or Meshcheriak estates lived in cantons responsible to the governor-general, while the rest of the province's population lived in counties supervised by the Ufa civil governor. As the steppe frontier came more fully under the tsar's authority, the need to mobilize militarily the region just northwest of the frontier decreased. The reduced threat from the steppe and the conquest of Central Asia meant that Bashkiria in general and Ufa in particular had less military significance. The pressure to have the Bashkirs perform military service in support of the Orenburg line now largely disappeared with the decline of the external threat in the region. As a result, in 1865, the Ministry of Internal Affairs made Ufa a separate province under a civilian governor with jurisdiction over the province's entire population. Ufa's position remained somewhat anomalous, however; the Orenburg governor-general continued to have substantial authority in Ufa.[67]

As pressure to have the Bashkirs perform military service on the frontier with Central Asia declined and the imperative to include Bashkirs in the civic order grew, the two forces combined to bring an end to the institutional isolation of the Bashkir estate from the peasant estate.[68] To this end, Tsar Alexander II issued the "Statutes on the Bashkirs" in May 1863, according to which, "the *inorodtsy* known by the name Bashkir, Meshcheriak, Teptiar, and Bobyl . . . are granted civil organization [*ustroistvo*] as free rural residents on the bases elaborated in these statutes."[69] Over the next two years, Bashkir cantons were eliminated completely. The Statutes on Bashkirs specified that the Bashkirs be granted all rights permitted peasants in 1861. They could enter into contracts, acquire property, run industrial and merchant establishments, enter trades, and change estate statuses as appropriate.[70] For the first time since 1818, the Bashkirs were permitted to sell their land. Rather than being subordinate to military command, the Bashkirs now fell under the jurisdiction of the Ministry of Internal Affairs. Like other peasants, they were organized into districts (*volosti*) under the leadership of an elected elder (*starshina*).[71] The Bashkirs' position remained somewhat different from peasants in that Bashkirs retained greater control over the distribution and inheritance of their land.[72] In most respects, however, the Bashkirs' status became identical to that of peasants in European Russia.

The stipulation that the Bashkir population should participate equally with Russian peasants in zemstvo affairs indicated the great extent to which their status had changed. The introduction of zemstvos only to Ufa Province in 1875 and not to Orenburg until the eve of the First World War indicated that the presence of nobles and educated men, not the presence of non-Russians, was the major difference in application of the Great Reforms. Bashkirs were more numerous in Ufa than Orenburg, but Ufa also had more nobles and educated non-nobles, both Orthodox and Muslim, than Orenburg. Since Orenburg had been more exposed to raids from the steppe in the period from 1770 to the 1840s, when nobles moved to Bashkiria in substantial numbers, noblemen preferred land in Ufa Province to land in Orenburg. As a result, officials in St. Petersburg considered Ufa to possess sufficient educated, cultured men to discharge the mission given to the zemstvo assemblies by the tsar, including the development of schools, postal services, and agronomical assistance. The zemstvos had a limited range of action. They were supposed to concern themselves only with local issues and not the larger affairs of state. They tended to be dominated by the same men, primarily nobles, who already dominated local affairs. Nonetheless, state officials and political activists attributed considerable importance to the zemstvos. Elections to them were organized in part by landholding rather than strictly by estate status, which distinguished them from other institutions. The major estate groups—nobles, merchants, and peasants—were all represented. Finally, since the zemstvos did have some legally recognized responsibilities, they have been interpreted as a first, if partial, deviation from autocratic principles and as the cradle of noble liberalism and civil society in Russia.[73]

In autumn of 1875, a zemstvo assembly was convoked in each of Ufa's six counties, and these bodies elected representatives to the provincial zemstvo that met later that year in the city of Ufa. Zemstvo institutions were one place where men of different estate statuses and religious groups met.

Since zemstvo statutes did not limit non-Orthodox participation, the Muslim population had substantial representation in zemstvo assemblies.[74] In the 1880s, Muslims made up 16 to 18 percent of the provincial assembly,[75] and in overwhelmingly Muslim Belebei County Muslim deputies ranged from approximately 30 percent to more than 50 percent of the total in 1887.[76] Furthermore, in Belebei, Muslims served as chairman of the zemstvo board three times.[77] The zemstvos thus fulfilled the government's intentions that they draw together various parts of local society, even though the performance of the Ufa zemstvos did not match the high expectations for these institutions.[78] They indicated a recognition that Ufa was similar to provinces of European Russia.

The final stage of Bashkiria's integration into European Russia occurred in the late 1870s and early 1880s. The effort to create an institutional apparatus that would increase the state's connection with a more responsible and civic-minded population had implications administrators neither locally nor in St. Petersburg fully appreciated. Improvements in communications and transportation, combined with the more educated, civic-minded society the Great Reforms sought to create, drew Bashkiria into the broader public sphere and the leftist politics of the capitals. New means of communications and the influx of migrants brought people, ideas, and goods from central Russia, as well as allowing local writers and activists to contribute more readily to the center's growing press.[79] By the 1870s, people from Ufa more regularly contributed articles to central newspapers. As they did so, they challenged the Europeanness of the activities of the local administration. By helping to expose the excesses of the local administration they made the administration out to be the force of darkness and backwardness in the region. The most marked result of their activity was the revelation that the local administration had worked to strip Bashkirs of their land in order to support themselves and friends of the governor-general. The scandal resulted in the elimination of the Orenburg governor-generalship and thus the end of Bashkiria's distinctive administrative structure.

The end of Bashkir isolation in 1865 had vast implications for both the Bashkirs and the region as a whole. The elimination of the Bashkir cantons required the review of laws applying to them. Nikolai Kryzhanovskii conducted such a review after he became Orenburg governor-general in 1865. Kryzhanovskii argued that the Bashkirs had been given civil status identical to that of the peasant estate with the exception of land ownership, and thus administrative arrangements regarding them should be the same as they were for other peasants.[80] The question of Bashkir landholding became central to state policy. Kryzhanovskii argued that the then-current ban on Bashkir land sales ran contrary to recognition of the Bashkirs as "landowners with full rights" (*polnopravnye sobstvenniki*) and should be eliminated. His proposal became law in February 1869 in the form of legislation that sought to regulate Bashkir land ownership patterns.[81] Many Bashkir lands had never been surveyed, and which Bashkir villages owned which land was uncertain. Moreover, Bashkirs had allowed some non-Bashkirs, called *pripushchenniki*, or "those let in," to lease some of their land, and the precise limits of such leases were not clear either. The 1869 law called for the surveying and demarcation of Bashkir land and specified that those who leased Bashkir land receive 15 desiatinas per household.[82] *Pripushchenniki* landholdings above that were supposed to be held in reserve by the state, supposedly for households with little land. At the same time, Kryzhanovskii sought to improve the position of "educated landowners" in Bashkiria, and to draw new men "who would be recognized as useful" to the region."[83] Upon the advice of Kryzhanovskii, in June 1871 the central government enacted legislation that permitted retired officials and officers to purchase from the state 150- to 2,000-desiatina parcels of state land.[84]

These two policies became a means to redistribute much of Bashkirs' land to the nobility and administrative elite that would implement the Great Reforms in Bashkiria.[85] In a sense, this became the final stage in a process begun in Catherine's reign—the grants of land or sales at advantageous prices to support an elite loyal to the tsar that would dominate Bashkiria. Now that the Bashkirs were allowed to sell their land, both Orthodox and Muslim nobles sought to take advantage of the Bashkirs' lack of mastery of the laws and bought large parcels of land for next to nothing. Others essentially stole land through manipulation and deceit.[86] A land fever developed, which one local observer likened to the "gold fever" during the California gold rush.[87] In all, between 1869 and 1878, Bashkirs lost 1,047,469 desiatinas of land through forced sales at extremely low prices.[88] The surveying of Bashkir land became a pretext to strip the Bashkir communities of "reserve" land. Rather than giving "excess" lands to *pripushchenniki* with little land as law stipulated, the province's Office of Peasant Affairs gave land to noblemen, local officials, and privileged or nonprivileged newcomers or sold it at extremely low prices. In the period 1876–1881 alone, 293 men purchased land in this manner, most of them servitors of high rank, including those in the local administration.

Kryzhanovskii received 6,294 desiatinas.[89] Many subsequently resold their land at great profit, often to migrants from central Russia. Kryzhanovskii's efforts to strengthen the ranks of "educated landowners" and to introduce a "Russian element" to the region through the promise of nearly free land initiated a land fever in Bashkiria that resulted in the "chaotic condition of landownership" in Ufa Province in particular.[90]

The expropriation of Bashkir lands engendered great discontent. Bashkir petitions protesting the local administration's actions flooded the government, and at least a few local landowners wrote to Petersburg about the dangerous, potentially explosive situation that the land policy had brought about. By 1878, petitions from Bashkirs and noblemen caused the government, with the support of Kryzhanovskii, to enact a law mandating that the sale of Bashkir lands be transacted only by way of public trade and in properly surveyed parcels. The upper ranks of the local administration were given the right to annul purchases of Bashkir land that had been acquired improperly.[91]

Such action failed to quiet discontent over the Orenburg administration's land policies. In 1880, articles began to appear in central newspapers such as *Nedelia* and *Golos* that exposed and criticized the practices of the Orenburg governor-general and the administrations in Ufa and Orenburg. In particular, Petr Dobrotvorskii, a *mirovoi posrednik* (arbitrator) in Birsk and Belebei counties, became a frequent contributor of articles on the plundering of Bashkir land. Some of Dobrotvorskii's pieces came to the attention of Count Loris-Melikov, the chair of the Supreme Executive Commission, and to Tsar Alexander II himself.[92] The Senate reacted to the reports from Ufa by redirecting M. E. Kovalevskii, a senator who had been assigned to conduct an inspection of eight provinces, including Kazan, Samara, and Saratov, to Ufa and Orenburg to investigate the accusations of corruption in Bashkiria.[93] A number of central newspapers followed the progress of the Kovalevskii's inspection closely in early 1881.[94] According to *Golos*, "The inspection provoked a terrific commotion among the ruling classes; and it is no wonder. In Russia there is hardly another place where the law is so slighted as in Ufa Province." Bashkirs gathered by the hundreds to present petitions to Kovalevskii for the return of their lands.[95]

Kovalevskii uncovered abuses of land policy in the region and reported them to St. Petersburg. A few land deals were annulled, but returning all illegally gotten Bashkir land to the Bashkirs was considered impractical, since Russians migrating to the area had settled on much of it. The inspection affected the local administration most of all. In 1881 Kryzhanovskii and much of his administration were stripped of their positions and the governor-general's post itself was eliminated.[96] Military administration ended in the region. Orenburg's governor became a civil one who no longer had authority over his counterpart in Ufa.[97] The scandal's effects were felt in Petersburg too. Although Minister of Internal Affairs Petr Valuev had not personally received Bashkir land, he had participated in the distribution of such land to high-ranking members of the bureaucracy. After a special commission accused Valuev of participation in the illegal distribution of land, Alexander III suggested Valuev retire. Valuev did so in late 1881.[98]

Although Alexander II's assassination in the midst of Kovalevskii's investigation overshadowed discussion of the scandal, the plundering of Bashkir land did not fade from Russian memory. The case of Bashkiria became firmly rooted in literature and political thought critical of the autocracy. During the 1880s, Bashkiria became the subject of numerous notes in "thick journals." A minor official and surveyor in the local peasant administration, Nikolai Remezov, wrote a book-length exposé of the politics of land in Bashkiria entitled *Ocherki iz dikoi Bashkirii: byl' v skazochnoi strane* (Sketches from Wild Bashkiria). First published in 1887, the book describes in great detail the actions of members of the local administration to take Bashkir land for themselves or to distribute it to their friends.[99] The prominent populist writer Gleb Uspenskii traveled to the region in 1889 and published a series of articles about his journey in the journal *Russkie vedomosti*.[100] Uspenskii cited Remezov's book prominently.

Remezov and Uspenskii, along with other writers critical of the administration of Orenburg and Ufa, such as Dobrotvorskii, helped identify Bashkiria as one of the empire's most backward areas in a manner echoed by the quote from *Golos* cited above. In doing so, these writers' interpretations of life in Ufa inverted the established cultural meaning of the imperial administration in Bashkiria. The local administration's attempt to redistribute land from the Bashkirs to political supporters of the autocracy differed little in practice from what had occurred since Catherine II's time. Rather than being a source of enlightenment and progress that would (supposedly) make the region more like European Russia, Remezov, Uspenskii, and others argued that the administration's activities reinforced Bashkiria's backwardness. Someone not knowing the subject of Remezov's book would very likely assume that "wild Bashkiria" was a statement on the lack of culture among local peoples. Rather, Remezov was commenting upon the behavior of supposedly "enlightened" administrators and noblemen who had stripped the Bashkirs of their lands. In a similar manner, Uspenskii described "deceit" (*podlog*) as the source of the Orenburg region's culture originating in central Russia. Deceit was that

> seed, which was first carried from the depths of our fatherland to the virgin soil of Bashkir land, and which, spreading the most slender and innumerable threads of its countless branches and shoots, having ensnared mutual relations of people of a predatory society, managed to grow also in the protecting law of institutions. It grew even here, and intertwined with shoots and branches into a unified, dark, dense . . . scandal.[101]

The scandal surrounding land policy in the 1870s and early 1880s thus had a dual effect. It caused the post of governor-general to be eliminated, and with it a major structural element that distinguished Bashkiria from the empire's European Russian core. At the same time, however, publicists depicted the local administration as a dark, obscurantist force and called into question the imperial administration's perceived identification with progress and European enlightenment.

Conclusion

By 1881, Bashkiria's western, most populous part, Ufa Province, had acquired the institutions of the European core of the empire. The place that had revealed the weakness of the tsar's authority through the Pugachev rebellion had now become part of European Russia. The change was not so much a question of conversion, the spread of Russian language and culture, or of economic development, though culture and economics certainly played a part. More importantly, the state had extended the essential political and administrative elements of the empire's central provinces that allowed civil administration by an elite of loyal men who could govern with less reliance on pure force of arms than their counterparts further east. A little more than a century of institution-building in Ufa had expanded the privileged stratum that identified with the autocrats, who, in turned identified themselves with Europe.

The process of Bashkiria's incorporation had begun in earnest under Catherine II. The demarcation of provincial and uezd boundaries and the increase in size and status of Bashkiria's administration strengthened its political and cultural connections with the capitals. This helped draw nobles to the region and increased the size of noble landholding. Given the overwhelmingly non-Orthodox, non-Russian speaking population of the region, the incorporation of Bashkiria required the recruitment of non-Orthodox elites who spoke enough Russian to work with the state bureaucracy and could connect the non-Orthodox community with the state. The Orenburg governor-generalship's persistence after most of central Russia had civilian governors, however, indicated the region's continued status as a frontier.

Alexander II's promotion of European ideals in politics after 1855, expressed in the Great Reforms, transformed the terms of inclusion in European Russia again. The reforms, along with the reduced military threat from the steppe, brought about the elimination of the Bashkir cantons and the introduction of a more powerful civilian governor in Ufa. The expansion of institutions and the expectations of greater participation in them increased the demand for educated, loyal men to staff institutions such as the zemstvos, city dumas, and legal institutions. Ufa Province's ability to meet such a demand depended upon a long-term process of elite formation and institution-building dating from Catherine's reign, as well as the actions of Orenburg's Governor-General Kryzhanovskii. His appeal to increase the number of such men in the region resulted in the stripping of much Bashkir land. The reformed institutions were built largely on the displacement of the native population. In 1875, zemstvos were established in Ufa, and in 1878, the legal reform was applied to the province as well.[102]

The extension of the Great Reforms to Bashkiria and the improvement of communications with the center changed Bashkiria in other ways, too. As local writers and activists contributed to the commercial press and participated in the public life of the capitals, the practices of the local administration were subject to greater scrutiny than ever before. Revelations surrounding the distribution of Bashkir lands to individuals in the local administration caused a scandal that even reached ministries in St. Petersburg. The elimination of the governor-general's post in Orenburg left Ufa without oversight from its neighboring province and put Bashkiria's administration on the same level with provinces of central Russia.

At the same time, the scandal that caused the end of the governor-general's governance in Bashkiria made apparent the changing nature of what was considered European in the period from the 1770s to the 1880s. The Europeanization of Bashkiria was always provisional. Catherine II cultivated noble and non-noble servitors who would represent the enlightened culture of St. Petersburg and incorporate Bashkiria into European

Russia. Under Alexander I and Nicholas I, the elaboration of ministerial institutions was the focus of governmental activity, and under Alexander II, the extension of new forms of governance based on European ideals and participation were the standard of the day. Toward the end of Alexander II's reign, however, central officials intervened on behalf of the Bashkir population who had lost land, rather than upholding the prerogatives of the privileged elite sponsored by Kryzhanovskii. What had been enlightenment under Catherine, the introduction of noble landholding to Bashkiria, was considered exploitation that threatened the region's stability under Alexander II. When writers such as Dobrotvorskii, Remezov, and Uspenskii published material critical of the region's administration after the 1880s, they registered considerable doubt regarding the Europeanness of Bashkiria and of the empire whose maps identified Ufa so clearly as part of European Russia.

Notes

1. Mark Bassin, "Russia between Europe and Asia: The Ideological Construction of Geographical Space," *Slavic Review* 50, no. 1 (Spring 1991): 1–9.

2. To cite only a few examples, Hugh Seton-Watson, *The Russian Empire, 1801–1917* (Oxford: Clarendon Press, 1967), 769–771; Ben Eklof, *Russian Peasant Schools: Officialdom, Village Culture, and Popular Pedagogy, 1861–1914* (Berkeley: University of California Press, 1986), xvi.

3. Mikhail Avdeev, "Gory," *Otechestvennye zapiski* 79 (1851), cited in M. G. Rakhimkulov, comp., *Bashkiriia v russkoi literature*, vol. 1 (Ufa: Bashkirskoe knizhnoe izd., 1989): 203. Konstantin Ton (1774–1881) also designed the Church of Christ the Savior in Moscow. This church was one of the most prominent and influential architectural projects of the nineteenth century. Ton designed it in 1832 as a memorial to the struggle with Napoleon. The church was consecrated in 1889, destroyed by Stalin in 1931 and rebuilt by the City of Moscow in the 1990s.

4. Although the characteristics of a local population factored into perceptions of Europeanness, before the late eighteenth century the Russian empire's elites had only begun to accumulate detailed knowledge of the empire's peoples. Peter Holquist, "To Count, to Extract, and to Exterminate: Population Statistics and Population Politics in Late Imperial and Soviet Russia," in Ronald Grigor Suny and Terry Martin, eds., *A State of Nations: Empire and Nation-Making in the Age of Lenin and Stalin* (Oxford: Oxford University Press, 2001): 111–144; Nathaniel Knight, "Science, Empire, and Nationality: Ethnography in the Russian Geographical Society, 1845–1855," in Jane Burbank and David Ransel, eds., *Imperial Russia: New Histories for the Empire* (Bloomington: Indiana University Press, 1998).

5. On the conquest of Bashkiria, see Alton S. Donnelly, *The Russian Conquest of Bashkiria, 1552–1740: A Case Study of Imperialism* (New Haven, Conn.: Yale University Press, 1968).

6. "Donoshenie orenburgskogo vitse-gubernatora D. V. Volkova imp. Ekaterine II ob osnovnykh voprosakh upraveleniia Orenburgskogo guberniei, 1763g. maia 26," in N. F. Demidova, comp., *Materialy po istorii Bashkirskoi ASSR,* vol. 4, part. 2 (1958): 451.

7. John P. LeDonne, *Ruling Russia: Politics and Administration in the Age of Absolutism, 1762–1796* (Princeton, N.J.: Princeton University Press, 1984).

8. John P. LeDonne, "The Territorial Reform of the Russian Empire, 1775–1796: II. The Borderlands, 1777–1796," *Cahiers du monde russe et soviétique* 24, no. 4 (1983): 427–428.

9. The local leadership reflected the cosmopolitanism of the tsarist servitors in the eighteenth century. Iakobii was the son of a Pole who had emigrated to Russia in 1711. Igel'strom was the son of a Lifland *Landrat,* well-connected with the Baltic aristocracy. LeDonne, *Ruling Russia:* 278, 285.

10. "Zapiski D. V. Mertvago," *Russkii arkhiv,* supplement (1867): 39.

11. Memoirs by those who lived and or served in Orenburg attest to the great influence governor-generals had on lives of the city's population. In addition to the often large suite of assistants and officers who accompanied a governor-general, the taste of the governor-general himself, his inclination to spend money on supporting the troops or large-scale social events determined much about both local life and state policy. For examples, see P. P. Zhakmon, "Iz vospominanii Orenburgskogo starozhila," *Istoricheskii vestnik* 100 (April 1905): 75–88; idem., ibid., 105 (July 1906): 75–79; N. G. Zalesov, "Zapiski N. G. Zalesova," *Russkaia starina* 114, no. 1 (1903): 41–64; ibid., no. 3 (1903): 267–289; ibid., no. 6 (1903): 527–542.

12. The governor-generals also presided over a period of institution-building. The first elections to noble assemblies were held in 1785; the first secondary school was built in 1790; and the Holy Synod created a bishopric in Ufa in 1800.

13. The Table of Ranks was created by Peter I in 1722 to regulate progress in service and the advance into the nobility. The figure does not include lower-status clerks. LeDonne, "The Territorial Reform of the Russian Empire, 1775–1796," 427–428, 432, 455–456.

14. V. A. Novikov, comp., *Sbornik materialov dlia istorii ufimskogo dvorianstva* (Ufa: n.p., 1879). Revised and expanded second edition, N. A. Gurvich, ed. (Ufa: n.p., 1904): 37–38.

15. The Tsardom of Muscovy expanded in large part because it co-opted various local elites. Kappeler, "Czarist Policy toward the Muslims of the Russian Empire," in Andreas Kappeler, Gerhard Simon, Georg Brunner, and Edward Allworth, eds., *Muslim Communities Reemerge: Historical Perspectives on Nationality, Politics, and Opposition in the Former Soviet Union and Yugoslavia* (Durham, N.C.: Duke University Press, 1994), 141; Marc Raeff, "Patterns of Russian Imperial Policy Toward the Nationalities," in Edward Allworth, ed., *Soviet Nationality Problems* (New York: Columbia University Press, 1972), 34.

16. *Polnoe sobranie zakonov Rossiiskoi imperii* [*PSZRI*], vol. 5, no. 2,734 (Nov. 3, 1713): 66–67, from Enikeev. Muslim nobles seemed to adopt a number of strategies to deal with the pressure to convert. Portions of some families converted and others did not. Some families appear to have led almost dual lives. The Tevkelevs are an interesting case in this regard. See G. G. Gudkov and Z. I. Gudkova, *S. T. Aksadov: sem'ia i okruzhenie* (Ufa: Bashkirskoe knizhnoe izd., 1991), 273–290; Ia. V. Khanykov, "Svedeniia

o rode Tevkelevykh i o sluzhbe general maiora Alekseia Ivanovicha Tevkeleva," *Vremennik Imperatorskago Moskovskago obshchestva istorii i drevnosti rossiiskikh* 13 (1858), 19–22.

17. The shift toward toleration has been noted in different ways by other historians, most notably Alan W. Fisher, Andreas Kappeler, and Dov Yaroshevsky. Alan W. Fisher, "Enlightened Despotism and Islam under Catherine II," *Slavic Review* 27, no. 4 (Dec. 1968): 542–553; Andreas Kappeler, "Czarist Policy toward the Muslims of the Russian Empire," 141–156; Dov Yaroshevsky, "Imperial Strategy in the Kirghiz Steppe," *Jahrbücher für Geschichte Osteuropas* 39 (1991): 221–224.

18. *PSZRI,* vol. 19, no. 13,996 (June 17, 1773): 775. Three years later, Catherine's *nakazy* restated this principle in a similar fashion, emphasizing the need for toleration in order to promote peace and security in a religiously diverse empire.

19. The only exception to this rule regarded the ownership of Christian serfs, which Muslims were denied. *PSZRI,* ser. I, vol. 22, no. 15,936 (February 22, 1784): 50–51.

20. The families listed by Novikov include the Avdeevs, Akchurins, Bikchurins, Biglovs, Diveevs, Enikeevs (princely and muza lines), Mansurovs, Maksiutovs, Suleimanovs, Sultanovs, Teregulovs, and Chanyshevs. Novikov, *Sbornik materialov,* 37–38.

21. RGADA, f. 16, op. 1, d. 934, ch. 5, pp. 81–82, cited in Danil D. Azamatov, "Orenburgskoe Magometanskoe Dukhovnoe Sobranie i dukhovnaia zhizn' Musul'manskogo naseleniia iuzhnogo urala v kontse XVIII–XIX vv," Kandidat dissertation, Russian Academy of Sciences Ufa Scholarly Center (1994), 37.

22. For a discussion of imperial ideology and the myth of empire in Catherine II's reign, see Richard S. Wortman, *Scenarios of Power: Myth and Ceremony in Russian Monarchy. Volume I, From Peter the Great to the Death of Nicholas I* (Princeton, N.J.: Princeton University Press, 1995), 86–88, 135–142, and Andreas Kappeler, *Russlands als Vielvölkerreich: Entstehung, Geschichte,* Zerfall (Munich, 1992), 135–138.

23. John LeDonne makes such a point about the local elite, though his focus is on their integration into military service and the spread of the principles of "Russian civilization." I emphasize integration into the nobility and non-military as well as military forms of service, and into a civilization that is not specifically Russian (recall that Igel'strom, the governor-general, could not write Russian) but part of a broader, European culture. LeDonne, *Ruling Russia,* 285.

24. Catherine began to support the regime-sponsored construction of mosques and schools for the Muslims in order to increase this influence and to "civilize" the Kirghiz (now Kazakh). "Arkhiv Grafa Igel'stroma," June 4, 1786: 355, November 12, 1786: 358; Arkhiv Turgaiskogo oblastnogo pravleniia, 1763: 43, cited in A. Dobromyslov, "Zaboty imperatritsy Ekateriny II o prosveshchenii kirgizov," *Trudy Orenburgskoi Uchenoi Arkheograficheskoi Komissii,* 9 (1902): 51–52.

25. Alan W. Fisher, *The Crimean Tatars* (Stanford, Calif.: Hoover Institution Press, 1978), 21, 71–78.

26. In April 1786 Igel'strom sent *Akhun* Husein and Mamat Girei Cherkaskii, an adjutant of Igel'strom's, on a mission to collect oaths of loyalty to the tsar from Kazakhs of the Small Horde. The emissaries secured such oaths from seven Kazakh sultans, 168 elders and "best people," with a total of 21,900 tents under their authority. *Kazakhsko-russkie otnosheniia v XVIII–XIX vekakh: Spornik dokumentov i materialov* (Alma-Ata: Nauka, 1964): 114–115. The Empress more than tripled the Akhun's pay, from 150 to

500 rubles, and authorized him to be named the "first *akhun*" in the region. "Arkhiv Grafa Igel'stroma," 353, 357.

27. The struggle with the Ottoman Empire manifested itself on the eastern frontier in early 1788. Igel'strom informed the Empress that he had received information that the Turks had begun negotiating with Bukhara in order to enlist the latter's armed support of the Ottomans in its conflict with Russia. Igel'strom sought to compete with Bukhara and its Ottoman allies for the allegiance of the Kirghiz (Kazakhs) on the steppe frontier. "Zapiski Dmitriia Mertvago," 43–44. Azamatov draws attention to the work of Husein and Muslim clerics as intelligence agents on the steppe. Azamatov, "Orenburgskoe magometanskoe dukhovnoe sobranie," 41.

28. *Arkhiv gosudarstvennogo soveta:* 812. According to the memoirs of an official in Igel'strom's administration, the Spiritual Assembly would "cut off the intrigues of the Bukharans . . . among the simple-minded Russian Muslims. "Zapiski Dmitriia Mertvago," 44–45.

29. The Russian word *mulla* was used to describe Muslim clerics of all types, but was used by Muslims in the OMSA's jurisdiction as an honorific indicating both clerics and wealthy notables who were not religious officials. The OMSA examined imams, the heads of mosques and Muslim congregations, as well as the *muezzins* (*mā'adhdhin* in Arabic, *azanchi* in Turkic), whose main job was to perform the call to prayer, and the *mudarris,* or teacher in the mosque. When a person with a specific title is indicated, I will use it. When referring to all such persons examined by the OMSA or when a person's specific function is not indicated, I will use "cleric" for simplicity's sake. I thank Allen Frank for his helpful suggestions regarding the Islamic nomenclature.

30. Muslims in Crimea and the western part of the empire remained under the authority of the mufti in Simferopol. *PSZRI* vol. 22, no. 16,710 (September 22, 1788): 1107; no. 16,711 (September 22, 1788): 1107–1108. *PSZRI* vol. 22, no. 16,759 (April 20, 1789): 20–21. For a more extensive discussion of the OMSA and the motivations behind its creation, see my dissertation, "Invisible Threads of Empire: State, Religion, and Ethnicity in Tsarist Bashkiria, 1773–1917," chapter 1. I have learned much from the work of Danil Azamatov. See Danil D. Azamatov, "Orenburgskoe magometanskoe dukhovnoe sobranie i dukhovnaia zhizn' musul'manskogo naseleniia iuzhnogo urala v kontse XVIII–XIXvv." Kandidat dissertation, Russian Academy of Sciences Ufa Scholarly Center (1994), 21–31, 41. Allen Frank's evaluations of the pattern of the administration's relations with the Muslim ulema leading up to the establishment of the OMSA also provide important context lacking in typical Western and Soviet explanations. Allen J. Frank, "Islamic Regional Identity," 18–48; idem., *Islamic Historiography and "Bulghar" Identity among the Tatars and Bashkirs of Russia* (Leiden: Brill, 1998).

31. See *Arkhiv Gosudarstvennogo soveta,* 849, for an example of the mufti's role.

32. As codified in 1837, residents of a Muslim "parish" (*prikhod*) chose their candidate by a two-thirds vote of the senior members of the households of the *prikhod,* under village authorities' the supervision. In Bashkir cantons, the *nachal'nik* supervised elections. Once a community chose a candidate for imam, he went to Ufa to be examined. The examination addressed primarily the candidate's knowledge of Islamic law. *PSZRI,* series 2, vol. 12, no. 10,594 (October 21, 1837): 801.

33. "Polozhenie o dukhovnom magometanskom sobranii, sostavlennoe simbirskim i ufimskim namestnikom O. A. Igel'stromom," December 4, 1789, and "Proekt

polozheniia o kompetentsii Dukhovnogo magometanskogo sobraniia, predlozhennyi simbirskim i ufimskim namestnikom O. A. Igel'strom na reshenie imp. Ekateriny II," December 5, 1789, in *Materialy po istorii Bashkirskoi ASSR*, vol. 5, 563. Fisher, "Enlightened Despotism," 550.

34. The tsarist administration appears to have intervened very little in the composition or administration of the examinations. Igel'strom mandated that all written matters of the Assembly be in Russian (*rossiiskii dialekt*) and translated into Tatar, and examinations of candidates be in Tatar translated into Russian. This bilingual administration enabled the governor-general and procurator to review the activity of the Assembly. Igel'strom ordered that the OMSA ensure that only the necessary number of clergy serve in a mosque and that they perform their duties correctly and soberly. Fisher, "Enlightened Despotism," 564.

35. The increased definition of the roles of the OMSA's judges (*chleny* or *zasedateli*) and their relationship to the mufti gave the OMSA the trappings of an institution rather than simply the administration of one man. In 1802, the Senate outlined the Assembly's decision-making procedures. Decisions were made by the mufti and judges. In the event of a disagreement they voted, and the majority prevailed. In case of an evenly divided Assembly, the vote of the man presiding prevailed. The decree mandated the creation of the position of senior judge, who presided over the Assembly in the absence of the mufti. *V pamiat' stoletiia Orenburgskago magometanskago dukhovnago sobraniia* (Ufa: n.p., 1891), 23. In a move unusual in tsarist administrative practice, the Senate allowed the election of three judges from among the Kazan Tatars, subject to the confirmation of Kazan's provincial governor. *PSZRI*, series 1, vol. 23, no. 17,146 (August 17, 1793): 452–454.

36. The mufti himself was appointed by the tsar upon the recommendation of the Minister of Internal Affairs. Legislation from 1832 specified that the mufti should be elected, but there is no evidence that a mufti was ever chosen in such a manner.

37. The staff included a secretary of 12th class, a translator of 12th class, two desk attendants of 14th class, a keeper of journals and archives of 14th class, four chancellery workers of middle salary (*sredniago oklada*), one of which had to know both Tatar and Russian, and four chancellery workers of lower salary. In 1843, a desk attendant and two chancellery workers of middle salary were added. In order to increase the prestige of service positions, the ceiling for advancement of some staff was raised as well. *PSZRI*, series II, vol. 18, no. 16,670 (March 30, 1843): 182; *PSZRI*, series 2, vol. 11, no. 8,780 (January 15, 1836): 47; Azamatov: "Orenburgskoe magometanskoe dukhovnoe sobranie," 104. *PSZRI*, series 2, vol. 11, no. 8,780 (January 15, 1836): 47.

38. In 1829, legislation allowed Muslim clerics to collect a 30-kopeck marriage fee. The fee, paid to the imam by the couple getting married and forwarded to the OMSA, provided the institution with a small but significant income. The OMSA used the fees to pay for clerical expenses, to supplement staff salaries, to construct more suitable quarters for the OMSA, and to provide aid for clerics in times of famine. *V pamiat' stoletiia*, 27; *PSZRI*, ser. 2, vol. 9, no. 7,351 (August 21, 1834): 827.

39. Among Russian speakers, the Conscience Court regularly dealt with family matters such as a case reviewed by the Senate in which a mother brought her daughters to Conscience Court because they had married without her permission. The parties involved knew neither the Russian language (*rossiiskii iazyk*) nor tsarist law, however,

and the court could not carry out its functions. Therefore, such cases were left to the Muslim clergy to resolve "according to their customs [*obriadam*] and laws." Only if these authorities could not resolve a matter could they be referred to a Conscience Court. *PSZRI,* series 2, vol. 10, no. 8,436 (September 30, 1835): 991.

40. The Governing Senate's opinion specified that the clergy of the OMSA had the right to "review and decide according to its law matters of private property arising from wills or the division of property among heirs." The law stated, however, that the clergy could become involved only at the request of the parties, and that parties unhappy with the decision of the clergy could submit their cases to civil authorities. *PSZRI,* series 2, vol. 11, no. 9,158 (May 11, 1836): 504.

41. The use of metrical books was expanded to include Catholics, Jews, and Lutherans in the 1820s and 1830s. For a discussion of metrical books and their significance, see Charles Steinwedel, "Making Social Groups, One Person at a Time," in Jane Caplan and John Torpey, eds., *Documenting Individual Identity: The Development of State Practices Since the French Revolution* (Princeton, N.J.: Princeton University Press, 2001).

42. In response to this deficit of information, the Senate resolved that each imam would receive two sets of books in order to record the time of each child's birth, the name of his or her parents, the death of each person, the names of those married and divorced, and the reasons for the latter. *PSZRI,* series 2, vol. 3, no. 2,296 (Sept. 21, 1828): 837–838.

43. The inclusion of the ruler in Muslim prayers had a long history within Islam. From the second half of the tenth century onward, the leader of Friday prayers in Muslim mosques inserted the name of the current ruler of the Muslim community after the name of the caliph. To be so mentioned in the Friday prayers became known as "the right of *khutba.*" The mentioning of authority in the *khutba* came to be an outward sign of the political orientation of the imam, the leader of prayers in the mosque. To omit a political leader from the *khutba* signified the non-recognition of the leader's political authority. Inclusion of the prayer signified that political authority was legitimate. Azamatov, "Orenburgskoe musul'manskoe dukhovnoe sobranie," 200; *Islam: Entsiklopedicheskii slovar'* (Moscow, 1991), 285.

44. "Perevod rechi, proiznesennoi Muftiem Abdussalamom k ego edinovertsam," *Kazanskii vestnik,* no. 9/10 (1826): 148–152. I thank Willard Sunderland for this reference. The prayers were controversial among both Russian officials and Muslim authorities.

45. In 1790, very shortly after the establishment of the OMSA, Mufti Husein was allowed to buy Bashkir land. *PSZRI,* series 1, vol. 23, no. 16,897 (August 13, 1790): 164–165; *PSZRI,* series 1, vol. 21, 15,936 (February 22, 1784): 51. In 1793 the Senate reaffirmed Mufti Husein's right to purchase Bashkir land and specified that the privilege extended to his heirs. *PSZRI,* series 1, vol. 23, no. 17,099 (January 26, 1793): 399. In recognition of Husein's service, Paul I presented him with a sable fur coat, increased his salary to 2,000 rubles, and gave him 4,000 rubles with which to build a house. Husein's salary became equal to that of the Mufti in Tauride. *Russkii arkhiv,* g. 24, no. 3 (1886): 491. Mufti Husein's elevated status received further confirmation in 1811, when Tsar Alexander ruled that allegations of wrongdoing on the part of the mufti would be judged by the Senate in St. Petersburg, raising the mufti's status well beyond

the level envisioned by Igel'strom. *PSZRI*, series 1, vol. 31 (October 18, 1811): 872. Alexander I ennobled Husein's successor, Abdulsaliam Abdrakhimov, in 1817, eight years before the latter became mufti. Nicholas I presented a sable fur coat to Abdrakhimov when he wrote a prayer for Nicholas's health at the time of his coronation. *V pamiat' stoletiia*, 42.

46. Martha Brill Olcott, *The Kazakhs* (Stanford, Calif.: Hoover Institution Press, 1987), 60–69.

47. The next mufti, Abdulvakhit Suleimanov, who presided over the OMSA from 1840 to 1862, made a career in the capital as St. Petersburg civil imam. For his service, he and eventually his three sons all were made noblemen, though he received only one gift, 1,500 rubles. Overall, Abdrakhimov's successor, Suleimanov, received less recognition as mufti, and the scorn of some, such as the missionary Nikolai Il'minskii. The patron of Suleimanov appears to have been Grand Prince Mikhail Pavlovich. Azamatov, "Orenburgskoe magometanskoe dukhovnoe sobranie," 66.

48. Imams in the Volga-Urals region did not belong to a separate religious caste before Russian conquest. As a result, their estate identity and the rights and burdens corresponding to it were determined by their status prior to assuming the role of imam. If they were commoners, they were subject to taxes, military service, and corporal punishment the same as other commoners. *V pamiat' stoletiia*, 20. The estate organization of the Crimean clergy may have been brought by the Russians to Crimea after their conquest of the peninsula.

49. *V pamiat' stoletiia*, 23.

50. In 1821, an imam in Penza province was convicted of counterfeiting by the Penza Criminal Chamber and sentenced to public knouting and then exile to Siberia. The OMSA disputed the sentenced and moved the Holy Synod, the Ministries of Justice and Education and the Senate to address the matter. The OMSA asserted that because the imams held the same rank and performed functions equal to those discharged by the Orthodox clergy, the imams should enjoyed the exemption from corporal punishment that the regime granted the Orthodox clergy. To do otherwise, the OMSA argued, meant treating an imam "just as one would a commoner." The Ministers of Justice and Education and the State Council agreed with the Senate and Synod. RGIA, f. 796, op. 1822, d. 528, ll. 1–3; f. 1149, t. 1, 1821, d. 11, l. 2ob, 3, cited in Schrader: 140. Schrader argues that the OMSA officials falsely believed that they were exempt from corporal punishment. It seems to me that the 1822 ukaz was a change in policy perhaps resulting from the jurisdiction of MNP over the Muslims in 1817. RGIA, f. 1149, t. 1, 1821, d. 11, l. 2, cited in ibid., 139.

51. RGIA, f. 1261, op. 1, 1848, d. 170, ll. 6–7-ob, cited in Schrader: 143–144.

52. In 1849, the State Council specified that the Orenburg Muslim Spiritual Assembly had direct authority over clerics, and that it had the right to supervise their activity. In the event of a cleric's misdeed, the OMSA had the authority to strip a cleric of his position temporarily or permanently. Although civil authorities retained the power actually to carry out a punishment, the opinion explicitly stated that the provincial administrations could not revoke the decisions of the Spiritual Assembly. Moreover, appeals regarding the decisions of the Spiritual Assembly were now directed to central authorities in St. Petersburg instead of the provincial governor. *PSZRI*, series 2,

vol. 24, no. 23,259 (May 21, 1849): 284. For an interpretation of this opinion which sees it as part of an effort to restrict the authority of the Assembly, see Rorlich, *The Volga Tatars*, 44.

53. *PSZRI*, series. 2, vol. 25, no. 23,932 (February 20, 1850): 126.

54. The Russian word *volost'* and the Bashkir *ulus* have common roots on the Eurasian plain, both indicating a group of people under the authority of one man. The exact etymology of the two words requires further research. For a discussion of the usage of these terms, see F. A. Shakurova, *Bashkirskaia volost' i obshchina v seredine XVIII-pervoi polovine XIX veka* (Ufa: Bashkirskii nauchnyi tsentr Ural'skogo otdeleniia Rossiiskoi akademii nauk, 1992).

55. Space does not permit even a cursory treatment of Bashkir organization. See Shakurova, *Bashkirskaia volost'*, for a thorough account.

56. The wealthiest Bashkirs managed to avoid service, so the Bashkir elders typically sent soldiers to the army who lacked horses, weapons, food, or all three. *PSZRI*, series 1, vol. 25, no. 18,477 (April 10, 1798): 189.

57. He insisted that the *iurts* correspond to the state's division of the province by county (*uezd*); *iurts* that fell into more than one county were reformed. Shakurova, *Bashkirskaia volost'*, 70.

58. A cantonal elder directed each of the eleven cantons and five Meshcheriak cantons. The cantons were not uniform in size but ranged from 4,000 to 30,000, and the number of *iurts* in each canton varied from 7 to 26. Shakurova, *Bashkirskaia volost'*, 70.

59. Clan-based organizations continued to exist. Shakurova, *Bashkirskaia volost'*, 71. Bashkirs required permission from the *iurt* elder to move within the canton, and permission from canton elders to move within the province. Elders could not authorize movement beyond the provincial borders. *PSZRI*, series 1, vol. 25, no. 18,477 (April 10, 1798): 193–194.

60. The *iurt* elders were to gather every year with information on the number of men between the ages of twenty and fifty under their command. One soldier would be drawn from about every four or five households, depending on the demand for troops. Igel'strom ordered that the troops be drawn more "systematically" (*po ocheredi*), rather than simply from the poorest and least influential village members. The soldier's community would be responsible for providing him with a horse, food, and equipment. *PSZRI*, series 1, vol. 25, no. 18,477 (April 10, 1798): 191. Bashkir and Meshcheriak troops fought in the wars of the empire as well as on the steppe frontier. Twenty-eight Bashkir companies and two Meshcheriak companies fought against Napoleon in 1812–1814, and many were decorated for their service. A. Z. Asfandiiarov, "Vvedenie kantonnoi sistemy upravleniia v Bashkirii," *Iz istorii Bashkirii (dorevoliutsionnyi period)* (Ufa: n.p., 1968): 159, 163.

61. Shakurova, *Bashkirskaia volost'*, 76–77.

62. Khamza F. Usmanov, *Razvitie kapitalizma v sel'skom khoziaistve Bashkirii v poreformennyi period, 60–90-e gody XIX v.* (Moscow: Nauka, 1981), 31.

63. Fazyl'ian A. Ishkulov notes a number of such cases. See *Sudebno-administrativnaia reforma v Bashkortostane* (Ufa: Kitap, 1994), 55–56.

64. The Sultanov family, that of the Orenburg mufti from 1885–1915, joined the nobility in the period 1818–1832 at a time when one of their members served as elder of the eleventh Bashkir canton. Bashkir cantonal leaders with the highest rank received

noble status after the elimination of the cantonal system, perhaps as a reward for their service and compensation for their lost position. Usmanov, *Razvitie kapitalizma*, 34.

65. Wortman, *Scenarios of Power*, 417.

66. For a discussion of governor-generals and their elimination, see Anatolii V. Remnev, "General-gubernatorskaia vlast' v XIX stoletii. K probleme organizatsii regional'nogo upravleniia rossiiskoi imperii," in Petr I. Savel'ev, et al., ed., *Imperskii stroi Rossii v regional'nom izmerenii (XIX–nachalo XX veka)* (Moscow: Transpechat', 1997), 52–66; and idem., *Samoderzhavie i Sibir': Administrativnaia politika vtoroi poloviny XIX–nachalo XX vekov* (Omsk: Omsk Universitet, 1997), 95–119.

67. The precise responsibilities of the two posts remained unclear. On the responsibilities of governors and governor-generals, see Anatolii V. Remnev, "Gubernatorskaia vlast' "; and idem., *Samoderzhavie i Sibir'*, 117–119.

68. Gregory Freeze presents an argument for the continued power of estate categories after 1860. He also asserts that the objective of reforms such as the zemstvo, city dumas, taxation, and military service was to "maximize resources and efficiency, not erase the separateness and isolation of individual groups." I would argue that the two objectives were perceived as inseparable in some cases, and that the intention to create a civil order that extended to nearly all was key to the reforms and should not be underestimated, even if it did not amount to a specific attack on estate distinctions. See "The *Soslovie* (Estate) Paradigm and Russian Social History," *American Historical Review* 91, no. 1 (February 1986): 11–36, and especially 25–27.

69. *Polozhenie o bashkirakh* (Ufa: n.p., 1912), 3.

70. Bulat S. Davletbaev, *Krest'ianskaia reforma 1861 goda v bashkirii* (Moscow, 1983), 109–110; *Polozhenie o bashkirakh*, 3–13.

71. In August 1863, pursuant to the Statutes on the Bashkirs, 808 villages and 130 districts were formed in Bashkiria. The change from cantons to peasant districts was somewhat tense. Cantonal elders feared the loss of their authority, and Bashkirs feared that loss of their lands, enserfment, or even Christianization would result from their change in status. Most cantonal elders were elected as district elders, in the end, and they continued to have considerable power over the Bashkirs. Davletbaev, *Krest'ianskaia reforma:* 110–111.

72. The Bashkirs, as a legally defined estate group, were given *votchinnik* rights to their land, that is, ownership with restrictions on the sale of the property. The *Polozhenie o bashkirakh* specified several limits on Bashkir land sales. The Bashkir community must have at least 40 *des.* of land remaining after the sale, the village assembly had to approve the sale of land, the district administration had to certify the sale, and the Orenburg governor-general needed to confirm it. These points are summarized in P. Shramchenko, "Zemel'nyi vopros v ufimskoi gubernii," *Russkii vestnik* 158 (March 1882): 463–464.

73. Marc Szeftel connected "a certain limitation of autocracy" with the zemstvo legislation, since the law delegated a limited amount of authority to the bodies. Marc Szeftel, "The Form of Government of the Russian Empire Prior to the Constitutional Reforms of 1905–1906," in John Shelton Curtiss, ed., *Essays in Russian and Soviet History* (New York, 1965), 116–119. Terence Emmons writes, "Together with the other reforms of the 1860s, . . . the zemstvo reform brought a cautious and partial dismantling of the old estate order with the lord-peasant relationship at its center." Terence Em-

mons, "The Zemstvo in Historical Perspective," in Terence Emmons and Wayne S. Vucinich, eds., *The Zemstvo in Russia: An Experiment in Local Self-Government* (Cambridge, UK: Cambridge University Press, 1982), 423.

74. In this respect the zemstvos included non-Russian groups on a more equal basis than other institutions such as the provincial administration and even the city council, or duma. The number of Muslim deputies allowed in the city dumas was limited to one-third of the total number of deputies, whereas the zemstvos had no such restrictions.

75. *Polnyi svod postanovlenii Ufimskago gubernskago zemstvo,* vol. 1, 19–24.

76. Statisticheskii otdel Ufimskoi gubernskoi upravy, *Istoriko-statisticheskie tablitsy deiatel'nosti Ufimskikh zemstv. K sorokoletiiu sushchestvovaniia zemstv Ufimskoi gubernii, 1875–1914* (Ufa: n.p., 1915), 226–228.

77. Muslims served as chairman from 1883 to 1885, from 1888 to 1892, and from 1906 to 1909.

78. Ufa's zemstvos were known for their backwardness and inactivity for their first twenty years. The relative inefficiency of the Ufa zemstvos resulted in large part from the province's comparative lack of men who would be likely to see in the zemstvo the means to invigorate local society or even press the government for further reform. The electoral franchise favored the large landowners, who already ran parts of the province virtually as personal fiefdoms. Boris Veselovskii, *Istoriia zemstva za sorok let,* vol. 4 (St. Petersburg, 1911), 404–417; A. I. Veretennikova, "Zapiski zemskogo vracha," *Novyi mir,* no. 3 (March 1956): 209, 219–220.

79. Steamship service first opened along the Belaia River, which connected the city of Ufa with the Volga and Kazan, in 1858. Such transportation remained rare until 1870, when a local company established a regular route. By the following year, three routes connected Ufa to Kazan and two to Nizhnyi Novgorod. R. G. Ganeev, V. V. Boltushkin, and R. G. Kuzeev, eds., *Istoriia Ufy: kratkii ocherk* (Ufa, 1981), 96.

80. Tsentral'nyi Gosudarstvennyi Istoricheskii Arkhiv Respubliki Bashkortostan, f. I-11, op. 1, d. 899, l. 4, letter from governor-general Kryzhanovskii to the Minister of Justice, dated January 15, 1871.

81. Shramchenko, "Zemel'nyi vopros," 465–466.

82. One *desiatina* was equal to about 2.7 acres of land. *PSZRI,* series 2, vol. 44, no. 46,750 (February 10, 1869).

83. The overall intent of the sales was to enhance the position of educated landowners and a vaguely defined "Russian element"—migrants from central Russia with agricultural skills superior to those of the local Bashkirs—who would make the region more productive and able to support the newly reformed institutions and break up the "closed mass of the Muslim population." Shramchenko, "Zemel'nyi vopros," 476–477.

84. Those wanting to purchase land were to declare their intentions to the governor-general, who would forward them to the Minister of State Domains for final approval. The average price per *desiatina* was about 1 ruble 80 kopecks, when the market price of land varied from 7 to 25 rubles per *desiatina*. Usmanov, *Razvitie kapitalizma,* 43.

85. Kryzhanovskii attacked policies of religious toleration, especially in Turkestan, in part to advance his candidacy for the post of governor-general of the new Russian colony. He was opposed, however, by influential officials such as Minister of War

Dmitrii Miliutin. Daniel Brower, "Islam and Ethnicity: Russian Colonial Policy in Turkestan," in Daniel R. Brower and Edward J. Lazzerini, eds., *Russia's Orient: Imperial Borderlands and Peoples, 1700–1917* (Bloomington: Indiana University Press, 1997), 118.

86. A landowner named Zavaritskii and the merchant Khor'kov purchased 20,000 desiatinas of land for the price of only one ruble per *desiatina*, in part by convincing the Bashkirs that their land would soon be surveyed and either lost or subject to high taxes. Force was used to get the last few to agree. Usmanov, *Razvitie kapitalizma,* 46.

87. *Orenburgskii listok* (February 15, 1876), cited in Usmanov, *Razvitie kapitalizma,* 45.

88. Usmanov, *Razvitie kapitalizma,* 47.

89. Ibid., 42.

90. Shramchenko, "Zemel'nyi vopros," 470.

91. *PSZRI*, series 2, no. 58,487 (May 9, 1878); P. I. Liashchenko, *Ocherki agrarnoi evoliutsii Rossii,* vol. 2: *Krest'ianskoe delo i poreformennaia zemleustroitel'naia politika* (St. Petersburg: n.p., 1913), 164–165.

92. On Petr Dobrotvorskii, "Moia ispoved'" in P. I. Dobrotvorskii, *V glushi Bashkirii: rasskazy, vospominaniia* (Ufa: Bashkirskoe knizhnoe izdatel'stvo, 1989), 192–193.

93. A copy of the instructions to M. E. Kovalevskii appears in the Bakhmeteff Archive, Columbia University, M. M. Kovalevskii collection, box 4. The instructions, undated, do not include Ufa Province, suggesting how rapidly and unexpectedly the subject of Bashkir lands had become a controversial issue.

94. See, for example, *Golos,* no. 2 (January 2, 1881): 2; no. 11 (January 11, 1881): 2; no. 26 (January 26, 1881): 2; no. 33 (February 2, 1881): 1; no. 34 (February 3, 1881): 2; no. 35 (February 4, 1881): 2; no. 42 (February 11, 1881): 3; no. 43 (February 12, 1881): 3; no. 45 (February 14, 1881): 3; no. 50 (February 19, 1881): 3; no. 51 (February 20, 1881): 4; no. 72 (March 13, 1881): 4; no. 103 (April 15, 1881): 3. Alexander II's assassination on March 1 resulted in less coverage for the scandal.

95. *Golos,* no. 72 (March 13, 1881): 4. Kovalevskii refused the petitions. Ibid., no. 103 (April 15, 1881): 3.

96. In 1882, a new law forbidding the sale of Bashkir lands except to the state and to peasant communes slowed the sale of Bashkir lands. The peasants also paid higher prices than the landowners had, from eight to fifteen rubles per desiatina. Usmanov, *Razvitie kapitalizma,* 48.

97. Orenburg would not receive zemstvos, however, until the eve of the First World War.

98. P. A. Zaionchkovskii, ed. and comp., *Dnevnik P. A. Valueva, ministra vnutrennikh del v dvukh tomakh,* vol. 1, 1861–1864 (Moscow: Akademiia nauk, 1961), 50–51.

99. Nikolai V. Remezov, *Ocherki iz zhizni v dikoi Bashkirii: byl' v skazochnoi strane* (Moscow: Kushnerov, 1887). Subsequent volumes appeared with the same main title, but different subtitles. His next book dealt with the question of resettlement to Bashkiria. See idem, *Ocherki iz zhizni dikoi Bashkirii: pereselencheskaia epopeia* (Moscow: Kushnerev, 1889). After Kovalevskii's inspection, Remezov was pressured into leaving Ufa Province. He held several positions in state service and ended up working for government newspapers in the Far East. His activity was considered hostile to the administration and he was exiled in 1904. He ended up working in Vladivostok as an admin-

istrative exile. The last volume of his work was published in Vladivostok under the title *Ocherki iz zhizni dikoi Bashkirii: sudebnaia oshibka ili sozdannoe prestuplenie?* (Vladivostok: n.p., 1900).

100. G. I. Uspenskii, "Ot Orenburga do Ufy," in G. I. Uspenskii, *Sobranie sochinenii,* vol. 8 (Moscow: Gos. izd. khudozhestvennoi literatury, 1957), 375–426.

101. Ibid., 375–376.

102. Alexander II decreed that legal reform should be implemented in Ufa and Orenburg provinces on May 2, 1878. However, only in March 1892 did the government create an *okruzhnii sud* in the provinces and introduce trial by juries (*prisiazhnye zasedateli*). N. I. Leonov, *Burzhuaznye reformy 60–70-x godov XIX v. v Bashkirii* (Ufa: Bashkirskii Universitet, 1993), 32–48.

4 Mapping the Empire's Economic Regions from the Nineteenth to the Early Twentieth Century

Nailya Tagirova

The history of regionalization in Russia is long, extending back to the empire's very foundation. Existence in a constantly expanding territory dictated the need to find an effective mode of administration for the state and its population. The results to a large extent depended on the availability of objective and accurate knowledge about the subject lands. Scientific knowledge of the territory made it easier to control.[1]

The term *raionirovanie* (regionalization) is one of those a priori concepts used to understand and to find the logic of complex socio-economic processes. In this sense, "regionalization" is not a fact of reality, but rather a scientific category employed by scholars. The history of regions and the process of regionalization is first and foremost the history of a branch of scientific inquiry. The criteria used in an administrative approach to regionalization may be completely different from those guiding a scientific approach. My goal here is to trace the evolution of Russian scientific thought on economic regionalization from the eighteenth to the early twentieth century, and to compare this evolution with the needs of the imperial state administration.

In the eighteenth century the *guberniia* (province) system, organized according to demographic principles, formed the basis for the territorial administration of the empire. But with the growth and complexity of economic relations and the formation of a Russian national market, such a system proved to be inadequate. The first scientific attempts at the designation of regions in the Russian empire began in the eighteenth century in connection with the study of territories that had been annexed and were gradually being assimilated. I. K. Kirilov and V. N. Tatishchev, two of the founders of Russian geography, led governmental expeditions, directed geographical research, collected cartographical materials, and compiled versions of plans for the construction of defense fortifications and trade routes.[2] These expeditions provided material for a "database" about soil and climate conditions, as well as the ethnographic make-up of the empire. This data laid the foundation for scientific efforts to designate regions in the Russian empire: three zones were formulated on the basis of climate conditions, with borders fixed by degrees of latitude.[3] These first scientifically designated regions were much larger than the guberniias.

In the second half of the eighteenth century, by decree of Catherine II (1763), the Imperial Academy of Sciences put together *Maps of Products of the Russians.*[4] This work necessitated an analysis of the economic aspects of life in the empire. The task proved to be unrealizable at this juncture, but a commission headed by M. V. Lomonosov was the first to note the differing geographical and commercial significance of various parts of the country. Lomonosov's commission designated the region between the Upper Volga and Oka rivers as the core of the Russian state.[5] Accompanying the growth of knowledge about geography and the economic conditions of different parts of the empire was the appearance of special terminology: scholars spoke of *prostranstva* (expanses), *statistika* (statistics) and *polosa* (zones).

At this time, the first maps of Russia's regions began to appear. Kh. A. Chebotarev was the first to group provinces not according to climate conditions, but in relation to their distance from Moscow Province, the "middle of Russia."[6] He divided these essentially economic regions into four groups: the northern, eastern, southern, and western provinces.

I. I. Zavalishin, S. I. Pleshcheev, E. F. Ziablovskii[7] and A. N. Radishchev,[8] among others, recorded their views on the empire's territorial diversity. For example, Radishchev precisely captures the empire's geographical and economic heterogeneity with his observation that within Siberia, the "birch-grove dweller, who feeds himself from a herd of deer" and the "peasant in Tomsk uezd," who "can only manage by farming . . . are as different from each other as an Englishman and a Frenchman," even though both are Siberians.[9]

In 1785 the General Land Survey of the Empire got underway, and the Imperial Free Economic Society (IVEO) compiled detailed descriptions of regions and economic appendices to the General Land Survey. The administrative reforms of the eighteenth century, the General Land Survey, and the government's charge to the Academy of Sciences all speak of the state's efforts to obtain more reliable information about the empire.

The first economic regions of the eighteenth century affected only European Russia: territories in the peripheries remained unstudied. The main criteria for delimitation were the designation of climate zones and, much less frequently, location in relation to the center of Russia—Moscow Province (Lomonosov and Chebotarev). Eighteenth-century scientific regionalization did not in any way coincide with the administrative division of the empire, since the two systems worked on different principles: demographic indicators and "ease of rule" underlay the guberniia system, while regions were organized primarily by climate.

In the early nineteenth century regionalization began to become an instrument of administration. In 1801 the territory of the empire was divided into twelve military inspectorates. The Postal Department of the Ministry of Internal Affairs created as a delimiter the postal and later postal-telegraph okrug (defining a total of 35 of these in the 1890s). Strategic considerations determined the territorial configuration of military and postal okrugs. By the mid-nineteenth century the empire had designated 12 judicial, 15 educational, and 9 water okrugs. These okrugs had their own configuration; only 62 religious dioceses generally coincided with guberniia borders. The central administrations of the various okrug departments had headquarters in different cities of the country. Only St. Petersburg, Moscow, Kazan, and Warsaw would be simultaneously water, educational, judicial, and transportation "capitals." The practice of regional (territorial) administration in the empire had become a reality.

Virtually every department began to experience a need for statistical and cartographical materials about their okrugs and often initiated their creation. The Imperial Russian Geographical Society (IRGO) and the Free Economic Society (IVEO) were enlisted to help with this. The study of geography and the economic, historical, and cultural life in the guberniia resulted in the multi-volume *Military-Statistical Survey of the Russian Empire* and *Materials for Geography and Statistics Compiled by Officers of the General Staff.* The 1840s witnessed the firm establishment of the practice of publishing maps and atlases. The *Atlas of Materials for Statistics on the Russian Empire* was published in 1839. There followed in 1842 the publication of the *Map of Industries of European Russia,* commissioned by the Ministry of Finance, with information about factories, manufacturing plants, and trade; administrative localities by manufacturing region; the most significant markets; water and land routes; and ports, lighthouses, custom houses, major wharves, and quarantine stations.[10] The Department of Agriculture of the Ministry of State Property, which was interested in grain-trading regions, conducted its own cartographical work.[11] The Ministry of Internal Affairs also carried out research for an atlas that was to reflect the "main characteristics" of the economy of European Russia, but it was not published.[12]

In 1847 the Ministry of Internal Affairs unveiled its variant of the division of the empire, according to which European Russia comprised twelve expanses, defined by climate conditions, "particularities of the population, tribal differences, ways of life, customs, and types of occupations."[13] The grid of regions bore geographical names. Only the lands of the Don Host and the Black Sea Cossacks did not receive designations ("neither guberniia nor oblast").

The scientific basis and experiments in regionalization during the first half of the nineteenth century were connected with the name K. I. Arsen'ev,[14] who headed the Statistical Committee of the Ministry of Internal Affairs from 1835 until 1853. Using government statistical materials, Arsen'ev put a large set of new data into scientific circulation. His 1818 *Survey of the Physical Conditions of Russia* divides the entire empire, not just its European core, into ten units.[15]

As in the past, the division was primarily based on "differences of climate and quality of soil," but Arsen'ev also introduced the innovation of detailed characterizations of each region, for example, information about the principal occupations of the population and an evaluation of the possible economic perspectives of all ten "expanses." Arsen'ev combined the tasks of acquiring knowledge about the empire and its transformation into a single enterprise.

Arsen'ev's ideas on regionalization drew a broad public response. Critics questioned whether the geographer was justified in "arbitrarily dividing the state into parts, however he chooses."[16] Among the constructive appraisals by historians of geography, we should note N. P. Ogarev's objections. Ogarev pointed out that Arsen'ev had underestimated the importance of a territory's economic specialization.[17] The socio-political views of Arsen'ev's contemporaries also reflected their different versions of regionalization.[18]

In his *Statistical Outline of Russia* (1848), Arsen'ev proposed a more refined territorial grid, and also included an outline of the history of the administrative-territorial division of the empire. The ten expanses he delimited were given the following physical-geographical names: (1) Northern, (2) Alaunskoe, (3) Baltic, (4) Lower, (5) Carpathian, (6) Steppe, (7) Central or Inner, (8) Urals, (9) Caucasus, (10) Siberia.[19]

The theoretical postulates of regionalization in the early nineteenth century varied fundamentally from those of earlier times and led to a delimitation of imperial territories differing from each other in a number of respects: geographical, demographical, and strictly economic. The number of these regions ranged from eight to twelve, and stipulated the existence of a hierarchy of inner (central) regions versus all the other regions. The concepts in use at this time were diverse; the terms *prostranstva*, (expanses), oblasts (districts), *zemli* (lands) appeared most frequently. According to Vladimir Dal's dictionary of the Russian language, these terms signified some "common aggregate in material or spiritual *byt* [customs, everyday life]," "space," "land, oblast, and people."[20] An inventory of regional particularities, based on scientific research, became a permanent attribute of state politics.

The 1860s represent a new stage in the history of the country—the era of the Great Reforms. The level of economic development in different parts of the empire varied greatly; in essence, the empire contained distinct "economic worlds." The annexation of Central Asia and the end of the prolonged war in the northern Caucasus made existing economic differences even more pronounced. The realization of market reforms now demanded a more complex inventory of regional differences. In order to transform the country into a "united and indivisible Russia," into a single economic space, it was first necessary to resolve issues regarding the optimal distribution of industrial enterprises, market infrastructures, new population settlements, and market centers. Here the railroad played a major role. The problem of regionalization had become part of the problem of the empire's economic modernization.

Geographers in this period based their scientific investigations on earlier premises and achieved major results in the study of the different component parts of the empire. In 1871 the eminent Russian geographer, P. P. Semenov-Tian-Shanskii, head of the Central Statistical Committee of the Ministry of Internal Affairs, proposed a variant for the division of the empire into regions or "natural oblasts." He designated 14 regions, grouped at the level of the uezd, not the guberniia.[21] He delimited four oblasts (Central Industrial, Black Earth Fertile, Black Earth Steppe, and Western Borderlands) as the core that made up the might of Russia and contained its major productive forces.[22] Regional and guberniia borders did not coincide in this grid.

In 1880 Semenov-Tian-Shanskii presented a new grid of regions based on guberniia borders. The principle of "homogeneous natural and economic indicators" served as the primary criterion in this instance: similarity of natural conditions and economic development, which manifested themselves in a dense population, systems of economy, and the territorial contiguity of the guberniias. The author accordingly designated twelve regions, which excluded the Kingdom of Poland, Finland, and the Don Province.[23] Later he divided Asiatic Russia and the Caucasus into seven regions, thus bringing the number of regions to nineteen.[24] This division recorded geographical differences among regions and the historical circumstances under which territories had entered the Russian state. The designation of regions on the basis of guberniia borders was convenient from the point of view of the government's administration.

Semenov employed both purely geographical and economic-geographical terms in naming the oblasts (e.g., Moscow Industrial Region, Central Agricultural Region). Economic specialization was designated only for the core of European Russia, where the degree of the social division of labor was higher than in the peripheries. Semenov noted that he determined the composition of the regions according to the principle of the territorial contiguity of guberniias, approximate homogeneity of natural conditions, and an apparent similarity of economic development. In this regard he took into account not only the territories' distinctive features, but also their internal similarities. Semenov's map thus represents a compendium of the state of the discipline of geography at the time. The map presented the government with a visual representation of the nationalities and economic distinctiveness of different parts of the empire. The Central Statistical Committee, the Ministry of State Property, and the Ministry of Finances adopted the map as their basic point of reference; it continued as such right up to 1917, remaining in use even later, in the 1920s. Semenov's regionalization served as the basis for statistical studies and research and official government reports. Even Lenin used this very same grid in his work "The Development of Capitalism in Russia" for a description of the regions' agricultural specializations.

Semenov's system of regionalization received both government endorsement and public recognition. As the nineteenth century drew to a close, a group of geographers under the leadership of Semenov and his son V. P. Semenov put together the publication, *Russia: A Full Geographical Description of Our Homeland,* a volume unsurpassed to this day.[25] The division of the country into regions in this publication virtually replicated the regionalization plan of 1880. Some twenty-two volumes were planned for publication, including nineteen devoted to individual regions. The authors expected their readers to be "travelers with trade, educational, and other goals" and therefore included information about the history of the settlement of territories, the ethnographic composition, industrial enterprises and markets, and communication routes. Contemporaries called *Russia: A Full Geographical Description of Our Homeland* an economic and geographical work.

In the era of modernization, the empire embarked on a course of industrial reorganization. The government now needed information that would assist it to map out an economic strategy. The dominant subject of study was no longer a simple description of diverse regions but an analysis of each region as part of an integrated whole, taking into account how regions cooperated with one another in order to create a single socioeconomic organism out of the country's diverse and distinctive parts. This fundamentally altered the methodological approach to the problem of regionalization and engendered different versions of the empire's territorial units, depending on the criteria used in mapping the regions.

At the end of the nineteenth century the terms *raion* (region) and *ekonomicheskie raiony* (economic regions) entered the scientific and political lexicon. The economic section of the Brokhaus-Efron *Encyclopedic Dictionary* included an article about the division of Russia into regions on the basis of natural characteristics and economic traits, which also provided a short history of regionalization, beginning with K. I. Arsen'ev.[26]

We can identify three main trends in the study of regionalization at the turn of the century. First, the traditional physical-geographical approach to regionalization, primarily based on climate conditions, finds reflection in the works of S. I. Korzhinskii, P. I. Brounov, V. V. Viner, I. I. Vil'son,[27] G. I. Tanfil'eva, and others.[28] A second approach was agricultural, focused on the soil and climate conditions of different territories—and the related particularities of agriculture, land use, and economic specialization, as well as the particularities of the market (e.g., N. G. Kuliabko-Koretskii,[29] A. I. Skvortsov,[30] A. N. Chelintsev, A. V.Chaianov, and N. D. Kondrat'ev). The agrarian specialization proceeded from a natural-geographical foundation; accordingly, "economic region" was in essence a synonym for "agricultural region."[31] Third, the "transportation-industrial" approach took as its base the theory of maximum utility, studying primarily the opportunities for the sale of marketable products and the conditions of their production and consumption (e.g., A. I. Chuprov and D. I. Mendeleev).

A. I. Chuprov (1842–1909) first introduced the theoretical scheme of dividing Russia into economic regions according to the principle of "maximum utility." As early as the 1870s, while engaged in the study of the country's railroad economy, he had noted the dependence of the intensity of economic life on proximity to new means of transportation—in particular, proximity to railroad lines and direct trade cargo routes. Chuprov also detailed four main traits that distinguished regions from one another: size, density of population, proportion of urban population to rural population, and type of region (or its industrial nature).[32] The main trait, the region's size, depended on the distance from which a certain branch of the railroad attracted local cargo at both terminal points. Chuprov correctly noted the absence of any general rule here, since each particular situation required its own study. The author believed that railroad construction led to a growth in the intensity of local economic life, and that the level of intensity depended on the distance from which a railroad station attracted trade cargo. This meant that active railroad construction would draw more and more of the new territories of Russia into the trade economy. Chuprov can be described as the founder of the multiple-factor analysis of local economic regions, which analyzed the value of the market, the cost of transportation, and demographic indicators.

D. I. Mendeleev advanced similar principles. In 1893 the Department of Trade and Manufacturing of the Ministry of Finances published the collection *Factory and Plant Industry and Trade in Russia* for the Columbus Exhibition in Chicago. The general introduction to the collection, written by D. I. Mendeleev, presented yet another variant of the division of the empire into fourteen economic "krais and oblasts," nine of which were located in European Russia, and the rest (Poland, Finland, the Caucasus, Siberia, Central Asia) in the peripheries. Three conditions important for factory and plant production formed the basis for this scheme: demographic indicators, convenient transportation routes, and a surplus of cheap fuel and raw materials.[33] Economists clearly did not agree on the level of economic development attained by the Russian empire in the early twentieth century; moreover, their estimations of Russia's economic development depended on the criteria (agricultural or industrial) used in their analysis.

In the late nineteenth century the scholarly publications of the IRGO and IVEO provided a forum for debates on the collection of data and the methodology of regionalization. The tendency to use an aggregate of traits and ignore administrative borders complicated the cartographic description of regions, while the number of regions fluctuated greatly (V. V. Viner proposed seven regions;[34] A. I. Skvortsov's plan designated thirty-four[35]). Complexity and methodological vagueness led to a compromise, forming around the use of several criteria for regionalization.[36] This found expression in the opinion that the regional grid bore a narrow "scientific-cognitive" significance, lacking in "practical" applications,[37] because "it is impossible to establish a division of Russia . . . that would satisfy the diverse demands that have been raised and that would unite the study of the country in all possible directions."[38]

A new approach to this problem was formulated by V. P. Semenov-Tian-Shanskii, the geographer's son. His conceptualization took shape gradually as he moved from the particular to the general and from concrete facts to theoretical generalization. In 1910 he published a work on the urban history and character of the settlement of European Russia and described its different types (zonal and azonal).[39] The zonal regions are characterized by the predominance of agriculture, azonal regions distinguished by urban industry. This typology laid the foundations for determining the level of the region's economic and cultural development.

V. P. Semenov-Tian-Shanskii next made a special study of the country's trade-industrial regions.[40] In his analysis of trade and industry in European Russia, V. P. Semenov-Tian-Shanskii noted that historical-cultural conditions and the location of transportation routes, especially railroads and paved roads, were among the most important factors.[41] A vast statistical inventory of materials, supplied by the Ministry of Trade and Industry (600,000 documents from the All-Russian Trade-Industrial Census of 1900), laid the foundation for Semenov-Tian-Shanskii's regionalization based on trade and industry. His proposed system utilized a completely different approach: "from the bottom up," that is, territories first considered independently and then in relation to European Russia as a whole. He designated twelve trade and industrial zones, each of which represented a certain aggregate of common trade or industrial attributes and could be regarded as a network of regions with a common type of production and trade circulation: (1) Northern Forest, (2) Northwest Agricultural, (3) Moscow Industrial, (4) Central Grain Trade, (5) Urals Grain Trade, (6) Southeast Cattle Raising and Fishing, (7) Predkavkazskaia, (8) Southern Grain Trade, (9) Southern Mining, (10) Southwest Agricultural and Industrial, (11) Woodlands, (12) Privislenskaia.

The trade and industrial regions of European Russia, V. P. Semenov-Tian-Shanskii noted, formed an almost unbroken band from Moscow to Petersburg, then followed the Volga, Kama, and Oka rivers, and included patches by those seas with suitable harbors and large railroad stations. In the remainder of the country the most active places were those contiguous to the scattered junctions of railroad, water, and land routes and the sites of certain local cultural centers. The trade and industrial regions of the Donets mountain region, the Urals, and the mountainous region of Poland were separate entities altogether.

Semenov-Tian-Shanskii's *Region and Country* (1928) represents a summary of the author's work on the theory, methodology, and classification of regionalization. Regionalization should proceed from a fragmented analysis to a summary and inclusive picture of regionalization. The scholar noted that there cannot be universal regions, that "regions live and are modified in *space* like everything else that exists on the earth's surface." Consequently, it is not possible to apply the regional grid from the 1870s to the conditions of the 1920s, because the changes in the natural, geographical, and economic environments that have taken place are too great.[42] Of all categories V. P. Semenov-Tian-Shanskii regarded climatological and economic regionalization to be the most complex and the most interesting, "because the factors on which they are based display maximal variations in magnitude and are as changeable as quicksilver."[43] Economic regions are unstable. "The more stable they are, the more strongly they exhibit the physical-geographical element. In general, . . . preference should be given the physical-geographical element in all questionable cases; it should play the guiding role."[44]

Although V. P. Semenev-Tian-Shanskii continued to argue for the supremacy of natural conditions and laws of development, the idea of acquiring knowledge about the country in order to facilitate the rational use of its riches flowed from the very logic of his scientific work. During World War I, he was an active member of the Commission for the Study of the Natural Industrial Forces of Russia (1915–1930).[45]

Interesting work on regionalization was carried out not only in Russia's capitals but also in the provinces, largely by local statisticians. The 1830s saw the creation of provincial statistical committees; in the 1860s statistical departments were established in the zemstvos. Ordinary zemstvo workers conducted surveys of districts in their provinces, performed soil analysis, and collected materials on peasants and landowners and their holdings. This work yielded a wealth of data. In the early twentieth century the Samaran statistician G. I. Baskin developed the so-called "remote" method, which he used to designate twenty-nine grain-trading regions in Samara Province. He based his method on the principle of maximum utility and the flow of corn harvests to certain trading points. In addition to the distance to the market, Baskin took into consideration other components: soil and climate conditions, density of population, the different systems of raising the crop, as well as the prices of the principal products.

During the first years of the Soviet regime Baskin headed the Provincial Statistical Committee, and his methods were widely implemented in, for example, the regionalization of the Middle Volga region and the country as a whole.[46] V. G. Groman in Penza and M. P. Krasilnikov in Ufa carried out similar work, analyzing the differences displayed by districts within a province.[47]

Conclusion

The economic regionalization of the Russian empire evolved over a long period, from the very early years of the eighteenth century when a "geographical inventory" of the land was undertaken. In the course of analyzing the statistical and topographical data collecting during the eighteenth and nineteenth centuries, investigators mapped the many differences and similarities in topographical, ethnographic, historical, and cultural conditions throughout the vast expanses of the Russian empire.

In fact, the research conducted in the eighteenth and nineteenth centuries and the early attempts at regionalization show that as scientific knowledge of the country increased, so too did the number of regions, reflecting the growing awareness of the distinguishing characteristics of individual regions. Consequently, while Lomonosov and Chebotarev designated three to four regions, by the late nineteenth century schemes of regionalization entailed a range of nineteen to thirty-four regions in the empire.

In the mid-nineteenth century new lines of inquiry (agriculture, transportation, industry) resulted in new schemes of regionalization. These new configurations of regionalization took into account not only a region's physical differences, but also economic, industrial and trade factors, thus mapping the empire in a completely new way. More importantly, this work was carried out not only in the capitals and by imperial institutions, but also on the local level by personnel in the zemstvos.

Despite their various orientations, sponsoring agencies and professional backgrounds, all regionalization analysts utilized data on demographics and transportation. While regional borders sometimes overlapped with administrative boundaries of provinces, perhaps for the government's convenience, many regionalization schemes ignored the state's boundaries, mapping a region by different criteria altogether. It was thus essential to define a region's economic centers and to trace the movement around those centers.

From the eighteenth century onward the state experienced a crucial need for accurate information about the space of the Russian empire. The first attempts at regionalization by the Academy of Sciences came about by state decree. Later Arsen'ev, Semenov-Tian-Shanskii, father and son, and Mendeleev worked in governmental ministries and made use of data collected by government agencies in their work. In the nineteenth century the military and the Ministry of Internal Affairs were those most interested in the problem of regionalization. By the early twentieth century this initiative had moved to the Ministry of Finance, and later to the Ministry of Trade and Industry. The publications of these ministries presented a forum for this new research, so essential to the administration of the state. With its basis in both scientific research and state administration, regionalization should be viewed as the precursor to economic planning.

Notes

1. D. A. Aleksandrov, "Nauka i imperializm," *Vtorye Peterburgskie kareevskie chteniia po novistike* (April 22–25, 1997); *Imperii novogo vremeni: tipologiia i evoliutsiia (XV–XX vv.); Kratkoe soderzhanie dokladov* (St. Petersburg, 1999), 39.

2. See Iu. N. Smirnov, *Orenburgskaia ekspeditsiia (Komissiia) i prisoedinenie Zavolzh'ia k Rossii v 30–40-e gg. XVIII veka* (Samara, 1997), 185–187.

3. The northern zone went from 57 degrees northern latitude to the White Sea; the middle zone from 50 to 57 degrees northern latitude; the southern zone from 5 degrees southern latitude to the Azov sea. See B. A. Val'skaia, "Obzor opytov raionirovaniia Rossii s kontsa XVIII v. po 1861," *Voprosy geografii* 17 (1950): 145.

4. N. P. Nikitin, "Zarozhdenie ekonomicheskoi geografii v Rossii," *Voprosy geografii* 17 (1950): 58. Volume 17 of the journal was a special issue on the history of geography.

5. Ibid., 66.

6. Kh. A. Chebotarev, *Geograficheskoe metodicheskoe opisanie Rossiiskoi imperii* (St. Petersburg, 1776), 540.

7. S. I. Pleshcheev, *Obozrenie Rossiiskoi imperii v nyneshnem i novoustroennom sostoianii* (St. Petersburg, 1787); E. F. Ziablovskii, *Noveishee zemleopisanie Rossiiskoi imperii,* part 1 (St. Petersburg, 1897).

8. A. N. Radishchev expressed his opinion on this question in correspondence with friends. See A. N. Radishchev, *Polnoe sobranie sochinenii* (St. Petersburg, 1907), 507–558.

9. A. N. Radishchev, cited in B. A. Val'skaia, "Obzor opytov raionirovaniia Rossii": 507–508.

10. A. I. Preobrazhenskii, "Ekonomicheskie karty v doreformennoi Rossii: Materialy k istorii russkoi ekonomicheskoi kartografii," *Voprosy geografii* 17 (1950): 105–138.

11. A. I. Preobrazhenskii, "Ekonomicheskie karty": 128.

12. V. K. Iatsunskii, "Neopublikovannyi statisticheskii atlas Ministerstva vnutrennikh del 1859 g., sostavlennyi N. A. Miliutinym," *Voprosy geografii* 17 (1950): 219.

13. The grid of regions was published in the journal of the Ministry of Internal Affairs in 1847. The article was anonymous. See B. A. Val'skaia, "Obzor opytov raionirovaniia," 168.

14. E. N. Pertsik. *K. I. Arsen'ev i ego raboty po raionirovaniiu Rossii* (Moscow, 1960).

15. K. I. Arsen'ev, *Obozrenie fizicheskogo sostoianiia Rossii i vygod, ot togo proistekaiushchikh dlia narodnykh promyslov* (St. Petersburg, 1818), 28–33. See also his *Nachertanie statistiki Rossiiskogo gosudarstva* (St. Petersburg, 1818) and *Kratkaia vseobshchaia geografiia* (St. Petersburg, 1818).

16. B. A. Val'skaia cites an anonymous review of K. I. Arsen'ev's work, published in the journal *Moskovskie vedomosti* in 1828. See B. A. Val'skaia, 152.

17. K. I. Arsen'ev included the Upper Volga industrial and Middle Volga agricultural territories in the composition of a unified Volga territory.

18. P. I. Pestel' proposed dividing Russia into 53 administrative units; N. Murav'ev into 14. See N. M. Druzhinin, *Dekabrist Nikita Murav'ev* (Moscow, 1933), 18. P. I. Pestel', *Russkaia pravda ili Zapovednaia gosudarstvennaia gramota velikogo naroda rossiiskogo, sluzhashchaia zavetom dlia usovershenstvovania gosudarstvennogo ustroistva Rossii i soderzhashchaia vernyi nakaz kak dlia naroda, tak i dlia vremennogo Verkhovnogo pravleniia* (St. Petersburg, 1906), 26, 42–43; B. A. Val'skaia, 164.

19. K. I. Arsen'ev, *Statisticheskie ocherki Rossii* (St. Petersburg, 1848).

20. V. I. Dal', *Tolkovyi slovar' zhivogo velikorusskogo iazyka,* vol. 2 (Moscow, 1991), 184, 593, 594.

21. P. P. Semenov, "Naselennost' Evropeiskoi Rossii," *Statisticheskii vremennik Rossiiskoi imperii,* series 2, vol. 1 (St. Petersburg 1871).

22. P. P. Semenov, "Naselennost' Evropeiskoi Rossii v zavisimosti ot prichin, obuslovlivavshikh raspredelenie naseleniia imperii," *Statisticheskii vremennik Rossiiskoi imperii* 1 (St. Petersburg, 1871), 128.

23. (1) Far North oblast (Arkhangel'sk and Vologda provinces), (2) Priozernaia (Olonetsk, St. Petersburg, Novgorod, and Pskov provinces), (3) Pribaltiiskaia, (4) Moscow Industrial oblast (Moscow, Tver, Iaroslavl, Kostroma, Nizhnii Novgorod, Vladimir oblasts), (5) Central Agricultural oblast (Riazan, Tula, Kaluzhsk, Orel, Kursk, Voronezh, Tambov, Penza), (6) Priural'e (Viatsk, Perm, Ufa, Orenburg), (7) Nizhnevolzhsk (Kazan, Simbirsk, Samara, Saratov, Astrakhan), (8) Little Russian (Khar'kov, Poltava, Chernigov), (9) New Russia (Ekaterinoslav, Taurida, Kherson, Bessarabia), (10) Southwest (Kiev, Volynsk, Podol'sk), (11) Belorussia (Smolensk, Vitebsk, Mogilev), (12) Lithuanian (Komensk, Vilnius, Grodnensk).

24. *Statistika pozemel'noi sobstvennosti i naselennykh mest Evropeiskoi Rossii* (St. Petersburg, 1880).

25. V. P. Semenov-Tian-Shanskii, P. P. Semenov-Tian-Shanskii, and V. I. Lamanskii,eds., *Rossiia. Polnoe geograficheskoe opisanie nashego otechestva. Nastol'naia i dorozhnaia kniga dlia russkikh liudei* (St. Petersburg, 1900–1907). The publication dates of the volumes were: Ozernaia oblast, 1900; Middle Povolzh'ia and Zavolzh'ia, 1901;

Middle Russian Black Earth oblast, 1902; Little Russia, 1903; Kirgizkrai, 1903; Upper Podneprov'ia and Belorussia, 1905; and Western Siberia, 1907.

26. F. A. Brokhaus and I. A. Efron, eds., *Rossiia: Entsiklopedicheskii slovar'* (1898; reprint ed., Leningrad, 1991), 54–55: 227–231.

27. I. I. Vil'son, *Ob'iasnenie k khoziaistvenno-statisticheskomu atlasu Evropeiskoi Rossii* (St. Petersburg, 1869).

28. G. I. Tanfil'ev, *Fiziko-geograficheskie oblasti Evropeiskoi Rossii* (St. Petersburg, 1896).

29. N. G. Kuliabko-Koretskii, *Raiony khlebnoi proizvoditel'nosti Evropeiskoi Rossii i Zapadnoi Sibiri* (St. Petersburg, 1903).

30. A. I. Skvortsov, *Khoziaistvennye raiony Evropeiskoi Rossii* 1 (Petersburg, 1914).

31. Ibid.

32. A. I. Chuprov, "Zheleznodorozhnoe khoziaistvo," *Uchenye trudy A. I. Chuprova v izdanii Imperatorskogo Moskovskogo Universiteta* 1 (Moscow, 1910), 320.

33. *Fabrichno-zavodskaia promyshlennost' i torgovlia v Rossii,* ed., V. I. Kovalevskii (St. Petersburg, 1893).

34. V. V. Viner, *Proekt organizatsii poraionnogo izucheniia sel'skogo khoziaistva* (St. Petersburg, 1908).

35. A. I. Skvortsov, *Khoziaistvennye raiony Evropeiskoi Rossii* 1 (Petrograd, 1914): 14.

36. D. I. Rikhter, "Opyt razdeleniia Evropeiskoi Rossii na raiony po estestvennym i ekonomicheskim priznakam," *Trudy Imperatorskogo vol'nogo ekonomicheskogo obshchestva,* 4 (1898).

37. D. I. Rikhter, "K voprosu o razdelenii Rossii po fizicheskim i ekonomicheskim priznakam," *Trudy IVEO* 1, no. 1(1909): 15.

38. Ibid., 19.

39. V. P. Semenov-Tian-Shanskii, "Gorod i derevnia v Evropeiskoi Rossii: Ocherk po eknomicheskoi geografii s 16 kartami i kartogrammami," in V. O. Struve, ed., *Zapiski Russkogo Geograficheskogo obshchestva po otdeleniiu statistiki* 10, no. 2 (St. Petersburg, 1910).

40. V. P. Semenov-Tian-Shanskii and N. M. Shtrupp, eds., "Torgovlia i promyshlennost' Evropeiskoi Rossii po raionam," *Ministerstvo torgovli i promyshlennosti,* nos. 1–12 (St. Petersburg, 1909–1911).

41. Ibid., no 1. Obshchaia chast', 12.

42. V. P. Semenov-Tian-Shanskii, *Raion i strana. Posobie dlia vysshei shkoly* (Moscow-Leningrad, 1928), 16–17.

43. Ibid., 23.

44. Ibid., 25.

45. A. V. Kol'tsov, *Sozdanie i deiatel'nost' Komissii po izucheniiu estestvennykh proizvodite'nykh sil Rossii, 1915–1930 gg.* (St. Petersburg, 1999), 171.

46. G. I. Baskin, "Rynok i ego rol' v organizatsii krestianskogo khoziastva," *Sbornik izbrannykh trudov G. I. Baskina,* vol. 4 (Samara, 1925).

47. V. Groman and K. Egorov, "Selskokhoziastvennyi obzor Penzenskoi gubernii za 1909–1911 gg.," *Vestnik Penzenskogo zemstva* (1914).

5   State and Evolution: Ethnographic Knowledge, Economic Expediency, and the Making of the USSR, 1917–1924

Francine Hirsch

Between 1917 and 1924 the Red Army pushed its way across thousands of miles, pro-Bolshevik forces waged successful uprisings in the peripheries, and the Soviet government marked the revolution's territorial gains with new borders and an official constitution. The Bolsheviks achieved the physical reconquest of most territories of the Russian empire, but the formation of the Soviet Union was just beginning. Even as the revolutionaries established formal political control over the former tsarist state's lands and peoples, expert consultants to the new regime (ethnographers, economists, and other holdovers from the imperial government) began the vital work of conceptual conquest. These experts compiled critical information about the diverse peoples within the fledgling state's expanding borders and helped the Bolsheviks make sense of their domain. Such processes themselves had transformative effects: through campaigns to label, classify, and map out the population, Soviet experts and administrators—sometimes unintentionally, but often purposefully—changed the conceptual categories that people used to define themselves and their communities.

The Soviet regime from the start found inspiration in the idea that modern governments could use scientific knowledge to revolutionize economic production, social structures, and individual consciousness. In particular, the regime wanted to use such knowledge to overcome the problem of "historical diversity" (*mnogoukladnost'*) and build socialism in an immense territory with lands and peoples "at the most diverse levels of historical development."[1] These ends were to be realized, in part, by reorganizing the lands and peoples of the former Russian empire. By establishing a rational administrative structure and a centralized economic plan, the regime would attempt to transform the former empire with its "under-developed expanses" into a "federation of cotton and flax, coal and metal, ore and oil, agriculture and machine industry."[2] By eliminating traditional institutions and ancient loyalties, it would attempt to speed up "evolutionary time," turning the nomads of the Kirgiz steppe, the indigenous tribes of Siberia, and the illiterate peasants of Central Russia into cultured socialist citizens.[3] The historian E. H. Carr has argued that "the disappearance of the old landmarks and the old names, the delimitation of new divisions and subdivisions, the arrival from Moscow of specialists and experts in planning, were a visible symbol of the consolidation of the revolution."[4] These measures were more than symbolic. With new landmarks, new administrative-territorial borders, and new ambitious economic plans, the Soviet regime would transform people's lives.

Concerns about time, geography, and the Revolution's future course converged in deliberations about the Soviet state's administrative form. Significantly, the regime's "specialists and experts in planning" did not have a unified vision for the administrative-territorial organization or regionalization (*raionirovanie*) of the new Soviet state. Instead, two paradigms vied for supremacy: the ethnographic paradigm and the economic paradigm. The former took the "ethnographic principle," or the "principle of nationality" as it was called in the Paris Peace Settlements, as its starting point.[5] Arguing that administrative divisions should conform to ethnographic boundaries, its advocates attempted to apply "the national idea" to a Soviet socialist context. The economic paradigm, by contrast, was motivated by "the principle of economic expediency" and drew inspiration from the European colonial empires and from proposals for the regionalization of the former Russian empire. Its advocates maintained that the socialist state should be organized into specialized economic-administrative units, based on a scientific evaluation of local "productive forces" (raw materials, instruments of production, and labor power).[6] Dismissive of "national rights," they argued that nationalism would dissipate once favorable economic conditions were established through the state-sponsored colonization of backward territories within Soviet borders. The regionalization debate was, in essence, a debate about the road to socialism. It closely paralleled discussions within the party about "the nationality question" and internationalism. Was a national stage of development necessary? Or could rapid economic development eradicate all traces of nationalism and speed the way to communism? Attempting to answer these questions, revolutionaries, administrators, ethnographers, and economists translated the ideals of the revolution into a program for state-building.

This chapter traces the evolution of plans to transform the Russian empire into a new Soviet state. It is addressed in part to a current discussion among historians of Soviet nationality policy about whether or not the Soviet Union was a colonial empire or a new type of state that "made nations." Most works that speak to this question use external criteria to judge Soviet policies and practices. This chapter takes a different approach and considers the extent to which contemporary ideas about nationality, colonization, and empire influenced the experts and administrators who participated in the formation of the Soviet Union. Part 1 situates the "principle of nationality" in the political landscape of World War I and shows how a group of late imperial ethnographers became consultants to the new Soviet government. Parts 2 and 3 focus on the regionalization debate by analyzing the two competing paradigms for organizing the Soviet state as well as the assumptions about progress and science that framed the debate. I conclude with a discussion of how the tension between the ethnographic paradigm and the economic paradigm became embedded in the Soviet Union's administrative-territorial form.

The Principle of Nationality: Ethnography, War, and Revolution

State interest in ethnography in Russia must be understood in the context of World War I. During the war, a slogan proclaiming "the right to national self-determination" gained popularity on all sides and galvanized interest in the "principle of nationality." In 1917, a few weeks before the February Revolution, ethnographers with the Imperial Russian Geographical Society learned that the German military had sent surveillance teams to research the ethnographic composition of the Western borderlands, including Lithuania, Poland, and Galicia.[7] The Germans were using ethnographic data to justify the establishment of German-sponsored national regions in occupied territories (such as the Belorussian-Lithuanian Land Ober Ost).[8] Russia's ethnographers decried their own government's ignorance of these territories, noting that ethnographic studies were of tremendous importance in a war that was being "conducted to a significant degree in connection with the nationality question."[9] They recommended the formation of "a special commission" of experts to support the war effort and the future peace. "The war continues, but it cannot go on without end," wrote Sergei F. Ol'denburg in a petition to the president of the Academy of Sciences in early February. In order to prepare for the "termination of war operations," the government must have a "clear understanding of the tribal [ethnic] composition" (*plemennyi sostav*) of those territories which "lie on both sides of our European and Asiatic borders" and which are "contiguous with the lands of our enemies."[10] With the Academy's backing, Ol'denburg petitioned state ministries for financial support and invited colleagues from Petrograd institutions such as the Russian Anthropological Society and the Linguistic Department of the Philological Society to join a Commission for the Study of the Tribal Composition of Russia and the Borderlands (KIPS).[11]

With the establishment of the Provisional Government in the aftermath of the February Revolution of 1917, the ethnographers continued their campaign for state-sponsored research. Tapping into the new government's anxieties about the strained wartime economy, the experts emphasized the value of ethnographic information for strategic planning. They used the language of economic and military necessity, describing *byt* (the customs of everyday life) as a fundamental indicator of "a population's economic capability" and "one of the most important factors for taking stock of the state's resources."[12] The ethnographers suggested that ethnographic information about the population might "help the state judge which peoples are most suitable for participation in the war and other state obligations."[13] Expanding on their original proposal, they recommended that an ethnographic commission examine not only the contested borderlands, but also "the peoples and territories of inner Russia." They argued that "objective" scientific data about Russia's ethnographic composition could be used to address "a whole number of questions" that might arise "during the convocation of the Constituent Assembly and its upcoming elections."[14] The Provisional Government responded with interest to the ethnographers' proposal; the fact that Ol'denburg was active in the new government and served for a short period as its Minister of Education helped the ethnographers' cause. With formal state approval, funds, and a sense of urgency, KIPS began to research the borderlands.

The new ethnographic commission's initial efforts to map out the peoples of Russia's borderlands provide an excellent example of how categories of classification are constructed within specific political, social, cultural, and institutional contexts. KIPS' cartographic efforts saw continuing disagreement among the ethnographers about the most effective means to determine "ethnographic type" or "nationality." These disagreements in part reflected the fact that ethnography (sometimes called ethnology) did not have a strong tradition as a separate academic discipline in Russia, but intersected with history, linguistics, anthropology, geography, and folklore.[15] The commission's members had backgrounds in different fields: Evfimii Karskii was a linguist, Veniamin Semenov-Tian-Shanskii was first and foremost a geographer, and Sergei Rudenko had been trained as a physical anthropologist. Rudenko expressed skepticism about his colleagues' proposal to rely on language to ascertain the population's tribal composition; such an approach was outside of his own competence. He suggested that KIPS also examine "physical type," a trait that is "of importance to the state," because it can illuminate "connections between different peoples" and "provide valuable data to resolve questions about the influence of environment, customs, nutrition, and prosperity" on different peoples' development.[16]

To further complicate matters of classification, ethnographers inherited from the imperial regime a high degree of confusion about the category "nationality."[17] The 1897 All-Russian Census had not included a separate question about "nationality"; to do so would have given ammunition to separatist movements. Instead, the census categorized most imperial subjects according to native language (*rodnoi iazyk*) and confessional group (*veroispovedanie*); ethnographers at the time suggested that these traits were essential signifiers of nationality (*narodnost'*). However, the 1897 census did not use these criteria to categorize most of the "indigenous" peoples of "Asiatic Russia"; it simply registered them as *inorodtsy* (aliens, or non-Russians).[18] The meta-ethnogeography of the All-Russian Census shaped KIPS' research agenda twenty years later. Beginning their work for the Provisional Government, the ethnographers had neither time nor resources to do extensive fieldwork in both the western and eastern borderlands. To map the western borderlands, the ethnographers decided to rely on data the about native language and confessional group from the 1897 census.[19] To map the eastern borderlands (parts of Turkestan and the Caucasus) and Siberia, by contrast, they also looked at "somatic type." They designated the eastern borderlands sites of new ethnographic fieldwork.[20] Some of the ethnographers who studied the eastern borderlands admitted to ignorance of local languages and dialects. (Almost all of KIPS' original members were from European Russia.) The ethnographers' predilection to categorize "European" peoples on the basis of language and culture and "Asiatic" peoples on the basis of a combination of traits that included physical type continued into the early Soviet period.

When the Bolsheviks took power in October 1917, the "principle of nationality" already reigned supreme in Europe. Indeed, the Bolsheviks' own promise of national self-determination was very much in keeping with the spirit of the times. Some 65 million of the 140 million people inhabiting Russia and its allied republics were non-Russians, and the Moscow-based government worried about the forces of national separatism.[21] Anxious to reinforce its tenuous hold on non-Russian regions, the Soviet regime assured all nationalities autonomy within a Soviet federation. Ironically, the same Bolshevik leaders who had written theoretical works about the "nationality question" before 1917 were not sure how to define "nationality" in its new political context. As Il'ia Trainin, the Deputy Commissar of the People's Commissariat of Nationalities (Narkomnats) later complained, declarations about the right to national self-determination issued by the Council of People's Commissars (Sovnarkom) and the Communist Party "did not concern themselves with a detailed analysis of the concepts nation [*natsiia*] and people [*narod*]."[22] At stake was the following: Which groups (nations, peoples, nationalities, national minorities) were entitled to "national rights"? The fact that there were different levels of "national consciousness" among the population added to the Bolsheviks' own uncertainty. Educated elites in many regions (such as Ukraine and Transcaucasia) were ardent nationalists and their support for the Revolution had been tied to the promise of self-determination.[23] By contrast, many peasants and nomads in Russian and non-Russian regions did not seem even to grasp the concept of "nationality," or at least did not give the "correct" type of response to administrators' questions.[24] As the Bolsheviks discussed plans to establish national republics and regions, attaining expert knowledge about "the nationality question" became a state priority.

The Petrograd ethnographers' initial reactions to the October Revolution were mixed. Most, however, perceived their disciplinary interests as compatible with the practical interests of the Soviet government. A regime that upheld the "principle of nationality" needed detailed ethnographic information. The ethnographers, for their part, were predisposed to participate in the affairs of government and empire. The imperial government had been conservative in its support for ethnographic research, characterizing the discipline as a "proponent of [national] separatism."[25] Through contact with colleagues in Western Europe the ethnographers understood the potential benefits to their discipline from an alliance between science and the state. There was another important point of confluence between the late imperial ethnographers and the Bolsheviks: a shared belief in progress and evolutionary development. Some of the same anthropological theories that shaped Russian ethnography in the late nineteenth century had also inspired Marx and Engels.[26] Bolsheviks and ethnographers alike believed that humankind evolved through discrete stages on a trajectory of development in time. Members of both groups were eager to wage a war on "backwardness" and facilitate the development of the population. Initially, Bolsheviks and ethnographers did not make an issue about whether "backwardness" should be defined in Marxist class terms or more generally. The introduction of a Marxist-Leninist vocabulary to discuss the processes of development would come later. Meanwhile, the KIPS ethnographers came to accept the October Revolution as an opening for partnership between themselves and a regime that had set out to govern by learning about and transforming its subjects' day-to-day lives.

In the context of the civil war, the KIPS ethnographers took on a key role as strategists in the Bolsheviks' struggle for conceptual conquest, helping Soviet administrators establish influence in non-Russian regions, delimit borders, and resolve "the fundamental questions of everyday life and politics."[27] In early 1919 the ethnographers briefed Narkomnats, the People's Commissariat of Enlightenment, and other institutions on their cartographic work and research. Later that year, Narkomnats and the All-Russian Central Executive Committee (VTsIK) of the government used KIPS' ethnographic maps (which were based on data about native language from the 1897 census) along with other sources to delimit the border between Ukraine and Russia.[28] The ethnographers also continued their fieldwork, conducting research in territories under Bolshevik control as well as in territories that resisted incorporation into the federation. The Caucasus and Central Asia became important sites of investigation. Soviet administrators argued that accurate facts and figures about these regions in particular were essential for the deployment of officials from Moscow who could effectively communicate the ideals of the revolution to local populations. The Revolutionary Military Council probably considered this argument when it granted the KIPS ethnographers official sanction to travel through front lines and closed zones to study local populations. The ethnographers in turn were expected to provide Bolshevik forces, including army intelligence, with ethnographic maps and reports about the populations' traditions, languages, economic practices, and religious beliefs.[29] The revolutionaries and ethnographers understood (and indeed may have learned from the German government's interest in ethnographic studies during World War I) that detailed ethnographic data could facilitate victories over recalcitrant regions and provide the rationale for including contested territories within a Soviet state. For example, Soviet leaders supported Aleksandr Samoilovich's trip to the eastern borderlands with the hope that ethnographic research on the Osman-Turks, Kurds, and Armenians would support Soviet claims for contested territories (e.g., Turkish Armenia) on the Turkish border.[30]

By the end of the civil war, the KIPS ethnographers were serving as consultants to numerous government institutions. As the Soviet regime turned its attention to state-building in 1921, the ethnographers worked especially closely with Narkomnats and the State Planning Commission (Gosplan). Gosplan and Narkomnats both sought ethnographic knowledge, but they saw the population differently. While Narkomnats characterized the population as a collection of ethno-historical groups, Gosplan described it as an integral part of the economic base that could be used to promote rapid modernization. KIPS worked with Gosplan on a large-scale project to research and inventory Soviet Russia's "human productive forces" or biopower. Taking a lead from nineteenth-century "race science," the ethnographers suggested that each nationality had a different economic orientation based on its natural abilities.[31] At the same time, KIPS continued to provide information and advice to Narkomnats, assessing the ethnographic composition of Soviet territories and recommending potential ethno-territorial regions. With different approaches to the nationality question, Gosplan and Narkomnats found themselves on opposites sides in what would become known as "the regionalization debate."

The Regionalization Debate

The creation of a Soviet multinational state was the subject of heated inter-institutional debate in the early 1920s. Throughout the civil war years the national idea gained support as self-described national leaders responded to the Bolsheviks' promise of national self-determination by organizing their own national territories. Yet as the Reds emerged victorious, revolutionaries and experts alike expressed ambivalence about relying on the "principle of nationality" to organize the state's administrative infrastructure. While VTsIK and Gosplan suggested that the socialist state should be subdivided into economic-administrative units, Narkomnats argued that administrative divisions should conform to ethnographic or "national" boundaries. Gosplan, VTsIK, and Narkomnats all aspired to build socialism and eliminate "backwardness." At issue was how best to do so. Narkomnats agreed with Gosplan that the ideal federation was one in which nationalities would disappear through a "great synthesis" and economic units would form "a large harmonious whole: the mighty socialist state." But Narkomnats administrators, such as Semen Dimanshtein, imagined that such an outcome would be the end result of a "long process, which will hardly come to a close before our planet dies off."[32] Alluding to Lenin's polemic against imperialism, Dimanshtein and his colleagues argued that disregard for the "ethnographic principle" in the interim would lead to the exploitation of backward peoples.

The establishment of official guidelines for the creation of a "rational" administrative-territorial framework became an official project in December 1919, when the Seventh All-Russian Congress of Soviets declared that VTsIK should "work out the practical question" of the regionalization of the Russian Soviet Federation of Socialist Republics (RSFSR).[33] Describing the existing system of administrative divisions as "anarchic," VTsIK officials such as Timofei Sapronov and Mikhail Vladimirskii recommended a major reform.[34] They called for the logical reorganization of communities, government organs, and institutions, such as schools, hospitals, and courthouses, into new clearly demarcated administrative regions. In the aftermath of the congress, VTsIK set up a subcommission to work out general principles for the regionalization of the RSFSR. VTsIK directed the subcommission to examine the borders of autonomous regions within the RSFSR and decide whether or not ethno-territorial subdivisions were a viable form of state organization. Shortly after the VTsIK subcommission began its work, Bolshevik leaders proposed a "single economic plan" for all territories of the federation—and economists and administrators began to discuss in earnest a form of regionalization based on the "economic principle."[35] Would economic and ethnographic regions coexist? Which factor would take precedence in the administrative framework of the Soviet state? The regionalization debate had begun.

In inter-institutional deliberations about state-building, Narkomnats presented "nationality" as "a fact," demanding primary consideration during the transitional period to socialism.[36] Up through 1920, Narkomnats continued to assume that the ethnographic paradigm would prevail. A *Zhizn' natsional'nostei* article celebrating the formation of the Mari, Votiak, and Kalmyk autonomous oblasts in November 1920 noted that the ethnographic principle reflected "the essence" of the regime's approach to "the nationality question." The author looked forward to the ethno-territorial regionalization of Siberia and the Caucasus (with recent civil war victories Soviet forces hoped to reconquer the Caucasus), but added that such a task awaited the completion of new ethnographic maps.[37] Despite Narkomnats' optimism, the formal institutionalization of the ethno-territorial principle was hotly contested. In December 1920, the Eighth All-Russian Congress of Soviets proposed an alternative to the Narkomnats vision: a federation organized solely on administrative-economic lines.[38] As if on cue, a front-page article in the Narkomnats journal stated what had just become obvious: "the federation is still far from having taken its final form!"[39] The timing of the December resolution was not accidental: Red forces had all but emerged the victors in Russia's civil war. With the defeat of the Whites, the return of Azerbaijan, Ukraine, and Belorussia to the Soviet fold, and the recognition that world socialist revolution was perhaps not imminent, the regime debated which model of administrative-territorial organization would best enable it to consolidate the state and promote economic recovery.

The most serious challenge to the ethnographic principle came from the offices of Gosplan. In May 1921, with the official incarnation of the New Economic Policy (NEP), Gosplan's Council of Labor and Defense established a Regionalization Commission and directed it to come up with a concrete plan for the economic-administrative organization of the Soviet federation; the Regionalization Commission was supposed to consult with the VTsIK subcommission, the People's Commissariat of Agriculture, and the Central Statistical Administration. It reviewed detailed reports of the RSFSR's lands and peoples—reports that had been compiled, in part, by the KIPS ethnographers. It also studied past recommendations for the regionalization of the Russian empire, including those produced by the geographers Dmitrii Rikhter in 1898 and Veniamin Semenov-Tian-Shanskii in 1911, and by the Academy of Sciences Commission for the Study of the Natural Productive Forces of Russia in 1920.[40]

The Gosplan Regionalization Commission sought a plan to promote the rational reorganization of the state's administrative infrastructure and the best use of Soviet Russia's "productive forces."[41] A number of commission members advocated that Russia adopt the model of the French administrative *département* and delimit regions to correspond with river basins. But others criticized the attempt to transfer "the French experience" with its "different economic and political conditions" to Soviet Russia.[42] The head of the commission, professor of economics Ivan Aleksandrov, proposed that the Soviet regime take a "completely new" approach to regionalization based on the "production trait": that it delimit economic-administrative units in accordance with their natural resources, potential economic specialization, and population (its physical type and *byt*).[43]

Ironically, Aleksandrov's "new" approach essentially involved adapting a colonial-type economy to a Soviet socialist context. He imagined Turkestan as a "cotton oblast," Arkhangel'sk as the base for a "forest operations colony," the Caucasus as an "oil and mineral procurement oblast," Moscow as the base for a "central-industrial oblast," Ekaterinburg as the base for a "Urals industrial oblast" and so on.[44] Aleksandrov spoke enthusiastically about the "natural division of labor" among agricultural, industrial, and natural resource oblasts.[45] He proposed that Moscow-based economists and administrators direct economic transactions among the different (agricultural, industrial, and trade) oblasts and plan production, trade, and consumption. Allowing for some local autonomy, Aleksandrov suggested that individual oblasts be delimitated according to the "principle of economic completeness": that each contain a "complex of resources" able to meet its inhabitants' basic needs. Thus, industrial oblasts and natural resource oblasts would have agricultural subregions to supply foodstuffs to workers, and each agricultural oblast would have a "proletarian" subregion, to exert a positive cultural influence on the rest of the population.[46]

The existence of autonomous national territories (republics, oblasts, and regions) that had been created during the civil war years presented a challenge to plans for economic-administrative regionalization. Aleksandrov and his colleagues at Gosplan viewed the Soviet state as one unified landmass, including not just the RSFSR, but also the allied national republics. Most of the economists assumed that existing national territories would be incorporated into economic-administrative units. This assumption had some basis. The economic unification of the RSFSR with the allied national republics was in progress in 1921. The Bolsheviks had negotiated treaties between the RSFSR and the Ukrainian, Belorussian, and Azerbaijani republics, which affirmed the autonomous status of the national republics, while calling for their inclusion in a centralized economy and military. But Aleksandrov and his colleagues imagined an even greater degree of unification, leaving an important question unanswered: How would national-territorial units preserve their autonomous status in a state that was organized on economic-administrative lines?

The Gosplan Regionalization Commission had a ready (if dismissive) response to the bothersome question of national rights. National-territorial units would *not* retain their autonomous status. Instead, their lands and peoples would be integrated directly into economic-administrative units. Aleksandrov acknowledged that this flew in the face of national self-determination. But, echoing Bolshevik internationalists, he argued that rapid economic development would eradicate the need for national territories altogether. "National tendencies were always quite limited" among the masses and "manifest themselves only when faced with unfavorable [economic] circumstances," Aleksandrov explained. Describing economic regionalization as a "revolutionary method of boosting the economy," he predicted that the "nationality question" would soon become irrelevant.[47]

In September 1921, Aleksandrov presented to Gosplan the Regionalization Commission's plan for the organization of the RSFSR and allied republics into 13 European and 8 Asiatic economic-administrative oblasts.[48] Each "economic-administrative oblast" would be "an actual administrative unit," and not just a "paper oblast" for statistics and economic planning. Each would represent "a link in the chain" of the national economy, a composite part of a "complete state organism."[49] Aleksandrov conceded that small national territories might remain intact upon their integration into the twenty-one economic-administrative oblasts. But he advocated that larger ethno-territorial units such as the Ukrainian SSR and the Kirgiz ASSR be broken up. For example, his plan called for the division of the Ukrainian national republic into the Southern Mining Oblast and the Southwestern Oblast, each with a different economic orientation. Demonstrating an awareness of Ukraine's ethnographic composition, Aleksandrov explained that these two parts of Ukraine were "ethnically" distinct from one another: that the projected Southwestern Oblast was dominated by Ukrainians, while the projected Southern Mining Oblast was comprised of "representatives of all the major *narodnosti* of Russia," including Great Russians, Ukrainians, Greeks, Bulgarians, Germans, Jews, and Tatars.[50]

Aleksandrov and his colleagues purported to take an innovative approach to the problem of backwardness, based on rational economic planning and "not on the vestiges of lost sovereign rights."[51] But Narkomnats and local elites viewed the commission's dismissal of "national rights" as an expression of imperialism. Aleksandrov insisted that economic-administrative regionalization would not interrupt "the development of the cultural and customary [*bytovye*] particularities of different nationalities."[52] But local national elites were not so sure. Nor were they only worried about culture. Ukrainian representatives protested that the division of Ukraine into two economic-administrative oblasts would mean the loss of its *political* autonomy. Narkomnats expressed similar concerns and felt

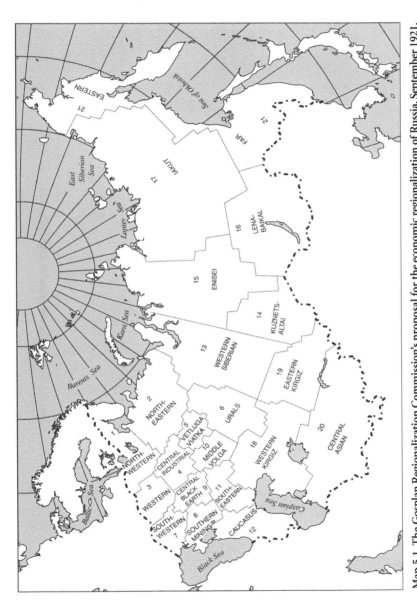

Map 5.1. The Gosplan Regionalization Commission's proposal for the economic regionalization of Russia, September 1921. (Based on map in A. F. Belavin, *Atlas Soiuza sovetskikh sotsialisticheskikh respublik, primenitel'no k raionam ekonomicheskogo raionirovaniia Gosplana SSSR* [Moscow-Leningrad, 1928], 13).

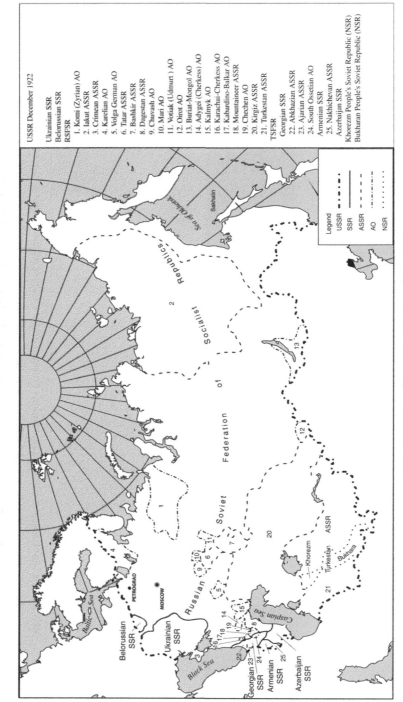

USSR December 1922

Ukrainian SSR
Belorussian SSR
RSFSR

1. Komi (Zyrian) AO
2. Iakut ASSR
3. Crimean ASSR
4. Karelian AO
5. Volga German AO
6. Tatar ASSR
7. Bashkir ASSR
8. Dagestan ASSR
9. Chuvash AO
10. Mari AO
11. Votiak (Udmurt) AO
12. Oirot AO
13. Buriat-Mongol AO
14. Adygei (Cherkess) AO
15. Kalmyk AO
16. Karachai-Cherkess AO
17. Kabardino-Balkar AO
18. Mountaineer ASSR
19. Chechen AO
20. Kirgiz ASSR
21. Turkestan ASSR

TSFSR
Georgian SSR
22. Abkhazian ASSR
23. Ajarian ASSR
24. South Ossetian AO
Armenian SSR
Azerbaijan SSR
25. Nakhichevan ASSR

Khorezm People's Soviet Republic (NSR)
Bukharan People's Soviet Republic (NSR)

Map 5.2. Union of Soviet Socialist Republics, 1922.

obliged to remind Gosplan that "Ukraine is an independent state."[53] The Narkomnats administrator Trainin cautioned that "the substance" of autonomy would be diminished for all nationalities if economic-administrative oblasts usurped the administration of autonomous national regions.[54]

The Regionalization Commission's recommendations were the catalyst for a protracted dispute between Gosplan and Narkomnats. In important respects, Gosplan and Narkomnats shared a common approach; both institutions looked outside Soviet borders for inspiration, and both relied on experts from the imperial regime for expert knowledge about the lands and peoples of the former Russian empire. Both institutions hoped to win central and local institutional support and both looked to validate their positions on scientific and ideological grounds. Both adjusted their proposals and arguments in response to each other's criticism. Reacting to the Narkomnats critique of the economic paradigm, Gosplan argued that its proposals were not "imperialistic" and made a small nod toward ethnographic considerations. Reacting to the Gosplan critique of the ethnographic paradigm, Narkomnats argued that the ethnographic model of regionalization was based in part on a concern for economic rationalism.

Narkomnats administrators such as Trainin argued that ethno-territorial regionalization was not a conciliatory measure taken at the cost of progress but was an approach with "maximum economic and cultural benefit." It would give "backward" nationalities the chance to thrive and participate in the Soviet campaign "on the economic front."

> We did not simply draw a line on the territory of each nation and say, "Please, here is your territory and its borders. Figure things out." No! We studied the economic situation of each oblast, its main economic and cultural centers, and set out to put things together in such a way that [people with similar] national-cultural particularities are settled in one autonomous region.[55]

Trainin acknowledged the practical advantages of an economic plan that placed all resources under a "central command." But he argued that such a plan need not forfeit the national principle. Gosplan could set overall "production targets" for the Soviet state, but allow the autonomous national-territorial units to use their "experiences and resources" to work toward plan goals.[56]

It was not just the Regionalization Commission's disregard for "national rights," but also its position on the "colonization question" that alarmed Narkomnats. As revolutionaries in late imperial Russia, the Bolsheviks had condemned all forms of colonization as exploitative. Not long after the Bolsheviks seized power, however, they began to argue that the state-sponsored colonization of resource-rich regions was critical for economic progress—and thus imperative for the transition to socialism. Bolshevik leaders explained that it was simply not possible for Soviet Russia to "do without the petroleum of Azerbaijan or the cotton of Turkestan."[57] The Gosplan Regionalization Commission reiterated this argument in the 1920s. Characterizing colonization as a program of state-sponsored agricultural and industrial development, it took for granted the regime's right to organize, use, and develop land, mineral deposits, forests, and water sources in Russia and the allied republics. Such an approach was consistent with Soviet law, which did not recognize the private ownership of property.[58]

Aleksandrov and his colleagues did not apologize for their colonization agenda, but instead insisted that colonization was not by nature exploitative. The Gosplan economists argued that late imperial efforts to colonize Turkestan and the Caucasus had provoked "anti-Russian sentiment" because they had been accompanied by a "crude Russification policy, with measures deeply insulting" for some of "Russia's *narodnosti*." According to Aleksandrov, "the sharp expression of national tendencies and the mobilization of the native population" in Turkestan before the revolution (for example, the revolt of the Kirgiz population in Semirech'e in 1916) had been "provoked" by "certain individuals in the Resettlement Administration" of the imperial regime who had mistreated the local Kirgiz population. Under different circumstances, "national feeling probably never would have taken such a sharp form," since "most natives in Turkestan" recognized that their connection with Russia meant "economic and cultural advances."[59] Aleksandrov did not consider the Gosplan recommendations to be economically or culturally oppressive, arguing that Russians and non-Russians alike would benefit from the full development of the country's productive forces.

As Narkomnats became embroiled in the regionalization debate, it looked to ethnography, and to KIPS in particular, to bring scientific authority to its arguments for the ethnographic paradigm of regionalization. The ethnographers, who also advised Gosplan, had divided loyalties. It was in this context in 1921 that Narkomnats drew up plans to establish its own Ethnographic Bureau. A Narkomnats-based bureau would initiate its own expeditions and work "in scientific unity" with KIPS and other institutions that engaged in "systematic ethnographic research." It would have a hands-on role in national-cultural construction. Its scholar-advisers would act as mediators between (primarily Russian-speaking) Soviet authorities and indigenous populations; they would bring information about local cultures to government institutions, while introducing agricultural techniques, healthcare and sanitation, and literacy in native languages to local populations. Thus conceived, the bureau would enable Narkomnats to "assist individual nationalities [*narodnosti*] striving to join European culture."[60]

The ethnographers endorsed the Narkomnats argument that attention to the ethnographic principle was not a "liberal, humanitarian" measure taken at the cost of progress, but was a rational approach that would establish a "solid, scientific foundation" for socialist construction.[61] An official Narkomnats memo about the proposed bureau characterized "the collection and analysis of information about the lives of the nationalities" of the RSFSR as having "enormous scientific, social, and administrative significance . . . Without scientific knowledge about geographical conditions and familiarity with national particularities IT IS IMPOSSIBLE TO GOVERN TO THEIR BENEFIT different peoples and not waste strength and resources on unneeded experiments.[62] "Not sentimentality but strict economic calculations" compelled the government to assist even the most "backward" peoples, affirmed the KIPS ethnographer Nikolai Iakovlev at an Ethnographic Bureau organizational session: "Every living person should be valued as a source of state revenue, as living capital which yields a determined amount of profit to the state through productive labor."[63]

If Narkomnats seemed to give the upper hand to Gosplan by arguing in economic terms, the commissariat continued to insist that its own version of regionalization was more in line with the party's nationality policy. Narkomnats administrators argued that the phenomenon of historical diversity was pronounced in Soviet territories because the imperial regime had stunted the development of "productive forces" in the empire's colonies (Turkestan, the Caucasus, Siberia) and had left the inhabitants of these regions "at backward historical stages." Within Soviet borders one could encounter the "closed" societies of "clans and tribes of the Caucasus, Turkestan, and Siberia" as well as peoples (*narody*) already "on the road to capitalism," explained Narkomnats administrator Georgii Broido in a 1923 article that set out the commissariat's position. Broido suggested that the ethnographic paradigm would further the goals of nationality policy by fostering the population's ethno-historical development from feudalism to capitalism to socialism to communism.[64]

Broido and his colleagues at Narkomnats went beyond the usual arguments for national self-determination and asserted that the Soviet regime should delimit national-territorial units for "backward" peoples lacking national consciousness. They advocated what might be described as a program of state-sponsored evolutionism: a Soviet version of the civilizing mission that combined Western European ideas about cultural evolutionism (which presumed that all peoples evolve through progressive stages of cultural development) with the Marxian theory of history (which presumed that all cultural forms correspond to particular stages on the historical timeline), and added to it the Leninist conceit that revolutionary actors could speed up historical progress. Ethnographic knowledge was absolutely critical to this endeavor. For example, Narkomnats representatives considered the ethno-territorial regionalization of Turkestan, even though the region's "three main peoples—the Uzbeks, Kirgiz, and Turkmen . . . have not reached that stage of political and economic development when it can be said with full certainty how their national interrelationships are developing."[65] The commissariat looked to ethnographers to determine which tribes and clans "belonged to" which nationality-in-formation.[66]

Between Two Paradigms

Between 1921 and 1923, regionalization remained a focal point in deliberations about the new Soviet state. As Narkomnats and Gosplan debated the connection between nationality and economic development, VTsIK attempted to find a compromise solution. In November 1921, VTsIK set up a commission under the leadership of Mikhail Kalinin to review the particulars of the Aleksandrov plan and evaluate Narkomnats' concerns. The new Kalinin Commission included representatives from Gosplan (including Aleksandrov), the NKVD, Narkomnats, the People's Commissariat of Agriculture, the Central Statistical Administration, and other central and local agencies. Its sessions became a forum for discussing the tension between economic-administrative regionalization and the nationality question, as it evaluated "written protests and verbal objections" to the Aleksandrov plan that had been presented by local national leaders.[67]

Representatives from groups that considered themselves "developed nations," like the Georgians, and members of former *inorodtsy*, like the Bashkir, characterized the Aleksandrov plan as a throwback to late imperial colonialism. Georgian Communists argued that the commission's proposal to combine the Georgian, Armenian, and Azerbaijani republics and the North Caucasus into a single economic-administrative oblast that specialized in oil and mineral procurement was an attempt to subordinate "the Georgian nation" to Moscow.[68] Bashkir representatives maintained that inclusion of the Bashkir ASSR in the proposed Urals economic-administrative oblast would promote a colonial relationship between Russian workers and Bashkir peasants.[69] Aleksandrov continued to insist that his plan had in mind the interests of the nationalities. He argued that underdeveloped nationalities (*narodnosti*) in particular would benefit from being attached to "existing and rising industrial centers": "cultured" workers would have a positive influence on these nationalities and help to "liquidate" their "age-old backwardness." To "raise the economic and cultural level" of the Bashkirs, Aleksandrov argued, it was critical to include them in the Urals Oblast.[70]

In February 1922, the Kalinin Commission produced a revised regionalization plan, which purported to honor the national principle within the general framework of economic-administrative regionalization. The new plan proposed twelve "European" and nine "Asiatic" oblasts. Like the original Aleksandrov plan, it was premised on the integration of national-territorial units into economic-administrative oblasts. But it differed in its recognition of the borders of national republics and oblasts as inviolable. No national republic or oblast would be divided between two or more administrative units. Small national-territorial units, which "due to their economic weakness" could not form separate economic oblasts, would constitute "internal subregions" in economic-administrative oblasts. Large, developed national-territorial units would constitute separate economic-administrative oblasts. The most expansive and diverse ethno-territorial units (such as Ukraine) would constitute two or more economic oblasts, but would be united in one administrative unit.[71] In short, ethno-territorial units would either overlap with or exist as subunits of economic-administrative oblasts. Kalinin acknowledged that the commission still had not worked out important "technical issues"—which had real political significance—such as which administrative bodies, those of the economic-administrative oblast or those of the national-territorial subunits, would have the authoritative voice on economic and political questions.[72]

For political elites in the allied republics and autonomous national regions, questions about the Soviet state's political and economic form were especially charged—and the Kalinin Commission's proposal did not satisfy their concerns. This became apparent as Aleksandrov discussed the new proposal with local national representatives in February 1922 and at a session with Narkomnats three months later.[73] Local national elites argued that even the revised plan compromised national rights and was "in fundamental contradiction" with the party's nationality policy. Narkomnats expressed particular concern about "weak nationalities," which "strong nationalities" might "swallow up" in the economic-administrative oblasts. Narkomnats administrators predicted that in the push for economic modernization, state resources would be focused on the "more developed subregions" of each economic-administrative oblast, and "backward nationalities" in "backward" subregions would be ignored and would fall "under the thumb" of their neighbors.[74]

The economic paradigm of regionalization and the "principle of nationality" proved difficult to reconcile. It was not clear, for example, how the two proposed Ukrainian economic oblasts (the Southwestern Oblast and the Southern Mining Oblast) would be integrated into a single Ukrainian administrative unit. Nor was it obvious how to subdivide the Caucasus into economically viable national territories. Meanwhile, Soviet leaders forged ahead with the formal political unification of the RSFSR and the national republics. In December 1922 the regime rejected a controversial proposal advocated by Stalin to include the national republics in an expanded RSFSR. Instead, on December 30 at the All-Russian Congress of Soviets, the RSFSR, Ukrainian SSR, Belorussian SSR, and Transcaucasian Soviet Federative Socialist Republic (TSFSR)—comprising the Georgian, Azerbaijani, and Armenian national republics—agreed to enter a new Union of Soviet Socialist Republics, centralized through Moscow.[75] As the republics were integrated into this union, the regionalization debate remained charged. The regime had to decide whether to delineate administrative subunits of the RSFSR and other republics on the basis of ethnographic or economic criteria.

Not just administrators and experts, but also Communist Party leaders, found themselves caught between two competing paradigms for administrative-territorial regionalization in the 1920s. The classic works on the formation of the Soviet Union describe a party that had clear aims and devised the Soviet Union's complicated administrative-territorial structure as a means to divide and rule.[76] In actuality, the Soviet state took shape as it did because party leaders were unable to control Soviet state-formation and regionalization. Party leaders could not reach a consensus in the early 1920s about how best to organize the Soviet state, let alone dictate all aspects of state-building in the RSFSR and republics.

High-ranking members of the Communist Party followed the regionalization debate at all stages; many participated in the deliberations through their positions in government institutions. But it was not until March 1923, once regionalization had been debated in local-level party and government organizations as well as at non-party peasant and national conferences, that the Politburo and the Central Committee formally weighed in on the issue. They approved the revised Aleksandrov plan "in principle," but urged "great caution."[77] Aleksei Rykov spoke about the party's position the following month at the Twelfth Party Congress. "In spite of its 'technical' name, the question of the administrative-economic division or regionalization of the state has colossal, gigantic significance" for "the entire transitional period of the October Revolution, for the entire transitional period from NEP to communism," asserted Rykov. In practical terms, regionalization would entail the complete reorganization of government and party organs. Arguing that the regime did not have enough "knowledge of local conditions" to endeavor such a major enterprise all at once, Rykov called the VTsIK-approved Gosplan proposal a "preliminary working hypothesis," which would have to be revised "on the basis of experience."[78]

The Party Congress deliberations on both regionalization and "the nationality question" are striking in their attempt to balance all-union (economic) and national (ethnographic) concerns. On the one hand, the party denounced prominent national elites for subordinating Soviet priorities to "local nationalist" interests.[79] On the other hand, the party affirmed the right of all "nationalities to their own state formations" and embraced the Narkomnats position on non-imperialistic development. Pointing to "colonial states such as Great Britain and old Germany," the party noted an "irreconcilable contradiction" between the "economic unification of peoples" (described as a progressive process which established the "material prerequisites for socialism") and the "imperialistic" practices often associated with economic unification (such as "the exploitation of less developed peoples by more developed peoples").[80] To differentiate the Soviet Union from the European colonial empires and from imperial Russia, party leaders recommended an "emancipatory nationality policy"—what Central Committee member Anastas Mikoian would later describe as a policy to help "tribes become nations."[81]

From Paradigms to Principles

By 1924, the Soviet regime had achieved the formal political unification of the territories within its borders. Soviet experts and administrators had begun the work of conceptual conquest and had elaborated a revolutionary approach to overcoming the problem of "backwardness." But neither Narkomnats nor Gosplan won the regionalization debate and much remained unresolved. In the aftermath of the Twelfth Party Congress, the regime directed Gosplan to oversee the regionalization of two trial economic-administrative oblasts in the RSFSR: the North Caucasus agricultural oblast and the Urals industrial oblast. At the same time, the regime upheld the national-territorial framework of the Soviet state (union republics, autonomous republics, autonomous oblasts, and national regions); it established a new Commission for the Regionalization of the USSR and directed it to evaluate existing national-territorial borders as well as the possible delimitation of additional national-territorial units.[82] The tension between the ethnographic paradigm and the economic paradigm became part of the structure of the Soviet Union.

In subsequent months and years, the ethnographic and economic paradigms for regionalization were reinterpreted as ethnographic and economic *principles* for border delimitation. Between 1924 and 1929 Gosplan worked toward the delimitation of economic-administrative oblasts throughout the Soviet Union. Its plans were compromised again and again as national oblasts and regions refused to be included in proposed economic-administrative oblasts. In almost all cases, the borders of proposed oblasts were redrawn in order to honor the national principle within the oblast, or to exclude national-territorial units altogether. For example, the Urals Oblast was supposed to include the Bashkir ASSR (in addition to the Ekaterinburg, Cheliabinsk, and Perm provinces). But Bashkir leaders argued for the exclusion of their autonomous oblast from the Urals Oblast, and the regime upheld the Bashkir position as a matter of national rights.[83] In this case and others national oblasts were integrated into the all-Union economic plan as separate units.

Even as Gosplan modified its plan for economic-administrative regionalization in order to take into account the national principle, TsIK and party organs adjusted the Union's national-territorial units with economic considerations in mind. As the TsIK regionalization commission investigated, proposed, and contested borders, it assessed the economic orientation of the population as well as all-Union economic concerns. Local national leaders who had worried previously that economic-administrative regionalization would facilitate a colonial relationship between Russians and non-Russians expressed anger as ethnographic precision was sacrificed to the regime's larger economic goals. The commission's first deliberations involved the borders between the Ukrainian SSR, Belorussian SSR, and autonomous national oblasts of the RSFSR.[84] A VTsIK subcommission (using KIPS' ethnographic maps) had drawn the initial borders on the basis of nationality determined by language. The TsIK regionalization commission reevaluated these borders for both ethnographic accuracy and economic viability.

With the formation of the Soviet Union, the KIPS ethnographers were thrust into a position of greater authority. The new Soviet constitution of 1924 dissolved Narkomnats and its Ethnographic Bureau. The Soviet of Nationalities, formerly an administrative organ within Narkomnats, became one of the Soviet government's two legislative bodies. As TsIK and the Soviet of Nationalities reviewed the Soviet Union's administrative-territorial framework, they looked to the KIPS ethnographers as experts who could further the work of conceptual conquest. The KIPS ethnographers would provide the TsIK regionalization commission with expert knowledge and would play a crucial role in other state-building projects—such as the First All-Union Census of 1926, which categorized the entire population under the rubric of nationality. The KIPS ethnographers, steeped in Western European and imperial Russian ideas about nationality and empire but with little formal training in Marxist thought, would continue to facilitate the process of internal transformation that shaped the new Soviet state.

Notes

1. G. I. Broido, "Nasha natsional'naia politika i ocherednye zadachi Narkomnatsa," *Zhizn' natsional'nostei,* no. 1 (1923): 5–13.

2. S. Dimanshtein, "Slozhnost' raboty novogo Narkomnatsa," *Zhizn' natsional'nostei,* no. 17 (74) (June 9, 1920): 1.

3. On "evolutionary time" and the Soviet project see Stephen E. Hanson, *Time and Revolution: Marxism and the Design of Soviet Institutions* (Chapel Hill, 1997). In some respects, Soviet-style modernization was similar to the French Republic's efforts "civilize" its peasants and imperial subjects. See Eugen Weber, *Peasants into Frenchmen: The Modernization of Rural France, 1870–1914* (Stanford, 1976).

4. E. H. Carr, *Socialism in One Country, 1924–1926,* vol. 2 (New York, 1959), 301.

5. For a discussion of the Paris Peace Conference and the national idea see C. A. Macartney, *National States and National Minorities* (London, 1934); Arno Mayer, *Wilson vs. Lenin: Political Origins of the New Diplomacy, 1917–1918* (Cleveland, 1964); and Mark Mazower, *Dark Continent: Europe's Twentieth Century* (New York, 1999).

6. For a discussion of Marx's use of the term "productive forces" see G. A. Cohen, *Karl Marx's Theory of History: A Defense* (Princeton, 2000).

7. On the origins of KIPS see Francine Hirsch, *Empire of Nations: Ethnographic Knowledge and the Making of the Soviet Union* (Ithaca, N.Y., 2005).

8. On the German example see Wiktor Sukiennicki, *East Central Europe During World War I: From Foreign Domination to National Independence*, vol. 1 (Boulder, Colo., 1984), and Vejas Gabriel Liulevicius, *War Land on the Eastern Front: Culture, National Identity, and German Occupation in World War I* (Cambridge, UK, 2000).

9. Rossiiskaia Akademiia nauk, *Ob uchrezhdenii Komissii po izucheniiu plemennogo sostava naseleniia Rossii, Izvestiia Komissii po izucheniiu plemennogo sostava naseleniia Rossii*, vol. 1 (Petrograd, 1917), 7–8.

10. St. Petersburg Branch of the Archive of the Russian Academy of Sciences (PFA RAN) f. 2, op. 1–1917, d. 30, l. 38; Rossiiskaia Akademiia nauk, *Ob uchrezhdenii Komissii*, 7.

11. PFA RAN f. 2, op. 1–1917, d. 30, ll. 38, 48–50.

12. Ibid., ll. 40–42.

13. Ibid.

14. Ibid., l. 52.

15. During the years leading up to 1917 the Russian Geographical Society's ethnographers made numerous attempts to define their discipline. See for example, "Zhurnal zasedaniia Otdeleniia etnografii I.R.G.O. 4 marta 1916 goda," *Zhivaia starina* 25, no. 2–3 (1916): 1–11.

16. PFA RAN f. 2, op. 1–1917, d. 30, ll. 40–42.

17. Census totals for 1897 included a table on occupation that was correlated according to "*narodnost*' based on native language"; the list included eleven main language groups (e.g., Russian, Romance, Turkish-Tatar), with corresponding subgroups (e.g., Russian: Great Russian, Little Russian, White Russian). G. G. Melik'ian and A. Ia. Kvasha et al., eds., *Narodonaselenie: Entsiklopedicheskii slovar'* (Moscow, 1994), 310, and A. I. Gozulov, *Perepisi naseleniia SSSR i kapitalisticheskikh stran* (Moscow, 1936), 189–201.

18. In some cases (but not all) census takers noted which "people" the *inorodtsy* belonged to in the same column—e.g., Ostiak, Tungus, Buriat. S. Patkanov, "Proekt sostavleniia plemennoi karty Rossii," *Zhivaia starina* 24, no. 3 (1915): 239–241.

19. PFA RAN f. 2, op. 1–1917, d. 30, l. 38.

20. Ibid., ll. 49–52.

21. George Liber, *Soviet Nationality Policy, Urban Growth and Identity Change in the Ukrainian SSR, 1923–1934* (Cambridge, UK, 1992), 26. The figure cited is from 1921.

22. I. Trainin, "O plemennoi avtonomii," *Zhizn' natsional'nostei*, no. 2 (1923): 19–26.

23. For a detailed discussion of early demands for self-determination see E. H. Carr, *The Bolshevik Revolution, 1917–1923*, vol. 1 (New York, 1950).

24. PFA RAN f. 135, op. 1, d. 11, ll. 134–137.

25. See D. Ianovich, "K voprosu ob izuchenii byta narodnostei RSFSR," *Zhizn' natsional'nostei*, no. 29 (127) (December 14, 1921): 1.

26. On Marx, Engels, and anthropological theories see John J. Honigmann, *The Development of Anthropological Ideas* (Homewood, Ill., 1976), 117, 121–122. On Tylor and Russian ethnography see "Zhurnaly zasedanii Otdeleniia etnografii Imperatorskago

russkago geograficheskago obshchestva: Zasedanie 28 oktiabria 1911," xxxi–xxxv. On the influence of Tylor and Morgan see N. M. Matorin, "Sovremennyi etap i zadachi sovetskoi etnografii," *Sovetskaia etnografiia,* no. 1–2 (1931): 3–38.

27. PFA RAN f. 135, op. 1–1917, d. 31, ll. 13–26; f. 135. op. 1, d. 3, ll. 1–6, 17–18. Also the Russian State Archive of the Economy (RGAE) f. 1562, op. 336, d. 8, l. 105.

28. PFA RAN f. 2, op. 1–1917, d. 30, l. 188. Also RGAE f. 1562, op. 336, d. 8, l. 105.

29. PFA RAN f. 2, op. 1–1917, d. 31, ll. 15–19.

30. Ibid., l. 39.

31. PFA RAN f. 135, op. 1, d. 3, l. 18.

32. S. Dimanshtein, "Slozhnost' raboty novogo Narkomnatsa," *Zhizn' natsional'nostei,* no. 17 (74) (June 9, 1920): 1.

33. *S"ezdy sovetov RSFSR v postanovleniakh i rezoliutsiiakh* (Moscow, 1939), 152. Cited in Carr, *Socialism in One Country,* vol. 2, 274. Also "Raionirovanie SSSR: Istoricheskaia spravka," in *Voprosy ekonomicheskogo raionirovaniia SSSR: Sbornik materialov i statei (1917–1929 gg.),* ed. G. M. Krzhizhanovskii (Moscow, 1957), 304. The Soviet regime inherited from the Russian empire a system of *sela* (villages), *volosty* (rural districts), *uezdy* (counties or regions), and *gubernii* (provinces). These were delimited without regard to ethnographic considerations. There were ninety-seven provinces in all.

34. K. D. Egorov, ed., *Raionirovanie SSSR: Sbornik materialov po raionirovaniiu s 1917 po 1925 godu,* (Moscow, 1926), 16.

35. The Bolshevik leaders made this announcement at the Ninth Party Congress in March 1920. Carr, *Socialism in One Country,* vol. 2, 274.

36. S. K., "Ekonomicheskoe raionirovanie i problemy avtonomno-federativnogo stroitel'stva," *Zhizn' natsional'nostei,* no. 25 (123) (November 12, 1921): 1.

37. I. Gertsenberg, "Natsional'nyi printsip v novom administrativnom delenii RSFSR," *Zhizn' natsional'nostei,* no. 37 (94) (November 25, 1920): 1.

38. *S"ezdy sovetov RSFSR,* 179. Also see Carr, *Bolshevik Revolution,* vol. 1, 275.

39. S. Kotliarevskii, "O razvitii federatsii," *Zhizn' natsional'nostei,* no. 41 (97) (December 24, 1920): 1.

40. Egorov, *Raionirovanie SSSR: Sbornik materialov,* 30–34.

41. Ibid., 12, 26–27. Also V. Ul'ianov (Lenin), "Polozhenie o gosudarstvennoi obshcheplanovoi komissii," in Gosplan R.S.F.S.R., *Ekonomicheskoe raionirovanie Rossii: Materialy podkomissii po raionirovaniiu pri Gosudarstvennoi obshche-planovoi komissii S.T.O.* (Moscow, 1921), 3–10, and G. M. Krzhizhanovskii, *Khoziaistvennye problemy R.S.F.S.R. i raboty Gosudarstvennoi obshcheplanovoi komissii (Gosplana),* vol. 1 (Moscow, 1921). Aleksandrov wrote chapter 6, "Sektsiia po raionirovaniiu."

42. I. G. Aleksandrov, "Ekonomicheskoe raionirovanie Rossii," in Gosplan R.S.F.S.R., *Ekonomicheskoe raionirovanie Rossii,* 31–32.

43. Ibid., 32.

44. Ibid., 38–42; and "Programmy razrabotki raionov," in Gosplan R.S.F.S.R., *Ekonomicheskoe raionirovanie Rossii,* 55–58.

45. Aleksandrov, "Ekonomicheskoe raionirovanie Rossii" 31–33. Also S. V. Bernshtein-Kogan, "K voprosu o programme i metode sostavleniia poraionnykh obzorov i khoziaistvennykh planov," in Gosplan R.S.F.S.R., *Ekonomicheskoe raionirovanie Rossii,* 25–26.

46. Aleksandrov, "Ekonomicheskoe raionirovanie Rossii," 32–33, 42, and Egorov, *Raionirovanie SSSR: Sbornik,* 39–42.

47. Cited in P. M. Alampiev, *Ekonomicheskoe raionirovanie SSSR* (Moscow, 1959), 133.

48. Aleksandrov's proposal was published in *Ekonomicheskaia zhizn'* in September 1921. There were several different versions of the plan. The initial version listed 14 European oblasts and 4 Turkestani oblasts; one published version listed 12 European oblasts and 8 Asiatic oblasts. See for example I. Trainin, "Ekonomicheskoe raionirovanie i natsional'naia politika," *Zhizn' natsional'nostei*, no. 21 (119) (October 10, 1921): 1. Also Alampiev, *Ekonomicheskoe raionirovanie SSSR*, chapters 3, 4, and Z. Mieczkowski, "The Economic Regionalization of the Soviet Union in the Lenin and Stalin Period," *Canadian Slavonic Papers* 8 (1966): 89–124.

49. Aleksandrov, "Ekonomicheskoe raionirovanie Rossii," 32, and Krzhizhanovskii, *Khoziaistvennye problemy R.S.F.S.R.*, 94, 97.

50. Aleksandrov, "Ekonomicheskoe raionirovanie Rossii," 38, 40–41.

51. Ibid., 33.

52. Ibid., 38.

53. S. K., "Ekonomicheskoe raionirovanie i problemy avtonomno-federativnogo stroitel'stva," 1.

54. Trainin, "Ekonomicheskoe raionirovanie i natsional'naia politika," 1.

55. Ibid.

56. Ibid.

57. Walter Russell Batsell, *Soviet Rule in Russia* (New York, 1929), 117.

58. This point is made in Allan Laine Kagedan, "The Formation of Soviet Jewish Territorial Units, 1924–1937," Ph.D. dissertation, Columbia University, 1985.

59. Aleksandrov, "Ekonomicheskoe raionirovanie Rossii," 35–36.

60. I. Borozdin, "Odna iz ocherednykh zadach Narkomnatsa," *Zhizn' natsional'nostei*, no. 28 (126) (December 3, 1921): 1.

61. The State Archive of the Russian Federation (GARF) f. 1318, op. 1, d. 17 (1), ll. 61–62.

62. Ibid. The memo was signed by the head of the Narkomnats Department of National Minorities Plich and the Moscow-based ethnographer Daniil Ianovich.

63. PFA RAN f. 135, op. 1, d. 1, ll. 222–223. Iakovlev was based in Saratov.

64. Broido, "Nasha natsional'naia politika i ocherednye zadachi Narkomnatsa," 5–6.

65. G. Safarov, "K voprosu o prisoedinenii Syr-Dar'inskoi i Semirechenskoi oblastei k Kirrespublike," *Zhizn' natsional'nostei*, no. 10 (16) (May 19, 1922): 4. In 1920, Lenin had mandated the preparation of a new ethnographic map of Turkestan that specified the region's Uzbek, Kirgiz, and Turkmen parts. "Zamechaniia na proekte Turkestanskoi komissii," *Leninskii sbornik* 34 (1942): 323–326.

66. GARF f. 1318, op. 1, d. 20 (4), ll. 218–225. Also PFA RAN f. 135, op. 1, d. 3, l. 43; f. 2, op. 1–1917, d. 30, l. 188.

67. GARF f. 6892, op. 1, d. 1, ll. 1–30. VTsIK also invited representatives from "national republics and autonomous oblasts" who happened to be in Moscow to participate in commission sessions. The commission held meetings between November 1921 and February 1922. Alampiev, *Ekonomicheskoe raionirovanie SSSR*, 106–107, 110.

68. Ibid., 128–129. It was called the Caucasus Oblast.

69. Ibid., 112, 128–129.

70. Ibid., 113.

71. Egorov, *Raionirovanie SSSR: Sbornik,* 47–50.

72. Ibid.

73. On the February meeting (of the All-Russian Conference of Local Regionalization Workers) see Alampiev, *Ekonomicheskoe raionirovanie SSSR,* 130–131. On the April
Narkomnats meeting see GARF f. 1318, op. 1, d. 9, ll. 4–7. On both meetings see Mieczkowski, "Economic Regionalization of the Soviet Union," 109–110.

74. "Iz deiatel'nosti Narkomnatsa," *Zhizn' natsional'nostei,* no. 10 (16) (May 19,
1922): 12.

75. Carr, *Bolshevik Revolution,* vol. 1, 396–397.

76. For examples of the "divide and rule" argument see Robert Conquest, *The Last
Empire* (London, 1962); Helène Carrère d'Encausse, *The End of the Soviet Empire: The
Triumph of the Nations* (New York, 1993); Olaf Caroe, *Soviet Empire: The Turks of Cen-
tral Asia and Stalinism* (London, 1953); and (more recently) Ahmed Rashid, *Jihad: The
Rise of Militant Islam in Central Asia* (New Haven, Conn., 2002).

77. Alampiev, *Ekonomicheskoe raionirovanie SSSR,* 137.

78. *Dvenadtsatyi s"ezd Rossiiskoi kommunisticheskoi partii (bol'shevikov),* Stenograficheskii otchet, 17–25 aprelia 1923 (Moscow, 1975), 429–431, 574, 651. Also Egorov,
Raionirovanie SSSR: Sbornik, 56–59, and Carr, *Socialism in One Country,* vol. 2, 279.

79. See for example the case of Mirsaid Sultan-Galiev. *Chetvertoe soveshchanie TsK
RKP s otvetstvennymi rabotnikami natsional'nykh respublik i oblastei v Moskve 9–12
iiunia 1923 g. (Stenograficheskii otchet)* (Moscow, 1923).

80. *Dvenadtsatyi s"ezd Rossiiskoi kommunisticheskoi partii,* 642–644.

81. This is from a 1925 speech by Mikoian, printed in Umar Aliev, *Natsional'nyi
vopros i natsional'naia kul'tura v Severo-Kavkazskom krae (Itogi i perspektivy): K pred-
stoiashchemu s"ezdu gorskikh narodov* (Rostov-on-Don, 1926). On the party's "emancipatory" nationality policy see *Dvenadtsatyi s"ezd Rossiiskoi kommunisticheskoi partii,*
644. Also see Yuri Slezkine, "The USSR as a Communal Apartment, or How a Socialist State Promoted Ethnic Particularism," *Slavic Review* 53, no. 2 (Summer 1994):
414–452.

82. This new Regionalization Commission was established under the auspices of
the new Central Executive Committee (TsIK) of the Soviet government. GARF f. 6892,
op. 1, d. 1, ll. 1–3, 12, 15–17.

83. Alampiev, *Ekonomicheskoe raionirovanie SSSR,* 128, 141–142. Most of the Bashkir ASSR was excluded, but a small part without a Bashkir majority was included on
ethnographic and economic grounds.

84. GARF f. 6892, op. 1, d. 1, ll. 15–16.

Part Two   *People*

6 Changing Conceptions of Difference, Assimilation, and Faith in the Volga-Kama Region, 1740–1870

Paul Werth

With its broad range of peoples, languages, and religions, the Russian empire was, by any standard, a diverse polity. Yet the ways in which that diversity was conceptualized and interpreted were far from consistent over the course of Russia's history. The purpose of this chapter is to trace a series of important shifts in the ways that state authorities, missionaries, and publicists conceptualized and confronted ethnic and confessional diversity in imperial Russia, from the mass conversion of non-Russians (primarily in the 1740s) through the era of the Great Reforms. Particularly in the mid-nineteenth century—from the beginning of the reign of Nicholas I in 1825 through the reform period under Alexander II in the 1860s—ways of distinguishing non-Russians from Russians and interpreting these differences underwent considerable change. Even as confessional status remained central both to the administration of the empire and to the taxonomies by which imperial authorities classified the empire's diverse population, officials and, increasingly, publicists began also to employ a newer taxonomy rooted in language and ultimately in ethnic origins.[1] This shift can be traced in changing terminological usage, more specifically in the expansion of the term *inorodtsy* (aliens; literally "those of other origin") from its initial referents in Siberia to many non-Russians in European Russia, who had to that point been classified principally in religious terms. Related to this shift were more frequent references to *obrusenie* (Russification), which implied a process of cultural assimilation more extensive and thorough than Christianization. Accordingly, missionaries offered novel arguments about the ways in which non-Russians' internalization of Christian values would facilitate the process of Russification and instill in them a sense of civic-mindedness (*grazhdanstvennost'*) crucial to their meaningful participation in the reformed order. "Faith," in this scenario, became less a matter of religious obligations, legal ascription, and authority than one of belief and religious conviction.

My emphasis in this chapter is on the interrelationships among these new modes of conceptualizing difference, assimilation, and faith, which I contend were part of a larger transformation in Russia culminating in the Great Reforms of the 1860s. Serf emancipation, judicial reform, the introduction of new forms of local self-government, and the elimination of many particularistic social categories placed the empire's subjects on a more equal footing in relation to the state. For these and other reasons to be considered below, the regime began to identify more closely with the Russian nationality in particular. Indeed, even as officials in substantial measure remained committed to the ideal of a non-national composite state, the regime also began to aspire to the creation of a more unified and efficient polity, which inevitably came to acquire national overtones. Officials were in effect forced to confront the question: What kind of political entity *was* the Russian empire? As I shall argue, the turn toward a national model—however partial and hesitant—required the definition of "alien" elements and contributed to the elaboration of more modern colonial ideologies. Yet these shifts were only partial, and these new layers of signification did not obliterate the old. In this sense, Russia from this point became a strange hybrid that simultaneously drew on several models of state organization: a traditional, dynastic, composite state; an emerging (incomplete) national state; and a modern colonial empire.

In addressing these larger issues, I focus particular attention on the region around the confluence of the Volga and Kama rivers—east of Moscow but west of Siberia—where the problem of ethnic, confessional, and even estate diversity was especially acute. This region stood at the intersection of three cultural worlds—the Slavic-Orthodox, the Turkic-Islamic, and the Finnic-animist—and its character casts into particularly sharp relief the tensions between imperial and national identity in Russian history. On the one hand, the non-Russians of the region were among the many peoples who had been incorporated into a state that was construed explicitly as an empire, and whose leaders therefore accepted the fact of ethnic and confessional diversity as a source of their legitimation.[2] On the other hand, the Volga-Kama peoples differed from colonial subjects in more distant regions, such as Transcaucasia, Siberia, Central Asia, or the Far East.

They were among the first to have been incorporated into Muscovy, and they inhabited a region that was no longer a borderland in the strict sense of the term. Conquered in 1552, integrated into the empire's administrative and socio-legal structures in the eighteenth century,[3] and having a substantial Russian population, the Volga-Kama region by the nineteenth century could not be construed as being alien to the same extent as the empire's outlying regions.[4] Instead it represented a transitional zone where the core lands of Muscovy shaded into the more distant and alien lands of the imperial periphery.[5]

From "New Converts" to "Aliens"

In the early-modern period non-Russians were most often referred to as specific tribes or were labeled by their religious confession or social status: for example, *tatarove, cheremisy, mordva, magometane, idolopoklonniki, teptiari,* etc.[6] Before the eighteenth century these designations were in effect simultaneously linguistic, confessional, and social. For example, *cheremisy* (Maris) were presumed to be "idolaters," were understood to speak their own language, and had a specific legal status in relation to the state. As Gregory L. Freeze has written, the social structure of pre-Petrine Russia "consisted of numerous, small groups and lacked collective terms for legal aggregation." The existence of nearly five hundred separate social categories underscores "the peculiar, fragmented structure of medieval Russian society."[7] At this time the term *inovertsy* (those of other faith) probably came closest to serving as a general term for non-Russian peoples, especially before the mass baptisms of the mid-eighteenth century.[8]

The introduction of the soul tax and transfer of tribute-payers (*iasachnye liudi*) to state-peasant status beginning in 1719 served to drain tribal designations of their socio-legal content, for now many non-Russians had the same privileges and obligations as Russian state peasants.[9] Furthermore, mass conversion of non-Russians to Orthodoxy from circa 1740 created a large pool of so-called "new converts" (*novokreshchenye*), which rendered *inovertsy* inadequate as a term for designating non-Russians collectively.[10] The result was a tripartite taxonomy of mutually exclusive categories: Orthodox Christians (Russians), *novokreshchenye,* and *inovertsy.* Implicit in this distinction between *novokreshchenye* and full-fledged Orthodox Christians was a recognition of the former's liminal position, even after several generations, at the edge of the Orthodox community. Latent doubts about the transformative power of baptism persisted, so that the *origins* of a convert, especially if he was one of a group of neophytes that had been inducted into Orthodoxy wholesale, remained an important part of his ascriptive identity and even that of his descendants. *Novokresh-chenye* remained in limbo, so to speak, between their old co-religionists and their new ones.[11]

Moreover, this term seems to have served simultaneously as both a religious distinction and a social one, for it was used in opposition both to "Orthodox Christian" and to "peasant" (*krest'ianin*), which in Russian explicitly signified a baptized person. Andreas Kappeler contends that non-Russians had begun to be referred to as "peasants" (*krest'iane*) by the second half of the eighteenth century or so,[12] but even in the 1820s at least one priest felt compelled to request that baptized Maris "no longer be called *novokreshchenye,* but peasants."[13] Moreover, because new-convert status could in certain contexts confer privileges, non-Russians themselves were sometimes eager to uphold the distinction. Baptized Udmurts in one instance insisted on calling themselves *novokreshchenye* "in order not to be deprived of the right they have received to brew *kumyshka* [an indigenous alcoholic drink] for domestic use."[14] In short, the term *novokreshchenye* operated as a kind of hybrid social and religious category that allowed both the state and indigenous communities to signify that the latter were formally Christian, yet still distinct from full-fledged Orthodox Christians.

The terminology of difference was to change in the second quarter of the nineteenth century, after the term *inorodtsy* made its debut in official usage in a new statute on the administration of native Siberians.[15] This designation encompassed *all* non-Russian Siberians, regardless of their religious affiliation, and thus implied that natives, while previously redeemable through baptism, had now become "congenital and apparently perennial outsiders."[16] The appearance of this term was rooted partly in purely administrative concerns, but should also be understood in terms of new Romantic conceptions of nationhood (*narodnost'*) that were making their way into Russia in the early nineteenth century.[17] At the foundation of the concept *narodnost'* was the idea that *each* people had its own national character and spirit, revealed in its language, songs, ballads, and religious beliefs.[18] The creation of an administrative category of *inorodtsy* in the Siberian Statute accordingly reflected a recognition that native Siberians were fundamentally distinct and that it was unrealistic to expect them to develop along Russian lines in the immediate future. Although the authors of the statute envisioned a kind of gradual and voluntary development in the direction of Russian social and cultural forms ("organic Russification," in Marc Raeff's phrase), at the base of the statute was the conviction that laws should reflect the spiritual character of the people, as well as local history, ethnography, and climatology.[19] One of the more remarkable features of the statute is that it provided no timetable for assimilation and offered no real route by which they might cease being *inorodtsy* and become something else.[20] In other words, difference here was construed as organic, and the adoption of the term *inorodtsy* was in part a product of this Romantic view of nations.

Only gradually did the term *inorodtsy* come to be applied to the non-Russians of the Volga-Kama region. If there are a few isolated cases of the term's use before the 1820s, its usage becomes more frequent only by the late 1840s.[21] Even then the term had clearly not yet been universally accepted, and its specific referents remained ambiguous. At times officials retained more cumbersome phrases, such as "state peasants of Mohammedan faith or pagans."[22] To a substantial degree, the term was initially used merely as a synonym for *inovertsy* and thus still contained a confessional component.[23] Over the course of the 1850s, however, the term *inorodtsy* was used more frequently as a shorthand for non-Russians regardless of the faith they practiced. The term gained notably wider currency in ethnographic accounts in the 1850s, and soon *inorodtsy* were being mapped, counted, and given history—all explicitly as *inorodtsy*.[24] The term gained a pervasive currency in the 1860s, in connection with educational reforms in the Volga-Kama region,[25] and by this time it clearly referred to non-Russians of any religious affiliation.[26] Even where the term *inovertsy* would surely have been more concise, authors now sometimes spoke of "unbaptized *inorodtsy*" (*nekreshchenye inorodtsy*).[27]

Meanwhile, those who were previously *novokreshchenye* now became simply "peasants" or "baptized [*kreshchenye*] *inorodtsy*," depending on the context. Indeed, the term *novokreshchenye* for the most part disappeared in the reform era as a social category, along with the many terms designating particularistic estates that had punctuated the region's social map and had now been largely collapsed into a single "peasant" category: *lashmany*, various peasant categories (state, crown, and manorial), and to a degree Bashkirs and Teptiars.[28] Indeed, it was perhaps the broad standardization of social identity associated with the Great Reforms—the elimination of a large number of particularistic social categories in favor of a simpler social taxonomy—that facilitated or even necessitated the ascendancy of newer epistemologies of difference.

Changing Conceptions of Difference, Assimilation, and Faith   173

If not entirely neutral, the term *inorodtsy* initially lacked the deeply pejorative connotation characteristic of terms used in the West to designate the Other, such as "savage" and "barbarian." Rather, as Nathaniel Knight argues, *inorodtsy* at this point "denoted an all-encompassing 'other' free from any gradations of hierarchy." In using the term *inorodtsy*, "Russians placed the emphasis on [non-Russians'] generic 'otherness' rather than their specific cultural identity and varying levels of development."[29] Petr Keppen, in his efforts to map and count non-Russians, applied the term not only to the Finnic and Turkic tribes of the eastern portion of the Empire, but also to Estonians, Finns, Germans, Swedes, and Jews.[30] And in fact the term could be used in entirely relative ways to include even Russians themselves. In 1854 the bishop of Simbirsk wrote that Chuvash in his diocese "shun interaction with *inorodtsy*," by which he seems simply to have meant that they avoided contact with anyone who was not Chuvash.[31] Notably, non-Russian authors (or at least authors of non-Russian origins), such as Spiridon Mikhailov (a Chuvash), Sergei Nurminskii (a Mari), and Petr Keppen (a German), themselves used the term without visible reservation and were in fact among the earliest to do so.[32] While Russians were reasonably convinced of their own cultural superiority—at least with respect to the peoples of the empire's east—the term *inorodtsy* itself did not baldly signify such hierarchy, as its extension to decidedly European peoples suggests. It was only later, in the early twentieth century, that the term became decidedly derogatory and polemical.[33]

What, then, is the significance of the fact that *novokreshchenye* became (or were becoming) baptized *inorodtsy*? In one sense, the significance seems actually to be quite limited. Both classifications discursively situated non-Russian Christians at the margins of the Russian Orthodox world, and both signified simultaneously inclusion and exclusion: formal incorporation through baptism, yet recognition of the partial and provisional nature of that incorporation through reference either to the novelty of the conversion or to ethnic origins. But at the same time the shift from *novokreshchenye* to *inorodtsy* was more than just semantic, for it implied that the process of assimilation and incorporation was now to occur along different lines and was to extend beyond the realm of religious confession alone. If previously the state's goal was that non-Russians become better Christians, then the goal now became "Russification" in a much more extensive and explicit sense. Undoubtedly, Orthodoxy remained linked to this goal, but its exact relationship to broader processes of cultural change became somewhat less certain. Nor was it clear that Christianization would produce with the requisite speed the transformations that many officials now desired. In short, just as the Great Reforms raised a series of questions about the relationship of state to society, the nature of the Russian peasantry, the place of law in society, and so on, they also raised crucial questions about how non-Russians, both in the Volga-Kama region and more generally, actually fit (or should fit) into the larger society.

National Minorities or Colonial Subjects?

As with the term *inorodtsy,* references to *obrusenie* (Russification) began to appear with much greater frequency in bureaucratic correspondence by the 1860s. Catherine II had used the intransitive verb *obruset'* as early as 1764, to mean centralizing and unifying the Empire's administrative and legal structure, and Nicholas I used the noun *obrusevanie* with regard to Congress Poland with much the same meaning in mind in 1835.[34] But however much officials in this earlier period sought to promote a deeper acquaintance among non-Russians with Russian language and outlooks, this enterprise was still not one that proceeded under the banners of *obrusenie* and "fusion" (*sliianie*), as it would by the 1860s. To be sure, Minister of Education Sergei Uvarov could speak in the 1830s of the need "to smooth over those sharp characteristic traits that differentiate Polish from Russian youth and . . . to bring them closer to Russian concepts and morals, to transfer to them the general spirit of the Russian people." And he could also refer to the desirable "rapprochement" (*sblizhenie*) of Jews with the Christian population.[35] But one would search in vain to find in the Nikolaevan age the ambitious aim that the curator of the Kazan educational district articulated for educational reform in 1869: "The final goal of the education of all *inorodtsy* living within the boundaries of our fatherland should unquestionably be [their] Russification and fusion with the Russian people."[36] Although the actual meaning of the term "fusion" remained unspecified, clearly the implied level of assimilation was much greater in the 1860s than it had been previously. Officials now began to point to the supposed "alienation" (*otchuzhdennost'*) of non-Russians from things Russian as being a matter of utmost significance. As Minister of Education Dmitrii Tolstoi wrote in 1867, undoubtedly with some exaggeration, *inorodtsy* remained "in the same ignorant condition as they were a few centuries ago." Accordingly, "the gradual enlightenment of *inorodtsy* and their rapprochement with the Russian people constitutes a task of the very greatest political significance in the future."[37]

Why had this matter now become so urgent? Broadly speaking, Russia's defeat in the Crimean War made clear to leading officials and many in Russian society that the country had to modernize more quickly and aggressively in order to remain competitive in the international arena. And because the nation-state was showing itself to be the most effective model for the organization and mobilization of a society's resources—a principle confirmed at this very time by the national unification of Italy, Rumania, and Russia's most important neighbor, Germany—it is not surprising that some officials began to look to the model of a unified national state. These tendencies had by no means been entirely absent under Nicholas I. His government had undertaken a number of measures designed further to centralize and to integrate his realms: the incorporation of the Uniate church into the Orthodox, the replacement of Lithuanian and Polish laws by the Russian imperial law code, the transfer of Ukrainian Cossacks to state-peasant status, and the abolition of the Jewish kahal (the executive agency of Jewish communities).[38] But these tendencies had always remained deeply qualified by Nicholas' continuing commitment to a non-national imperial model and to the principle that any reform be decidedly measured and limited. Nor, for the most part, did these policies have a significant ethnic or linguistic dimension, as they were principally administrative and institutional in nature. The Great Reforms represented a much more extensive overhaul of state institutions and existing social structure, which could not fail to have significant implications for non-Russians. As the legal historian A.D. Gradovskii wrote in retrospect, "It is not difficult to see that as soon as Russia took the first steps on the path toward the equalization of social status [*k uravneniiu soslovii*] and toward the development of personal and public liberty, the idea of nationality as the foundation and standard of policy made significant progress."[39]

Sviatoslav Kaspe has stated the problem succinctly: "Even so moderate a democratization as the Great Reforms inevitably rendered more urgent the question of the nature—national or imperial—of the Russian state system then under renovation."[40] And the state's partial dismantling of the system of social hierarchy that lay at the foundation of the old imperial orientation suggested that the regime, willy-nilly, would take a substantial step in the direction of the national model. In effect, Russia's further modernization and indeed liberalization implied the adoption of a model of a national state—a more thoroughly integrated, if still not ethnically homogeneous, entity.[41] It needs to be stressed that this did not necessarily mean the adoption of brutal and heavy-handed policies of cultural

Russification. But to the extent that Russians were now being identified as the "core population" (*korennoe naselenie*) and even the "ruling popula-tion" (*gospodstvuiushchee russkoe naselenie*), the new orientation *did* rep-resent a potential threat to non-Russians, who were in danger of being re-duced to the status of ethnic and confessional minorities.[42]

The Polish insurrection of 1863 was another seminal factor in the state's reorientation along these lines and can indeed be regarded as a major turn-ing point in the empire's history. Construed by officialdom as a traitorous "mutiny," the insurrection contributed to a climate of counter-reform al-ready developing in the mid-1860s and cast into doubt the loyalty of other ethno-religious groups.[43] In response to the insurrection, the regime took a number of steps representing a significant deviation from traditional policies. In contrast to its long practice of ruling through local elites, the state focused its repression above all on the Polish nobility, who were un-derstood to be the leaders of the insurrection, and even sought to foster antagonism among the peasantry against their landlords in the process of implementing emancipation in Poland in 1864. The state also retreated from its policy of cooperation with recognized non-Orthodox clergy by attacking the Catholic Church in Poland.[44] Once again, although these measures were not entirely without precedent, they had a much greater national and cultural dimension than, for example, the state's repression of the 1830 Polish insurrection, which was sooner administrative and insti-tutional in character. Officials began also to act on the long-held proposi-tion that the western provinces—the area adjacent to the former Kingdom of Poland and inhabited primarily by Lithuanians, Belorussians, Ukrain-ians, and Jews—had been Russian and/or Orthodox from the oldest times. It was of course the government's self-appointed task to make this "fact" clear to the local population through the energetic promotion of Russian language and culture at the expense of alternatives.[45] It should be stressed that similar policies did not extend to other portions of the empire, or did so only considerably later, and we should therefore be careful not to exag-gerate the scale of the shift.[46] But it seems beyond dispute that a crucial reorientation had taken place in the ways that many officials and segments of Russian society regarded the character of their state.

By the 1860s there was also another important implication of the shift just described: namely, the emergence of a more coherent and explicit ideology of imperialism, especially in relation to Russia's eastern territo-ries. Mark Bassin has identified a strong sense of imperial mission that emerged in the 1840s with regard to the Amur region—a vision that Russians were uniquely qualified, given their location between East and West, to bring European civilization and enlightenment to the peoples of Asia. Austin Jersild likewise sees a "rethinking of empire" in the 1840s and 1850s, whereby society in both metropole and the Caucasus, drawing on categories of enlightenment, progress, and "Europe," contemplated the nature of Russia's multi-ethnic community and the role of Russia in the east. Thomas Barrett contends that the capture of the rebel Shamil in the North Caucasus in 1859, after almost thirty years of imperial warfare against native mountain people, represented a clear confirmation of Russia's Westernness and its role in the forward march of civilization. And finally, Russia's conquest of Central Asia in the 1860s seemed to offer a clear example of the victory of civilization and prosperity over barbarity and fanaticism, and thus reinforced Russia's European status still more.[47] The fact that Russia now found itself faced with "fanatical" Muslims (and could therefore assign itself the task of subordinating them to reason and civilization) established it as a functional equivalent of other colonial European powers, which of course had their own Muslim "fanatics" to deal with.[48] In short, Russia was now participating in the larger European project of modern colonialism. Thus, in the context of educational reform in the 1860s, one publicist could write,

> If in general it is characteristic for a state, in which one people, by its numbers and its historical significance, decisively prevails over all alien elements, to aspire to their complete merging with the element that constitutes its main strength, then such an aspiration for Russia with respect to the *inorodtsy* of her eastern outskirts is an obligation that is doubly holy: assimilating these *inorodtsy* to its predominant nationality, the Russian state would simultaneously fulfill its calling of a Christian and European-educated power and would render a true service both to the Christian church, and to the matter of general civilization.[49]

Similarly, the historian S. Eshevskii, identifying Russia's "predominant Russo-Slavic element" as "European," could therefore conclude in 1857 that "each step forward of Russian *narodnost'* at the expense of other tribes is a victory for Europe."[50] That Russians now viewed their imperial project as essentially a colonial one is underscored by the fact that educators studied British and French school policies in India and Algeria before drawing up the 1870 statute on education of non-Russians.[51]

This new colonial orientation can be seen in the very ways that missionary work was now being organized. The state had of course long under-stood itself to be a promoter of civilization in its realms, and at times quite actively promoted the conversion of non-Christians to Orthodoxy. But now missionary work was being undertaken, at least ostensibly, in the name of the Russian people and even with their participation. Though subordinate to the Holy Synod, the Orthodox Missionary Society in Mos-cow was established as a non-state institution that would draw, in the spirit of the times, on the participation of Russian society. In promoting mis-sionary activity in the empire—above all in Siberia—the Society's partici-pants indicated that it was the task of the Orthodox Russian people, per-haps even more than of the state, to spread their faith among the empire's benighted non-Christians. Though subordinate to the Holy Synod, the Orthodox Missionary Society in Moscow was established as a non-state institution that would draw, in the spirit of the times, on the participa-tion of Russian society in seeking to acquaint Russians with missionary activity in the empire—above all in Siberia—and to enlist their support for this enterprise. In short, the Society's participants indicated that it was the task of the Orthodox Russian people, perhaps even more than of the state, to spread their faith among the empire's benighted non-Christians.[52] Thus Count A. V. Bobrinskii, a member of the Society's board, complained in 1875 that in a number of dioceses local committees had not been estab-lished, despite the presence of "a native Orthodox Russian population that is capable of regarding the missionary cause with just as much love" as had Russians in other dioceses.[53] The Bishop of Perm, speaking at the opening of the Society's Perm Diocesan Committee in 1872, also saw missionizing as a task for the Russian people:

> I submit that Russian Orthodox Christians do not need to look to the
> example of other Christian states of Europe, from which proselytes go
> in great numbers to the American deserts and across the burning sands
> of Africa and to the maritime states of Asia, China, and Japan in order
> to proclaim the Gospel to the wild Americans, the Negroes, or those
> who revere Brahma and Mohammed . . . The Russian heart does not
> sympathize with the spread of the faith of Christ any less.[54]

He thus called on church servitors and laymen, people of all ranks and calling, men and women, to contribute in any way they could. Particularly given the Siberian and Asian focus of the Society's work, these perspectives reflected a new colonial consciousness, according to which the Russian Orthodox population represented the empire's "core," while everybody else, to one degree or another, represented the periphery.[55]

Viewed in this context, the term *inorodtsy* gains broader significance. It now represented a conceptual tool for a changing state and society to define who, in fact, constituted the "core population" of the empire, and who, in effect, made up the residual. John Slocum has described the broadening of the term's application, from its use in Siberia to the inhabitants of Central Asia, to Jews, to the peoples of the Volga region, and eventually—principally for polemical purposes—to virtually all the empire's non-Russian groups.[56] But if the term eventually was to signify "insurmountable" difference, as Slocum argues, I would contend that this was not yet the case in the period of the Great Reforms. At this stage, it seems to me, the concern was not merely to ascertain who was Russian and who was not, but also to determine which groups could realistically be expected to participate in a process of national construction, and which would be excluded from direct participation in this project.[57] By the 1860s the term *inorodtsy* was being used to signify *both* "national minorities" (those who were understood to be different from Russians but amenable to assimilation) and "colonial subjects" (who were so different and/or uncivilized that they should be administered in a particularistic fashion). Thus state officials could energetically promote *obrusenie* among some *inorodtsy,* such as the smaller Finnic groups, while refusing to incorporate others even into the state's system of social classification (let alone set out to assimilate them culturally), as was the case for the native populations of Central Asia. Similarly, the state could extend to some provinces with substantial non-Russian populations the major institutions of the Great Reforms—for example, zemstvos and the judicial reform—while postponing or indeed rejecting their introduction to other non-Russian provinces, especially those further from the center.[58]

The Volga-Kama region was one of the places where the task of distinguishing core from periphery proved especially difficult. If we attempt to classify the peoples here as either national minorities or colonial subjects, along the lines described above, it is difficult to avoid the conclusion that they were both at once. Missionaries and some state officials increasingly came to regard Muslims in the region as being alien, unassimilable, and ultimately hostile to Christianity and the Russian state. Simultaneously, most officials maintained hope that the Finnic peoples and Chuvash could be assimilated, as long as the state adopted the appropriate policies. Indeed,

Islam—understood by officials not merely as a religious confession, but as a larger cultural complex of dispositions and attitudes that rendered its adherents "fanatical" and hostile to reason and civilization—seems to have been a crucial factor in drawing such distinctions.[59]

Thus, even as state officials continued to espouse older conceptions of dynastic loyalty and to emphasize social distinctions that in principle encompassed the entire population, alternative orientations were now beginning to appear, as a result of both the state's own promotion of change in the context of the Great Reforms and the challenges presented by non-Russians (most importantly, in Poland and the western provinces). The appearance of a modern ideology of colonialism represented a corollary to the new aspirations of creating a national state, since not all of the empire's far-flung and diverse territories could realistically be included in a project of national construction. Accordingly, while all of those distinct from "the core population of the empire" (Russians) would gradually be labeled *inorodtsy*, only some of those *inorodtsy* would actually be considered objects for assimilation.

Confession, Assimilation, and Belief

The spread of the concepts *inorodtsy* and *obrusenie* clearly implied important shifts in the significance of religious confession in Russia as well. In Muscovite times and well into the imperial period—notwithstanding the mass conversions of the mid–eighteenth century—Orthodoxy and Russianness were intimately, if not organically, linked in the minds of most people. Indeed, as Theodore Weeks has contended, this connection remained salient and in some sense insurmountable until the very end of the old regime.[60] Even so, clearly discernible from about mid-century is a certain decoupling of ethnicity and faith. Already by the early nineteenth century the empire had expanded to include non-Slavic peoples with long historical attachments to Orthodoxy, most notably Georgians and the Rumanian-speaking population of Bessarabia.[61] By mid-century still other possibilities for the development of non-Russian Orthodoxies were appearing, thus further disrupting the neat equation of Orthodoxy and Russianness. In the midst of the conversion of more than 100,000 peasants in Lifland province from Lutheranism to Orthodoxy in the 1840s, the church began to perform services in Estonian and Latvian, translated and printed an Orthodox catechism and prayer book, and ordained local residents as deacons and priests. Thus, as A. V. Gavrilin has written, in the late 1840s one begins to see "the development of Latvian and Estonian variants of Orthodox culture."[62]

Almost simultaneously (in 1847), as a means of combating persistent "apostasy" in the Volga-Kama region, Nicholas I ordered the translation of Orthodox religious books into Tatar, with the goal of eventually performing church services in that language. While this effort enjoyed little immediate success, it contributed by the 1860s to a missionary reform in which non-Russians and their languages would figure much more prominently. Organized and implemented by the lay missionary Nikolai Il'minskii, this reform promoted Orthodoxy using native vernaculars and enlisted native cadres as priests and teachers, thereby reinforcing the proposition that Orthodoxy was not an intrinsically Russian faith. By 1867, Il'minskii had obtained from the Synod a directive that authorized the training and ordination of *inorodtsy* clergy and exempted them from the normal seminary course. By 1869 the Orthodox service had been translated into Tatar using this new approach, and the Kazan diocesan authorities were encouraging the use of native languages in religious discussions and for the most oft-used prayers and songs. In 1883 the Synod authorized the conduct of services in non-Russian languages wherever there was "a more or less substantial population" of non-Russians.[63] To be sure, it was only in the early twentieth century (and especially after 1905) that ideas about non-Russian Orthodoxy received fuller articulation by devout *inorodtsy* who saw their spiritual development being sacrificed to the imperatives of Russification. But such ideas were beginning to find expression some decades earlier.[64] In short, it became increasingly possible to be piously, even zealously Orthodox *without* being (or becoming) Russian.

Moreover, just as Orthodoxy could begin to appear in non-Russian forms, at the possibility was now raised that "foreign" (non-Orthodox) confessions could appear in a Russian idiom. In the aftermath of the Polish insurrection, the state began to consider the idea of giving the Russian language a more prominent place in non-Orthodox church services and liturgies. In the 1860s state authorities initiated efforts not only to introduce the Russian language into Catholic churches of the northwest provinces, but also to translate the service of the small Reformed (Calvinist) Church into Russian. The principal goal of this effort was to prevent the further "Polonization" of Catholic "Russians" (primarily Belorussians) in the northwest provinces, and thus to "revitalize the Russian nationality in that region."[65] One publicist, noting that Protestantism had enjoyed a substantial presence in Lithuania during the Reformation, even went so far as to argue for "the resurrection of Protestantism in Lithuania on the basis of the Russian nationality."[66] By no means were officials entirely certain that combining the Russian language and "foreign" confessions in this way was either truly possible or a good idea. Aside from the danger that translation made "foreign" confessions accessible to Russians and thus might increase the incidence of "seduction" and "apostasy" from Orthodoxy, there was great uncertainty about whether it was actually *Polishness* or *Catholicism* that represented the danger to be combated (and indeed how the two were actually related to one another).[67] Nor was it clear whether official Russia really accepted that there could be such a thing as a Russian Catholic—i.e., that Catholicism did not render a person Polish almost by definition.[68] Still, the very fact that such proposals and questions could arise suggests that the comfortable equation of ethnicity and faith was now in some doubt.

How, then, did Orthodoxy view the promotion of Russification in such circumstances? On the one hand, it now became possible to contemplate Russification without Orthodoxy. In the case of the education of Muslim Tatars, for example, there was no possibility of attracting them to institutions in which Orthodoxy played a visible role. Instead, imperial administrators planned to make language the main vehicle for Russification, by introducing Russian language instruction into Tatar schools and eventually requiring mullah-teachers to have some knowledge of Russian.[69] On the other hand, many still saw Russification in primarily spiritual terms.[70] Frequently cited is Il'minskii's statement, "As soon as an *inorodets* has internalized Orthodoxy consciously and with conviction, with his mind and heart, he already has become Russified [*on uzhe obrusel*]."[71] Undoubtedly even those, like Il'minskii, who emphasized the importance of native languages and cadres also envisioned the *complete* cultural assimilation of *inorodtsy* at some point in the future. And many clerics, like Kazan Archbishop Antonii, were careful to emphasize that missionaries' efforts to translate religious texts into indigenous languages would not result in a complete non-Russian literature, thereby obviating the need for non-Russians to study Russian. Rather, missionaries would publish "only those books in *inorodtsy* languages that contain the most necessary elementary ideas, especially religious-moral ones." This would render them "capable of further education, which generally will then take place in *inorodtsy* schools in the Russian language."[72] In this formulation, spiritual enlightenment took a back seat to Russification.

Changing Conceptions of Difference, Assimilation, and Faith   183

Nonetheless, the reliance on native languages and cadres would undoubtedly uphold and even promote ethnic particularity—even if only temporarily. Il'minskii's statement on Russification may perhaps best be understood as a tactical stance designed to disarm critics who regarded Russification in more straightforward (linguistic) terms. In one sense, as Robert Geraci has remarked, "Il'minskii did want to create a 'Tatar church' [within Orthodoxy], not just new members of a Russian church." And both he and those who shared his outlook "seem not to have wanted the *inorodtsy* to give up their original identities."[73] The claim of Il'minskii and his supporters that their project served the larger goal of Russification was thus legitimately open to contestation.

Rather than justifying their efforts in terms of Russification alone, missionaries also adopted a more universal language and argued that Orthodoxy's principal benefit was its contribution to larger processes of civilizing in Russia's eastern provinces. Thus in 1866 Evfimii Malov wrote, "One or another religion, confessed by a given people or tribe, can, by its essence and character, present favorable or unfavorable conditions for the internalization by that tribe of education and civic-mindedness [*grazhdanstvennost'*]. The example of European peoples unquestionably accords to Christianity in this respect the best and highest significance."[74] In other words, non-Russians' internalization of Christian values would render them amenable to the sensibilities that secular authorities considered essential in the reform era. In a similar fashion, the Bishop of Perm in 1872 listed numerous benefits "for our Fatherland here on earth" that would appear once non-Christian peoples both "among us" and on the empire's periphery "become sons of the Orthodox church":

> Then in place of the unbridled arbitrariness of wild passions, to which unenlightened people usually submit, there will appear law and legality; instead of rapaciousness and pillage, to which people alien to Christian civilization are inclined, respect for their fellow man's property will come into force, and the laws of both state and family will become inviolable; instead of interminable wars, as there are among the various tribes of barbarous peoples, there will emerge peace and tranquillity; instead of vagrant and aimless life will appear life attached to a permanent place, and there will appear order in family and public life. The cross and the Gospel bring with them all these worldly blessings.[75]

In such cases, missionaries and clerics were intent on emphasizing the contribution that they could make to the fulfillment of the secular government's larger goals.

The more explicit association between Orthodox Christianity and ideas such as "civic-mindedness" was to have one other repercussion that we must note here: the appearance of new standards for measuring "faith." If non-Russians' internalization of Orthodoxy was to provide all the benefits that missionaries claimed, then of course that internalization had to be genuine and thorough-going. Accordingly, clerics by the 1860s began to focus much more of their attention on the actual *convictions* of baptized non-Russians, and somewhat less attention on external rituals of practice that had been the principal standard for judging their religiosity theretofore. In the eighteenth and early nineteenth centuries, Russian authorities had construed religion above all as "law" (*zakon*)—a set of rules and prescriptions governing behavior, worship, rites, hygiene, and appearance. What the putative believer actually believed was less important than whether he submitted to the religious authority of his clergy. Likewise, when new converts showed an inclination for "apostasy" and "deviation," the principal concern of both state and church was to ensure their submission to the authority of the church by compelling them to sign statements promising to abandon "Mohammedanism" and "delusions."[76] Central to this older conception was the performance of prescribed rituals, the assumption of the appropriate external appearance, the proper display of designated religious objects (such as crosses and icons)—in short, orthopraxy more than orthodoxy.[77] This is not to deny that ritual represented a way for believers to express and maintain their religious beliefs, nor to suggest that the church was entirely indifferent as to what its adherents actually believed. My point is rather to underscore the relative significance of external display vis-à-vis internal conviction in the church's and state's conception of what constituted religious affiliation.

As concerns conversions, in the eighteenth century, church and state had not refrained from using material incentives and even force to secure mass conversions. Potential converts had been offered tax breaks, exemptions from military service, even payment in cash and goods to draw them to the baptismal font. Converts could also be freed from prosecution for lesser crimes, or have their sentences lightened in more serious cases. By no means was the church entirely indifferent to the motivations for conversion, even in the eighteenth century. Aware of the cash nexus in many conversions, the Synod remarked in 1746 that the Christian faith "should be accepted not deceitfully and not by pretense, that is, not for the sake of money, and not for the sake of any other temporary profit, but with one's entire soul, exclusively for the love of God and for one's own eternal salvation."[78] Moreover, when non-Russian complaints began to appear in the wake of the mass conversions in the 1740s, the Synod required local religious authorities to collect "written voluntary petitions" from those desiring baptism and to confirm that the candidates had been adequately instructed in the essentials of Christianity.[79] Yet despite this apparent concern for the sincerity of conversion, material incentives were retained well into the nineteenth century. As late as 1853, the Bishop of Orenburg stated openly that "idolaters can be more conveniently stimulated to religious acceptance of the saving Christian faith by means of material encouragements."[80]

Only in the mid-nineteenth century did the state dismantle most of the provisions that were apt to promote disingenuous conversion. In 1837 the Ministry of Finance argued that direct payments to Muslim and pagan converts in cash and clothing, as established by an ukaz of 1740, should be terminated, primarily because it "is not in accord with its goal and the essence of the very matter."[81] Furthermore, a law of 1861 established clearer guidelines governing the baptism of non-Christians into Orthodoxy, whereby both clergy and local secular authorities were to ascertain "thoroughly" that the candidate was accepting baptism voluntarily "and with the necessary understanding"; "without this conviction in no case is the baptism to be performed or permitted."[82] In 1865, the Synod's chief procurator, D. A. Tolstoi, obtained the elimination of the provision that lightened the punishment of those who converted to Orthodoxy during investigation or trial, since "[p]ractice had shown that those making use of this provision were immoral people."[83] Thus by 1870 or so, the state had terminated most of the provisions that could generate aspiritual motivations for conversions. Accordingly, the last mass conversions—i.e., conversions involving several hundred or more converts at once under suspicious circumstances—occurred in the Volga-Kama region in the 1840s and 1850s, prior to the majority of these changes.[84]

Indeed, a more modern consciousness concerning the issue of conversion appeared among missionaries themselves. If the missionaries of 1830 gauged conversion by whether or not *novokreshchenye* signed statements promising to abandon indigenous traditions, then by 1850 Il'minskii dismissed precisely this standard with scorn: the earlier missionaries considered it to be a "very great success," he wrote with irony, "when they managed, in one way or another, to get a few signatures from the Tatars for the fulfillment of Christian rites, although these signatures *did not in the least vouch for the sincerity of conversion.*" Il'minskii doubted the effectiveness of itinerant missionaries, because "a person's religious convictions, naturally, cannot change quickly as a result of merely verbal admonitions."[85] Likewise, Evfimii Malov articulated a forceful criticism of earlier missionary methods—mechanical "admonitions," resettlement of "apostates," etc.—for being too "external" and "official," for attempting merely to demonstrate the illegality of apostasy, rather than "strengthen[ing] the internal bond between the baptized-Tatar apostates and the Christianity they had accepted." It was now time, Malov insinuated in these works, to focus on the convictions of baptized Tatars, on the nature of their "internal bond" with Christianity—in short, to abandon "forceful" and "external" measures in favor of "purely spiritual ones."[86] To be sure, missionaries were hardly indifferent to external manifestations of religious affiliation. But the very explicit contrast Malov drew between the "internal" and the "external" suggests the appearance of a more faith-based, even individualized, notion of confessional affiliation.

Broadly speaking, this shift can be attributed to two principal factors. On the one hand, apostasy vividly demonstrated the limits of the older standards. As long as baptized non-Russians feared the consequences of apostasy, the old standards were sufficient to keep the edges of the Orthodox community reasonably firm, even when spiritual commitments to Christianity remained weak. But once the situation became more fluid in the 1860s,[87] it became clearer that only an "internal" commitment to Orthodoxy would allow baptized non-Russians to resist the temptations of apostasy. On the other hand, aspirations in the reform period to create a more inclusive civil order, one that would draw on the initiative of the empire's population and entrust them with crucial responsibilities of administration and justice, required that subjects no longer merely submit passively to the dictates of secular and ecclesiastical authorities, but instead actively engage in the process of reform and improvement of the empire. This active engagement could of course not be created by simply gathering signatures or through force. As Malov wrote, "At the present time, in light of the newly arising civil changes in our fatherland and even partly of political calculations, forceful measures in the matter of faith and conscience are being abandoned."[88] Faith was no longer to be just a matter of constituting difference and securing subordination to authority, but was now more explicitly to help shape a virtuous populace for a transformed imperial Russian polity.

And yet, even as many recognized the significance of religious conviction, virtually no one in this period was prepared to allow non-Russians' own self-definitions to determine their religious status. The deferential petitions of baptized Tatars for recognition as Muslims were all categorically rejected. Change would come only in 1905 and even then would be significantly conditioned by provisions designed to defend the predominance of Orthodoxy and Christianity.[89] Most officials seem to have implicitly agreed with Malov's contention that formal Christian status was the indispensable precondition for Christian enlightenment and therefore was not negotiable.

It is crucial not to exaggerate the scale of the shifts I have described here. Many of these "new" outlooks and practices clearly had significant precedents, especially in the period of Nicholas I. Likewise, older conceptions—the dynastic and non-national character of the empire, the role of religion as a crucial sign of cultural identity, the state's refusal to accept its subjects' expressions of religious confession—all persisted, to one degree or another, until the end of the old regime. And as Richard Wortman has shown, the monarchy began to identify with the Russian people explicitly only in the reign of Alexander III (1881–1894).[90] But with all these caveats in place, we may nonetheless posit a series of important shifts in the way the state marked cultural difference, the ways in which both officials and members of educated society understood their polity, and the criteria that many people employed for measuring religiosity and confessional affiliation. It was now up to the state, the church, and the citizens of Russia to grapple with the consequences of this reorientation.

Notes

This chapter represents a modified version of chapter 5 of my book, *At the Margins of Orthodoxy: Mission, Governance, and Confessional Politics in Russia's Volga-Kama Region, 1827–1905* (Ithaca, N.Y., 2002).

1. Yuri Slezkine has documented how these novel modes of classification began to appear among scholars in the eighteenth century. See Yuri Slezkine, "Naturalists versus Nations: Eighteenth-Century Russian Scholars Confront Diversity," in *Russia's Orient: Imperial Borderlands and Peoples, 1700–1917*, ed. Daniel R. Brower and Edward J. Lazzerini (Bloomington, 1997), 27–57. The present chapter in effect documents how these modes gained a broader currency, albeit in new and different contexts.

2. On the issue of empire as legitimation, see Richard S. Wortman, *Scenarios of Power: Myth and Ceremony in Russian Monarchy, Volume One: From Peter the Great to the Death of Nicholas I* (Princeton, N.J., 1995), 6, 135–139.

3. This process was more drawn out in the eastern part of the region, as Charles Steinwedel finds in his contribution to the present volume.

4. Accordingly, this region generated far less Romantic fascination with the exotic or sense of imperial mission than has been documented for other regions. See, for example, Galya Diment and Yuri Slezkine, eds., *Between Heaven and Hell: The Myth of Siberia in Russian Culture* (New York, 1993); Susan Layton, *Russian Literature and Empire: Conquest of the Caucasus from Pushkin to Tolstoi* (Cambridge, 1994); Adeeb Khalid, *The Politics of Muslim Cultural Reform: Jadidism in Central Asia* (Berkeley, 1998); Mark Bassin, *Imperial Visions: Nationalist Imagination and Geographical Expansion in the Russian Far East* (Cambridge, 1999).

5. The problem of ascertaining where empire "begins" geographically was not restricted to Russia. Recent scholarship on European colonialism has revealed that distinctions between metropole and colony were far more problematic than they might appear on the surface. In Britain, moreover, there was the problem of "internal colonialism." See Ann Laura Stoler and Frederick Cooper, eds., *Tensions of Empire: Colonial Cultures in a Bourgeois World* (Berkeley, 1997); Michael Hechter, *Internal Colonialism: The Celtic Fringe in British National Development, 1536–1966* (London, 1975).

6. Michael Khodarkovsky, " 'Ignoble Savages and Unfaithful Subjects': Constructing Non-Christian Identities in Early Modern Russia," in *Russia's Orient* (Bloomington, 1997), 14; S. V. Sokolovskii, "Poniatie 'korennoi narod' v rossiiskoi nauke, politike i zakonodatel'stve," *Etnograficheskoe obozrenie* 3 (1998): 76.

7. Gregory L. Freeze, "The *Soslovie* (Estate) Paradigm and Russian Social History," *American Historical Review* 91 (1986): 15.

8. Andreas Kappeler, *Russlands erste Nationalitäten: Das Zarenreich und die Völker der Mittleren Wolga vom 16. bis 19. Jahrhundert* (Cologne, 1982), 356.

9. On the tax reform, see Kappeler, *Russlands erste Nationalitäten*, 245–291; and E. V. Anisimov, *Podatnaia reforma Petra I: Vvedenie podushnoi podati v Rossii, 1719–1728 gg.* (Leningrad, 1982), esp. pp. 179–189. Bashkirs and Teptiars were the exception in this regard, because they continued to signify distinct social groups.

10. There had been some missionary activity in the Volga-Kama region prior to 1740, but in that year a curious institution, the Office for the Affairs of New Converts, was created near Kazan and oversaw the baptism of more than 400,000 non-Russians over the next two decades. See E. A. Malov, *O Novokreshchenskoi kontore* (Kazan, 1878); A. Mozharovskii, *Izlozhenie khoda missionerskogo dela po prosveshcheniiu kazanskikh inorodtsev s 1552 po 1867 goda* (Moscow, 1880); Michael Khodarkovsky, " 'Not by Word Alone': Missionary Policies and Religious Conversion in Early Modern Russia," *Comparative Studies in Society and History* 38, 2 (1996): 267–293.

11. Khodarkovsky makes this point in " 'Ignoble Savages and Unfaithful Subjects,' " 18, 20–21. The notion that a convert's origins in one or another community trumps his or her own profession of religious conviction is a central theme in Gauri Viswanathan's exploration of conversion in colonial India, *Outside the Fold: Conversion, Modernity, and Belief* (Princeton, N.J., 1998), esp. pp. 75–117.

12. Kappeler, *Russlands erste Nationalitäten,* 357.

13. Gosudarstvennyi Arkhiv Kirovskoi Oblasti (GAKO), f. 237, op. 131, d. 1283, ll. 82ob–83.

14. "Istoriko-statisticheskaia zapiska o sele Sviatitskom v severo-zapadnoi chasti Glazovskago uezda," *Viatskiia gubernskiia vedomosti* 41 (1851), p. 345. Udmurts, as a tribe, had been granted a special right to brew this drink, and these *novokreshchenye* evidently believed that they would no longer be considered Udmurts if they were regarded as full-fledged Orthodox Christians.

15. *Polnoe Sobranie Zakonov Rossiiskoi Imperii* (PSZ), first collection, vol. 38, no. 29126 (1822). Khodarkovsky and Sokolovskii have both contended that this term appeared well before the nineteenth century, but neither offers any specific examples of its use before 1822 or indicates where precisely the term was applied. Robert Geraci at least provides concrete evidence for the term's existence before 1822; see Robert P. Geraci, *Window on the East: National and Imperial Identities in Late Tsarist Russia* (Ithaca, 2001), 31. My focus here, however, is on patterns of usage rather than the mere existence of the term. Restricting myself to the Volga-Kama region, I therefore concur with Kappeler and John Slocum, who argue that the term gained broad currency only in the 1850s. Kappeler, *Russlands erste Nationalitäten,* p. 481; and John W. Slocum in "Who, and When, Were the *Inorodtsy*? The Evolution of the Category of 'Aliens' in Imperial Russia," *Russian Review* 57, 2 (1998): 176. Notably, in his most recent publication, Khodarkovsky has stated that non-Christians "were systematically referred to" as *inorodtsy* "by the early nineteenth century," thus placing the term somewhat earlier than in his previous publications. Michael Khodarkovsky, *Russia's Steppe Frontier: The Making of a Colonial Empire, 1500–1800* (Bloomington, 2002), 188.

16. Yuri Slezkine, *Arctic Mirrors: Russia and the Small Peoples of the North* (Ithaca, N.Y., 1994), 53.

17. On the appearance of this term, see Nathaniel Knight, "Ethnicity, Nationality and the Masses: *Narodnost'* and Modernity in Imperial Russia," in *Russian Modernity: Politics, Knowledge, Practices,* ed. David L. Hoffmann and Yanni Kotsonis (New York, 2000), 41–64.

18. Nathaniel Knight, "Constructing the Science of Nationality: Ethnography in Mid–Nineteenth Century Russia" (Ph.D. diss., Columbia University, 1994), 84, 87–119.

19. Marc Raeff, *Siberia and the Reforms of 1822* (Seattle, 1956), 112–128.

20. Slezkine, *Arctic Mirrors,* 80–92.

21. For example, an 1841 ethnographic description of Kazan province, which offered ample opportunity to use the term *inorodtsy,* did not actually do so. "Etnograficheskoe opisanie Kazanskoi gubernii," *Zhurnal Ministerstva vnutrennikh del* 39 (1841): 350–410.

22. Rossiiskii Gosudarstvennyi Istoricheskii Arkhiv (RGIA), f. 383, op. 7, d. 6109b, ll. 22–23.

23. Notably, even the Siberian Statute itself seems to have used the terms *inovertsy* and *inorodtsy* indiscriminately at times.

24. S. M. Mikhailov, *Trudy po etnografii i istorii russkogo, chuvashskogo i mariiskogo narodov* (Cheboksary, 1972); V. A. Sboev, *Issledovaniia ob inorodtsakh Kazanskoi gubernii* (Kazan, 1856); V. M. Cheremshanskii, *Opisanie Orenburgskoi gubernii v khoziaistvenno-statisticheskom, etnograficheskom i promyshlennom otnosheniiakh* (Ufa, 1859);

Petr Keppen, *Ob etnograficheskoi karte Evropeiskoi Rossii* (St. Petersburg, 1852); *Etnograficheskii sbornik*, vyp. 4 (1858); M. Laptev, *Materialy dlia geografii i statistiki Rossii, sobrannye ofitserami General'nago shtaba: Kazanskaia Guberniia* (St. Petersburg, 1861); P. I. Keppen, *Khronologicheskii ukazatel' materialov dlia istorii inorodtsev Evropeiskoi Rossii* (St. Petersburg, 1861); Nikolai Firsov, *Inorodcheskoe naselenie prezhniago Kazanskago tsarstva v novoi Rossii do 1762 goda i kolonizatsiia zakamskikh zemel' v eto vremia* (Kazan, 1869).

25. Slocum, "Who, and When, Were the *Inorodtsy*?" 185.

26. See, for example, P. D. Shestakov, "Soobrazheniia o sisteme obrazovaniia inorodtsev, obitaiushchikh v guberniiakh Kazanskogo uchebnago okruga (3 dekiabria 1869)," RGIA, Pechatnye zapiski, folder 3103, which counted Latvians, Estonians, and (provisionally) Germans as *inorodtsy*.

27. E. V–N, "Soobrazheniia o sposobakh k uspeshneishemu privlecheniiu nekreshchenykh inorodtsev k vere khristovoi," *Pravoslavnyi sobesednik* 1 (1871): 50–72.

28. Bashkirs retained, after their transfer to civilian rule in 1863, the distinction of being recognized as the owners of land they used (*votchinniki*). For details on Bashkir status after 1863, see Charles Steinwedel's contribution to the present volume.

29. Knight, "Constructing the Science of Nationality," 340–341. Boris Mironov concurs that the term *inorodtsy* "did not convey anything belittling or insulting." Mironov, *Sostial'naia istoriia Rossii (XVIII–nachalo XX v.)*, vol. 1 (St. Petersburg, 1999), 32.

30. Keppen, *Ob etnograficheskoi karte*, esp. pp. 29–40; and idem, "Ob inorodcheskom, preimushchestvenno nemetskom naselenii S.-Peterburgskoi gubernii," *Zhurnal Ministerstva vnutrennikh del* 32 (1850): 181–209.

31. RGIA, f. 802, op. 6, d. 17303, l. 1.

32. See the works by Mikhailov and Keppen cited above, as well as S. Nurminskii, "Inorodcheskie prikhody," *Pravoslavnoe obozrenie* 12 (1863): 243–263; and "Inorodcheskie shkoly," ibid. (1864): 201–226.

33. Slocum, "Who, and When, Were the *Inorodtsy*?" 185–190.

34. Edward Thaden, ed., *Russification in the Baltic Provinces and Finland, 1855–1914* (Princeton, N.J., 1981), 7; S. Kh. Alishev, *Istoricheskie sud'by narodov srednego povolzh'ia, XVI–nachalo XIX v.* (Moscow, 1990), 246.

35. Quoted in Cynthia H. Whittaker, *The Origins of Modern Russian Education: An Intellectual Biography of Count Sergei Uvarov, 1786–1855* (DeKalb, Ill., 1984), 191, 193. On Uvarov and the Jews, see Michael Stanislawski, *Tsar Nicholas I and the Jews: The Transformation of Jewish Society in Russia, 1825–1855* (Philadelphia, 1983), 59–69.

36. Shestakov, "Soobrazheniia o sisteme obrazovaniia inorodtsev," 20.

37. *Sbornik postanovlenii Ministerstva narodnago prosveshcheniia*, vol. 4, no. 172 (1867), 415. For more on this problem of assimilation and non-Russian schooling, see Geraci, *Window on the East*; and Wayne Dowler, *Classroom and Empire: The Politics of Schooling Russia's Eastern Nationalities, 1860–1917* (Montreal, 2001).

38. See Andreas Kappeler, *Russland als Vielvölkerreich: Entstehung, Geschichte, Zerfall* (Munich, 1992), 204–207, as well as Thaden, *Russification*, 15–24; Stanislawski, *Tsar Nicholas I*, 123–127; Zenon E. Kohut, *Russian Centralism and Ukrainian Autonomy: Imperial Absorption of the Hetmanate, 1760s–1830s* (Cambridge, Mass., 1988).

39. Quoted in Sviatoslav Kaspe's article in the present volume.

40. Ibid.

41. As Geoffrey Hosking has written, "Probably the Russian government had no alternative but to pursue some kind of Russification policy in an era when economic growth required greater administrative unity and coordination, and when national solidarity was establishing itself as a paramount factor in international relations and in military strength." Geoffrey Hosking, *Russia: People and Empire, 1552–1917* (Cambridge, Mass., 1997), 397.

42. In the present volume, Leonid Gorizontov thoroughly analyzes the problem of defining "interior Russia" in the nineteenth century.

43. Theodore R. Weeks, *Nation and State in Late Imperial Russia: Nationalism and Russification on the Western Frontier, 1863–1914* (DeKalb, Ill., 1996), 94–96; W. Bruce Lincoln, *The Great Reforms: Autocracy, Bureaucracy, and the Politics of Change in Imperial Russia* (DeKalb, Ill., 1990), 168; and S. Frederick Starr, *Decentralization and Self-Government in Russia, 1830–1870* (Princeton, N.J., 1972), 256–260.

44. Kappeler, *Russland als Vielvölkerreich*, 208–209.

45. Ibid., 210–211. On Ukraine specifically, see A. I. Miller, *"Ukrainskii vopros" v politike vlastei i russkom obshchestvennom mnenii (vtoraia polovina XIX v.)* (St. Petersburg, 2000).

46. Kappeler, *Russland als Vielvölkerreich*, 211–215; Thaden, *Russification,*, 27–28; idem, *Russia's Western Borderlands, 1710–1870* (Princeton, N.J., 1984), 144–168, 236; John Doyle Klier, *Imperial Russia's Jewish Question, 1855–1881* (Cambridge, 1995), 145–158; Tuomo Polvinen, *Imperial Borderland: Bobrovnikov and the Attempted Russification of Finland, 1898–1904,* trans. Steven Huxley (London, 1995).

47. Bassin, *Imperial Visions,* esp. 37–68 and 182–205; Khalid, *The Politics of Muslim Cultural Reform,* 15–16, 50–53; Austin Jersild, *Orientalism and Empire: North Caucasus Mountain Peoples and the Georgian Frontier, 1845–1917* (Montreal, 2002), 8–11; and Thomas Barrett, "The Remaking of the Lion of Dagestan: Shamil in Captivity," *Russian Review* 53 (1994): 353–366.

48. Patricia M. E. Lorcin, *Imperial Identities: Stereotyping, Prejudice, and Race in Colonial Algeria* (London, 1995), 53–75; and David Edwards, "Mad Mullahs and Englishmen: Discourse in the Colonial Encounter," *Comparative Studies in Society and History* 31 (1989): 649–670. For more on changing attitudes toward Islam, see Werth, *At the Margins of Orthodoxy,* chapter 7; Elena Campbell's contribution to the present volume: and Robert D. Crews, "Allies in God's Command: Muslims Communities and the State in Imperial Russia" (Ph.D. diss., Princeton University, 1999), chapter 6.

49. "K voprosu ob ustroistve," 79.

50. S. V. Eshevskii, "Missionerstvo v Rossii," in *Sochineniia S. V. Eshevskago,* vol. 3 (Moscow, 1870), 670.

51. *Sbornik postanovlenii Ministerstva narodnago prosveshcheniia,* vol. 5, no. 167 (1872), 760.

52. See "Pravoslavnoe missionerskoe obshchestvo," *Pravoslavnyi blagovestnik* 20 (1894): 149–159. The Society for the Restoration of Orthodoxy in the Caucasus, formed in 1860, operated in a similar fashion (Jersild, *Orientalism and Empire,* 42–47).

53. Quoted in "Pravoslavnoe missionerskoe obshchestvo," 152.

54. Quoted in Evgenii Popov, *Ob userdii k missionerskomu delu* (Perm, 1874), 9.

55. And of course societies were central to the colonial missions launched from west-

ern European states in Africa and Asia. See for example Peter Van Rooden, "Nineteenth-Century Representations of Missionary Conversion and the Transformation of Western Christianity," in *Conversion to Modernities: The Globalization of Christianity,* ed. Peter van der Veer (New York, 1996), 65–88; Antony Copley, *Religions in Conflict: Ideology, Cultural Contact and Conversion in Late-Colonial India* (Delhi, 1997).

56. Slocum, "Who, and When, Were the Inorodtsy?" 189–190.

57. Sviatoslav Kaspe makes a similar point in the present volume.

58. Kappeler, *Russland als Vielvölkerreich,* 227. Jörg Baberowski traces the differential implementation of the 1864 judicial reform in *Autokratie und Justiz: Zum Verhältnis von Rechtsstaatlichkeit und Rückständigkeit im ausgehenden Zarenreich 1864–1914* (Frankfurt am Main, 1996), 339–427.

59. Kappeler likewise notes that in Transcaucasia, the Christian peoples became the object of Russification, while the Muslims did not (*Russland als Vielvölkerreich,* 218).

60. See, for example his works, *Nation and State;* and "Defending Our Own: Government and the Russian Minority in the Kingdom of Poland, 1905–1914," *Russian Review* 54 (1995): 539–551.

61. And of course, though the imperial government did not recognize them as peoples distinct from Russians, Ukrainians and Belorussians also had long histories of adherence to Orthodoxy beyond Muscovy and the Russian empire.

62. A. V. Gavrilin, *Ocherki istorii Rizhskoi eparkhii* (Riga, 1999), 118–119, 140–143, 159 (citation from page 182). By 1905, in Riga the Orthodox service was even performed in German. See "Bozhestvennaia liturgiia na nemetskom iazyke v kafedral'nom sobore," *Rizhskiia eparkhial'nyia vedomosti* 6–7 (1905): 28–45.

63. This missionary reform has been analyzed at greater length in Geraci, *Window on the East,* 47–85; and Werth, *At the Margins of Orthodoxy,* 223–235. Austin Jersild notes that native-language instruction in Orthodoxy was also being developed in the Caucasus region at this time. See *Orientalism and Empire,* 47–56.

64. See Geraci, *Window on the East,* 223–263; and Paul W. Werth, "*Inorodtsy* on *Obrusenie:* Religious Conversion, Indigenous Clergy, and the Politics of Assimilation in Late-Imperial Russia," *Ab Imperio* 2 (2000): 105–134.

65. "O vvedenii russkago iazyka v katolicheskoe bogosluzhenie," *Russkii arkhiv* 5 (1874), p. 1262. This issue has been treated at greater length by Theodore Weeks, in "Religion and Russification: Russian Language in the Catholic Churches of the 'Northwest Provinces' after 1863," *Kritika: Explorations in Russian and Eurasian History* 2, 1 (2001): 87–110. The issue of the Reformed liturgy is addressed in RGIA, f. 821, op. 5, d. 1594.

66. A. Vladimirov, "O vvedenii russkago iazyka v bogosluzhenie katolicheskoi i protestantskoi tserkvi v severo-zapadnom krae," *Vestnik Evropy* 3 (1881): 374.

67. This dilemma is stated directly in I. Kornilov, *Stoit li vvodit' russkii iazyk v kostely zapadnykh gubernii?* (St. Petersburg, 1897), 3. Leonid Gorizontov has found that in practice state officials often resorted to a simple equation—Catholic=Polish—despite their recognition that this was not entirely accurate. See L. E. Gorizontov, *Paradoksy imperskoi politiki: Poliaki v Rossii i russkie v Pol'she* (Moscow, 1999), 100–118.

68. Weeks, "Religion and Russification," p. 98.

69. *Sbornik postanovlenii Ministerstva narodnago prosveshcheniia,* vol. 5, no. 168.

For a broad consideration of these questions, see Geraci, *Window on the East,* 116–157; and Isabelle Teitz Kreindler, "Educational Policies Toward the Eastern Nationalities in Tsarist Russia: A Study of Il'minskii's System" (Ph.D. diss., Columbia University, 1969), 169–170.

70. This distinction between linguistic and spiritual *obrusenie* is central to Geraci's discussion of these educational issues (*Window on the East,* 116–157).

71. Quoted in A. H. Grigor'ev, "Khristianizatsiia nerusskikh narodnostei, kak odin iz metodov natsional'no-kolonial'noi politiki tsarizma v Tatarii," *Materialy po istorii Tatarii,* vyp. 1. (Kazan, 1948), 262.

72. RGIA, f. 796, op. 149, d. 102, ll. 4ob–5.

73. Geraci, *Window on the East,* 74–75.

74. E. A. Malov, "Statisticheskie svedeniia o kreshchenykh tatarakh Kazanskoi i nekotorykh drugkikh eparkhii, v volzhskom basseine," *Uchenyia zapiski Kazanskago universiteta,* vyp. 3 (1866): 313. Such a formulation was not entirely new. Officials like Uvarov and Kiselev had likewise contended in the1830s that Christianity and "civic-mindedness" were inherently linked, the former constituting the purest manifestation of the latter. See Whittaker, *Origins of Modern Russian Education,* esp. 205–206, and Stanislawski, *Tsar Nicholas I,* 66.

75. Quoted in Popov, 9–10. Perm diocese itself had many non-Christians, including almost 89,000 Muslims, almost 13,000 "idolaters," roughly 300 "fire-worshippers" (*ognepoklonniki*), and even 250 Jews (ibid., 3).

76. On these efforts, see Werth, *At the Margins of Orthodoxy,* 44–73, 96–123.

77. I adopt this distinction from Clifford Geertz, " 'Internal Conversion' in Contemporary Bali," in *The Interpretation of Cultures* (New York, 1973), 177.

78. *Polnoe sobranie postanovlenii i rasporiazhenii po vedomstvu pravoslavnago ispovedaniia Rossiiskoi Imperii,* series 2, vol. 3, no. 984 (St. Petersburg, 1912), 53–55.

79. *PSZ,* first collection, vol. 13, no. 9825.

80. RGIA, f. 796, op. 129, d. 1542, l. 172ob.

81. The Synod agreed and cash payments were terminated. *PSZ,* second collection, vol. 12, no. 10135 (1837); RGIA, f. 796, op. 118, d. 1806.

82. *PSZ,* first collection, vol. 36, no. 37709 (1861). An attempt was made to extend these new rules, in a modified form, to cases of non-Christians wishing to convert to other (non-Orthodox) Christian religions. The Polish insurrection of 1863 intervened to prevent resolution of this question, but the materials of that file (RGIA, f. 821, op. 10, d. 253) show clearly that the state was committed to preventing disingenuous conversions.

83. RGIA, f. 1405, op. 63, d. 4952, ll. 3–3ob.

84. I analyze these cases in *At the Margins of Orthodoxy,* 86–94. The largest case of conversion to Orthodoxy in the nineteenth century occurred in Lifland province, where over 100,000 Latvians and Estonians became Orthodox in 1845–1848. See Gavrilin, *Ocherki istorii Rizhskoi eparkhii,* 109–182.

85. Natsional'nyi arkhiv Respubliki Tatarstana (NART), f. 10, op. 1, d. 5964, l. 17ob., 18ob. Emphasis added.

86. E. A. Malov, "Prikhody starokreshchenykh i novokreshchenykh tatar v Kazanskoi eparkhii," *Pravoslavnoe obozrenie* 17 (1805): 449–494; 18 (1865): 283–308, 499–513.

87. In the 1860s rumors began to appear that baptized Tatars could return to Islam

if they so desired. By the late 1860s a mass apostasy had developed in the Volga region, in which over ten thousand baptized Tatars openly abandoned Orthodoxy. See chapter 6 of *At the Margins of Orthodoxy.*

88. Malov, "Prikhody," 451.

89. Werth, *At the Margins of Orthodoxy,* 245–254.

90. Richard S. Wortman, *Scenarios of Power: Myth and Ceremony in Russian Monarchy, vol. 2: From Alexander II to the Abdication of Nicholas II* (Princeton, 2000), 161–195, 235–270.

7 Thinking Like an Empire: Estate, Law, and Rights in the Early Twentieth Century

Jane Burbank

In the eighteenth and nineteenth centuries, Russian emperors and ruling elites strove to apply contemporary European strategies of governance to their expansive realm. Attempting to standardize authority within Russia's borders, Catherine the Great divided territory into provinces, each with its governor, its districts, and, in theory, its clearly defined place in the administrative hierarchy of the polity.[1] European models were also emulated in the borderlands. In the mid-nineteenth century, officials of the Russian General Staff applied lessons from the French military's experience in Algeria to Russian campaigns in the Caucasus and Central Asia.[2] In social policies as well, Russia's rulers undertook initiatives in education, health, and law that corresponded to concerns of their rivals in Western Europe. But a central achievement of the revolutionary era in Western Europe, the abolition of legal estates, was never attempted by the Russian imperial government. Only after the fall of the Romanov monarchy was the legal category of estate abolished. In March 1917, the liberal Kadets who dominated the Provisional Government achieved their long-held goal of ending the *soslovie* system.

The abolition of status as source of particular rights in and particular obligations toward the state did not last long in Russia. As Mark Vishniak, a Socialist Revolutionary, observed in 1920, the new Bolshevik government of Soviet Russia reintroduced the estate principle by making class membership a source of rights, duties, and claims upon the state.[3] Essays in this volume address imperial ways of thinking that were carried into the Soviet period, and one effect of the long retention of *soslovie* in tsarist Russia may have been to privilege the idea of group-based rights, and penalties, in the Soviet Union.[4] In this article, I raise a different question: What were the effects of the *soslovie* system and, more generally, of governance based on group-held rights and duties upon the prospects for social and political reform of the old regime? How did this central element of imperial rule—the division of the governed into status and other groups with particular rights and duties—affect efforts to construct inclusionary and equal citizenship in Russia, a project that began in full force in the 1860s and continued by fits and starts until the collapse of the tsarist imperial system? More specifically, did the *soslovie* system structure the ways that members of the largest estate of the realm—peasants—imagined their place in the polity, both in the present and the future?

One setting for the examination of these questions, and for study of people's relation to the state and to each other, is the court. In this article, I draw upon the history of the most local and most used judicial instance in the empire, the township court, to investigate the attitudes of rural people toward imperial law and legal reform. I begin with an overview of the *soslovie* system, its place in late imperial public discourse and its significance for subjects of the empire. I then turn to the history of the township courts, an estate-based instance introduced for peasants by imperial reformers in the 1860s. I conclude with a consideration of the reception of a 1917 reform intended to establish non–estate-based governance of the countryside.

Soslovie as an Imperial Category

Soslovie was a typical strategy of Russian imperial rule, one of the several registers through which the polity was governed. The vast majority of the population in the mid-nineteenth century belonged to the noble, church, merchant, townsperson, or peasant estates; these legal status groups were cross-cut by other classifications and affiliations. The most important of these other categories were defined by religious confession, ethnicity (nationality), geographical-political units, and state service. Each of these attributes could become the source of claims upon the state, or of obligations placed upon the subject. These collective designations were not all mutually exclusive, or at least not at all times; individuals could manipulate their group identifications to assert various rights, defeat rivals, avoid duties, or undertake any number of other actions.[5]

Confusion, rather than clarity, about who and what comprised the nation was characteristic of late imperial discourse. To take one example, a 1912 compilation of statistics on the empire was titled *Russia in Numbers:*

Country. People. Estates. Classes (*Rossiia v tsifrakh. Strana. Narod. Sosloviia. Klassy*), as if to suggest that several estates and classes (these words are in the plural) composed a single "people [*narod*]" and country (both in the singular). In his introduction to *Russia in Numbers*, N. A. Rubakin asks the perennial question, "What is Russia?" and answers as follows: "Russia— this is above all the Russian people [*russkii narod*] and other peoples [*narody*], living on the territory of the present Russian [*russkoe*] state—in other words—the population of our country." Thus, "our" country includes many peoples [*narody*], Russians and non-Russians. Rubakin, like others before and after him, rejoices in the variety and particularity of his intended readers—"people of the most various positions, occupations, estates, classes, people of different sexes and ages, of different degrees of education"—and his answer, ultimately, to who "we" are is "numbers, which speak for themselves, and are above any tendentiousness." The rest of the book provided readers with compilations of statistics about the population of the empire divided by religion, class, *soslovie*, sex, occupation and other categories.[6]

Adding to the complexity of legal and social divisions within the country was the insistence of many educated contemporaries in late imperial Russia that the "real" divisions in Russian society were based on class, not estate. In the second half of the nineteenth century *soslovie* came under attack from both liberals and Marxists. For the author of *Russia in Numbers, soslovie* was not a Russian idea, but an import from the West. In his view, the imperial government had introduced the *soslovie* principle in the eighteenth century in order to divide the population into European-style estates—aristocracy, clergy, city dwellers, and peasants—each with distinct rights and a corporate identity. Rubakin observed that with the exception of a few aristocratic privileges, the estate system had disappeared in Europe itself, while in Russia the state had preserved this outmoded structure. The failure of Russian rulers to abolish this borrowed and alien principle put "contemporary Russian legislation . . . in a strange contradiction with the factual conditions of Russian life."[7]

As much as some members of the educated classes might want to disavow it, *soslovie*, precisely as a legal category, was a vital fact of Russian life. Estate status, in addition to religion, geographic locality, gender, age, and nationality, was the source of an individual's legally defined rights and duties. The polity was based upon the principle of subjects' rightful obligation to the state, with both rights and obligations assigned to people, not directly as individuals, but through their status as members of collective bodies.[8] The empire's legal codes spelled out the rules for social life by addressing individuals through their group status. It was by belonging to a collective, with its particular regulations, or by being ascribed rights that earlier had been assigned to members of another collective, that an individual gained the possibility of engaging legally in many of the most fundamental aspects of social life. Marriage, buying property, changing one's place of residence, bequeathing land and goods were not simply regulated, but regulated according to the estate, religious, ethnic, or regional status of concerned individuals.

The reformers of the 1860s made a considered choice in the retention of the estate system after the abolition of serfdom. Marriage laws were altered in 1861 to allow unions between people of different estates,[9] but the principle of rights accorded to groups and the division of the population by social status persisted as mechanisms of governance.[10] A new "Regulation on the Rural Estate" was compiled and attached as a "Special Appendix" to the codification of Laws on Estates. This Regulation contained the rules for land tenure established by the emancipation decree and modified by later legislation, defined the institutions regulating rural life, and communicated the usual massive number of special statutes for particular territorially and ethnically defined groups. Most important for the peasants of the empire was book 1 of the Regulation on the Rural Estate, titled the *General Regulation on Peasants.*[11]

This detailed code was the source of rights for most of the empire's peasants. The first statute addressed the critical issue of the family: "To peasants are extended the general decrees of the civil laws on family rights and obligations." Based on the terms of the emancipation decrees, the *General Regulation on Peasants* provided for the right of individuals of peasant status to marry legally under the same limitations and rules applied by the Civil Code to people of other statuses. This single-sentence statute was modified by two columns of exceptions. Other statutes in this section titled "On the rights of peasants" granted peasants the right to carry on trade and industry, to register themselves in other estates and societies according to the Rules on Estates, to be taxed and represented in regulated ways. Most critical to individual peasants making their lives in the empire, the last statute in this section on "personal and estate rights" declared, "Peasants may not be deprived of the rights of the estate or limited in these rights otherwise than by a court or by a verdict of a society [*obshchestvo*], confirmed according to the rule established in this Regulation."[12] This statute underscores that estate was a source of rights in the polity. To understand the significance of estate in rural life and for rural people, it is important to set aside the liberal critique of the estate system as a foundation of inequality and unequal rights and to focus instead on how subjects attained rights of any kind in the Russian Empire. Both the Civil Code and the *General Regulation on Peasants* indicate that the estate system was, for better or worse, the established way of having legal status, of having rights, of being among the governed. Correspondingly, a peasant could only lose his or her estate-based rights through legal process.

Imperial law, as a source of rights and obligations, and legal process, as a means of determining access to status-based rights, were fundamental to the imperial polity and its subjects.[13] Nowhere is the intersection of *soslovie* with the polity clearer than in the courts of late imperial Russia, where disputes between individuals, with their estate-based rights, were settled in accord with imperial law. The next section of this essay examines a controversial legal instance, the lowest-level rural court, established for the peasant estate after 1861. I look first at elite debates over this court; second, at the use of the court by rural people; and finally at the attempted replacement of this "peasant" instance with a more inclusive, territorially defined court. Each of these arenas displays the long-term impact of imperial governance through particular collectivities, in this case, estates. The habit of estate-based, differentiated rights and powers was deeply ingrained in the ways that intellectuals envisioned their society, and in the ways that peasants employed the law. The outcome of efforts to erase legal status from the rural courts suggests that estate-based imaginaries and practices constituted a barrier to creating equal citizenship in the empire. In this sense, both elites and peasants were thinking like an empire.

Law by Peasants

The history of the township (*volost'*) court has been made part of Russian studies not by legal historians but by scholars working on Russia's peasants. This lower-level legal instance established after the emancipation to deal with small crimes and civil suits among peasants has been linked, inextricably it would seem, to issues of rural tradition, development, custom, backwardness—in short, to what was known in late imperial times as "the peasant question."[14] Let me provide an overview of the court's jurisdiction.

The framers of the emancipation felt obliged to provide some kind of legal institution to ex-serfs after their liberation from the authority of their former owners. The result was the creation of a very localized court system, which relied, as did so much imperial governance, upon the principles of self-administration and central oversight. After the 1861 reform, peasants in their status as members of the rural estate were bound by the *General Regulation on Peasants* to two collective bodies. First, every peasant was a member of a "rural society" (*sel'skoe obshchestvo*), which possessed and regulated use of common economic resources.[15] For the most part, these rural societies of post-emancipation Russia were descendants of the peasant collectives, also known as communes, which had controlled the cultivation of land in common either on a serf-owner's estate or on state-controlled domains.[16] Second, above the rural society, with its economic responsibilities, the *General Regulation on Peasants* established the township (*volost'*) as the local authority over peasants' administrative and judicial affairs. Modeled on the church parish, a township combined several rural societies with their contiguous territories and settlements.[17]

The *General Regulation on Peasants* instantiated a court at the administrative center of each township. The law assigned the township court the task of adjudicating "quarrels and suits about property" and "misdemeanors" for the rural population. In its original incarnation, the court was to decide cases involving peasants exclusively; after 1889, its jurisdiction was expanded to include people of several other, but not all, estates, resident in the township. People of noble status were not obliged to appear when called by the court, while members of other estates—"townspeople, tradespeople, craftspeople, and guildspeople"—were made subject to the regulations of the township court, "retaining, however, all the personal and estate rights conferred upon them."[18] In the beginning of the twentieth century—the period examined in this article—the overwhelming majority of the people using these courts were ascribed to the peasantry.

The procedures for choosing judges reflected the estate-based origins of the township court and were never changed to admit non-peasants. The judges were peasant men, heads of households, over thirty-five years old, never convicted of major crimes, and "enjoying the respect of their co-villagers." Each rural society elected a single candidate judge; these elected representatives formed the roster from which judges and their substitutes were chosen for terms of three years at the court.[19] After 1889, the township courts were linked to a hierarchy of appeals instances through a regional official, the *zemskii nachal'nik*. This official (usually translated as Land Commandant) was responsible for supervision of township court activity and for forwarding reports and records on up the imperial legal ladder. It is was his duty to call for regular elections for township judges and to choose a three-year roster of judges and substitute judges from among the candidates elected by the rural societies in each township.[20]

The township court provided accessible, rapid, and formal justice. Normally cases were heard and decided by three or four judges, sitting in the presence of a scribe who recorded the proceedings. There was no jury. No lawyer or other advocate would be present at the court, for litigants presented their own cases. Testimony was oral, but documents and witnesses were summoned when appropriate to a suit or charge.[21] The township judges were instructed to decide cases "according to conscience, on the basis of the evidence contained in the case." In civil cases, particularly those involving peasant inheritance, the court was to be "guided by local customs," a clause that gave rise to a long-sustained representation of the township court as a site of customary law.[22]

A sharp distinction between "custom" and "law" was ingrained in nineteenth-century Russian legal thought and provided grounds for both attacks and defenses of the township court.[23] While populists, liberals, and conservatives took different positions on the value of peasant tradition—some ethnographers argued that it could provide a basis for a new Russian state law applied to all citizens—all participants in the debate viewed the township courts as an irregular sort of judicial body. Township court procedures were regarded as inferior to those of the circuit courts established in 1864, with their juries, lawyers, and, from the perspective of Russian elites, "real" statute law. As I have argued elsewhere, these notions of what constituted law and what was peasant custom blinded Russian elites to the rigorous legalism of the township courts—to their adherence to the statute law, their formal procedures, and their meticulous, written record-keeping.[24] The instruction to township judges to decide cases "according to conscience, on the basis of the evidence contained in the case" was unexceptional, but somehow the similarity between this principle of township court adjudication and the process of the circuit courts, where lawyers routinely appealed to conscience and evidence, was forgotten.

What can explain the long-term adherence of Russian educated elites to the idea of a strict division between law and custom, between township courts and "real" ones, between peasant and non-peasants in Russian society? In her seminal book *Peasant Icons,* Cathy Frierson describes various stages in the interpretation of the "peasant question" after the emancipation; she concludes that Russian educated society's self-produced relationship to the peasantry in the 1890s was essentially the same as that of the

1860s—the village was a world apart, the peasant was "other," and the intelligentsia alone was capable of modernizing initiatives.[25] A variety of functionalist approaches might explain the intellectuals' desires to lead the backward of the polity, but why in the face of the rapid diffusion of people of peasant origin into cities, factories, businesses, and even universities, and at a time of rapid communications between large towns and surrounding villages, did intellectuals continue to classify peasants as a separate sort of people with different ideas of justice and everything else?

Here I think an imperial explanation is in order. Even during the explosive growth of Russian cities in the early twentieth century, in circumstances that fostered individual mobility, the habit of estate thinking prevailed. Elites were by no means immune to this way of thinking; after all, estate rights for people of noble status meant privileges unavailable to others. In the late nineteenth century, professionals created new occupational organizations, labeled them *sosloviia* (estates) and called upon the government to grant them, through these organizations, their own *soslovie* rights and privileges.[26] *Soslovie* was a primary way to relate to the polity; rights were demanded for collectives; the "peasantry"—whether you saw it as backward or as authentic—was an "it." Even those members of the Russian public [*obshchestvo*], as it defined itself, who wanted to put an end to the distinctions among estates found themselves caught in a way of thinking about society that was imbued with collectivizing assumptions and with the particularism endemic to imperial governance.[27]

During the many discussions of rural reform undertaken by the Russian government and public, critical voices did pose the question of separate estates and separate cultures. Take, for example, the positions articulated at a meeting of a subcommittee of the venerable Free Economic Society on April 5, 1904. The committee's task was to review a draft law intended to reform the township court. Members of the committee noted that the proposed legislation made peasants even more subject to distinct and separate rules, courts, and punishments than the regulations in effect. The presiding officer, V. E. Varzar, proposed that the committee address the general issue of "the estate-distinct juridical position of the peasants," but only a minority of the committee supported the idea that there was no need for special courts for peasants.[28]

In subsequent meetings on this issue, the subcommittee returned to the question of estate status (*soslovnost'*), and at session on April 19–20, the question of customary law—linked to the question of separate courts for separate estates—exploded once again.[29] Infuriated by the assertion that the draft law could not be examined without "knowledge of customary law," A. I. Ventskovskii asserted that "customary law played an insignificant role in the life of the people [*narod*] . . . We cite customary law when we have nothing else to say or when we need it to cover this up. Customary law is a fiction, created by populism." This outburst gave rise to a long and heated discussion; perhaps this is why the committee meeting continued into a second day. Some experts cited the need to understand customary law in order to draft a law code that would meet the needs of "the village"; others regretted the all too frequent clashes they had witnessed between peasant custom and real law. Ventskovskii held his own with a strong defense of the need for general laws and general citizenship: "Legal questions must be the same for all citizens and equally applicable in all places and all circumstances. The life of a peasant is not limited by the village, and besides, when he moves to the city, he is subject to other laws and other punishments. This is logically and legally absurd."[30]

The meeting ended with the request for yet another report on customary law by one of the committee members, but not before the presiding officer tried to smooth over differences with these despairing comments:

> For anyone familiar with the draft law, all its technical imperfections are obvious, the degree to which it does not take into account, although they are mentioned, the multiple particularities of Russian [*rossiiskii*] imperial life and the conditions in which *tsarane, chetverniki*, Cossacks, etc., live. In our life there's chaos, a muddle of conceptions and relations; in local areas you can't figure anything out, everything happens arbitrarily. We call this the application of customary law. But it's necessary, finally, to create something general.[31]

Intellectuals debated the merits and, from their perspective, the many demerits of the township court system right up until the revolution against the autocracy in 1917.[32] While this extended controversy raged, the courts went about their business of deciding minor civil and criminal suits for hundreds of thousands of people. From the 1870s, the township courts attracted increasing numbers of litigants in provinces throughout the empire, according to both government statistics and reports of commissions on the courts.[33] By the early twentieth century, the township courts in Moscow Province, for example, processed 47,761 cases in a single year. An average township court in Moscow Province decided 484 cases in 1905.[34] A study of inheritance cases at township courts of other provinces suggests that the Moscow region was by no means exceptional.[35] The township courts were in a literal sense the most "popular" courts of late imperial Russia, in part by virtue of their authority over the most numerous estate in Russia, in part because peasants used the courts with zeal. A rough estimate of the township courts' place in the legal system, cited by advocates of further legal reform in the first decade of the twentieth century, is that the township courts decided "80 percent of all cases from 80 percent of the population."[36]

What accounts for this outpouring of litigiousness on the part of people presumed to be outside the law? As the state's regulations indicate, the township instance was a small claims and petty crimes court. Its procedures were relatively simple. A case was initiated by filing a straightforward complaint form at the township administration; for most cases, this was all a plaintiff had to do before showing up at court. The court was physically nearby; decision-making was usually rapid; and enforcement of verdicts was enhanced by local networks of acquaintance and knowledge. These features of this local instance provided rural people with an easy way to try to settle accounts with their neighbors in a legal forum.[37]

Most important, as court record books make clear, rural people used the courts effectively to solve problems that were central to their daily lives.[38] The bulk of civil cases were suits for very small amounts—less than 30 rubles.[39] The township courts enabled rural people to enforce contracts, to pressure employers to pay for their labor, or to recover losses, for example, when a neighbor's animals trampled crops. The courts also regularly dealt with inheritance,[40] guardianship, and wardship cases.[41] In addition to these civil matters, peasants used the township courts to punish offenses against personal dignity.[42] Insults—verbal, physical, verbal and physical—were considered crimes in Russian law and were the subject of the majority of criminal cases heard in the township courts.[43]

The issues settled in the township courts—the defense of individual dignity, disputes over property and labor, the reallocation of property from one family, individual, and, overall, generation to another—were important to rural society, even if no one cared about such cases outside the village. That the township courts could provide rapid resolutions to local problems may explain the enormous success—unrecognized by elites—of this legal instance as an institution. Moreover, almost every participant in a township court was of peasant status.

Even if the law permitted or in some circumstances required people of other estate groups to participate in township courts in various capaci-

Table 7.1. Estates of Plaintiffs and Defendants 1905–1916 Cases (Civil and Criminal) from Case Records of 10 Township Courts in Central and Northern Russia

Estate	Plaintiffs		Defendants	
	Frequency	Percent	Frequency	Percent
Dvorianstvo	3	0.4	0	0.0
Krestianstvo	540	75.8	664	96.5
Meshchanstvo	35	4.9	21	3.1
Official, No Estate	133	18.7	3	0.4
Clergy	1	0.2	0	0.0
Total	712	100.0	688	100.0

ties, the vast majority of cases before the township courts involved people of peasant estate, and people of peasant estate alone. Nobles generally stayed away from the township court, in accord with their estate privileges. In my survey of cases heard between 1905 and 1916 from ten township courts in central or northern Russia, people of peasant estate accounted for 97 percent of all plaintiffs in civil cases and 81 percent of the plaintiffs in criminal cases. Peasants accounted for 94 percent of the defendants in civil cases, and 96 percent of the defendants in criminal cases in this same period. Peasants made up 98.5 percent of witnesses called in civil cases, and 93 percent of the witnesses in criminal cases. These figures under-represent peasants' presence in the township courts. The non-peasant plaintiffs in criminal cases were usually policemen, whose estate status was not registered, and most of the police and other officials who filed cases for aggrieved parties or appeared as witnesses would have been themselves of peasant estate. Many of the non-peasant plaintiffs and defendants belonged to the merchant estate (see table 7.1), and these individuals could well have their origins in local peasant families before they attained merchant status.[44] Most important, the judges at the township court were peasant men who had been elected by villagers in the township and who were thoroughly familiar with rural life. Peasants in early twentieth-century Russia enjoyed access to a local court, where people of non-peasant status rarely appeared and where justice was administered by men of their own estate.

The particular process of the township court—the possibility of legal judgment rendered by one's peers yet legitimated by the state—exemplifies the strategy of self-administration typical of the empire and suggests the power of estate-based governance. The court was a forum that empowered peasants as litigants and judges to employ the law in ways that both satisfied local sensibilities and conformed to the rules of a law-based empire. Through the township court, peasants exercised their rights to legal process and established a connection to the polity beyond their obligations to pay taxes and provide service. The absence of uniformity in legal process for all subjects did not mean chaos or unlawfulness, but rather the engagement of people with distinct rights in legal fora adapted to their desires and needs. The township courts were indeed "separate" from other courts, but their separateness was a characteristic and effective means of imperial governance.

Taking Estate Out

The Provisional Government established by Russian liberals and socialists after the fall of the monarchy set about dismantling the old regime. The new governors began this transformation immediately. Contrary to commonly held views, they did not wait for the Constituent Assembly to put their dearest objectives into law. Many of the Provisional Government's initiatives reversed the defeats liberal reformers had suffered in earlier, long-term struggles against the autocracy. Quotas on Jews were removed along with all restrictions based on religion or nationality; press censorship was abolished; freedom of assembly was declared. Other radical measures reflected less united struggles from the past: feminists saw their moment and won from their liberal colleagues the right to vote for the Constituent Assembly and to participate in all other elected institutions. Three reforms in particular bear directly on the subject of this essay: the abolition of estate distinctions, the creation of a non-estate administration at the township level, and the abolition of the township court.[45]

The attempt to institute a new kind of governance at the township level, embodied in a township zemstvo elected by, and theoretically comprised of, residents regardless of their former estate status, challenged the earlier distribution of power in the empire. Liberal reformers believed deeply that a main culprit for the backward condition (as they saw it) of the countryside was the administrative system that ran from peasant judges and other elected township officials up through the *zemskii nachal'nik* to the central government. What they thought would correct this ladder of corruption and patronage—again, from the elite perspective—would be a new local government, modeled on the zemstvo organs that already supervised education, medicine, transportation, and other community affairs at the district (*uezd*) and provincial levels.

For years, leading figures in the zemstvo organizations had argued that a township-level zemstvo, with representatives from all estates, was a requirement for justice and progress in the countryside. Such an institution, elected by people of all ranks resident in the township, could raise taxes from all estates to pay for local welfare. It would thus be fairer than the existing system, which taxed only peasants, and not nobles, for the expenditures on local welfare. Reformers saw the injustice of the old regime of estate-based taxation, whereby peasants organized in their societies (*obshchestva*) within each township were required to pay taxes to the district level zemstvo, where the township as such had no designated representatives. The township-level zemstvo, also known as the "small all-estate entity" (*melkaia vsesoslovnaia edinitsa*), was intended to "bring the zemstvo closer to the population, in order both to reveal needs and to better satisfy them." The justification for the new institution was straightforwardly developmentalist: an all-estate zemstvo would "develop self-awareness and self-enterprise among the population," and "collaborative work with more developed elements" would bear "educational significance for the peasantry." Finally, the creation of an all-estate township zemstvo was seen as a way to overcome the disabilities of the estate system, by "gradually attracting the whole population without differences of estate into local activity."[46]

A similar kind of reasoning informed liberal thought about the township court. Would it not be more fair to establish a local court that would include all estates and be governed by the same regulations as those used by the justices of the peace courts, with their educated judges, or by the circuit courts, with their judges, lawyers, and juries? An all-estate court would mean that peasants, nobles, and all other estates would be subject to the same legal regulations, be sanctioned with the same legal penalties, and have access to the same legal process.[47]

In the aftermath of the February revolution, the Provisional Government found the opportunity to put both of these reforms in place, giving substance at the local level to the abolition of estates. A new administrative unit, the township zemstvo, was established by decree in May 1917; a local (*mestnyi*) court was to replace the township court. These reforms were interlocking. The local court was to be headed by a three-person college—one presiding justice of the peace, elected by the residents of the township, and two "members of the courts" elected by the township zemstvo assembly. Both men and women could be elected to these positions. A justice of the peace had to be at least twenty-five years old and either a graduate of a secondary school or a person with at least three years practical experience in the judicial system. The two "members" of the college were required to be literate. The old township court was abolished in the same decree.[48]

In the liberal press these initiatives were presented as unquestionably progressive and essential to the new democracy. Moscow's major centrist newspaper welcomed the abolition of the township court and of the position of township judge and their replacement by the new local court:

> The reorganization of the local courts is as imperative as other reforms that touch upon the arrangements of local life. The strengthening of the bases of law in local life is now one of the pressing tasks advanced by the present epoch. This task can be fulfilled only by a court that will command the complete confidence of the population. The new justice of the peace court, which is close to the population and which is organized on the principle of election by a wide stratum of the population, will be able to fulfill this lofty task . . . [49]

A new pamphlet-size magazine called *The Township Zemstvo* [*Volostnoe zemstvo*] was produced in Petrograd to popularize these initiatives and to encourage rural people to vote in the elections to the new institution. This publication, addressed to peasants and populists alike, recounted the thwarted struggles under the autocracy to establish the township zemstvo and the great significance of this reform: "without it [the township zemstvo] the village cannot stand on its legs, cannot leave its wretched life behind." [50] The elections to the township zemstvo began July 30, 1917, and were completed by mid-September.[51]

The results were not what reformers had expected. Even the editors of *The Township Zemstvo* were forced to confess their disappointment. According to these enthusiasts of local power, almost everywhere peasants were indifferent to the elections—"busy with agricultural work and badly informed about what the township zemstvo is." Let it be noted that these elections were organized at the peak of the year's agricultural labor, the season when peasants worked extremely long days and nights to get the harvest in. One observer noted, "The general mass of the peasants is completely passive; it [the mass] is busy with the harvest and relates to the township zemstvo as if to something foisted on it, like a boss or a lord."

Others noted that factory workers, dacha owners, and craftsmen showed interest in the elections, while the intelligentsia stayed away. According to the journal's reporters, peasants, if they voted, tried to send "useless, superfluous" people—those who could not work—or those with little land, in the hope that the township zemstvo might give them new territory.[52]

The discussion of the township zemstvo exposes once again the vast distance between intellectual reformers and the peasant population they sought to reconstruct. Democracy, for the editors of *The Township Zemstvo*, could not be other than tutelary and collectivizing. In brochures intended to drum up support for the government's reforms, rural people who had formally lost their estate status were referred to as "the benighted village [*derevenskaia temnota*]"[53] and at the same time expected to welcome the democratizing measure of the township zemstvo.

The disappointing outcome of the township zemstvo reform indicates how difficult it was for reformers to stitch the polity together in a new way. Parallel but separate systems of administration had been the rule, and these encouraged estate-like thinking on everybody's part. Peasants were quite right to see the township zemstvo as a usurpation of their previously legitimated administrative practices. Now not just one nobleman—the *zemskii nachal'nik*—would supervise their township administrations and their courts, but a raft of specialists, estate owners, teachers, and women would take over the local institutions that had been theirs to control. It was hardly likely that peasants could outmaneuver better-educated people in the elections to the township zemstvo. People voted by submitting a list of names to the electoral commission, an open-ended concept to be sure, but one that guaranteed a huge advantage to literate, organized, mobilized voters, and in any case to those who did not have to bring in the harvest. Elected representatives to the township zemstvo did not even have to live in the province, let alone the district or township that they were to govern. This "broadening" of the electorate undermined the principles of local knowledge and local responsibility under which the old township court had functioned so effectively.

While activists declared that the township zemstvo would be the "liberation of the peasantry from its burdensome wardship," peasants with reason might have seen the same reform as vastly increasing the number of their guardians. In the place of the township headman and the township scribe, the township zemstvo assembly composed of "twenty to fifty elected people, the township representatives [*glasnye*]" would decide "all matters of local economy and administration" and appoint all local authorities. The threat to the legalized autonomy of the former township judges was clear: they would be replaced, enthused populist propaganda, with "people who could help the peasantry carry on court affairs and understand the laws."[54]

Contrary to the elite notion that peasants had no legal culture, rural people continued to turn to the township courts after the fall of the monarchy. Throughout the revolutionary year, these courts were used by peasants, not resisted.[55] When the Provisional Government proposed to institute an all-estate, or non-estate, court, one whose costs would be paid for by the whole population of the area, not just by peasants, peasants did not welcome the new institution. Their right to rule themselves was threatened by the abolition of their estate-based empowerment as judges. Russian peasants' political imagination was formed imperially. Even after being granted the new universalizing status of "citizen," they strove not to eradicate estate boundaries but rather to preserve their bounded yet empowered judicial space.

Imperially Minded People

This essay has looked at political imagination—both of would-be state reformers, and of people who would be subject to their reforms. Both liberal reformers and peasants "thought like an empire." Commonalities established through the procedures of imperial rule structured really existing realms of power even for lowly people, and the separations established by those same procedures enforced social and ideological distance among imperial groups. These established communities—established through imperial law—provided the basis for political imagination, and for its limits.

The history of the township court provides an example of the empowering and constraining effect of estate-based governance. The "peasant" court was attacked by liberals precisely for its separateness, but the estate principle was critical to the way that legal culture took shape in the countryside. Peasant litigants in the township courts did not confront a 12-member jury; they instead were judged by their peers—by peasant judges elected by rural societies. An imperial principle of community self-rule fostered an extensive inclusion of peasants in the legal system of the polity, in their separate but very law-bound courts. A culture of respect for law could develop among Russian peasants, alongside elite society's firm conviction that peasants were devoid of legal consciousness. Both peasant legality and its critique were framed by an imperial mode of thinking.

This kind of thinking, based on estate and other imperial classifications, inclined people to see other groups not only as distinctive but as threats to their own rights in the polity.

In the late imperial period, conservative nobles made this imperial political imaginary clear in their explicit campaigns to preserve estate distinctions. Most scholarship on Russia treats noble defense of *soslovie* as a logical expression of class interest. What I argue here is that it was imperial governance that encouraged estate-based thought and that provided the language and the context in which a claim for noble and other rights could be sustained and seen as important. When we see peasants preferring their own local courts and their own local, and locally elected, judges against a new definition of universal justice that would include nobles and peasants in the same legal structure, we are seeing not just class interest—this is definitely part of the explanation—but also a claim to maintain status-based rights in the state. *Soslovie* was not, as the author of *Russia in Numbers* asserted, "in a strange contradiction with the factual conditions of Russian life." It was instead a familiar foundation of authority, deployed to determine those factual conditions. "Better separate than equal" was a pragmatic response to the new non-estate and indirect suffrage that would have undermined peasants' estate-based rights to select their own judges.

Intellectuals, for all their discourses of equality, were also thinking imperially and, more specifically, in estate-based terms. For them, the peasantry seemed never able to dissolve into peasants, and their plans for reform continued to treat rural people as a mass, with its distinctive needs, even if shorn of its distinctive rights. That states create nations has become a convention of our scholarship, but perhaps we should entertain a more open notion that empire-states create collectivities with distinctive, group-based claims upon the state. Imperial Russia created not just estates (*sosloviia*), but *soslovnye liudi*—estate-minded people. An egalitarian evolution before and after 1917 was hindered by the long-term practice of group-defined access to group-defined rights and duties.

Notes

1. On the provincial reform and Catherine's intentions, see among others, Aleksandr B. Kamenskii, *The Russian Empire in the Eighteenth Century: Searching for a Place in the World,* trans. and ed. David Griffiths (Armonk, N.Y.: M. E. Sharpe, 1997), 203–224; George L. Yaney, *The Systemization of Russian Government: Social Evolution in the Domestic Administration of Imperial Russia, 1711–1905* (Urbana: University of

Illinois Press, 1973), 68–72. On the governmental goals of Russia's rulers, see Marc Raeff, *The Well-Ordered Police State: Social and Institutional Change through Law in the Germanies and Russia, 1600–1800* (New Haven, Conn.: Yale University Press, 1983.

2. Peter Holquist, "To Count, To Extract, To Exterminate: Population Statistics and Population Politics in Late Imperial and Soviet Russia," in Ronald Suny and Terry Martin, eds., *A State of Nations* (New York: Oxford University Press, 2001), 116, 122.

3. Marc Vishniak, *Le régime soviétiste* (Paris: Union, 1920), 26.

4. On the meaning of class in the early Soviet period, see Sheila Fitzpatrick, "Ascribing Class: The Construction of Social Identity in Soviet Russia," *The Journal of Modern History* 65 (December 1993): 745–770.

5. For an example of such manipulation, see Willard Sunderland, "An Empire of Peasants: Empire-Building, Interethnic Interaction, and Ethnic Stereotyping in the Rural World of the Russian Empire, 1800–1850s," in Jane Burbank and David Ransel, eds., *Imperial Russia: New Histories for the Empire* (Bloomington: Indiana University Press, 1998), 174–198.

6. N. A. Rubakin, *Rossiia v tsifrakh* (St. Petersburg: Izdatel'stvo "Vestnik Znaniia," 1912), cover, 3–4. On the "display of peoples" notion of the Russian Empire at an earlier period, see Kevin Tyner Thomas, "Collecting the Fatherland: Early-Nineteenth-Century Proposals for a Russian National Museum," in Burbank and Ransel, *Imperial Russia*, 91–107. For an analysis that emphasizes fluidity and uncertainty as well as legal categorization as critical to Russian society and governance, see Elise Kimerling Wirtschafter, *Structures of Society: Imperial Russia's "People of Various Ranks"* (DeKalb: Northern Illinois Press, 1994).

7. Rubakin, *Rossiia v tsifrakh*, 52–53. See Gregory L. Freeze's discussion of the liberal attack on *soslovie* in his provocative article, "The *Soslovie* (Estate) Paradigm and Russian Social History," *American Historical Review* 91, no. 1 (February 1986): 11–36. Note that Rubakin's perspective implies a critique of the state from two opposite directions: first, for having adopted an alien (European) principle as a principle of rule and, second, for not keeping up with European standards through in its failure to abolish estates.

8. "Rightful obligation" is my term, coined to capture the reciprocity between duties and rights of imperial subjects.

9. *Svod zakonov grazhdanskikh* (hereafter SZG), st. 1, (a) notes. SZG is vol. 10, part 1 of the *Collected Laws of the Russian Empire* (*Svod zakonov Rossiiskoi imperii, Sobranie tret'e* [hereafter SZRI]).

10. For a summary of the legal position of ex-serfs after the emancipation, see Daniel Field, "The Year of Jubilee," in Ben Eklof et al., eds., *Russia's Great Reforms, 1855–1881* (Bloomington: Indiana University Press, 1994), 40–53.

11. *Obshchee polozhenie o krest'ianakh* (hereafter OPK). The *General Regulation on Peasants* was issued as book 1 of *The Regulation on the Rural Status* (*Polozhenie o sel'skom sostoianii*). All eight books of the *Polozhenie o sel'skom sostoianii* constitute the "Special Appendix to the Ninth Volume" of the *Collected Laws of the Russian Empire* (*SZRI*, 9, Osoboe Prilozhenie). I am using the 1902 edition of *The Regulation on the Rural Status*, updated to 1912, published in *Svod zakonov Rossiiskoi imperii v piati knigakh*, 5 vols., ed. I. D. Mordukhai-Boltovskii (St. Petersburg: Deiatel', 1912). This edition of *The Regulation on the Rural Status* incorporates various revisions of the

township court rules, the most substantial of which was enacted in 1889. It also includes the extensive modifications to the legal code concerning peasant landholding (the "Stolypin" reforms) promulgated in 1906 and 1910.

12. OPK, st. 1–7.

13. The law as a subject of inquiry has only recently become a focus of interest among historians. Before the 1990s, Russian historiography shared the anti-law mentality typical of the Russian intelligentsia as conventionally defined. See Andrzej Walicki, *Legal Philosophies of Russian Liberalism* (Oxford: Clarendon Press, 1987), 9–103, on the critique of "western" law in nineteenth-century Russia. A major exception to the neglect, before 1991, of the law in the history of imperial Russia is Richard S. Wortman's *The Development of a Russian Legal Consciousness* (Chicago: University of Chicago Press, 1976). For examples of the revival of interest in imperial law, see Peter Solomon, ed., *Reforming Justice in Russia, 1864–1994: Power, Culture, and the Limits of Legal Order* (Armonk, N.Y.: M. E. Sharp, 1997), and E. A. Pravilova, *Zakonnost' i prava lichnosti: Administrativnaia iustitsiia v Rossii (Vtoraia polovina XIX v.—oktiabr' 1917 g.)* (St. Petersburg: SZAGS: Obrazovanie-kul'tura, 2000).

14. For a discussion of the historiography on the township courts and the "peasant question," see Jane Burbank, *Russian Peasants Go to Court: Legal Culture in the Countryside, 1905–1917* (Bloomington: Indiana University Press, 2004), 10–16, 245–251, 257–260.

15. OPK, st. 47.

16. On the functions of the commune, see Steven L. Hoch, *Serfdom and Social Control in Russia: Petrovskoe, a Village in Tambov* (Chicago: University of Chicago Press, 1986), esp. 133–159.

17. OPK, sts. 50–52. In theory, each township was to have authority over no fewer than 300 and no more than 2,000 male "souls," a taxation unit that counted all males in an area, thus roughly 600 to 4,000 people. In practice, townships varied in size; by the early twentieth century, over half of all townships were larger than the upper limit prescribed by law. The township administration was to be located within 12 *versts* (12.7 kilometers) from the most distant settlement of peasants subject to it. For the parish model and exceptions to it, see st. 50, note 2. On the size of townships, see S. Latyshev, "*Volost'*," in *Entsiklopedicheskii slovar'*, ed. I. E. Andreevskii (Leipzig and St. Petersburg: F. A. Brokgauz and I. A. Efron, 1890–1904), vol. 13: 95.

18. OPK, sts. 77, note 1; 124–131. The estate groups added to the township court's jurisdiction are "*meshchane, posadskie, remeslenniki, i tsekhovye*" with permanent residence in the settlements of the area.

19. OPK, sts. 113–115.

20. For regulations on the *zemskii nachal'nik*'s office, see SZRI, 9, Osoboe Prilozhenie, Polozhenie o sel'skom sostoianii, kn. 3: "Polozheniia ob ustanovleniiakh, zaveduiushchikh krest'ianskimi delami," raz. 1: Polozhenie o Zemskikh uchastkovykh nachal'nikakh, gl. 2: Poriadok naznacheniia i uvol'neniia Zemskikh uchastkovykh nachal'nikov. On the selection of judges, see Burbank, *Russian Peasants Go to Court*, pp. 167–173.

21. For descriptions of township court procedures, see V. V. Tenishev, *Pravosudie v russkom krest'ianskom bytu* (Briansk: Tipografiia L. I. Itina i Ko., 1907), esp. chapters 4–6, and Cathy A. Frierson, "'I Must Always Answer to the Law . . .': Rules and Re-

sponses in the Reformed Volost' Court," *Slavonic and East European Review* 75, no. 2 (April 1997): 308–334.

22. OPK, st. 135.

23. The distinction between customary law and formal law was "universally" accepted in Russia in the nineteenth century, see Cathy A. Frierson, *Peasant Icons: Representations of Rural People in Late Nineteenth-Century Russia* (New York: Oxford University Press, 1993), 55. For a critique of the way customary law has distorted discussions of legal culture in Russia, see Jane Burbank, "Legal Culture, Citizenship, and Peasant Jurisprudence: Perspectives from the Early Twentieth Century," in *Reforming Justice in Russia, 1864–1996: Power, Culture, and the Limits of Legal Order*, ed. Peter H. Solomon, Jr. (Armonk, N.Y.: M. E. Sharpe, 1997), esp. 85–94.

24. Burbank, *Russian Peasants Go to Court*, 245–261.

25. Frierson, *Peasant Icons*, 194.

26. On lawyers and their *soslovie*, see Jane Burbank, "Discipline and Punish in the Moscow Bar Association," *Russian Review* 54, no. 1 (January 1995): 44–64.

27. See Yanni Kotsonis, *Making Peasants Backward: Agricultural Cooperatives and the Agrarian Question in Russia, 1861–1914* (New York: St. Martin's Press, 1999), for a related argument about estate-thinking. In his study of the cooperative movement Kotsonis identifies the refusal to see peasants as responsible individuals as informing the ways that professionals and governors constructed imperial policy in the countryside.

28. *Trudy Imperskogo vol'nogo ekonomicheskogo obshchestva*, 1904, t. 2, kn. 4–5, 94.

29. Ibid., 95–97.

30. Ibid., 96.

31. Ibid., 96–97.

32. On the effort to replace the township court with an all-class local court in the early twentieth century, see L. N. Zyrianov, "Tret'ia duma i vopros o reforme mestnogo suda i volostnogo upravleniia," *Istoriia SSSR* no. 6 (1969): 45–62.

33. Cathy A. Frierson, " 'I Must Always Answer . . . '," 327–331.

34. *Obzor Moskovskoi gubernii za 1905* (Moscow: Gubernskaia tipografiia, 1906), pp. 79–131. The judicial instances covered by the statistics of this yearly survey are those described by Eroshkin as subject to *"pravitel'stvenno-dvorianskii nadzor"*—the hierarchy of supervision established for the township courts after 1889 (N. P. Eroshkin, *Istoriia gosudarstvennykh uchrezhdenii Rossii do velikoi oktiabr'skoi sotsialisticheskoi revoliutsii* [Moscow, 1965], 267–268).

35. Gareth Popkins, "Popular Development of Procedure in a Dual Legal System," *Journal of Legal Pluralism and Unofficial Law* 43 (1999): 57–87.

36. Tenishev, *Pravosudie*, p. 4. On the increase in the use of the courts in the late nineteenth century, see Frierson, " 'I Must Always Answer . . . '," 327–329.

37. See Burbank, *Russian Peasants Go to Court*, 49–73 on township court procedures.

38. This conclusion is based on my reading of several hundred case records from township courts in Moscow, Petersburg, and Novgorod provinces; see Burbank, *Russian Peasants Go to Court*, for a fuller discussion of how and why peasants used the township courts. See Gareth Popkins' dissertation for a study of courts in other provinces of European Russia for a longer period of time: "The Russian Peasant *Volost'* Court and Customary Law 1861–1917," (D. Phil. Diss, Oxford University, 1995).

39. Although the township courts were empowered to hear cases for up to 300 rubles, rural litigants were concerned for the most part about much smaller sums of money. At the Iaguninskii township court in Moscow province in 1916, for example, 128 of the civil cases (out of a total of 208) were "suits" for various amounts of money, for damages, payments, or other property matters. Of these 128 suits, 74 were for under 30 rubles, and 29 were for less than 10 rubles. Tsentral'nyi istoricheskii arkhiv Moskvy [TsIAM], f. 749, op. 1, d. 38. The amount specified in these suits would have been affected by wartime inflation, and thus the claims are even smaller than they appear from the ruble standards of the prewar period.

40. On inheritance cases at the township courts, see Popkins, "Popular Development of Procedure in a Dual Legal System."

41. For examples of guardianship cases, see TsIAM, f. 74, op. 1, d. 52, ll. 17–20; TsIAM f. 749, op. 1, d. 38, ll. 27–28, and d. 33.

42. See Jane Burbank, "Insult and Punishment in Rural Courts: The Elaboration of Civility in Late Imperial Russia," *Etudes rurales* 149–150 (January–June 1999): 147–171.

43. For small crimes, punishments were of three kinds: a reprimand in the presence of the court; a fine ranging from 25 kopecks to 30 rubles; or arrest of up to fifteen days. OPK, sts. 143, 144.

44. For a discussion of this survey, see Burbank, *Russian Peasants Go to Court,* 16–18, 273–278, 290–291 and http://www.nyu.edu/projects/burbank/. The numbers of defendants and plaintiffs in the survey and the table differ because some cases involved uncontested matters, such as requests to be confirmed as the inheritor of peasant property.

45. Volume 1 of the collection of documents edited by Robert Paul Browder and Alexander F. Kerensky—*The Russian Provisional Government 1917* (Stanford: Stanford University Press, 1961)—provides a sense of the radical nature of the Provisional Government's first months. For the texts of civil rights and local court decrees, see 210–215, 226–239. On the feminists' victory, see Linda Harriet Edmondson, *Feminism in Russia, 1900–1907* (Stanford, Calif.: Stanford University Press, 1984), 165–168.

46. See Count Uvarov's passionate pleading for the township zemstvo in *Moskovskoe gubernskoe zemstvo v poluvekovuiu godovshchinu osnovaniia zemskikh uchrezhdenii, 1864–1914* (Moscow: 1917), 28–34. For a later example of this position, see *Volostnoe zemstvo,* no. 3 (1917): 85.

47. See, among many sources, *Ob uchastii narodnogo elementa v mestnom sude* (St. Petersburg: tip. M. M. Stasiulevicha, 1911); M. M. Mogilianskii, "Zemstvo i mestnyi sud," in *Iubeleinyi zemskii sbornik. 1864–1914* (St. Petersburg: O. N. Porova, 1914), 86–96; E. S. Kots, *Mestnyi sud i ego reforma* (St. Petersburg: Zemledelets, 1913). A law setting forth a reform of the local court was issued by the imperial government on June 15, 1912, but a decree putting the law into effect in some regions of the realm did not follow until September 16, 1914. See N. Rudin, *Zakon 15 iiunia 1912 o preobrazovanii mestnogo suda. Vremennye pravila o volostnom sude* (St. Petersburg: Sotrudnik, 1912).

48. Browder and Kerensky, *Provisional Government,* 1: 234–236.

49. Browder and Kerensky, *Provisional Government,* 1: 236. Translated from *Russkie vedomosti,* no. 106 (May 13, 1917): 3.

50. *Volostnoe zemstvo,* no. 3 (1917): 83.

51. *Volostnoe zemstvo,* nos. 17–18 (1917): 343.
52. *Volostnoe zemstvo,* nos. 17–18 (1917): 343–345.
53. *Volostnoe zemstvo,* nos. 17–18 (1917): 343.
54. *Volostnoe zemstvo,* nos. 9–10 (1917): 262, 263, 266, 267.
55. Burbank, *Russian Peasants Go to Court,* 228–244.

8 From Region to Nation: The Don Cossacks 1870–1920

Shane O'Rourke

The striking biblical metaphor "flesh of one flesh, bone of one bone"[1] aptly expresses the widely held belief about the Cossacks[2] before and after the 1917 revolution concerning their familial but dependent relationship with the Great Russian people and the Russian state. According to the point of view of the commentator, the emphasis could be on either the people or the state.[3] Both interpretations assumed that the Cossacks were linked inextricably to one or the other, and that outside of these two polarities the Cossacks had no existence. Yet as an explanation of Cossack identity, such a categorization is simplistic at best and wholly misleading at worst. It cannot account for Cossack behavior in the revolution and civil war that did not fit into either a populist or a statist narrative. During that conflict the Cossacks identified themselves neither with the Russian people nor with the Russian state in whatever guise it was offered to them.

To understand their behavior a different explanation is required, which must take into account the deep-rooted collective identity of the Cossacks that distinguished them from the Great Russian population. A combination of a discrete collective identity and acute political, economic and social crisis, beginning in the 1870s but accelerating dramatically in 1917–1920, created the circumstances for a Cossack nation to emerge on the Don steppe. The transition to a nation was a complex, ambiguous and contradictory process that remained incomplete. Nor was it inevitable. Cossack collective identity could have manifested itself in many forms during the last fifty or so years of its existence. But the conjunction of long-term trends in Cossack society and the short-term events of revolution and civil war eliminated other possibilities, leaving for most Cossacks only a stark choice between their destruction as a distinct community and independent nationhood.

Collective identity is a protean and sometimes elusive belief. Categorizations of collective identity are legion: national, ethnic, regional, religious, caste, communal, occupational and so on. Each category is accompanied by a list of attributes that help discern the particular form of collective identity under discussion. Thus ethnic identity usually involves some combination of factors, such as language, culture, and religion, while a national identity adds a territorial and political dimension to these elements.[4] In theory, each form of collective identity can be reduced to its constituent parts and assigned its correct categorization. Of course, in practice such taxonomies are never so neat, not only because there are no universally accepted definitions of such concepts as nationalism and ethnicity, but also because some forms of collective identity do not fit easily into any of the standard categories. This is particularly marked in cases of claims for national recognition when a group appears to lack many if not all of the standard attributes that are normally used to justify that claim. Often they appear to have little more to sustain them than the group's insistence that they are indeed a nation, attracting derision and not infrequently violence from outsiders who reject these claims and have something to lose if they are realized.[5]

Even those who do not have a vested interest in the rejection of such claims reject them because they are based solely on subjective criteria and have none of the usual so-called objective features distinguishing one national group from another, such as religion, language, or culture. Whatever differences exist between two groups are so minor that for one of them to seek to claim a separate nationality on the basis of these differences is evidently misguided at best, or downright mendacious at worst. Yet as Max Weber pointed out, ethnic and national claims do not depend on the quantity of cultural differentiation: "Any cultural trait, no matter how superficial, can serve as a starting point for the familiar tendency to monopolistic closure."[6] By emphasizing subjective rather than objective factors, claims judged to lack any basis in objective reality suddenly become much more understandable. In other words, the critical issue becomes what people believe about themselves.[7] Although developed by anthropologists, this approach offers much to the historian as well. It has relevance not only in contemporary Eastern Europe, but also for our understanding of ethnic and national difference in imperial Russia.

Arguments that Cossack collective identity went deeper than the corporate one provided by the imperial state have been given short shrift by Western historians. Peter Holquist, the most sensitive of recent investigators, has argued that attempts to create a Cossack ethnicity were largely a literary construction of post–civil war Soviet and émigré writers: "Lacking the corporate structures that had previously given a concrete institutional identity to the Cossacks, a central leitmotif in Cossack attempts to elaborate their past over the course of the twentieth century has been the tendency in the Soviet Union and in emigration to ethnologize their history."[8] Robert McNeal concluded that the Cossacks were a *soslovie* (estate) that had become an anachronism by the beginning of the twentieth century.[9] Peter Kenez, referring to the Cossacks during the civil war, writes, "In order to justify themselves in their own eyes, they created a bogus nationalism based on a mythical past."[10] Essentially these arguments assume that Cossack difference rested on the *soslovie* system, which defined and regulated identity. Since the state eroded Cossack institutional autonomy to the point of nonexistence by the end of the nineteenth century, the only thing separating the Cossacks from the rest of the Great Russian population was the artificial barriers of the *soslovie* system maintained by the state. Once the state disappeared, the disappearance of the Cossacks was only a matter of time.

Russian approaches to Cossack identity have become more complex since the demise of the Soviet Union. The rigid Leninist models defining Cossack identity through the standard tripartite division of Cossack society into rich, middle, and poor layers has been abandoned for more complex and varied explanations. Cossack ethnicity and nationalism have now become legitimate if highly contested academic subjects. The debate revolves around the relationship of the Cossacks to the Great Russian people. Some adopt the traditional line that the Cossacks were an extension of the Great Russians. One eminent historian accepted the view that in the early years of their existence the Cossacks did indeed constitute a separate ethnos, but that by the second half of the nineteenth century "the Cossacks as a *soslovie* has already become an unconditional reality."[11] Others have argued that the Cossacks were unconditionally a separate ethnos.[12] Majority opinion at the moment has settled around the argument that the Cossacks formed a sub-ethnos of the Russian people.[13]

The case for a Cossack collective identity, separate and opposed to a Russian identity, can at first sight appear fragile. The Cossacks spoke Russian and were Christians of either the Orthodox or sectarian rites; many had originated from Russia.[14] In all, such differences as there were between the Cossacks and the wider Russian culture seem too marginal for a separate collective identity to be constructed. This, however, ignores the Cossacks' own beliefs about themselves and their community.

Cossack identity was rooted in their perception of themselves as different from other peoples, and in the perception of other people that they were different. The first definite information we have about their existence identifies the critical elements that were to constitute Cossack identity. In 1549 Khan Iosef of the Crimean Tatars complained to Ivan the Terrible that Cossacks living on the Don were raiding his territory.[15] Thus a particular name, a particular place and a particular way of life were identified. In this lay the origins of Cossack collective identity; these core elements shaped a self-conscious community that had already coalesced in 1549. The community had a common name, way of life, and sense of place. To this was added an ideology that celebrated and contrasted Cossack freedom with the oppression of the surrounding states, a set of institutions that stabilized and reinforced identity and a profound sense that the land of the Don itself, *Zemlia Voisko Donskogo*, was an inextricable part of Cossack identity. Muscovy's only contribution was a negative one, in that it provided something for the community to define itself against. The formation of Cossack identity took place outside the control of Muscovy and was created in defiance of that state.

Perhaps most remarkable was the Cossacks' ability to give institutional expression to their beliefs about themselves and the nature of their society. At the highest level, the *Krug*, or general assembly, of the Cossacks became their sovereign body, electing the ataman or leader annually. Once a decision had been taken, the will and authority of the Krug were uncontested in the Voisko, in theory at any rate.[16] At a local level, each Cossack *stanitsa* (village) had its own mini-krug, the *sbor*, which elected its own *ataman*. These practices became part of the fabric of everyday life for the Cossacks, woven into their group identity.[17] Together the institutions at the local level and at the highest articulated Cossack self-consciousness and solidified the bonds between the individual members. Even the later abolition by Peter the Great of the symbols of Cossack freedom, the Krug and the election of the ataman, in the early eighteenth century, did not erase the memory of that time. The Cossack state lived on not only in the collective memory of the Cossacks through their tales and songs, but also more tangibly in the institutions of the stanitsa, where the sbor and the election of the local ataman continued unchanged. As long as that memory endured, the Cossacks could never be completely integrated into the imperial State.

None of this is to suggest that the Cossacks remained untouched by the more interventionist attitude of the state. Many Cossacks took pride in their relationship with a strong and successful state in which their service was constantly extolled. Military exploits in the service of the empire did indeed become a part of Cossack identity. During the Napoleonic Wars in particular, the regime was unstinting in its praise of Cossack service.[18] But in the end all the state had really achieved in its relationship with the Cossacks was to overlay a strong pre-existing identity with a new layer, which, as events were to show, had shallow roots. When the bureaucracy after the Great Reforms began to plan seriously for the incorporation of the Cossacks into the wider society, it was the last two emperors themselves who decisively blocked these reforms on the grounds that Cossack peculiarity was a direct expression of their special relationship with the throne.[19] Yet a persistent economic crisis due to military service and increasing resentment at the use of the Cossacks for internal repression undermined this relationship.[20] In 1917, when the Cossacks were called upon to repeat their repression for the tsar, they refused, breaking their final ties with the regime.

Cossack separateness cannot be equated solely with the degree of administrative autonomy that its institutions enjoyed, important though this was; a number of customs, habits, and traditions maintained and reinforced Cossack identity, regardless of the attitude of the state. These have been consistently ignored in both Western and Soviet histories of the Cossacks, yet they formed the invisible cordon that policed the boundaries of group identity, preventing dissolution or dilution of the group. Cossackness was woven into the fabric of everyday life—from clothes, food, and land usage to stories and celebrations. Endogamous marriage, fictive kinship, godparentage, blood-brotherhood, *odnosumstvo*, and *polchaniki* are some of the relationships that knitted the society together, constantly identifying who was a Cossack and who was not.[21] The stanitsa was the pivot around which all these relations revolved, but it did not exclude the wider identity of Don Cossack. None of these relationships depended upon the state for its existence.[22] They are of the utmost importance in understanding the cohesiveness of Cossack society, even though their ordinariness and banality rendered them invisible to most outsiders, obsessed with political, economic, or institutional matters.

Of course, Cossack society was not monolithic. Like any human collective, the Cossacks were divided in a number of ways, including divisions between the upper and lower Don, between the Orthodox and the sectarians, between the elite and the rank and file, between rich and poor, and so on. War and revolution also created differences, all of which would affect the course of the civil war in the Don. Yet as we shall see, in no way did they erode the primary identity of being a Cossack. Even in the midst of the most fratricidal struggle, those who fought continued to identify themselves as Cossacks first and foremost.

Until the Emancipation of the Serfs in 1861, the boundaries separating the Cossacks from the rest of the population were rather ill-defined. On the eve of emancipation, the total number of peasants in the Cossack territory was 306,699.[23] These were serfs on noble land, overwhelmingly concentrated in the Rostov and Taganrog districts. Within a few years of the Emancipation, a steady flow of migrants from Russia and the Ukraine moved into the Don territory. This group, known as the *inogorodnie*, first appeared on the registers in 1865, when 28,101 were recorded.[24] By 1914 that number had grown to 684,024.[25] Although they settled throughout the Don, like the peasantry they were concentrated in the lower Don. Many of them lived and worked in Cossack stanitsas as hired laborers. It was against this group that Cossack identity became ever more sharply defined. They were impoverished, outsiders, and potential competitors for the same economic resources as the Cossacks. The sense of threat was far greater in the lower Don than in the upper, for the simple reason that far more *inogorodnie* lived there.[26]

On the eve of the First World War, Cossack collective identity was not dissolving or becoming diluted, but was actually becoming stronger. The regime had failed to impose a new, imperial identity on the Cossacks, and its limited success in this area was receding by 1914. The influx of outsiders into the Don had hardened boundaries between the two communities rather than softened them. Yet as the political and administrative framework in which Cossack identity had expressed itself for the past two hundred years collapsed, there was no consensus on how that identity could be expressed in a new context. The Cossacks themselves were divided and would be even more so by the experience of the First World War.

When news of the February Revolution reached the Don, the Cossacks sloughed off their imperial identity, abandoning the dynasty without a backward glance.[27] A group of officers meeting in Novocherkassk stanitsa issued an appeal to all the stanitsas and regiments to send delegates for a Cossack Conference to be held in Novocherkassk at the end of April. They were concerned that the Don Executive Committee was insufficiently robust in defending Cossack interests. On April 26, the Conference opened and immediately proclaimed itself the supreme authority within the Voisko, unceremoniously pushing aside the Don Executive Committee. The main business of the Conference was the organization of elections for a new

Krug by the Cossack population. Over seven hundred delegates were selected; on May 26 the Bol'shoi Voisko Krug opened, the first Krug in nearly two hundred years.[28]

The election of the Krug and its appointment of General Kaledin as ataman restored the constitutional position of the Don to approximately what it had been under Peter the Great. Then, however, the Krug had been confronted by a dynamic, expansionist state extending its authority in all directions. Now the Krug faced a very different type of central government. The Krug's first act was to define its new relationship with this government. The Krug demanded the widest possible autonomy for the separate parts of the state, while insisting that the Don Voisko was an indivisible part of the new republic.[29]

The Provisional Government accepted this new definition of the constitutional relationship between itself and the Voisko, since it approximated its own policy of allowing wide local autonomy while maintaining the territorial integrity of the old empire. The Krug had expressed no desire for independence, wanting only to be master in its own house. In addition, it affirmed the policy of war until final victory, supported peace without annexations or indemnities, and called for military discipline to be maintained.[30] The basis for a successful relationship between the center and this particular section of the periphery appeared to have been laid.

The implosion of the Provisional Government in the summer and autumn of 1917 destroyed any chance of this. Kaledin and the Voisko government watched with dismay as the Provisional Government proved powerless to halt the collapse of state authority and the deepening of revolution. The steadily mounting criticism from the Voisko reached a crescendo during Kaledin's speech at the Moscow State Conference. Moving from words to deeds, Kaledin sought alliances at the national level with forces of the right, concluding an electoral bloc with the Kadets.[31] Secret contacts were established with more shadowy organizations that were committed to the overthrow of the Provisional Government by force.[32] During the Kornilov coup, Kaledin openly revealed his hand, cutting the rail links between the Don and Moscow. For better or worse, the Don had emerged as the center of counter-revolutionary activity in Russia. Following the seizure of power by the Bolsheviks in October, Kaledin announced the temporary secession of the Don from Russia. The Don was now in effect at war with Russia.

In the past the right to declare war and conclude peace had been the prerogative of the Krug, and its decision had been binding on all Cossacks. Kaledin's actions had followed Cossack tradition. The Krug had given him its overwhelming support.[33] Their actions, however, assumed that the Krug enjoyed the same degree of authority over the territory and its people that its predecessors had done. But the Krug was already in a much weaker position than any of its predecessors. More than half the population were non-Cossacks who had no desire to be part of a Cossack state in which they would be second-class citizens at best. The Krug's problems, however, ran deeper. Since it regarded itself as the heir to the earlier Krugs, it assumed that it would enjoy the same level of authority as the previous Krugs. But this was an untested assumption. The level of participation in the election had been rather low, which, given the circumstances and speed with which they were organized, was not surprising.[34] Nevertheless, it was a slender platform from which to launch the Voisko into a second major war. Everything now depended on the reaction of the Cossacks in the stanitsas and *khutora* (villages).

Information about ordinary Cossacks and their attitudes in 1917 is sparse. Nevertheless, it is reasonable to assume that the overwhelming concern must have been the safety of relatives at the front. Keeping the farm going in the absence of so many men would have been another constant worry.[35] There were signs that ripples from the great storm raging in Europe were reaching deep into the Don. The traditional patriarchal order was openly challenged by women and the young.[36] It is likely that these were not isolated problems, since every belligerent country experienced them.[37] Most corrosive of all was the unprecedented increase in the consumption of alcohol, which appeared to be affecting everyone.[38] There was little evidence of a desire to make any more sacrifices for the common good. The Voisko government asked the population to hand over surplus agricultural products and animals for the sake of the war effort. Everywhere its commissioners met with polite but firm refusals.[39] These were the people who were now expected to fight another war, but this time much closer to home.

If the political attitudes of the Cossacks at home were hard to determine, there was more information about those at the front, the *frontoviki*, a distinct group bonded by the shared experiences of a terrible war. Like millions of frontline soldiers in Europe, those Cossacks who fought at the front were radicalized by their experiences and were deeply alienated from the societies that had sent them to war. The horrors of the war had produced a profound shift in the worldview of the *frontoviki*.[40] Older loyalties, habits, and traditions were eclipsed by new ideas, new explanations, and new solutions. For some these changes would be temporary, dissolving on their return home, but for a significant minority they would be permanent, creating a new division in Cossack society. These men did not deny their Cossackness, but they identified Cossack interests with the new regime.

The radicalization of the rank and file in the Russian army is well documented. While the radicalization of the Cossack *frontoviki* took place more slowly, it eventually became just as pronounced. The 1st and 4th Don Cossack regiments, those who had refused to open fire on demonstrators during the February Revolution, showed little desire to take an oath of loyalty to the Provisional Government, provoking the Krug to issue a stern reminder about their duty.[41] This did not turn out to be an isolated incident.[42] Despite the very public calls for the restoration of order from the Cossack elite and high-ranking Cossack officers, more and more *frontoviki* were drifting leftward toward Bolshevik positions. A Conference of Front-Line Cossacks in Kiev in the summer exposed this rift. Later political events, such as the electoral alliance with the Kadets proposed by Kaledin and, above all, the complicity of Kaledin in the Kornilov coup, intensified the alienation of the *frontoviki*.[43] Some of these attitudes were shared in the upper Don.[44] By the time these units began to arrive back in the Don at the end of 1917, their attitudes were virtually indistinguishable from those of the rest of the army. Report after report came through to Novocherkassk describing the Bolshevization of the *frontoviki* and their political unreliability.[45]

The October Revolution cruelly exposed the divisions within Cossack society. The Voisko government and the Krug regarded the Bolshevik seizure of power as wholly illegitimate and wanted to use the Don as a base to overthrow the Bolshevik regime. Kaledin immediately announced the temporary secession of the Don from Russia.[46] A de facto state now existed on the Don for the first time since the swearing of the oath to Alexis in 1673. If ever a favorable climate for the creation of an independent Cossack nation existed, it was now. State institutions were in place, Russia was in chaos, and the Voisko had at its disposal significant armed forces. In addition, political and military refugees arrived in the Don determined to assist in the anti-Bolshevik struggle.

Almost immediately, however, it became apparent that large sections of the Cossack population had no enthusiasm for this course of action. Relations between the Cossacks and the non-Cossack refugees crowding into the Don were very poor.[47] The formation of the Volunteer Army in early November was particularly badly perceived among the Cossack population. The overwhelming desire among the Cossack population was to stay out of the approaching conflict. This was so even in the southern stanitsas, where the atmosphere between Cossacks and the peasantry was much more tense. A year later an article in the anti-Bolshevik paper *Donskaia volna* accurately summed up the mood in the stanitsas and khutora:

> However, there was no noticeable desire to participate in the struggle, and the question was often heard, "How do we know whom to support? Kaledin or the Bolsheviks?" But the Cossacks gave this question a particular meaning. What strictly concerned them was who would be victorious and which would be the least dangerous policy to support. They themselves had no interest in the direction either of Kaledin's policy or that of the Bolsheviks.[48]

Other contemporary observers concurred in this analysis of the general mood of the population, although few were as frank (or as accurate) in their evaluation of the Cossack mood.[49] Evidence of the refusal of the Cossacks to support their elected government came from all sides. Scarcely any Cossacks participated in the fighting to retake Rostov in early December after a seizure of power by the city soviet.[50] A mobilization order that same month was ignored. Worse was to follow. As the *frontoviki* began to return home at the end of the year, they showed themselves willing to fight, but for Soviet power, against the Cossack government. Due to these circumstances, the Cossack state collapsed largely through its internal weakness. The Bolshevik army was approaching the Don, but Kaledin's government was in complete disarray before it even arrived. Kaledin recognized that his position was hopeless; on January 30, 1918, he shot himself. A few days later, pro-Soviet forces entered Novocherkassk and the Don Soviet Republic was proclaimed.

An independent Cossack nation had lasted barely twelve weeks. At first sight its ignominious collapse suggested that the Cossacks had little conception of themselves as a separate community, let alone a separate nation. The majority of the population wanted to avoid conflict altogether, while the *frontoviki* were overwhelmingly sympathetic to the Soviet regime. No one had been prepared to fight for the independence of the Don. The difference between the Cossacks and the rest of the population appeared to be crumbling as the structures that had supported it vanished. Yet Cossack identity had neither weakened nor dissolved. As far as we can tell, the overwhelming desire for most Cossacks was to avoid fighting at almost any cost. The Bolshevik regime made strenuous appeals to the Cossacks to convince them that it posed no threat to the interests of ordinary Cossacks. Its Decree on Land specifically exempted the land of ordinary Cossacks from confiscation.[51] Its quarrel was with the Cossack elite who had aligned themselves with anti-Soviet forces. As yet there was no tangible evidence that the Bolsheviks did threaten Cossack interests. Kaledin's policy, on the other hand, was leading directly to bloody conflict with the regime in which the Cossacks would be the cat's paw for all the anti-Bolshevik old guard. It seemed particularly pointless in the upper stanitsas where there was only a minimal threat from the *inogorodnie*. Even in the lower stanitsas where the threat was much more real, most appeared to give the regime the benefit of the doubt. The Cossacks as a community rejected Kaledin and his policy of confrontation with the Bolsheviks. They had not, however, ceased to see themselves as Cossacks. In a situation fraught with danger, they opted for the path that promised the least risk.

The Don Soviet Republic was not created on a wave of popular support. It enjoyed the active support of a significant minority of Cossacks, the *frontoviki*, but beyond that it was widely seen as better than most available options. The neutrality or tolerance of the Cossacks was given on the assumption that the regime would not interfere with their lives or make any demands on them. Such assumptions were unrealistic given the enormous expectations that the October Revolution had aroused among the peasantry and *inogorodnie*. Decades of resentment, poverty, and humiliation made restraint and moderation difficult. Somehow the new regime in the Don, headed largely by Cossacks, had to manage these expectations. At the same time, the authority of the new republic over its subordinates at the local level was weak. Many of these people were from outside the Voisko and were ignorant of local conditions; they regarded Cossacks, as a group, as enemies of the people.

The Don Soviet Republic sat uneasily on the top of Cossack society. The basic structures of that society remained intact. The sense that they were a community remained strong in all groups, whatever their political beliefs. For those Cossacks who actively supported soviet power and became officials, it was extremely difficult to ignore the ties of community and kinship with their stanitsa. *Donskaia volna* reported, "Almost everybody knew one another from childhood and almost all were related to one another. To arrest a counter-revolutionary meant to put in jail the husband of your aunt. To confiscate the property of another meant to rob the godfather of your sister. This restrained the commissars and did not allow them to deepen the revolution to the necessary degree."[52] Bolshevik appeals acknowledged a basic fact of life—namely, that the Cossacks represented a distinct group and that this distinction must be recognized if the Cossacks were to be successfully mobilized.[53] This, however, had dangers for the Cossacks, since such categorization could take extremely negative forms. Given the suspicion that existed within the Party toward the Cossacks, it would not be difficult to characterize the Cossacks as counter-revolutionary by the fact of their being Cossacks. This was a tension that remained at the heart of Bolshevik policy toward the Cossacks.[54]

Institutionally, Cossack society preserved its ability to run its own affairs. Stanitsa sbory continued to meet and to maintain links with all their khutora. The Soviet regime found it extremely difficult to gain a foothold in these rural institutions. Shortage of personnel, vast distances, and the general chaos were all contributing factors. More important, however, was the refusal of the Cossacks to allow outsiders to impose control over their way of life. Information is sketchy, but what there is confirms this pattern and fits in with peasant tactics everywhere. Demands that the Cossacks abandon their old institutions for Soviet ones were ignored. When it became too difficult to ignore, they complied—but in a way that made it meaningless. Only in March, after a series of categorical demands and the arrival of delegates from the Okrug conference, did the sbor decide to bow to necessity and elect a soviet. But there and then it was decided to reelect the previous structure of administration, changing the ataman into the chairman of the soviet, his assistants into comrades, and the *pisar'* into the soviet secretary.[55]

Only in those stanitsas with substantial *inogorodnie* populations did it prove possible for the administration to come under effective Soviet control. *Donskaia volna* observed that in these areas,

> a Sovdep was created in which the Cossacks made about half the number. In the beginning they attempted to make up an opposition and to vote against several decrees which touched directly on the interests of the Cossacks population. But the threatening cries of "c[ounter]-revolutionaries," "Kadets" and so on and the constant threat of arrest sharply discouraged them from real opposition. The Cossacks decided to evade their obligations and stay at home. In this way all power in the stanitsa was transferred to the *inogorodnie* population.[56]

However, the Cossacks retained control over their local administration in most stanitsas, which became obvious when the revolt against Soviet power broke out in the spring of 1918.

Soviet power collapsed in the lower Don in the spring of 1918. Although both sides were initially restrained in their behavior to each other, this fragile truce was easily broken. In Velikokniazhskaia stanitsa, the uneasy standoff was broken when some Cossacks welcomed the partisan detachment of General Popov into the stanitsa. In reprisal the Soviet authorities carried out an indiscriminate shooting of the Cossack population.[57] Such actions became more common as tensions rose.[58]

A series of revolts against Soviet power broke out in March 1918 in the lower Don. These isolated and unconnected revolts were transformed into a general rising by the Cossack ability to conceive of themselves as a community extending beyond their immediate environment and the administrative capacity to give substance to this vision. The revolt began in Suvorovskaia stanitsa with a decision in the stanitsa sbor. Messengers were dispatched to neighboring stanitsas who then mobilized through their stanitsa sbory.[59] An account of the revolt from Migulinskaia stanitsa in the upper Don corroborated these examples from the lower Don. A sbor had been called to discuss the attempt by the authorities to mobilize the Cossacks into the Red Guards. In addition to the stanitsa itself, fifty-five khutora participated in the meeting. As the meeting was going on, news arrived that a punitive expedition had been sighted on its way to the stanitsa.

> The news put an end to any doubts, and the sbor unanimously decided to forestall a bloody battle and disarm the Red Guards. To do this it was decided to proclaim a general mobilization of everyone from 20 to 55 years old . . . a military staff of the stanitsa council, or as it called itself a military section, was formed in the *sbor*. Two officers and two NCOs who were in the staff were elected commander of the unit and its chief of staff. These men were granted full authority and commissioned to lead military operations. Couriers flew through the quiet, warm April night with the mobilization order.[60]

This capacity for organization between and within stanitsas was the critical element in the success of the revolt. Without it, Cossack revolts, whatever their initial success would have been as isolated and as vulnerable as peasant revolts.

After the success of the rising, the Krug for the Salvation of the Don met and elected General Krasnov ataman. The new Cossack administration was now openly committed to a policy of independence for the Don.[61] Under Kaledin this had always been muted, and he had declared independence only when his hand had been forced by the Bolshevik seizure of power. The real change, however, was the reaction of the Cossack population to this new attempt to create a nation-state. This time they were willing to fight for it. A regular army of 50,000 men had been created by July 1918.[62] This did not mean that all Cossacks were irrevocably divided from the Bolsheviks. Some, such as Filipp Mironov, remained loyal to them, while others, particularly in the north, continued to waver. Nonetheless, a sea change in Cossack attitudes had taken place. The creation of a large army was made possible only by the willingness of the Cossacks to join it. In the aftermath of the rebellion, the central authorities did not have the coercive machinery to conscript people against their will. Later on that machinery would exist, with harsh punishments for desertion.[63] But even this was only possible because the majority of the population was willing to support it. When that support was withdrawn in the upper Don later on in 1918, the government was once again powerless to keep the army together. But the aftermath of the rebellion witnessed a much closer convergence of interests of institutions at the state level, those at the local level, and the mass of the Cossack population.

But this did not mean that there was identity of interests. Few Cossacks showed enthusiasm for service beyond the borders of the Don, nor did they show any interest in a wider strategy to link up with Admiral Kolchak in the east. A senior Don officer despaired of what he termed "the border illness" of the Cossacks.[64] (The Bolsheviks also began to pick up these signals and act upon them.[65]) This in itself was a manifestation of Cossack nationalism. A willingness to fight for the independence of the Don was not the same as a willingness to rid Russia of the Bolsheviks. Any sense of an overarching Russian identity was rapidly giving way to a much more limited commitment to the homeland of the Don. In the northern Don, in particular, there was a deep reluctance to serve outside the Don. The Bolsheviks grasped this attitude early and strove to exploit it with all their energy and skill.[66] By the late autumn, Cossacks of the upper Don began to abandon the front; Cossacks from Veshinskaia, Migulinskaia, and Kazanskaia returned home, leaving a gaping hole in the front.[67] The Bolshevik army entered the Don a second time. Meanwhile, the withdrawal of the German army had exposed the Don Voisko in the West. By early 1919 the collapse of the Don Voisko once again appeared imminent.

The Cossacks of the northern stanitsas had opened the front to the Bolsheviks from a combination of war weariness, suspicion of Krasnov's government, and a willingness to take the Bolsheviks at their word.[68] A report from one Bolshevik official noted the exhaustion of the population and the terrible losses caused by the civil war. In Eryzhinskaia stanitsa 17 had died in the First World War, but 320 had been killed in the civil war; for Annenskaia the figures were 22 and 413.[69] These give some indication of the savagery of the civil war. Once more the Cossacks were searching for the least risky way to secure their identity and way of life. Krasnov's policy, like Kaledin's, was involving the Cossacks in an endless war that was bleeding the community to death. Victory, if ever it came, would be Pyrrhic. Continued existence under vague and preferably distant Bolshevik auspices seemed a better bet.

The prospects for a successful consolidation of Soviet power were incomparably brighter than the previous spring. Report after report from Soviet officials on the ground confidently predicted the imminent collapse of the whole anti-Bolshevik struggle in the south.[70] Their optimism was not misplaced. The end of the Don Voisko was indeed imminent. All the Bolsheviks had to do was to continue the policies of encouragement, reassurance, and relative moderation which had brought such positive results. However, another tendency, which had been evident earlier during the spring of 1918, gained the upper hand; namely, to treat the Cossacks as an undifferentiated mass solidly committed to counter-revolution.[71] At first this expressed itself in a series of petty measures, such as forbidding the Cossacks to wear the famous red stripe on their trousers; the administrative break-up of the Voisko; and the replacement of the name stanitsa with *volost'*.[72] Such measures targeted the Cossacks for being Cossacks and made no distinction between those who had fought for or against Soviet power. Far worse, however, was the formulation this policy was given in Moscow in January 1919. Proceeding from the principle that the Cossacks were a distinct group who were inveterate counter-revolutionaries, the Orgburo followed this policy to its logical conclusion and issued an order that amounted to a directive for genocide:[73]

> Based on the experience of the civil war with the Cossacks, it must be recognized that the only correct policy in this most merciless struggle with the entire upper stratum of all Cossacks is to exterminate them to a man. No compromises or half-heartedness whatsoever are acceptable. Therefore it is necessary:
>
> > 1: To carry out mass terror against wealthy Cossacks, exterminating them to a man: to carry out merciless mass terror against all Cossacks who have taken part in any way, directly or indirectly, in the struggle against Soviet power.[74]

Subsequent articles made it clear that the whole Cossack way of life was to be destroyed, so that they would cease to exist as a distinct people. The policy was put into effect with devastating results. Thousands of Cossacks were shot by revolutionary tribunals amidst scenes of the most appalling brutality.[75] The terms of reference of the decree were so wide that it embraced virtually the entire Cossack population. Once again the Cossacks were being targeted for who they were, not for what they had done. Those implementing the policy made full use of the latitude given them. This was not a clinical exercise in removing inveterate opponents of the Soviet regime, but the wholesale slaughter of a people. Few Cossacks could have any doubts that not just their way of life, but their physical survival was at stake. Exhausted and war-weary as they were, there were still sufficient reserves of strength within the society to rise against their enemies. Uprisings against Soviet power began in those stanitsas that had been most pro-Soviet.

Whatever divisions existed among the Cossacks were sealed by this policy of terror. In the upper Don it had become clear as never before that there was no place for the Cossacks in the Soviet order. The regime had demonstrated in the most graphic manner possible that it recognized no distinctions among the Cossacks, but regarded them all as enemies to be exterminated. As the rebellion developed, Bolshevik policy, if anything, became even harsher. The Revvoensoviet of the 8th Army issued an order that encapsulated the new Bolshevik attitude to the Cossacks:

> The Don Cossack traitors have once more shown themselves to be the eternal enemies of the laboring people. All Cossacks who have risen in arms in the rear of the red armies must be exterminated to a man; all those who have had any connection whatsoever to the rebellion and to anti-Soviet agitation must be exterminated, not stopping at a percentage of the population of stanitsas and the burning of stanitsas and khutora which have risen in arms against us in the rear. No pity for the traitors.[76]

In the upper Don the rebels were determined to eject the Communists from the Don and to have no more truck with them. They were still not explicitly committed to a nation-state of their own, but it was the only realistic possibility left for them.[77] Paradoxically, the regime had started the transition to nationhood in a section of the Cossack population that doubted that it was necessary for them.

The rising of the northern Don was one of the most dramatic events of the civil war. It was possible only because of the cohesion of Cossack society and their conception of themselves as an ethnic group. Caught completely by surprise, the Bolsheviks were ejected from the Don, ushering in the climatic phase of the civil war. Commitment to the anti-Bolshevik cause was not unlimited, but a unified society acting in concert with its political institutions was now well on the way to being a nation-state. A war of national liberation had begun on the Don.

The civil war marked the transition of the Don Cossacks from a separate but subordinate community to a nation. To see them as just another *soslovie* of the imperial regime engaged in a desperate defense of anachronistic privileges is to completely misunderstand the nature of their society. They were a distinct group and had been for centuries. Only this allows us to understand their behavior in the civil war. Without that sense of collective identity, the Cossacks would have been as atomized and disoriented as all other sections of imperial Russia, at the mercy of events. At the start of the civil war few Cossacks were convinced that an independent nation-state was the only means of securing their own existence. There was little doubt that they were a distinct group rooted in the Don, but there was no consensus on what was the best political structure for them. The collapse of the old regime confronted the Cossacks with that question in an unavoidable form. Tradition and memory allowed the institutions of a Cossack state to be created with remarkably little difficulty.

Yet the difference between what the elite in Novocherkassk and the mass of ordinary Cossacks wanted led to the destruction of the Cossack state without a shot being fired in its defense. This was not due to the unraveling of an identity that had only been sustained artificially, but came from the belief that the elite was serving interests other than those of the mass of ordinary Cossacks. For most, some form of coexistence with the Bolsheviks seemed the least risky option in late 1917. Only the experience of Bolshevik rule convinced most sections of Cossack society that a nation-state was the only safeguard for their existence. The Bolsheviks' deep suspicion of the Cossacks and their readiness to subject them to the most brutal treatment were essential elements in the transition to nationhood. For the southern stanitsas this shift took place in 1918, and for the northern ones in 1919. The commitment to fight was only half the struggle. Cossack institutions, above all the stanitsa, had survived tsarist rule intact and gave them the institutional means to mobilize their society. The ability to conceive of themselves as a people and a nation lifted their horizons beyond the immediate locality. Institutions at the state level and the local level then allowed that commitment to be turned into reality.

Of course, a Cossack nation did not emerge fully armed like Athena from the head of Zeus. Nation-building is a process, not an event, and much still needed to be done, particularly in the upper Don. Nevertheless, that process had started among the Cossacks and had achieved critical mass by 1919. That the Cossack bid for nationhood was stopped by defeat in civil war should not obscure the reality that a bid for nationhood was taking place. The Cossacks were neither the first nor the last to have had their hopes for an independent nation smashed by defeat in civil war.

Notes

I would like to thank the British Academy, which generously funded some of the research necessary for this chapter.

1. S. Nomiskosov, ed., *Statisticheskoe opisanie Oblasti Donskago* (Novocherkassk, 1884), 297.

2. Unless otherwise explicitly mentioned, this chapter refers exclusively to the Don Cossacks.

3. An example of the former is S. G. Svatikov, *Rossiia i Don (1549–1917) Issledovanie po istorii gosudarstvennago i administrativnago prava i politicheskikh dvizhenii na Donu* (Belgrade, 1924); and of the latter, A. P. Savel'ev, *Trekhsotletie Voiska Donskogo 1570–1870* (St. Petersburg, 1870).

4. See, for example, A. Smith, *National Identity* (Harmondsworth, 1991), 14; A. Hastings, *The Construction of Nationhood: Ethnicity, Religion and Nationalism* (Cambridge, 1997), 167.

5. Macedonia is a good example. Greece, Bulgaria, and Serbia either currently or in the past have denied that a Macedonian nation exists, using as a pretext precisely these "objective" tests of language, religion, and history. See L. M. Darnfort, *The Macedonian Conflict: Ethnic Nationalism in a Transnational World* (Princeton, N.J., 1996).

6. M. Weber, *Economy and Society* (Berkeley, Calif., 1978), 388.

7. F. Barth, *Ethnic Groups and Boundaries: The Social Organization of Cultural Difference* (Norway, 1969), 6. "Ethnic identity is a matter of self-ascription and ascription by others in interaction, not the analyst's construct on the basis of his or her construction of a group's 'culture.'" This seems to me to have even more relevance for national claims than ethnic ones.

8. P. Holquist "From Estate to Ethnos: The Changing Nature of Cossack Identity in the Twentieth Century," in N. Schleifman, ed., *Russia at a Crossroads: History, Memory, and Political Practice* (London, 1998), 33.

9. R. McNeal, *Tsar and Cossack 1855–1914* (London, 1987), 220.

10. P. Kenez, *Civil War in South Russia, 1919–1920* (Berkeley, Calif., 1977), 112.

11. A. I. Kozlov, "Kazaki—Natsiia i Sosloviie," in A. P. Skorik, ed., *Vozrozhdenie kazachestva: Istoriia i sovremennost'* (Novocherkassk, 1995), 14.

12. See, for example, V. V. Glushchenko, *Kazachestvo Evrazii* (Moscow, 2000), 80.

13. L. Gumilev, *Ot Rusi do Rossii* (Moscow, 2000), 238.

14. The main exception to this were the 30,000 Kalmyk Don Cossacks living in the trans-Don steppe who were Mongol in origin and Buddhist by religion.

15. Svatikov, *Rossiia i Don,* 13.

16. Ibid., p. 37.

17. See, for example, E. Kotel'nikov, *Istoricheskoe svedenie Voiska Donskogo o Verkhne-Kumoiarskaia stanitse* (Novocherkassk, 1886), 16–20.

18. V. M. Bezotosnyi, *Donskoi generalitet i Ataman Platov v 1812 godu* (Moscow, 1999), 6–7.

19. McNeal, *Tsar and Cossack,* 4–5.

20. For the former see S. O'Rourke, *Warriors and Peasants: The Don Cossacks in Late Imperial Russia* (London, 2000), 82–101. For the latter see O'Rourke, "The Don Cossacks in the 1905 Revolution: The Revolt of Ust-Medveditskaia Stanitsa," *Russian Review* 57, no. 4 (1998): 583–598.

21. O'Rourke, *Warriors and Peasants,* 167–169.

22. Even though the Law of 1835 stipulated Cossacks could marry only other Cossacks, this was less strict than the Cossack tradition of marrying within the stanitsa. See M. Kharuzin, *Svedenie o kazatskikh obshchinakh na Donu: Materialy dlia obychnago prava* (Moscow, 1885), 113.

23. Gosudarstvennyi arkhiv Rostovskoi oblasti (GARO), f. 353, op. 1, d. 209, l. 1.

24. GARO, f. 353, op. 1, d. 209, l. 1.

25. Rossiiskii gosudarstvennyi voenno-istoricheskii arkhiv (RGVIA), f. 330, op. 61, d. 222, ll. 29–30.

26. O'Rourke, *Warriors and Peasants,* 59.

27. G. Ianov, "Revoliutsiia i Donskie kazaki," in *Donskaia letopis': Sbornik materialov po noveishei istorii Donskogo kazachestva so vremeni Russkoi revoliutsii 1917 goda,* 3 vols. (Belgrade, 1923) vol. 2: 7.

28. K. Kaliugin, "Organizatsiia vlasti na Donu v nachale revoliutsii," *Donskaia letopis',* vol. 2: 67–97.

29. *Postanovlenie Donskogo Voiskogo Kruga: Pervyi sozyv. 26 maia–18 iunia 1917 g.* (Novocherkassk, 1917–1918), 2.

30. Ibid., 1.

31. A. V. Venkov, *Antibol'shevisstkoe dvizhenie na iuge Rossii na nachal'nom etape grazhdanskoi voiny* (Rostov-na-Donu, 1995), 18.

32. Gosudarstvennyi arkhiv Rossiiskoi federatsii (GARF), f. 1255, op. 1, d. 4, l. 8.

33. *Postanovleniia Bol'shogo Voiskovogo Kruga voiska Donskogo tret'iago sozyva. 2–12 dekabria 1917 goda* (Novocherkassk, 1917), 6.

34. Holquist, "From Estate to Ethnos," 94.

35. V. P. Trup, *Kazachii izlom* (Rostov-na-Donu, 1997), 68–69.

36. GARF, f. 1255, op. 1, d. 4, l. 178. See also GARF, f. 1255, op. 1, d. 4, l. 197.

37. See, for example, R. Bessel, *Germany After the First World War* (Oxford, 1993), 23–26; A. Marwick, *The Deluge: British Society and the First World War* (London, 1965), 113–119.

38. GARF, f. 1225, op. 1, d. 39, ll. 1–2.

39. GARF, f. 1225, op. 1, d. 4, ll. 218–220.

40. Trup, *Kazachii izlom,* 66–67.

41. *Postanovleniia Donskogo Voiskogo Kruga: Pervyi sozyv. 26 maia–18 iunia 1917 g.* (Novocherkassk, 1917-1918), 6.

42. GARF, f. 1255, op. 1, d. 4, l. 155.

43. Ianov, "Revoliutsii i Donskie Kazaki," 13–19; Venkov, *Antibol'shevistskoe dvizhenie,* 18.

44. M. Astapenko, *Istoriia Kazachestva* (Rostov-na-Donu, 1998), 29.

45. GARF, f. 1225, op. 1, d. 57, l. 2. *Postanovlenie Chastnago soveshchaniia deputatov Voiskogo Kruga Voiska Donskogo 3 ianvaria-5 fevralia 1918* (Novocherkassk, 1918), 2–12.

46. Kaliugin, "Voiskovoi Ataman A. M. Kaledin i ego vremia," *Donskaia letopis',* vol. 2:148.

47. Not only for political reasons. Many petty Cossack functionaries complained that rents were soaring under pressure from the refugees. GARF, f. 1255, op. 1, d. 4, ll. 399–400.

48. *Donskaia volna,* May 12, 1919.

49. G. Ianov, "Don pod Bol'shevikami vesnoi 1918 goda i vosstanie stanits na Donu," *Donskaia letopis',* vol. 3: 14.

50. Kaliugin, "Voiskovoi Ataman," 149.

51. Y. Akhapkin, *First Decrees of Soviet Power* (London, 1970), 26. For an account of Soviet policy to the Cossacks in general immediately after the October Revolution, see I. Ia. Kutsenko, *Kubanskoe kazachestvo* (Krasnodar, 1993), 310–311.

52. *Donskaia volna,* September 2, 1919.

53. GARF, f. 1235, op. 82, d. 10, l. 193.

54. For differing views of debates within the Party, see B. Murphy, "The Don Rebellion March–June 1919," *Revolutionary Russia,* 6 (1993): 315–350, and P. Holquist, "'Conduct Merciless Mass Terror': Decossackization on the Don, 1919," *Cahiers du Monde Soviétique* 38, nos. 1–2 (1998): 127–162.

55. *Donskaia volna,* May 12, 1919.

56. *Donskaia volna,* February 10, 1919.

57. Ibid.

58. Kaliugin, "Stepnoi pokhod v zadone v 1918 godu i ego znachenie," *Donskaia letopis',* vol. 3: 17; Ianov, "Don pod Bol'shevikami," 17.

59. Ianov, "Don pod Bol'shevikami," 23.

60. *Donskaia volna,* May 12, 1919.

61. Kaliugin, "Donskoi Ataman P. N. Krasnov," *Donskaia letopis',* vol. 3: 70–71.

62. V. Dobrynin, "Vooruzhennaia bor'ba Dona s bol'shevikami," *Donskaia letopis',* vol. 1: 103.

63. GARF, f. 1235, op. 82, d. 15, l. 286. *Doklad Komissii Bol'shogo Voiskogo Kruga po oborone* (Novocherkassk, 1919), 10.

64. Dobrynin, "Vooruzhennaia bor'ba," 106–107.

65. See, for example, GARF, f. 1235, op. 82, d. 15, l. 67.

66. See, for example, the appeal in GARF, f. 1235, op. 82, d. 10, l. 193.

67. Kaliugin, "Donskoi Ataman P. N. Krasnov i ego vremia," *Donskaia letopis',* vol. 1: 132.

68. Murphy, "The Don Rebellion," 319–320.

69. GARF, f. 1235, op. 82, d. 15, l. 121.

70. See, for example, the reports in GARF, f. 1235, op. 82, d. 15, ll. 120–123; f. 1235, op. 82, d. 15, ll. 67–68; f. 1235, op. 82, d. 15, ll. 95–99.

71. Murphy, "The Don Rebellion," 323–324; Holquist, "'Conduct Merciless Mass Terror,'" 130–133.

72. GARF, f. 1235, op. 82, d. 36, ll. 212–213.

73. Article 2 of the U.N. Convention on the Prevention and Punishment of the Crime of Genocide states: "Genocide means any of the following acts committed with intent to destroy, in whole or in part, a national ethnical, racial or religious group, as such: (a) Killing members of the group; (b) Causing serious bodily or mental harm to members of the group; (c) Deliberately inflicting on the group conditions of life calculated to bring about its physical destruction in whole or in part."

74. Rossiiskii gosudarstvennyi arkhiv sotsial'noi i politicheskoi istorii (RGASPI), f. 17, op. 65, d. 35, l. 216.

75. Communist officials described the implementation in graphic detail. GARF, f. 1235, op. 82, d. 15. ll. 74–75. V. Danilov and T. Shanin, eds., *Filipp Mironov. Tikhii Don v 1917–1921* (Moscow, 1997), 204–208 and 223–225.

76. Danilov and Shanin, *Filipp Mironov,* 164 ff.

77. See, for example, the appeal "To all the toiling people of the Don," issued by the rebels. "The uprising has been undertaken not against Soviet power or against Soviet Russia, but only against the Communist party who have seized power in our native land," in Danilov and Shanin, *Filipp Mironov,* 159–161.

9   Bandits and the State: Designing a "Traditional" Culture of Violence in the Russian Caucasus

Vladimir Bobrovnikov

This chapter explores the culture of violence that emerged among the highlanders of the Caucasus during the state reforms in the nineteenth and twentieth centuries. By "culture of violence" I mean a set of practices—from blood revenge and the seizure of a debtor's property (*ishkil*) to seasonal raids by bands of young men and the guerrilla warfare waged by the so-called *abreki* (Russian plural form from the word *abrek*), whose practices have been described by Russian ethnographers and politicians as the "traditional manners and customs" of the Caucasian highlanders. These activities had both criminal and legal functions in the pre-conquest context. Highlanders used the threat of violence to prevent the escalation of violence and, ultimately, to support the social order in their communities. The main agents of this culture were professional bandits, known in the region by the name of *abrek,* and regarded as noble and pious outlaws in the manner of Robin Hood.

I explore the emergence and meanings of this "culture of violence" by drawing on both my ethnographic fieldwork in the north Caucasus and on a variety of historical sources in Russian and Oriental languages.[1] In this chapter I will explore the following paradox: the more the Russian imperial and Soviet regimes "pacified" the Caucasus, the more this produced professional banditry among the mountaineers.[2] I consider these questions: When and why did the *abrek* appear in the Caucasus? What was their position in highland society before and after the nineteenth-century Caucasian war? How did the highlanders and their neighbors treat the bandits? What was the relationship between power holders and bandits? How were the latter linked with highland society? How did the *abreki* change over the course of 150 years of Russian rule? Why have the Russian authorities failed to eradicate banditry and other criminal practices in the Caucasus? Did these bandits have an effect on society and culture in the Russian Caucasus from the mid-nineteenth century to the present? My purpose here is to seek answers to these questions within the broader historical context of state reforms.

"Predatory Highlanders" Orientalized

The Orientalist idiom of Caucasian "predatory highlanders" was common in accounts of travelers, traders, and missionaries who passed through this region, frequently depicted as a den of robbers. In these accounts, highlanders are pictured as "natural thieves" and "robbers." For example, the fifteenth-century Italian traveler Giorgio Interiano reports the custom of the Circassian princes to "hunt . . . domestic [animals] and even people" on their estates.[3] In his *Journey across Three Seas*, the Russian merchant Afanasii Nikitin, a contemporary, blamed the people from the Dagestani *utsmiyat* (principality) of Qaytag for pirating on the coast of the Caspian Sea.[4] According to the seventeenth-century Ottoman traveler Evliya Zelebi, the Adygs did not allow their daughters to marry "a man who was not a robber, and therefore could not be considered a brave person [*jigit*]."[5] While Evliya Zelebi's writings are known to be inaccurate, similar accounts were widespread.

Hajji-Ali, from the Avar village of Chokh, was secretary to Imam Shamil, political and religious leader of anti-Russian resistance among Muslim tribes of the northern Caucasus. Hajji-Ali, who subsequently deserted to side with the Russian army, wrote that his fellow "highlanders are as wild as the nature around them, and are no less predatory than wild animals."[6] Russian historiography of this time also tended to view any Caucasian highlander in a negative light. Even such objective writers as S. M. Bronevskii believed that the mountaineers "respect property acquired by force . . . , esteem their freedom as the richest gift, but use it for evil ends, carrying out raids on each other and in the surrounding areas."[7] Russian writers during the period of the Caucasian war (1817–1864) labeled this alleged inclination of the highlanders toward crime and violence "preying" (*khishchnichestvo*).[8] Bandit raids, robbery, and murder were considered the main means of subsistence in the local rural economy.

In order to understand the sentiments of the above-mentioned writers, one should keep in mind the political situation in the pre-colonial Caucasus, and, indeed, the fact that some of these authors had been victims of highlander banditry. On the eve of the Russian conquest, any stranger traveling without a local guide across the Caucasian mountains, especially in its northern areas, could have been kidnapped, sold into slavery, or even murdered. The rulers of small Muslim khanates of Dagestan pirated along the Caspian coast. Russian geographer S. Gmelin, who visited Dagestan to carry out fieldwork, fell prey to one of them, the Utsmy of Qaytag, and died in captivity in 1774.[9] The Circassian princes (*pshi*) organized seasonal raids (*zekwe* in Kabardian; *naezdnichesto* from the Russian word *naezd*, "raid") by the mounted aristocracy against their enemies and rebellious vassals in the northwest Caucasus. In the beginning of the nineteenth century, Russian military writer F. Tornau spent two years as a Circassian prisoner.[10]

Furthermore, during the prolonged Caucasian war, both Russian military authorities and *imams* of Dagestan and Chechnya saw terror as the only means to spread their power over highlands. Both sides carried out devastating raids on the enemy villages, plundering civilians and burning down their dwellings. Ironically, there was hardly any difference in this regard between the famous Chechen *abrek* Bey-Bulat Taymiev and Russian generals. For instance, in the first half of the nineteenth century, A. P. Yermolov organized a series of punitive expeditions against "non-pacified highlanders" (*nemirnye gortsy*) during which whole villages were burnt, their populations executed, and the livestock taken. Note that such violent practices of both non-pacified highlanders and Russian army were referred to by the term "raid" (*nabeg*) in the nineteenth-century Russian historiography. For instance, the Russian General Potto reported that he organized "raids . . . executing the people and taking *amanat* [Arabic for hostages]" in Chechnya.[11]

On his part, Imam Shamil brutally suppressed mountaineers who did not obey his power. In 1843 he demolished the village of Qhunzaqh, resistant capital of the Avar khanate in highland Dagestan. Two years later, his generals completely destroyed another Avar village of Chokh.[12] During his subsequent imprisonment in Russia, Shamil confessed to Colonel Runovsky: "I used cruel repression against the highlanders. Many people were executed according to my orders . . . I killed mountaineers from Shatoy, Andi, Tad-Burti."[13] Some well-known bandits, such as the famous *abrek* Hajji-Murad of Avariia, served in his army and military administration as *na'ib*—deputies of the *imam* in the districts (*wilayat*) of his state.

Yet, it is much more important to note that all the above-mentioned authors exaggerated the importance of professional banditry in the Cau-

Figure 9.1. Circassians in a raid on the Russian Caucasian border.
From *Utverzhdenie russkogo vladychestva na Kavkaze*
(Tiflis, 1903, volume 3, part 2).

casus. The first criticism of the discourse on "predatory highlanders" appeared in the works of Baron P. K. Uslar, the prominent mid-nineteenth century Russian scholar and the founder of the linguistic school in Caucasian studies. As he put it, "In the period of Romanticism the nature and the people as they exist in the Caucasus had been misunderstood . . . We could imagine the highlander only as a madman, an inflamed mind, chopping [with his sword] his enemies right and left . . . until he is himself slaughtered by the next generation of madmen. There was a time, when some in the Russian readership were simply fascinated by this wild creation of our literary imagination! Others . . . did not express much fascination with such characters . . . [but] proposed a complete eradication of these tribes."[14]

Ethnographic studies, which started in highland Dagestan in the early twentieth century, revealed that these raids performed social rather than economic functions. Youths took part in them chiefly to gain the position of a brave and noble *jigit* in their village. The main income of a mountain household was based not so much on a booty plundered in military

Figure 9.2. Circassian raider (*naezdnik*).
Drawing by G. Engelman. From *Voyage dans la Russie méridionale et particulièrement dans les provinces situées au delà du Caucase fait depuis 1820* (Paris, 1826, volume 2).

raids as on peaceful activities such as farming, cattle-breeding, gardening, handicrafts, and trade.[15] As I. Pantiukhov observed in 1901, "Understanding the Lezghis [the Dagestani highlanders] only as daring robbers while being unfamiliar with their family life, chroniclers and historians have taken the Lezghis for savages and bandits. However, the proper social organization of the Lezghi communities, the honesty of their interrelations, and their sedentary rural culture do not permit us to regard the Lezghis as savages. They lived mainly from agriculture and cattle-breeding, and not from bandit raids."[16]

Detailed field and archival research of the Soviet era supports this argument. Historians and ethnographers established that violence—especially in the form of the highland raids—was not as regular as it seemed, that it was limited to a small number of highland communities, and that it was often protective in character. For instance, warriors of different village confederations from Avariia united in order to resist the invasion of the famous Iranian conqueror Nadir-shah in the mid-eighteenth century. In the 1830s, highlanders from the Georgian village Shaitli beat off an attack of Shamil's troops from Dagestan.[17] Nevertheless, historians and anthropologists of the Caucasus, Russian and Western alike, still tended to exaggerate the role of *abrek* in the highland society.

There were two separate yet fundamentally similar approaches to the highlanders' violence in Russian historiography. The first one treated *abrek* banditry as a social reaction of primitive highland society to the challenges of the Russian conquest. This view dominated works of pre-revolutionary writers and scholars. It was rejected as a "legacy of the tsarist colonial regime" in the early Soviet period but was revived between the late 1930s and 1950s, and again in the 1980s. Attempting to make the highland societies fit the Soviet Marxist theory of social formations, scholars argued that *abrek* terrorist activities corresponded to a primitive "highland feudal formation" whose foundation was the "economy of raids."[18] This view is still shared by the Ossetian historian Marx Bliev and a number of his followers. They consider the *abrek* banditry an example of "the expansion of primitive pastoral tribes of the highlands against a civilized lowland population." Accordingly, the nineteenth-century Caucasian war was seen as a protective reaction of the "progressive" bourgeois Russian state against the mountaineers' banditry.[19]

The majority of historians and ethnographers from the north Caucasus have criticized Bliev's approach. They did so, however, from the point of view developed in the early Soviet period that portrayed *abrek*-bandits as agents of the national liberation movement in the colonial Caucasus. Devastating raids were considered "natural" highlanders' resistance against the "expansion of Russian colonialism." Yet in excusing the highland banditry, these Soviet scholars, ironically, subscribed to some of the nineteenth-century stereotypes. While the raids organized by bandits coming from lower classes were treated favorably as peasant guerrilla warfare, the military actions of the highlanders' noblemen, including the Dagestani khans or Circassian princes, were labeled "reactionary and anti-popular preying." This legacy of pre-revolutionary historiography can be found in works by the eminent Russian historian N. I. Pokrovsky,[20] and in those of his Kabardian colleague V. K. Gardanov, who reported that "predatory actions were committed only by the feudal chiefs and never by the people."[21]

Some Western historians of the Cold War period drew on this early Soviet approach,[22] extending it, not unexpectedly, to not merely the imperial but also the Soviet periods. For them, the *abrek* robbery and raids constituted a specific social form of anti-colonial resistance. The most prominent followers of this approach were Alexandre Bennigsen and his daughter Maria Bennigsen Broxup.[23] They contributed much to the study of banditry in the post-conquest Caucasus. However, they—like the Soviet scholars—examined banditry disregarding its specific historical context, and saw it as an eternal, essential characteristic of Caucasian highland societies. They assumed an unchanging historical continuity of local village societies and their cultures. Some historians combined data of different historical periods and even projected the present-day ethnographic materials into the past or vice versa.[24] Moreover, a great number of the above-mentioned studies relied exclusively on secondary and inaccurate sources.

I propose instead to examine first-hand sources related to the period when *abrek*-bandits really existed. I argue that the Caucasian banditry emerged in reaction to, and in the context of, the Russian imperial/socialist legacy. It is not difficult to show that the majority of witnesses concerning local banditry date back to the nineteenth and twentieth centuries. In reality, the very term *abrek* has considerably changed from the 1830–1840s on. In addressing the *abrek* issue, I attempt to shift the focus from concerns about anti-Russian resistance toward the problem of hybrid culture and society in a colonial and a socialist polity.[25]

On the Term *Abrek*

What does the word *abrek* mean? F. I. Leontovich, the Russian historian of Caucasian customary law who surveyed data collected by pre-Soviet ethnographers, proposed the following explanation of this term: "An *abrek* is a person expelled from his family and clan . . . In highland society *abreki* were homeless vagabonds for whom theft was a question of subsistence. In a common legal usage an *abrek* was an outlaw without any rights and support of the law."[26] Similarly, the eminent Soviet linguist V. I. Abaev, in his *Etymological Lexicon of the Ossetian Language*, rendered the word *abrek* "A person in exile due to a committed assault."[27] Yet the term *abrek* was not used in this sense invariably. With linguistic and ethnographic evidence, one can track the following episodes of its very long odyssey in the Caucasus.

According to Abaev, the term originates in the Ancient Iranian *aparak*, signifying "vagabond" or "highwayman" (from the Middle Iranian; cf. also the New Iranian word *avara* of the same meaning).[28] In the early Middle Ages the term was introduced into the Caucasian languages through the Turkic tongues. In a number of contemporary Dagestani and Nakh languages, it had kept its original form (*aparag*, plural *aparagzabi* in Avar) but not its pejorative meaning. In the later stages, the term designated free strangers who fled their communities for the fear of blood revenge.[29] Their descendants were also called *aparagzabi*. Among the highlanders of Dagestan and Checheno-Ingushetiia, they occupied a midway position between free men of common origin (*uzden*) and domestic slaves (*lag, lay, kuli, qazaq*). An old Avar proverb reported: "The house of the stranger is on the village outskirts" (*Aparagasul ruq roso ra'alda*).

The mountaineers of the northwest Caucasus used this term to define local noblemen expelled from their communities for murder, rape, or any other major criminal offense. Hence the terms *abrej,* and an older form *abreh,* in Kabardian; *abyreg* in Abkhaz, Abaza, and Ossetian; *abragi* in Mengrel and Swan dialects of Georgian.[30] It is significant that the term *abrej/aparag* did not mean a homeless vagrant who had to live off banditry. Expatriated princes of the Adyg and Ossetian tribes could easily find refuge in houses of their vassal noblemen either on the left side of the Kuban River or in Small Kabarda (in the territory of contemporary Krasnodar region, Karachay, and the Chechen Republic). Village communities (*jama'at*) and clans (*tuqhum*), to which the host of Chechen and Dagestani *aparag* dwellers belonged, protected the latter from blood revenge.

During the Caucasian war of the nineteenth century, highland deserters both to the Shamil and the Russian side were also called *abrek*. They had to flee from their homeland, losing their former social position, property, and power. Such deserters often served in the troops of the Imamate or in the Russian irregular cavalry called "highland police" (*gorskaia militsiia*). Some of them became real highwaymen at the same time. Such a modification of the term is attested to in an interesting talk that occurred between Colonel Runovsky and Shamil in Kaluga:

When I asked him what the word *abrek* means, Shamil explained to me
that this is the same thing as an emigrant, exile, or refugee:

[Shamil:] Do you know the Dagestani *militsiia*?

[Colonel Runovsky:] I do.

[Sh.:] These are *abreki* . . . And do you know that some of your "peace-
able highlanders" deserted from you and came to me?

[C.R.:] I do.

[Sh.:] These are *abreki* too. There are no others.[31]

The term *abrek* was introduced into the Russian vocabulary from the
Circassian (Adyg) language in the second half of the nineteenth century.
In the pre-revolutionary Russian usage, this word became equivalent to
bandit or robber. It was applied to all non-pacified highlanders.[32] On the
other hand, *abrek* received a distinct and quite negative connotation that
was linked to the notion of Muslim terrorist. Such a negative anti-Islamic
interpretation of the term is found first in the *Russian Encyclopedic Lexicon*
of F. G. Toll (1863),[33] and, later, in the second (1880) edition of the famous
Dictionary of the Russian Language of Vladimir Dal. Here Dal retained its
new negative meaning, signifying both "bandit" and "Muslim fanatic":
"*abrek*—a fearless highlander who devoted his life to the [holy] war against
infidels; in addition, a vagrant who entered highlanders' band for the purpose of robbery."[34] Under the impact of the Russian usage the term *abrek*
received the notion "bandit" even in a number of Caucasian languages at
that time. It became equivalent to the Turkic word *kachak* ("robber" or
"outlaw").[35]

By the beginning of the twentieth century, the meaning of the term
changed again, albeit not so radically. It lost its pejorative connotation and
received the notion "noble and religious bandit from the Caucasus." This
is best illustrated by an extract from unpublished memoirs by B. N. Polozov, who had been Lieutenant-General of the Russian military administration in the Elizavetpol province (*guberniia*), in the territory of contemporary northern Azerbaijan, and who, after the establishment of Soviet rule,
emigrated to the United States. Assigned to fight against highland banditry
in pre-Soviet times, Polozov in his memoirs treated his former adversaries
with strong respect:

Some criminal people are called either *abrek* . . . in the north Caucasus
or *kachak* in the south, in Transcaucasia. Both terms mean a man in
exile. *Abrek* and *kachak* outlaws do not resemble Russian criminals,
namely thieves and robbers. However, all of them were under threat of

[deportation to] Sakhalin [in eastern Siberia] or even hanging, and, indeed, some of them had been exiled to labor camps [*katorga*] but escaped, with fantastic adventures, and fled . . . back to the Caucasus where they entered the band of a famous criminal chief (*kharambash* in Azeri). This is why they became outlaws living in the criminal underground in remote woods and mountains of the old Caucasus. This kind of men, about eighty percent of them at least, were sent to labor camp for murders committed according to the ancient Asiatic custom of blood revenge (or *kanly* in Turkic).[36]

Finally, changes in the usage of the term *abrek* occurred during Soviet times, when it received a two-dimensional official interpretation signifying "a member of anti-colonial/anti-Soviet resistance from the Caucasian mountaineers." This notion can be found in the well-known *Dictionary of the Russian Language* composed in the late 1920s by S. I. Ozhegov: "In the period of the Russian conquest of the Caucasus, *abrek* meant a highlander taking part in the struggle against the tsarist administration and the Russian army."[37] A comparable definition was included in all historical lexicons and encyclopedias published in the Soviet period. For example, the *Great Soviet Encyclopedia* stressed the archaic character of the word, connected with the pre-revolutionary past and not the socialist present: "After the revolution of 1917, the *abrek* resistance disappeared, with the surviving usage being confused with a prosaic criminal banditry."[38]

At the same time, socialist scholars and writers continued to glorify "the heroism of pre-Revolutionary bandits." During the twentieth century, an imagined glorious past of the Caucasus was commonly evoked by a number of ethnographic and literary clichés, including that of *abrek* who were said to have sided with poor highlanders against their "feudal and capitalist exploiters." In accord with this quasi-historical fiction about *abrek*, which has been taking shape since the mid-1920s, in 1926 the Ossetian historian and writer Dzakho Gatuev published a novel about the *abrek* Zelim-khan Gushmazukaev (1871–1913), whose band devastated the lands of Chechnya and Dagestan in the beginning of the twentieth century. This story became very popular in the Caucasus and later was retold by another Chechen writer and historian, M. A. Mamakaev.[39] In 1929 a film was made about Zelim-khan, with a screenplay written by Gatuev. A novel about Data Tutashkhia, a Georgian bandit of the late nineteenth century, by Georgian writer Chabua Amirejibi, and a 1977 film from the novel, contributed much to the construction of an image of Caucasian

Robin Hoods.[40] Other contributions include those of Abkhaz writer Fazil Iskander and the Avar poet Rasul Gamzatov.[41]

Abrek Banditry Historicized

This gradual change in the meaning of the term *abrek* highlights profound social transformations in the Caucasus after the Russian conquest that I will outline below. Let me begin with the examination of pre-conquest practices of violence, to which the Caucasian banditry was often related. These practices included irregular armed forces of highland youths, the cult of the brave warrior (*jigit*), customs of blood feud and hospitality (*kunachestvo*, from the Turkic word *kunak,* meaning both "guest" and "host").

Before the Russian conquest, armed forces of mountaineers (*jaish* in Arabic, *bo* in Avar, *hurebo* in Darghi, *iha* in Andi, *eri* in Georgian) included all able-bodies males in highland village communities and their confederations and khanates. They were neither bandits nor professional soldiers; this can be deduced from size of military forces in north Caucasian principalities reported in medieval Arabic sources. For instance, the will (*wasiya*) of the fifteenth-century Avar khan Andunik reported that collected forces of Dagestani highlanders included 250,000 men (*rijal*).[42] The army was formed on the basis of associations of unmarried youths (so-called *batirte* in the Dagestani village of Kubachi, *sehbat* among the Rutuls, *qoqabi* among the Andis, *sidar bakhru* among the Tsezes, etc.). Their members spent winter in a military tower or a fortress (*gulala qhali* in Kubachi, *ghorqo ruq* in Avar, *sapekhno* in the Khevsur dialect of Georgian), whose social function was comparable to the long houses of the Pacific and African societies. There they were occupied with religious rituals, military exercises, and feasts. In spring, youth associations of village community or village confederation conducted raids against their lowland neighbors.[43] Their task was also to protect their communities in case of outside aggression, and to conduct some agricultural and construction work.[44]

Independent village communities of highland Dagestan and Chechnya used to elect their military leaders. They called them *khan, shah, tsewe-khan* (in Avar), or *bikt-khalel* (in Kubachi). The Adyg tribes of the northwest Caucasus were ruled by hereditary warlords called *pshi* ("prince" in Kabardian) and *uzden* ("nobleman"). Before the mid-eighteenth century, the main functions of the prince (*pshi*) included peace- and war-making, gathering *uzden* armed forces, and organizing military raids. As a rule, *zekwe* (raids) were more often preventive than aggressive.[45] It was not easy to be a prince among the Adygs. A *pshi* was not only a commander but also a warrior who fought in every battle.

It is noteworthy that there were no stable borders between social classes in societies of Dagestani highlanders, Chechens, and some groups of Ossetians and Adygs. As the nineteenth century Russian traveler N. Berzenev stated, "To be known as a brave man means to become an aristocrat in the Highlands."[46] Participating in, and especially guiding, military raids was a means to acquire honor and power among the highlanders. A widespread image of the brave warrior (*jigit* in the northwest Caucasus or *kant* among the Chechens and Ingushes) was imitated by all male youths for generations. Some fortunate military leaders succeeded in capturing an enormous, if temporary, power.

In the eastern Caucasus, successful military leaders founded many local ruling dynasties, as in the case of the *bek* clan from the Rutul village confederation in southern Dagestan who were said to have originated from "the former chiefs of raids."[47] Kh. Steven, who lived in a Chechen village confederation, notes that "they elected their chieftains among descendants of the family, which was the source of able military leaders for generations."[48] Arabic chronicles and oral histories from Dagestan and Chechnya demonstrate that the village *jama'at* used to murder family members of their successful war chiefs to prevent them from becoming their hereditary rulers.[49] From time to time, the highland confederations invited outside noblemen (*bek* and their descendants born by common women and known under the title *chanka/janka*) to be chiefs of their armed forces. Thus, in the period between the fourteenth and the seventeenth centuries, the *bek* clans originating from the dynasty of Muslim princes or *shamkhal* from the Lak village of Ghazi-Ghumuq diffused throughout central and northern areas of highland Dagestan.

Another important element of the pre-conquest culture of violence was the blood feud. In response to the rape or kidnapping of a woman, the capture of land, murder, or wounding, the highlanders were to kill the aggressor. Customary law (*'adat/rasm*) established the principle of collective responsibility for all these offenses. In theory, blood revenge covered the whole clan of a person held responsible for a crime and called *kanly*. In cases of rapes or other major family insults, blood revenge between highland clans could last for centuries, until the full eradication of one of them. For instance, in the Dagestani village of Qadar two *tuqhum*-clans were divided by the blood feud for about two hundred years, from the seventeenth till the mid-nineteenth centuries.[50]

In reality, however, the development of blood revenge was restricted by the so-called system of compensations, that is, to monetary and in-kind penalties in accordance with the norms of customary law. As a result, the blood feud was used as an important legal tool preventing warfare. The nineteenth-century traveler L. Lulie, who lived among the Adygs of the northwest Caucasus for a long time, reported: "Unlike the vendetta of the Corsicans, the blood revenge of the [Caucasian] highlanders is not comparable with the unlimited spontaneous sentiment. It is, rather, a re-strained duty imposed by honor, public mood, and the principle 'blood for blood.'"[51] The existence of a similar principle is also attested by the Bezhta proverb from northwest Dagestan: "Blood cannot be washed by blood" (*He heyd botsona baqhaas*).[52]

The social hierarchy was virtually reflected in the *adat* system of compensation through the amount of blood-money (*diyat*) to be paid to relatives of a killed person. Among the Kabardians of the northwest Caucasus and in lowland Dagestan, the highest penalty was to be paid for any physical damage inflicted to representatives of the local mountain elite. According to the early eighteenth-century Kabardian customary law, "Deliberate killing of a prince-*pshi* entailed *diyat* equal to between 6,000 and 8,000 bulls, while the amount of blood-money inflicted for killing of a common free man was only 160 bulls."[53] The murder of a slave was evaluated according to his usual price. Legal norms of customary law strictly prohibited blood revenge against persons belonging to higher social classes. This principle supported law and hierarchical order in the highland societies of the pre-Russian Caucasus. As the contemporary Kabardian historian Valerii Kazharov rightly points out, "a high amount of blood-money which was to be paid for killing a prince strengthened the social security of his people."[54]

The position of an expelled "blood enemy" and even of a man traveling outside his home territory was secured by the custom of hospitality widespread throughout virtually all the Caucasian highlands. As the early nineteenth-century English traveler John Longworth reported, "There are three properties which grant a highly regarded reputation to anyone in these areas [in the Caucasus] and these are courage, eloquence and hospitality."[55] Sergey Kuchera, the nineteenth-century Cossack officer who studied customary law of the Adygs, also stated the importance of hospitality among them before the Russian conquest: "The Circassians consider hospitality the highest virtue, and every guest, whoever he might be, is regarded as a sacred and immune person."[56]

Highlanders used to treat any accidental visitor as an honorable guest of their family and community. Both guest and host were considered *kunak* (after the Turkic verb *konak*, "to lodge," "to pass a night under somebody's roof"). On his part, the guest was to receive his host or anybody belonging to his clan as a revered *kunak* in his own house. The attitude of highlanders to the guest was based on two principles. First, the hospitality ties linked the host with any visitor, including even expelled criminals and excommunicated *kanly* (if not those of his own clan). Secondly, the host was to guarantee the personal security of his guest, even at the risk of losing his life in defense of his *kunak*.[57] These norms of behavior saved the life and property of a great number of highlanders outside their home communities, and sometimes even among their foes.

The combination of all the elements of the culture of violence I have analyzed above, including military male associations, veneration of brave warriors, blood revenge, and hospitality to expatriated persons, allowed the highlanders to survive in the difficult conditions of constant local wars and invasions from the south and the north. In the absence of a centralized state, these practices were used basically to support local power and prevent criminal violence and political anarchy. The systematic threat of violence worked well to prevent it in the pre-conquest highland society. Besides blood feud and raids(*zekwe*), mountaineers used to employ another violent practice, namely *ishkil* or *baranta*. This word meant a forcible capture of the debtor's relatives or his co-villagers' property to make him pay the debt. A village community or even village confederation often threatened to apply the *ishkil* penalty against another community or khanate for various political and economic reasons. There are several hundreds of *ishkil* letters dating back to the eighteenth and the early nineteenth century in the Collection of Manuscripts of the Institute of History, Archaeology, and Ethnology in Makhachkala.[58]

The attitude of highlanders toward violence was rather contradictory. On the one hand, they admired the courage of the young who acquired the *jigit* glory and honor in raids. Avar songs about raids composed in the eighteenth and nineteenth centuries included a repeated refrain at the end of every verse: "Let every mother give birth to such a son!" (*Hedinal haregi ebelatl wasal*).[59] Of course, there were bandits in the highlands as elsewhere. Some of them, like the famous Avar *abrek* Khochbar, who is said to have lived in Hidatl in the eighteenth century, were glorified in people's songs and epic stories. On the other hand, the highland folklore also celebrated severe attacks against participants of bandit raids and robbers. This attitude can be found in popular songs about bandit raids of the "heretic Shi'a troops" into southern Dagestan organized by the Iranian Safawi dynasty.[60] There was also a popular genre of lamentation songs weeping about victims of the devastating raids of mountaineers. Such a complicated attitude toward violence is reflected in the just-mentioned song of Khochbar. It describes how the perfidious khan of Qhunzaqh was severely punished for sentencing to death his guest *abrek*. Khochbar jumped into a fire with two of the khan's babies, thus leaving him no heir.[61] It was "God's revenge" for violation of the sacred custom of hospitality.

Highland Response to State Reforms

Following the Russian conquest of the Caucasus, local highland society and mentality experienced a deep crisis from which professional *abrek* banditry emerged. Though regarded by highlanders, ethnographers, and politicians as a continuation of brave raids of *jigit* (warriors) or their "predatory actions," in fact *abrek* banditry was a product of the interaction between local society and imposed Russian power. I argue that *abrek* banditry appeared as a specific answer of mountaineers to challenges originating from drastic Russian reforms. How did such an interaction take place?

In order to "pacify predatory highlanders," the tsarist military administration applied the so-called "siege policy." Under the reign of Catherine the Great, in 1777 the administration began construction of a Caucasian fortified line in the northwestern and central Caucasus, consisting of a series of forts and Cossack settlements aimed at establishing a barrier between submissive (*mirnye*) and independent or non-pacified (*nemirnye*) highlanders.[62] Irregular armed forces of village communities and highland noblemen were prohibited, first in Kabarda and later in Chechnya and Dagestan. According to state decrees issued between the 1820s and the 1850s, Adyg warlords lost almost all their former privileges, including peace- and war-making, gathering *uzden* armed forces, and organizing military raids.[63] Deprived of all their usual sources of income, these princes and nobleman had to choose between Russian military service and professional banditry.

Though outlawed, village youth associations survived in many highland Dagestani villages up to the mid-twentieth century, although they lost their principal military functions. Dagestani ethnologist A. G. Bulatova offers the following evidence for their decline.[64] First, from the second half of the nineteenth century, they ceased to include all the village youth. In contrast, married men of thirty to fifty years old entered these gatherings. By Soviet times, youth associations were turned into village male clubs that spent the winter organizing banquets and athletic competitions.

At the same time, tsarist military authorities tried to eradicate blood feud and *ishkil* as illegal criminal practices against the law of the Russian empire. In 1793, they issued a law prohibiting the resolution of blood revenge cases according to local customary law and the taking of *baranta*. From this time onward, the cases that previously caused blood revenge were settled according to the Russian Penal Code, initially in the Highest Frontier Court in Mozdok and subsequently in the Kabarda Temporary Court established by General Yermolov in 1822.[65] Having achieved the submission of northeast Caucasus, General-Adjutant Prince A. I. Bariatinskii initiated the legal reform in highland Dagestan and Chechnya in the 1860s. Highlanders were allowed to settle their criminal and land cases according to their customary law, leaving family and inheritance trials under the jurisdiction of the *Shari'a*. *Ishkil* penalty was strictly prohibited. The blood feud cases were, however, to be settled in the Russian military courts as major criminal offenses. Some norms of blood revenge were legalized, albeit with significant modifications. From this time, the *kanly* were to be exiled to convict labor companies in Siberia and other remote provinces of the Russian empire for a period from three to ten years. In 1913 a new bill was brought into force that extended the duration of their exile up to twenty years.[66]

Believing that the independent (*nemirnye*) highland elite was a natural antagonist of the Russian state in the Caucasus, General-Protector Yermolov attempted to deprive them of their former legal privileges. His special decree, issued in 1822, abolished the well-known *adat*, which prohibited blood revenge against members of higher social classes: "I order *uzdens* [noblemen] and common people [of the Kabarda] to use arms when they meet a traitor. You must abandon your foolish rule not to fire at princes if they shoot at you . . . if the common people do not fire, the population will be severely punished."[67] The authorities thus allowed, if not encouraged, murders of princes who were deprived by the Russian state of their former noble position.

Trying to restrict the old custom of hospitality that helped independent highlanders and other enemies of the state find shelter in Russian territory, the military Russian authorities introduced the so-called *bilet* (internal-passport) system. From the end of the eighteenth century, any person passing through the Caucasian fortified line had to carry this *bilet* issued by Russian officers and local Caucasian rulers under the Russian command. In the first half of the nineteenth century, the passport regime attaching highlanders to the land of their village communities was reinforced. Highlanders were prohibited from providing lodging to any guest who had no *bilet*. They were also to inform the Russian governors about their neighbors' unauthorized guests. As Yermolov's recommendations to the Kabarda Temporary Court put it, "If any Kabardian is found guilty of receiving a guest who arrived from the lands on the other side of the rivers Kuban and Terek as well as from the [territory] of the Nazranis [Ingush] and wasn't registered by the Russian governor, or if this guest had no *bilet*, [the host] will be penalized; in the case that the host provides unlawful people or *abreks* with lodging, the former will be severely persecuted in accordance with the Russian laws."[68]

Later, a similar *bilet* system was imposed over Chechnya and Dagestan. The harsh internal passport regime remained in force for the Caucasian mountaineers until the end of the nineteenth century. After a short period of liberalization, begun in the period of the two Russian revolutions, a strict passport system accompanied with political persecutions was revived under Stalin's rule and lasted up to the mid-1950s. The socialist state affirmed the punitive policy of late Empire as far as non-peaceful highlanders was concerned.

On the one hand, the administrative measures described above allowed imperial Russia to control most of the highland Caucasus and centralize its administration. As a result, by the end of the nineteenth century, the social and criminal situation in the area became much more stable than in the turbulent period of the great Caucasian war. Turned into Russian subjects, the highlanders had to adapt to the Russian imperial context. On the other hand, the foundation of professional banditry had been laid. The former legal practices of violence, including military associations, warlords, blood feud, and hospitality, were outlawed. They were gradually reclassified as illegal, criminal practices. The change in the social context of violence caused modifications of people's attitudes to *abrek* activities. As the Kabardian historian Valerii Kazharov argued, the Russian imperial authorities turned a segment of the former military leaders and warlords of the mountaineers into outlaw bandits deprived of rights and protection in the Russian Caucasus. But the highland society never expelled them.[69] Deprived of their status, chieftains and warlords became the principal actors of anti-Russian Caucasian banditry.

It is not a coincidence that many famous nineteenth century *abreki*, such as the Kabardian prince Tau-Sultan Atazhukin, originated from this social class. Some of them, such as Daniyal-Bek, ruler of the Ilisu sultanate in south Dagestan, or Hajji-Murad, originating from a family close to the Avar khans and the Kabardian nobleman Muhammad Anzorov, sided with the Imam Shamil in the Caucasian war.[70] On the other side, local village society supported them in their struggle against the "infidel Russians." As Russian archival files inform us, highlanders used to treat outlaws as their *kunak*-guests and did not inform Russian authorities about them. If the arrival of an *abrek* was discovered by authorities, his hosts often fled with him to the mountains.[71] For example Lieutenant-General Gramotin reported to the head of the center of the Caucasian fortified line that "a lot of people whose sentiments and behavior are not certain often come from different places to Kabarda and other tribes of the center of the Caucasian line directed by me. Frequently neither I nor even *pristavy* [bailiffs] and *ekzekutory* [policemen] are informed about their arrival."[72]

Russian judicial statistics of the 1830s demonstrate that the pacification policy paved the way for the development of *abrek* banditry. Highlanders strove to conceal serious crimes committed in their villages from Russian authorities. This concerned mainly murders and rapes that could provoke blood revenge according to the norms of customary law. As Russian pre-revolutionary observers showed, such cases were settled by Kabardians, Chechens, and Dagestani highlanders according to the principles of local *adat* without appealing to village or district court.[73] Cases of horse-stealing and plundering that occurred close to highlanders' villages were also hidden by the local highland population. Reports of Russian civil and military courts revealed a great number of cases related to buying and gifts of cattle captured in raids—*zekwe*.[74]

Effects of the reprisals organized by Russian troops can be seen in the fascinating account of these events written by the famous Russian poet Alexander Pushkin. He passed through the Caucasus on his way to Erzerum in 1829, that is, at the very point when the *abrek* banditry appeared in the region. "Circassians hate us," he confessed; "we deprived them of free pasture-lands, ruined their *auly* [highland villages], slaughtered whole tribes. They seek shelter far in the mountains and prepare their raids from there. Friendship of *mirnye* [pacified] highlanders is untrustworthy. They are always ready to help their violent confederates."[75]

Sporadic Revivals of "*Abrek* Banditry"

As a specific post-conquest form of banditry in the Russian Caucasus, *abrek* banditry emerged sporadically during the last two centuries. When centralized power strengthened, *abrek* disappeared, but it reappeared again when the center weakened. I distinguish four principal periods in the history of Caucasian banditry: first, that of the Caucasian war (1817–1864) and anti-Russian revolts of 1877–1878; second, the period between the two Russian revolutions of 1905 and 1917; third, the period of Civil War (1918–1921) and early Soviet reforms up to the mid-1940s; and finally, the turbulent post-socialist era with its two Russian-Chechen wars. Though some parallels may be drawn between periods of return of the *abrek* banditry, there were important differences between the four.

During the first period, Caucasian banditry retained a number of features of the pre-conquest culture of violence. It was located in the areas where highlanders' raids had been conducted, including the Alazan Valley in the east of Georgia and the valleys of the Terek and Sunzha rivers, inhabited by Cossacks. Like the former military associations, *abreki* organized gangs comprising dozens, if not hundreds, warriors. They started their raids in the late spring and stopped them every autumn and winter. Their actions consisted of attacking lowland villages, seizing cattle and other livestock, and kidnapping.[76] The outlaws often confronted their blood enemies. Some of them even perished due to blood revenge. This was the case of the famous Chechen *abrek* Bey-Bulat Taymiev (or Taymazoghly, b. 1779), killed by his *kanly* in 1832.[77] Another famous Chechen *abrek*, Vara, from the village of Gekhi, was handed over to Russian dragoons by his blood enemy Murad Gudanat.[78] These were professional bandits deprived of their former social status and living off robbery. Members of *abrek* groups did not participate in the peasant life of mountain communities.[79] They became real homeless outlaws.

At that time, local banditry was linked to the anti-Russian military activities in the highlands. As mentioned above, many *abrek* outlaws served in the army of the Imam Shamil. Nazir *abreki* from Chechnya, Vara and Atabay of Karachay, fell in battle with the Russian troops. Shortly after the military defeat of the imamate, *abrek* groups participated in a series of local anti-Russian revolts and in the all-Dagestani uprising of 1877. Besides raids and robbery, bandit activities of that period included attacks on Russian garrisons in the highlands and murders of Russian officers.[80] For example, in 1872 they killed the Russian chief officer of the Khasavyurt district (*okrug*) in north Dagestan. Nevertheless, *abreki* cannot be considered real actors of the national liberation movement as the early Soviet and the late Sovietologist historiography argued. They concentrated mainly on violent criminal activities, while their alliances with the leaders of anti-colonial movements had only a tactical character, as is well-documented by both highland and state sources.[81]

The next explosion of bandit violence supported by mountaineers occurred in 1905–1913. It was stimulated by the defeat of the Russian army in the Russian-Japanese war and a subsequent degradation of Russian military administration in the Caucasus. The criminal situation of this period was best described by Lieutenant-General Polozov:

> The revolution of 1905–1907 had some specific features in the Caucasus. Here the situation was quite different than in other regions of the Empire . . . Chechnya, Ingushetiia, Kabarda, Dagestan, and other Muslim areas didn't support the political claims of the Russian revolutionary parties . . . They [even] volunteered themselves to the police as cavalrymen [in units] that were formed in central provinces (*gubernii*) at that time . . . However, the number of *abrek*-bandits grew considerably in Terskaia province (*oblast'*) where famous Zelim-khan was operating. Having no political claims, they decided to use the opportunity to plunder and kill their blood enemies. In reality, the police and army were weakened, the former occupied with disturbances of workers in oil companies, the latter having lost troops that were sent to the war against Japan in Manchuria.[82]

In this second period, the most famous Caucasian *abreki* included the just mentioned Zelim-khan Gushmazukaev (1871–1913) from the Chechen village of Kharachoy, his comrade Salambek Garavodzhev from the Ingush village of Sagopsh, Buba from the Lezghi village of Iqra, Hamzatkhan from the Kumyk village of Buglen, and Shih-zade and Dali-Ali from the north of Azerbaijan. The character of Caucasian banditry changed greatly by the turn of the century. Its location shifted from the highlands to towns and villages that grew up in the lowland and hill areas. But *abreki* still used to escape into remote highlands of south Chechnya and northwest Dagestan or into Karachay or north Azerbaijan. For example, Zelim-khan, having stolen eighteen thousand rubles from the state bank in the town of Kizlyar, fled to highland Chechnya in March 1910. At that time his band comprised sixty men.[83]

Bandits had no contacts with town revolutionaries from Transcaucasia, but they began to control town businessmen. In 1905 Buba of Iqra, who was the head of a gang of twenty bandits, collected tribute from all fish traders, rich proprietors of gardens, and merchants who lived on the sea coast between Baku and Port-Petrovsk (the contemporary Makhachkala, Dagestan). Though his raids occurred in the countryside, he bought arms and munitions in towns. The support of local highland populations al-lowed him to increase his band to two hundred people and to escape pur-suit by the police.[84] Russian authorities continued to oppose the *abrek* ban-ditry with raids and punitive expeditions, which was very expensive but not very effective. The military administration of Dagestan and Terskaia provinces had to patrol areas where *abrek* gangs acted, such as the Kaytago-Tabasaran and Temir-Khan-Shura districts of Dagestan, with Russian troops and irregular militia of highlanders. By 1913 the most eminent bandits, such as Buba, Zelim-khan, Salambek, and Shih-zade, were killed or executed,[85] and the region was again "pacified"—but not for long.

The *abrek* banditry revived from the beginning of the Russian Civil War in 1918. Rural bands, groups of the so-called red or green partisans, dev-astated all the Caucasus. Khasavyurt and some other small towns were completely destroyed by them and ceased to exist by 1921. Between the two Russian revolutions, the *abrek* movement established links with radi-cal revolutionary and Islamic political movements who opposed the domi-nation of imperial Russia in this region. By the beginning of the 1920s, heads of bandit groups were the only real power in towns and countryside. In Dagestan, Chechnya, Kabarda, and some other Caucasian republics, So-viet power was established thanks to alliances between Bolsheviks and bands of red partisans such as *kachak*-'Omar, Girey from the village of Kuppa, or Kara Karaev, who for their part sided with radical Islamic lead-ers such as Ali-Hajji of Akusha in Dagestan.[86]

At the same time, village bands terrorized Soviet and Party officials all over Dagestan, Chechnya, North Ossetia, Kabarda. They seemed to im-plement the famous slogan of the serious enemy of Soviet power in Dage-stan Uzun-Hajji (d. 1920) who proclaimed the intention "to lynch . . . all those who write from left to right [i.e., non-believers writing in Rus-sian, not in Arabic] such as commissars, engineers, and teachers."[87] Rural gangs escaped to the mountains even at the end of the 1930s and during the unstable times of the Second World War. They continued to conduct from there daring, devastating raids in the countryside. To "abolish the roots of banditry," the highland population of Chechnya, Dagestan, and Kabarda, with the exception of red partisans, were prohibited from carrying firearms and even, from the mid-1940s on, daggers. In 1926, the OGPU forces supported by Red Army troops seized 60,000 pieces of firearms in highland Dagestan.[88] In February 1944 whole mountain peoples—the Chechens, Ingushes, Karachais, and Balkars, from whom the majority of pre-revolutionary and early Soviet *abrek* outlaws had originated,[89] were forcibly deported by NKVD forces from the north Caucasus to Kazakhstan and Central Asia.[90] As a result, the criminal situation in the area became more stable for half a century.

The recent eruption of banditry, which appeared again in the "traditionally *abrek* areas" of north Dagestan and Chechnya, was caused by the breakup of the Soviet Union and the crisis of power structures throughout the country. In the local writing of the socialist era, the cult of the *abrek* as the national hero of the nineteenth-century Caucasian war played an important role in disseminating these criminal practices. A noble image of the *abrek*, comparable to a kind of Caucasian Robin Hood, had been planted in the local collective memory of post-war times.[91] Following the first Russian-Chechen war (1994–1996), banditry diffused in the postsocialist north Caucasus and some areas of Transcaucasia. After the war, the local population retained a great number of contemporary firearms. To my knowledge, some highland collective farms sold all their communal property and then bought arms and pieces of ammunition to protect themselves against local bandits and marauders from the Russian Federation troops. In September 1999, the Dagestani People's Assembly passed a bill allowing citizens of the republic to keep registered firearms.[92] Similar draft bills were discussed in other north Caucasian republics.

At the present time, small terrorist groups led by Chechen and Dagestani field commanders such as Arbi Baraev (1973–2001) or the Ahmadov brothers have terrorized the republics of Chechnya, Dagestan, Ingushetiia, and north Ossetia, as well as Krasnodar and Stavropol. They may well be regarded heirs of the *abrek* of the nineteenth—early twentieth centuries, although there are some important differences. Post-socialist bandits are occupied with robbery, the capture of cattle, kidnapping, and terrorist actions against local police and the Russian Federation army. They are usually located in the lowland and most populated areas of the region but escape into mountain valleys of Chechnya, Dagestan, and northeast Georgia. According to my field materials, these bands include mainly unmarried or just married males, twenty to fifty years old. Many of them graduated from Caucasian and Moscow special technical colleges and higher schools. Their chiefs maintain close links with illegal traders of arms and drugs as well as town criminal groups.[93] My field materials collected in 1995–2001 provide evidence of their participation in blood feud and other local violence practices which revived in the post-socialist Caucasus.

Some Final Remarks

I have argued that *abrek* banditry emerged among the Caucasian mountaineers under the impact of Russian conquest and administrative reforms. The analysis of this phenomenon allows us to make some interesting generalizations about the relationship of violence, power, and historiography in the Oriental margins of imperial and socialist Russia. To conclude this work, I'd like to stress some important theoretical and methodological points. First of all, we should rethink the myth of the traditional nature of the *abrek* banditry. Of course it was formed on the basis of such pre-conquest violence practices as the old cult of the warrior (*jigit*), blood feud, and raids of male associations and armed forces headed by highlanders' chieftains. But as a whole it was the result of a complicated interaction between the state, local highland communities, and their military leaders. The history of Caucasian *abrek* can be divided into four main periods: the great Caucasian war of the nineteenth century and the last anti-Russian uprisings; the first Russian Revolution; the Civil War and the early Soviet period; and the post-socialist decade, which includes two Russian-Chechen wars. There is a continuity in forms and strategies of criminal violence between the pre-conquest, colonial, and socialist Caucasus. Guerrilla-type warfare in the countryside hasn't changed much. But the idea of continuity in criminal practices of the Caucasian mountaineers is also problematic. There are many differences between nineteenth- and twentieth-century professional banditry and pre-conquest violence practices. They concern the actors, the location, the ideological and political dimensions of the violence, its global characteristics. The Russian state has failed to eradicate *abrek* banditry by punitive military and administrative measures. *Abrek* banditry reappeared in the times of political instability provoked by the great revolutions and local civil wars from the nineteenth century onward. Moreover, it became a new Caucasian "tradition" reconstructed by anthropologically influenced state reforms. One should take into account the influence of ethnographic concepts on the hybrid mountain societies in the Russian Caucasus.

Translated by Nikolai Ssorin-Chaikov

Notes

1. This study is based mainly on first-hand fieldwork and archival data that I collected among the Muslim highlanders of the eastern Caucasus in the 1990s. I am grateful to the Wenner-Gren, MacArthur, Ford, and Soros Foundations for supporting my field and archival studies on the anthropology of violence in the Caucasus and my work in libraries of the United States from 1992 to 1998 (grants W92/114, ZZ5000/022, 24-History/1996, 1072/1996). These organizations might disagree with conclusions of this chapter. Published sources include materials concerning relationships between banditry and state that are kept in libraries of Makhachkala and Moscow; the Bakhmeteff Archive of the Rare Books and Manuscript Collection of the Butler Library at Columbia University in New York; rare periodicals issued by Russian and Caucasian emigrants in the 1930s–1970s; newspaper interviews with bandits in post-socialist Chechnya and Dagestan.

2. In this formulation of the relationship between state social reforms and its "outside," I draw on Nikolai Ssorin-Chaikov, "Stateless Society, State Collectives, and the State of Nature in Sub-Arctic Siberia: Evenki Hunters and Herders in the Twentieth Century" (Ph.D. dissertation, Stanford University, 1998). Based on Ssorin-Chaikov's description of Siberia, my work suggests parallels with the Russian Caucasus and the case of ethnographically designed reforms to make "wildness."

3. *Adygi, karachaevtsy i balkartsy v izvestiiakh evropeyskikh avtorov XIII–XIX vv.* (Nalchik, 1974), 48.

4. *Dagestan v izvestiiakh russkikh i zapadnoevropeiskikh avtorov XIII–XVIII vv.* (Makhachkala, 1992), 44.

5. Evliya Zelebi, *Kniga puteshestvii* (Moscow, 1979), fasc. 2, 59.

6. Gadzhi-Ali (Hajji-Ali), *Skazanie ochevidtsa o Shamile* (Makhachkala, 1995), 21.

7. S. M. Bronevskii, *Istoricheskie vypiski o snosheniiakh Rossii s Persieiu, Gruzieiu i voobshche s gorskimi narodami, na Kavkaze obitaiushchimi so vremen Ivana Vasil'evicha donyne* (St. Petersburg, 1996), 28.

8. For a detailed description of the colonial discourse of "predatory highlanders" see Bobrovnikov, *Musul'mane Severnogo Kavkaza: obychai, pravo, nasilie* (Moscow, 2002), 16–24.

9. *Dagestan v izvestiiakh,* 5, 49–50; S. M. Bronevskii, *Istoricheskie vypiski,* 112, 116.

10. F. F. Tornau, *Zapiski russkogo ofitsera* (Moscow, 2000). Cf. Khan-Girey, *Zapiski o Cherkessii* (Nalchik, 1976), 299.

11. The Central State Historical Military Archives (hereafter TsGVIA. Moscow), f.VUA (Voenno-Uchetnyi Arkhiv), d. 6438; For materials about the Russian punitive raids in the nineteenth-century Caucasus, see also: The Central State Historical Ar-

chives of the Republic of Georgia (hereafter TsGIA RG Tbilisi), f. 2, op. 1, d. 2540, 103, d. 9173, l. 1; *Akty, sobrannye Kavkazskoi arkheograficheskoi komissiei* (hereafter AKAK. Tiflis, 1880), vol. VI, part 2, 541; A. P. Ermolov, *Pis'ma* (St. Petersburg, 1826); A. M. Elmesov, *Iz istorii russko-kavkazskoi voiny* (Nalchik, 1991), 184.

12. Muhammad-Tahir al-Qarakhi, *Blesk dagestanskikh sabel' v nekotorykh shamilevskikh bitvakh* (Makhachkala, 1990), part II, 12–13, 20–22; P. I. Takhnaeva, *Chokh v blistatel'nuiu epokhu Shamilia* (Makhachkala, 1997), 40–45, 88–92.

13. Quoted from the work by the contemporary Russian historian D. I. Oleinikov, "Shamil'," *Rodina* no. 1/2, 64 (Moscow, 2000); the cited names belong to different Dagestani and Chechen village confederations. Tad-Burti was the Avar name of the Cheberloy village confederation in southern Chechnya.

14. P. K. [Uslar], "Koe-chto o slovesnykh proizvedeniiakh gortsev," *Sbornik svedenii o kavkazskikh gortsakh* (hereafter SSKG. Tiflis, 1868), fasc. I, 4–5.

15. M.-Z. O. Osmanov, *Formy traditsionnogo skotovodstva narodov Dagestana v XIX–nachale XX v.* (Moscow, 1990), 52–60.

16. I. Pantiukhov, "Sovremennye lezginy," *Kavkaz* no. 228 (Tiflis, 1901).

17. E. M. Shilling, "Kubachintsy i ikh kul'tura," *Trudy Instituta etnografii* 8 (Moscow, 1949) 174–175.

18. A. Bagirov, "Miuridizm i Shamil'," *Bol'shevik* 13 (1950), 21–37; N. A. Smirnov, *Reaktsionnaia sushchnost' dvizheniia miuridizma i Shamilia na Kavkaze* (1952); A. V. Fadeev, "O vnutrennei sotsial'noi baze miuridskogo dvizheniia na Kavkaze XIX v.," *Voprosy istorii* no. 6 (1955), 67–77.

19. M. M. Bliev, "Kavkazskaia voina, sotsial'nye istoki, sushchnost'," *Istoriia SSSR* no. 2 (1983); M. M. Bliev, V. Degoev, *Kavkazskaia voina* (Moscow, 1994), 37–109. See also V. B. Vinogradov, *Vmeste k edinoi tseli* (Grozny, 1987), 9.

20. N. I. Pokrovskii, *op. cit.,* 188. See also his doctoral dissertation published almost a half century after his death, N. I. Pokrovskii, *Obzor istochnikov po istorii imamata Shamilia* (Moscow, 1939).

21. V. K. Gardanov, *Obshchestvennyi stroi adygskikh narodov (XVIII–pervaia polovina XIX v.)* (Moscow, 1967), 56.

22. See a fascinating survey of Soviet studies of the ex-socialist Islamic regions in Alan J. Frank, *Muslim Religious Institutions in Imperial Russia: the Islamic World of Novouzdensk District and the Kazakh Inner Horde, 1780–1910* (Leiden-Boston-Cologne, 2001), 5–16.

23. With some variations this argument can be found in the following works: A. Bennigsen, Ch. Lemercier-Quelquejay, *Le soufi et le commissaire. Les confreries musulmanes en URSS* (Paris, 1986); M. Bennigsen Broxup, "Caucasian Muridism in Soviet Historiography," in Jemaleddin of Kazikumukh, *Naqshbandi Treaty* (Oxford, 1986), 5–6, 14; M. Bennigsen Broxup (ed.), *North Caucasus Barrier. The Russian Advance toward the Muslim World* (London, 1992), 112–117. Cf. M. Gammer, *Muslim Resistance to the Tsar: Shamil and the Conquest of Chechnia and Daghestan* (London, 1994), 250–252.

24. For example see M. A. Aglarov, *Sel'skaia obshchina v Nagornom Dagestane v XVII–nachale XIX v.* (Moscow, 1988), 18–21, 141, 143.

25. My position in this regard has been much influenced by Paul W. Werth, "From

'Pagan' Muslims to 'Baptized' Communists: Religious Conversion and Ethnic Particularity in Russia's Eastern Provinces," *Comparative Study of Society and History* 42, no. 3 (2000), 497–523.

26. F. I. Leontovich, *Adaty kavkazskikh gortsev* issue I (Odessa, 1882), 360.

27. V. I. Abaev, *Istoriko-etimologicheskii slovar' osetinskogo iazyka* (Moscow–Leningrad, 1958), vol. I, 25–26. See also: A. K. Shagirov, *Etimologicheskii slovar' adygeiskogo (cherkesskogo) iazyka* (Mosow, 1977), vol. 1, 56.

28. *Etimologicheskii slovar' russkogo iazyka* (Mosow, 1963), vol. I, pt. 1 (A), 17.

29. Yu. D. Anchabadze, "'Ostrakizm' na Kavkaze," *Sovetskaia etnografiia* no. 5, (Moscow, 1979), 137; M. A. Aglarov, *op. cit.,* 101–104. A great number of records of customary law norms in Arabic treating the position of *aparag*s in the highland Muslim society have come down to us in private, mosque, and state archives. See for example, the document from the Avar village of 'Urada in the Collection of Manuscripts of the Institute of History, Archaeology and Ethnography (hereafter RF IIAE. Makhachkala), f. 5, op. 1, d. 57, 3.

30. V. Kh. Kazharov, *Traditsionnye obshchestvennye instituty kabardintsev i ikh krizis v kontse XVIII–pervoi polovine XIX v.* (Nalchik, 1994), 337–338. See also similar use of these terms in archival files from the Caucasus kept in the Archives of the Foreign Affairs of Russia (hereafter AVPR. Moscow), f. 115 (Kabardian affairs), op. 1 (dated 1754), d. 6, l. 218.

31. "Dnevnik polkovnika Runovskogo, sostoiavshego pristavom pri Shamile vo vremia ego prebyvaniia v Kaluge," AKAK (Tiflis, 1904), vol. XII, 1422–1423.

32. V. Kh. Kazharov, *op. cit.,* 337.

33. F. G. Toll, *Nastol'nyi slovar' dlia spravok po vsem otrasliam znaniia (spravochnyi entsiklopedicheskii leksikon)* (St. Petersburg, 1863), vol. I, 9.

34. V. Dal', *Tolkovyi slovar'* (St. Petersburg, 2nd ed., 1880), vol. I, 2; see also the article "Abrek" in F. A. Brokgaus and I. A. Efron (eds.), *Entsiklopedicheskii slovar'* (St. Petersburg, 1891), vol. I, 41.

35. For example, see the contemporary social vocabulary of Dagestani languages in M. S. Saidov, *Avarsko-russkii slovar'* (Makhachkala, 1967), 524; N. S. Dzhidalaev, *Russko-lakskii slovar'* (Makhachkala, 1994), 20; M. Sh. Khalilov, *Bezhtinsko-russkii slovar'* (Makhachkala, 1995), 153; P. T. Magomedova, R. Sh. Khalilova, *Karatinsko-russkii slovar'* (St. Petersburg–Makhachkala, 2001), 178.

36. [B. N.] Polozov, *V debriakh Zakavkaz'ia,* Bakhmeteff Archive of the Collection of Manuscripts and Rare Books of the Library of the Columbian University (hereafter BAR. New York), 1–2.

37. 'Abrek', in S. I. Ozhegov, *Slovar' russkogo iazyka* (Moscow, 4th ed., 1960).

38. 'Abrek', in *Bol'shaia sovetskaia entsiklopediia* (Moscow, 1st ed., 1926), vol. 1, 83.

39. K. (Dz.) Gatuev, *Zelimkhan* (Rostov-on-Don–Krasnodar, 1926); M. A. Mamakaev, *Zelimkhan* (Grozny, 1990).

40. Ch. Amirejibi, *Data Tutashkhia* (Moscow, 1990).

41. R. Hamzatov (Gamzatov), *T'asa rishcharal asaral k'uchdul* [Selected poetry, in Avar] (Makhachkala, 1970), vol. 1, 3; F. Iskander, *Stoianka cheloveka* (Moscow, 1991).

42. See M. G. Gadzhiev, O. M. Davudov, A. R. Shikhsaidov, *Istoriia Dagestana s drevneishikh vremen do kontsa XV v.* (Makhachkala, 1996), 322, 324.

43. For a detailed ethnographic description of the male youth associations in the pre-Russian Caucasus see Iu. Iu. Karpov, *Jigit i volk. Muzhskie soiuzy v sotsiokul'turnoi traditsii gortsev Kavkaza* (St. Petersburg, 1996).

44. See I. M. Shamanov, "Skotovodstvo i obshchestvennyi byt karachaevtsev v XIX–nachale XX v.," in *Kavkazskii etnograficheskii sbornik* issue 5 (Moscow, 1972), 86–87; S. Kh. Mafedzef, *Obriady i obriadovye igry adygov v XIX–nachale XX v.* (Nalchik, 1979), 37–52.

45. AVPR, f. 115. *Kabardinskie dela,* op. 1, d. 6, ll. 243, 246 rev., 248 rev., 251; *Kabardino-russkie otnosheniia XVI–XVIII vv. Dokumenty i materialy* (Moscow, 1957), vol. 2, 263, 274.

46. N. Berzenov, "Iz vospominanii ob Ossetii," *Kavkaz* no. 92 (Tiflis, 1851).

47. L. B. Panek, "Materialy po etnografii rutul'tsev," RF IIAE, f. 3, op. 36, d. 2, 59.

48. Kh. Steven, "Zhurnal puteshestviia po zemle Voiska Donskikh kazakov, k Kavkazu i v Astrakhan'," *Severnyi arkhiv* t. 12, no. 24 (St. Petersburg, 1824), 260.

49. Iu. Iu. Karpov, *op. cit.,* 132.

50. A. V. Komarov, "Adaty i sudoproizvodstvo po nim," SSKG (Tiflis, 1868), fasc. I, 43–49.

51. L. Ia. Lulie, "Uchrezhdeniia i narodnye obychai shapsugov i natukhaitsev," in L. Ia. Lulie, *Cherkesiia* (St. Petersburg 1859), 40.

52. S. A. Luguev, D. M. Magomedov, *Bezhintsy v XIX–nachale XX v.* (Makhachkala, 1994), 144.

53. V. K. Gardanov, *op. cit.,* 233.

54. V. Kh. Kazharov, *op. cit.,* 406.

55. *Adygi, balkartsy i karachaevtsy,* 516.

56. Cited from above-mentioned the work by F. I. Leontovich, *op. cit.,* issue I, 125.

57. See examples of hospitality norms from the seventeenth and eighteenth century 'adat records in V. Kh. Kazharov, *op. cit.,* 321.

58. RF IIAE, f. 16, op. 1, d. 1260–1310. On *ishkil* in the pre-colonial northern Caucasus see Bobrovnikov, *Musul'mane Severnogo Kavkaza,* ch. 3.

59. A. A. Ahlakov, *Geroiko-istoricheskie pesni avartsev* (Makhachkala, 1968), 49–59, 181–202.

60. *Pesni gortsev* (Makhachkala, 1990), 22–26, 209–216.

61. P. K. [Uslar], "Koe-chto o slovesnykh proizvedeniiakh gortsev," pp. 39–41.

62. On the 'siege policy' see M. Gammer, *op. cit.,* 45–49.

63. V. Kh. Kazharov, *op. cit.,* 182, 189.

64. A. G. Bulatova, *Traditsionnye prazdniki i obriady narodov Nagornogo Dagestana v XIX–XX vekakh* (Leningrad, 1988), 115.

65. P. G. Butkov, *Materialy dlia novoi istorii Kavkaza s 1722 po 1803 g.,* ed. L. Brosse (St. Petersburg, 1869), pt. 2, 263–265, 267.

66. "Resolution No. 2288 issued by the chairman of the Dagestani People's Court on September 1911," in Central State Archives of the Republic of Dagestan (hereafter TsGA RD. Makhachkala), f. 21, d. 7, l. 18.

67. Quoted from F. I. Leontovich, *op. cit.,* issue I, 261.

68. The Central State Archives of the Kabardino-Balkar Republic (hereafter TsGA KBR. Nalchik), f. 23, op. 1, d. 48, vol. 1, ll. 11, 11 rev.

69. V. Kh. Kazharov, *op. cit.*, 338.

70. For more details see M. Gammer, *op. cit.*, 251.

71. See for example the relevant case of Jambulat Nemirov discussed in the monograph by V. K. Gardanov, *op. cit.*, 300–301.

72. TsGA KBR, f. 23, op. 1, d. 48, vol. 2, 52.

73. [B. N.] Polozov, *V debriakh Zakavkaz'ia*, 5–6; V. Kh. Kazharov, *op. cit.*, 421; Bobrovnikov, "Obychnoe pravo v poreformennom Dagestane (1860–1917)," in R. I. Seferbekov, ed., *Nauka i molodezh'* issue 1 (Makhachkala, 1997), 26.

74. TsGA KBR, f. 23, op. 1, d. 48, vol. 2, 59. See also: E. M. Shilling, *Malye narody Dagestana* (Moscow, 1993), 104.

75. A. S. Pushkin, "*Puteshestvie v Arzrum vo vremia pokhoda 1829 goda*," in A. S. Pushkin, *Polnoe sobranie sochinenii v 10-ti tomakh* (Moscow, 1964), vol. VI, 647.

76. T. M. Aytberov, Kh. A. Omarov, Iu. U. Dadaev, eds., *Vosstaniia dagestantsev i chechentsev v posleshamilevskuiu epokhu i imamat 1877 goda* (Makhachkala, 2001), 49–64; A. Kh. Ramazanov, "Bor'ba dagestanskikh narodov protiv kolonializma v posleimamatskii period," in R. I. Seferbekov, ed., *Nauka i molodezh'* issue 1 (Makhachkala, 1997), 58, 62.

77. S. K. Bushuev, *Bor'ba gortsev za nezavisimost' pod rukovodstvom Shamilia* (Moscow–Leningrad, 1939), 62.

78. K. Gatuev, *op. cit.*, 15.

79. For a more detailed account of the first bandits (*abreks*) in the northern Caucasus see my article "Abreki i gosudarstvo: kul'tura nasiliia na Kavkaze," *Acta Eurasica* no. 1, (Moscow, 2000), 38–40.

80. T. M. Aytberov, Kh. A. Omarov, Iu. U. Dadaev, eds., *Vosstaniia dagestantsev i chechentsev*, 41–43, 66–68.

81. See for example TsGVIA, f. 400, d. 31, 3; *Checheqler: Qumuq literaturany almanakhy* (in Kumyk), (Makhachkala, 1939), 279–280.

82. [B. N.] Polozov, *1905 i 1906 gody v Zakavkaz'e*, in BAR, 1.

83. K. Gatuev, *op. cit.*, 99–105; S. K. Berdiaev, *Chechnia i razboinik Zelimkhan* (Paris, 1930).

84. TsGA RD, f. 2, op. 4, d. 5, 2–4, 5. See also V. Kozachkovsky, *Razboi na Kavkaze* (Vladikavkaz, 1913), 79.

85. K. Gatuev, *op. cit.*, 124; S. K. Berdiaev, *Razboi na Severnom Kavkaze* (Paris, 1936), 5–16.

86. K. R. Karaev, *Vospominaniia* (Makhachkala, 1968), 23, 36.

87. TsGA RD, f. r-268, op. 1, d. 5; *Krasnyi zemlerob*, 1.04.1925.

88. TsGA RD, f. r-1, op. 3, d. 149; K. R. Karaev, *op. cit.*, 74.

89. A. D. Daniialov, *Vospominaniia* (Makhachkala, 1992), 68; cf. S. K. Berdiaev, *Razboi na Severnom Kavkaze*, 25.

90. TsGA RD, f. 2, op. 4, d. 5, 2–4, 5.

91. See for more details in my article: "Sovetskaia natsional'naia politika i izmenenie identichnosti gortsev severo-zapadnogo Dagestana," in A. V. Malashenko, M. B. Olcott, eds., *Faktor etnonatsional'noi samobytnosti v postsovetskom obshchestve* (Moscow, 1998), 125–126.

92. *Dagestanskaia pravda* (Makhachkala), 24.09.1999.

93. These data are based mostly on my first hand field materials collected in highland Dagestan in 1992–1997 and partly published in my article "Abreki i gosudarstvo,'" 19–46. Data of regional Caucasian mass media were also used. See, for instance, *Novoe delo* (Makhachkala), Feb. 7, 1997; Feb. 21, 1997.

10 Representing "Primitive Communists": Ethnographic and Political Authority in Early Soviet Siberia

Nikolai Ssorin-Chaikov

Let me begin with a photograph (Figure 10.1) taken in 1926 on the banks of the Podkamennaia Tunguska, a northern tributary of the Yenisei River basin. The photograph, taken by ethnographer and reformer Innokentii Suslov, bears the following caption: "All participants of the communal meeting [*suglan*] perform the Evenki national dance, *iokhor'io.*" In the 1970s, Suslov donated this photograph, together with some other field materials, to the museum in Tura, the administrative center of the Evenki Autonomous District. From Suslov's commentaries to the photo, which are also in the museum archives, we learn that the "circle dance" was performed on the occasion of communal meetings of nomadic "clans" of Evenki hunters and reindeer herders, when several tents were pitched together in a larger camp for a communal meeting. He concluded his comments, however, by pointing out that the photo of the dance was not "ethnographically correct":

> On the Baikit shot, the ethnographic veracity of the *iokhor* or *osukhai* (in the Yakut language) is somewhat distorted: the tarpaulin tent is not removed, and the figure of M. I. Osharov is in the center of the circle dance. [Osharov] . . . began the *iokhor,* and could not hear my request to leave the center and join the circle. I was calling him from atop a birch tree, from where I took this unique shot. Because of this, Comrade Grishikhin, the photographer of the Museum of Ethnography of the Peoples of the USSR [in Leningrad], at my request, removed from the negative both the tarpaulin tent and the figure of Osharov. The negative thus was made *ethnographically correct.* [. . .] I took this shot

Figure 10.1. Participants in a communal meeting perform
the Evenki national dance.
Reproduced courtesy of the Kraievedcheskii musei Evenkiiskogo avtonomnogo
okruga [Regional Museum of the Evenki Autonomous District].

from atop a tall birch tree, where I was hidden in the branches. June
1926. Baikit (emphasis added).[1]

The photo and commentaries reveal the fabric and the fabrication of
the Soviet ethnographic canon. What makes this event not sufficiently
"ethnographic" for Suslov are the signs of "modern" life: the tarpaulin tent
does not fit the image of "authentic" Evenki traditions. The most important target of Suslov's editing, however, are the signs of the staging of this
event. Once the photograph is edited and Osharov is removed from the
center of the dancing circle, we see Suslov secretly observing a supposedly
spontaneous social gathering.

This photograph reveals the construction of ethnographic fact "in its
fabricated originality," to use the words of Michael Ames.[2] Not only ethnographic representations were staged on the banks of the Podkamennaia
Tunguska in the 1920s and early 1930s. When Suslov rafted down the Podkamennaia Tunguska in 1926, the dual purpose of his trip was both to

collect ethnographic data and to organize the new Soviet state institutions in this area. Suslov chaired the provincial branch of the Soviet State Committee for the Assistance to the Peoples of the Northern Borderlands (hereafter referred to as the Committee for the North), which between 1924 and 1935 administered the integration of Siberian aborigines into Soviet society. He participated in drafting the key document of this Committee, the Provisional Statute of Administration over Native Peoples and Tribes of the Northern Borderlands (1926). The goal of his trip was to set up local soviets among the Evenki of the Podkamennaia Tunguska in accordance with this statute.

The mid-1920s represent a peculiar historical moment when political and ethnographic representations collided in the cultural construction of their designated object—the "primitive-communist" social(ist) organization, which, according to the Provisional Statute of 1926, should have been both socialist and "ethnographically correct." These social projects were to follow indigenous social organization "organically" in terms of "locality" and "genealogical" differences, despite the fact that Suslov and other reformers knew very well that Siberian indigenous societies in the early twentieth century did not exist in their "pure" primitive communist form. Just as a random photo of the Evenki traditional practices revealed the Russian presence, indigenous clans and local communities were said to exhibit the presence of the tsarist colonial system. The organization of the clan soviets followed, as I show below, the logic of making "ethnographically correct" photographs—it was to proceed by clearing up the picture from "contaminating" elements of the old tsarist regime.

My goal in this chapter is to explore the micro-politics of this vision. I read the state reforms of the 1920s and early 1930s as a location for the Soviet ethnographic imagination, and, vice versa, early Soviet anthropology as a site of state reforms in the indigenous North. I look, first, at the making of facts in the materials from Suslov's trips to the Podkamennaia Tunguska River; then, at the broader ethnographic and policy debates that drew on materials such as these; and, finally, at regimes of micro-politics that were socially produced through these practices of knowledge.

Two points underscore the narrative that I present below.

First, I would like to historicize the notion of "clan-based community," which gained considerable currency in post-Soviet Siberian indigenous politics. In the 1990s, "clan-based community" emerged as an ubiquitous and controversial institution that coexists with and, in parts of Northern Siberia, replaces state collective farms. In late- and post-Soviet literature and legislation, the indigenous "clan-based community" was conceived as an institution that would provide a viable economic alternative to the nearly bankrupt state collectives, an "organic" alternative to the "imposed" collective farm order. The purpose of this chapter vis-à-vis these debates is to deconstruct the opposition between "imposed" and "organic" policies and institutions. Current ethnographic literature in Russia tends to romanticize the policies of the Committee for the North as collectivization's more humane yet not completely realized alternative, genuinely (at least, in intent) "accounting for" (*uchityvaia*) differences between indigenous societies and the emerging Soviet social order.[3]

In this chapter, I demonstrate that, if anything, organic institutions of the 1920s were as "staged" and "imposed from above" as the collective farms that followed. Furthermore, I argue that power technologies employed in the cultural production of both reveal a continuity rather than a break. Both depended on an ethnographic understanding of what indigenous social structures "really" implied, and both expanded, therefore, through social science discourses. I will not focus here on collectivization, yet, as I argue elsewhere, both the "organic" institutions of the 1920s and, later, the collective farms sought to establish a form of government that constitutes analytically and politically autonomous indigenous collectives and voices through practices of surveillance and reporting.[4]

My second goal is to examine the operation of the category of the "real" in these research and reform practices. The problem with "ethnographically correct" facts is not merely that they are "incorrect," or that policies based on these facts do not, as they claim, "account for" real cultural forms. The real problem is, rather, the regime of social relations that operates with, and within, these notions of "correctness" and "accounting for" reality. I argue that without examining this operation, a mere deconstruction of "ethnographically correct" facts simply reproduces the opposition between "imposed" and "organic."

Early Soviet indigenous reforms articulated several meanings of the real that I will chart here. First of all, the "real" stands for "ethnographically correct" facts, that is, what, in the view of Suslov and other ethnographers and reformers, indigenous societies "really" are. In these discussions, the "real" also refers, however, to the deep underlying structure—"the real socio-economic foundations," as in Marxist discourse. In this sense, the "real" is invisible, since it is posited in opposition to the "overt" form or "appearance" of social relationships. Finally, particularly in the terms of the Committee for the North and scholars who were associated with the

Committee, the "real" invokes "natural," as in "natural selection." As one of the members of the Committee for the North put this,

> The [Siberian] peoples have accumulated thousands of years of experience . . . this is the practice [*byt*] that was formed through long-term natural selection . . . In this case we have the *organic approach*, really grounded in life experience. We take what was formed by *natural selection*, by the very way of life [*putem zhizni*], by experiments that took place over thousands of years, which we do not destroy but out of which we *breed the basis for the future* of the Northern borderlands (emphasis added).[5]

My focus in this chapter is on the relationships between these meanings of the "real" in ethnographic and policy debates over a very short period of time, namely from 1925 to 1928. I argue that these meanings articulate Russian/Soviet macro-narratives of power. The politics of representation of the mid-1920s are an episode in the long-term transformation of forms and meaning of statehood in northern Siberia from tributary frameworks to ones based on ideologies of social science. During the tsarist period, Tungus identities within the Russian empire were formed by tributary formulas that marked them as "aliens" in contrast, for example, with Siberian peasants who paid regular tax (*obrok*). The term "tribute" (*iasak*), with its old Turkic roots, evoked an older Mongolian vocabulary of power in which "tribute" distinguished conquered "others" from the tax-paying "us," but also signified "law" and "state" (cf. the term for Chingis-Khan's empire, and for its legal code, *Iasa*, which comes from the same root as the word *iasak*[6]). After Speranskii's reforms of the 1820s, and, more fully, under the Soviet system, this connotation also acquired a new meaning of "law" as "science," which glossed over the older usage of "law" as "tribute." From the early nineteenth-century reformers who sought to ground indigenous administration in "history, ethnography, and climatology"[7] to Soviet discourses on "primitive" and "scientific" socialism, Siberian governance expanded as the management of a "natural history" that constructed the Siberian peoples as its "savage slot."[8]

Yet the micro-historical reading of one of the episodes of this transformation allows us to see what a broader perspective obscures. I shall argue that, while the meanings of the "real" articulate the meanings of state order as "science," they do not operate as closed discursive formations or points of view. The textual and political elaboration of these meanings did not purify them, but on the contrary, revealed others. In the 1920s and early 1930s, the "organic" and orthodox Marxist approaches to socialism and indigenous social organization traded places several times. The administrative and ethnographic elaborations of these points of view did not take the form of a developmental sequence from "primitive" to "scientific" socialism, as later Soviet historiography would have us believe.[9] Rather, this elaboration accumulated the asystematic ("rhizomic"[10]) totality of an archive, much like, for example, the *Complete Essays by Marx and Engels,* where for each canonic text there is always a draft of that same text or a letter that negates it. Therefore, to the extent that these visions can be systematized as "points of view," they form points of their own discursive displacement.

Technologies of Vision

In conducting Sovietization meetings, initiating agents removed themselves from the close-up shot in a fashion similar to that by which the ethnographers were deleted from ethnographic pictures. What was made "real" by this act of removal? Suslov's report on the Podkamennaia Tunguska meetings starts with him at the center of the events: "The delegates of the Tungus *suglan* sat down in a circle in a forest glade. The head of the Committee for the North [Suslov] sat in the middle of the circle, read the statute, explained it point by point, and opened the discussion." Note how the circle stands for the communal meeting and for the community itself, and particularly for the new, socialist ways of governance: "After 300 years the natives were asked for the first time how they wanted to be governed!"[11] The meeting concluded with a round dance, similar to the one that Suslov photographed. In this report, however, the dance manifests not the Evenki "old ways" but a new collectivity. It affirms the reality of the newly established "clan soviet," as Suslov observes from outside of the circle of the dance how the Evenki take turns singing:

> It was Shaman Barkaul's turn to sing. His art of singing is known widely. . . .
> All listen carefully to his voice. And "the Big Russian master" [*Bol'shoi russkii nachal'nik*], having just now conducted the first [Soviet] *suglan* on the Chunia [tributary of the Podkamennaia Tunguska], gladly hears words of the shaman who is well respected in the area [*vo vsei okruge*]—the evaluation of all decisions of the *suglan*. This evaluation is very favorable . . .

And Suslov wrote in his field diary: "Barkaul told in his song all that had happened at the meeting. Oh, if only we had a phonograph! How many truthful, healthy, sincere opinions we hear about the measures that we are taking among the natives [*tuzemtsev*]." [12]

A report used in this publication was authored by Suslov. Suslov also took the minutes of the meetings, recording the indigenous voices in writing: "We . . . the Tungus, illiterate but deeply feeling, deeply honor the Soviet power" and "all as one offer up our gratitude . . . for the help provided to us." [13] From these minutes, however, we cannot understand exactly where Suslov was at the meeting, and what role he played. He did not chair the meeting; in the minutes he lists local Evenki activists as assuming this role. In one of his later publications, Suslov mentions that he was elected to the presidium of the meeting at the suggestion of one of the Evenki elders. [14] But in the minutes themselves we find that he was "simply" one of the speakers who just "joined the circle," to use the language of the commentary to the "circle dance" photograph.

If Suslov himself is *not visible* in these notes, he makes sure that readers *see* that the new soviets are based on "genealogical clans." His diary specifies that "Pankagir, Kurkagir, and Chemdal clans," whose members came out to form the Chunia Clan Soviet, "are not administrative units but blood-related clans, whose Tungus founders were Chemdal, Kurga, and Panka," and that these clans are local to the Podkamennaia Tunguska area: they "live in concord, marrying their daughters to one other." We learn that, in the past, all three were registered together to pay fur tribute in Kezhma, a Russian village on the Angara River, and therefore constituted a single "Kezhma county." The Pankagir clan joined them relatively recently, however, having migrated from the Nizhniaia Tunguska River. This signaled "real" ("ethnographic") differences between them, and the Pankagirs were to form the soviet separately from the other two clans. [15]

As in the case of the photo, however, this vision of indigenous social organization did not present itself easily. Evenki "genealogical clans" had long been integrated into Russian administrative ones, and clan ideology was controlled by the local elite—rich reindeer herders and former "princes," who were appointed before the Revolution to govern administrative clans and collect fur tribute.

It is interesting to note that in Soviet writing the solution to this problem also comes from the members of the indigenous communities themselves. In an historical novel that describes the early Soviet reforms among

Evenki of the Podkamennaia Tunguska, an old Evenki man, Girmancha, took the floor at one such meeting and spoke of how the new "elementary cooperation" would, in fact, be in harmony with the old Evenki traditions. He first criticizes the uses of the clan in socio-economic domination: "The strength of the rich is in the poverty of the herders. Where would one go if the prince promises reindeer in exchange for labor? . . . The rich princes yell: 'We are all kinsmen. We have *gnimat*, the law of clan mutual aid' . . . [but] pastures are in their 'clan ownership.' The princes are not stupid: if there is joint herding—they would have fewer herders. They want small herds by the poor households." Then he reminds the audience of the "old ways": "Long ago, however, there was a good custom—joint herding. Have you forgotten? Yes, the young don't remember . . . " Finally, Girmancha asks the assembly if the "new laws don't return us to the old custom of joint herding."[16] In doing so, he leads those at the meeting to "clean" these traditions from the overt layer of recent colonial and capitalist appropriations, to recover the "old ways" in their pure, yet socialist, form.

The "Real" as the Form: Siberian Social Organization in Early Soviet Scholarship

The recipe for this social technology was made available to early Soviet reformers in 1924 when the Moscow journal *Arkhiv Marksa i Engelsa* published an 1881 letter that Marx wrote to the Russian peasant socialist Vera Zasulich. The Russian peasant commune, Marx argued in this letter, is not an obstacle for socialist development but "a fulcrum of social revival in Russia." The socio-economic crisis of capitalism that "must end with its elimination" will also be "a return of modern societies to the 'archaic' type of communal property, or, to quote an American writer [Lewis Henry Morgan] . . . 'the new system' towards which modern society is tending 'will be a revival in a superior form' of an archaic type of society."[17] In order for such a commune to serve as a fulcrum for Russia's social revival, Marx goes on to say, it "should be, first, cleansed of the pernicious influences to which it is exposed from all sides and, then, provided with normal conditions of free development."[18]

While this passage bears a striking similarity to the technology of vision that Suslov deployed in his 1926 trip, the connection between the two is not obvious. The Committee for the North did not use Marx's letter to Zasulich in their discussions of socialism among Siberian hunter-gatherers and reindeer herders. This passage does not appear in ethnographic publications until the mid-1930s.[19] If anything, ethnography of the 1920s made often very insightful uses of the more mainstream Marxist methodology: the critique of the *form* of clan organization as a colonial product. From within, it was seen as analogous to the operation of the commodity form: mutual help and sharing within clan-based communities was theorized as masking class-like social inequalities in these communities. From without, clan organization was seen as analogous to the operation of "circle binding" (*krugovaia poruka*) among the peasantry, which created collective responsibility before the state or landlord.

For example, the ethnographer and head of the Novonikolaevsk branch of the Committee for the North, Lidiia Dobrova-Iadrintseva, argued that the clan was an administrative construct created for the purposes of taxation; moreover, an administrative unit that was "newly created yet *resembling* the relationship of blood relatives" (emphasis added).[20] The Krasnoiarsk scholar Dmitri Lappo emphasized the importance of Speranskii's Statute of Alien Administration (1822) in this social construction. The Tungus and other indigenous people in the early twentieth century, he argued, accepted the "rules of the Statute [of 1822] . . . as their national [common] law, although such institutions as the native headquarters [*inorodcheskaia uprava*] and the communal meeting of clansmen were created in accordance with the rural administration of the peasants." In the course of the nineteenth century these norms remained practically intact (unlike the peasant legislation), so that "attempts on behalf of the government to reform the indigenous administration [in the late 1800s] met with resistance on the indigenous side; the natives saw every attempt of change or reform as a threat to their nationality, . . . placing them on the same footing as the peasantry" and, ultimately, "Russianization."[21] Drawing on his earlier work in south Siberia, he even suggested that underlying the administrative and legal regime of Speranskii's statute, a historically informed ethnographer could discern not some kind of organic community but the legal code of a *defeated* empire. "Indigenous groups accepted the older codes of various states, to which they abided before the Russians came, as their common law," submitted Lappo: "underneath" the 1822 Statute was the 1640 Steppe Code of the Oirat Mongols, with Chingis-Khan's *Iasa* further "underneath" the Steppe Code.[22]

This is an early example of an approach that emphasized state and colonial construction of indigenous communities and identities, and it easily incorporated the Marxist vision of inequalities on the capitalist periphery. For Lappo, kinship connections between members of a given unit were "fictitious": *kniaz'* (prince), is "the governor of a clan," and he "is accepted [by the clan] as an elder, as if this clan were a single family; whereas . . . state officials transferred indigenous families from one clan to another by issuing certificates of resignation and reinstatement . . . "[23] Yet for Lappo and other Siberianists, this "administrative clan" also worked as a "trading post in miniature,"[24] in which local kinship identities and loyalties masked social inequalities that were the products of the colonial fur trade.

Due to the distance between hunting grounds and trading posts, hunters without reindeer acquired hunting equipment and supplies not from Russian traders but from a "clansman who is wealthier in reindeer, to whom the hunter has to trade his furs, often for a symbolic price, and to whom, because of this, he becomes increasingly indebted."[25] Furthermore, "for the purposes of avoiding competition with the Russian traders, the Tungus hunters who are quite influential among their clansmen, take measures to prevent an ordinary hunter from coming out to the trading post."[26] These authors observe a social encapsulation of the fur-hunting periphery within this fur-trade economy. Thus, the social structure within local groups replicated patterns of class relations between the forest and the trading post: the indigenous population "gravitated" economically to trading bases just as, within the local communities, hunters and small-scale herders formed a social periphery of rich reindeer holdings. These relationships *appear* as "a single web of these [kinship and marriage] connections." But reindeer and products are "leased" to poorer herders and hunters in exchange for labor and fur. It *appears* that "the large-scale reindeer holding is . . . supported by *rodniki*, 'relatives.' "[27] Social relationships within clan-based communities appeared as a non-monetary political economy that existed within larger market relations, which ethnographers and reformers describe in terms of "credit" and "debt," despite the non-monetary meanings of these transactions.[28] Yet in these analyses, the logic and vocabulary of monetary transactions were present not as such, but as an *analogy* between structures within local communities and the relationships between these communities and Russian traders and tax officers. These relationships "resemble" serfdom where "the serf doesn't receive payment [wages] from the landowner, but, on the contrary, the landowner receives tribute from the serf." In reindeer-herding communities, this tribute is paid in labor "to maintain and expand the [rich herd's] livestock."[29]

From this point of view, the round dance of the Evenki, recorded by Suslov, and the argument of the elder Girmancha about "joint herding" manifest not the cleansing from the commune "of the pernicious influences" of capitalism, as Marx put it in his letter to Zasulich, but also a recovery, in the spirit of *Capital,* of the implicit "social relations between people," which underscore the overt, "fetishized" forms of clan organization as administrative units and "trading posts in miniature." The categories of the Polar Census of 1926 followed the Marxist language of social differentiation in the village: it classified northern hunters and herders into "poor," "middle" and "rich" groups (*bedniaki, sredniaki,* and *kulaki*). The "Resolution on Class Stratification in the Yenisei North," adopted by the Krasnoiarsk branch of the Committee for the North in 1927,[30] singled out reindeer herding as the material base for social inequality in indigenous communities. In this context, the narratives of Suslov and others represent the ethnographic equivalent of socialist realism, as they follow the idiom of socialist construction that *made* visible and real the implicit forms of socialized labor, which existed hitherto as underlying structural principles rather than overt social forms. Yet, as I will demonstrate, it is this point of explication that introduced a rupture in this ethnographic socialist realism, and a displacement of these underlying structural principles into "nature."

The "Real" of Underlying Structure

What I call rupture in this ethnographic socialist realism relates to a contradiction in these constructivist approaches. Dobrova-Iadrintseva and Lappo posited economic cooperation in indigenous communities as following a different logic than the one fetishized in administrative form and trade exchange. In contrast to her constructivist vision of "administrative clans," Dobrova-Iadrintseva argued, for example, that the clan had "features of a mere overt . . . legislated . . . unit only at the beginning." But "over a long period of time and due to the bond that naturally developed [*estestvenno slozhivsheisia spaiki*], based on tradition, on the foundations of economic character, and on the practices of everyday life," this unit became "a newly established form of clan community" (*zanovo slozhivsheisia formoi rodovoi upravy*).[31] In turn, Lappo distinguished the administrative clan as a "legislated norm," sanctioned by the tsarist regime to forge and, at the same time, to mask social inequalities, as well as "a form of autonomous foraging [*promyslovyi*] communism of tribes associated on a particular territory." The overt "legislated" norm is opposed in Lappo's text to "the unwritten rules" that underscore a "practical," "social-juridical form" of indigenous communities, and it is the latter that was to be uncovered by "the solid revolutionary legality."[32]

I argue that this rupture constitutes a site of displacement of the constructivist approach onto an evolutionary one that undoes the constructivist vision as it is elaborated using this rupture as a starting point. Let us turn now to the 1925 conference of the Committee for the North, which discussed working drafts of the Provisional Statute of Administration over Native Peoples and Tribes of the Northern Borderlands. Drawing on the experience of Sovietization in the lower parts of the Yenisei River basin (the Turukhansk District), Lappo proposed to create local soviets among the indigenous population, precisely where this "practical" foraging communism could be found—in *tundras*, the territorially bound groups. *Tundras* were to form soviets "according to the locality of their migration routes, mutual economic relations and uniformity of language."[33] The chief criterion in identifying such a local group was the fact of "economic gravitation" of the indigenous population to the trading posts where they used to come for trade and tribute payment. Such posts were to become offices of these soviets and, later, centers of settlement and "cultural development" of nomadic groups. We can see these points of economic gravitation and the related *tundras* on the map that he enclosed with his proposal.

Lappo saw the *tundras* as spatial units of his "autonomous foraging communism of tribes associated on a particular territory." Although this draft was submitted by the Krasnoiarsk branch of the Committee, it was the chair of this branch, Suslov, who found fault with this territorial criterion. From his point of view, the main fault of this proposal was that it drew on the "old divisions of [administrative] 'clans' and 'headquarters,'" which were tied to the centers of political and economic gravitation and the south-bound trade routes. To accept this plan would legitimize in the new political conditions the power of the "old clan organization," that is, the old administrative forms in which personality was subordinated to the authority of "elders as well as local bosses, such as the former princes" and where "clans' headmen or princes assumed the authority of the father, with the right to call one to court in the light of the tribe's customs." To create local soviets on the basis of economic gravitation was to take "a princely [*kniaz*'] measure, because it is the same as the old prince."[34]

In order to isolate "purely ethnographic" borders, Suslov distinguished the "genealogical clan," that is, "an overgrown extended family," from the "artificial" clan, that is, "a conglomerate of cults and pieces of different clans, brought together by some overt circumstance," such as tsarist taxation. Armed with his ethnographic facts, Suslov commented on the names of the Tungus clans that are mentioned by Lappo: "Such names as 'Miroshko' or 'Liutok' are arbitrary nicknames, like 'Chingo' (this was a nickname of an old man from the Chapagir clan)." These arbitrary nicknames should be omitted from the list of genealogical clans which are to serve as a basis for local Soviets.[35]

Lappo and Tugarinov responded that "ethnic principles cannot be applied" to the local administrative organization, "because clans of different peoples wander and hunt in the same areas."[36] Dobrova-Iadrintseva made a similar point. The indigenous peoples of the Turukhansk district, she wrote, never "divided their lands between clans." In the course of annual migrations, "indigenous tribes do not take borders into consideration," their migration routes "come together, run parallel, diverge, cross" and so on.[37] She contended that to draw lines between clans and tribes was "in some cases absolutely impossible, in others—quite difficult but, most importantly, this does not serve any practical purpose."[38]

Despite this criticism, the Committee considered "the *tundra* organization of the clan soviets impossible in the conditions of existing social differentiation of various natives of the Province" and supported "further organization of the clan soviets on tribal principles."[39] In the end, the Committee backed another proposal, submitted by the Tomsk branch and authored by D. T. Ianovich.[40] In both Suslov's critique and this proposal, the political isolation of indigenous social organization meant recovering "genealogical clans" from deconstructed "administrative" ones. For these scholars, ideology apparently ended where genealogy started, with the latter built around the social and territorial "atom" of clan organization— the extended family. According to the organizational scheme advanced for the local Soviets, organic social units of the northern areas of the Ob River—genealogical clans of Nentsy and local bands (*vatagi*) of Khanty— are clearly viewed as "the prime order" of the Soviet grid of administration.

Both of these drafts of the Provisional Statute followed the guidelines of the Soviet government in leaving the "ground level" of indigenous social organization "the way it is."[41] But the two have very different understandings of the meaning of "reality." In the first plan, the "real" group is a community which, for Lappo, is literally on the ground: it is an area on the map. In the second plan it is a structure—a scheme of relations that isolates clans analytically and subordinates them politically to federal administrative networks. The author of this plan, Ianovich, along with Bogoraz, was one of the chief advocates of isolated reserves for protecting Siberian aborigines from mainland influences and contacts.[42] Genealogical and other ethnographic methods here are a means to achieve this isolation and "to create the second level of government above the clan, drawing not merely on the ethnographic notion of tribe, but also on the notion of the migration area, . . . if they [i.e., individual households] were detached from the clan."[43]

Here, the same move that analytically isolates indigenous social organization displaces indigenous societies to "nature" and Soviet reforms onto the imaginary landscape of management of natural history. The clan soviets should, according to Ianovich's plan for the statute, "establish and change the regulations of land tenure . . . , accept new members to society and resolve issues of resigning from it . . . , organize social mutual help among its members." They should do so, however, because "existing clan-based societies . . . compose *natural [estestvennye]* divisions of the native tribes" (emphasis added) and because in their practices of decision-making they already do so "at their meetings and gatherings."[44]

This displacement into nature is particularly visible in discussions of the indigenous land tenure at the 1928 Moscow Plenum of the Committee for the North. The head of the Committee, Petr Smidovich, gave a paper that provided an ethnographic vision for incorporating indigenous ecological experience into the Soviet system. "Natives," he argued, are so well adapted to a given territory with "their nerves, eyesight, visual memory, and sense of space," because they have put a "tremendous effort in subsisting on a given territory, and in doing so they have undergone *natural selection* [emphasis added] to a much greater extent than the rest of humanity."[45] This experience translates directly into various forms of knowledge: "the native knows each path [in the forest] and, moreover . . . each family in a clan knows its own path, . . . they [all] know well who belongs to what clan, who does what [in the clan], for the clan does not wander together . . . ,"[46] and they know the relationships between clans and communities. If there is a lack of squirrel or sable "on a given clan territory," the whole clan turns to relatives, joins them, and starts wandering together. "All this is done on the basis of common law," which is based both on sharing and on the "great respect for the actual use of the land." With examples from various parts of Siberia, he concludes: "This is the basis of primitive communism."[47]

At this point, the constructivist narrative of colonial social organization is disrupted completely: "The rights and duties of the natives in regard to land use are contingent upon their legal consciousness [*pravosoznaniem*]," which Smidovich understands here as formed not by colonial policies and mercantile inequalities but by "natural environment and primitive hunting techniques." The development of a "new organization and rationalization of labor in the conditions of the Soviet power"[48] on the basis of these techniques "would create the ground for awakening the practice of self-building [*samodeiatel'nost'*] and agency [*aktivnost'*] of the native population, for involving the native in the work of local Soviets and executive committees, for using his primitive-communist habits in collective, planned work . . . creating the soil for the rationalization and multifaceted development of the native economy."[49]

The Return of Political Economy as a Specter of the "Real"

The drafting of the Provisional Statute in 1925–1926 and discussions of indigenous land-tenure in 1927 should be seen in the broader context of the uses of the so-called "ethnographic principle" in early Soviet reforms, particularly in creating ethnicity as an identity-marker among Soviet subjects and as a basis of the administrative parceling of the former Russian empire into Soviet socialist federal republics and autonomous districts.[50] (See also the article by Francine Hirsch in this volume.) In Suslov's opinion, for example, Lappo's plan was riddled with "ethnic mistakes," which "soon will surface because the organization of clan soviets on the basis of historical and ethnographic materials will significantly change the borders of the districts."[51] In the context of Siberian aboriginal policies, however, the ethnographic map that the Soviet reforms were to match was much more detailed. In this context, the "ethnographic principle" also concerned the level of local soviets and collective farms, and it revealed a vision that, by the mid-1920s, was strikingly systematic. "Organic" clan soviets were to exist within "organic" ethnic autonomies; "genealogical kinship" as a foundation for the former correlated to the sense of common ethnic origin as a basis for the latter. "Organic" local soviets were not merely the smallest instances of "national self-determination," but also the "elementary units" of a new socialist social structure.

The "organic" era in indigenous politics was very short, however. In 1929, references to indigenous "common law" in the Provisional Statute were among the first to fall prey to "the Stalinist counter-revolution" of the late 1920s that institutionalized an orthodox Marxist vision of collectivization across the Soviet Union. Nevertheless, by examining the micropolitics of the implementation of this "organic" vision, I will argue now that this change should also be understood in the context of difficulties that its implementation encountered. I argue that these difficulties falsified "organic" policies (in the eyes of the reformers) in favor of orthodox Marxist policies without changing—but, rather, reinforcing—the structures of ethnographic and political authority that enabled both.

If the structure of this ethnographic and political authority was contingent on erasing the traces of the "initiating agent" (like Suslov) from the ethnographic and political close-up, materials on the 1926 clan soviet meetings convey a fierce competition to occupy this very center within the framework of the highly decentered politics of that time. In Resolution 10 of the Baikit Clan meeting (1926), for example, Suslov finds it important to state the following "on behalf of the Tungus":

> Because many [Soviet] organizers were recently noticed in the area calling the Tungus to come out to the meetings at the same time but to different places, because of which the Tungus, fearing to be accused of "disobeying the master" [*nepodchinenii nachal'niku*], exhaust their last remaining reindeer, leave hunting and other activities, but nevertheless try to make it to all meetings that cannot be legitimate without a quorum, [the meetings resolves] to petition the Committee for the North to influence through related institutions those enthusiasts [*liubitelei*] that call meetings and to allow only the authorized persons to call meetings, and only at important junctures, and during the time free from hunting and other activities, in accordance with the everyday economic [*khozaistvenno-bytovym*] conditions of the Tungus.[52]

In that same year, ethnographer Glafira Vasil'evich also reported that the Evenki were very confused about the rush with which they were registered and re-registered in different local soviets. "There was some kind of *suglan*," the Evenki in the upper part of the Podkamennaia Tunguska basin complained to her,

> but for what purpose it was called, the Tungus [from Taimba and Bachin tributaries] themselves could not say. Even the head of the Clan Soviet, Semen Kureiski, said about his new post: "I shall be a master too, but the devil knows [*chert ego znaet*] to what purpose." Some [of the Tungus] recalled that they were supposed to have another *suglan* in

winter, on Epiphany, and asked me what would be the aim of this other meeting. . . . [53]

One of Vasil'evich's informants wondered, "why do various masters drop in only for one hour?"[54]

Various masters were in a rush to call as many meetings as possible during the summer—the most comfortable time to travel—in order to promote competing interests. Vasil'evich went to the Podkamennaia Tunguska from the Chadobets village on the Angara River, and she reported to the Committee for the North about the boss of a local cooperative, a certain Comrade Skotnikov who, "with a revolver" and an enthusiasm comprised of both "revolutionary and alcoholic agitation," wanted to prevent her field trip from proceeding unless the expedition was registered in the Chadobets Soviet. "This fellow," commented Vasil'evich about Skotnikov, "cannot live without moonshine; and he clearly would not hesitate to make money out of it" among the Evenki of the Podkamennaia Tunguska.[55] Writing the minutes of the first Soviet *suglan* in Baikit, Suslov made sure to record the Tungus request "to miss the *suglan* called by the Angara River District Executive Committee on St. Peter's Day on the Mutorai River, a tributary of the Chunia." This call for a *suglan* that the Evenki were to ignore was issued on Yenisei Union of Cooperatives stationery. The union, based in the villages of the Angara River, was competing with the Krasnoiarsk Committee for the North for the allegiances of the Podkamennaia Tunguska Evenki.[56]

For all interested parties, however, the trouble was that the newly established clan soviets virtually disappeared once the reformers/observers were gone. The teacher and ethnographer Tatiana Petrova, for example, came to the watershed of the Podkamennaia Tunguska and the Angara rivers in 1927 expecting to start a school at the Komo Clan Soviet. But she was not able to do so because there was no soviet to work with: "It fell apart . . . after the instructor, Comrade Volkov, left." She wrote that the previous year the Tungus of that area were "organized" in a Komo Clan Soviet with its center at the trading post at Komo. The instructor moved to the post, and "offered to teach literacy to whoever would be willing to learn, but warned that they should bring their own food." She quoted the Evenki as having replied, "If the state wants to teach them, it should feed them too, because to come with their own bread in their pocket is not convenient." For the same reason, Petrova was unable to reestablish the clan soviet. The person calling the meeting was supposed "to treat the Tungus, in accordance with the custom" with food and drink, and for this she "did not possess any resources."[57]

This does not imply, however, that the Evenki generally proved hostile to the reformers. For example, Petrova reported that the Evenki of the Komo and Kamenka rivers have heard that "the kind master Suslov" was supposed to help them against the encroachments of the Russian fur hunters upon their territories. When she was leaving the area, Petrova was approached by the Evenki of the Tokhomo tributary, who asked her "to elect a master [*nachal'nik*] among them, in order to settle arguments, because otherwise they had too much trouble among themselves."[58] For other Evenki, however, the rare visits by the "masters" from the Committee for the North were obstacles. Materials of the Committee cite, for example, one clan soviet secretary from the Khatanga River basin as saying: "in my horde I am the master, and you [the Committee for the North representative] are just an instructor."[59]

Regardless of whether these instructors were favorably received, the Soviet substitution of local political forms with "scientific" (and therefore, supposedly, politically neutral) ones generated even more contentious politics. A clan soviet secretary from Baikit, for example, dictated a report in which he accused Suslov of endorsing traditional patriarchy by depriving Evenki women of the right to vote in the clan soviet meetings.[60] The secretary of the Katonga Soviet, on the contrary, took a more traditionalist position by using the power of the soviet to condemn a low-income Evenki who did not have enough income to pay *kalym*, the bride ransom.[61] At any event, the heads of new soviets faced difficulties similar to those of the ethnographers and reformers: in a letter that one of the new heads of soviets addressed to the Turukhansk Executive Committee, he asked for help in calling the next *suglan*, "in such a way that all the rich people would attend it." He finished the letter with a note of despair: "Would you explain to everyone, both rich and poor, that the *suglan* decisions are obligatory for all."[62]

The "initiating agents" next returned in the summer of 1928, when an instructor from the Committee for the North came to draw boundaries between different "family and clan territories." To the request "to draw a map on which all hunting lands and borders of family territories would be marked," the Evenki replied that

> before, there were no borders between different households, or between different hunting and fishing territories and reindeer-herding pastures;

one would go wherever one wanted to wander, if the lichen was exhausted in one place, then he would go to another place with his tent and his reindeer, if there was poor fishing in a given lake, he would go to another—even if there were other tents on that lake it is not forbidden to come over and catch fish . . . [63]

The archives of the Committee for the North are full of similar responses from various meetings across Siberia.[64] Participants at one meeting acknowledged that richer reindeer herders "have more certain routes of wandering, which are divided on winter and summer pastures . . . In general, [however], the native does not live at the same place, he is wandering all the time, and does not return to the same place the next year." The Clan Soviet resolved "not to define the borders of the family territories, because the population does not pursue nomadic lifestyle in any regular manner along any routes . . . [*naselenie ne vedet reguliarno kochevoi obraz zhizni po kakomu-libo marshrutu*]."[65]

The campaign to parcel land in accordance with the "organic" vision of indigenous "clan-based communities" also revealed "land quarrels" of sorts. As Suslov, who visited the basin of Nizhniaia Tunguska River in 1928, reports,

> [in the spring of that year] . . . two Tungus from the Mukta clan went chasing moose to the Iringa River, where the Tungus Oikodon hunted, and started a row with him. In the end Oikodon declared that he was a member of the Strelka-Chunia Clan Soviet (which is true [Suslov personally founded that soviet]), and demanded that they leave the Iringa at once and leave him the bodies of two killed moose. So they gave him the game, and left the Iringa. Now these two complain to a certain "Skipidonych" [the head of the Yerbogachen Soviet] in the hope that Oikodon will be punished.

Suslov pointed out that *neither* side of this conflict hunted on "their" proper clan territories: "The clan lands of Oikodon are the upper part of the Taimura River area, and not by the Iringa. And the clan lands of these two Mukta are the lower Taimura basin and the [Nizhniaia] Tunguska River down to the mouth of the Uchami tributary. Evidently, all three started a scandal by being outside their own hunting territories."

Suslov obtained this information from a member of the Yerbogachen Clan Soviet whom he interviewed at the mouth of the Limpe River. That member was also keen to point out that "the Chapagir clan has no place here, so let it go away back to its [native] Tura." Yakuts, who periodically came over from the Vilui River basin, should also have been driven away, according to this activist, "because one of them stole the moose carcass from a cache and ran away to Vilui."[66] "We can see here," wrote Suslov, "the doubtless tendency to settle personal scores and show off one's authority." This made him feel manipulated: "A small group of Tungus, assisted by semi-literate L., . . . writes various minutes and memos, and sends them to 'Skipidonych' . . . with a firm belief that the 'government' will do anything for them."[67]

*　*　*

As the reformers and ethnographers struggled with the predicaments of their own approach, the overall political climate in the Soviet Union began to change. The February 1928 Plenum of the Committee for the North, which set the course for the rationalization of indigenous experience as rooted "in centuries of natural selection," took place just before the orthodox political-economic vision of social differentiation in the countryside made a dramatic comeback as the "line on collectivization."

However, as my materials suggest, this political-economy approach reappears before and quite independently of this change—in the predicaments of the attempts to implement the "organic" approach, "really grounded in life experience," as Smidovich put it. The visibility of genealogical clans was hard to maintain, and attempts to introduce the structural principles of indigenous land tenure into indigenous communities failed. These failures, however, had important socially productive effects. Failures of "organic" clan-based communities affirmed the correctness of the orthodox Marxist vision. In 1929, the Baikit Executive Committee reported: "The poor do not have their own consciousness at all; they dwell under the influence of the rich [kulaki] and the strong middle-wealth [seredniaki]. This year we had to carry out work on the differentiation of the native population through the organization of the poor and women. . . ."[68] On the Podkamennaia Tunguska River (as elsewhere in rural parts of the Soviet Union) the local elections of 1929 were based on class quotas. "Clan" Soviets were renamed "Native" (tuzemnye) and "Nomadic" (kochevye), and references to "customary law" were dropped from the articles of the Provisional Statute. In 1931, local cooperatives of this area were transformed into "Elementary Production Units" (PPO) and, in 1938, into standard Soviet collective farms.

These failures also legitimized the Soviet narrative of social reforms. As historian and Party *apparatchik* V. N. Uvachan put it, the "clan principle" of Soviet construction "did not achieve the separation of 'the eldest' and 'the best' members of clans. Although the old clan division was abolished, in the eyes of the population the former leaders preserved their authority and power even if they lost their administrative posts."[69] This view is echoed by reformer and ethnographer M. A. Sergeev, the author of the key Soviet indigenous policy statement, "The Non-Capitalist Development of the Peoples of the North." Among many examples, he cites the following report from the Nizhnaia Tunguska area: "The rich herder Chapagir . . . claimed: ' . . . all Tungus are equal; [the Russians] want to cause us to quarrel, to divide us into rich and poor . . . ' Adjusting to the new circumstances, the rich were representing their group interests as the general interests of their clan or tribe."[70]

Finally, the predicaments revealed in the micro-history of the "organic" wave of Soviet reforms in the North indicate the limits of the usefulness of the "invention of tradition" approach that gained theoretical currency in the understanding of imperial social and administrative visions in Eastern Europe and Russia.[71] Failures in the "invention of tradition" indicate, as Mark Bassin points out, limits to an approach that grants the " 'gaze' of the observer a sort of hegemonic license in regard to the object region, a license that suggests a kind of absolute power and control."[72] I have approached this "invention" not as a process of "formalization and ritualization, characterized by reference to the past" and "by imposing repetition" on new social forms,[73] but rather as a process of signification which, according to Slavoj Zizek, "ultimately always fails," making "the real" return "in the guise of spectral apparitions."[74] The "real" of the constructivist approach of Dobrova-Iadrinsteva and Lappo, the "real" of the "natural history" of Suslov and Smidovich, and the "real" of the Marxist orthodox political economy are affirmed, rather than challenged, by the failures of state reforms. In this particular context, the failures of signification of the clan-based communities in the mid-1920s made the "real" return as a specter of orthodox political economy and conditioned identity politics in northern Siberian collective farms.

Notes

1. Kraievedcheskii muzei Evenkiiskogo avtonomnogo okruga, f. I. M. Suslova, fotografiia 54.

2. Michael M. Ames, *Cannibal Tours and Glass Boxes: The Anthropology of Museums* (Vancouver: University of British Columbia Press, 1992), 42.

3. For example, A. I. Pika and B. B. Prokhorov, *Neotraditsionalizm na Rossiiskom severe: etnicheskoe vozrozhdenie malochislennykh narodov severa i gosudarstvennaia regional'naia politika* (Moscow: Institut narodnokhoziaistvennogo planirovaniia, 1994), 30, 49–53; E. G. Fedorova, "Natsional'naia kul'tura segodnia: problemy i perspektivy," in Ch. M. Taskami et al., eds., *Kul'tura narodov Sibiri* (St. Petersburg: Muzei antropologii i etnografii RAN, 1997); V. V. Karlov, "Malye narody severa: sovremennoe sostoianie i al'ternativnost' putei razvitiia," in A. I. Martynov et. al., eds., *Etnicheskie i etnokul'turnye protsessy u narodov Sibiri: istoriia i sovremennost'* (Kemerovo: KemGU, 1992).

4. Nikolai Ssorin-Chaikov, *A Social Life of the State in Sub-Arctic Siberia* (Stanford, Calif.: Stanford University Press, 2003).

5. Gosudarstvennyi arkhiv Rossiiskoi federatsii (hereafter GARF), f. 3977, op. 1., d. 279, l. 141. The context for this quote is the discussion of clan-based land-tenure in 1928. I examine this discussion below.

6. S. V. Bakhrushin, "Iasak v Sibiri," in *Nauchnye trudy,* vol. 3, part 2 (Moscow: AN SSSR, 1955).

7. Yuri Slezkine, *Arctic Mirrors: Russia and the Small Peoples of the North* (Ithaca, N.Y.: Cornell University Press, 1994), 80.

8. To use the terms of Michel-Rolf Trouillot, "Anthropology and the Savage Slot: The Poetics and Politics of Otherness," in Richard G. Fox, ed., *Recapturing Anthropology: Working in the Present* (Santa Fe, N.M.: School of American Research Press, 1991).

9. M. A. Sergeev, *Nekapitalisticheskii put' razvitiia malykh narodov severa* (Moscow and Leningrad: AN SSSR, 1955); V. N. Uvachan, *Gody ravnye vekam: stroitel'stvo sotsializma na Sovetskom severe* (Moscow: Mysl', 1984).

10. "Rhizome" is the concept of Deleu Gilles Deleuze and Felix Guattari which "connects any point to any other point . . . and [which] brings into play very different regimes of signs, and even nonsign states" (*A Thousand Plateaus: Capitalism and Schizophrenia* [Minneapolis: University of Minnesota Press, 1987], 21).

11. N. I. Leonov, "Tuzemnye sovety v taige i tundrakh," in P. G. Smidovich, *Sovetskii sever 1* (Moscow: Kom. Sod. narodnostiam severnykh okrain, 1929), 219. This publication quotes from Suslov's report on his trip to the Podkamennaia Tunguska.

12. Ibid., 224.

13. Gosudarstvennyi arkhiv Krasnoiarskogo kraia (hereafter GAKK), f. 1845, op. 1., d. 23, ll. 3–10, 36.

14. I. M. Suslov, "Suglan na Strelke," in I. M. Bublishenko and O. A. Khonina, eds., *Evenkiia v serdtse moem* (Krasnoiarsk: Krasnoiarskoe knizhnoe izdatel'stvo, 1980), 60.

15. Krasnoiarskii Kraievedcheskii muzei (hereafter KKM), o/f 8119-1/PI 286, zapisnaia knizhka 9; GAKK, f. 1845, op. 1., d. 23, ll. 36.

16. Zhores Troshev, *Bol'shoi Oshar* (Krasnoiarsk: Krasnoiarskoe knizhnoe izdatel'stvo, 1981), 67.

17. Karl Marx and Friedrich Engels, *Sochineniia* (Moscow: Gosudarstvennoe izdatel'stvo politicheskoi literatury, 1955), 19: 251. This is a gloss of the concluding pages of Morgan's *Ancient Society:* "[t]ime will come . . . when human intelligence will rise

to the mastery over [private] property . . . " and this historical point "will be a revival, in a higher form, of the liberty, equality and fraternity of the ancient gentes [clans]": Lewis Henry Morgan, *Ancient Society* (Cleveland: World Publishing Company, 1963 [1877]), 561–562.

18. Marx and Engels.

19. For example, A. F. Anisimov, *Rodovoe obshchestvo evenkov (tungusov)* (Leningrad: Izdatel'stvo Instituta narodov severa, 1936), 156–157; S. A. Tokarev, *Dokapitalisticheskie prezhitki v oirotii* (Leningrad: Sotsial'no-ekonomicheskoe izdatel'stvo, 1936), 140.

20. L. I. Dobrova-Iadrintseva, *Tuzemtsy Turukhanskogo kraiia* (Novonikolayevsk: Izdanie Sibrevkoma, 1925), 5.

21. D. E. Lappo, "Obychnoe pravo Sibirskikh tuzemnykh narodnostei," manuscript, Krasnoiarskii Kraievedcheskii Muzei (n.d.), 79.

22. Ibid., 81.

23. Ibid., 80.

24. KKM 7886/195, l. 11.

25. Dobrova-Iadrintseva, 26.

26. A. Ya. Tugarinov, *Turukhanskie inorodtsy i kooperatsiia* (Krasnoiarsk: Tipografiia Eniseiskogo Gub. soiuza kooperativov, 1918), 7.

27. N. N. Bilibin, "Batratskii trud v khoziaistve koriakov," *Sovetskii sever* 1 (1933): 44.

28. The language of "debt" and "credit" was used by the Polar Census of 1926–1927.

29. Bilibin, 45–46; P. Maslov, "Opyt perepisi trekh raionov krainego severa (leto 1933 goda)," *Sovetskii sever* 3 (1934): 53. This inequality emerged in the context of the fur trade, but it was sanctioned by common law—that is, according to Lappo, by the *Steppe Code* of 1640 recorded in 1822 as indigenous common law. The administrative construction of clan-based communities from the outside legally encapsulated these hierarchies in the following formula of 1822 *Statute:* "Impoverished debtors shall be given to their creditors and remain in their hands until by their labors they shall have paid the debt; or money shall be taken from them over a set period, depending on their conditions": see R., "O zakonakh Sibirskikh inorodtsev," quoted in Valentin A. Riasanovsky, *Customary Law of the Nomadic Tribes of Siberia* (Tientsin: 1938), 73.

30. KKM PI (r) 8471/415, l. 80–81.

31. GARF, f. 3977, d. 81, l. 143–144.

32. Lappo, "Obychnoe pravo," 88, 93.

33. GARF, f. 3977, op. 1, d. 28, l. 65.

34. Ibid., l. 19–22.

35. Ibid., l. 20.

36. GAKK, f. 1845, op. 1, d. 9, l. 61.

37. GARF, f. 3977, op. 1, d. 65, p. 11.

38. Ibid., d. 81, p. 143.

39. Ibid., d. 65, l. 2.

40. See *The Project of the Statute on the Administration over the RSFSR Territories Occupied by Northern Peoples* by D. E. Lappo and *The Project of the Northern Code* by I. S. Ianovich; these two drafts were published in the journal *Severnaia Aziia,* 1–2 (1925): 123–130, and 3 (1926): 94–101.

41. GARF, f. 3,977, op. 1, d. 45, l. 36.

42. D. T. Ianovich, "Zapovedniki dlia gibnushchikh tuzemnykh plemen," *Zhizn' natsional'nostei* 4 (1922); V. G. Bogoraz (-Tan), "Podgotovitel'nye mery k organizatsii malykh narodnostei," *Severnaia Aziia* 3 (1925).

43. GARF, f. 3977, op. 1, d. 45, l. 36.

44. Ibid., d. 63, ll. 11–15.

45. Ibid., d. 279, ll. 88–89.

46. GAKK, f. 1845, op. 1, d. 183, l. 44; GARF, f. 3977, op. 1. d. 279, l. 90.

47. Ibid., ll. 90–93; GAKK, f. 1845, op. 1, d. 183, ll. 44–46.

48. Ibid., l. 48.

49. Ibid., l. 42.

50. Yuri Slezkine, "The USSR as a Communal Apartment, or How a Socialist State Promoted Ethnic Particularism," *Slavic Review* 2 (1994): 414; Francine Hirsch, "The Soviet Union as a Work-in-Progress: Ethnographers and the Category *Nationality* in 1926, 1937, and 1939 Censuses," *Slavic Review* 2 (1997); on the role of ethnography in Siberian ethnic construction, see David G. Anderson, *Identity and Ecology in Arctic Siberia: The Number One Reindeer Brigade* (Oxford: Oxford University Press, 2000), 74–96; and Debra L. Schindler, "Theory, Policy and the Narody severa," *Anthropological Quarterly* 2 (1991).

51. GAKK, f. 1845, op. 1, d. 183, l. 19.

52. Ibid., d. 23, l. 39.

53. Ibid., d. 156, ll. 29, 30.

54. Ibid., l. 30.

55. GAKK, f. 1845, op. 1, d. 156, ll. 22–23.

56. Ibid., d. 23, l. 39.

57. GARF, f. 3977, op. 1, d. 138, ll. 1–4.

58. Ibid.

59. GAKK, f. 769, op. 1, d. 306, l. 3.

60. Ibid., f. 1845, op. 1, d. 199, l. 38 (see the resolution of the Katonga Soviet, in which, "according to the customary law, those women who attended the meeting do not take part in the vote": GAKK, f. 1845, op. 1, d. 23, l. 36).

61. Ibid, f. 1845, op. 1, d. 199, l. 81.

62. GAKK, f. 1845, op. 1, d. 23, l. 45.

63. GAKK, f. 1845, op. 1, d. 62, ll. 224–227.

64. The area of the Podkamennaia Tunguska and Nizhniaia Tunguska rivers is discussed in GAKK, f. 1845, op. 1, d. 62, ll. 223–227, 176, 14–15.

65. GAKK, f. 1845, op. 1, d. 62, ll. 224–227.

66. KKM o/f 8119–1/PI 301, ll. 185–186.

67. Ibid.

68. GAKK, f. 1845, op. 1, d. 199, l. 82.

69. Uvachan, *Gody ravnye vekam,* 89; Sergeev, 294.

70. Sergeev, 299.

71. Larry Wolff, *Inventing Eastern Europe: The Map of Civilization on the Mind of the Enlightenment* (Stanford, Calif.: Stanford University Press, 1994); Mark Bassin, "Inventing Siberia: Visions of the Russian East in the Early Nineteenth Century," *American*

Historical Review June (1991); see also Daniel R. Brower and Edward J. Lazzerini, *Russia's Orient: Imperial Borderlands and Peoples, 1700–1917* (Bloomington: Indiana University Press, 1997).

72. Mark Bassin, *Imperial Visions: National Imagination and Geographical Expansion in the Russian Far East, 1840–1865* (Cambridge: Cambridge University Press, 1999), 277.

73. Eric Hobsbawm, "Introduction: Inventing Traditions," in Eric Hobsbawm and Terence Ranger, eds., *The Invention of Tradition* (Cambridge: Cambridge University Press, 1983), 4.

74. Slavoj Zizek, "The Spectre of Ideology," in Slavoj Zizek, ed., *Mapping Ideology* (London: Verso, 1994), 21.

Part Three   *Institutions*

11 From the Zloty to the Ruble: The Kingdom of Poland in the Monetary Politics of the Russian Empire

Ekaterina Pravilova

The study of the rise, development, and fall of empires is an inexhaustible project. Even as researchers continue to adopt new approaches and raise new questions about the organization and functioning of imperial states, the number of unresolved issues and unexplored topics barely seems to diminish because the subject is so complex. Indeed, just as old "blank spots" in the history of empires are filled in, new ones emerge, while other important problems remain persistently under-examined. One enduring "blank spot" of imperial history concerns the vital question of money, or, more generally, the question of the working of imperial financial systems. What, after all, could be more important to understanding how empires work than determining the costs for an empire of acquiring or losing a given piece of territory, the general economic consequences of imperial growth and decline, the influence of financial factors on the nature of imperial administration, culture, and social life, and the underlying principles that informed the drafting of imperial budgets? Despite their obvious importance, however, questions of this sort have not usually been taken up by historians.

In the case of tsarist Russia, the organization of state finances reflected some of the complexities that characterized the broader administration of the state. The management of the Russian empire in the eighteenth and nineteenth centuries rested both on a toleration of diversity and on the pursuit of standardization. Consequently, in Russia perhaps more than elsewhere, the life of the state was defined by an interweaving of the particular and the universal. Nowhere was this more noticeable than in the realms of economy and finance. On the one hand, the Russian government routinely adopted measures that were tailored to address the special economic needs and circumstances of its disparate regions; on the other, it also routinely sought to bring these particular policies into alignment with general principles governing the empire's business and economic life. This already implicitly contradictory situation was made all the more complicated by the fact that the empire's regions varied strikingly in terms of their general level of economic development. Many of the imperial borderlands were markedly less developed than the Russian center in terms of industry or manufacturing. Consequently, their "maintenance" proved to be quite costly for the imperial treasury. At the same, the empire also included the much richer territories of Poland and Finland, whose economies were oriented toward Western Europe and many of whose financial institutions and practices were based on European models.

These differences in development as well as the equally diverse financial cultures of the empire's regions led Russian administrators to adopt an extremely broad range of budgetary, taxation, custom, and credit policies. At the same time, there was no question that these same administrators ultimately aspired to integrate the financial systems of the borderlands into a common imperial framework. Naturally the existence of a unitary financial space of this sort presupposed the existence of a single currency—the Russian ruble—that would circulate throughout the whole of the state's territory. The road to a single currency was complicated, however, and the process of incorporating newly acquired territories into the empire's financial system often dragged on for decades. War, the incompatibility of Russian and non-Russian accounting practices, and the preference of local peoples for the currencies already in circulation in their regions prior to the advent of Russian power all helped to make the complete elimination of non-Russian currencies in the borderlands extremely difficult.

Of course, the most obvious and important hurdle standing in the way of monetary standardization was the incompatibility of Russian monies with the currencies of foreign states circulating in the empire's newly acquired territories. The Russian government encountered this problem repeatedly as it expanded to the west. Polish-Lithuanian and Western European coins that circulated in areas such as Little Russia, the Baltic provinces, Belorussia, and Poland were much easier to use for accounting purposes and tended to be better minted than Russian kopecks, which were full-weight (that is, undebased) but small and difficult to use.[1] The inhabitants of the Ukrainian lands incorporated into the Russian state in 1654 were unfamiliar with Russian coinage and preferred to use the monies they knew best rather than adopt Russian ones. As a result, two fundamentally different currency regimes—one Ukrainian, the other Russian—evolved within the confines of a single state. In 1686–1687, in an attempt to establish some kind of link between these two currencies, the Muscovite government issued new coins known as *Sevskie chekhi* because they were minted in the town of Sevsk. These coins were intended to circulate solely in Ukraine and the Polish Commonwealth and were designed to resemble the Polish monies of Sigismund III, though with the Polish markings replaced by Russian ones, notably the image of the Russian two-headed eagle and the names of Great Princes Ivan and Peter Alekseevich.[2] Perhaps not surprisingly, the results of this "imitator coin" fell short of expectations. The new coinage was boycotted by the local population, and in 1689 the *chekhi* were withdrawn.

In subsequent periods the Russian government frequently minted what was known as "extraordinary coinage" (*monety chrezvychainykh obstoiatel'stv*), whose usual purpose was to serve as a medium of exchange for Russian troops on foreign campaign. Thus coins known as *shestaki* and *tinfy* were issued in 1707–1709 for Russian armies on campaign in Lithuania, Poland, Saxony, and Prussia; in 1759–1762, during the Seven Years' War, Prussian thalers were minted bearing the image of tsarina Elizabeth; and in the early 1770s, *pary* were issued to troops in Moldavia, displaying the monogram of Catherine II and the Russian coat of arms.[3] Russian officers were expected to use these monies to purchase supplies for troops in newly conquered areas and to make up for shortfalls in the supply of Russian coins, while the Russian heraldry and imperial portraits that usually figured on the coins symbolized the new imposition of tsarist power.[4]

In certain cases when special monies were issued, political and ideological motivations were clearly more at issue than financial ones. For example, in 1787 the mint in Feodosiia in the Crimea issued bronze and silver coins known as Tavrians. These coins were completely analogous to standard Russian coins, though the silver Tavrian included the inscription "Empress of Khersones and the Tauride" beneath an image of Catherine's monogram.[5] The new monies were designed to commemorate the annexation of the Crimea, though much like the Prussian and Moldavian coins, their minting was envisioned as a temporary measure.

The minting of such "extraordinary coinage" did not mean that the government reconsidered its basic desire to introduce Russian notes and bills into newly acquired regions. In some cases, the government attempted to introduce the ruble but recognized that it was unprofitable or simply impossible. In 1710, for example, the circulation of the ruble was formally instituted in Lithuania, but most transactions continued to occur in Swedish currency, and local residents sold the newly introduced Russian coins abroad to be melted down as metal. Acknowledging this situation, the Monetary Office (*monetnaia kantseliariia*) ordered a halt in 1756 "to the circulation [of Russian money] in this province," a move intended both to keep Russian monies from entering Lithuania and to prevent Lithuanian ones from entering the rest of the empire.[6] As a result, special *livonezy* were minted for circulation in Lithuania and Estonia in 1756–1757. At the same time the use of Polish, Swedish, Prussian, and even Russian currency continued to be permitted on a temporary basis. The government ultimately stopped minting *livonezy* a year after their introduction due to the onset of the Seven Years' War, but the number of *livonezy* in circulation was in any case extremely limited and foreign coinage remained widely used.[7] Despite repeated bans on the circulation of foreign money within the empire, it was not until 1846 that Prussian and other international currencies were finally completely prohibited in Lithuania. In Transcaucasia, where the Ministry of Finance had similar concerns over the sale of Russian coinage for melting abroad, foreign currencies continued to circulate until the middle of the 1850s. St. Petersburg was simply forced to accept the fact that despite its minting of a special coin—the *abaz*—for use in Georgia in the early nineteenth century, foreign coinage remained in wide use in the region, even the coinage of former ruling powers.[8]

The Russian empire clearly did not possess a single, unitary currency system in the eighteenth and nineteenth centuries. The peoples of newly incorporated territories often reacted indifferently to the introduction of Russian money, preferring foreign coinage, and even in those areas where Russian coins did become firmly established, Russian paper money was practically nonexistent. In still other regions, the government ultimately decided against introducing the ruble and chose instead to mint special regional coins that would be more familiar to the empire's new subjects in terms both of appearance and of denominations.

Making the Russian Zloty

The rulers of Russia's finances encountered the whole welter of these monetary problems in the late eighteenth century as the empire engulfed the territories of eastern Poland. Following the Polish partitions, each of the three new powers—Russia, Prussia, and Austria—introduced its own currency into its newly acquired domains. The ruble thus began to circulate in Russian Polish territory, but, despite this fact and not surprisingly, the local population continued to use Polish coins. In fact, the government had a difficult time organizing the transition to an exclusively Russian monetary regime in the Polish lands because Polish coins were based on the silver standard and on Prussian units of weight, while in Russia there was no real equivalent. The Russian silver ruble had not yet emerged as the empire's standard coin; and the Polish monetary system was better organized than Russia's, which was plagued by a surfeit of devalued treasury bills.

The discrepancy between the empire's financial system and that of its newly acquired western provinces was duly noted by Russian statesmen and helped to prompt thoughts of domestic monetary reform. In 1810, Mikhail Speranskii argued that it was imperative to institute "a monetary order based on the silver ruble" so that it would be possible "to immediately ban the circulation in Lithuania and Poland of any other currency," a measure that he saw as "the sole means for uniting the financial system of these provinces with that of Russia and thus putting an end at last to the harm and offense currently suffered by our finances."[9] Speranskii was ahead of his time, however, and the full transition to a silver ruble standard did not occur in Russia until after the monetary reforms of 1839–1841.

By the early nineteenth century, a variety of factors, including the Polish partitions, the wars of the period, and frequent changes in government, helped to make the monetary situation in the Polish lands all the more confusing. Beginning in 1810, in addition to the variety of Polish and foreign monies already in circulation, non–interest-bearing treasury notes (*besprotsentnye assignatsii*) issued in Dresden by the Saxon monarchy also began to circulate in the former Duchy. By the time that the Duchy regime fell and the transitional supreme provisionary council came to power, some five million *zlotys* worth of these notes were in circulation—though the exact sum was not even known at the time, since the Duchy government managed to cart out of the country not only the metallic reserves supposedly backing up these notes but also all the records pertaining to their issue. Though still widely circulating, the notes declined in value by 20 percent, and their continued use threatened to further destabilize the currency system because they could be (and were) easily counterfeited. It was thus clear to the Russian financial leadership that the notes had to be completely removed from circulation as soon as the political fate of the Duchy was determined and the Polish territories were reintegrated into the empire. A decisive step was taken to this end when the Ministry of Finance established December 1, 1814, as the final deadline for transactions involving the Saxon notes.

This measure was a clear reflection of the government's fear of the notes' potentially deleterious effect on the empire's monetary system and its desire to put an end to the flood of notes being traded for gold and silver on the Russian exchange. In order to safeguard imperial finances, Minister of Finance D. A. Gur'ev proposed not just banning the import and export of the notes to and from Germany but also immediately putting common Russian coinage and paper bills into circulation in Russia's Polish territories. Insisting on the need to introduce Russian money into Poland, the minister noted the case of Hungary, where Austrian currency was put into circulation shortly after the territory was incorporated into the Austrian empire.[10] On November 19, 1815, the Russian government issued a decree on the monetary situation in Poland that amounted to something of a compromise with Gur'ev's position.[11] This decree, one of the earliest and most important relating to Russian power in the Polish territories, mandated that the zloty was to remain the basic Polish currency and the essential principles of the Polish monetary system were to be left intact. At the same time, the decree linked Polish money to the Russian currency at a fixed rate of 15 silver kopecks per 1 zloty, directly tying Polish finances to those of the empire. The Polish mint would also issue new coinage: gold coins in denominations of 25 and 50 zlotys, silver coins of 1, 2, and 5 zlotys, and silver and bronze pennies of 10, 5, 3, and 1 *grosh* (penny) denominations. A number of the grosh coins were issued as silver and bronze alloys known as billons. The fact that the Ministry of Finance chose to permit the minting of the alloyed billons represented a departure from Russian practice and was intended as a cost-saving measure. The use of a bronze-silver alloy was seen as a way to reduce the quantity of silver used in the smaller value coinage and thus recoup some of the expenses involved in the issue of the new currency.

The gold and larger denomination silver zlotys were minted with a portrait of Alexander I accompanied by the name and herald of the Kingdom of Poland. Alexander initially opposed including his portrait on the new coins, since representations of the tsar did not appear on Russian coinage. It was later determined that putting the portrait on the zloty was necessary so that "when Polish people looked at their coins, they would see the image of their monarch," and feel "bound" to him.[12] The lettering on the coins (that is, the rendering of the emperor's title and the coin's value) was all in Polish. In 1826, following the accession of Nicholas I, the Polish viceroy proposed replacing Alexander's portrait with that of the new tsar. Nicholas objected, noting that his older brother's image should be "maintained forever" on the coins of Poland as a means of commemorating the ruler "to whom Poland owes her existence."[13] Indeed, according to a decree later that year, only the inscription on the zloty was ordered changed. The phrase "Resurrector of the Kingdom of Poland" was now to be added to Alexander's imperial title, while Nicholas I's title was to appear on the reverse side of the coin. The design of the smaller denomination coins was left unchanged.[14]

While the new zloty introduced in 1815 was envisioned as the basic currency of the kingdom, it was never intended to be the only money in use in the territory. The decree on the Polish monetary system that established the new zloty also permitted the unlimited circulation of Russian currency. Yet even the combined circulation of Polish and Russian monies could not meet the region's need for coins, especially smaller value coinage, and consequently foreign coins also continued to circulate. At the same time, the new Polish coins intended for use in the kingdom ended up being used beyond the kingdom as well, spreading quickly to other formerly Polish provinces and to Russia's Baltic territories.

The endemic shortage of coinage and the concomitant toleration of the use of foreign currency were not unique to the Polish case. In fact, this situation was found across the empire's borderlands. In Bessarabia and the Crimea, for example, Ottoman monies were broadly used.[15] Prussian coins and paper notes circulated widely in western and Baltic provinces, even despite their having been supposedly banned in 1815. The introduction of the new zloty led to a partial reduction in the quantity of foreign monies circulating in western and Baltic provinces, but for Russia, of course, the new zloty was itself a foreign currency. Furthermore, at least as far as the Russian Minister of Finance Egor Kankrin was concerned, monetary practices in Poland were simply "incorrect." He noted, for example, that the alloy of the billon coins made them easier to use but also easier to counterfeit, and he therefore considered the issuing of the coins to be an unfortunate deviation from Russia's "correct monetary system."[16]

The circulation of Polish monies in Russian territories beyond the Kingdom of Poland offered certain advantages. Most importantly, it helped to meet the need for coinage in the empire's western and Baltic provinces. Without the Polish coins, monetary exchange in these areas would have been considerably more difficult. The Ministry of Finance, however, was not impressed and sought to ban the circulation of Polish coins as well as all other foreign currencies in the region, pledging to provide all the specie required without recourse to monies from abroad.[17] In 1827, the issue of the ban was taken up by the State Council. In the ensuing debate, the Ministry of Finance proposed completely outlawing the circulation of all smaller denomination foreign coinage in the western and Baltic provinces. The region's governors—the Marquis F. O. Pauluchchi, Duke M. S. Vorontsov, Duke M. I. Palen, as well as N. Novosil'tsev—then responded that Polish billons represented virtually "the only means of exchange used by local residents" and that all prior attempts to exclude the use of foreign monies had failed dismally. Acknowledging the concerns of the governors, the State Council decided against banning the circulation of small denomination foreign coinage and "to permit, or rather, to tolerate" the billon, though it did reiterate a ban on importing billons from abroad.[18] From this point the Polish billon thus began to circulate completely legally within the western provinces, though the imperial customs service, while permitting the introduction of gold and silver zloty from the Kingdom of Poland, steadfastly guarded against the removal of any silver or bronze grosh coins.[19]

In 1828, a new shift occurred in Poland's monetary landscape with the introduction of banknotes issued by the Polish Bank. Given that the kingdom's mint was placed under the authority of the Committee of Finance and the Treasury rather than the bank, the bank was not technically involved in currency policy. Still, in its 1828 statute, it was granted the right to issue bills that could theoretically be exchanged at any time for coinage, with the bank required to hold one-seventh of the total value of the issue in coin reserves. The bills that were ultimately issued were printed in rather high denominations (notes of 5, 10, 50, 100, 500, 1000 zlotys), but they were nonetheless widely used, largely because they could be freely exchanged for metallic currency. The notes, in effect, fulfilled the role of paper money and thus greatly facilitated the kingdom's currency exchange.

Thus, between 1815 and 1830, a new currency regime was established in the Kingdom of Poland that reflected both the kingdom's autonomous status within the empire and the relative financial independence that the kingdom enjoyed at the time. This system was only superficially linked to the broader currency system of the empire. The zloty gradually began to squeeze out foreign currencies circulating in the kingdom; at the same time it remained itself a foreign currency in the eyes of the Russian government. The largely autonomous currency regime in Poland was poised to become still more established in the coming decades, but things changed markedly with the rebellion of 1830.

Making the Zloty Russian

One of the first actions taken by the insurgent government in 1830 was to place the mint under the authority of the Polish Bank, a move intended to make it easier for the bank to finance the military operations of the rebellion.[20] The leaders of the rebellion had access to a generous supply of metallic reserves that the bank had just secured through a foreign loan. As of March 1831, the rebellious government began minting new 2- and 5-zloty silver coins as well as Dutch ducats made from imported gold.[21] The government quickly ran through its reserves, however, and the neutral Prussian government declined to allow needed transfers of precious metal and arms to the Polish insurgents. By the end of the rebellion, the regime's principal form of currency was the 1-zloty banknote. Still, as the Polish historian Władysław Terlecki has suggested, the combined activities of the Polish Bank and the mint did manage to provide the regime (and the country) with a sufficient supply of currency, though this in itself was not enough to stave off the ultimate defeat of the rebellion.[22]

After the suppression of the revolt, the Provisional Administration of the Kingdom of Poland quickly moved to abolish all the fiscal rulings of the mutinous government. The coinage that had been minted in 1831 was to be withdrawn from circulation and melted down for reminting, and the mint was to be placed once again under the authority of the Committee of Finance and the Treasury. The head of the Polish Bank, Józef Lubowidzki, managed to have the reassignment of the mint postponed for four months, however. This was not based on a recognition of the obvious advantages of continuing close cooperation between the mint and the bank, but rather on the fear that the value of the banknotes might fall in the event of a rapid administrative transfer.[23] Not surprisingly, it was politics rather than fiscal concerns that weighed most in the decision to remove the mint from the bank's control, since it is clear that the bank would likely have been more than able to manage the country's monetary needs. Indeed, some two years after the decision to transfer the mint, R. F. Furman, the head of the Commission of Finance and the Treasury, motioned to have the Warsaw Mint returned to the bank's authority. He argued that this was necessary because the mint was currently failing to produce a profit for the Treasury despite the fact that it was issuing debased coinage. Furman's proposal was sternly rejected by Kankrin, the Russian finance minister, who noted that the reform was entirely unnecessary and was more a matter of "speculation or perhaps ambition [on the part of the bank] to raise its own weight, influence, and authority over private speculators."[24] The Minister of Finance was not particularly partial to the Polish Bank.

The real fact of the matter, however, was that leaving the mint under the purview of the bank would have been at odds with the new direction of Russian financial policy. Beginning in 1831, the Russian government began to markedly curtail the kingdom's former autonomy in fiscal affairs,[25] and one of the first steps taken in this direction was the move to reform the prevailing currency regime in the region. In November 1831, Kankrin was ordered by the tsar to review the question of introducing Russian currency in Poland. His response was to propose issuing Russian monies with a Polish-language inscription and "to require all accounting [in the kingdom] to be conducted in Russian rubles rather than in florins [i.e., zlotys]."[26] As the new medium of exchange, Kankrin suggested introducing a new Russian-Polish coin, the silver 15-kopeechnik, whose value would be equal to 1 zloty.

Kankrin's proposal ran into some resistance. I. F. Paskevich, the Polish viceroy, for one, argued that the introduction of Russian currency was likely to be an extremely difficult task, one far more difficult than introducing the Russian system of weights and measures. He noted that introducing Russian currency would mean not only replacing Polish coins but also "some 30 million" banknotes issued by the Polish Bank as well as mortgage notes issued on the basis of real estate collateral by the Land Credit Society (*zemskoe kreditnoe obshchestvo*). As Paskevich saw it, "a sudden change-over" in the currencies of these securities would lead to problems in accounting and result in the general paralysis of the kingdom's financial system. The viceroy's principal argument against proceeding with Kankrin's plan, however, turned on the fact that the empire's currency system was deficient and that insistence on its introduction in Poland would therefore be counterproductive. Paper rubles no longer bore their initial value, and thus tying the zloty to the paper ruble made no sense at all. On the other hand, merely issuing a new Russian-Polish 15-kopeck coin equivalent to the value of 1 zloty would not change much, since accounts in the region, in Paskevich's view, would continue to be conducted in zlotys rather than rubles.[27]

In the viceroy's opinion, if the government wished to move immediately toward monetary reform, it should begin by exchanging Polish monies for Russian ones, halting the issue of bank and mortgage notes, and issuing securities in ruble denominations. Then, beginning in 1834, it should order government offices to begin keeping their accounts in rubles and by the following year require commercial enterprises to do the same. (After all, as Paskevich noted, moving to require ruble-based accounting in the kingdom prior to the time that Polish monies could be exchanged for rubles would make no sense.) The new coins to be minted in Poland could have either Russian or Polish inscriptions, but in the viceroy's view it was absolutely necessary that they "bear Russian names and display the same images that appear on Russian coinage."[28]

Kankrin rejected Paskevich's objections by noting that the Ministry of Finance indeed intended to maintain the zloty as the basic unit of accounting in the kingdom, though it would do so by minting coins with a double ruble/zloty denomination. Thus, the minister proposed minting silver and gold coins that would display both a zloty and a ruble value (15 kopecks/1 zloty; 5 kopecks/$\frac{1}{3}$ zloty; 1 ruble/$6\frac{2}{3}$ zlotys, etc.). In addition, the billon would be completely withdrawn because the minting of debased coinage would undermine the new currency system. According to Kankrin, these measures were sufficient "to obtain the [government's] goal of integrating the monetary systems of the Kingdom and the Empire."[29] The only complication that the minister perceived had to do with the fractional value of some of the coinage. As a result, the Ministry of Finance ultimately refrained from minting a ruble coin equivalent to $6\frac{2}{3}$ zlotys. Thus, curiously, one cannot truly speak of the Russian government introducing the ruble into Poland, because the ruble coin as such was not supposed to be minted. In fact, because of anticipated accounting problems surrounding the use of fractional denominations, Tsar Nicholas decided to limit the new minting to just the 15-kopeck piece.[30] Plans for the rest of the coins were left on the drawing board.

On May 26, 1832, Kankrin submitted the design of the new coins to the tsar for review. The design, in accordance with Nicholas's decree of 1826, prominently displayed the portrait of Alexander I, but times had changed and Alexander's profile no longer fit entirely well with the new political situation in the kingdom. For one, having Alexander's image on the Polish coin seemed to suggest the uniqueness of Polish money within the empire (no other Russian coins displayed Alexander's portrait); and, secondly, the visage of the deceased tsar also provided an unwelcome reminder of the autonomy that he had formerly granted to the Poles. Nicholas thus reversed his earlier opinion and ordered his brother's portrait removed, to be replaced by the standard image of the Russian imperial seal that appeared on all Russian coinage.[31] (Nicholas's "forever," in other words, had lasted less than ten years.) The new design was approved and the St. Petersburg Mint was directed to prepare a mold for the 15-kopeck piece. Upon reviewing the new casting, the tsar then ordered the small image of the Polish seal appearing on the wings of the two-headed eagle to be rendered "as clearly as possible."[32] Later, he ordered one more revealing change: the word "Polish" in the inscription "Polish zloty" was to be struck, leaving the word "zloty" to appear on its own.[33] The coin was then confirmed for circulation in Poland in the fall of 1832[34] and minted, displaying on one side the imperial seal and on the other the coin's parallel values: 15 kopecks, written in Russian at the top, and 1 zloty, written in Polish at the bottom.

The 15-kopeck/1-zloty coin marked the first step toward integrating the Polish and Russian currency regimes. Yet it was still premature to speak of the introduction of the ruble in Poland because as yet no ruble coin was being introduced. The introduction of Russian coinage approved by the tsar was largely symbolic, an ideological statement that in fact did little to change the terms of Polish monetary exchange. The tsar himself recognized the primarily symbolic function of the new coinage. Two weeks after the minting of the 15-kopeck/1-zloty coin, he wrote to Kankrin to ask him whether he thought it might also be wise "to mint a 20-zloty or 3-ruble coin in order to introduce the name of the ruble in Poland? Or perhaps *imperialy* with a value of 12 rubles or 80 zloty?"[35] Kankrin responded by listing a variety of potential denominations, and the tsar ordered designs for two silver coins (¾ ruble and 1½ rubles) and one gold coin (3 rubles). In January 1833, a decree followed ordering the creation of new 5- and 10-zloty gold coins with a design based on that of the 15 kopeck/1 zloty issue. In May 1834 permission was given for the new coins to be minted, though no longer in St. Petersburg but in Warsaw.[36] A new 3-ruble coin was confirmed in the same imperial decree, and the Warsaw Mint was also instructed to begin issuing a 30-kopeck/2-zloty silver coin. Coins that had been produced on the basis of the decrees of 1815 and 1826 were no longer to be minted.

Thus from the 1830s through 1841, a variety of monies circulated in

Poland: the new ruble/zloty coins, earlier Polish coinage minted in accordance with the decrees of 1815 and 1826, monies issued by the Polish insurgent regime that continued to circulate until 1838, and Polish and foreign *billony*. The introduction of the ruble/zloty coinage in the early 1830s marked, in effect, the true onset of a transition toward unifying the monetary systems of Poland and the empire. The coins were supposed to familiarize the population with Russian money and with the image of Russian power, while at the same time allowing them to continue using their traditional currency. It was probably with this ideological objective foremost in mind that Nicholas ordered the minting of a 10-zloty coin in 1835 with an image of the imperial family. The emperor had been impressed by a thaler that his ambassador to Bavaria had sent him displaying a portrait of the Bavarian king and his family. The Russian mint was now to prepare something similar: on one side of the coin would appear Nicholas's profile, on the other the profile of the empress and the imperial children.[37] Beginning that same year changes were also made to the silver and bronze grosh coins. In contrast to the larger denomination coins, establishing equivalent values between Polish and Russian monies at the penny level was impossible without resorting to complicated fractions. It was just as impossible to inscribe the billons and *groshi* with both Russian and Polish lettering because the coins were simply too small.[38] As a result, the Russian authorities decided to make the design of the billon adhere as much as possible to that of Russian penny coinage. In 1835 and 1836, new billons with this design began appearing, their lettering noticeably stripped of the words "Kingdom of Poland" and "Polish."[39]

From the Zloty to the Ruble

If the introduction of the dual zloty/ruble marked the beginning of a bona fide transition toward monetary unification, unification itself came in 1841 following the Russian empire's adoption of the silver standard and the removal of the last obstacles standing in the way of a currency merger. On January 7, 1841, Kankrin instructed the Department of Mines and Salt Production to prepare designs for gold and silver coinage with Russian and Polish inscriptions. The castings produced were identical to those of coins circulating in interior Russian provinces and, in an important break with precedent, the new coinage was not adjusted to accommodate zloty-based accounting. The 5-ruble gold coin was valued at 33⅓ zlotys, 1 ruble equaled 6⅔ zlotys, one half-ruble equaled 3⅓ zlotys, and so on. Two weeks later, on January 21, 1841, the Polish viceroy issued a decree establishing a single monetary regime between the Polish Kingdom and the rest of the empire.

Poland's full integration into the empire's currency system was made possible by the major reform of Russian finances that had been inaugurated by the manifesto of July 1, 1839, and whose principal achievement was the Russian adoption of the silver standard. In the viceroy's decree, the Russian silver ruble was declared "the single denomination and legal tender" of the region; all government and private accounts were required to be held in rubles; and holders of the paper notes of the Polish Bank were ordered to exchange them for "notes in Russian rubles" with inscriptions in Polish and Russian. All old monies, with the exception of the dual language Russian coins, were to be reminted as Russian rubles. The decree also called for Polish grosh coins to be gradually withdrawn from circulation, though their continued minting was permitted "until further notice" because the government simply did not have enough smaller denomination coinage available for use in the kingdom.[40]

A decree issued a few months later, in April 1841,[41] extended the merger between the Polish and Russian currency regimes by ordering that the former standard unit of weight for Polish monies—the Cologne mark—be abandoned in favor of the Russian pound (*funt*). The Warsaw Mint was now to produce 5-ruble gold coins as well as silver coins in denominations of 1 ruble and 50, 25, 20, 15, 10, and 5 kopecks. The gold and large denomination silver coins were to be virtually identical to their equivalents circulating in the empire. Only the mark of the Warsaw Mint (MW) would provide any hint of the coins' relationship to Poland. The value in groshi was indicated on some of the larger denomination silver kopeck coins, but most displayed only the Russian value. As for the dual zloty/rubles with inscriptions in Russian and Polish, most ceased to be minted, the only exception being the 25-kopeck piece. The Polish Commission on Finances and the Treasury proposed introducing new silver and bronze groshi displaying a portrait of Alexander I and including the inscription "Kingdom of Poland," but the project was rejected by St. Petersburg. Instead, the central government took the opposite approach and elaborated a proposal to change the design of the Polish billon so that it fully resembled Russian petty coinage.[42]

With the decree of 1841, the unification of the two monetary systems was essentially complete. The Russian ruble had eclipsed the zloty. Only one inconsistency remained: the Polish billon. In addressing the question of what to do about the billon, the central government had to reconcile its political goal of establishing a single empire-wide currency with the need to safeguard the money supply and provide for viable currency exchange. According to the government's rulings, the billon should have been gradually withdrawn from circulation. Yet even in 1841, the year that Poland was supposed to join the world of the ruble, the viceroy of Poland was granted permission to mint 450,000 rubles worth of billons. This minting obviously directly contradicted the 1841 decree, but the authorities got around this uncomfortable fact in ingenious fashion by having the billons marked with the year 1840.[43] Indeed, "1840" billons continued to be produced by the Warsaw Mint through 1865. The mint also minted bronze kopecks during this period, but the overall value of billons that it issued was considerably greater.[44]

The basic explanation for the billon's longevity was that the bronze-silver alloy was at once cheaper to mint than silver coins and easier to use than bronze coins. These were the reasons cited by the Polish viceroy in 1857, for example, when he ruled "to allow the continued circulation of the billon in the Kingdom of Poland." The use of the billon, as the viceroy saw it, was a good thing both for the local population and especially for the government; the cost of producing one billon amounted to just 66 percent of the coin's nominal value, allowing the government to save on the difference. Furthermore, starting in 1815, the viceroy calculated that the government had minted some 2 million rubles worth of billons, whereas there were no less than 1,300,000 rubles worth of billons in circulation at the time. Removing the coins would mean, in effect, losing 700,000 rubles, a loss that threatened to seriously affect the kingdom's finances. Moreover, removing the billon would lead to further problems because the government did not have enough petty Russian coinage to exchange for the billons, and thus the broader goal of replacing Polish with Russian coinage would not be met. Indeed, it was more than likely that the population of the kingdom would compensate for the lack of billons by resorting to Prussian or other foreign pennies instead. The Minister of Finance agreed with the viceroy and approved retaining the billons, though he advised against any further mintings, a position that was subsequently endorsed by Alexander II.[45] Even after all this, just one year later, in 1858, the Minister of Finance completely reversed himself and sought the tsar's permission to issue some 100,000 rubles worth of new billons. The minister justified the request by noting that "all the measures taken to this point have been unable to resolve the shortages of petty coinage [in the kingdom] and as a result these coins are in constant need by the local population, especially the working class."[46] In 1859, permission was granted to issue billons to the additional amount of 300,000 rubles.[47]

Repeated requests for new mintings of billons were indicative of the crisis then unfolding within the Polish money supply. Between 1846 and 1852, the Ministry of Finance routinely allowed the Polish administration to mint new bronze kopeck coinage at the Warsaw Mint despite the fact that it generally preferred not to allow so much independence to regional mints. Its preference would have been to send to Poland coins already minted in Russia.[48] The shortage of petty coinage and even larger denomination coinage in Poland was so great, however, that this special concession was made. The reasons for the deficit of coinage were many, but the most important had little to do with Poland's broader integration into the empire's currency regime. Because of the relative autonomy of Polish finances prior to the merger, the merger itself did not produce much instability in the exchange rate of Polish currency on foreign markets. Instead, by far the most important factor, the one that marked a true turning point in the history of Poland's finances, was the introduction to Poland of Russian banknotes.[49]

The Russian Paper Ruble and Its Consequences

The first appearance of paper rubles in Poland was tied to the momentous events of 1848. The revolutions of that year led to severe shortages of coinage in many of Poland's neighboring states, and Polish banknotes began flowing abroad in huge quantities. Hoping to make up for this flight of Polish currency, the Polish viceroy, I. F. Paskevich, took the unilateral and (incidentally) illegal move of permitting government offices in Poland to accept payments in Russian banknotes. Paskevich's measure was envisioned as "temporary," to be rescinded once the revolution was suppressed and the currency situation stabilized, but, as the finance official S. A. Starynkevich later observed, the 1848 revolution was soon followed by "the Hungarian campaign, then the Eastern Question returned to the fore, and soon there was the Danube campaign and the Crimean War."[50] In other words, one thing quickly led to another and the banknotes continued to circulate. The financial crisis that unfolded in the empire as a result of the Crimean conflict led to an inundation of ruble bills throughout the empire, including Poland. Things became so bad that the open exchange of bills for coinage was banned in 1854. The large military presence in Poland meant that the region was awash in paper money. In 1854 alone, the Polish Treasury processed approximately 71 million silver rubles worth of paper rubles. By 1856, in order to see that the notes retained their value, the government announced that they would be considered legal tender for all treasury payments in the kingdom. This measure not surprisingly led to the hoarding of effective coin and the virtual disappearance of coinage from the economy.

In addition to their negative impact on the Polish monetary system, the influx of paper rubles, which increased notably following the removal of the customs barrier between the kingdom and the empire in 1850, also greatly impaired the fiscal operations of the Polish Bank. Foreseeing the potential for problems of this sort as early as 1847, M. Biernacki, who headed the Commission on Finances and the Treasury, and W. Niepokoj-czycki, the head of the Polish Bank, had implored Viceroy Paskevich to secure permission for Polish notes to be accepted for payment by treasury houses within the empire. The two men feared that if this permission were not granted, paper rubles, which were required by law to be accepted every-where, would simply squeeze the Polish notes out of circulation. If this happened and a stampede then developed to exchange the Polish notes for coinage, the Polish Bank, being short of the necessary reserves, would find itself on the brink of collapse. As Biernacki and Niepokojczycki saw it, there were only two ways to avoid this potential catastrophe: either re-establish a separate currency regime in Poland, or permit notes of the Pol-ish Bank to be accepted by Russian treasuries as legal tender.[51]

Paskevich approved the proposal and forwarded it to St. Petersburg, where the matter was taken up by the Ministry of Finance's Committee on Finances in April 1848. As a conciliatory gesture, Paskevich suggested allowing the Polish notes to be accepted by Russian institutions at a pre-mium, but even this concession did not sway the Minister of Finance or his lieutenants. They steadfastly rejected the proposal, arguing that the Polish notes were easily counterfeited and that in any case they were not designed to function in the same way as the state's ruble bills. Therefore, they noted, allowing the Polish notes to be used as "circulating currency would be contrary to [the principles of] our monetary system."[52]

While these discussions were unfolding, the demand for metal coin-age in the kingdom only continued to increase. With each passing day, ever growing quantities of the kingdom's paper credits were sold on for-eign exchanges to pay down the kingdom's foreign debts.[53] Their sale re-quired coming up with over 2 million silver rubles. Another approximately

600,000 silver rubles were required to provide for exchanging the bank's notes. Niepokojczycki was dispatched to St. Petersburg to confront the Ministry of Finance with the urgency of the bank's need for additional coin reserves. He argued to his superiors that if the bank did not receive more coinage, it would not be able to meet its many obligations, including its foreign debts, all of which had been assumed "with supreme approval" —that is to say, on the basis of the emperor's personal guarantee.[54]

Niepokojczycki was convinced that the kingdom's troubles stemmed entirely from its integration into the monetary system of the empire. As he saw it, prior to 1841, when Poland's currency was separate from that of the empire and the kingdom possessed the authority to mint its own money, and even in the first years following the introduction of the ruble regime, the Polish Bank and the Treasury "were able to continue to make payments in metallic currency." But the introduction of ruble bills that began in 1848, Niepokojczycki explained, drained the treasury's metal reserves to the point that it could no longer supply metal to the bank. This situation then led the kingdom's administration to turn to the Ministry of Finance for additional metal reserves that could then be used to cover the exchange of notes tendered by the population and to process debt payments. Petitioning for a yearly infusion of some 2.2 million rubles, Niepokojczycki stressed that "the Polish Bank's recurrent need for support from the empire's reserves would only cease if the current price of promissory notes were to increase . . . or if the paper rubles were withdrawn from circulation since their inordinate supply has led to a complete shortage of coinage in the empire and in Poland."[55] Reviewing the petition, the Minister of Finance subsequently agreed to provide the Polish Bank with a yearly installment of 1,600,000 gold and 600,000 silver rubles.

As it turned out, even massive yearly infusions of coinage were not enough to resolve the ongoing crisis in Polish finances. In 1858, the Polish viceroy M. D. Gorchakov appealed to the Minister of Finance to permit the kingdom's offices to cease accepting payments in Russian paper rubles and to establish a six-month period during which they would be removed from circulation and surrendered for exchange.[56] P. F. Brok, then Minister of Finance, pledged in response to provide the kingdom with the necessary metal reserves and allocated 400,000 in gold rubles to cover foreign debt payments, as well as 100,000 silver rubles to provide for exchanging paper currency. Just a few months later, however, Gorchakov appealed once again to the minister for a significant new tranche of coinage. This time the minister agreed to meet only part of the requested sum and made plain that his ministry would not be able to provide such substantial infusions of effective coin in the future. Given the generally sound condition of Polish business, the minister suggested that the exchange of paper rubles in the kingdom should be performed not in coinage but in promissory notes.[57]

By the end of the 1850s, the monetary crisis in Poland was acute and its effects could be seen in a variety of ways. Foreign monies again began to circulate in border areas. High demand for petty coinage was such that small coins were traded at a 5 percent premium versus paper rubles, Polish banknotes, and even undebased silver coins. Though it was in violation of their statutes, the Land Credit Society as well as the Polish bank were also forced to accept paper rubles and even to use them to make their own payments. The local population, despite the obvious illegality, began to make popular coinage—marks (*marki*)—either out of metal or other materials, while commercial houses, agricultural wholesalers, and even church institutions began issuing bearer bonds (*bilety na pred"iavitelia*) in values from 5 to 50 kopecks. According to the local administration, the total amount of "money" of this sort circulating in the kingdom reached 1 million rubles. The mayor of Warsaw even suggested allowing the city administration to issue small bills so that it could protect the city's population from speculators.

In November 1861, the Polish situation was taken up by the State Council. In the discussion that ensued, the Finance Minister M. Kh. Reitern was forced to acknowledge that the "difficult" financial circumstances in the kingdom were the result of an excessive issuance of paper money, in particular of ruble bills. At the same time, Reitern explained that the Ministry of Finance had done all that it could to alleviate the situation by providing the kingdom with annual deliveries of metal currency, permitting continued minting of the billon, and issuing lower denomination bills in exchange for larger ones.[58] The State Council ultimately ruled in March 1862 that the Polish administration should open provisional exchange offices in the kingdom to allow users to trade in their large banknotes for smaller denomination bills. If necessary, the smaller notes were to be issued on the basis of reserves provided by the State Bank.[59]

In 1863, a new initiative came to the fore as the Kingdom's Ruling Committee (*Sovet upravleniia*) proposed printing four series of interest- and non-interest-bearing bonds for a total sum of 4 million rubles. The issue of these notes, as the committee saw it, would help alleviate the kingdom's continuing problems with the supply of petty coinage while at the same time providing revenue to the treasury. Not surprisingly, however, the Financial Committee of the Ministry of Finance categorically rejected this proposal. While the Finance Minister and his advisors felt that the printing of interest-bearing notes was inappropriate for the time being, their more strenuous objection concerned the issue of the non–interest-bearing notes, which were seen as tantamount to the issue of a new Polish paper currency. As far as the Financial Committee was concerned, "the issue of notes of this sort would have a most negative effect on the empire's paper ruble," whose value would inevitably fall as a result of the Polish printing.[60]

As the kingdom's currency woes continued, a special committee was established within the office of the Polish viceroy in 1864 under the chairmanship of Lieutenant General Gegevich. The committee reviewed the kingdom's financial situation and proposed a series of measures to address the situation, including a new request to the Ministry of Finance for additional silver coinage, permission to allow the viceroy to direct the Warsaw Mint to issue requisite quantities of billons without obtaining prior approval from St. Petersburg, the introduction of new strictures against the issue of illegal "marks" by the general population, and permission to print small denomination treasury notes in order to meet (at least partially) the high demand for petty coinage.[61] Once these proposals reached the Polish Committee (*Komitet po delam Tsarstva Pol'skogo*), however, they too met with resistance. The Polish Committee endorsed the new measures against illegal monies, but, much as the Ministry of Finance had done earlier and in similar terms, it vigorously opposed the issuing of non–interest-bearing Polish notes. The committee concluded that if the Kingdom of Poland were to issue notes of this sort, "then [it] would be in a position to develop its own paper currency separate from our ruble bill. Given the indivisibility of the kingdom and the empire, this eventuality cannot be permitted."[62]

The Polish Committee approved the last issue of 500,000 silver rubles worth of billons in January 1865, though the end of the billon did not mark the end of Poland's financial troubles. Russian paper rubles continued to flood the kingdom, and the finance official Starynkevich, writing that same year, saw only three possible courses to completely resolve the situation. One was to formally legalize the circulation of paper rubles in the kingdom (this measure ironically had never actually been taken) and thus ensure that the central treasury would be bound to provide the Polish treasury with the appropriate coinage reserves; another was to ban the circulation of paper rubles within the kingdom as Gorchakov had proposed earlier; and a third possible solution was to establish a direct equivalence (*vzaimnost'*) between lending practices in Poland and in the empire. Inasmuch as the Polish treasury as well as individual Poles were obligated to accept payments in Russian securities, it followed that Polish banknotes should also begin to circulate in the same way, with the value of the notes themselves guaranteed by commensurate reserves from the imperial treasury. Starynkevich viewed this last solution as the best of the three, because "by easing the relations of commerce, it would be of interest to both countries, that is, to both parts of the same state . . . and in time could provide the basis both for establishing a single consolidated budget . . . and for easing the burden of the kingdom's foreign debt. . . . This material rapprochement [between the kingdom and the empire] would perhaps serve as the best and most reliable road to an eventual spiritual union, that is, to the effective merging [of the two territories] into a single state."[63]

The following year the Polish and Russian budgets were indeed consolidated, though the harmonious joining of interests suggested by Starynkevich was not much in evidence. The Polish Bank was not accorded the right to issue banknotes; consequently the merger of the currency systems of the two territories ultimately came down to a situation in which Russia's financial system simply swallowed the Polish one. Currency reform in Poland thenceforth became part of a broader series of policies undertaken to normalize the imperial monetary system in the aftermath of the Polish rebellion of 1863, a rebellion that incidentally also prompted stirrings of monetary reform in Russia itself.

Conclusion

It would be an exaggeration to say that the financial crisis brought on by the introduction of the paper ruble alone led to the end of Poland's financial autonomy. To be sure, political concerns were always paramount and leeway for financial autonomy under Russian power was always limited. Between 1830 and 1866, Poland's finances were gradually incorporated into the financial orbit of the empire. The first and most important step in this direction was the decision taken after the rebellion of 1830 to deny the administration of the kingdom the authority to develop its own fiscal and budgetary policies. Forced to align their financial operations with the directives of the Ministry of Finance, the kingdom's rights of maneuver on European capital markets were also severely curtailed. The foreign loans concluded by the kingdom in 1835 and 1844 were likewise dictated not only by the particular needs of the Polish treasury, but also quite clearly by the broader financial and strategic goals of the empire. Over time Poland lost access to a variety of potential sources of revenue, which were instead directed toward the central Russian treasury. In 1850, the kingdom lost its customs service and the autonomy afforded by its own customs regime. By the 1860s, an independent Polish budget had for all intents and purposes ceased to exist, with the Polish treasury completely subordinated to the dictates of the Ministry of Finance.

Given these developments, it was clearly impossible for Poland to maintain and develop a monetary system of its own in the nineteenth century. To possess one's own currency is a basic condition of state sovereignty. The Ministry of Finance was well aware of this and consequently took steps beginning in the 1830s to eliminate "regional" currencies (especially in cases where their elimination did not directly affect its revenue) and merge them gradually into a single, empire-wide currency regime. The Ministry's policies in Poland in the 1830s and 1840s were entirely consistent with this approach. The development of a single state-wide currency system represented one of the "universal principles" underlying Russia's otherwise diverse platform of imperial policies.

In response to the question of typicality, one would have to say that the empire's financial policies in Poland in the nineteenth century were indeed typical, though only partially so. The empire's actions in Poland were influenced by a variety of factors largely unique to the Polish case, such as the essentially Western European orientation of the Polish economy and Polish financial institutions, and the existence in Poland of a "financial culture" and financial traditions that were somewhat unfamiliar to the Russian financial leadership. Overall, despite great efforts toward creating a single, empire-wide system of finance, St. Petersburg was not able to achieve total uniformity in its fiscal policies, not even when it came to currency matters. Indeed, if the viability of a separate Polish currency was seriously undermined by the crisis of the 1850s and its circulation stopped altogether in the 1860s, this was not the case everywhere. In Russian Finland, for example, the monetary crisis had the opposite effect of actually helping to launch a separate Finnish currency—the Finnish mark—whose issue was approved by imperial decree in the spring of 1860. The introduction of the new Finnish currency is a vivid reminder of the fact that while the Ministry of Finance may have aspired to and even vigorously pursued "universal principles," it also never developed an entirely consistent conceptualization of regional fiscal policy.

More often than not, Russia's financial politics were dictated by geopolitical concerns and by the need to ensure (as much as possible) a certain legal and administrative uniformity to imperial governance. The case of Poland was something of an exception in this respect. Poland briefly enjoyed a measure of fiscal autonomy alongside the political autonomy that it had been granted by Alexander I. Following the rebellion of 1830, both the kingdom's political and fiscal autonomy came to be seen as suspect and dangerous, and in the financial sphere, a clear and radical shift occurred in Poland's position within the imperial monetary system. The gradual transition from the zloty to the ruble can thus be seen as a process that mirrored larger changes in the political relationship between Poland and the empire in the nineteenth century. At the same time, the Polish case also reveals something of a broader imperial dynamic in the financial sphere. The imperial borderlands presented St. Petersburg with compelling diversities, and St. Petersburg responded by pursuing (or at the very least hoping for) standardization; but the fiscal relationship between center and region was always complex and shifting. As a result, the road to a uniform Russian currency and financial field within the empire proved to be long and difficult.

Translated by Willard Sunderland

Notes

Research for this chapter was made possible through the generous support of a Young Researcher's Grant provided by the Science Support Foundation of the Russian Federation.

1. V. N. Riabtsevich, *Rossiisko-"Pol'skie" monetnye emissii epokhi Petra I* (Tol'iatti, 1995), 33.

2. Ibid., 7–103.

3. Ibid., 104–215; "Monety, chekanennye dlia Prussii," in Georgii Mikhailovich (Great Prince), *Russkie monety, chekanennye dlia Prussii 1759–1762, Gruzii 1804–1833, Pol'shi 1815–1841, Finliandii 1864–1890* (St. Petersburg, 1893) (hereafter *Russkie monety*); P. fon Vinkler, *Iz istorii monetnogo dela v Rossii: Moldavo-Valakhskaia moneta (1771–1774)* (St. Petersburg, 1899); I. G. Spasskii, *Russkaia monetnaia sistema* (Leningrad, 1970), 219.

4. Russia's enemies also engaged in similar extraordinary mintings. In 1788, for example, the Swedish government minted Russian *piataki* for use by the Swedish Army in its campaign against the Russians in Finland. See Spasskii, *Russkaia monetnaia sistema*, 222.

5. Fon Vinkler, *Iz istorii monetnogo dela v Rossii: Tavricheskaia moneta 1783–1788* (St. Petersburg, 1899); Spasskii, *Russkaia monetnaia sistema*, 219–220.

6. Fon Vinkler, *Iz istorii monetnogo dela v Rossii: monety dlia Estliandii i Lifliandii (1756–1757)* (St. Petersburg, 1898); Spasskii, *Russkaia monetnaia sistema*, 219.

7. Rossiiskii gosudarstvennyi istoricheskii arkhiv (hereafter: RGIA), f. 1152, op. 1 (1812), d. 112.

8. For almost two decades in the late eighteenth century, special regional coins were also minted in Siberia. On the circumstances of this minting, see Spasskii, *Russkaia monetnaia sistema*, 205.

9. M. M. Speranskii, "Plan finansov," *Sbornik imperatorskogo russkogo istoricheskogo obshchestva*, 45 (1885): 28–29.

10. RGIA, f. 560, op. 10, d. 69, ll. 7–9 (ob).

11. "O monetnoi sisteme Tsarstva Pol'skogo," *Russkie monety*, 3.

12. "Predstavlenie direktora Varshavskogo monetnogo dvora ministru finansov Tsarstva Pol'skogo," *Russkie monety*, 13.

13. "Otnoshenie ministra st.-sekretaria S. Grabovskogo k namestniku Tsarstva Pol'skogo," *Russkie monety*, 12; RGIA, f. 1101, op. 1, d. 321, ll. 31–33.

14. *Russkie monety*, 15.

15. RGIA, f. 560, op. 10, d. 282.

16. RGIA, f. 1142, op. 1 (1827), d. 78, l. 20(ob).

17. RGIA, f. 1152, op. 1 (1827), d. 78, l. 5.

18. Ibid., ll. 25–28.

19. RGIA, f. 37, op. 20, d. 1818, ll. 1–4.

20. "Postanovlenie vremennogo pravleniia (revoliutsionnogo): o peredache monetnogo dvora v vedenie Pol'skogo banka," *Russkie monety*, 15.

21. "Postanovleniia narodnogo pravleniia, 23 marta 1831 g. i 29 marta 1831 g.," *Russkie monety*, 16.

22. Władysław Terlecki, "Polityka monetarna Banku Polskiego w dobie Powstania listopadowego," *Wiadomości numizmatyczne* 4, no. 1 (1962).

23. "Predstavlenie pol'skogo banka, 22 dekabria /2 ianvaria 1831 g.," *Russkie monety*, 17.

24. Archivum Główne Akt Dawnych (hereafter: AGAD), Osobennaia kantseliariia ministerstva finansov, no. 2, 50.

25. See E. A. Pravilova, "Rossiia i Tsarskoe Pol'skoe: mekhanizmy biudzhetno-finansovykh otnoshenii v imperskoi sisteme (1815–1866)," in B. V. Anan'ich and S. I. Barzilov, eds., *Prostranstvo vlasti: istoricheskii opyt Rossii i vyzovy sovremennosti* (Moscow, 2001), 235–263.

26. RGIA, f. 37, op. 18, d. 92, ll. 4–4(ob).

27. Ibid., ll. 10–10(ob).

28. Ibid., l. 12.

29. Ibid., ll. 23–25.

30. Ibid., l. 19.

31. Ibid., l. 32.

32. Ibid., l. 52.

33. Ibid., l. 74.

34. *Polnoe sobranie zakonov rossiiskoi imperii* (hereafter: PSZ), series 2, vol. 7, no. 5678 (1832): 713. See also Georgii Mikhailovich (Grand Prince), *Monety tsarstvovaniia Nikolaia I* (St. Petersburg, 1890), 46.

35. RGIA, f. 37, op. 18, d. 92, l. 82.

36. *PSZ*, series 2, vol. 9, no. 7032 (1834): 341; *Monety tsarstvovaniia Nikolaia I*, 52.

37. "Pis'mo gr. Kankrina upravliaiushchemu Departamentom gornykh i solianykh del, 12 sentiabria 1835 i dr. dokumenty," *Monety tsarstvovaniia Nikolaia I*, 59.

38. "Otnoshenie namestnika Tsarstva Pol'skogo k ministru stats-sekretariiu Grabovskomu, 20 marta (1 aprelia) 1835," *Russkie monety*, 19.

39. W. Terlecki, "System monetarny Królestwa Polskiego po powstaniu listopadowym (1832–1842)," *Wiadomości Numizmatyczne*, 10, no. 1 (1966): 4–5.

40. *Monety tsarstvovaniia Nikolaia I*, 82.

41. Ibid., 83.

42. Terlecki, "System monetarny Królewstva Polskiego," 9.

43. "Otnoshenie ministra st.-sekretaria I. Turkula k namestniku Tsarstva Pol'skogo o vysochaishem soizvolenii na otchekanku billona na 450,000 r.s. pod starym shtempelem i 1840 g.," *Russkie monety*, 25.

44. On the "1840" *billony*, see W. Terlecki, "Mennica Królestwa Polskiego w okresie jej likwidacji (1842–1867)," *Wiadomości Numizmatyczne* 11, no. 1 (1967): 2; and *Monety tsarstvovaniia Nikolaia I*, 116. See also RGIA, f. 583, op. 4, d. 252, ll. 338–345(ob); f. 583, op. 4, d. 254, ll. 22–28(ob); and f. 583, op. 4, d. 256, ll. 92–98, 181.

45. RGIA, f. 583, op. 4, d. 258, ll. 128–134.

46. Ibid., d. 260, ll. 340–347.

47. Ibid., d. 263, l. 7.

48. "O predpolozhenii namestnika Tsarstva Pol'skogo chekanit' na Varshavskom monetnom dvore novuiu mednuiu monetu i o mnenii ministra finansov otklonit' eto predpolozhenie," *Monety tsarstvovaniia Nikolaia I*, 141.

49. I. S. Poznanskii, *Istoricheskii ocherk ekonomicheskogo polozheniia Pol'shi* (St. Petersburg, 1875), 25.

50. RGIA, f. 869, op. 1, d. 611, l. 85 (ob).

51. AGAD, Komisja Rządowa Przychodów i Skarbu, no. 2351, page number not indicated.

52. Ibid.

53. On the question of Polish foreign loans, see E. A. Pravilova, "Imperskaia politika i finansy: vneshnie zaimy Tsarstva Pol'skogo," *Istoricheskie zapiski* 4, no. 122 (2001): 271–316.

54. RGIA, f. 583, op. 4, d. 256, ll. 395–397.

55. Ibid., l. 400 (ob).

56. RGIA, f. 869, op. 1, d. 611, l. 85 (ob).

57. Ibid., l. 86.

58. Ibid., l. 90.

59. Ibid., l. 90 (ob).

60. RGIA, f. 563, op. 2, d. 177, ll. 61–61(ob).

61. RGIA, f. 1270, op. 1, d. 6, ll. 5–9.

62. RGIA, f. 869, op. 1, d. 611, ll. 93(ob)–94.

63. Ibid., l. 99 (ob).

12 The Muslim Question in Late Imperial Russia

Elena Campbell

In the second half of the nineteenth century a series of "questions" came to occupy a prominent place in the Russian political lexicon. While some questions concerned a political and social issue across the empire as a whole (for example, the woman question), others, such as the Jewish question, the Ukrainian question, and the Baltic question (*ostzeiskii vopros*), pertained only to non-Russian subjects of the empire. While it problematized not a specific nationality or region, but rather a religion with adherents of many various ethnicities and places of residence, the Muslim question was regarded by contemporaries as one of the so-called "alien questions" (*inorodcheskie voprosy*).

The importance attached to issues concerning non-Russians by both ruling circles and the public is evidence of the spread of nationalist ideas in the empire at this time. Nationalist ideas challenged dynastic and estate-based imperial loyalty, on which the autocracy had theretofore relied,[1] and gave a particular poignancy to the problem of maintaining the empire's integrity. If the Romanovs had accepted nationalism as a state ideology, it would have meant a radical transformation of both the social and the political order. At the same time, they were compelled to react to the nationalistic challenge—to find ways of integrating their subjects into the empire and maintaining the state's unity. As for political order, the tsars hesitated to delegate political power to a representative body. Instead, Alexander III and later Nicolas II accepted the concept of "popular autocracy" as the ideology of their rule. However, the slogan of unity between the tsar and the people was not sufficient for legitimizing the regime and securing the integrity of the empire. The nationalist way of thinking promoted a reconceptualization of the character of the empire, and of the goals of imperial policies. While imperial authorities considered state unity a condition necessary for successful competition with other countries, they came to view the traditional heterogeneous character of the empire as a political problem.

Scholars have noticed that from the second half of the nineteenth century, and especially at the beginning of the twentieth century, imperial institutions and political elites used more often the category of ethnicity while describing the differences between imperial subjects. (Other fundamental categories in use at the time were estate and confessional affiliation).[2] Attempts to establish Russianness (*russkost'*) as the cornerstone of the empire were challenging the traditional perception of the politically centralized dynastic multinational empire.[3] An important sign of change was the gradual expansion of the legal category of "aliens" (*inorodtsy*). Originally this category was applied to nomadic and semi-nomadic tribes of Siberia, but later it began to include all of the non-Russian population of the empire (excluding Ukrainians and Byelorussians who were considered as a part of the Russian nation).[4] Concepts of "rapprochement" (*sblizhenie/sliianie*) of aliens with Russians and of a "united and indivisible" state received particular emphasis in Russian imperial rhetoric at this time. While Russian nationality was given an integrative role in the state, aliens began to be associated with separatism and potential threats to state integrity and the Russians' dominant role in the empire. However, the degree, the pace, and the results of rapprochement had not been clearly formulated into a program by the imperial authorities. A template to be applied to the different nationalities did not exist. Partly, this had to do with the asymmetrical character of the empire in the spheres of administrative, legal, economic, social, and cultural life. The continued expansion of the empire and the increase of the non-Russian population made the development of uniform policies unrealistic.

Initiative in the reformulation of the alien questions belonged to the public, as well as to local church and civil authorities. An important factor facilitating debate on these questions was the development of the press after Alexander II's liberal reforms. Stressing the importance of state unity, central authorities made attempts to discourage active public discussion of certain alien questions, because this discussion was not just a way of articulating existing problems, but also a discourse about the instability of the empire. But gradually, central authorities became involved in this discussion and had to develop measures aimed at solving these questions.[5] The present chapter seeks to ascertain who formulated the "Muslim question" and the circumstances in which they did so. In the end, the Muslim question acquired a distinctly ethnic tint and was merged into the "Tatar-Muslim question."

From the 1860s on, Orthodox clerics were especially active in problematizing Islam and bringing the Muslim question to the attention of the imperial authorities and the Russian public. This took place in the context of a new wave of missionary activity launched in the Volga region in response to the apostasy of the baptized Tatars to Islam.[6] Initially local ecclesiastical authorities regarded this phenomenon as a temporary delusion rooted in baptized Tatars' ignorance of and inability to understand Christianity. With time, however, this view of the conversion of baptized Tatars to Islam changed. Orthodox clergy began to attribute the steady flow of cases of apostasy to Muslim propaganda and to Islam's intrinsic strength, which was opposed to Russian cultural influence. The apparent spread of Islam to the neighboring non-Muslim peoples began to generate serious misgivings, especially since this was taking place in the empire's internal provinces, where Russian power and the Orthodox church were assumed to have a long-standing and solid position.

Local civil authorities were not inclined to ascribe any serious political significance to these apostasies, which they regarded as disorders, and those responsible were considered to be merely individuals spreading nonsensical rumors among the Tatar population.[7] The actions of the local administration, which desired merely the speedy re-establishment of order, took the form primarily of locating and then exiling "instigators."

Ecclesiastical authorities regarded the phenomenon of "apostasy" in more dramatic terms. In 1867 Kazan Archbishop Antonii (Amfiteatrov) presented a report to the Holy Synod, in which he drew attention to the strengthening in the Kazan region of the "Mohammedan spirit" [*magometanskii dukh*], whose main source of support, he believed, were the mullahs and mosques.[8] The Archbishop compared "Mohammedanism" in the eastern part of the empire with "Latinism" in the western provinces and called upon authorities to take restrictive measures with respect to Muslims. Antonii's report was forwarded to the Department of Religious Affairs of Foreign Confessions (under the Ministry of Internal Affairs) for consideration by the consultant on Muslims affairs, A. K. Kazem-Bek, who, not sharing the majority of the Archbishop's apprehensions, expressed the hope that the government would exercise caution in its relation to Muslims.[9] The latter position was supported by the department's director, E. K. Seivers, in a letter to Antonii (1876). Responding to the Archbishop's demands to apply repressive measures in the matter of apostasy, Seivers wrote of the impossibility of combating religious beliefs by means of punitive measures.[10]

From the 1870s on, the problem of the "apostasy" movement became a frequent subject in the Orthodox press. The authors of these articles, usually missionaries and priests, blamed their failures on Islam.[11] In the absence of a Muslim mission and the right of Muslims to proselytize Islam openly in Russia, the missionaries viewed the success of Muslim propaganda to be the result of the broad dissemination of Muslim schools and mosques.[12] According to the missionaries, the development of Muslim propaganda had been made possible in part by the "mistaken" policy of Catherine II, which, in their opinion, had been directed toward the support of Islam in Russia.[13] The missionaries believed that religious confession was connected to the idea of nationality. As Orthodoxy was viewed as the Russian faith, so Islam was considered the Tatar faith. In 1897 the priest I. A. Iznoskov wrote, "Among Tatars the idea of a Tatar and a Muslim are contemplated inseparably. Propagandizing Mohammedanism, they propagandize Tatarness as well. He who accepts Islam also accepts the [Tatar] nationality."[14] Thus Tatars, devoted to their faith, appeared to missionaries as influential "Kulturträgers of the Muslim East,"[15] and they saw the rivalry between Orthodoxy and Islam as a battle for cultural domination in the empire.

Associating baptism with the acceptance of Russian values—that is, values propagated by the state—clerics regarded the apostasy of baptized Tatars and the spread of Islam among pagans as a serious political problem that merited the government's attention. The problem of apostasy and Muslim propaganda became a subject of attention for the Committee of Ministers in conjunction with the discussion of an 1881 report from the governor of Kazan region. In his conclusion on the matter of apostasy, Chief Procurator of the Holy Synod Konstantin Pobedonostsev, drawing on the authoritative opinion of the Kazan missionary Nikolai Il'minskii, wrote, "the apostasy movement is a chronic calamity characteristic not only of Kazan Province, but almost everywhere in Russia. It is difficult to define with precision the true reason for this long-standing and stubborn aspiration for Mohammedanism, which constantly appears among baptized Tatars, but one may suppose that it in all likelihood is chiefly the result of the mechanical and hasty baptism of Tatars, who did not have a deep conviction in Christianity's truth and salvation."[16] Expressing his support for missionary activity, Pobedonostsev also considered that to be successful it would be necessary "to paralyze forces hostile to Christianity," that is, to institute restrictive measures with regard to Islam.

Surveying the situation in the Kazan region in 1884, the Committee of Ministers noted that the return of baptized Tatars to Islam had become a mass phenomenon after the peasant emancipation of the 1860s. Since then the degree of control exercised by the center had weakened, and the power of both rural communities and the Muslim clergy had grown. Recognizing the strength of Muslim religious convictions, the Committee decided that at the present stage there could be talk only of keeping within Orthodoxy those people who were officially Orthodox but had begun to go over to Islam. For this purpose it was appropriate to develop missionary activity and schools among apostates.[17]

Another important factor contributing to the rise of Islam as a matter of particular attention was the empire's annexation of expansive territories inhabited by Muslims in the second half of the nineteenth century. As a result, by the end of the century Muslims had become the largest non-Christian religious group in the empire. The religion and way of life of these new subjects represented a significant obstacle to the policy of rapprochement. The state was now facing the question of how to incorporate the Muslim population into the structure of a Russian Orthodox state. The unfamiliar world of Muslims concealed within itself a potential danger for Russians.

In 1867, Orenburg governor-general N. A. Kryzhanovskii wrote to Minister of Internal Affairs P. A. Valuev, "After the advance into the depths of Central Asia and the annexation of Turkestan to the empire, the entire boundless space from Kazan to the Tian-Shan mountain range represents an uninterrupted Muslim population. . . . The image of such a mass of people confessing a religion according to whose dogmas we, Christians, are regarded as the natural and irreconcilable enemies of all true believers, should automatically draw the government's attention, all the more so since this same Islam has provoked at the present time in neighboring China such a degree of fanatical barbarity that holy war for the faith has been declared, and continues beyond our borders still further."[18] This circumstance, in the governor-general's view, allowed one to speak of a "Muslim question" in the eastern part of Russia. Valuev, on the other hand, regarded the situation in less dramatic terms and considered the weakening of Muslim fanaticism to be a matter of time.[19]

In 1899–1900 the Turkestan governor-general S. M. Dukhovskoi posed the Muslim question. Dukhovskoi had expressed his thoughts on this problem in various papers and reports to St. Petersburg, as well as in the press. The cause for raising the question was the uneasy situation in Turkestan, in particular, the attack by a group of Muslims on the Andijan garrison in the Ferghana Valley in 1898. Based on the opinion that Islam was incompatible with all Christian culture and had developed in its adherents an extreme intolerance toward other religions, Dukhovskoi considered the subjugation of Turkestan's Muslims to be illusory.[20] According to the governor-general, the European advance into the East had "awakened the Muslim world" and had facilitated its solidarity under the slogan of Pan-Islamism. Looking to the anti-European manifestations in China at the time (the Boxer Rebellion), Dukhovskoi considered an "all-Muslim *ghazawat*" to be an entirely realistic possibility.[21] He criticized the tendency of the central authorities to regard the Muslim question as purely religious, devoid of any political tinge, and proposed establishing a general state plan for the resolution of what he saw as a crucial problem.

The governor-general's view of Islam as a "force hostile to Russian state interests" did not find support in governmental circles. Minister of Finance S. Iu. Witte acknowledged the existence of a Muslim question, but unlike Dukhovskoi did not consider the problem to be particularly dangerous. Witte evaluated internal policy with regard to Muslims in connection with Russia's foreign policy in the Muslim East. From this perspective, the state's acceptance of Dukhovskoi's views would constitute "a decisive change in policy concerning Muslim subjects. And this, in turn, would offer a basis for accusing Russia of intolerance to Islam and would generate a hostile mood toward her throughout the Muslim world, which would inevitably affect Russia's position in the east."[22] As far as Dukhovskoi's apprehensions about the spread of Pan-Islamism among Russian Muslims were concerned, Witte considered the facts presented by the governor-general to be insufficient for drawing any conclusions. And Pan-Islamism itself, as a new phenomenon, required extensive study, in Witte's opinion. Witte suggested that the religious-political unification of Russian Muslims would scarcely be possible in practice, since ethnic and cultural differences among Muslims would hinder this. On the whole, Witte considered Muslims to be sufficiently loyal subjects.[23]

Recognizing the strength of Muslim religious convictions, central authorities at the end of the nineteenth century regarded the Muslim question as merely a religious problem and were not inclined to ascribe to it any political significance. Some local officials, for example, Turkestan Governor-

General K. P. von Kaufman, maintained the position that, as long as they were not intruded upon, Muslim religious convictions would not necessarily represent an obstacle to a policy of integration.[24] At this time ruling circles considered far more politically dangerous "ideas about distinctive nationality and the attainment of independence," with which Russian Muslims, according to the Ministry of Internal Affairs (MVD), "were not yet infected."[25] Therefore, for the time being central authorities did not see any grounds for fearing "any kind of difficulties, at least as concerns the majority of Muslims," considering them to be entirely loyal subjects. Important factors defining the official position with regard to Muslims were international relations and the foreign interests of Russia in the East. With this in mind, authorities tried not to over-dramatize the situation inside the country and sought instead to maintain relations with Muslim subjects that would appear peaceful externally. In its policy toward Muslims, the authorities accordingly attempted to avoid everything that could seem to represent an encroachment on Muslims' religious convictions.

But for others, the presence in the empire of a widespread Muslim culture based on principles interpreted as hostile to state ideology and European civilization (of which Russia considered itself to be a part), the resistance of Muslims to rapid assimilation, and the spread of Islamic influence among non-Muslim peoples constituted the "Muslim question" and a serious one. In the view of its proponents, the Muslim question represented both a political and a religious problem. First of all, unassimilated Muslims, in their eyes, were unreliable subjects who threatened Russia's security and state unity. Second, the influence of Islam on non-Muslim peoples was regarded as a threat to Russian cultural dominance. Interpreted in this way, the Muslim question was not a problem restricted to any one particular region, but was relevant for the empire as a whole. For these reasons, missionaries and some local officials repeatedly requested that the Muslim question be addressed at a more general level, believing that it could only be resolved as a problem that concerned the entire empire.

Differences in the views of missionaries and central authorities in regard to the Muslim question gave rise to quite different approaches to the realization of rapprochement of Muslims with Russians. The Orthodox clergy and missionaries in particular began from the proposition that Muslims were staunchly devoted to their faith and would always be hostile to Christians. Therefore, only Orthodoxy was capable of making a heterodox person into a "reliable" subject. "Aliens" should accordingly "come together" [*sblizit'sia*] with Russians through Christianity. Moreover, missionary activity should serve civilizing goals, introducing principles of "higher" culture into the Muslim world. These ideas found their incarnation in projects for the religious-moral enlightenment of Muslims. Thus one sees in the nineteenth century the establishment of the Orthodox Missionary Society, anti-Muslim missions, and religious brotherhoods with missionary goals. At the Kazan Ecclesiastical Academy a missionary division was created and special missionary courses were established.

The Volga region was to serve as the beachhead for the realization of these missionary plans.[26] The missionary project of enlightenment was closely connected with the system of N. I. Il'minskii, which consisted of Christianizing aliens in their native languages with the help of missionaries, teachers, and priests drawn from alien communities. With this goal in mind, missionaries promoted the publishing of religious books in "alien languages" with the use of the Cyrillic alphabet. In practical terms this system was realized at the Central Baptized-Tatar School in Kazan and in other alien schools in the Russian East.

Despite some successes in the Christianization of a segment of Turkic and Finnic peoples of the Volga region, ruling circles acknowledged more than once that the acceptance of Christianity did not draw aliens closer to the Russian world; that Orthodoxy, when compared to Islam, occupied a rather weak position; and that missionary work merely rendered the situation more strained.[27] Missionaries themselves acknowledged that in a religious sense it was more than difficult to struggle with Islam. The state tried to avoid missionary activity in its policy with regard to Islam. Without rejecting Orthodox priorities on an official level, from the second half of the nineteenth century the government emphasized the spread of the Russian language and attracting Muslims to state schools.

An important aspect of the Muslim problem was the existence of a Muslim clergy in Russia, which exerted influence on the Muslim population. As a result of the policy of religious toleration and the regulation of the spiritual life of non-Orthodox subjects established in the eighteenth century, religious administrations were eventually created for Muslims of Crimea, Transcaucasia, and the eastern part of European Russia. The Muslim clergy was thereby integrated into the structure of state administration. For decisions concerning family affairs, marriages, property concerns, and matters of ritual, the application of Muslim religious law (*shariat*) was permitted. But in the views of Orthodox clergy and some local administrators in Muslim regions, mullahs were "anti-Russian" elements who hindered the policy of rapprochement between Muslims and Russians. From their perspective the official recognition of Muslim spiritual organizations supported the "seclusion" and "fanaticism" of the Muslim population and thus represented a mistake on the part of the state. They considered it necessary to restrict to a maximum degree the activities and rights of Muslim religious figures. Ruling circles ascribed considerable importance to their relations with the Muslim clergy. Fearing manifestations of religious fanaticism, state authorities rejected radical measures with regard to existing religious institutions and conducted a policy that was geared toward the further bureaucratization, Russification, and subordination of officially existing institutions to state control. A different approach was adopted in other Muslim regions—north Caucasus, Turkestan, and the steppe region. Here, religious life was not subjected to clear forms of regulation, and Muslim religious figures did not receive official status as a "clergy." In judicial affairs preference was given to customary law (*adat*), which authorities saw as offering a more convenient foundation than did shariat for transition to all-empire institutions.[28]

At the beginning of the twentieth century the thinking on Muslims in Russia began to change. Unexpectedly for Russians, the "ignorant and fanatical Muslim world . . . had awakened." The director of the Tashkent Teachers' Seminary, N. P. Ostroumov, called the twentieth century the century of the "awakening of Muslims," describing this as "a conscious movement of Muslims toward universal [*obshchechelovecheskoe*] enlightenment and toward forms of life that are in accord with modern conceptions of culture and progress."[29] In Ostroumov's view, this movement, which had begun in the 1870s among the foremost segments of the Tatar population, had not been immediately noticed by Russian authorities, who had paid attention to it only once it acquired a political character.[30]

The "awakening" about which Ostroumov wrote was connected to Jadidism, a movement manifested in an especially vivid fashion among the Tatar intelligentsia and directed toward the modernization of Muslim life through the reform of the system of religious education, the introduction of European achievements into Muslim culture, and the creation of a single Turkic language.[31] The first in Russia to pay attention to this phenomenon were missionaries. On the one hand, they viewed with skepticism Muslims' efforts to modernize Islam, considering Islam and progress incompatible. On the other hand, missionaries saw in this movement national ideas, which, from their point of view, were facilitating the strengthening of the insularity of the Muslim population and thus complicating the Muslim question by transforming it into a "Tatar-Muslim question." In this regard N. I. Il'minskii wrote to Pobedonostsev that under the guise of "cultured progress" [*intelligentnyi progress*] the Muslim intelligentsia, including "Gasprinskii & Co.," had begun to adopt a "national-political" point of view in place of "the usual awkward and unseemly fanaticism," and were seeking to establish a Muslim cultural center in Russia.[32] Il'minskii indicated that it was precisely in Russian educational institutions that Muslims had acquired national ideas,[33] which in his view were much more dangerous than the notorious "fanaticism." Concerned about the spread of "progressive ideas on a Mohammedan foundation," Il'minskii repeatedly underscored the complication of the Muslim question in Russia in his letters to Pobedonostsev.[34] Similarly, Ostroumov wrote, "We understand and value the movement among Russian Muslims for education, which expresses itself in the aspiration to improve methods of instruction and certain textbooks, but we do not understand their inclination for insularity, which allows us to regard the Tatar question as having been born in Russia." This question, he believed, "should be a cause of concern for the Russian government."[35] In Ostroumov's opinion, this movement was deepening an already-existing insularity of Muslim culture. The declarations by progressive Muslims of their aspiration to draw closer to Russia on the basis of Islam and Turkish culture did not earn Ostroumov's sympathy.[36]

At the beginning of the twentieth century governmental institutions became more interested in the awakening of Muslims. The staff of the Main Administration for Press Affairs, analyzing the Muslim press, acknowledged the appearance of "new influences" in Tatar literature, which "threatened to shatter the entire centuries-old style of life of a Muslim population in Russia." Describing Gasprinskii's newspaper *Tercüman*, the head of the administration, N. V. Shakhovskoi, noted the "duplicitous" orientation of that paper, which he saw in its approval of the Russian government, on the one hand, and its praise of the Turkish sultan and of the European enlightenment of the Tatars, on the other.[37] In Shakhovskoi's view, the Muslim movement had turned into an effort to foist Turkish culture on Muslim peoples.[38] According to information from the Department of Police, at first these new influences among Muslims appeared in the "innocent" form of the spread of Gasprinskii's new method of instruction. Thereafter it turned into "an intellectual and social movement" that divided Muslims into two sides: "traditionalists" and "progressives." The Department of Police was hard-pressed to predict which of these two parties would emerge victorious, and how far the victors would go. Nonetheless, evaluating the issue from the standpoint of "Russian state interests" (*interesy russkoi gosudarstvennosti*), the department recognized both sides as equally "unreliable" due to their "alienation from Russia" (*otchuzhdenie ot Rossii*).[39]

The revolutionary situation in Russia in 1905, as well as the government's promise of reform, not least in the realm of religious policy, were conducive to the politicization of the Muslim movement in the country. Recalling that time, the priest S. Bagin wrote, "The liberation movement roused Muslim Tatars . . . Everywhere there were meetings, gatherings, conferences, unions, circles, new publications and publishers, journals, newspapers, etc."[40] The largest Muslim political organization became Ittifak, founded by representatives of the liberal wing of Jadidists. The party's program united the political slogans of the Kadets with Muslim religious and cultural demands. Muslims participated in the work of the State Dumas, where they united to form a special Muslim fraction that stood on Ittifak's platform.[41]

Muslim political activity was a surprise for the Russian public. Reporting on the Second Congress of Muslims (January 1906), the periodical *Niva* noted the error of viewing Tatars and Bashkirs as representing "sluggishness and inertia."[42] *Novoe vremia* wrote about the congress: "A few years ago that mass of Russian Muslims were striking for their stagnation, mistrustfulness, and their immunity to universal cultural ideas and influences . . . [Now] the mass of the Russian Muslims, 15 million strong, has awakened, has become discontented, is seeking renewed forms of life, is concerned with its unification, without regard to ethnic distinctions, and on the basis of Pan-Turkism is attempting to establish ties, for now merely moral, with the entire Muslim world." The newspaper regarded this phenomenon as "worthy of sympathy and interesting to a high degree."[43]

Muslims' pretensions to participation in the discussion of political questions generated anxiety on the part of the government, which began to relate to Muslim political activists with suspicion. The Third Muslim Congress (August 1906) was viewed negatively by the authorities. Their principal accusation was that the congress's participants had deviated from their program and had touched on questions supposedly not subject to discussion. In particular, they had criticized the dissolution of the Duma, accused the government of oppressing Muslims, and demanded that Muslim religious issues not be discussed until the calling of the next Duma. The delegates had also expressed their support for the establishment of a constitutional regime in Persia. An article written under the direction of the Ministry of Internal Affairs and published in the newspaper *Rossiia* spoke of "the violation of the government's trust" and about the necessity of evaluating the numerous requests for various congresses more carefully.[44]

Despite the suspicion engendered by the Muslim congresses, the authorities were still not inclined to accuse the entire Muslim population of anti-state activity and thus to raise the Muslim question at this time. In governmental circles, the prevailing opinion was still that the overwhelming mass of Muslim subjects were "loyal to the throne and fatherland."[45] In all likelihood, such a view was facilitated by the fact that, in comparison with other nationalities, the direct participation of Muslims in the revolutionary events of 1905–1907 had been very modest. Moreover, in the opinion of the authorities, the awakening was a local phenomenon and had not seriously influenced the entire Muslim population, which, so it still seemed, was more concerned with questions of religion than ones of politics.

By 1907 the revolution of 1905 had suffered defeat, and one peculiarity of the new political regime that was installed after the coup of June 3, 1907, was the strengthening of the nationalist mood in Russian society. This mood began to exert a significant influence on the country's political course. On the one hand, "aliens" earned the authorities' mistrust of their political activity, and, on the other, they became the targets of the attacks of Russian nationalists, who worried about "alien dominance" [*inorodcheskoe zasil'e*] in Russia. In the atmosphere of fear that was part of the social and political crisis of the last years of empire, the Muslim question gained new relevance.

As before, the question was most actively discussed in missionary circles. Traditionally, missionaries had viewed this problem as a matter of Islam's "attack" on Christian culture. To this missionaries now added new arguments that confirmed the existence and, most importantly, the danger of the Muslim question. First, Muslims had demonstrated their disloyalty, since some among them had created an opposition party and had thus entered the struggle against the government. They were also attempting to gain religious and cultural autonomy, which was regarded as "separatism." Second, missionaries believed that Russian Muslims were infected with Pan-Islamic ideas, which oriented them toward political rapprochement with Turkey rather than Russia. Regarding the Muslim question not just as a religious problem, but as a political one as well, missionaries accused the authorities of "overlooking" Muslims, of trusting them excessively. They accordingly demanded the resolution without delay of the Muslim question.

The clergy increased the pressure on governmental circles, calling their attention to the Muslim problem. The Kazan missionaries were especially active in this regard. In 1908 at a missionary congress in Kiev, Andrei, Bishop of Mamadysh and the chairman of the Kazan Brotherhood of St. Gurii, raised an initiative to call a special conference for the study of the Muslim question in the Volga region.[46] At the same time he sent a note to the Ministry of Internal Affairs, calling attention to the development of "Tatar-Mohammedan" propaganda in the Volga region."[47] Speaking of "the invasion of Islam," Bishop Andrei argued that the weakening of Islam itself would scarcely be possible. His main concern was those non-Russian peoples who, in light of their territorial and ethnic proximity to Tatar Muslims, were under the influence of Muslim propaganda and were converting to Islam and becoming Tatars. In his note Andrei proposed a set of measures that, he believed, could "protect aliens" from Tatar-Muslim influence. The bishop saw the firmness of the Muslim religious community as one of the main reasons for the strength of Islam. He therefore concluded that for the successful "Russification of aliens" it was necessary to strengthen the Orthodox parish and to develop the "national-patriotic enthusiasm" of the Russian population. The bishop proposed developing missionary activity among baptized aliens on the basis of the Il'minskii system and with the state's support. He contended that the development of the national particularities of the small peoples would not hinder their "merging" with Russians, at the core of which should be religious unity. Thus Bishop Andrei called upon the government to draw a distinction between baptized aliens and Muslim Tatars, since only the first merited the government's trust, while the latter represented "loyal enemies."[48]

The missionaries' concerns about "Mohammedan propaganda" attracted the attention of central authorities. In this connection, P. A. Stolpyin, the Minister of Internal Affairs and the Chairman of the Council of Ministers, wrote to Chief Procurator S. M. Luk'ianov in 1909 about the danger of the Muslim question in Russia.[49] The cooperation of the government with missionaries elicited a negative reaction from "progressive" Muslims, who believed that the missionaries were "intentionally frightening" the authorities with the specter of Muslims.[50] The government's increased attention to the Muslim question was expressed in its organization of a special inter-ministerial conference in January 1910, under the auspices of the

Ministry of Internal Affairs. The official name of the meeting was the "Conference for the Elaboration of Measures to Counteract Tatar-Muslim Influence in the Volga Region." A. Kharuzin, the director of the Department of Foreign Confessions, was named the conference's chairman. The rector of the Kazan Ecclesiastical Academy, Bishop of Chistopol Aleksei, the chairman of the Brotherhood of St. Gurii, Bishop of Mamdysh Andrei, representatives of the Ministry of Education and the Holy Synod, and the governors of Kazan and Viatka provinces all participated in the conference.

The reason for calling the conference, recorded in the sessions' minutes, was "the exacerbation of the Muslim question." According to the conference's participants, this exacerbation was reflected, on the one hand, in the mass conversions of baptized Muslims and some pagan peoples to Islam and the increase of Muslim propaganda, and, on the other, in the "awakening of Russia's Muslims," which had taken a political character. These phenomena were evaluated by the conference's participants as "separatist"—geared in the long run to the destruction of the integrity of the Russian state. The participants also linked the exacerbation of the Muslim question with the democratization of the political regime in 1904–1905, and thus with the development of the liberation movement, as well as with the growth of Pan-Islamic propaganda among the world's Muslims, especially after the Young Turk revolution of 1908.[51] The conference was to study the Muslim question and to specify government measures that could facilitate the question's resolution.

Having defined the essence of the problem, the participants acknowledged its complexity and the difficulty of finding an all-encompassing resolution. On the one hand, governmental circles recognized the heterogeneity of Russia's Muslims, i.e., the differences in nationality and conditions of life among the empire's Muslim peoples. Such a view required a differential approach to the resolution of the Muslim question. On the other hand, there was a conception of a unified Muslim world. The Islamic religion was regarded as a "completely distinctive cultural phenomenon," which, having its particular historical traditions, possessing its international spiritual centers, and introducing into world politics its own distinctive principles of life, unified Muslims into a single whole, leveling their national peculiarities. The habit among the majority of Muslims of identifying religion with nationality made Islam the factor that isolated them from non-Muslims and simultaneously unified various peoples confessing Islam into a single cultural community. This particularity allowed one to speak of the existence among Muslims of a distinctive "religious nationalism" opposed to European "ethnic nationalism."[52] The view of Muslims as a single whole demanded a general approach to the resolution of the Muslim question. Although the conference participants shared both views of Muslims, for the resolution of the question they decided to restrict themselves initially to a discussion of the situation in the Volga region, where, they believed, the Muslim problem appeared in especially sharp relief.[53]

According to the participants, it was the situation in the Volga region that demonstrated the existence of the Muslim question. Precisely here, over the course of almost a century, there had been a mass "apostasy" movement among baptized Muslims. It was precisely the Volga Tatars who had become renowned as the most successful disseminators of Islam among neighboring non-Muslim peoples. Finally, it was precisely the Volga Tatars who had become the most active participants in the Jadid movement and had been the initiators in the early twentieth century of the political movement among Russia's Muslims. The Tatars' clear leading role allowed one to speak of a Tatar-Muslim question.

The exacerbation of this problem was connected with the spread of the ideologies of Pan-Islamism and Pan-Turkism. Bishop Aleksei considered the modern movement of Russian Muslims as part of a Pan-Islamic trend, which had as its goal the political unification of the world's Muslims under the aegis of Turkey. In his view, the other goals that Muslims had officially declared, such as the raising of the religious, moral, and cultural level of Muslims and the attainment of religious and political freedoms, were secondary to this Pan-Islamic goal.[54] The evidence for this conclusion was the politicization of the Muslim movement—the establishment by Muslims of an opposition party and their participation in the movement against the government. Thus, in Aleksei's interpretation, Islam's "primordial" hostility was now further burdened by the Muslims' political movement, which had Pan-Islamic goals. All of this made the Muslim question even more dangerous.

However, conference participants held differing views about the dimensions of the threat. Thus A. A. Ostroumov, the assistant curator of the St. Petersburg educational district, did not ascribe political significance to Pan-Islamism. He contended that it was only the youth, rather than the entire Muslim population, that had become interested in such ideas.[55] Nor did all participants consider Islam to be a hostile force and conflate the cultural opposition of Islam and Orthodoxy with the Muslim movement into a single problem. For example, the governor of Viatka Province, P. K. Kamyshanskii, expressed the opinion that the Muslim revolutionary movement appeared on the basis of religion's "decomposition," and that the government should therefore concern itself with upholding the purity of Islam.[56] The Conference's chairman, Kharuzin, likewise did not consider Islam, by itself, to be a political problem. Although Islam could not be equated with Christianity in terms of its rights, it represented a source of morality that should not be shaken. In Kharuzin's opinion, the basic mass of the Muslim population could be considered entirely "reliable." The source of concern was the anti-governmental activity of specific groups of Muslims.[57]

Despite the view of the Orthodox clergy, who considered Islam and Muslims in principle to be dangerous for the state, at the conference a different view prevailed, according to which the basic mass of Muslims were recognized as loyal. However, the loyalty of Muslim subjects, as well as of Baltic Germans and Finns, was characterized as "formal." The loyalty of Muslims was explained not by a true sense of devotion on the part of the Muslim population to the throne and fatherland, but rather by their "inertness" and "ignorance."[58] Precisely this "ignorance," in the view of the conference's majority, was the reason why Muslims turned out to be "unprepared" to accept revolutionary ideas.[59] The Muslim problem was the product of the anti-governmental activity of only some Muslims, primarily Tatars, who made use of religious slogans in their attempt to tear Muslims away from Russia and reorient them toward Turkey.[60] The participants in the conference linked Muslims' anti-governmental movement, which appeared with the greatest force in Kazan, with the program of Pan-Islamism, which had gained currency among Muslims all over the world. In Russia, they believed, the Pan-Turkic program, which envisioned the unification of all Turkic peoples, represented a transitional stage toward the realization of Pan-Islamic goals.[61]

For a long time Muslims' "ignorance," which was associated with their devotion to their religion, was regarded as an obstacle to their integration into the Russian empire. Therefore education had been an important part of the policy of "rapprochement." After the revolution the authorities discovered that precisely this "ignorance" was the reason for the loyalty of the basic mass of Muslims. In opposition to the government were those Muslims who had received Russian education, but had not been assimilated by Russians and instead became proponents for Muslim religious-national autonomy. This agenda was communicated to the Muslim masses through the reformed confessional schools, which operated outside of the government's control. The participants of the conference realized very well all of the advantages and threats coming from the spread of literacy among the population. Therefore, it was precisely educational policy (that is the subjugation of the general schooling system to the government and state interests) that they saw as the answer to the Muslim question. To achieve this, the conference's participants recommended a strict division between confessional and general schools, and the banning of general subjects (including Russian language) from the curriculum of religious schools.[62] In order to weaken the influence of Tatars on other Muslims, the conference proposed the dismemberment of the Orenburg Muslim Spiritual Assembly.

Having recognized the significance of the Muslim question, the conference nonetheless noted the government's insufficient familiarity with the problem and with Muslims in general. In this regard the Conference worked out a program for the study of Muslims and the Muslim question, which would include the organization of courses in Islamic studies for the preparation of servitors in Muslim regions, as well as the publication of a special printed organ, which would gather information on the Muslim question. Because the resolution of the Muslim question required joint action of various ministries, the conference also suggested that periodically convened inter-ministerial conferences on the Muslim question would organize study and discussion of the problem. After the close of the conference, its materials were transferred to the Council of Ministers, where they lay without further discussion until 1913, when preparation began for yet another conference on the Muslim question.[63]

The journals of the conference also were sent to the Ministry of Foreign Affairs for its consideration. Russian politicians had long ago noted that the government's policy with regard to its Muslim subjects influenced its relations with the Ottoman Empire, just as the latter influenced the mood of Russia's Muslims. To the extent that in the previous century the "Eastern Question" had been among the most important in international relations, the Muslim card had become very significant for the foreign relations of the European powers, including Russia. In considering the issues raised by the conference, the Ministry of Foreign Affairs noted that Russian Muslims and the events that occurred in their lives could not be regarded as an exclusively Russian phenomenon. To the extent that Muslims' international connections made the Muslim question relevant, the ministry believed that this problem must take into account events occurring in the Muslim world as a whole.[64] At the same time, the Foreign Ministry was not inclined to equate the "Muslims' awakening"—in the sense of their aspirations for European culture—with Pan-Islamism.[65] Because both of those phenomena had an international character, the ministry considered the Muslim question to be a problem not only for Russia, but also for Great Britain, France, and other countries. Accordingly, the ministry suggested studying the methods of ruling Muslims in various countries and possibly unifying the actions of the European powers in the resolution of the Muslim question.[66]

In contrast to secular authorities, the clergy looked at the Muslim question much more broadly, considering it to entail not only the appearance among Muslims of anti-state orientations, but also an attack by Islam on Christian culture. Missionaries considered it possible and indispensable to struggle against Islam. Because, in their view, the essence of the Muslim question concerned Islam itself, missionaries believed that the government's policy of non-interference in Muslim religious affairs was a mistake, and that the hopes that the religion would die off (*otomret*) of its own accord to be unfounded.[67] At the same time, missionaries criticized the forced introduction of the Russian language, which, as they saw it, did not facilitate rapprochement, but, on the contrary, stirred up national sentiments.[68]

The missionary discussion of the Muslim question unfolded at a missionary congress held in Kazan in 1910.[69] As was the case with the Special Conference, particular attention was paid at the congress to the Volga region, where the opposition of Islam and Orthodoxy seemed particularly tense. At the same time discussions of Turkestan and the Caucasus were not excluded, since missionaries regarded the Muslim question to be relevant there as well. The principal speakers in the "anti-Mohammedan" section of the congress were a professor of anti-Muslim missionary studies at the Kazan Theological Academy, M. A. Mashanov,[70] and the director of the Tashkent Teachers' Seminary, N. P. Ostroumov.[71] Although the specific goal of the congress concerned the discussion and elaboration of a set of missionary measures that had not become a part of the Special Conference, the speakers did not limit themselves to that task and discussed the Muslim question more generally.

In his report, Ostroumov presented the Muslim question as being no less dangerous than the Polish, Finnish, and Jewish questions. He argued that although the Muslim question, which he saw as a problem of opposition between Islam and Orthodoxy, had a history of many centuries in

Russia, it was precisely in recent years that it had attained such serious political significance and had begun to threaten the foundations of Russian
statehood. In his view the government's policy was not consistent. Thus,
for example, the government had long been in error concerning the loyalty of Muslims. Ostroumov considered Muslims' political activity to represent proof of the fact that the Muslim population "was not so innocent or tranquil" as many were inclined to think. Ostroumov believed that
the government should take a more clearly defined position with regard to
the Muslim problem, basing its actions on both religious toleration and the
superiority of Orthodoxy and Russian culture.[72] Ostroumov contended
that the struggle with Islam should be a matter not only for the church,
but for the state and all of Russian society as well.

The congress's participants noted Islam's remarkable firmness, which
they saw as the result of several factors. To missionaries' traditional "enemies"
—mullahs and schools—were now added the Muslim press, which had recently begun to play an important role in Islamic propaganda and the "isolation" of Muslims. The difficulty of drawing Muslims closer to Russians
derived also from the fact that Russians themselves did not attempt to
draw them closer and often related with hostility to aliens. The missionaries' tasks accordingly included not only "work" with the aliens, but also
efforts with the Russian population as well. Concrete measures worked out
in the anti-Mohammedan section of the congress involved efforts to improve religious life in the Orthodox parishes, to strengthen the religious
dimension in alien schools established according to the Il'minskii system,
to translate Orthodox literature into alien languages, and to publish literature critiquing Islam.[73] Considering Christian education to be one of the
principal means of solving the Muslim question, the congress's participants came out in favor of the development of missionary activity not only
in the Volga region, but also in Turkestan. This initiative did not, however,
meet with approval from the administration of Turkestan, which traditionally viewed relations with Muslims as a prerogative of secular authority, and missionary activity in the region as impermissible.[74]

Raising the Muslim question in government, missionary, and public
circles, and—most importantly—interpreting that problem as a danger
supposedly coming from Muslims, encountered condemnation from Muslim liberals. S. Maksudov, a member of the Muslim fraction in the Third
State Duma, declared, "Our nationalists . . . acquire prestige among a certain public when they raise the Polish and the Jewish questions. But those
two questions—the Polish and the Jewish—have been played out, and

therefore it is necessary to create a new one . . . some kind of new alien question [*inorodcheskii vopros*]. Now they are trying as much as possible to create a Muslim question in Russia."[75]

Once again the Muslim question became a subject for discussion in government circles at an inter-ministerial conference on Muslim issues convened at the Ministry of Internal Affairs in 1914, under the chairmanship of the Deputy Minister of Internal Affairs I. M. Zolotarev. Among the participants were representatives of the Holy Synod, the Ministries of Education, Internal Affairs, and War, the representatives of all the regions of the empire inhabited by Muslims, and several orientalists. Representatives of Muslim religious institutions were also invited, although they were allowed to attend only sessions concerning issues of the Muslim clergy's staffing and salary. Discussion of the Muslim question occurred without their participation. Discussing the mood of the Muslim population in various parts of the empire, the conference's participants noted that the Pan-Islamic and Pan-Turkic movements, which they had feared in 1909–1910, had not enjoyed substantial success among Russia's Muslims. In their opinion, individual manifestations of religious solidarity, as well as the energetic political activity of a certain group of Muslims during the revolution of 1905, had not changed the attitude toward the basic mass of the Muslim population as loyal citizens. Moreover, the very idea of Muslims' religious unification was recognized by the conference as being unrealistic to be implemented in the Russian empire.[76] Far more real and more dangerous for the Russian authorities was "Pan-Tatarism," which was understood to mean the religious-national revival of Volga Tatars and their aspiration to subordinate other Muslim peoples to their cultural influence. At the time of discussion that phenomenon had appeared only in the Volga region, where Tatars had assimilated primarily Finnic peoples. Thus the Muslim question at the 1914 conference was regarded as a Tatar-Muslim question, which for the time being was relevant only in a single region. Because the concern was with the spread of Tatar national culture on neighboring Muslim and pagan peoples, the resolution of the Tatar-Muslim question appeared to entail a struggle against "Tatar domination" [*tatarskoe zasil'e*]. Fearing the "denationalization" of other peoples under Tatar influence, the conference's participants nonetheless considered no less dangerous the strengthening of those people's *own* national consciousness.[77] In short, a dilemma had arisen: how to protect those other peoples from being swallowed by Tatars without promoting in them their own national sentiments.

In this connection a question arose concerning the relationship of the state to Islam and its religious institutions. Those religious institutions, along with religious schools and the Muslim press, were regarded as the basic weapon of Tatar influence.[78] To the extent that national (Tatar) ideas had already made headway among the other Muslim peoples, shared religion and the undeveloped character of national consciousness among those peoples established the conditions for their rapid Tatarization. Because Islam was seen to be the conductor of Tatar ideas, the conference was faced with finding measures for the struggle with "Tatarness" [*tatarizm*] that would, on the one hand, limit the spread of Tatar culture, and, on the other, weaken Islam. From this point of view, the conference's participants examined the problem of the relations between the government and the existing organs of Islamic religious administration. The conference suggested a policy of weakening existing muftiats by way of reducing their authority and strengthening state control over them. Concerning those regions where state-sanctioned Muslim institutions were absent, the conference recommended retaining the existing state of affairs and by no means regulating Muslims' religious affairs. For all intents and purposes the conference did not make major changes in the already existing system of Muslim administration. The conference also discussed the question of the educational requirements for the Muslim "parish clergy." If at the end of the nineteenth century the knowledge of the Russian language was understood to represent a means of enlightening and attracting "the ignorant Muslim clergy" to Russian norms, now, in the view of the conference's participants, knowledge of the Russian language had facilitated the penetration of revolutionary ideas into Muslims' minds. For this reason and also because in some regions there were still few or no mullahs who knew Russian, the conference considered it possible to require only that mullahs be able to speak and understand Russian. The conference recommended elimination of this requirement in certain regions, which were to be identified by the Ministry of Internal Affairs.[79]

Although the conference's participants decided to convene similar conferences at least once every two years, the conference of 1914 was the autocracy's last attempt to discuss the Muslim question in a specially established governmental organ. The beginning of the First World War drew the attention of the authorities away from the Muslim question. Given the military actions occurring on the western frontier, the Polish and Ukrainian questions became much more important. The recommendations of the special conferences on the Muslim question received neither further legislative movement nor realization in practice.

The authorities refused to promote rapprochement between Muslims and Russians by eliminating limitations on rights that were based on religious confession, as had been promised in the decree on religious toleration in 1905. Of the concrete problems concerning Russian Muslims that had been identified in the program of the Committee of Ministers in 1905 and that had been discussed in various special conferences, only one of these had been resolved by legislation: the emancipation of the Muslim clergy from military service. The authorities' failure to fulfill their promises called forth the criticism of deputies in the State Duma, who insisted on the complete elimination of all forms of national and confessional discrimination.[80] Discussing this demand in 1916, all the ministers considered its realization at the given moment to be "unacceptable," and put off the resolution of that question until after the war, when "it will become clear to what extent those measures are well-timed and correspond to the internal political situation."[81]

The government's tactics can be illustrated by a report put together by the order of Minister of Internal Affairs A. N. Khvostov in 1916 in conjunction with the Duma's impending budget discussion. That report suggested a possible response of the ministry if the Muslim fraction were to speak out in the Duma. The report pointed to the complexities of the Muslim question, which were caused by the heterogeneity of Russia's Muslims and the war—that is, to "the lack of clarity of Muslims' possible positions depending on the outcome of the war." In such conditions that review of all legislation concerning Muslims had become "inappropriate at the present time." The Ministry of Internal Affairs recommended that the government "refrain from defining any strictly formulated promises in one or another direction, limiting itself to the declaration that the government recognizes the urgency of the question and that in its resolution the needs of Muslims will be taken into account."[82] Thus, once again, the government did not undertake any major reforms concerning Muslims and postponed resolution of the Muslim question until a later time.

Despite the fact that Russian authorities had been interacting with Muslim subjects since the sixteenth century, the Muslim question appeared as a political problem in Russia only in the second half of the nineteenth century—that is, only then was it recognized and formulated as such. The missionaries were among the first to draw attention to the Muslim question. Evaluating Islam from the standpoint of its dogmas, missionaries a priori regarded Islam as a hostile force and Muslims as unreliable subjects. Therefore, in the missionaries' eyes, the Muslim question represented first and foremost a religious problem and would exist as long as Islam itself existed. Following the missionary logic, the resolution of the Muslim question would, in the end, mean the victory of Christianity over Islam. Missionaries accordingly insisted on the Christianization of Muslims or, more modestly, on keeping within Orthodoxy those Muslims who had already been baptized and on measures that would limit the activities of Islamic institutions.

Secular authorities, having inherited the tradition of religious toleration and pragmatic politics from the eighteenth century, did not regard the religious question as a problem of the state and therefore were not inclined to participate in a religious struggle against Islam. Their imperial project included the rapprochement of Muslims with Russians through secular education and the Russian language. With regard to Islamic religious affairs, the authorities practiced two policy variants: (1) cooperation with religious figures and the legislative regulation of Muslim religious life; and (2) complete non-interference in Muslim religious affairs and, in essence, disregard of the religious factor.

Central authorities began to pay serious attention to the Muslim question only at the beginning of the twentieth century, as a result, principally, of the appearance among Muslims of a political movement with national overtones. Recognizing the religious dimension of the Muslim question, the authorities regarded it as analogous to other similar alien questions and saw in it above all a separatist movement of Volga Tatars. These were understood to be spreading their cultural influence over neighboring non-Russian populations by means of religion, thereby creating a threat to Russian cultural dominance in Russia's East and the unity of the empire. The government responded to the Muslim question with inter-ministerial discussions on ways of integrating Muslims into the empire and securing the threatened state unity. The Ministry of Internal Affairs (the principal designer of Islamic policies) recognized that interference in the religious lives of Muslims caused disturbances among these populations, which resisted any governmental reforms, interpreting them as attempts at Christianization. In practice, priority was given to civil order and political stability in the empire rather than to grand projects of cultural transformation for the implementation of which the imperial authorities had neither enough resources nor determination. "To avoid disturbances among Muslims" was the primary consideration that often directed Russian policies toward Islam. The absence of a proactive and consistent course toward the Muslim population met criticism from the right, as well as from the left.

S. N. Maksudov, a liberal Muslim delegate to the Third State Duma, offered a quite exact characterization of the approaches of missionaries and government to the Muslim question: "Missionaries seek to resolve the Muslim question by eliminating it altogether, they say to us: there should be no Muslims in Russia. And the government goes back and forth; sometimes it is compelled to resolve the question in accord with the missionary view, and sometimes in accord with state concerns. But I must say that very rarely does the state character become manifest: it is like spaces of light in the government's behavior, and we experience them like happy eras."[83]

Of the active alien questions, the Muslim question did not garner as much attention in the circles of the central government as, for example, the Polish, Finnish, and Jewish questions. Possibly this is connected with the fact that, in comparison to other such questions, the Muslim question was long regarded as a religious problem and did not appear to the government to be dangerous in a political sense. The national dimension of the Muslim question, which was what disturbed the government, appeared rather late. Moreover, in the view of the authorities, Muslims' national "awakening," even though it had a certain political character, was nonetheless weakly expressed and had an insignificant influence on the mass of Muslims, as a result of the latter's "ignorance." Following this logic, it turned out that this same ignorance, which the authorities proposed to overcome by means of enlightenment in the nineteenth century, became the very reason why the Muslim question did not disconcert ruling circles to the same extent that other alien questions did. Recognizing this, the authorities in essence refused to take any decisive reforms in regard to the Muslim population, as if hoping to stop time and restrain Russia from modernization.

Translated by Paul Werth

Notes

1. A. Kappeler, *Rossiia—mnogonatsional'naia imperiia. Vozniknovenie, istoria, raspad* (Moscow, 1997), chapter 6.

2. Charles Steinwedel, "To Make a Difference: the Category of Ethnicity in Late Imperial Russian Politics, 1861-1917," in *Russian Modernity. Politics, Knowledge, Practices,* ed. David Hoffmann and Yanni Kotsonis (New York, 2000), 67.

3. B. Anan'ich, Gatrel, "Natsional'nye i vnenatsional'nye izmereniia ekonomicheskogo razvitiia Rossii, 19-20 vv.," *Ab Imperio* 4 (2002): 74, 82.

4. J. Slocum, "Who, and When, Were the *Inorodtsy?* The Evolution of the Category of "Aliens" in Imperial Russia," *The Russian Review* 57 (April 1998): 173-190.

5. E. I. Campbell (Vorobieva), " 'Edinaia i nedelimaia Rossiia' i 'inorodcheskii vopros' v imperskoi ideologii samoderzhaviia," *Prostranstvo vlasti. Istoricheskii opyt Rossii i vyzovy sovremennosti* (Moscow, 2001), 204-217.

6. On the connection of apostasy to emerging conceptions about Islam and the reevaluation of Islam by missionaries, see Paul W. Werth, *At the Margins of Orthodoxy: Missions, Governance, and Confessional Politics in Russia's Volga-Kama Region, 1827–1905* (Ithaca, 2000), 178-182.

7. See, for example, "Vypiska iz dela ob 'otpadenii' krest'ian vtorogo stana kazanskogo uezda i o soprotivlenii ikh mestnym vlastiam" (dated not earlier than July 26, 1866), in *Materialy po istorii narodov SSSR, vyp. 6: Materialy po istorii Tatarii vtoroi poloviny XIX veka: Agrarnyi vopros i krest'ianskoe dvizhenie 50–70-kh godov XIX veka,* part 1 (Moscow and Leningrad, 1936), 239.

8. Rossiiskii gosudarstvennyi istoricheskii arkhiv (hereafter RGIA), f. 821, op. 8, d. 743, ll. 31-31ob.

9. RGIA, f. 821, op. 8, d. 743, l. 47 ob.

10. Ibid., l. 62 ob.

11. See, for example, E. N. Voronets, "K voprosu o svobode very i o sovremennykh, vnutri Rossii, otpadeniiakh ot khristianstva v magometanstvo," *Pravoslavnyi sobsednik* 1 (1877): 226-258.

12. See, for example, N. Ostroumov, "Zapiska o znachenii mokhammedanstva v istorii khristianstva i v istorii chelovechestva," *Pravoslavnyi sobesednik* 3 (1872): 22.

13. Voronets, "K voprosu," 252.

14. I. A. Iznoskov, "Inorodcheskie prikhody Kazanskogo uezda," *Pravoslavnyi blagovestnik* 21 (1897): 225.

15. Cited in S. Rybakov, *Islam i prosveshchenie inorodtsev v Ufimskoi gubernii* (St. Petersburg, 1900), 14.

16. RGIA, f. 821, op. 8, d. 743, l. 142 (For Il'minskii's report to Pobedonostsev on these issues, see op. cit., ll. 81-98ob.).

17. RGIA, f. 821, op. 8, d. 743, ll. 181-189.

18. *Materialy po istorii narodov,* 190-191.

19. RGIA, f. 821, op. 8, d. 594, l. 62ob.

20. *Vsepoddanneishii doklad turkestanskogo general-gubernatora Dukhovskogo. Islam v Turkestane* (Tashkent, 1899).

21. Arkhiv vneshnei politiki Rossiiskoi imperii (hereafter AVPRI), f. 147, op. 485, d. 1256, ll. 5-7.

22. RGIA, f. 821, op. 150, d. 409, ll. 13-15.

23. Ibid., l. 11ob.

24. Missionaries criticized this view. See, for example, N. Ostroumov, "Kolebaniia vo vzgliadakh na obrazovanie tuzemtsev v Turkestanskom krae," in *Kaufmanskii sbor-*

nik, izdannyi v pamiat' 25 let, istekshikh so dnia smerti pokoritelia i ustroitelia Turkestanskogo kraia K. fon Kaufmana (Moscow, 1910), 139–140.

25. RGIA, f. 821, op. 150, d. 406, ll. 1ob.-2.

26. For an analysis of missionary activity in this region, see Werth, *At the Margins of Orthodoxy.*

27. See, for example, Rossiiskii gosudarstvennyi voenno-istoricheskii arkhiv (RGVIA), f. 400, op. 1, d. 2689, l. 3.

28. E. Campbell, "The Autocracy and the Muslim Clergy in the Russian Empire (1850s–1917)," *Russian Studies in History* 44, no. 2 (Fall 2005): 8–29.

29. N. Ostroumov, *Islamovedenie* (Tashkent, 1910), 3.

30. N. Ostroumov, "Kolebaniia vo vzgliadakh," 148–149.

31. On the *Jadid* movement and its inspirer I. Gasprinskii, see, for example, Serge Zenkovsky, *Pan-Turkism and Islam in Russia* (Cambridge, Mass., 1967).

32. *Pis'ma N. I. Il'minskogo K. Pobedonostsevu* (Kazan, 1895), 2, 64–65 (letters from February 11, 1882, and February 10, 1884).

33. Ibid., 74 (letter from February 29, 1884).

34. Ibid., 61, 338 (letters from February 10, 1884, and February 1, 1890).

35. N. Ostroumov, *Koran i progress: Po povodu umstvennogo probuzhdeniia sovremennykh rossiiskikh musul'man* (Tashkent, 1901–1903), 244.

36. N. Ostroumov, "Magometanskii vopros v Rossii v nastoiashchee vremia," *Khristianskoe chtenie* (September 1905).

37. RGIA, f. 821, op. 8, d. 1194, ll. 8ob.-9.

38. Ibid, l. 18.

39. RGVIA, f. 400, op. 4, d. 14, ll. 2–3ob.

40. S. Bagin, "O propagande islama putem pechati," *Pravoslavnyi sobesednik* 2 (1909): 248.

41. On Muslims in the State Duma, see D. Usmanova, *Musul'manskaia fraktsiia i problemy "svobody sovesti" v Gosudarstvennoi Dume, 1906–1917* (Kazan, 1999).

42. *Niva* 7 (1906): 112.

43. "Izvestiia i zametki: Musul'manskii s"ezd (iz *Novago vremeni)*," *Pravoslavnyi blagovestnik* 15 (1906): 336.

44. *Rossiia* 238 (September 14, 1906).

45. RGIA, f. 821, op. 8, d. 1198, l. 68ob.

46. Ibid., d. 801, l. 73.

47. Episkop Andrei, *O merakh k okhraneniiu Kazanskogo kraia ot postepennogo zavoevaniia ego tatarami* (January 14, 1908), in RGIA, f. 1276, op. 4, d. 815, ll. 1–4.

48. Ibid., ll. 3, 8.

49. See I. Shpitsberg, "Tserkov' i rusifikatsiia buriat-mongol pri tsarizme," *Krasnyi arkhiv* 4, no. 53 (1932): 102.

50. Translation of an article from the Tatar newspaper *Iuldyz* [Star] 520 (1910), in *Sotrudnik Bratstva sv. Guriia* 22–23 (1910): 355–58.

51. "Predstavlenie A. N. Kharuzina v Sovet ministrov 'O merakh dlia protivodeistviia panislamistskomu i panturanskomu (pantiurkskomu) vliianiiu sredi musul'manskogo naseleniia' (January 15, 1911)," Biblioteka RGIA, Pz. 747, 1.

52. "Zhurnal osobogo soveshchaniia po vyrabotke mer dlia protivodeistviia tataromusul'manskomu vliianiiu v Privolzhskom krae," ibid., 7.

53. "Predstavlenie A. N. Kharuzina," 6.

54. Episkop Aleksei, *Sovremennoe dvizhenie v srede rossiiskikh musul'man* (Kazan, 1910), 6–8. This report was revised with new material and published again as a brochure titled *Voinstvuiushchii islam* (Moscow, 1914).

55. RGIA, f. 821, op. 8, d. 801, l. 166ob.

56. Ibid., l. 152.

57. Ibid., ll. 154–154ob.

58. Ibid., l. 167.

59. Ibid., ll. 167–167ob.

60. "Predstavlenie A. N. Kharuzina," 14.

61. Ibid., 2.

62. For an analysis of the discussion of the schooling issue at the 1910 conference that situates this issue in the broader transformation of the view of Russian authorities concerning the possibility of assimilating Muslims, see Robert Geraci, "Russian Orientalism at an Impasse: Tsarist Education Policy and the 1910 Conference on Islam," in *Russia's Orient: Borderlands and Peoples, 1700–1917*, ed. Daniel R. Brower and Edward J. Lazzerini (Bloomington, 1997), 138–161. Geraci interprets the discussion at the 1910 conference on education as a manifestation of "Orientalism" (i.e., the idea that Russian authorities preferred ignorant Muslims to enlightened ones, and thus did not wish to disrupt the barrier between East and West). I would rather interpret the position of the conference's participants (especially the opinion of Kharuzin about formal loyalty of Muslims, Baltic Germans, and Finns) as a fear of non-Russian nationalism—a force that authorities believed could destroy the empire.

63. RGIA, f. 1276, op. 7, d. 9, l. 48.

64. AVPR, f. 147, op. 485, d. 1258, ll. 48–50.

65. Ibid., ll. 122–122ob.

66. Ibid., l. 50ob., l. 146.

67. See, for example, "Politika ignorirovaniia," *Sotrudnik Bratstva sv. Guriia* 43 (1911): 689–692, 45 (1911): 719–723.

68. "Russkii iazyk v Kavkazskikh shkolakh," *Sotrudnik Bratstva sv. Guriia* 3 (1911): 39–43.

69. In his correspondence with the Ministry of Internal Affairs, Bishop Andrei insisted that the congress be closed, since he saw a danger that Muslims would counter with their own enterprises and did not want Orthodoxy to expose its weaknesses before Muslims.

70. M. A. Mashanov, *Sovremennoe sostoianie tatar-mukhammedan i ikh otnoshenie k drugim inorodtsam* (Kazan, 1910).

71. N. Ostroumov, "Kolebaniia russkogo pravitel'stva vo vzgliadakh na missionerskuiu deiatel'nost' pravoslavnoi russkoi tserkvi," *Sotrudnik Bratstva sv. Guriia* 42, 43 (1910) 676–679. The report was also published as a separate offprint, with a few minor changes, in the same year.

72. Ibid., 678–679.

73. N. V. Numerov, "Kazanskii missionerskii s"ezd," *Pribavlenie k tserkovnym vedomostiam* 13 (1910): 1816.

74. AVPRI, f. 147, op. 485, d. 1258, ll. 99ob.-100.

75. *Gosudarstvennaia Duma. Tretii sozyv. Stenograficheskie otchety. Sessiia IV. Zasedanie 67 (February 26, 1911),* part 2, 2936.

76. RGIA, f. 821, op. 133, d. 576, ll. 120ob.–122.

77. Ibid., ll. 254–254ob.

78. Ibid., ll. 134ob.-135ob.

79. Ibid., ll. 309, 311 ob.

80. RGIA, f. 1276, op. 12, d. 3, ll. 7ob.-9.

81. Ibid., l. 1ob.

82. RGIA, f. 821, op. 133, d. 638, ll. 11–11ob., 15ob.

83. *Gosudarstvennaia Duma. Tretii sozyv. Stenograficheskie otchety. Sessia IV,* part 1, (Zasedanie 5; October 23, 1910), 375.

13 The Zemstvo Reform, the Cossacks, and Administrative Policy on the Don, 1864–1882

Aleksei Volvenko

The implementation of the Manifesto of February 19, 1861, entailed changes in the administration of the Russian empire, setting off, in the expression of B. G. Litvak, "a chain reaction of reform."[1] The introduction of the zemstvo represented one of the links in this chain. The goal of the zemstvo reform was the creation of local organs of self-government on an elected basis. The zemstvo was to be elected by all estates and was to possess sufficient authority and independence to resolve local economic problems.

The creation of the zemstvo by the Law of January 1, 1864, came about as a result of the government's desire to bring some order to local administration, which was thought to be in a far from satisfactory state. The government also hoped through this reform to deflect a wave of discontent among the nobility, who had virtually been deprived of power in the provinces after the emancipation. The government's policy regarding the zemstvo was extremely circumspect and cautious, causing the institution to be introduced gradually: in 1865 zemstvos were opened in nineteen provinces, and between 1866 and 1876 another sixteen were established.[2] The Don oblast was included in the second group.

The introduction of the zemstvo into the Don was an unusual event in the history of the zemstvo. First, the zemstvo had to be adapted for a province in which a large part of population belonged to the military estate, i.e., the Cossacks. The zemstvo generally has been regarded as a positive development, but the Don was the only case in its 50-year history where it collapsed. After only six years the zemstvo in the Don was abolished due to Cossack opposition.

The Don region remains a "blank spot" in the history of the zemstvo.

The absence of serious studies of the Don zemstvo, combined with its short existence, has led historians of the zemstvo simply to note its existence, without detailed commentary as a rule,[3] or to ignore it altogether.[4] Some have even denied that the zemstvo ever existed on the Don.[5] The present essay is an attempt to lay the groundwork for a history of the Don zemstvo. I analyze this as a process in which local self-government was established in the Don and in which public opinion played an important role.

The Land of the Don Host (*voisko*), which became an oblast in 1870, had an exceptional place in the Russian empire. This was not so much on account of its size, seventh among the provinces of European Russia, but more the result of the population's peculiar social structure, its unique system of administration, and its low level of economic development. Cossacks made up two-thirds of the total population of the Don. Both hereditary and life nobles as well as ordinary inhabitants of a *stanitsa* (large village) were counted as Cossacks. Each Cossack by law received an allotment of communal land in return for his military service; the size of the allocation depended on his rank. If a Cossack reached the rank of commissioned officer in the military service or the ninth grade in the Table of Ranks in the civil service, he became a noble for life. He received a temporary allotment of land, which he did not have the right to turn into his hereditary property. Those who had such temporary allotments, along with horse ranchers and those running coal mines, were exempt from any taxes, unlike the hereditary nobles and the inhabitants of stanitsa communes. The latter paid taxes in kind, which by ancient custom excluded direct personal taxation. The Don peasantry, "temporarily obligated" since 1861, represented a third of the population; they were scarcely distinguishable by their way of life or legal status from peasants elsewhere in the empire. Land in the Don oblast was regarded as property of the Don Host, and buying and selling it was illegal. The number of *inogorodnie,* i.e., people who were not Cossacks, was insignificant.

The whole structure of life in the Don oblast, the rights and obligations of every estate, was consolidated by the Law on the Administration of the Don Host of May 26, 1835. The Law also codified the peculiar system of administration, envisaging the separation of civilian and military authority and the concentration of all power in the hands of the Nakaznyi Ataman, who was appointed by the War Ministry. The system of civil administration was distinguished from the rest of the empire not only by different institutional structures and different names, but also by a completely different method of appointing the staff of these institutions. The essence of this difference was the appointment of officials by election. This system was based on the existence among the Cossacks, the majority of the population, of a tradition of self-government in the form of stanitsa assemblies (*sbory*) and noble assemblies. The administrators of the seven districts (*okrugi*) were elected by these assemblies. As a rule, posts in the voisko administration were held by members of the hereditary nobility.[6] The Law of 1835 had made the Cossacks a closed caste, isolated its system of administration, and separated the Don Host from the rest of the empire, which had not led to a cultural and economic renaissance in the territory. According to the testimony of contemporaries, the War Ministry was well aware that stagnation was the rule everywhere—in the economy, the administration, and daily life.[7] Serious reform of the existing state of affairs had become a matter of urgency for both central and local authorities.

In 1860 local committees were opened in all the Cossack territories in order to review the voisko statutes. The original task given to the committees by War Minister N. O. Sukhozanet was limited to a simple codification of the laws.[8] When D. A. Miliutin became War Minister the situation changed radically. In early 1863 the Main Administration of the Cossack Armies sent a secret memorandum to all appointed atamans. The memorandum, titled "A Common Program of the Main Principles of Host Statutes," proposed the replacement of universal military service with volunteers, free entry and exit from the Cossack estate, and the separation of military from civil matters and the judicial system from the administration through the introduction of imperial law in legal proceedings.[9] In fact, the memorandum called for a fundamental transformation of the Cossack host. The zemstvo reform, which aimed to improve and systematize local government, fitted neatly with the new policy of the War Ministry. In the opinion of senior bureaucrats, the basic principle of the reform—local self-government—was not in opposition to the Cossack way of life.[10] Indeed, the principle of universality embodied in the zemstvo could lead to the end of Cossack parochialism, and enhance tolerance and respect for the rest of the population of the empire.

In a memorandum dated January 25, 1864, Miliutin asked the head of the Administration of Irregular Armies "to obtain the preliminary opinions of the Nakaznyi Ataman of the Don and senior local officials who had jurisdiction over the other Cossack hosts regarding the zemstvo reform." The memorandum was based on an *ukaz* of February 29, which shortly afterward was sent to all the Cossack territories. The purpose of the *ukaz* was to find out "whether it was possible to introduce the zemstvo reform into the [Cossack] territories" and "what changes were necessary in the aforementioned law."[11] Nakaznyi Ataman of the Don P. Kh Grabbe entrusted this task to the local committee reviewing the laws on the Cossacks. In late April 1865, all the proposals of the committee that had been drafted during its five-year existence were forwarded to the War Ministry for review. Among these were matters related to the zemstvo reform (i.e., rough drafts rather than completed proposals). Grabbe personally presented the proposals of the Don committee and those of the other hosts to the War Ministry. However, in the opinion of senior officials in the War Ministry and in other interested departments, these proposals "did not correspond in either their contents or direction to the spirit of the most recent legislation."[12] From the perspective of the Minister of Justice, the basic articles of the committee's proposed law "would cut the voisko off from the rest of the empire, surround it with an impenetrable barrier and within this closed circle create an entirely separate internal administration."[13] Negative public reaction possibly influenced the committee in making such proposals, since representatives of the Cossacks were invited to its meetings. Early in 1863 rumors swept through Novocherkassk "that there was a proposal in the government to transform the Cossacks into *muzhiks* [peasants]."[14] The chief of staff of the Don Host, A. M. Dondukov-Korsakov, confirmed in a letter to Miliutin that these rumors gave rise to "exaggerated fears among all estates on the Don about the government's desire to destroy the host. There had been *sbory* in the stanitsas, speeches in the noble assemblies, and a widespread feeling of anger in the territory."[15]

It fell to the Main Committee for the Review of Cossack Law, which had been introduced on October 2, 1865, under the auspices of the Department of the Administration of Irregular Armies, to correct the shortcomings of the original proposals. The establishment of the committee signaled that the War Ministry had decided to place the drafting of the necessary reforms directly under its own supervision. This ruled out any deviation from the course the ministry had already decided upon; in fact, the regulation did remain unchanged. The committee was charged with prioritizing "the improvement of the civil life of the Cossacks rather than the military organization."[16] This meant, above all, introducing the zemstvo and judicial reforms. Alexander II fully approved the plans of the War Ministry. Speaking to the deputies of the Main Committee, the emperor expressed his desire that "the military service of the Cossacks be compatible as much as possible with the benefits of civil life and economic well-being in the organization of the Cossack host.[17]

The transfer of drafting the reform from the Don to the capital annoyed local authorities, who until this time had made all the changes. In October 1865, Grabbe, the aged Nakaznyi Ataman, was appointed Voisko Ataman by imperial order. In order "to ease his onerous burdens" an assistant was appointed to be responsible for civil matters with the title of Nakaznyi Ataman.[18] Major-General Potapov was assigned to this position. Before his posting to the Don, Potapov had been head of the Corps of Gendarmes and head of the Third Section of His Imperial Majesty's Own Chancellery. From 1864 he had been an assistant to the Governor-General of Vilensk with responsibility for civil affairs.[19]

Before setting out for the Don, Potapov submitted a memorandum to the Administration of the Irregular Armies (October 15, 1865) in which he expressed doubts that the Main Committee could successfully draft a law for the zemstvo in the Don, since "it did not have the necessary local data." He then "proposed setting up a special temporary committee in Novocherkassk to draft a law on the zemstvo for the Don." Taking into account the wishes of the Don nobility, Potapov also proposed that the personnel of the committee be elected from all estates within the territory. Furthermore, he suggested the participation of an expert from the Ministry of the Internal Affairs who was "well acquainted with the [zemstvo] law."[20] The Voisko Ataman supported Potapov's initiative, and on March 1, 1866, the Military Council agreed to create a local committee to draft a law on the zemstvo in the Don.[21]

Careful preparations were made for the committee that would determine a great deal of the future development of the Don. More than half of the committee was to be made up of elected deputies from the different estates. Potapov and the specialist in zemstvo affairs, Court Councillor Eremeev, drew on the negative experience of the committee that had earlier reviewed voisko law. The Cossacks had made clear to the Committee their hostility to any radical changes in their lives. Potapov and Eremeev worked out a detailed agenda for the future zemstvo committee.[22] Some deputies and some members of the voisko administration were to be acquainted with the agenda before the committee started work in order to give their preliminary approval. Subsequent changes were to be forbidden. In the preliminary meeting, however, three of the deputies, P. I. Pavlov, voisko elder and holder of a temporary allotment, and P. B. Aver'kov and A. I. Zhidkov, representatives of the Cossack Trading Society, spoke out against the articles that planned to give legal status to towns in the Don. They also objected to accepting the program as a whole before the committee had officially begun to work. In their words, "this would infringe upon the rights of those members who had been elected by their estate but had not been invited to the preliminary meeting. Such a decision would restrict a large number of deputies from expressing their opinion."[23] Pavlov, Aver'kov, and Zhidkov in turn suggested their own agenda, the contents of which can be judged by an extract from the report of Nakaznyi Ataman Potapov to the War Ministry. The ataman believed that the changes proposed by the three deputies amounted to "a petition to transfer to the zemstvo all voisko property, including the budget. If the property of the voisko was transferred to the zemstvo, then it would become desirable to exclude the peasantry and the *inogorodnie*, both official estates of the Don territory, from the zemstvo." This violated "the first principle of the zemstvo, namely, the right of the whole population to have a voice in its decisions."[24]

The three deputies accepted the possibility that the zemstvo might exist in the Don, but they attempted to fix the terms of reference of the committee. At the very least this would allow them to establish a platform from which they could guide the drafting of the reform along the lines of the principle "the zemstvo for the Cossacks alone." The proposal to hand over all voisko property, including the voisko budget, to the zemstvo could help achieve this, since the non-Cossack population had no legal right to a share in voisko property and still less the budget.

There is no doubt that Pavlov, Aver'kov and Zhidkov were voicing not only their own interests, but also the interests of a particular section of society. Pavlov had risen from sergeant to the position of host elder through military service. His defining characteristic was a deep respect and veneration for tradition. His outlook had been shaped by military service into a rigid set of beliefs that emphasized Cossack uniqueness above all else. It is hardly surprising, then, that Pavlov was unwilling to share power with the peasantry in the zemstvo, let alone with the *inogorodnie*. In addition, the desire for a purely Cossack zemstvo can be explained by the direct personal losses Pavlov would suffer if the zemstvo went ahead on an all-estate basis. Like the majority of those who held temporary allotments awarded to them for their military service, Pavlov received in addition a meager salary that he supplemented by renting out his land. Even this did not produce enough money to live in the manner appropriate to his status in society. A compulsory zemstvo tax not only violated the Cossack privilege of exemption from taxes apart from military service, but also would reduce his standard of living. The new tax would be based primarily on land, which would be a double insult for Pavlov since the land was not even his own property. Therefore, the Cossack zemstvo was a way for Pavlov to shape zemstvo policy in line with his own interests.

Aver'kov and Zhidkov were representatives of the local Cossack Trading Society, which in the mid-1860s numbered around 800 people. Like other Cossack merchants, members were exempted from military service in return for paying a small sum to the state treasury. Members of the trading society also enjoyed significant advantages in trade over non-Cossack and peasant merchants. The legal incorporation of towns in the Don on the same principles as the rest of the empire would give legal standing to the activities of non-Cossack merchants. This would make them equal members of the local trading society. Moreover, it would open up other trading centers and allow competition to flourish. In accord with their rejection of the legal incorporation of towns in the Don, Aver'kov and Zhidkov supported other ideas that would have led to a purely Cossack zemstvo. By personally representing the trading society in the zemstvo, the Cossack merchants would obtain new leverage against their competitors by removing them from any discussions on local economic matters. Furthermore, they would be able to influence zemstvo policy by easing any compulsory tax.

The opinion of the three deputies, however, was ignored (subsequently two of the three were removed from the committee at Potapov's insistence), and their views were not even considered in the committee's preparatory work when it met in full session in 1867. The deputies of the committee successfully dealt with the tasks given to them by Nakaznyi Ataman Potapov. These were to reconcile the reform "with the exceptional position of the Don territory, brought about by its historical evolution and military tradition . . . while preserving the military capacity and organization of the estate and by not violating Cossack privilege."[25] The principle of universal participation in the zemstvo and in payment of taxes, including monetary taxes, was almost fully achieved in the seventh draft (three of the drafts envisaged the legal incorporation of towns and the creation of an urban electorate). The vexed question of monetary taxes was avoided with the aid of the stanitsa communes. Monetary taxes were levied not directly on each inhabitant of the stanitsa but on communal income as a whole.[26] The committee proposed the election of 264 deputies to the okrug zemstvos and 44 to the voisko zemstvo. The majority of deputies would be drawn from the nobility, the stanitsas were to have 73, while the peasantry and the urban areas would have 39 and 20 respectively.[27] By equalizing the rights of hereditary owners of land with those of temporary allotments as far as representation in the zemstvo was concerned, the leading role in the zemstvo was given to the Don nobility as the committee had intended.

The tough and consistent position of Nakaznyi Ataman Potapov, who had become the sole holder of power in the Don at this time, had contributed to the successful outcome of the committee's work. In addition the first private newspaper, *Donskoi vestnik*, which began publication in 1866, supported the Ataman's policy. The liberal intelligentsia, who were mostly of noble origin, were grouped around this paper. The first issue of the paper announced its role as "influencing public opinion in favor of the zemstvo."[28] This message was reflected in practically every issue right up to the closure of the newspaper in 1869.

By the end of 1867 the zemstvo had every chance of being successfully implemented. The committee had paved the way by including representatives from all estates in the territory. The reform enjoyed the support of the most active section of society and possessed a real tool for influencing public opinion.

The discussion of the committee's work in government circles coincided with an aggravated struggle for power at court between Miliutin and the new Minister of Internal Affairs A. E. Timashev, a member of the so-called "party" of Count P. A. Shuvalov. Timashev had wished to bring the Don zemstvo under his own ministry's jurisdiction, something Miliutin categorically rejected. Timashev then enlisted the support of the Minster of Justice. Timashev interfered with the project at every stage and in every possible way. In particular, he found it necessary to review the proposals for the legal incorporation of towns in the Don.[29] The statement of the new Nakaznyi Ataman, Major-General M. I. Chertkov, about the passage of the reform was a real stab in the back for the War Ministry. Chertkov spoke out against the introduction of the zemstvo in the Don, saying that "even now there had been little preparation of the territory for such an important transformation." Among the reasons for his opinion, Chertkov singled out two: "The obligation of paying taxes would be so new and shocking to the mass of the Cossacks that they would have absolutely no sympathy for the reform," and second, "If the reform transferring temporary allotments into the private property of nobles actually took place, then the owners of such allotments would have no solidarity with the interests of the nobility."[30] In addition, Chertkov fully approved the conclusions of a special commission working under his supervision about the applicability of a new urban law to Novocherkassk. The members of the committee unanimously rejected the introduction of the law because it "would bring with it various taxes and turn the Cossacks into an urban estate ... which would make them very angry."[31] This combination of circumstances boded ill for the reforms and left the War Ministry without any hope of successfully piloting them through government circles.

In August 1870, however, Chertkov produced a new report. The Ataman pointed out the significant changes that had taken place since 1867 and proposed that the work of the old committee "be subjected to a radical review and amendment" by a new committee created for this purpose.[32] The changes referred to had profoundly transformed the socio-economic situation on the Don. In a single year (1870) the temporary allotments of the Don nobility had been handed over to them as their private property; a new law on the Communal Administration of the Cossack Host had been passed that improved stanitsa self-government; and, to mark the 300-year jubilee of the Don, the region was given a new official title, the Oblast of the Don Host. The oblast administration was reformed as well; the gradual changes in the old structure of the Voisko administration would eventually transform it along the lines of the gubernatorial model. The elected element of the old system was abolished; now many key posts in the administration were held by people who were not native to the Don, but were appointed by the Nakaznyi Ataman from other provinces. The number of provincial bureaucrats who were not from the Don but were making successful careers in the Don was gradually growing.

Chertkov's initiative was approved by the War Ministry, and in late 1871 a commission made up exclusively of officials from the oblast administration had prepared its own project of zemstvo reform for the Don.[33] The members of the commission recognized the necessity of restricting themselves to drafting supplementary rules to the general zemstvo law that would give due emphasis to the idiosyncratic nature of the territory. The main difference from earlier rules was the reduction in the number of deputies: it was proposed that 302 deputies be elected to the okrug zemstvo meetings and 55 to the voisko meetings. The number of representatives from the stanitsas and the nobility were almost identical, 121 and 120 respectively. The remaining deputies were drawn from the peasantry and the merchant estate (including the urban electorate), who numbered 47 and 14 respectively.[34] Possibly the increase in the number of stanitsa deputies impelled the committee to impose the monetary taxes "as a *personal* [emphasis added] obligation on each stanitsa inhabitant." Such a decision was justified on the grounds that "the Cossacks through paying taxes for the needs of the Don territory would be interested in knowing how these monies were spent and, consequently, in the work of the zemstvo."[35] The supplementary rules thus envisaged the predominance of the Cossack element in the zemstvo. It seemed initially, at least to the authorities, that this predominance along with the absence of an urban electorate and the transfer of the temporary allotments to private property would minimize the risk that Cossacks—whether merchants, nobles, or in the stanitsa— would be hostile to the reform.

The zemstvo reform was reviewed for more than three years by the War Ministry and the government. The Minister of Internal Affairs again sought to have the Don zemstvo brought under his own jurisdiction. Miliutin was helped in overcoming the obstructionist tactics of his opponent by the unexpected support of Potapov, who had become Chief of Gendarmes and head of the Third Section. On the eve of the meeting of the State Council on April 6, 1875, which would decide the fate of the Don zemstvo, Potapov convinced Alexander II in a private conversation to favor reform based on "Miliutin's proposals rather than Timashev's."[36]

Corrections had been made to the reform at every stage of its passage. Repeating the efforts made by the War Ministry to cut expenditures, the voisko administration wanted to remove from the voisko budget the collection of monetary taxes and a series of expensive items paid for by the voisko and transfer them to the zemstvo.[37] The War Ministry approved this initiative, but by so doing significantly restricted the zemstvo's financial freedom of action. The following detail is of interest in this regard. In later documents, which had no connection with the reform, it was claimed that the request of the voisko authorities for the introduction of the zemstvo had "as its main aim the transfer to the zemstvo of some of the expenditure from the voisko budget which was not in a very satisfactory state."[38] This should be kept in mind when speaking of the real interests of local authorities in connection with the zemstvo.

The approval of the zemstvo reform for the Don marked the long-awaited end of laborious efforts "to put the civil organization of the Cossack Host, as far as possible, on the same basis as the rest of empire."[39] The Ministry urged the new Nakaznyi Ataman, N. A. Krasnokutskii, to implement the reform as quickly as possible. Despite the best efforts of the local authorities (such as the election of deputies, which was rushed through without the necessary preparations), the meetings of the zemstvo at the voisko and okrug level only began in spring 1876.[40]

In the six years of the zemstvo's existence on the Don the key factor was not so much the concrete results of its activity (although this should not be ignored.) The zemstvo achieved little largely because of the attitude of the Cossacks and the local administration to the idea of the zemstvo as a whole.

The first two years of the zemstvo's existence showed that the deputies and administration quickly found a common language in dealing with the complex problems of the regional economy as envisaged by the zemstvo law. Nevertheless, there was a sharp divide between those who supported the principle of equality of all estates in rights and duties without distinction and those who represented the interests of the Cossacks and their traditions. The latter insisted on the legitimacy of estate privilege. The majority of zemstvo decisions favored the former group, largely thanks to the liberal intelligentsia. Matters touching on the Cossacks directly were not regarded as primary concerns and were taken into account only on their intrinsic merits. The main problem for the zemstvo was drawing up the budget and the later additions that were made to it. The possibility that the zemstvo would remain only on paper after the law had been passed due to a lack of financial resources forced the zemstvo to impose monetary taxes, as had been foreseen by the law. In addition, the zemstvo demanded money from the voisko budget, as in their opinion several items of obligatory expenditure had been unjustifiably transferred to the zemstvo. This laid the ground for future conflict with the voisko administration.

The fate of the zemstvo, its success or failure, depended to a large degree on the population's recognition of its significance and goals and the willingness of the taxpayers, two-thirds of whom were Cossacks, to fund the new expenditure. Their attitudes quickly became clear. There was a furious reaction as soon as the stanitsas became aware of the new land tax, compulsory insurance, payments for a grain reserve, and other measures. Taken together, the reforms would change the Cossack economy, way of life, and traditions and would in effect deprive them of their privileges. There had already been unrest in several stanitsas in Donets, Khoper, and Ust-Medvedets okrugs in early 1878. The administration had attempted to implement a new law controlling the use of stanitsa woods. The anger that this had caused was now redirected against the zemstvo.[41] G. V. Plekhanov, an eyewitness to these events, stated: "The Cossacks fought not only for the return of the old ways of using the stanitsa woods but against the zemstvo. The Cossacks could see no difference between the government and the zemstvo and attributed the wood law to the zemstvo."[42]

At first the stanitsas fought the zemstvo by delaying payment of zemstvo taxes. Exhortations to pay these taxes and propaganda about the aims of the zemstvo by the voisko administration had no effect.[43] By autumn 1878 it had become clear that practically all the stanitsas in Khoper Okrug and several in Ust-Medvedets had refused to pay the taxes or even assign them.[44] By the beginning of 1879 the shortfall had grown to such an extent that the zemstvo assembly petitioned the Nakaznyi Ataman to cancel the previous year's assessment and to pay the zemstvo directly from the voisko treasury.[45]

Matters worsened in the winter of 1878–1879, when the authorities in Khoper Okrug attempted to recover the arrears owed by the worst non-payers. They made an inventory of their properties and tried to sell them in the stanitsa *sbory* that had been called to hold elections for the zemstvo. The host authorities had not given permission for local authorities to proceed in this way,[46] and these actions unleashed a storm of protest, some of it physical, from the Cossacks. Twenty-two out of twenty-five stanitsas refused to hold elections for the zemstvo deputies. The Cossacks declared, "Our grandfathers and fathers have performed military service and paid taxes in kind, and we will continue to do so. But any tax paid in cash is a burden." Moreover, they believed that the continuation of the zemstvo was pointless.[47]

A meeting of the zemstvo with representatives of the administration failed to reach a consensus on the reasons for the Cossacks' anger. The zemstvo believed the refusal of the stanitsas to pay the arrears and to elect deputies was not due to activity of the zemstvo. Instead, they blamed unfavorable circumstances: for example, the damage done to the economy by the military tradition of the region, the harvest failure of 1878–1879, a severe cattle plague, the costs of the recent Russo-Turkish war, etc. While not denying the impact of unfavorable conditions, the oblast authorities blamed the zemstvo. They accused the zemstvo of not understanding the Cossack way of life and costing too much to run. At the same time, the authorities removed policing powers from the zemstvo.[48] Consequently, a campaign to overcome Cossack opposition, based on the administration and the zemstvo acting in concert, did not take place. In addition, the authorities dropped prosecutions for the non-payment of taxes in stanitsas where there had been unrest to avert an even more sweeping protest.[49]

The War Ministry regarded the events in the Don with the greatest concern. In his evaluation of the situation, Miliutin largely blamed the zemstvo. The minister agreed with the administration's proposal to set up a commission for a detailed investigation of the affair. In particular it was to look at the extent to which the existing zemstvo arrangements were acceptable or whether a cheaper, simplified zemstvo was preferable. The War Ministry was emphatic that "there could be no question of reducing the military obligations of the Cossacks or changing the ways in which the voisko budget was spent."[50]

The commission was formed from representatives of the administration and the zemstvo under the chairmanship of the assistant to the Nakaznyi Ataman for Civil Affairs, Major-General Maslakovets. The commission worked from November 1879 to May 1880. The discussions in the meeting turned bitter, even personally abusive. The zemstvo accused the local authorities of poor administration and taking bribes. The local authorities in turn accused the zemtsvo of complete incompetence and lack of experience.[51] The personal beliefs of the chairman, "a fervent opponent of the zemstvo," determined the outcome of the commission, namely, defeat for the zemstvo. Under Maslakovets's supervision a series of changes to the zemstvo rules was prepared using the work carried out by the commission. The abolition of the okrug zemstvo and the replacement of the zemstvo board by officials were proposed. Since all zemstvo business would now be concentrated at the oblast level, it was further proposed that policy on a local level could be carried out by special plenipotentiary delegates.[52] Nakaznyi Ataman Krasnokutskii approved the proposals and suggested the creation of a new committee made up of all estates to review them. Maslakovets himself would travel to St. Petersburg to present the proposals on behalf of the Nakaznyi Ataman.

However, the supporters of the zemstvo refused to admit defeat. They actively campaigned to turn public opinion in their favor. The protocols of the commission, named the Maslakovets Commission, were distributed to the main newspapers and journals with a request to comment on them objectively and in an unprejudiced manner.[53] Soon many articles appeared in various publications. The articles, on the whole, favored the zemstvo.[54] In practically every okrug during the summer of 1870, resolutions were passed in village assemblies that expressed "gratitude to the zemstvo and hope for its continued existence." Several stanitsa communes added their support to that of the peasantry, a big victory for the zemstvo.[55] Every resolution of support for the zemstvo was published in the newspaper *Donskoi golos,* which acted as a mouthpiece for the zemstvo. When this newspaper began publication in 1880, the supporters of the zemstvo finally received a public platform for their case. They could now answer their opponents in the official paper *Donskie oblastnye vedomosti*, where anti-zemstvo articles had regularly appeared since the beginning of the crisis.

However, after an extensive analysis of the crisis, the zemstvo deputies were forced to recognize that they did not enjoy the support of a significant section of society. The Cossacks viewed the zemstvo tax as a type of poll tax and understood the activity of the zemstvo as part of a gradual transformation of the Cossacks into a tax-paying estate. No less unhappy with the reform were private landholders, holders of temporary allotments, homeowners, and trading and industrial people. This was because their liability for zemstvo taxes was considerably more than they had previously paid. Their supporters used their influence in the stanitsa *sbory* to incite the ordinary Cossacks against the zemstvo.[56]

Declarations were heard urging the zemstvo to continue the struggle. Obviously wishing somehow to influence Maslakovets's review of the zemstvo reform in the War Ministry, the oblast zemstvo board asked the okrug zemstvo to compile short accounts of all the work they had done since the beginning. They were also asked to give their opinions on Maslakovets's work as a whole. Without exception all the okrug zemstvos criticized it sharply.[57]

However, the War Ministry rejected the requests of the zemstvo, even without the prompting of Maslakovets. In effect, the Don zemstvo was now on a slippery slope. As the internal situation in the country became more complex, the suggestion of closing the zemstvo was raised in the Ministry. Ataman Krasnokutskii had so far maintained a position of strict neutrality between the voisko administration and the zemstvo. When he arrived in St. Petersburg he gave his backing to the zemstvo. The Ataman realized that closing the zemstvo "would be extremely difficult." He was able to obtain the Tsar's approval for his previous initiative in a new guise: the creation of a commission made up of all estates to discuss the problems raised by the zemstvo reform.[58]

From the very first days of his ascension to the throne after the tragic death of his father, Alexander III pursued conservative policies. Nevertheless, in spite of his readiness to exercise autocratic power, Alexander III did not dare to begin his reign by ignoring the vital interests of the largest Cossack territory. On March 17, 1881, he gave permission for the committee to begin work.[59]

The election of the ninety-six members of the commission (plus ten representatives appointed by the voisko administration) took place against the background of the dismissal of the War Minister and Nakaznyi Ataman Krasnokutskii. Miliutin had been the original driving force behind the zemstvo, and Krasnokutskii was a supporter. Inevitably this had an effect on the fate of the zemstvo. When the new ataman, Major-General Sviatopolk-Mirskii, arrived in St. Petersburg, he put forward for the emperor's personal review an agenda for the proposed commission. It was decided that the discussion of whether or not there would be a zemstvo in the Don would take place not in the full commission but in three subcommissions. These would be estate-based, made up of deputies drawn from nobles, stanitsa communes, peasants and merchants, and would meet separately.[60] Such a division was justified by the heated emotions that threatened personal relations, and by the proposition that "the intelligentsia members of the commission who were skilled in debate would stifle the representatives of the ordinary people."[61]

The opinions voiced in the commissions in November–December 1881 caught the government by surprise. The stanitsa delegates who were against the zemstvo in its existing form nevertheless supported the basic principle of the reform, self-government. They suggested a "different type of zemstvo that would control the territory's entire economy" and would in turn entail the reestablishment of the old voisko krug as the sovereign body in the voisko. Peasant members of the commission declared that if the government abolished the zemstvo on the Don, the peasants would ask to be resettled in other provinces. The majority of the noble members thought that the only way out of the mess was the preservation of the zemstvo, but on the condition that the civil and military authorities worked with it, not against it.[62]

As a result the fate of the zemstvo, far from becoming clearer, had become more confused than ever. The zemstvo now threatened to break out of the conservative framework constructed by the administration into a much broader democratic institution. This was completely unacceptable to the government. Finally, Alexander III decided to ignore public opinion as expressed by the committee. On March 24, 1882, the Don zemstvo was closed on the grounds that "it did not correspond to the spirit of the Cossacks."[63]

Against a background of complete success elsewhere in the empire, the zemstvo failed in the Don. Unlike other zemstvos, the Don zemstvo had no broad base of support among the population, which did not see the advantages of the new form of self-government. The Don nobility and the Cossacks, at whom the reform was aimed, regarded it first and foremost as a means to abolish their privileges and introduce new taxes. The responsibility for the substance of the reforms lay primarily with the central and local authorities, but the zemstvo bore some responsibility as well. The War Ministry regarded the reform as a means to integrate the Cossacks into the general economic and cultural life of the empire and to overcome the Cossacks' isolation and parochialism. The dogmatic principles of the supporters of the zemstvo prevented a more flexible and cautious approach. This would not have been to everyone's liking, but it might have satisfied a majority of the population. The local authorities were interested in the zemstvo only to the extent that it coincided with their own interests. As far as civil society on the Don was concerned, its divided reaction to the reforms put the government in a difficult position. With its closure of the zemstvo, the administration acknowledged its own powerlessness to resolve the difficult questions of ongoing regional politics.

Translated by Shane O'Rourke

Notes

1. B. G. Litvak, *Perevorot 1861 goda: pochemu ne realizovalas' reformatorskaia al'ternativa* (Moscow, 1991), 213.

2. B. B. Veselovskii, *Istoriia zemstva za 40 let,* vol. 3 (St. Petersburg, 1911), 47–48.

3. N. M. Pirumova, *Zemskoe liberal'noe dvizhenie. Sotsial'nye korni i evoliutsiia do nach. XIX v.* (Moscow, 1997), 34; G. A. Gerasimenko, *Zemskoe samoupravlenie v Rossii* (Moscow, 1990), 12; F. A. Petrov, "Organy samoupravleniia v sisteme samoderzhavnoi Rossii: zemstvo v 1864–1879 gg.," in L. G. Zakharovoi, B. Eklof, Dzh. Bushnell, eds., *Velikie reformy v Rossii 1856–1874* (Moscow, 1992), 205.

4. L. A. Zhukova, *Problemy vzaimodeistviia vlastnykh struktur i zemskogo samoupravleniia v poreformennoi Rossii 1864–1918 gg. Problemnaia lektsiia dlia studentov vsekh spetsial'nostei* (Moscow, 1995), 14; *Zemskoe samoupravlenie v poreformennoi Rossii (1864–1918 gg). Dokumenty i materialy: uchebnoe posobie* (Mosocw, 1995), 6; N. G. Koreleva, *Zemstvo na perelome (1905–1907 gg.)* (Moscow, 1995), 19.

5. *Istoriia Rossii s nach. XVIII do kontsa XIX vv.* (Moscow, 1997), 397; A. P. Korelin, *Dvorianstvo v poreformennoi Rossii 1861–1904 gg.* (Leningrad, 1979), 213.

6. N. Kranov, ed., *Materialy dlia geografii i statistiki Rossii sobrannye ofitserami general'nogo shtaba. Zemlia voiska Donskogo* (St. Petersburg, 1863), 226, 428, 433.

7. N. Korshikov, "Svoevremennye sovety iz proshlogo," *Don* 5 (1995): 41; *Materialy dlia geografii i statistiki Rossii,* 439.

8. Gosudarstvennyi Arkhiv Rostovskoi Oblasti (hereafter GARO), f. 802, op. 1, d. 1, l. 2.

9. S. G. Svatikov, *Rossiia i Don (1549–1917). Issledovanie po istorii gosudarstvennogo i administrativnogo prava i politicheskikh dvizhenii na Donu* (Belgrade, 1924), 340.

10. Rossiiskii Gosudarstvennyi Voenno-Istoricheskii Arkhiv (hereafter RGVIA), f. 330, op. 1, d. 33, ll. 379.

11. Ibid., ll. 4, 8.

12. *Stoletie Voennogo ministerstva 1802–1902* (St. Petersburg, 1902), 412.

13. RGVIA, f. 330, op. 1, d. 47, l. 101.

14. *Donskoi vestnik* 4 (1869).

15. Citation from A. I. Agrafonov, *Oblast' voiska Donskogo i Priazov'e v doreformennoi period* (Rostov-na-Donu, 1986), 119.

16. *Stoletie Voennogo ministerstva,* 415.

17. RGVIA, f. 330, op. 1, d. 111, ll. 40–41.

18. Ibid., op. 9, d. 37, ll. 21–23.

19. *Gosudarstvennye deiateli Rossii XIX–nach. XX vv. Biograficheskii spravochnik* (Moscow, 1995), 149–150.

20. RGVIA, f. 330, op. 1, d. 33, l. 119.

21. GARO, f. 46, op. 1, d. 754, l. 101.

22. RGVIA, f. 330, op. 1, d. 33, ll. 215–225.

23. Ibid., ll. 235–236.

24. Ibid., l. 242.

25. GARO, f. 55, op. 1, d. 836, l. 6.

26. Ibid., l. 7.

27. Ibid., l. 23.

28. *Donskoi vestnik* 42 (1867).

29. RGVIA, f. 330, op. 1, d. 33, l. 238.

30. Ibid., ll. 352, 353–538.

31. Ibid., ll. 474–475.

32. Ibid., l. 437.

33. GARO, f. 46, op. 1, d. 1183.

34. Ibid., l. 78.

35. Ibid., ll. 84–85.

36. D. A. Miliutin, *Dnevnik,* vol. 1 (Moscow, 1947), 185.

37. RGVIA, f. 330, op. 1, d. 34, l. 298; d. 35, ll. 3, 51, 105.

38. *Ob"iasnitel'naia zapiska k proektu Polozheniia o Donskom zemskom upravlenii (materialy komissii gen.-maiora Kuteinikova)* (Novocherkassk, n.d.).

39. RGVIA, f. 330, op. 1, d. 35, l. 304.

40. GARO, f. 52, op. 1, d. 1, l. 67; *Sbornik oblastnogo voiska Donskogo zemstva za 1876 god* (Novocherkassk, 1877), 65.

41. V. P. Krikunov, *Krest'ianskoe dvizhenie na Donu i Severnom Kavkaze v 60–70-e gg. XIX veka* (Groznyi, 1965), 185–187; GARO, f. 46, op. 1, d. 1566, ll. 10–12.

42. G. V. Plekhanov, *Sobranie sochinenii,* 3d ed., vol. 1 (Moscow, n.d.), 29–35; E. D. Osklovka and N. A. Kazarova, "Plekhanov o Donskom Kazachestve," *Izvestiia SKNTs Vsh.* 4 (1996): 78–87.

43. GARO, f. 46, op. 1, d. 1697, ll. 6–7.

44. Ibid., f. 301, op. 5, d. 31, ll. 17–37.
45. RGVIA, f. 330, op. 23, d. 630, l. 4.
46. GARO, f. 301, op. 5, d. 33, l. 35.
47. Ibid., f. 46, op. 1, d. 1697, l. 13.
48. Ibid., ll. 18–28.
49. Ibid., f. 301, op. 5, d. 33, l. 19.
50. Ibid., f. 46, op. 1, d. 1697, ll. 40–49, 65.
51. *Trudy Komissii, uchrezhdennoi v g. Novocherkasske dlia rassmotreniia voprosov, kasaiushchikhsia prakticheskogo primeneniia polozheniia o zemskikh uchrezhdeniiakh v Oblasti voiska Donskogo* (Novocherkassk, 1880).
52. N. A. Maslakovets, *Ob"iasnitel'naia zapiska k voprosu o primenenii k OVD zemskoi reformy na osnovaniiakh sootvetstvuiushchikh mestnym usloviiam kraia i bytovym osobennostiam glavnoi (kazach'ei) massy ee naseleniia* (Novocherkassk, 1880).
53. GARO, f. 378, op. 1, d. 52, ll. 30–31.
54. *Novoe vremia* 1634, 1637, 1638 (1880); L. Borisov, "Donskoe zemstvo," *Iuridicheskii vestnik* 1 (1881); S. Eremeev, "Zemstvo i kazachestvo," *Russkoe bogatstvo* 11 (1880).
55. GARO, f. 46, op. 1, d. 1697, ll. 158–214; f. 378, op. 1, d. 84.
56. Ibid., f. 378, op. 1, d. 1, l. 4–6; *Sbornik Oblastnogo voiska Donskogo zemstva za 1880 god* (Novocherkassk, 1881), Postanovlenie No. 17, December 15, 1880.
57. GARO, f. 448, op. 1, d. 6; f. 449, op. 1, d. 2; f. 450, op. 1, d. 2; f. 451, op. 1, d. 3; f. 452, op. 1, d. 1; f. 453, d. 1; f. 454, op. 1, d. 1, 2.
58. Ibid., f. 46, op. 1, d. 2151, ll. 1–3.
59. Ibid., d. 1697, l. 193.
60. Ibid., d. 2151, ll. 317, 334.
61. *Donskoi golos* 86 (1881).
62. *Donskoi golos* 30 (1882).
63. GARO, f. 46, op. 1, d. 1697, l. 193.

14 Peoples, Regions, and Electoral Politics: The State Dumas and the Constitution of New National Elites

Rustem Tsiunchuk

The Russian empire at the beginning of the twentieth century constituted a unique and multidimensional system of "center and regions." For a scholarly understanding of this system it is important to consider it from various points of view—in the context of power and of political relations, and by tracing changes in the system of "center–regions" during transformations in political and social life.[1] It is also apparent that the history of the Russian state principle (*gosudarstvennost'*) fostered and set against each other traditions of centralism and unitarianism as well as traditions of regionalism, federalism, and self-administration.[2] The unitary Russian empire at the end of the nineteenth and the beginning of the twentieth century was characterized by multiple variations in the political-administrative status of territories and regions. Russian central authority had on the one hand to be guided by the idea of a great power and, on the other, to acquiesce to a certain degree of independence for some regions and peoples.

When describing the evolution of ideas and the search for a political model of state-building in the nineteenth and early twentieth centuries, it should be noted that right up to the revolution of 1905–1907 ideas of decentralization and parliamentarism, regionalism, and self-administration existed and were disseminated only in the milieu of the educated minority; these notions had been developed in the framework of urban, Europeanized civilization. The underdevelopment of the political consciousness of the masses, the absence of democratic freedoms, and the presence of political censorship impeded a wider understanding of these ideas. At the end of the nineteenth and the beginning of the twentieth century, the land-owning and financial-industrial elites were interested in the preservation of their privileged position both in the politics and in the economy of the empire, even though they recognized the necessity of decentralizing part of the Great Russian bureaucracy. Therefore, they very selectively and carefully supported only certain democratic demands: the broadening of territorial self-administration—yes; the granting of autonomy to peoples—no; the establishment of democratic rights and freedoms and of an all-Russian representative institution—necessary; the establishment of civic equality for non-Russians (*inorodsty*) and the guarantee of representation in an elected institution—not necessary.

The Duma and Relations in the "Center–Regions" System: A New Chance for the Modernization of Authority

The Russian "center–regions" system became noticeably more complex and multidimensional in connection with the beginning of political modernization and the creation in Russia of the first all-imperial representative institution—the State Duma—in 1906. The beginnings of Russian parliamentarism made it possible for representatives of regions and peoples of the empire for the first time to enter into an elected all-imperial institution and permitted legal expression of national and regional interests in the course of an electoral campaign and from the Duma rostrum. Parliamentarism allowed national and regional political organizations and political elites to take shape, aided the growth of the political culture of society and the development of regional and national self-consciousness, and favored the diffusion of democratic ideas of national self-determination and regional self-government. The oppositional zemstvo regarded the upper legislative chamber, the State Council, precisely as a possible chamber for electoral representatives of the regions. To the extent that half of the Council's members (around 100 people; in 1914, there were 188 members) were appointed by the emperor, it could appear as such only to a small degree. Sixty-one representatives were chosen individually from provincial zemstvo assemblies, and from special assemblies in provinces of European Russia and Polish provinces not having zemstvos.

The question of limitations on institutional competence became another ethno-regional problem connected with the Duma's changes to relations in the center–regions system. Having taken the first steps in the direction of the division of authority horizontally, and having allowed the existence of elected representation, the autocratic government did not want vertical decentralization. Article 10 of the Fundamental Laws of the Russian Empire (1906) proclaimed that "the authority of administration in all its scope belongs to the Sovereign Emperor within the boundaries of the entire Russian state."[3] The tsar appointed ministers and governors and defined the regional policies of the state. The right to declare individual localities under martial law or in a state of emergency belonged to the emperor. The Russian language was declared "the state language and obligatory in the army, the navy, and in all state and social institutions," and the use of local languages and dialects in "state and social institutions" had to be defined by "special laws."[4]

The Duma did not have the power to change on its own the political or administrative system of relations of center and regions. On the contrary, the establishment of the State Duma of 1906 and the Fundamental Laws of 1906 presented the Duma with the opportunity to promote the preservation of vertically centralized authority, especially in the areas of budget and finance. Items requiring the publication of laws and regulations, budgetary income and expenditures, and control over them were placed in its jurisdiction. Separately, it was specified that "estimates and the apportionment of land taxes in localities in which zemstvo institutions had not been introduced, and likewise matters of raising of zemstvo or city taxes contrary to the rate specified by zemstvo assemblies and city dumas" were subject to the competence of the Duma.[5] At the same time, local organs of state institutions of various departments had to pass through the Duma questions concerning disbursement of local resources and staff appointments; this requirement created a constant flow of so-called "legislative vermicelli." For instance, the third session of the Third State Duma resolved the question of the distribution of resources for the maintenance of the keeper of the Shepelev Lighthouse and the establishment of two positions of deliverymen in the Evalakh police district of Elizavetpol' Province.[6]

Duma Electoral Legislation: National-Regional Particularities

Duma electoral laws were not fully democratic. Elections were not universal insofar as they excluded women, those younger than twenty-five years old, students, and those in active military service. Elections were also not equal insofar as the vote proceeded by curia (landowning, city, peasant, and worker); this system gave multiple advantages to the first two categories. Elections were indirect and multi-tiered. The basis of the electoral system had been laid by the zemstvo statutes of 1864. However, as is well known, by 1905 the zemstvo structure had been extended only to the three dozen provinces of European Russia. Regional asymmetry in local administrative structure and governance constitutes the *first regional particularity*.

The *second ethno-regional particularity* was connected with the electoral restrictions for non-Russian peoples noted in the Statues on Elections to the State Duma. Article 6 in point "d" completely deprived a number of peoples of the empire (the so-called wandering *inorodtsy—* hunter-gatherer peoples of the North) of the right to participate in elections, and article 55 indicated that "persons not knowing the Russian language may not be elected deputies to the State Duma."

The problem of an undesirably weighty non-Russian representation worried the creators of the Russian electoral system. Even before the Manifesto of October 17, 1905, S. E. Kryzhanovskii, preparing legislation on the Duma, the State Council, and elections in the Ministry of Internal Affairs, wrote to the Chairman of the Special Conference of the State Council, Count D. M. Sol'skii:

> In Russia, the predominant nationality (*natsional'nost'*) on which the government stands comprises only about 66 percent of the overall population, and alien nationalities (*chuzhdye narodnosti*) 34 percent, that is, a percentage not seen in a single Western European power other than Austria . . . Therefore, the interests of greatest state importance urgently require that the voice of the Russian people, on which alone stands firm both the strength of state authority and the very throne of the Russian sovereign, unconditionally prevail in institutions concerned with the preparation of legislation . . . A strong majority inconvenient for the government may form in the Duma on questions touching on the interests of non-Russians.[7]

A third group of *regional-national electoral particularities* of the Russian empire was reflected in the order in which the ten separate legislative documents on the conduct of elections in ten different regions of the country were considered and in the nature of discussions regarding them. The first, the "Bulygin" Statutes on Elections, were taken up on August 6, 1905. They regulated districts and the number of electors and deputies for 51 provinces and 20 cities of European Russia. Afterward, regional electoral laws began to be worked out by higher organs of authority and in the Special Conference of Count S. M. Sol'skii. Then, on October 11, 1905, the rules on the application of the statutes on elections for 10 provinces and 2 cities of the Kingdom of Poland were adopted. On October 20, 1905, the rules on elections in 4 Siberian provinces and the city of Irkutsk were published. On February 2, 1906, the rules on elections in 6 Caucasian provinces, 5 areas (oblasts), 2 districts, and 2 cities were promulgated. On February 22, 1906, rules on elections in 4 areas (oblasts) of Kazakhstan were issued. On March 25, 1906, a decree on the confirmation of rules for elections by nomadic non-Russians (*inorodtsy*) of Astrakhan and Stavropol provinces came out. Finally—the last—on April 22, 1906, already on the eve of the convocation of the first Duma, four decrees on the order of elections were adopted. These were rules on elections in 3 oblasts of the Far East, statutes on elections in Iakutsk oblast, rules on the application of statutes on elections in 4 oblasts of Central Asia and the city of Tashkent, and rules on the order of election of members of the Duma from the Orthodox population of Siedl'tse and Liublin provinces. The lack of simultaneity in the adoption of electoral rules and orders bore witness not only to the chronic tardiness of legislative organization, but also to the government's maneuvers directed toward the goal of forming a more loyal Duma.

The most important question of the elections' political geography concerned electoral districts, their territory and the density of population, and the social and national-religious composition of the population. Provinces and oblasts and also major cities were defined as electoral districts. The *fourth ethno-religious* particularity of the elections was that, in national regions in the borderlands, separate territorial-ethnic, territorial-confessional, or territorial-estate electoral districts were formed with a fixed representation of deputies in the Duma, in order to strengthen the role of the Russian, Orthodox, or Cossack population living "in non-Russian [*inorodcheskii*] surroundings." If in central Russia existing provincial administrative boundaries were used for electoral districts, in the Caucasus districts were created for political purposes, including groups of administrative territorial units (Kuban oblast and Chernomor Province, Batum oblast and Sukhum okrug, Dagestan oblast and Zakatal okrug). Territorial-ethnic districts that separated the non-Russian population were created in all areas of Kazakhstan, Central Asia and in the city of Tashkent, and also for the *inorodtsy* of oblasts beyond Lake Baikal. As a rule, representatives of all local peoples living in a region were united in the category of non-Russian (*inorodtsy*) by district (okrug). According to the same principle, "nomadic non-Russians (*inorodsty*)" of two provinces, Astrakhan and Stavropol, were united in a special territorial-ethnic district, which consolidated representatives of two peoples—the Kirghiz (Kazakhs) and Kalmyks—into one seat each in the Duma. The Orthodox population of the two provinces of the Kingdom of Poland constituted a territorial-confessional district. Territorial-estate districts were specified for the Cossacks, who were guaranteed twelve deputy mandates.

In connection with the issue of rates of representation from the provinces, the explanatory notes compiled by the Ministry of Internal Affairs proposed that the distribution of deputy positions in the future Duma be determined by the total population—for central provinces, one deputy per 250,000 residents.[8] Reconstruction of the actual ratio of Duma positions from the various regions, provinces, oblasts, and cities, indicating the quantity of population and ethno-confessional composition of the residents of the regions, makes it possible to see the problem of the formation of the first all-Russian parliament in regional and ethno-regional perspective. (See table 14.1.)

The total number of deputies to the first and second convocations of the State Duma, set at 524 deputies, was distributed among the five groups of regions of the Russian empire in the following manner: 414 positions (79%) for the population of European Russia (75% of the population of the empire); 37 positions for Poland (7.1% of the deputies of the empire for 7.5% of the empire's population); 29 positions for the population of the Caucasus (5.5% for 6.7%); 21 positions for the inhabitants of Siberia and the Far East (4% for 4.6%); and 23 positions for the inhabitants of Kazakhstan and Central Asia (4.4% for 6.2%).

For the empire, the average number of people per deputy in the first and second Duma convocations was 239,800 people, at a time when the average figure per province of European Russia was 12,000 less—227,800 people per deputy. At that time the ratio in all other groups of regions exceeded the overall ratio for the empire: in Poland 14,300 more, in Siberia and in the Far East 34,400 more, in the Caucasus 50,400 more, and in Central Asia and Kazakhstan 97,000 people more. Thus, the average rate of representation for the national borderland regions was almost 100,000 higher, and the most extreme ratios—121,300 people per deputy (Olonetsk Province) and 786,100 people per deputy (Fergana oblast)—shows a difference of 664,800 people (six and one-half times). The explanatory note of the Ministry for Internal Affairs argued for increased representation from provinces larger in territory but sparsely settled (such as, for instance, northern

Table 14.1. Regional Representation of the Population of the Russian Empire in the First through Fourth State Dumas[1]

Name of Province (oblast or city)	Number of Residents (oblast or city) (in thousands)*	Number of Deputies (oblast or city)		Ratio of Representation (number of residents to one deputy) (in thousands)	
		I-II Dumas	III-IV Dumas	I-II Dumas	III-IV Dumas
EUROPEAN RUSSIA					
1. Arkhangelsk prov.	346.5	2	2	173.2	173.2
2. Astrakhan prov.	10003.5/890.7	3 (1 from Cossacks)	4 (1 from Cossacks)	296.9	250.9
From the nomadic population of Astrakhan and Stavropol provs.	**	1 (from the Kalmyks) 1 (from the [Kazakh] Kirgiz)	—		
City of Astrakhan	112.8	1	—	112.8	—
3. Bessarabia prov.	1935.1/1826.7	8	9	228.3	215
City of Kishinev	108.4	1	—	108.4	—
4. Vilno prov.	1591.2/1436.7	6	7 (2 from the Russian pop.)	239.4	227.3
City of Vilno	154.5	1		154.5	—
5. Vitebsk prov.	1489.2	6	6	248.2	248.2
6. Vladimir prov.	1515.7	6	6	252.6	252.6
7. Vologda prov.	1341.8	5	5	268.3	268.3
8. Volyn prov.	2989.5	13	13	229.9	229.9
9. Voronezh prov.	2531.2/2450.6	11	12	222.7	210.9
City of Voronezh	80.6	1	—	80.6	—
10. Viatka prov.	3030.8	13	8	233	378.9
11. Grodno prov.	1603.4	7	7	229	229

		11 (1 from the Cossacks)	12 (1 from the Cossacks)		
12. Oblast of the Don Host	2564.2/2444.8			222.2	213.7
City of Rostov-on-Don	119.4	1	—	119.4	—
13. Ekaterinoslav prov.	2113.7/2000.8	9	10	223.3	211.3
City of Ekaterinoslav	112.8	1	—	112.8	—
14. Kazan prov.	2170.6/2040.6	9	10	226.7	217
City of Kazan	130	1	—	130	
15. Kaluga prov.	1132.8	5	5	226.5	226.5
16. Kiev prov.	3559.2/3311.5	15	13	220.7	254.7
City of Kiev	247.7	1	2	247.7	123.9
17. Kovno prov.	1544.6	6	6 (1 from the Russian population)	257.4	257.4
18. Kostroma prov.	1387	6	6	231.1	231.1
19. Kurland prov.	674	3	3	224.6	224.6
20. Kursk prov.	2371/2295.3	10	11	229.5	215.5
City of Kursk	75.7	1	—	75.7	—
21. Lifland prov.	1299.3/1017.1	4	4	254.2	254.2
City of Riga	282.2	1	2	282.2	141.2
22. Minsk prov.	2147.6	9	9	238.6	238.6
23. Mogilev prov.	1686.8	7	7	240.9	240.9
24. Moscow prov.	2430.6/1392	6	6	232	232
City of Moscow	1038.6	4	4	259.1	259.1
25. Nizhnii Novgorod prov.	1581.8/1491.8	6	7	248.6	226
City of Nizhnii Novgorod	90	1	—	90	
26. Novgorod prov.	1367	6	6	227.8	227.8
27. Olonetsk prov.	364.2	3	3	121.3	121.3

Continued on the next page

Table 14.1. Continued

Name of Province (oblast or city)	Number of Residents (oblast or city) (in thousands)*	Number of Deputies (oblast or city)		Ratio of Representation (number of residents to one deputy) (in thousands)	
		I-II Dumas	III-IV Dumas	I-II Dumas	III-IV Dumas
28. Orenburg prov.	1600.1	7 (1 from the Cossacks)	6 (1 from the Cossacks)	228.5	266.7
29. Orel prov.	2033.8/1964	8	9	245.5	226
City of Orel	69.7	1	—	69.7	—
30. Penza prov.	1470.4	6	6	245	245
31. Perm prov.	2994.3	13	9	320	377.1
32. Podol'sk prov.	3018.2	13	13	322.1	322.1
33. Poltava prov.	2778.1	12	12	231.5	231.5
34. Pskov prov.	1122.3	4	5	280.5	224.4
35. Riazan prov.	1802.1	8	8	225.2	225.2
36. Samara prov.	2751.3/2661.3	12	13	221.7	211.6
City of Samara	90	1	—	90	—
37. St. Petersburg prov.	2112/847.1	3	4	282.4	211.8
City of St. Petersburg	1264.9	6	6	210.8	210.8
38. Saratov prov.	2405.8/2268.7	10	11	226.9	218.7
City of Saratov	137.1	1	—	137.1	—
39. Simbirsk prov.	1527.8	6	6	254.6	254.6
40. Smolensk prov.	1527.3	6	6	254.5	254.6
41. Stavropol prov.	873.3	3	3	291.1	291.1
42. Tauride prov.	1447.8	6	6	241.2	241.7
43. Tambov prov.	2684	12	12	223.6	223.6
44. Tver prov.	1769.1	8	8	221.1	221.1

45. Tula prov.	1419.4/1304.7	5	6	260.9	236.5
City of Tula	114.7	1	—	114.7	—
46. Ufa prov.	2196.6	10	8	219.6	274.6
47. Khar'kov prov.	2492.3/2318.4	10	11	231.8	226.6
City of Khar'kov	n173.9	1	—	173.9	—
48. Kherson prov.	2733.6/2329.8	10	10	231.9	231.9
City of Odessa	403.8	1	2	403.8	201.4
49. Chernigov prov.	2297.8	10	10	229.8	229.8
50. Estland prov.	412.7	3	3	137.6	137.6
51. Iaroslavl prov.	1071.3/999.7	4	5	249.9	214.2
City of Iaroslavl	71.6	1	—	71.6	—
Total for European Russia	94316.2	414	403	227.8	234

Poland

1. Warsaw prov.	1931.9/1248.2	5	1	249.6	1248.2
City of Warsaw	683.7	2	2 (1 from the Russian population)	341.8	341.8
2. Kalish prov.	840.6	3	1	280.2	840.6
3. Kiel'tse prov.	762	3	1	254	762
4. Lomzha prov.	579.6	2	1	289.8	579.6
5. Liublin prov.	1160.6	5	1	232.1	1160.6
6. Pietrokov prov.	1403.9/1089.9	5	1	218	1089.9
City of Lodz	314	1	1	314	314
7. Plotsk prov.	553.6	2	1	276.8	553.6
8. Radom prov.	814.9	3	1	271.6	814.9
9. Suvalki prov.	582.9	2	1	291.4	582.9

Continued on the next page

Table 14.1. Continued

Name of Province (oblast or city)	Number of Residents (oblast or city) (in thousands)*	Number of Deputies (oblast or city)		Ratio of Representation (number of residents to one deputy) (in thousands)	
		I-II Dumas	III-IV Dumas	I-II Dumas	III-IV Dumas
10. Siedl'tse prov.	772.1	3	1	257.3	772.1
From the Orthodox Population of Liublin. and Siedl'tse provs.	**	1	1	—	—
Total for Poland	9402.2	37	14	254.1	671.6
CAUCASUS					
1. Baku prov.	826.7/714.8	2	2 (from Baku, Elizavetpol, and Erevan provs.)	357.4	1267.3**
City of Baku	111.9	1	—	111.9	—
2. Batum obl. and Sukhum okrug	144.6 (without Sukhum okr.**)	1	1 (from Kars and Batum obl. and Sukhum okrug.)	144.6	435.2***
3. Dagestan obl. and Zakatal okr.	571.1 (without Zakatal okr.**)	2	1	285.5	571.1
4. Elizavetpol prov.	878.4	3	—	292.8	—
5. Kars obl.	290.6	1	—	290.6	—

6. Kuban obl. and Chernomor prov.	1976.3	6 (3 from the Cossacks)	2 (1 from the Kuban, Cossacks, 1 from the non-Cossack population of Kuban and Tersk obl. and Chernom. Prov.	329.4	**
7. Kutais prov.	913.6	3	1	304.5	913.6
8. Tersk prov.	933.9	3 (1 from the Cossacks)	1 (from the Tersk Cossacks)	311.3	**
9. Tiflis prov.	1051	3	1	350.3	1051
City of Tiflis	159.6	1	—	159.6	—
10. Erevan prov.	829.5	3	—	276.5	—
From the Russian population of the Caucasus	**	—	1	—	**
Total for the Caucasus	8416	29	10	290.2	841.6

SIBERIA

1. Amur oblast	120.3	1	1	120.3	120.3
2. Enisei prov.	570.1	2	1	285	570.1
3. Zabaikal obl.	672	3 (1 from the Cossacks, 1 from the inorodtsy, 1 from the rest of the population)	2 (1 from the Cossacks)	224	336
4. Irkutsk prov.	514.2/463.2	1	1	463.2	514.2
City of Irkutsk	51	1		51	—
5. Primorsk obl.	223.3	1	1	223.3	223.3

Continued on the next page

Table 14.1. Continued

Name of Province (oblast or city)	Number of Resident (oblast or city) (in thousands)*	Number of Deputies (oblast or city)		Ratio of Representation (number of residents to one deputy) (in thousands)	
		I-II Dumas	III-IV Dumas	I-II Dumas	III-IV Dumas
6. Sakhalin	28.1	—	—	—	—
7. Tobolsk prov.	1433	4	3	358.2	477.7
8. Tomsk prov.	1927.7	6	4	321.3	482
9. Iakutsk prov.	269.9	1	—	269.9	—
From the Amur and Ussurii Cossacks	**	1	1	**	**
Total for Siberia	5788.8	21	14	274.2	411.3
CENTRAL ASIA					
1. Akmolinsk obl.	682.6	2 (1 from the inorodtsy)	—	341.3	—
2. Zakaspiisk obl.	382.5	2 (1 from the inorodtsy)	—	191.2	—
3. Samarkand obl.	860	2 (1 from the inorodtsy)	—	430	—
4. Semipalatinsk obl.	684.6	2 (1 from the inorodtsy)	—	342.3	—
5. Semirechensk obl.	987.9	3 (1 from the Cossacks, 1 from the inorodtsy, 1 from the rest of the population)	—	369.3	—

6. Syr-Daria obl.	1478.4/1322.7	2 (1 from the inorodtsy)	—	661.3	—
City of Tashkent	155.7	2 (1 from the inorodtsy)	—	77.8	—
7. Turgai obl.	453.4	2 (1 from the inorodtsy)	—	226.7	—
8. Ural obl.	645.1	1 (from the Cossacks), 2 (1 from the inorodtsy 1 from the rest of the population)	1 (from the Ural Cossacks)	322.3	—
9. Fergana obl.	1572.2	2 (1 from the inorodtsy)	—	786.1	—
From the Cossacks of Akmolinsk and Semipalatinsk obl. and Tomsk prov.	**	1	—	**	—
Total from Central Asia and Kazakhstan:	7746.7	23	1	336.8	—
TOTAL:	125640	524	442	239.8	284.2

*the indicated population of the province excludes the residents of a provincial city with separate representation. **an accurate count is unavailable. ***the indicated ratio in the framework of new okrugs.

1. The table is compiled from material of the official statutes on elections of 1905–1907 and from information from the 1897 census of population, cited in 4 supplemental half-volumes of the *Encyclopedic Dictionary* of Brokhaus and Efron (F. A. Brokgaus and I. A. Efron, eds., *Entsiklopedicheskii slovar'*, 51 vols. [St. Petersburg: Tipo-litografia I. A. Efrona, 1890–1907]).

Arkhangelsk, Vologda, and Olonetsk provinces) with an indication that otherwise "diverse local interests . . . will not be sufficiently expressed."[9] The increased representation of Russians relative to the composition of the population of the provinces of European Russia was also explained by "the significance to the state of the native Russian provinces in the general structure of the empire."[10]

Considerable ethno-regional particularities can be traced in the city electoral districts that had separate representation in elections to the First and Second Dumas. One of the initial electoral legislative projects proposed the presentation of separate city status to 19 cities of the empire having populations greater than 100,000 people. At a minimum, 13 of these cities (Warsaw, Odessa, Lodz, Riga, Kiev, Khar'kov, Tiflis, Tashkent, Vil'no, Kazan, Ekaterinovslav, Baku, and Kishinev) had substantial non-Russian and non-Orthodox populations. It therefore was decided to expand the list of cities with separate representation to 26 and "include in this list several purely Russian cities, closely resembling in size those located on the list."[11] Thus, 7 additional provincial capitals received separate representation, although their selection was in no small measure arbitrary. For example, while Nizhnii Novgorod and Samara, with populations of 90,000 people, received representation, the multinational provincial center of Minsk, with the same number of residents, did not. Of the cities with higher populations than that of Orel (69,700) with its separate electoral district, multinational Nikolaev (92,000), Kokand (81,000), Orenburg (72,400), and Kovno (70,900) did not receive separate representation. The smallest provincial capital of the empire that received representation was Irkutsk (51,000). The rate of representation of major cities likewise differed in no small measure. Of all the cities of European Russia, Odessa (403,800 residents per deputy) had the highest ratio of representation, followed by Riga (282,200), then Kiev (247,700). Moscow had an elevated rate of representation (259,100 per deputy) by comparison with St. Petersburg (210,800). The proportional rates of representation from Warsaw (341,800) and Lodz (314,000) were much higher than that for the whole empire and higher than for Poland. Noticeably lower than the general proportion for the empire and the lower proportion in the Caucasus were the average norms of representation for Baku (111,900) and Tiflis (156,600), which were similar to the proportions of cities of central Russia. The average index of Tashkent was equal to 77,800, but was appreciably higher for the non-Russian population of the city than for the Russians.

The law on elections of June 3, 1907, which was adopted by circumventing the Duma, lowered the number of members of the Duma (the third and fourth convocations) by 82 deputies, that is, from 524 to 442 persons. The new electoral law set as its goal the sharp reduction of representatives of national regions. The Manifesto of June 3, 1907, on the dissolution of the State Duma and the change in electoral procedure, stated:

> Created for the strengthening of the Russian state, the State Duma must be Russian also in spirit. Other nationalities (*narodnosti*) under our authority must have representatives of their needs in the State Duma, but must not be present in numbers giving them the possibility of being decision-makers in purely Russian questions. In those border regions of the state where the population has not attained sufficient development of civic consciousness (*grazhdanstvennost'*), elections to the State Duma must be temporarily halted.[12]

The asymmetry of the electoral system was noticeably strengthened. At the time when the representation of provinces of European Russia was reduced by 11 deputies, the representation of Polish provinces was reduced by 23 mandates, the Caucasus lost 19 of 29 deputy positions, representation of Siberia and the Far East was reduced by 5 deputy positions, and of 23 deputies from Central Asia and Kazakhstan autocratic lawmakers left only one position for representatives of the Ural Cossacks. Under the new rules, the provinces of European Russia sent to the Duma 91.2 percent of the deputies, Polish provinces had 3.2 percent of the overall Duma complement of deputies, the Caucasus—2.2 percent, Siberia and the Far East—3.2 percent, Central Asia and Kazakhstan—0 percent, Ural Cossacks—0.2 percent of the members of the Duma.

In connection with the reduction of the number of Duma deputies by 82 persons, the average proportion of representation according to the law of June 3, 1907, increased by 44,400 people (from 239,800 to 284,200). The overall norm of representation for provinces of European Russia in connection with the loss of 12 positions increased insignificantly—by 6,800 persons. In the majority of these provinces, norms of representation remained as they had before. In 14 provinces and one oblast (Astrakhan, Bessarabia, Vil'no, Voronezh, the oblast of the Don Host, Ekaterinoslav, Kazan, Kursk, Nizhnii Novgorod, Orel, Samara, Saratov, Tula, Khar'kov, and Iaroslavl), the average proportion of representation fell owing to the liquidation of separate city electoral districts and the inclusion of these deputy positions in the general quota of deputy positions from the province.

Representation from the Ural provinces was reduced (Viatka from 13 to

8, Perm from 13 to 9, Ufa from 10 to 8, Orenburg from 7 to 6), and likewise that of Kiev Province (from 15 to 13, with the transfer of one position to Kiev). Separate representation of the nomadic *inorodtsy* of Astrakhan and Stavropol provinces was abolished. However, the number of deputies from Odessa, Kiev, and Riga was increased to two, thereby reducing the average proportion. The proportion of residents per deputy in Kiev (123,900) and in Riga (141,200) became among the lowest absolute rates in the country.

In elections to the Third Duma, national electoral districts were created in the provinces of European Russia for the first time: in Vil'no Province for the election of two Russian deputies and in Kovno Province for the election of one deputy from the Russian population. It was decided also to divide county electoral congresses of electors by nationality. After June 3, 1907, in connection with the sharp reduction in representation from the Polish provinces, the norm of proportional representation decreased by 2.6 times (from 254,100 to 671,600). The greatest increases (by five times) were for the norms of representation from two of the largest Polish provinces—Warsaw and Pietrokov. One of Warsaw's two deputies was elected from the Russian population.

A radical re-division of the electoral districts was carried out in the new electoral system in the Caucasus, the districts of which were reduced by half, to 6, while 3 districts replaced former separate okrugs that had lost their representation—Dagestan oblast merged with Zakatal okrug and Kutais and Tiflis provinces. The cities of Tiflis and Baku lost separate representation. Baku, Elizavetpol, and Erevan provinces were united and, having lost 6 places all in all, now could elect only 2 deputies (1 each from the Muslim and non-Muslim populations). Kars oblast lost separate representation and was joined with the electoral district of Batum oblast and Sukhum okrug. The non-Cossack populations of Kuban oblast and Chernomorsk Province were united into a common electoral district with Tersk oblast and the representation of this population reduced from 5 deputies to 1. The separate representation of the Kuban Cossack and Tersk Cossack hosts was maintained, but the Kuban Cossacks were to elect 1 deputy instead of 3.

The Russian population of the Caucasus made up a separate electoral district and elected one deputy. The statutes determined that "with respect to the conduct of elections to the State Duma (article 4), persons of Russian origins—Orthodox, Old-Believer, and Lutheran—are counted among the Russian population of the Caucasus. The immediate decision (*ukazanie*), in individual cases, of who in particular should be counted as a person of Russian origin is to be made by the Governor-General . . . "[13] The understanding of "national," apparently not unintentionally, in practice became mixed up with or was even replaced by "confessional," which must have promoted an amorphousness on the part of some nations (especially non-Russian peoples practicing Orthodoxy), and accordingly to some degree may have impeded national consolidation and national movements.

The Ethno-confessional Composition of the Russian Parliament, 1906–1917

Elections to the State Duma of the Russian empire promoted the development of political parties among the peoples of Russia and the making of political culture. Questions of national-state construction and regional life were expressed in the political programs of the overwhelming majority of political parties.[14] In the course of elections, the Polish National-Democratic Party, the Polish Party of Practical (*Real'noi*) Policy, the Estonian People's Party of Progress, the Latvian Constitutional-Democratic Party and Latvian Democratic Party, the Armenian Revolutionary Union (Dashnaktsutiun), the Union of Muslims (Ittifak al-Muslimin), Ukrainian, Georgian, and Jewish political parties and organizations actively declared themselves and gained Duma representation. On the eve of elections, the Second All-Russian Congress of Muslims (Petersburg, January 1906) spoke out for the formation of an electoral bloc with the Constitutional-Democratic Party,[15] which influenced the results of elections in the Volga, Ural, Crimean, and Caucasus regions. At a minimum, twenty-five deputies from the western, multinational provinces passed into the First Duma in a bloc with the Kadets.[16] The main result of the first elections was that for the first time the country's regions and peoples received electoral representation.

For a more thorough understanding of the political, regional, and national processes in the Russian empire, it is possible to collect, count, and analyze the national and confessional composition of all four convocations of the State Duma and to trace the dynamics, trends, and order of these processes in the context of the national-confessional structure of the entire population of the Russian empire in the early twentieth century (see tables 14.2 and 14.3).

The parliament of such a multinational country as the Russian empire,

Table 14.2. National Composition of Deputies to the First through Fourth State Dumas of Russia[1]

| Nationalities | Number and Percent of Deputies in the State Dumas, Convocations I-IV | | | | Percentage in the composition of the Russian empire |
	Duma —%	II Duma —%	III Duma —%	IV Duma # —%	
Russians	289-58.3	328-63.4	377-77.4	366-83.4	44.3
Ukrainians	62-12.5	47-9.1	28-5.8	9-2.1	17.8
Poles	51-10.3	46-8.9	22-4.6	17-3.9	6.3
Belarussians	12-2.4	8-1.5	12-2.5	5-1.1	4.7
Jews	13-2.7	6-1.2	4-0.8	3-0.7	4
Kazakhs (Kirgiz)	5-1.0	7-1.3	—	—	3.4
Tatars	7-1.4	13-2.5	4-0.8	5-1.1	1.7
Germans	4-0.8	4-0.8	13-2.7	9-2.1	1.4
Uzbeks (Sarts)	—	3-0.6	—	—	1.3
Lithuanians (and Zhmuds)	10-2.0	8-1.5	5-1.1	5-1.1	1.1
Azerbaijanis	6-1.2	5-1.0	1-0.2	1-0.2	1.1
Georgians	7-1.4	7-1.3	2-0.4	3-0.7	1.1
Bashkirs	5-1.0	4-0.8	4-0.8	—	1.1
Latvians	6-1.2	6-1.2	2-0.4	2-0.5	1.1
Armenians	5-1.0	7-1.3	4-0.8	4-0.9	0.9
Moldovans	1-0.2	1-0.2	2-0.4	3-0.7	0.9
Mordvinians	2-0.4	1-0.2	—	—	0.8
Estonians	4-0.8	5-1.0	2-0.4	2-0.5	0.7
Chuvash	1-0.2	1-0.2	—	—	0.6

Table 14.2. *Continued*

Nationalities	Number and Percent of Deputies in the State Dumas, Convocations I-IV				Percentage in the composition of the Russian empire
	Duma —%	II Duma —%	III Duma —%	IV Duma # —%	
Lezgins	—	2-0.4	1-0.2	1-0.2	0.4
Udmurts	1-0.2	—	—	—	0.3
Buriats	—	1-0.2	—	—	0.2
Turkmen	—	1-0.2	—	—	0.2
Chechen	1-0.2	1-0.2	—	—	0.02
Kalmyks	1-0.2	1-0.2	—	—	0.01
Greeks	—	2-0.4	2-0.4	1-0.2	0.01
Finns	—	1-0.2	—	—	0.01
Abkhaz	1-0.2	—	1-0.2	—	0.01
Komi (Zyrian)	—	—	1-0.2	—	0.12
Bulgars	1-0.2	—	—	—	0.14
Czechs	—	1-0.2	—	—	0.04
Karaim	1-0.2	—	—	1-0.2	0.01
Izhorts	—	—	—	1-0.2	0.01
Swedes	—	—	—	1-0.2	0.01
Total	496	517	487	439	

1. On the first Duma, see N. A. Borodin, "Lichnyi sostav pervoi Gosudarstvennoi dumy, ee organizatsiia i statisticheskie svedeniia," in *Pervaia Gosudarstvennaia duma, vyp 1, Politicheskoe znachenie pervoi Dumy* (St. Petersburg, 1907), 1–39. The calculation of the deputies in the first Duma by N. A. Borodin, widely cited in the literature, is incomplete (it has information on only 448 members of the Duma) and contains errors in percentages. Therefore, information on 48 more deputies elected from the eastern borderlands included in the official lists of members of the Duma is added to the calculations of N. A. Borodin. See also *Pamiatnaia kniga I Gosudarstvennoi dumy*, vyp. 1–3 (St. Petersburg, 1906) and "Prilozhenie—Obshchii spisok chlenov Gosudarstvennoi

Continued on the next page

Table 14.2. *Continued*

dumy I, II, III, IV sozyvov," in vol. 14, *Novyi entsiklopedicheskii slovar' F. A. Brokgauza i I. A. Efrona*. On the Second Duma see: *Gosudarstvennaia duma. Ukazatel' k stenograficheskim otchetam. Vtoroi sozyv, 1907* (St. Petersburg, 1907). On the Third Duma, see: *Obzor deiatel'nosti Gosudarstvennoi dumy tret'ego sozyva 1907–1912*, part 1 (St. Petersburg, 1912), where in a list according to nationality (page 8) there is also a typographical error. On the Fourth Duma, see: *Gosudarstvennaia duma, IV sozyv, 1 sessiia. Spravochnik, 1913*, vyp. 6 (St. Petersburg, 1913). The overall percentage of peoples in the composition of the Russian empire is given according to the census of 1897 (excluding Finland, deputies from which were not in the Duma). In the overall number of deputies in the First Duma are included all those elected and appearing in official lists; in the Second Duma—all elected and present in the Duma and included in official lists, including those who left; in the Third Duma—all elected and officially appearing members of the Duma (including those refused, excluded, deceased, likewise those whose elections are recognized as improper); in the Fourth Duma—all elected and officially appearing members of the Duma (including those who departed). Nationality is indicated, as a rule, on the basis of notes of deputies in personnel questionnaires. All materials at the disposal of the author were used and studied, although individual discrepancies with calculations cited in the literature are possible.

Table 14.3. Composition of Deputies of the First through Fourth Dumas according to Religious Denomination[1]

Religious Denomination	Number and Percentage of Deputies in the State Duma, Convocations I-IV								Percentage in the Composition of the Russian Empire
	I Duma		*II Duma*		*III Duma*		*IV Duma*		
	#	(%)	#	(%)	#	(%)	#	(%)	
Russian Orthodox	371	(74.8)	396	(76.6)	414	(85)	384	(87.4)	69.4
Old Believer	4	(0.4)	2	(0.4)	6	(1.2)	2	(0.5)	1.8
Edinoverie	—		2	(0.4)	1	(0.2)		—	*
Catholic	63	(12.7)	54	(10.4)	27	(5.6)	21	(4.8)	9.1
Lutheran	14	(2.8)	14	(2.7)	20	(4.1)	15	(3.4)	2.8
Muslim	25	(5.1)	36	(7.0)	10	(2.1)	7	(1.6)	11.1
Jewish	11	(2.2)	4	(0.8)	3	(0.6)	4	(0.9)	4.2
Baptist	1	(0.2)		—		—		—	*
Buddhist	1	(0.2)	2	(0.4)		—		—	0.3
Armiano-Gregorian	5	(1.0)	7	(1.3)	4	(0.8)	3	(0.7)	0.9
Mennonite		—		—	1	(0.2)	2	(0.5)	*
Molokan		—		—		—	1	(0.2)	*
Evangelical		—	2	(0.4)	1	(0.2)		—	*
Free convictions	1	(0.2)		—		—		—	*
Total	496		517		487		439		

*precise data are unavailable

1. From calculations based on the sources indicated above.

where the non-Russian peoples constituted more than half the population, inevitably had to be multinational. However, the number of non-Russian peoples represented in the Duma and the level of representation varied, expressing the general tendency toward reduction. The overall number of non-Russian deputies decreased from 41 percent in the First Duma to 17 percent in the Fourth Duma. In the general list of members of all four convocations of the Duma one finds deputies of 35 nationalities. But only 14 peoples became "Duma peoples," that is, they were consistently represented in all four Dumas. These were the major ethnicities of the Russian empire, which according to the census of 1897 numbered from 55 million to 1 million: Russians, Ukrainians, Poles, Belarussians, Jews, Tatars, Germans, Lithuanians, Azerbaijanis, Georgians, Latvians, Armenians, Moldovans, and Estonians. However, the Kazakhs and Kirghiz, with populations of almost 4 million, were represented only in the First and Second Dumas. More than a million Bashkirs were represented only in the First, Second, and Third Dumas. The Mordva population, also numbering more than 1 million people, had deputies only in the First and Second Dumas. The Chuvash (800,000) also had representatives only in the First and Second Dumas. Deputies of the Lezgin (610,000) and Greeks (180,000) were in three convocations of the Duma (II, III, IV). Chechens (220,000) and Kalmyks (190,000) were able to make it into two convocations of the Duma (I, II). In the First and Second Dumas the same Abkhaz deputy was elected; in the First and Fourth Dumas the same Karaim was elected. Representatives of the Uzbeks, the Udmurts, the Turkmen, the Buriats, the Komis, Izhorts, and also the Bolgars, Czechs, and Swedes entered the Duma in only one of its convocations.

The percentage of Russians in the Dumas substantially exceeded their percentage in the population of the empire. The Fourth Duma was the most Russian in composition, with a rate in excess of that for the empire by almost two times. The overall percentage of Russians in the Dumas constantly increased: from 58.5 percent in the first Duma to 83.4 percent in the Fourth Duma. The share of Russians changed especially sharply in the composition of the Third Duma, in connection with the new electoral law of June 3, 1907, the reduction of deputies from Poland and the Caucasus, and the loss of representation from the areas of Central Asia. It should be noted that deputies indicating Russian in their questionnaire were in many cases Russified (and Orthodox converts) representatives of traditional noble national elites (chiefly Ukrainians, Belarussians, and Germans), who had settled throughout the empire and who had been incorporated into the imperial aristocratic elite and bureaucracy. Another portion of those who counted themselves among the Russians were people (mostly Orthodox Ukrainians and Belarussians living in the western provinces) who had started to identify themselves as Russian under the influence of intensified great power and Russification policies.

The Moldavians and Germans were two peoples whose representation increased in the Third and Fourth Dumas in comparison with the First and Second Dumas. The Moldavians went from 1 representative in the First and Second Dumas to 3 in the Fourth Duma. The Germans went from 4 in the First and Second Dumas to 13 in the Third Duma and 9 in the Fourth Duma. Moreover, if in the first two convocations of the Duma German deputies were settler-colonists from the provinces of south Russia and the Volga region, in the Third and Fourth Dumas German representation increased thanks to Baltic German representation, the majority of which was made up of nobles—large landowners and officials.

The quantity and numerical majority of ethnic groups in the Fourth Duma decreased dramatically by comparison with the first Duma convocation. The percentage of Azerbaijanis in the First Duma compared to the Fourth Duma was reduced by 6 times, Jews and Ukrainians by 4 times, Poles and Latvians by 3 times, Belarussians, Lithuanians, Georgians, Estonians by 2. The overall percentage of Tatars and Armenians also declined. Eleven peoples—Kazakh, Uzbek, Kirghiz, Bashkir, Mordva, Chuvash, Udmurt, Buriat, Turkmen, Kalmyk, and Chechen—were among the nationalities of the Russian empire numbering not less than 200,000 people that earlier had had their own deputies but that were not represented at all in the Fourth Duma. Comparing the proportion of ethnic representation in the Fourth Duma with the composition of the empire, it should be noted that the Duma rate was lower for the overwhelming majority of peoples, among them Ukrainians by 5 times, Jews and Azerbaijanis by 6, Belarussians by 4, and Latvians by 2.

Data on confessional adherence can supplement this analysis of tendencies in the national composition of deputies, since religion defined ethnosocial status and the formal grouping of subjects of the Russian empire to a larger extent than native language and nationality. In all four Dumas, the empire's seven basic confessional groups were represented—the Orthodox (Russian, Ukrainian, Belarussians, Georgians, Moldovans, Mordva, Chuvash, and others), and also Old Believers (Russians), Catholics (Poles and Lithuanians on the whole), Lutherans (Germans, Latvians, and Estonians), Armenian-Gregorian, Jewish (Jews, Karaim), and Muslims (Tatars,

Azerbaijanis, Bashkirs, Kazakhs, Kirghiz, Uzbeks, peoples of the Caucasus). Other religious denominations (Buddhists, Evangelicals, Mennonites, Baptists, Molokans, and Edinoverites) were represented in the first and second convocations of the Duma. The percentage of Orthodox in all Dumas noticeably exceeded their percentage in the population of the empire. The percentage of Catholics exceeded the all-imperial rate in the First and Second Dumas, but noticeably decreased in the Third and especially in the Fourth Duma. The percentage of Muslims, Jews, and Old Believers did not once exceed the all-imperial rate. The percentage of Armenian-Gregorian exceeded the all-imperial rate in the First and Second Dumas, and then was somewhat less. The percentage rate of Lutherans, to the contrary, was close to all-imperial rates in the First and Second Dumas and sharply increased in the Third Duma, and then exceeded the all-imperial rate also in the Fourth Duma. Thus, in the Fourth Duma the percentage of representation of Catholics was lower than the all-imperial percentage by 2 times, Old Believers and Jews by 4.5 times, and Muslims by 7 times. At a time when the peoples of the empire more and more actively strove to be included in political life, the ethno-confessional composition of the Russian parliament became less and less representative.

The State Duma and the Formation of New National Political Elites

The Duma became a consequential factor in the formation of new national political elites. The demarcation (and at the same time consolidation) of these deputies had already taken place on the eve of the opening of the First Duma on April 27, 1906, and during its first sessions, in connection with the formation of fractions and groups. Deputy to the First Duma and journalist V. R. Obninskii drew attention to the ethno-regional picture of the first all-imperial representation:

> Nearly 500 people have come together in Petersburg and have taken their seats on the benches of the Tauride Palace instinctually, as groups, according to affinity of language, tribe, or faith. Deputies had to notice on the very first day that here sits the "Polish kolo" alongside them— Lithuanian deputies, Ukrainians crowd together with southerners, skull caps of Tatars are visible alongside the characteristic profiles of representatives of the eastern borderlands, the black curls of the Caucasians huddled together on the far left, and, finally, the wide center of Russia,

with its two capitals, here also occupied the entire middle of the hall. A true ethnographic map of Russia! . . . Later, when they took seats according to party, this grouping was completely destroyed, but the first impression cannot be erased. This was how an imperial parliament of an autonomous-constitutional state looked; here, besides the common state cause, and even dominating it, although for the moment in hidden form, local, regional and national interests held the minds of those present."[17]

Deputy associations formed in the Russian Duma were of two types: *party fractions and groups* (constitutional-democratic, trudovik, peaceful renewal, social-democratic, etc.) and *national-regional groups*. National-regional Duma fractions were not identical and were formed according to several indicators and principles: *ethno-territorial* (the Polish *Kolo*, the Ukrainian *Hromada*, Latvian, Lithuanian, and Estonian groups); *confessional* (Muslim); *ethno-estate* (the Cossack group); and *regional* (the group of the western borderlands—the Polish-Lithuanian-Belarussian group; the Siberian group). These groups, as a rule, set as their goal the presentation of national and regional interests in an all-imperial political arena, supported the democratization of imperial national policy, demanded national and confessional equality, and proposed the development of local self-government and the realization of decentralization.[18] As a counterweight to these fractions, the Russian national fraction was created according to the national-political principle in the Third and Fourth Dumas. This rightist-monarchist group of deputies, together with other extreme conservative forces in the Duma, spoke out in favor of the continuation of imperial policy and the preservation of the privileged position of Great Russians and the Orthodox Church.

National deputies, starting with the First Duma, defined themselves in parliament in different ways. One part of these deputies entered the Duma under already formulated national slogans and consistently associated themselves with national parties. For example, members of the Polish National-Democratic Party played a leading role among deputies of the Polish *Kolo* group of all convocations. The Polish *Kolo* was distinguished by the organization and the stability of its membership. Activists of the Democratic Party of Lithuania and the Lithuanian Social-Democratic Party entered the Lithuanian group, members of the Latvian Democratic and Latvian Constitutional-Democratic parties into the Latvian group, the Estonian People's Party (of progressives) into the Estonian

Table 14.4. National Parties and Associations in the First through Fourth Dumas[1]

Name of Party	Number of Deputies			
	Duma I	Duma II	Duma III	Duma IV
Party of "Nationalists" (All-Russian National Union)/ Russian/	—	—	24	33
Ukrainian Democratic-Radical Party	>30	*	*	*
Polish National-Democratic Party	33	27	10	9
Polish Party of Realistic Policies (Ugodovtsy)	2	2	*	*
Union for the Achievement of Equality for Jews	6	*	—	—
Jewish People's Group	—	2	—	—
Baltic Constitutional Party (German)	*	*	2	*
Latvian Democratic Party	*	2	—	—
Latvian Constitutional-Democratic Party	1	1	—	—
Lithuanian Christian-Democratic Party	*	*	*	1
Democratic Party of Lithuania	4	2	*	2
Social Democratic Party of Lithuania	*	5	1	*
Estonian People's Party	3	2	2	2
Revolutionary Party of Socialist-Federalists of Georgia	1	*	1	—
Armenian Revolutionary Union (Dashnaktsutiun)	3	3	—	—

*Data are unavailable.
1. Information for the table is taken from materials summarized by L. M. Spirin in his book *Krushenie pomeshchich'ikh i burzhuaznykh partii v Rossii* (Moscow, 1977).

group. Other deputies simultaneously entered both a national party and an all-Russian party fraction. According to N. A. Borodin, there were up to forty such deputies in the membership of the Kadet fraction and not a few in the Duma toilers group.[19] Finally, a third part of the national deputies, although also sympathizing with national movements, did not register in national fractions and entered all-Russian Duma political fractions.

Caucasian deputies entered the Social-Democratic and Trudovik groups in the First through Fourth Dumas; Baltic Germans joined the Octobrist fraction in the Third and Fourth Dumas.

The first two Dumas were distinguished not only by the multinational composition of the deputies, but also by the greater number of formal national groups. The overall number of national fractions and their members reached the highest rate in the First and Second Dumas (up to eight national-regional groups: the Polish *Kolo*, Ukrainian, Muslim, Latvian, Lithuanian, Estonian, Cossack, western borderlands). After that it fell to three and five in the Third and Fourth Dumas respectively (the Polish *Kolo*, Polish-Lithuanian-Belarussian, Muslim, Cossack, and Siberian groups).

Thus, even a formal ethno-confessional analysis of the composition of the Dumas demonstrated the existing juridical and factual inequality of peoples and regions of the Russian empire. It bore witness to the strengthened imperial content of the political system of the third of June, at the same time when processes of national and regional development and national self-consciousness strengthened in society. The first two convocations of the Duma are of great interest for their display of ethno-regional and national representation and especially of the activity of national Duma elites. These Dumas were quite democratic and multinational in composition; they expressed national-religious interests and attitudes; and they revealed national and political problems that required urgent resolutions. National fractions in the subsequent Dumas continued efforts to force authorities to democratize the sphere of ethno-confessional life.[20]

Deputies from national regions, as a rule, enjoyed special authority in their provinces and oblasts. Therefore it is not surprising that among the eight deputies who were members of all four Dumas, seven represented multinational provinces and oblasts of the empire. Three were from the Kingdom of Poland—Ia. Garusevich, A. Parchevski, and L. V. Jaronski. Two were from the Kuban and Don oblasts—K. L. Bardizh and V. A. Kharlamov. A. K. Dem'ianovich was from Bessarabia Province and K.-M. B.-G. Tevkelev was from Ufa Province. Many of the deputies of the Duma, appearing as representatives of national political elites, acquired their first parliamentary experience and became political activists precisely in the Duma. A significant part of the elite of Poland (V. Grabski, R. Dmovski, A. Lednitski, M. Zamoyski, Ia. Stecki, L. Petrazhycki and others) took shape and showed itself in the Duma. Member of the First, Second, and Third Duma V. Grabskii—the leader of the Polish National-Democratic

Party—occupied the post of prime minister of Poland in 1920 and in 1923–1925. Another leading activist of this party, deputy to the Second and Third Dumas R. Dmovskii, was the leader of the Polish *Kolo* in these Dumas and, in 1919–1923, was a member of the government of Poland.

Duma deputies actively participated in the political life of Baltic states after independence. Chairman of the Constituent Assembly and President Ia. Chakste, Prime Minister P. Jurashkevski, minister Ia. Goldmanis as well as Ia. Kreitsberg and K. Ozolin of Latvia served in the Duma. Minister P. Leonas and A. Bulota of Lithuania did as well. Ia. Tenisson (Tynisson) and T. Iurine of Estonia served in the Duma. The founder of the Estonian People's Party of Progress and a deputy to the First Duma, Tennison was the prime minister of Estonia. He was later a deputy to the Constituent Assembly and the State Assembly (Duma) of Estonia. Tennison was also a professor of Tartu University; in 1940 he was arrested and perished in the camps.

The consolidation of Ukrainian deputies had already taken place in the First Duma. Many of them, such as V. M. Shemet, I. L. Shrag, Ia. K. Imshenetski, P. I. Chizhevski, A. G. Viazlov, and F. I Shteingel, played an important role in the Ukrainian national movement and in Ukrainian state institutions in 1918–1919.

Cossack deputies K. L. Bardizh, M. A. Karaulov, V. A. Kharlamov, I. N. Efremov, N. A. Borodin, S. A. Taskin, T. I. Sedel'nikov participated in local government. M. A. Karaulov became a commissar of the Provisional Government, was chosen ataman of the Tersk Cossack Host, and also participated in the organization of the Southeastern Union of Cossack Hosts, Mountain Peoples of the Caucasus, and Free Peoples of the Steppe. After October 1917 he declared the Tersk Cossack Host a sovereign unit of the Russian Federal Republic, and in December 1917 he headed the Tersk-Dagestan government. He was killed at the end of 1917.

Former deputies played an active role in the organization of governments of Transcaucasian states: in Armenia, M. I. Papadzhanov; in Georgia, the director of the provisional parliament and directory of the government N. P. Zhordaniia, deputy I. G. Tsereteli, chairman of the Transcaucasian Sejm and chairman of the national Constituent Assembly I. S. Chkheidze, ministers A. I. Chkhenkeli, E. P. Gegechkori, and I. I. Ramishvili; in Azerbaijan, chairman of the parliament A.-M. A. Topchibashev, prime minister of the Azerbaijani Democratic Republic F. I. Khoiskii (Khan-Khoiskii), ministers I. I. Gaidarov, Kh. G. Khas-Mamedov, and L. M. Dzhafarov.

Members of the Duma from Kazakh areas A. N. Bukeikhanov, M. M.

Tanyshpaev, A. K. Beremzhanov appeared as organizers of Kazakh national-territorial autonomy Alash-Orda.

After the February Revolution of 1917, many Muslim deputies, including S.-G. Sh. Alkin, I. A. Akhtiamov, Kh. M. Atlasov, M. M. Biglov, S. S. Dzhantiurin, K. G. Khasanov, S. N. Maksudov, M. M. Ramiev, became leaders of the struggle for national autonomy of the peoples of the Volga and Urals region. S. N. Maksudov, a jurist and publicist, deputy to the Second and Third Dumas from Kazan Province, was the leader of the Muslim fraction of the Third Duma. In 1918, he was chairman of the national parliament of the Muslims of Inner Russia and Siberia (*Millet Medzhelisi*) in Ufa; of the collegium on the formation of the Idel-Ural state; and of the administration for the realization of cultural-national autonomy of the Muslims of Inner Russia and Siberia (*Milli Idare*), and he took part in the Versailles Conference. After the Russian civil war, he became a deputy in parliament in Turkey, a member of the Turkish delegation to the League of Nations, and a professor at Istanbul University.

The role of former Duma deputies S. Ia. Rozenbaum, G. Ia. Bruk, Sh. Kh. Levin in the making of the state of Israel should also be noted.

At a time when ideas of constitutionalism and parliamentarism began to be assimilated by the public and to be realized in political life, ideas of national autonomy and federalism did not find support among Great Russian ruling elites. These conservatives did not want to undermine the monopoly of authority of the imperial center with respect to the regions. The imperial and national principles emerged sharply opposed to each other.[21] Attempts just to maintain, much less strengthen, the imperial principle at the expense of the national weakened parliamentarism. By conducting an imperial policy, the Duma, rather than becoming a factor for the unification of the democratic movements of various nations, became a factor in its own uncoupling through the national principle.

One can, however, suppose that a gradual overcoming of unitary, imperial qualities through the development of parliamentarism, and through the creation of national self-government and cultural-national autonomy, remained a potential of the Duma period. Although the Russian model of Duma parliamentarism was truncated in comparison with more developed European systems, the step toward reform made in 1905–1907 by the pragmatically thinking portion of the Russian power elite opened up real possibilities for the principle of constructive development of the Russian state principle and the constitution of civil society and indicated a pathway toward democratic relations between center and region. The Duma factor became significant for the formation of the bases of parliamentarism and a multi-party system and for the development of a corresponding political culture in Russian society in the early twentieth century.

The appearance of the legal possibility and the inevitability of the struggle for representation appreciably stimulated the establishment of the Russian multi-party system (including national parties). An appreciable expansion of the political elite in the Russian empire took place as a result of the creation of an all-Russian elected legislative institution and the organization of political parties and party fractions in the Duma. Earlier electoral mechanisms had operated in the strictly limited frameworks of zemstvo and city self-administration. Elections to the all-imperial Duma for the first time made it possible for representatives of non-privileged estates—urban strata, peasants, and workers—to enter the political elite (or counter-elite). Representatives of non-Russian peoples also had the opportunity to participate in the legislative organ of Russia through their associations formed in the Duma. The oppositional Duma political elite, oriented toward European examples and maintaining a connection with the electorate, formed a Russian parliamentary political culture, resisting autocratic-bureaucratic tradition and national-religious isolation. National-regional fractions in the Duma coordinated the activity of political forces in the regions and attracted supporters of evolutionary transformations of the political and cultural life of non-Russian peoples of the empire. They promoted the consolidation of the liberation movement not only in the Russian empire, but also in neighboring multinational empires.

Translated by Charles Steinwedel

Notes

1. See R. A. Tsiunchuk, "Rossiiskaia imperiia kak sistema 'tsentr–regiony': genezis, razvitie, krizis," *Puti poznaniia Rossii: novye podkhody i interpretatsii,* vyp. 20 (Moscow, 2001): 126–144. For a fuller discussion of the subject of this article, see my monograph, *Dumskaia model' parlamentarizma v Rossiiskoi Imperii: etnokonfessional'noe i regional'noe izmereniia* (Kazan, 2004).

2. See R. G. Abdulatypov, L. F. Boltenkova, Iu. F. Iarov, *Federalizm v istorii Rossii,* books 1–2 (Moscow, 1992–1993); R. A. Tsiunchuk, *Idei federalizma v rossiiskom politicheskom protsesse (XIX–nachalo XX vv.),* in Z. R. Valeeva, ed., *Federalizm—global'nye i rossiiskie izmereniia* (Kazan', 1993), 104–108; M. von Hagen, "Writing the History of Russia as Empire: The Perspective of Federalism," in *Kazan, Moscow, St.Peterburg: Multiple Faces of Russian Empire. Kazan', Moskva, Peterburg; Rossiiskaia imperiia vzgliadom iz raznykh uglov* (Moscow, 1997), 393–410; Petr Savel'ev, ed., *Imperskii stroi Rossii v regional'nom izmerenii (XIX–nachalo XX veka)* (Moscow: MONF, 1997); A. V. Remnev,

"Imperskoe upravlenie aziatskimi regionami Rossii v XIX–nachale XX vekov.: nekoto-rye itogi i perspektivy izucheniia," *Puti poznaniia Rossii: novye podkhody i interpretatsii,* vyp. 20 (Moscow, 2001): 97–125.

3. *Zakonadatel'nye akty perekhodnogo vremeni (1904–1906 gg.)* (St. Petersburg, 1907): 572.

4. Ibid., 571.

5. F. I. Kalinychev, *Gosudarstvennaia duma v Rossii. Sbornik dokumentov i materialov* (Moscow, 1957), 118.

6. *Obzor deiatel'nosti Gosudarstvennoi dumy tret'ego sozyva, 1907–1912,* part 1, appendix 5 (St. Petersburg, 1912): 269, 302.

7. S. E. Kryzhanovskii, Zapiska "K preobrazovaniiu Gosudarstvennogo soveta," Rossiskii gosudarstvennyi istoricheskii arkhiv, f. 1544, op.1, d. 16, l. 76.

8. V. A. Demin, *Gosudarstvennaia duma Rossii (1906–1917): mekhanizm funktsionirovania* (Moscow, 1996), 14.

9. *Materialy po uchrezhedeniiu Gosudarstvennoi dumy* (St. Petersburg, 1905): 126.

10. Ibid., 127.

11. Ibid., 30.

12. F. I. Kalinychev, *Gosudarstvennaia duma v Rossii. Sbornik dokumentov i materialov* (Moscow, 1957), 273.

13. Ibid., 385–386.

14. See R. A. Tsiunchuk, "Prezentatsiia etnokonfessional'nykh i regional'nykh inter-esov v politicheskikh programmakh i predvybornykh platformakh partii i obshchetvenno-politicheskih ob"edinenii Rossiiskoi imperii 1905–1912 gg.," in B. V Anan'ich and S. I. Barzilov, eds., *Prostranstvo vlasti: istoricheskii opyt Rossii i vyzovy sovremennosti* (Moscow: MONF, 2001), 288–316.

15. "Postanovleniia vtorogo musul'manskogo s"ezda," Natsional'nyi Arkhiv Respubliki Tatarstana, f.199, op.1, ed. khr. 772, l.14ob.

16. T. Emmons, *The Formation of Political Parties and the First National Elections in Russia* (Cambridge, Mass., 1983), 370.

17. D. Shakhovskoi, Viktor Petrovich Obninskii, *K 10-letiiu 1-oi Gosudarstvennoi dumy. 27 aprelia–27 aprelia 1916* (Petrograd, 1916), 212–213.

18. See Z. Lukawski, *Kolo Polskie w Rosyjskiej Dume Panstwowej w latach 1906–1909* (Wroclaw, 1967); E. Chmielewski, *The Polish Question in the Russian State Duma* (Knoxville, 1970); O. W. Gerus, "The Ukrainian Question in the Russian Duma, 1906–1917: An Overview," *Studia Ucrainica* 2 (Ottawa, 1984): 157–173; R. A. Tsiunchuk, "Deputaty natsional'nykh raionov Povolzh'ia v Gosudarstvennoi dume," *Natsional'naia zhizn' i mezhnatsional'nye otnosheniia* (Kazan', 1993); R. A. Tsiunchuk, "Razvitie politicheskoi zhizni musul'manskikh narodov Rossiiskoi imperii i deiatel'nost' musul'manskoi fraktsii v Gosudarstvennoi dume Rossii 1906–1917 gg.," in Savel'ev, ed., *Imperskii stroi Rossii v regional'nom izmerenii,* 176–223; *Musul'manskie deputaty Gosudarstvennoi dumy Rossii 1906–1917 gg. Sbornik dokumentov i materialov,* compiled by L. A. Yamaeva (Ufa, 1998); D. M. Usmanova, *Musul'manskaia fraktsiia i problemy "svobody sovesti" v Gosudarstvennoi dume Rossii (1906–1917)* (Kazan', 1999).

19. N. Borodin, "Lichnyi sostav Gosudarstvennoi dumy, ee organizatsiia i statisticheskie svedeniia o chlenakh," *Pervaia Gosudarstvennaia duma, vyp. 1, Politicheskoe znachenie pervoi Dumy* (St. Petersburg, 1907): 24.

20. See the second chapter of the volume edited by V. Iu. Zorin, S. V. Kuleshov, D. A. Amanzholova, *Natsional'nyi vopros v Gosudarstvennykh dumakh Rossii: opyt zakonot-vorchestva* (Moscow, 1999).

21. On the opposition of imperial and national principles in the Duma itself, see my "Imperskoe i natsional'noe v dumskoi modeli rossiiskogo parlamentarizma," in *Kazan, Moscow, St.Petersburg: Multiple Faces of Russian Empire,* 92–103.

15 The Provisional Government and Finland: Russian Democracy and Finnish Nationalism in Search of Peaceful Coexistence

Irina Novikova

The period between the February and October revolutions of 1917 was one of the most tense and dramatic times in the history of Russian-Finnish relations. During these few months the Provisional Government, a new political entity that had appeared on the ruins of the autocracy, undertook a series of desperate attempts to preserve the unity of the Russian empire. In this chapter, I analyze relations between the Russian Provisional Government and Finnish political parties; my goal is to clarify why Russian liberals and democrats in 1917 were unsuccessful in "domesticating" Finnish nationalism.

Finland was joined to the Russian empire as a result of the Russo-Swedish War of 1808–1809. By the peace treaty signed in 1809 in the Finnish city of Fredrikshamn (Hamina), Sweden gave up the Grand Duchy of Finland to Russia.[1] Finland subsequently developed as an autonomous state with its own system of national administrative self-governance. Although a part of the Russian empire, it was nonetheless governed by the rules of Swedish administration, and over the course of the nineteenth century the parameters of the Duchy's autonomy tended to expand persistently. The Duchy received its own legislative organ, the Sejm, whose approval was required for the introduction of new laws and taxes. Finland likewise had its own legislative organ, the Senate, independent from St. Petersburg with regard to the Duchy's internal matters. Finland's autonomous status was also manifest in its own system of government, with an exclusively Finnish bureaucratic apparatus. Nor did Russian military structures extend to the Duchy, which was freed from providing recruits for military service and, beginning in 1878, was also permitted to have its own modestly sized army. This army became a symbol of Finland's special status within the empire.[2] The Duchy also enjoyed a national postal service with its own stamps; a rail system with a gauge different from that in the rest of the empire; and distinct systems of customs, finance, and credit. The only thing common to Finland and the empire proper were the head of state (the Russian Emperor was simultaneously the Grand Duke of Finland), foreign relations, and the matter of the Duchy's strategic defense.[3] On the whole, the Grand Duchy of Finland enjoyed more rights and powers within the Russian empire than any constituent part of the Russian Federation today.

However, the atmosphere of mutual understanding and cooperation between local and imperial elites that characterized Russo-Finnish relations throughout the nineteenth century was irretrievably lost toward its end. The rise of separatist orientations in the Duchy has correctly been linked to the so-called "policy of oppression," or Russification, whose causes historians have analyzed in detail.[4] On the whole, the active separatism of Finland's residents was the consequence of the Russian center's departure from its traditional principles of administration in its western territories. As Andreas Kappeler has shown, in Finland the Russian government had employed three methods of governance with great consistency: the maintenance of the administrative and political status quo, cooperation with local elites, and religious tolerance.[5] In the Duchy, the revision of Russia's Finnish policy under Nicholas II was regarded as a violation of the promises made by preceding Russian monarchs. Nicholas himself, who had promised upon his ascension not to violate the rights and privileges of the Duchy, earned among Finns the ignoble distinction of being a perjurer.

Moreover, at the turn of the century the Finnish national movement itself ceased to be modest and restrained. Finnish nationalists, due either to political inexperience or to a desire to obtain quick popularity in the eyes of their countrymen, underscored their national exclusivity importunately and unceremoniously, and began to promote an extreme vision of isolationism. The absence of moderation in the proclamations of the leaders of the Finnish national movement gave Russian officials reason to interpret the natural aspiration of a small people to a certain degree of insularity and the preservation of its privileges, language, and culture as a criminal form of separatism. By the beginning of the twentieth century the interests of Finland's national development were starkly juxtaposed to the imperatives of Russia's imperial development.

World War I subjected the Russian empire to a colossal test. In 1915–1916—although many Russian officials and military figures could not bring themselves to believe it—a number of Finnish volunteers joined the German army as the 27th Royal Prussian Jäger Battalion (*Kuninkaalinen Preussin Jääkäripataljoona 27*).[6] Attempts to play down this unpleasant fact could not change its essence: a number of recently loyal Finns, who in the previous century had been considered among the non-Russians most devoted to the Russian crown, were now on the other side of the front, rendering aid to Russia's military enemy.

The fall of the monarchy in the February Revolution opened the way for Russia's transformation from a coercive empire to a voluntary union of equal peoples. The fate of the revolution's democratic gains depended on the success of this transformation.[7] The national question turned out to be no less urgent than issues of power, land, and peace. And a fundamental component of that question was the problem of the Grand Duchy's future status.

The February Revolution did not signify any essential change in the country's foreign policy. The Provisional Government continued the war, and in this context maintaining control over the strategically important Finland retained great significance.[8] Members of the Provisional Government were informed that ideas about the Duchy's secession from Russia were beginning to appear in radical circles in Finnish society—with either open or indirect support from Germany. In part, these ideas were being promoted by the extreme nationalist "activist" movement, whose leaders lived abroad in Berlin and Stockholm. It was they who had organized the recruitment of Finns for the Finnish Jäger Battalion formed on German territory with the support of Berlin. They hoped that in opportune circumstances—for example, in the case of a German naval landing—this subunit could serve as the kernel of a Finnish army of national liberation.[9] No less than before February, the possibility of a German landing in the Duchy and a Finnish mutiny represented a substantial threat to Petrograd.

At the same time, the Provisional Government was well aware of the autocracy's earlier attempts at the forceful unification of Finland with Russia. It had been precisely the liberals and socialists now so prominent in the new government who had sharply condemned those actions earlier. The promises made by the Constitutional Democrats (Kadets) and the socialists during their opposition to the autocracy now awaited their fulfillment. In this regard, the Provisional Government's policy on Finland had to secure the loyalty of the Duchy's population to Russia's new democracy, bring them into active cooperation with central authorities in Petrograd, and compel them to reject secret relations with Germany. The Provisional Government's first steps with regard to the "Finnish question" were geared toward these tasks.

On March 16 (3) the commander of the Baltic Fleet, Admiral Andrian Nepenin, invited representatives of the leading Finnish political parties aboard the flagship Krechet and informed them of the revolution in Russia, the establishment of the Provisional Government, and the arrest of the most odious figures personifying the autocracy's policy of Russification—Finland's governor-general Franz A. Seyn and vice-chairman of the Finnish government Mikhail Borovitinov.[10] After this meeting, a delegation of the Duchy's leading political figures departed for the Russian capital to conduct negotiations with the Provisional Government. The Finns requested that Petrograd establish a parliament (sejm), appoint a new governor-general, and grant the Duchy its previous privileges of autonomy. At the same time, as delegation member Karl Gustav Idman recalls in his memoirs, the Finns expressed neither the hope nor the demand that Petrograd recognize Finland's full independence.

The new Russian government actively responded to the wishes of the Finnish delegation, and on March 20 (7) published the Act of Confirmation of the Constitution of the Grand Duchy of Finland and Its Full Implementation. This document resurrected the Duchy's previous rights of autonomy that had been revoked by the autocracy's centralizing policy. Mikhail A. Stakhovich, a former member of the State Council well known for his defense of the Duchy's autonomy, now became the governor-general. In place of the reactionary Vladimir A. Markov, Karl Enckell, a native of Finland who was fluent in Russian, became the minister state secretary. All those who had fought against the autocracy's measures of centralization, as well as those who had participated in the Finnish Jäger Battalion in Germany, were amnestied.

The first task of the Provisional Government in Finland was to appoint a new government, or Senate. Now Finns themselves gained the right to elect its members, although this fact hardly made matters easier to resolve. In the 1916 elections the Social Democrats had gained an absolute majority in the Parliament—103 of 200 seats—but at that time it was still the Senate, with Russian members, that governed the country. The SDs did not discuss the possibility of taking on the responsibilities of governing.[11]

After the Revolution, Finnish Social Democrats could have tried to form a government consisting only of their own members. The SDs would have secured tremendous power for themselves in light of their absolute majority in parliament, but they were also frightened by this power. They turned out to be unprepared to take upon themselves such a heavy responsibility. They had much experience in forming an opposition, but no experience in governing. Consequently, negotiations between the bourgeois parties and the SDs produced a coalition government. The SD's Oskari Tokoi was selected chairman of the Senate, while five other SDs and six representatives of bourgeois parties entered the government as well. As before, the chairman of the Senate remained the governor-general. On March 26, 1917, the Provisional Government confirmed the Finnish Senate.[12] Finland now had a government whose members were not Russians but Finnish citizens, representing all the political groups of the country.

Having reestablished Finland's previous autonomy, the Provisional Government expected reciprocity from the Finnish population. The Finnish politician and Helsinki University professor Edvard Hjelt recalls in his memoirs a curious conversation with the new commander of the Baltic fleet, Admiral A. S. Maksimov. In the course of their discussion, Maksimov unambiguously noted that as a sign of thanks for the freedoms it had been granted, Finland should demonstrate its solidarity with Russia by offering volunteers for the army. In the admiral's opinion, "a sense of duty should have obligated the Duchy to enter the war more ardently on the Russian side."[13]

The effective restoration of the Grand Duchy's autonomy initiated after the February Revolution in fact had generated a surge of sympathy for the new Russia among the majority of Finnish citizens and politicians.[14] Finnish society simultaneously hoped that it could make use of the transfer of power in Russia for the benefit of its own country, and ascribed particular significance to the establishment of strong, civilized contacts with Russian authorities. The popular Finnish poet and activist Eino Leino wrote on this subject in the journal *Sunnuntai* [Sunday]. In a speech in March 1917, J. R. Danielson-Kalmari, the spiritual leader of the bourgeois-conservative party (the "old Finns" [*starofinny*]), compared the February Revolution to the French Revolution of 1789. He noted that the Eastern powers had now entered an important historical period through which the Western powers had passed after the French Revolution.[15] The Finnish politician Juho Kusti Paasikivi meanwhile called upon Finns to maintain a line of cooperation with the empire, a strategy he referred to as a "policy of conciliation" (*myöntymyyksen politiikka*). He argued that no large changes should occur in the Duchy's political development, and he called upon Finns not to risk the opportunities that had already been attained, especially since Russian military regiments were located in the country.[16] On the whole, most representatives of the bourgeois parties considered it essential to conduct a policy of cooperation with the Provisional Government. The further broadening of the Duchy's autonomy in the framework of the Russian state appeared to be attainable by constitutional means, through a dialogue with the Provisional Government.

Representatives of the separatist activist movement took a rather different position, however. At the outset of the war they had declared the principal goal of their movement to be the attainment of Finland's complete political independence.[17] But in a practical sense the leaders of the movement viewed the idea of "independence" less in terms of the country's acquisition of state sovereignty than in terms of its secession from Russia. Many of them did not exclude the possibility of Finland becoming a German protectorate.[18] The revolution in Petrograd generated confusion for the activists; the murky, unexpected, and awkward situation required a reevaluation of the existing political line. But they were not prepared for this reevaluation and were unwilling to abandon the proposition, which was convenient from a propagandistic standpoint, that Russians were "hereditary enemies."[19] Germanophiles by conviction, they bowed before the might of the German empire; their faith in German arms was total. Therefore, individual concessions could not change their attitude toward Russia, which they still regarded as the oppressor of the Finnish people. Not without reason, Edward Hjelt, one of the activists already mentioned, wrote in his diary after his trip to Petrograd: "It seems to me that we have been striving for a different 'freedom' than the one that the Russian 'freedom' can give us. It must be created on reliable German soil, without remaining dependent on Slavic emotions."[20] The leader of the émigré "activist" committee in Stockholm, Alexis Bonsdorf, was reported by German authorities to have dismissed the Provisional Government's manifesto of March 20 as "mere peanuts" (*Linsengericht*), for which one must not give up the aspiration for complete independence.[21] From his perspective there were now greater possibilities to realize secession from Russia than at anytime previously.

In a report to German Chancellor Theobald von Bethmann-Hollweg, the German ambassador in Sweden, Helmuth Lucius von Stödten, reported on a meeting of the Finnish separatists in Stockholm devoted to developing a strategy for the movement after the February Revolution. The participants called upon Finns not to trust Petrograd's promises.

Without denying the importance of the March Manifesto, they nonetheless did not consider it a decisive resolution of Russo-Finnish relations. The leitmotif of those who spoke was the idea that the Finnish question could not be resolved by the directive of the Provisional Government.[22]

In April 1917 Herman Gummerus, one of the "activist" leaders, sent a memorandum to the German foreign minister in which he proposed two solutions to the "Finland problem." The first involved the advance of German regiments on the Russian capital; the second foresaw the possibility of a peace agreement between Germany and Russia that would guarantee Finland's independence. In the latter case Finland would become an ally of Germany.[23] In the memorandum, which was written in German, Gummerus used the German concept *Unabhängigkeit* (independence). Previously he had preferred to express the final goal of the activist movement as *Selbständigkeit*, whose Finnish equivalent (*itsenäisyys*) signified merely autonomy within the empire, or self-governance. This was perhaps the first time since the beginning of the war that a member of the activist movement used the term *Unabhängigkeit* in the sense of full state sovereignty (though without rejecting close ties with Germany). Thus, partially under the influence of the February Revolution, previously diffuse understandings of Finland's future were becoming clarified and more concrete in the minds of the separatists.

As regards the labor movement, the revolution in Petrograd took Finnish workers almost entirely unawares.[24] It was viewed initially as a return to the situation of 1905–1907, with the only difference being that the fall of the autocracy had made deeper changes possible. Finnish SDs at first did not demand the termination of relations with the Provisional Government.[25] At the same time, like the bourgeois parties, they strove to limit the power of the Provisional Government in the territory of the Duchy.[26] To be sure, the goals of these actions on the part of the bourgeois parties and SDs were different. The former regarded the broadening of the Duchy's autonomy as indispensable to restraining the revolutionary anarchy spreading from Petrograd. The latter viewed this demand as an essential precondition for the introduction of social reforms that had until then been blocked by both the imperial center and the conservative elements in Finnish society.

In the spring of 1917 at party meetings and in the Finnish press two questions were discussed in detail: the future status of the Duchy and the mechanisms of relations with central authorities in Petrograd. Above all, it had to be determined to whom supreme power over the Duchy had passed after the abdication of the Russian monarch. According to the March Manifesto the Provisional Government considered itself to be the heir of the supreme rights over Finland that had previously belonged to the Russian emperor—at least until the Russian Constituent Assembly, yet to be convened, could resolve the issue conclusively. But many Finnish legal specialists contested this proposition. Two points of view were advanced on the question of supreme power in the Duchy. The first, put forward by P. A. Vrede and Robert Hermanson, representatives of the Old Finnish Party, held that Finland continued to constitute an indivisible part of the Russian empire. Accordingly, relations between the empire and its "national borderlands" should be rooted in the recognition that the bearer of supreme power in Russia was simultaneously the bearer of supreme power in Finland. From this position, the Provisional Government *temporarily* possessed the right of supreme power in Finland. The second view was presented by the lawyer and activist Rafael Erich, a professor of law at Helsinki University. Erich, residing abroad at the time, tried to demonstrate to his fellow countrymen that with the fall of the autocracy, the union between Russia and Finland, personified in the person of the Grand Duke (the Russian emperor) was now dissolved. Therefore, no Russian government had the right to rule the Duchy. The Provisional Government thus did not represent the bearer of supreme power in Finland, nor could that power be transferred to the Constituent Assembly.[27]

In one of his articles Erich wrote, "For the inclusion of Finland in a Russian federal state there are neither historical, nor ethnographic, nor national-psychological conditions. All the Russo-Finnish institutions that were introduced or established by Russia became baneful for state life in Finland. . . . Even the position of a qualified state within a Russian federal union cannot satisfy Finland's rightful pretensions."[28] What did Erich propose as a solution? Even though he belonged to the cohort of activist leaders, in spring of 1917 Erich nonetheless did not yet speak categorically in favor of Finland's complete state sovereignty. As an expert on the Duchy's fundamental law, he proposed to solve the problem of Russo-Finnish relations by granting Finland the special status of a state-appendage (*gosudarstvo-pridatok*). In this case Finland would remain in union with the Russian state, but would preserve the broadest possible rights of self-governance. The most important thing, in Erich's opinion, was to prohibit Russian interference in the definition of Finland's state status without the latter's consent. He proposed that Russian authorities agree to a referendum in the Duchy on the question of its future state status, even if this might lead to the severance of Finland's union with Russia. Erich thus considered the establishment of normal relations of trust between the two countries to be more important than the imperial ambitions of the central authorities.[29]

On March 31 the Finnish Senate established a Constitutional Committee, with Finland's subsequent first president, Karl Stolberg, at its head. Among its tasks was the preparation of a new treaty on Finland's status with respect to Russia. Stolberg was a realist who understood that the authority of the Russian tsar in Finland had been transferred to the Provisional Government: it was thus impossible to change this situation without either an agreement or a revolt.[30] The Constitutional Committee worked out a draft treaty, according to which a substantial portion of the prerogatives previously belonging to the Russian emperor—such as the power to convene and disband the Sejm, and the approval of Finnish laws—were transferred to the Finnish Senate. The Senate would become the focus of real power in the Duchy. The Provisional Government would retain the prerogative of appointing the highest officials in Finland, as well as deciding issues of defense and foreign policy. On April 7 this proposal was sent to Petrograd, where, in the course of the negotiations with the Provisional Government, it was rejected. As K. G. Idman, the secretary of the Constitutional Committee, remarked in response, dialogue with the Provisional Government "demonstrated the impossibility of establishing a common denominator."[31] In general, the Provisional Government did not permit even an element of doubt concerning its competence to serve as Finland's temporary curator. It regarded as its duty to keep the state whole until the Constituent Assembly could be convened. Its determination to continue the war with new energy similarly required that it oppose everything that could weaken "unified and indivisible Russia."[32]

Meanwhile the Finnish Senate sought to appropriate the basic prerogatives of the monarch in the Duchy. This desire was motivated, in part, by the aspiration of bourgeois members of the government to counteract the Finnish parliament, where the majority of the votes belonged to the SDs. Furthermore, members of the Constitutional Committee were surprised by the Provisional Government's different attitudes toward the Finnish and Polish questions. News of Petrograd's recognition of Poland's independence, should such a decision be approved by the upcoming Constituent Assembly, quickly made its way into the pages of the Finnish press. In response to demands that the Duchy's autonomy be broadened, the Provisional Government declared that "recognizing Poland's independence is the same as giving a promise to the moon, since the territory of that country is occupied by the German military."[33] Still unoccupied by the Germans, Finland was clearly in a different situation. In general, increasing disappointment with the Provisional Government led to greater support in the Duchy for refusing to recognize the Provisional Government's supreme rights in Finland.

The April Crisis in Russia led to the dismissal of a number of more conservative ministers and to the first coalition Provisional Government. Finnish SDs succumbed to the temptation of using the changes in the Provisional Government to demand further concessions from Russia.[34] Also in April the Finnish parliament began its work. Due to the preponderance of SDs, this parliament has gone down in history as the "Red Sejm." The left-SD Kullervo Manner was selected as its chairman. For the delegates, the speech of the Senate's vice-chairman O. Tokoi on April 20 was a sensation. Tokoi declared the necessity of attaining full political independence:

> With time the Finnish people has developed and become sufficiently mature to be a sovereign people, independent in everything that concerns its rights, problems, and plans. In terms of its history and its economic and social development, Finland differs sharply from Russia. There can be no talk of their rapprochement. The neighbor of a new and free Russia must also be an independent people.[35]

Although Tokoi's speech made no mention of the specific way in which independence was to be realized, his speech was consistent with the political line of those who refused to recognize the Provisional Government as the legal successor to the Grand Duke with supreme power in Finland.

Many of the SDs' declarations about the Provisional Government were imprinted with populism. In actual practice, in the spring of 1917 the leaders of that party, as before, did not rule out the possibility of a constructive dialogue with the Petrograd leadership. In an unofficial appeal to Aleksandr Kerenskii, the head of the Provisional Government, the prominent SDs Edvard Güllig, Otto Kuusinen, and Karl Wiik formulated the basic principles of a social-democratic variant of a state treaty between Finland and Russia. In its capacity as an "independent state" Finland was to form an "indissoluble union" with Russia. Questions of foreign policy would be decided by Russia, but elements of even that policy directly concerning Finland would go into effect only after their approval by its parliament. Further, Finland would receive complete independence in internal affairs and an organ of supreme power independent of the empire. Defense would likewise be Finland's internal affair; in times of peace Russia would not have the right to station troops there. Finally, Russian citizens in Finland would enjoy equal rights and freedoms with the residents of Finland.[36]

The appeal was secret and was designed to test the waters for a possible agreement with the Provisional Government. Moreover, its authors were open to the possibility of reconsidering certain of the draft's points. Anticipating the central authorities' likely objection that signing such an agreement would result in Finland's practical independence, the SDs noted, "Finland is too small to scorn the interests and wishes of Russian state power." They were furthermore prepared to acknowledge that the Duchy's position in union with Russia was more advantageous for Finland than its status as an independent country, whose inviolability was not guaranteed by anyone.[37] Thus the Finnish SDs had in mind the application of principles of independence and sovereignty primarily in regard to internal affairs, with the goal of securing a maximum degree of autonomy while maintaining some form of union with Russia. In all likelihood, if the Provisional Government had reacted to the SDs' proposal more attentively and had not rejected a dialogue with them, an acceptable compromise would have been found, which in turn would have prevented the SDs from adopting a policy of open struggle with the central Russian authorities.

In its most direct form, a demand for the Duchy's state sovereignty in the spring of 1917 was advanced only by the student movement, whose leaders held activist views. On May 12 a joint meeting of the students of Helsinki University and the Higher Technical School adopted the following appeal: "Finland has now matured to the point that it may occupy a place among sovereign peoples. We are convinced that the hour will soon come when our country acquires full state sovereignty. In order to attain this goal, we wish to employ all our energy and means."[38] The leaders of the student movement considered it their most immediate task to influence public opinion in the Duchy in order to prove the incompatibility of Finland's interests with its attachment to the Russian state. Students made similar declarations during Kerenskii's visit to the Duchy in the spring of 1917.

The war minister clearly voiced the position of the Provisional Government on the question of Finnish sovereignty when he stated, "As an independent state Finland would represent a constant danger to Petrograd, and the satisfaction of Finnish demands can be realized only on an equal basis with the demands of other non-Russian nationalities populating the

Russian empire.[39] As Kerenskii and other members of the Provisional Government contended, "Today Finland will secede, tomorrow Siberia and Ukraine. Thus, of Great Russia only Moscow will remain."[40]

In the spring and summer of 1917 the Finnish activists undertook an attempt to draw the Duchy's largest party—the SDs—into cooperation. On June 4 in Stockholm representatives of Finnish activism and the SDs conducted a joint meeting, during which the question of preparation for an armed uprising in the Duchy with the goal of secession from the Russian state was raised. The SDs insisted that in the current conditions it was possible to achieve independence by peaceful means. The activists gave preference to armed forms of struggle.[41] The two sides could not find a common ground; nonetheless, in the spring and summer of 1917 some ties between the two were established in the form of personal contacts of the parties' leaders and the creation of "guard detachments" (the so-called *Schutzkorp*), which were officially called upon to maintain internal order in the Duchy. The Activist Committee began forming these guards in the spring and summer of 1917.[42] Almost simultaneously "guards of order" appeared from among workers. Initially there were no sharp conflicts between the two armed organizations. It was not rare for them to conduct exercises together. Workers sometimes joined the *Schutzkorp,* an action that did not meet with protests from the SDs.[43] The Activist Committee sought to strengthen these cooperative relations. Instructions for the organizers of the *Schutzkorp* spoke of unrestricted admission of workers, so that the "guard detachments" would not obtain a "class character" in the eyes of the population.[44] Russian counterintelligence at the initial stage of the creation of the *Schutzkorp* and the workers' guards of order did not see a fundamental distinction between the two.[45]

Gradually, however, differences became more apparent. The primary goal of the *Schutzkorp* was the preparation of armed cadres for a national revolt in the case of a German invasion of the Duchy. The Finnish Jägers arriving from Germany took active part in the organization of the *Schutzkorp.*[46] The workers' guards, on the other hand, did not plan any actions against Russia. Russian military leaders rightly regarded the formation of the *Schutzkorp* with greater anxiety.[47]

Indeed, the rapprochement between the activists and the SDs in the spring and early summer of 1917 lacked a solid foundation not only because of the different social constituency of the two movements, but also because of differences in their understandings of "independent Finland." The SDs regarded Finland's sovereignty as a necessary precondition for social transformation, which had been hampered by central officials and local Finnish authorities. Moreover, they hoped for the support of their Russian colleagues in bringing about this transformation.[48] Russian revolutionary activity in Finland, in the form of the Regional Executive Committee of the army, fleet, and workers, offered grounds for hopes of this kind. The leading role in this organization was played by the Helsinki Soviet and the Central Committee of the Baltic Fleet. On June 2 (May 20) the Second Regional Congress of Soviets promised to support the demand for an independent Finland, should it be endorsed by a majority of the region's population.[49] In contrast to the SDs, the activists were principally bourgeois nationalists, and the slogan of independence for them meant complete secession from the Russian state. For the realization of this goal the activists considered their allies to be not the revolutionary parties of Russia, but the movements of Russia's other national minorities.[50]

Relations between Russia and Finland were complicated further by a currency crisis. In 1917 Russia found itself in such a sorry financial state that it was forced to turn to Finland for a loan. The Provisional Government needed Finnish marks in order to pay its troops and for state orders. Three-quarters of Finland's workers were occupied fulfilling these orders and thus delay in these payments threatened to promote unrest. Making use of this circumstance, the Finnish Sejm linked the question of a loan to the granting of full autonomy to the Duchy.[51] In one of his interviews Tokoi declared that Finland could provide 100–200 million Finnish marks on the condition that the Duchy be declared independent in its internal affairs and that the resolution of the Finnish question be transferred to an international congress of the Great Powers.[52] After its unsuccessful inquiry with the Finns, the Provisional Government turned for a loan of $75 million to the U.S., which turned out to be more compliant. Having received this American loan, the Provisional Government began in the summer of 1917 to purchase Finnish marks in Finland with American dollars, with the goal of paying for Russia's military orders in Finland.[53] This operation established a crucial precedent for Finland. By appealing to Finland for a state loan and then paying Finland in U.S. dollars—that is, in foreign currency—the Provisional Government in fact had recognized the complete sovereignty of the Finnish currency market, a recognition that Finland had specifically sought to achieve.[54] Finnish entrepreneurs were entirely satisfied with the condition of Russo-Finnish relations in the early summer of 1917.

Meanwhile, in early July in Petrograd yet another political crisis broke out, and the authority of the Provisional Government was left hanging by a thread. In this context on July 18 (5), with a vote of 136 to 55, the Finnish Sejm approved a Law on Supreme Power, by which the prerogatives previously belonging to the Russian monarch, with the exception of foreign-policy and military spheres, were transferred to the parliament.[55] This was a significant step on the road toward complete internal sovereignty of the Duchy. The law was passed at the height of the July crisis, when the outcome of the struggle in Petrograd was not yet clear and when information coming to Finland about events in the Russian capital was incomplete and contradictory. Many deputies of the Sejm believed that the Provisional Government had been overthrown and wished to make use of the resulting anarchy.[56]

News of the Sejm's passage of the Law on Supreme Power called forth a storm of indignation in the Russian press. The newspaper *Den'* published an interview with M. A. Stakhovich, the governor-general of Finland, who laid all the blame for what had occurred on the Russian Social Democrats and called on the next Congress of Soviets to condemn the Finns' actions.[57] The Kadet paper *Rech'* published an article by Dmitrii Protopopov, who called the Sejm's decision "an act of great political tactlessness" and "near-sightedness." He proposed instituting harsh political and economic sanctions against Finland.[58] Famous for its anti-Finnish pronouncements, the newspaper *Novoe vremia* greatly exaggerated Finland's dark ingratitude and perceived hidden German support behind the Sejm's decision. Mensheviks and Socialist Revolutionaries (SRs) also criticized the law; in their opinion it injured the interests of the Russian state.[59] The actions of the Finnish parliament were unconditionally supported only by the Bolsheviks,[60] although, according to the English historian Robert Service, at this time the Bolsheviks were not playing the "national card" very actively and preferred to allow the grievances of the national regions against the Provisional Government to accumulate and to await further developments.[61]

The development of the Russo-Finnish conflict occurred against the background of rumors about a coming German landing in the Duchy. Military intelligence uncovered facts of activists preparing for an uprising in Finland. In the opinion of the new commander of the Baltic Fleet, Dmitrii N. Verderevskii, the Provisional Government had therefore to act with the necessary circumspection.[62] At the same time, military circles discussed their options should disorders break out in Finland. V. N. Klembovskii, commander of the 42nd Army Corps stationed in Finland, proposed concentrating the mass of troops around Vyborg for the protection of Petrograd, bringing together troops scattered in small groups throughout Finland into larger contingents, and warning the local civil administration that if any rebellious activities should occur, then large cities—first and foremost Helsinki—would be sacked.[63] It became clear that Russia's armed forces intended to retain Finland at all costs.

On July 31 (18) the Provisional Government issued a manifesto dissolving the Finnish Sejm.[64] This was, it seems, one of its fatal mistakes. Despite all of its passion in asserting national sovereignty, the Sejm had in fact sought to attain for the Duchy the broadest possible internal autonomy, but not separation from Russia. As historian Vitalii Startsev notes, Russia's strategic interests were not even touched by the Law on Power. The Sejm did not concern itself with foreign policy and did not demand the withdrawal of Russian troops.[65] The Finnish parliament, in which the majority of votes belonged to the SDs, dreamed of appropriating for itself supreme power in the internal affairs of Finland, thus pushing into the background the Senate, where members of the bourgeois parties blocked the passage of many important social reforms. The SDs lacked practical experience in legislating, and if the Provisional Government at this juncture had refrained from hasty and abrupt measures with regard to the Finnish parliament, the two sides possibly would have come to a mutual compromise. The Sejm, after receiving reports from Petrograd about the Bolshevik defeat and the victory of the Provisional Government in the July Days, had swiftly prepared the necessary documents to clarify its position on the question of Finland's internal sovereignty.[66] But the Provisional Government did not even begin to look them over. Instead of engaging in dialogue, it preferred to disband the obstinate Sejm.

The SDs left the government to protest the disbanding of the Sejm, leaving only bourgeois senators, with Professor E. Setälä at its head. The SD majority of the Sejm, not recognizing the supreme rights of the Provisional Government in Finland, nonetheless attempted to call the dissolved parliament on August 29 (16). But Governor-General Stakhovich summoned soldiers and closed the meeting hall. As the Finnish historian Pentii Luntinen notes, this was the last time that "the army defended imperial interests in Finland. Soon revolutionary agitation penetrated all military elements, once and for all shattering their discipline and fighting spirit."[67] With the dissolution of the Sejm, a new and complicated stage in Finland's internal political development began. Now not only did the SDs demand complete internal sovereignty for the Duchy, but practically all the bourgeois parties supported this as well.[68]

The shift of the Duchy's ruling elite to a more radical position was conditioned by the Provisional Government's destruction of many of the political and administrative structures that had supported the multinational state, based on the naïve hope that society would preserve the empire in its new, democratic form.[69] It had seemed that the democratization of society would, by itself, remove all the problems of the multinational state, and that with the strengthening of democracy the national question would disappear on its own. However, with the disintegration of the institutions that had bound the empire together and the worsening of Russia's military, foreign-policy, and internal situations, national elites that had initially taken a moderate stance were now more and more inclined to the idea of complete secession.

Moreover, the Finnish political elite became seriously concerned about the strengthening of Russian revolutionary sentiment in the Duchy. After the Kornilov Affair (an unsuccessful right-wing coup attempt in Russia proper), trust in the Provisional Government had been undermined, while the influence of the Bolsheviks had grown. The Bolsheviks prevailed at the Third Regional Congress of the army, fleet, and workers of Finland in September of 1917.[70] The Bolshevik Ivan T. Smilga was selected chairman of the Regional Committee's Executive Committee, and under his leadership on October 3 (September 20) that organ took charge of all the Russian governmental institutions in the Duchy. No directives from the Provisional Government could be carried out in the region without the approval of the Regional Committee. For example, the Regional Committee countermanded the Provisional Government's order that forces not ready for combat be brought out of Finland and replaced with new formations.[71] In general, the Regional Committee acted in accordance with the instructions of Lenin, who ascribed great significance to the maintenance of pro-Bolshevik forces in Finland.[72] On October 10 (September 27) the Regional Committee took control of the Russian security service, the so-called "guards of people's freedom." According to the Finnish historian Eino Ketola, this amounted to a revolt against the Provisional Government.[73]

Indeed, the Regional Committee systematically interfered in the internal affairs of the Duchy, supporting the actions of the Finnish SDs that were directed against the Provisional Government and the Finnish bourgeoisie. The Finnish workers' guards were provided with arms, to the chagrin of the local population.[74] In the fall of 1917, due to fears of a German naval landing and flashes of separatist disorders, the number of Russian forces in the Duchy, together with the Baltic squadron, amounted to approximately 125,000 men.[75] But these forces suffered from a decline in discipline and general demoralization.

The Russian side recognized the interference of Russian forces in the internal affairs of the Duchy, although in comparison to 1914–1916, the Russian forces in Finland represented the sad result of the Provisional Government's policy of "democratizing the army." A report on the Finnish question prepared by a member of the Baltic Fleet's counter-intelligence indicated that "Russian forces regularly support various disorders and interfere in the directives of local authorities. Through such actions they incite the residents, who endure great losses as a result of maintaining the forces (the felling of forests, illegal requisitions, and so on). A very difficult situation has been created."[76]

The increased German military presence in the Baltic region also played a role in the radicalization of Finnish national aspirations. In an attempt to weaken its eastern opponent internally, Germany had adopted a "policy of revolutionizing" (*Revolutionierungspolitik*), which included support for the secession of national minorities from the Russian empire. The February Revolution gave a second wind to this policy of revolutionizing Finland. On March 15 the head of the German Ministry of Foreign Affairs, Arthur Zimmermann, requested that the Stockholm activist center "make use of the current situation for energetic activity" in the Duchy, declaring that "the moment for the declaration of independence, it seems, has arrived."[77] Alongside the German Ministry of Foreign Affairs, the political division of the German General Staff, headed by Ernst von Hülsen, also took an active part in the program of "revolutionizing" Finland. On March 20 von Hülsen requested the ministry to support an appeal that 1 million marks be given to the Finnish separatist movement.[78] This sum constituted one-fifth of the funds that the Secretariat of Foreign Affairs had requested from the German imperial treasury in March 1917 for revolutionary propaganda in all of Russia. As documents from the archive of the German Ministry of Foreign Affairs show, the imperial treasury granted 5 million marks on April 3 for the realization of this task.

On April 23, 1917, the German leadership met in Kreuznach to define the tasks related to the conduct of the war.[79] At this meeting the German Supreme Command exhibited a rather cool attitude toward the requests of Finnish activists concerning direct military support in the form of a naval landing in the Duchy. But the activists were promised arms so that they would not sheathe their swords.[80] In May a German U-boat brought the first batch to Finland.[81] In the summer of 1917 the number of Finnish Jägers sent to Finland to form the *Schutzkorp* began to grow. In a telegram to Erich Ludendorff, head of the German Supreme Command, Zimmermann noted, "We are now sending many Finns who have received a military education to Finland and are assisting the country in its creation of a military organization. True, the fact of our help should remain secret."[82]

The future of the Provisional Government's June offensive against the Central Powers, Russia's internal instability, the reduction of the combat-readiness of its army and fleet all helped to convince the German Supreme Command that further annexations in the East would meet little or no resistance. At the beginning of September, German forces captured Riga, and in October they occupied the islands of Esel, Dago, and Moon along the eastern Baltic coast. These new annexations in the Baltic region served to reinforce Finnish public opinion that Germany was prepared to begin military action on the Duchy's territory. The Germans themselves eagerly spread such rumors.[83]

The Russian military command noted with bitterness the growth of Germanophile sentiments among Finland's population and contended that in the case of a German landing in Finland the population would most likely provide assistance. The Duchy's residents often idealized Germany's aspirations for the "liberation of small nations"; moreover, they hoped that Germany would help solve the extreme food crisis in Finland.[84] However, it would be naive to reduce the whole range of factors serving to radicalize Finnish national demands merely to a theory of a German conspiracy.

A significant role in the radicalization of the national aspirations of the Finnish bourgeoisie was played by its conflict with local Social Democracy. Growing social discontent was regarded by the political elite of the Duchy less as a result of the natural dissatisfaction of thousands of Finnish workers than as a consequence of revolutionary agitation coming from Russia. Finland's ruling circles, displaying their strong authoritarian tradition, saw only two possible alternatives for the Duchy's future development—either strengthening the status quo or opening the floodgates of revolution. In the opinion of historian J. Paasivirta, liberalism did not wield much influence on the Finnish political scene and was ultimately unable to establish a basis for social compromise.[85] The general attitude of the Duchy's political elite was based on a sense of urgency. Finland should make use of the moment to take another step toward state independence. And in this regard the country had two advantages: the instability of the central authorities in Russia and the strengthening of the German military presence in the Baltic region.

In early October 1917, elections were held to the Finnish Sejm. The bourgeois parties, united in a single bloc, managed to win a majority of the seats—108 out of 200. In Petrograd negotiations on the question of broadening the Duchy's internal sovereignty recommenced. Stolberg's Constitutional Committee proposed strengthening the connection between Russia and Finland by accepting a Law on Relations of Mutual Rights, a draft of which was to be ratified in both the Finnish Sejm and the future Russian Constituent Assembly. Finland would be declared a republic in which supreme executive power would belong to a ruler (*valtakunnan pääies*), elected from among Finland's citizens, who would hold all the powers of the Russian monarch in Finland with the exception of hereditary rule and permanent office. Foreign policy would remain in Russia's hands, but Finnish delegates would participate in those international conferences that touched on Finland's interests. Russian forces would remain in the Duchy until the creation of the latter's own army, which in times of war would be under joint command with the Russian army but would operate only within Finnish borders. Provisions were included for Russia and Finland to turn to the international tribunal in The Hague in the case of disagreement.[86]

The notion of Finland's internal autonomy did not raise misgivings in the Provisional Government, but its extent was a source of distress. Petrograd objected to the stationing of Russian forces on Finnish territories only at times of war, the idea of having issues resolved in an international court of arbitration, and the excessively broad range of powers of the ruler. Russian legal experts also considered indispensable that all draft laws passed by the Finnish Sejm also be confirmed by the supreme Russian power.[87]

The Finnish side solicitously entertained the Provisional Government's remarks and agreed to certain concessions. The Constitutional Committee proposed transferring powers, aside from those pertaining to the military sphere and the status of Russian citizens, to the Finnish Senate. The position of governor-general of the Duchy would be eliminated. On November 7 (October 25) the new Finnish governor-general, Nikolai V. Nekrasov, and State Secretary Enckell left for Petrograd in order to lay out these proposals to the Provisional Government. Their realization would have prevented the sharing of power with the socialists in the Sejm. But this solution was proposed too late. At the train station on the Russian border Nekrasov and Enckell were informed that the Provisional Government no longer existed.[88]

A retrospective consideration of the Provisional Government's policy on the Finnish question reveals distinct parallels with the collapse of the USSR—between the actions of the Provisional Government with regard to Finland in 1917 and the USSR's policy under Gorbachev with respect to the national regions in 1989–1991. Both instances involve attempts to democratize public life and a surge of regional nationalism. And in both cases compromise with national elites was probably possible, though the opportunity for this was allowed to pass. In both 1917 and in 1989–1991, a fledgling Russian democracy preferred a policy of postponement and procrastination in the hope that *with the strengthening of society's democratization, national problems would solve themselves automatically.* This may help to explain why in 1917 Russian liberals and democrats were unable to find a *modus vivendi* with the Finnish elite. In the course of the February Revolution, the mechanisms of power holding the empire together were destroyed, and the framework on which the empire had been constructed was eliminated. As a result, the regions experienced a vacuum of power that threatened catastrophe. The Finnish political elite was simply left with no alternative but to fill that vacuum and to assume some of the prerogatives of the central authorities. The leaders of the new Russia, however, remained captives of an imperial understanding of national interests of the country and did not wish to offer an acceptable compromise to national elites.

Translated by Paul Werth

Notes

All the dates in this essay are provided in New Style, with dates in Old Style given in parentheses where appropriate. The term "Finnish" is used to refer to the citizens of Finland, who could be Swedes as well as ethnic Finns.

1. Finland received the status of Grand Duchy in the sixteenth century, under the Swedish King Johann III. In practice, however, this was in large measure merely a pleasant-sounding declaration, lacking any real content.

2. In 1901 a new law was passed, on military service, which was supposed to elimi-

nate the Finnish forces and to obligate the residents of Finland to serve in the regular Russian army. However, this law was not realized in practice. The majority of recruits boycotted the new provisions, and as a result St. Petersburg merely demanded that the Finnish authorities, by way of compensation for Finland's exemption from providing recruits, pay a so-called "war tax." Initially, the annual payment of the tax amounted to 2 million Finnish marks, rising subsequently to 15 million. Rossiiskii Gosudarstvennyi Istoricheskii Arkhiv (hereafter RGIA), f. 1538, op. 1, d. 2, l. 2ob. (Dokladnaia zapiska V. K. Pleve Nikolaiu II ot 28.03.1902.)

3. Andreas Kappeler, *Russland als Vielvölkerreich: Enstehung, Geschichte, Zerfall* (Munich, 1992), 77; A. B. Beloglazov, "Federalizm v 'tiur'me narodov': Velikoe kniazhestvo Finliandskoe," in *Federalizm: Problemy formirovaniia* (Kazan, 1994), 47–48; and I. N. Novikova, "Velikoe kniazhestvo Finliandskoe v imperskoi politike Rossii," in *Imperskii stroi Rossii v regional'nom izmerenii, XIX–nachalo XX veka* (Moscow, 1997), 134.

4. See Novikova, 134–136; T. Polvinen, *Derzhava i okraina* (St. Petersburg, 1997), 20–46; *Venäläisten sortokausi Suomessa* (Porvoo and Helsinki, 1960), 19–23; J. Paasivirta, *Pientet valtiot Europassa* (Helsinki, 1987), 350.

5. Kappeler, 88–90.

6. A total of 1,897 persons fought on the German side in the Finnish Jäger Battalion. See M. Lackmann, *Jääkärimuistelmia* (Keuruu, 1994), 12. For more on the Finnish Jäger Battalion, see O. Apunen, *Suomi keisarillisen Saksan politiikassa* (Helsinki, 1968) and M. Lauerma, *Kuninkaallinen Preussin Jääkäripataljoona 27* (Helsinki, 1966).

7. V. Iu. Cherniaev, "Revoliutsiia 1917 goda i obretenie Finliandiei nezavisimosti," in *Padenie imperii i novaia organizatsiia Evropy posle Pervoi mirovoi voiny. Rossiisko-finliandskie gumanitarnye chteniia* (St. Petersburg, 1993), 14.

8. The border of the Grand Duchy passed within 32 kilometers of Petrograd. Finland thus protected the approaches to the Russian capital from the north. Finland, moreover, was home to the main base of Russia's Baltic Fleet.

9. Politischen Archiv des Auswärtigen Amts [hereafter PAAA], Grosses Hauptqwartier (GrHq), Finnland, Bd. 1., L 084155/68 (F. Wetterhoff, Über eine militärische Aktion in Finnland vom 24–25 August 1915).

10. Rossiiskii Gosudarstvennyi Arkhiv Voenno-Morskogo Flota (henceforth RGAVMF), f. r-29, op. 1, d. 153, l. 92 (M. E. Zinger, 1917 god v Baltiiskom flote).

11. V. Rasila, *Istoriia Finliandii* (Petrozavodsk, 1996), 142.

12. V. Rasila, E. Jutikkala, and K. Kuhla, *Suomen polittinen historia, 1905–1975* (Porvoo, Helsinki, and Jyvä, 1980), 64.

13. Cited in E. Hjelt, *Vaiharikkailita vuosilta. Muistelmia,* vol. 2 (Helsinki, 1919), 34. As we have seen, the general military draft did not extend to Finland. With the start of the First World War, authorities in Petrograd had hoped that the surge of patriotism evident in Russia would extend to Finland as well, and that the latter would send volunteers to the Russian army. But the results of this enlistment were unimpressive: in 1914 only 400 Finns entered the Russian armed forces, in 1915 only 40, and in 1916 a mere four. In all only 544 Finns served in the Russian army. See O. Turpeinen, *Keisarillen Venäjän vironomaisten suhtautuminen jääkäriliikkeeseen* (Helsinki, 1980), 262. Admiral Maksimov, like many other representatives of the Russian liberal elite, thought that the resurrection of Finland's autonomy would automatically lead to a change in the attitude of young Finns toward service in the Russian military.

14. See, for example, RGIA, f. 229, op. 4, d. 2039, l. 235 (Poslanie finnskikh grazhdan F. I. Rodichevu ot 10.03.17).

15. J. Paasivirta, *Finland and Europe, 1914–1939* (Helsinki, 1988), 65.

16. K. Ikonen, *J. K. Paasikiven polittinen toiminta Suomen itsenäistymisen murrosvaiheessa* (Helsinki, 1991), 354.

17. Herman Gummerus, *Jääkärit ja aktivistit* (Porvoo, 1928), 34.

18. PAAA. Der Weltkrieg (hereafter Wk.) 11c, Bd. 7, A18546 (F. Wetterhoff an Moltke vom 9.04.1915); Sweden 56:1, Bd. 3., H 055177 (F. Wetterhoff an A. Zimmermann vom 17.05.1915).

19. V. V. Pokhlebkin, *SSSR-Finliandiia: 260 let otnoshenii, 1713–1973* (Moscow, 1975), 174.

20. Cited in Hjelt, 41.

21. PAAA. Wk. 11c., Bd. 19, Bl. 135 (Lucius an Bethman-Holweg vom 22.03.1917).

22. Ibid., Bd. 20, Bl. 340–346 (Finnländisches Memorandum, ohne Datum).

23. Ibid.

24. J. Paasivirta, *Finland and Europe,* 68.

25. Ibid.

26. Thus one of the leaders of Finland's Social Democratic Party, Yrjö Mäkelin, publicly expressed the hope for the development of an independent Finnish political activity (*aktivnost'*) that would be free from intrusive limitations of the center.

27. K. G. Idman, *Maamme itsenäistymisen Vuosilta* (Porvoo and Helsinki, 1953), 24; Rasila, Jutikkala, and Kuhla, 65.

28. Arkhiv Vneshnei Politiki Rossiiskoi Imperii [hereafter AVPRI], f. 135, op. 474, d. 374/245, l. 3.

29. Ibid.

30. Rasila, 144.

31. Idman, 127.

32. T. Polvinen, "Oktiabr'skaia revoliutsiia i stanovlenie nezavisimosti Finliandii," *Rossiia i Finliandiia, 1700–1917: Materialy VI sovetsko-finliandskogo simpoziuma istorikov* (Leningrad, 1980), 13.

33. E. Ketola, "Revoliutsiia 1917 goda i obretenie Finliandiei nezavisimosti," *Otechestvennaia istoriia* 6 (1993): 29.

34. V. I. Startsev, "Vremennoe pravitel'stvo i Finliandiia v 1917 godu," *Rossiia i Finliandiia v XX veke* (St. Petersburg and Lichtenstein, 1997), 10.

35. Cited in R. N. Dusaev, "Obrazovanie nezavisimogo Finliandksogo gosudarstva," *Vestnik Leningradskogo gosudarstvennogo universiteta,* vyp. 1 (1975): 89.

36. Rossiiskii Gosudarstvennyi Arkhiv Sankt-Peterburga, f. 7384, op. 9, d. 320, ll. 18–19.

37. Ibid.

38. PAAA, Wk. 11c., Bd. 21 (Bericht über die Lage in Finnland vom 31.05.1917).

39. RGIA, f. 1093, op. 1, d. 88, l. 8.

40. AVPRI, f. 135, op. 474, d. 395/245, l. 47.

41. Gummerus, 467.

42. For details, see O. Manninen, *Kansannoususta armejaksi* (Helsinki, 1974), 25.

43. E. E. Kaila, "Suojeluskuntatyö Suomessa sodan puhkeamiseen," *Suomen Vapaussota* 2 (Jyväskylä, 1922), 100.

44. RGIA, f. 1093, op. 1, d. 88, l. 44.

45. See for example the reports of the head of the counter-intelligence unit at the Sveaborg fortress, A. Simonich, in RGAVMF, f. 1356, op. 1, d. 278, ll. 8–8ob.

46. Kaila, 99.

47. By August of 1917 Russian military circles had excluded the possibility of joint actions by the *Schutzkorp* and the Finnish workers' guard, and they contended that, most likely, hostility would emerge between the two formations. In such a case, they supposed that Finnish society might well fall into civil war. See RGAVMF, f. 418, op. 1, d. 549, l. 9.

48. Ibid., f. 1356, op. 1, d. 278, ll. 44–45ob. (Tuo 21.07.1917).

49. V. Iu. Cherniaev, "Revoliutsiia 1917 goda i obretenie Finliandiei nezavisimosti," 40.

50. PAAA. GrHq., Bd. 1, L084179/80. On the cooperation between Finns and the Baltic peoples, see S. Zetterberg, *Die Liga der Fremdvölker Russlands, 1916–1918* (Helsinki, 1978); and O. Hovi, *Interessensphären im Baltikum* (Helsinki, 1984), 25–32.

51. Cherniaev, 41.

52. RGAVMF, f. 418, op. 1, d. 2859, l. 114 (*Åland* 18.07.1917).

53. Startsev, 22; Pokhlebkin, 177.

54. Pokhlebkin, 177.

55. Startsev, 15–16; Rasila, Jutikkala, and Kuhla, 68.

56. *Työmies* [Worker], July18, 1917.

57. AVPRI, f. 135, op. 474, d. 395/245, l. 30 (*Den'*, July 9, 1917).

58. Ibid. (*Rech'*, July 12, 1917).

59. RGAVMF, f. 418, op. 1, d. 2859, l. 23ob. (Obzor pressy za 30.07.1917).

60. V. Antonov-Ovseenko, *V semnadtsatom godu* (Kiev, 1997), 152–153.

61. R. Servis [Robert Service], "Gosudarstvo i revoliutsiia," *Sovremennye metody prepodavaniia noveishei istorii* (Moscow, 1996), 329.

62. RGAVMF, f. 418, op. 1, d. 342, l. 32 (V. N. Verderskii to A. P. Kapnist, July 7, 1917).

63. Ibid., d. 278, l. 13 (V. N. Klembovskii to D. N. Verderskii, July 18, 1917).

64. RGIA, f. 1276, op. 14, d. 23, l. 122 (Manifest o rospuske seima ot 18 [31].07.1917).

65. Startsev, 17.

66. Ibid, 18.

67. P. Luntinen, "Razluka bez pechali," *Rodina* 12 (1995): 29.

68. RGAVMF, f. r-315, op. 1, d. 86, l. 1 (Obzor finliandskoi pressy).

69. For more on this process, see Mark von Hagen, "The Russian Empire," in *After Empire: Multiethnic Societies and Nation-Building* (Boulder, Colo., 1997), 67–68.

70. Antonov-Ovseenko, 199–202.

71. In part, the matter concerned the removal of the 128th division, which had pro-Bolshevik sympathies, and its transfer to the Revel section of the front. Already at the time of the June offensive, this division had refused to submit to the orders of the Provisional Government. See *Novoe vremia* (July 14, 1917).

72. In a letter of September 27, 1917, to Smilga, Lenin wrote, "It seems that the only thing that we can have entirely in our own hands and that plays a serious military role are the troops in Finland and the Baltic fleet . . . Under no circumstances can we allow the transfer of [those] troops out of Finland—this is clear. It is better to do everything else, an uprising or the seizure of power." Cited in I. I. Siukiianinen, "Gel'sing-

forsskii seim rabochikh organizatsii v 1917–1918 gg.," *Skandinavskii sbornik,* vyp. 5 (Tallin, 1962): 101–102.

73. At the 11th Finnish-Soviet Historians' Symposium in 1987, Ketola offered the thesis that the uprising in Finland represented a strategic prerequisite for the October Revolution and was simultaneously that revolution's first successful operation. (Ketola: Suomen sotilaskapina-Lokakuun vallankumouksen strateginen edellytys," *XI Suomalais-Neuvostoliitolainen Historioitsijoiden Symposio, 1987* (Helsinki, 1988). In contrast another Finnish historian, P. Luntinn, questioned the high degree of Bolshevization among the sailors of the Baltic Fleet. Opposition to the Provisional Government, in his view, derived not from ideational positions, but from war fatigue (ibid.).

74. RGAVMF, f. 353, op. 1, d. 127, l. 12ob. (Reshenie Oblastnogo Komiteta ot 19.10.1917).

75. O. Rinta-Tassi, "Lokakuun vallankumous ja Suomen itsenäistyminen," *Lenin ja Suomi* II (Helsinki, 1989), 98; P. Huttunen, *Venäläisten linnoitustyöt Suomen sisämaassa ensimmäisen maailmansodan aikana* (Oulu, 1989), 274.

76. RGAVMF, f. 418, op. 1, d. 549, ll. 35–35ob. (V. Sadovskii v General'nyi morskoi shtab ot 26.09.1917).

77. PAAA, Wk. 11c., Bd. 19 (Zimmerman an Lucius vom 15.03.1917); M. Menger, *Die Finnlandspolitik des deutschen Imperialismus, 1917–1918* (Berlin, 1974), 55; I. Schubert, *Schweden und das Deutsche Reich im Ersten Weltkrieg* (Bonn, 1918), 124.

78. PAAA, Wk. 11c., Bl. 104 (von Hülsen an AA vom 20.03.1917).

79. W. Schuman, *Weltherrschaft im Visier* (Berlin, 1975); Fritz Fischer, *Griff nach der Weltmacht* (Düsselddorf, 1994), 290.

80. T. Polvinen, *Venäjän vallankumous ja Suomen* 1 (Porvoo and Helsinki, 1987): 138.

81. P. Luntinen, *Saksan keisarillinen laivasto Jtämerella* (Helsinki, 1987), 130.

82. PAAA GrHq., Finnland, Bd. 1 (Zimmermann an Lersner vom 04.08.1917).

83. Upon the seizure of the island of Esel, the local population was informed that the next object would be Finland. RGAVMF, f. 418, op. 1, d. 549, l. 67 (Oberkvartirmeister 42-go armeiskogo korpusa K. Berens v General'nyi rossiiskii shtab ot 29.10.1917).

84. For more on Germany's Finland policy in 1917, see I. N. Novikova, "Rol' Germanii v protsesse provozglasheniia Finlandiei nezavisimosti i vykhoda iz sostava Rossiskoi imperii (fevral'—dekiabr' 1917 g.)," *Rossiia i Finlandiia v XX veke* (St. Petersburg, 1998), 34–47.

85. Paasivirta, *Finland and Europe,* 95.

86. RGIA, f. 1361, op. 1, d. 68, ll. 19–26ob. (Zakon o vzaimnykh pravovykh otnosheniiakh Rossii i Finlandii ot 16 [29] oktiabria 1917 g.).

87. Ibid., ll. 26–27ob.; Idman, 166.

88. Polvinen, 96–100.

Part Four   *Designs*

16 Siberia and the Russian Far East in the Imperial Geography of Power

Anatolyi Remnev

By virtue of its complexity and diversity, the Russian empire requires a regional analysis. Individual regions with distinctive characteristics (e.g., the time of their entry into the empire, geographical, natural, and climatic factors, distance from the imperial center, ethnic and confessional composition, level of socio-economic development, foreign influences) represented different variants of imperial processes. An interdisciplinary approach to the study of the territorial organization of society presupposes an interaction between historical (temporal) and geographical (spatial) aspects, examined through a complex investigation of the temporal dynamics of the evolution and transformation of the empire.

My investigation is focused on explaining the functional logic of empire, which provides an excellent opportunity to resolve a number of problems associated with research on the Russian empire. From an administrative point of view, the Russian empire represented an intricately organized state space. The prolonged stability of the Russian empire can be explained by the polyvalent power structures, the diversity of judicial, state, and institutional formations, the asymmetry of the connections between various ethnic groups and territorial formations. The greater the success achieved by the government in centralizing and unifying the administration (doubtlessly one of its goals), the more inflexible it became, and thus unable to react effectively and adequately to quickly changing political and socio-economic conditions, and to respond to the challenges of nationalism and modernization.[1] The renowned Russian jurist B. E. Nol'de was forced to acknowledge that Russian law "never systematically investigated what it had created here [i.e., in the periphery—A.R.]; our law only knew individual lands and characterized individually their relation to the Russian state as a whole." The path to find "the realization of one and the same idea in state and legal contexts," Nol'de suggested, "must follow the study of each autonomous land, taken separately."[2] This highlights the need to take into account the peculiarities of the borderlands at the time of the organization of their administration, while clearly understanding that the administrative policy of the autocracy in the periphery was distinguished by a number of general principles that were characteristic of the Russian state administration as a whole. "As flesh and bone of the general state administration," emphasized the scholar of the history of the administration of Siberia S. M. Prutchenko, "the administrative system in Siberia was directly dependent upon the extent to which difficulties that were inseparable from the organization of the administration of the emerging state seemed to have been solved in the core regions of the state."[3]

Power, like any real object and process, has its own temporal and spatial characteristics and is influenced by natural-climatic and socio-cultural factors.[4] To describe these factors, I have suggested the term *geography of power* (spatial distribution, institutional structure, and administrative hierarchy in the dichotomy "center–periphery," and in territorial dynamics of power). As an empire, Russia was continuously expanding and annexing to its space new territories and peoples, who were distinguished by numerous socio-economic and socio-cultural parameters. After the initial military and political tasks of imperial policy were resolved, the goals of the administrative organization and the subsequent integration of the region into the imperial space followed.

Along with the rationalization, modernization, and institutional differentiation of state power in the center and in the regions, this power developed extensively, fed by the inclusion of new territories within the empire. This process shaped regional administrative differences: the "geography of power" had a complex political administrative landscape based on the repetition (sometimes transplantation of models already tested in other regions) of archaic institutions of power ("non-Russian," "military-people's administration") and different models of administrative behavior.

My method of exploring the imperial theme is based upon two main approaches: *regional* and *administrative*. These two approaches embrace important spheres of imperial regional policy: imperial ideology and imperial practice in a regional reading; the establishment of external (including state), as well as internal (administrative) boundaries of a region; the dynamics of administrative organization in intra-regional space (powerful administrative-territorial and hierarchical structures of regional space, the administrative centers and their migration.)

Following from the above, it would seem sufficient to define *empire* as a large geopolitical community ("world-empire" in the words of F. Braudel and I. Wallerstein), a historical means to overcome the global isolation of small communities, the establishment of internal peace and interregional economic and cultural ties, even if by force. In accordance with Braudel's definition, the world-empire entails the presence of a "center" and a "periphery." The internal space of the world-empire has its own hierarchy, which presumes the presence of different types of inequality among the peripheral regions with respect to the center, the space where strong state power was to be found—privileged, dynamic, simultaneously inspiring fear and respect.[5]

Andreas Kappeler forcefully emphasizes the promise of the regional approach: "It seems to me that in the future, a regional approach to the history of empire will become particularly innovative. By overcoming the ethnocentrism of the nation-state tradition, it permits the study of a polyethnic empire on different spatial planes. Unlike national histories, ethnic and national factors are not absolutized; alongside ethnic conflicts, it examines the more or less peaceful coexistence of different religious and ethnic groups."[6]

The regional approach to the study of the imperial theme focuses attention on the concept "center–periphery," theoretically developed by E. Shils and S. N. Eisenstadt. A significant number of imperial conflicts revolved around the main axis of relations between center and periphery. The center represented a special symbolic and organizational formation, which not only sought to extract resources from the periphery, but also to penetrate into the periphery and to transfer its own spiritual-symbolic principles to these areas and, organizationally, to mobilize the periphery for its own goals.[7] The Russian empire demonstrated in this system of relations a relatively high degree of penetration by the center into the periphery, in order, as Eisenstadt notes, "to mobilize the resources, to consolidate the periphery's attachment to the center and identification with it, and to control those types of activity that involved all of society."[8] The enormous expanse of the Russian empire, poor communication links, and the fragmented economic and demographic appropriation of the new territories in the east required formation of second-order centers along the lines of center–periphery and translated the functions of the main imperial center to distant regions, which had potentially important political significance.

The theme of imperial administration has a long scholarly tradition. As V. V. Ivanovskii, professor of Russian state law, had already noted in 1899, "questions of centralization and decentralization of government activity are as old as the life of the state itself; yet at the same time they are eternally young, inexhaustible questions, to which it is apparently impossible to give one definite answer, equally appropriate for all eras and all peoples."[9] Moreover, the topicality of the problem of the interdependence of the center and regions remains, and tends to become aggravated in the conditions of modernization. Michael Hechter, who suggested the term "internal colonialism," relegated this problem to eternity, and noted that the conditions for a partial integration of the periphery and the state core "are perceived more and more by the peripheral group as unjust and illegitimate."[10]

The concept "center" has its own concrete historical understanding. K. I. Arsen'ev, a statistician and geographer of the first half of the nineteenth century, understood the center of Russia to be "the expanse [prostranstvo] —the heart of the empire, the true fatherland of the Russian people, the center of all of European Russia, the repository of all treasures attained through education, disseminated by industry and extensive internal trade."[11] Central or inner space, according to Arsen'ev's classification, designated the common mores of the population, the unity of language, the unity of a judicial and administrative system, one religion and approximately the same level of education of the people. This defined the "true fatherland of the Russians, the most solid or main support of the Russian state; it is the great circle to which all other parts of the empire are attracted like radiuses in different directions, some closer, some farther away, and which more or less promotes its indissolubility."[12]

Similar definitions of the center are given by contemporary authors who, noting the unevenness and non-universality of innovations, formulate the term as follows: "The concept 'center' fixes the place of their generation, while 'peripheries' are the site of their dissemination, the course of which depends on contacts with the center." In addition, "the contrasts between the centers and the periphery constitute the most elementary and at the same time powerful impulse for the emergence and reproduction of territorial inequality."[13] The center, as defined by the contemporary French sociologist Pierre Bourdieu, represents "a place in physical space in which are concentrated the highest positions of all fields [political, economic, social, cultural—A.R.] and the largest number of agents occupying these dominant positions."[14]

Center and region are terms that describe, first and foremost, the geography of power. From the administration's point of view, the center is the capital—the location of higher and central state institutions, where strategic administrative decisions are made. In this sense, the spatial structuring of power becomes a promising direction for the study of the imperial administration.

In the course of the historical development of the Russian empire, large territorial communities (regions) took shape within its enormous and highly diverse geographical space. These regions had distinctive identities and possessed fundamentally different socio-economic, socio-cultural and ethno-confessional profiles, which were reinforced by a certain regional identification. In this instance, by region I mean not a political and administrative space, but a historical and geographic one. "*Oblast'*" (the source of the name of the Siberian social-political movement *oblastnichestvo*) may be considered the pre-revolutionary equivalent of the contemporary term "region." D. N. Zamiatin notes, "Historical-geographic space, in contrast with geographical space, is structured primarily by precise spatial localization, representations, and interpretations of corresponding historical events, which took place (or are taking place) in a defined geographical area (region)."[15] In this connection, the process of the genesis of a new mental-geographic spatial object is important, separating it into a particular subject of social geopolitical consciousness and of the segmentation of government policy.

The geography of power has its own historical dynamics. As we survey the physical space of Siberia and the Russian Far East, it is not difficult to see how its administrative/bureaucratic configuration changed over time, how administrative lacunae were gradually filled and how the initial state vacuum and the territorial thinness of state power disappeared. The state administratively structured new imperial space by demarcating its external and internal boundaries. At the same time, the administrative-territorial grid, inevitably imposed on the geographic landscape, attempted to account for the historical contours of settlements of ethnic groups and to bring them in line with an effective imperial political administration and economic regionalization. The administrative-territorial division of the state was primarily subordinated to the realization of two main functions: securing the central power's control over the local authorities and the collection of taxes.[16] However, in the peripheral regions these usual functions needed to be coordinated with other needs—for example, foreign policy concerns, local military-political and economic controls.

When the empire annexed one or another of the territories in the east it initiated, first of all, its forceful conquest and integration into the imperial administrative-political space. Subsequently, the empire used the boundary regions as military-economic beachheads for further expansion— Okhotsko-Kamchatskii krai for North America, Transbaikal for the Amur region, the Amur Region for Manchuria, and western Siberia and the Orenburg region for Kazakhstan and Central Asia.

The process of imperial integration had a significant temporal duration and a definite sequence of events.

First, a process of initial assimilation. This involved the "discoverers" who guarantee "historical" rights to the given territory, the creation of supporting military-industrial bases, and the establishment of the perimeters (zones, borders) of the external frontiers that guaranteed state security and formed the imperial rear (including natural barriers, low accessibility and paucity of natural and labor resources, the unattractiveness of the borderlands). Finally, the process promoted the creation of defensive borders and state boundaries and the stationing of armed forces (regular and irregular troops, Cossack lines, naval bases) along the border. This stage was characterized by a high degree of individual initiative in the borderlands, merely coordinated and directed by the government, and a symbiosis of military-economic functions and the creation of quasi-administrative institutions (private companies, expeditions).

Second, an attempt to "center" the new territories by creating regional centers of state power. At first, military-administrative and fiscal interests would predominate, followed by economic ones. We then witness the start of economic colonization of the regional rear (often this process goes from the borders of the region to the heart of the territory). Changes in foreign and domestic policy, the economic assimilation of the region, and demographic processes lead to frequent migration of regional centers.

Third, the assignment of the region's administrative and political status (*namestnichestvo,* governor-generalship, guberniia, or oblast) and finding the optimal model for relations between the regional power and the center—a combination of the principles of centralization, deconcentration, and decentralization. This stage includes organizing the imperial infrastructure in the region (communications, post, telegraph), providing for cultural reinforcement (churches, schools, hospitals, scholarly institutions), and creating combined organs of local administration and justice ("non-Russian," "military-civilian administration").[17]

Fourth, the imperial "absorption" of the region by means of creating uniform administrative structures. These concern administrative-territorial divisions (including special departmental administrative-territorial formations: military, judicial, mining, and other districts) as well as the specialized institutional organization of different levels of the administration and courts. The sphere of activity of traditional institutions is reduced and the system of administrative communications is improved. This stage also includes the "Russification" (*obrusenie*) of the territory through intense agricultural and industrial colonization, the dissemination into the borderlands of reforms tested in the country's center, and economic and sociocultural modernization.

Thus the empire's *regional policy* pursued the goal of political and economic integration and the establishment of social, juridical, administrative, and even demographic (*narodnonaselencheskoe*) uniformity. However, the concrete needs of the administration forced the government to continue to take into account the regional specifics of the territories, which augmented the contradictory nature of administrative policy in the border regions, and, in turn, was reflected in the relationship between central and local authorities, resulting in serious administrative conflicts. The transition from a polyvalent administrative structure (as it was in the early stages of the empire) to an internally complicated monovalent model inevitably led to the growth of the centralization and bureaucratization of the administration. This allowed for only a limited deconcentration of power in the regions. Administrative centralization was a powerful instrument not only of administration, but also of political reform.

As it carried out its policy aimed at the political-administrative and economic integration of the Asiatic borderlands into a unified imperial space, the autocracy adhered to a definite sequence during the transition from military-administrative oversight of the traditional institutions of power to their replacement with a Russian bureaucratic system of state institutions. The governor-general of Eastern Siberia, D. G. Anuchin, succinctly identified this process in the early 1880s:

> During any expansion of our territory, be it through the conquest of
> new lands or through personal initiative, the newly annexed regions did
> not immediately enter the general structure of the state and thus were
> not governed by the same administration that operated throughout the

rest of Russia; instead they were connected to the empire through *namestniki* or governors-general, who acted as representatives of the supreme power. Moreover, at the frontiers of our periphery regions, only the most essential Russian institutions were introduced in their most basic form, according to the needs of the population and country, and often many of the former organs of administration were preserved. Such was the case in the Caucasus, Siberia and all of Central Asia. . . . [18]

The administrative structure of Asiatic Russia in the nineteenth century was viewed as a "transitional form," which according to the official position must have as a final goal "bringing by means of successive reforms the regions into that stable administrative structure, typical of the provinces of European Russia, which allows for freedom and development within the limits of regional interests and supports unification in the hands of central institutions." [19]

Regional administrative policy was the aggregate (often neither a system nor even a complex) of government measures aimed at the preservation of the integrity of the empire, the economic assimilation of regions, a response to ethnic, confessional and socio-cultural demands, as well as an acknowledgment of administrative and juridical traditions (while eliminating any political claims). The administrative problem of the center and the region included a dialog of two sides (central and local state agents) whose positions often did not coincide. The steady flow of instructions from the center could be dampened successfully by their non-fulfillment in the periphery. The difference in views on regional problems of central and local powers is of significant interest. As is well known, the latter, especially in the Asiatic lands of the empire, strove to conduct their own autonomous policy, which often did not coincide with the intentions of the center.

Administrative policy was aimed not only at the creation of an effective and inexpensive administrative mechanism, but also at finding the optimal relationship of power between central departments and the higher territorial administration as represented by governors-general and governors, and surmounting at the regional level problems engendered by the absence of a single power in the center and the periphery. At higher and central levels, it was possible to create special territorial organs (e.g., Siberian, Western, Caucasian, the Committee of the Kingdom of Poland, the Committee of the Siberian Railway, the Committee of the Far East, the Committee for the Settlement of the Far East).[20] However, as contemporaries noted: "The territorial character of central institutions to a certain degree masked the complete absence of anything resembling a regional structure."[21]

In its organization of the regional administration the autocracy maneuvered between the Scylla of centralization and the Charybdis of federalism. In this regard official Russian state opinion asserted,

> If, in the provinces, we give power only to representatives of the central government, without any participation of local society, then a time of severe despotism will come about, notwithstanding the most liberal form of government rule. But if we remove representatives of the central government, who serve as a link between the provinces and the center, and leave everything to local society, then the state will cease to be a unified whole and, in the best case, will be transformed into a federation of provinces.[22]

The despotism of a nearby power seemed even a greater burden than the despotism of the center. It was essential not only to free the central organs from the excessive burden of administration and to hand over a part of these functions to local authorities, but also necessary to find a reasonable combination of centralization, deconcentration, and decentralization of power. At the same time, when the interests of the central authorities in the Asiatic regions continued to bear an impulsive imprint, intensified above all by foreign policy ambitions or threats, the local administration was most interested in stability, in precise guidelines and priorities (and even the systematic nature) of assimilation. The presence of a governor-generalship made it possible to go beyond the strict boundaries of a centralized administration, and to allow a certain degree of administrative autonomy.

However, the existence of the governor-generalship somehow reinforced the idea that this part of the empire had been exempted from the jurisdiction of general legislation. In the words of the Russian legal scholar A. D. Gradovskii, it was difficult for the governor-general to relinquish the presumption "that the region was something separate from the rest of the state."[23] Juridical isolation, behind which loomed political isolation, threatened the desired unification of the empire. The personal nature of the governor-general's power, especially given the frequent change of governors-general, inevitably imparted a discrete character to government policy with respect to one or another region. The replacement of governors-general often had a defining impact on the direction and success of government measures. In conflicts between the departmental and territorial principles of administration, the governors were considered by the central ministers as less dangerous and more dependent on the central powers.

The city played a significant role in regional processes. As a region-forming factor, the city brought the territory together not only administratively (as was chiefly the case in earlier periods), but also economically.[24] It was precisely the city that became the center of modernizing influences and initiatives. The process of including the regions in the communications network of the empire took place via the cities. At the same time, as A. I. Herzen wrote, there were some peculiar cities "that for the most part had been invented and existed for the purposes of the administration and the bureaucrat-conquerors."[25] The peripheral city was first and foremost a center of imperial power of the second or third order, connected to the main imperial center. It is thus understandable why so much attention was given to the selection of the administrative center and why these centers migrated so frequently, especially on the empire's frontier.

The border regions occupied a special place in the administrative-territorial structure of Asiatic Russia. In these regions a simplified system of administration existed alongside traditional institutions of self-rule and justice; military authority was given priority over civilian authority for an extended period; external borders were amorphously defined and, therefore, highly mobile. Given these conditions, the local administration became responsible not only for the internal organization of the region, but also for defining its borders, including state borders, for the purposes of foreign policy.

One of the most important features of regional power in Asiatic Russia at the turn of the twentieth century was the lack of any firm boundary between domestic and foreign policy, since the state borders were still in the process of being determined. In the case of Asia the state boundary bore a specifically frontier aspect characteristic of mobile zones of occupation and assimilation. For a long time, the territory between the empires (as, for example, between the Russian and Chinese empires) represented a half-wild buffer territory, sparsely populated by nomadic groups, a no man's land, despite the fact that it formally belonged to one or the other empire. The "Asiatic border" from the European perspective represented a huge barrier zone between empires, upon which various local power structures continued to exist.[26] However, any administrative border, especially a state one, once drawn, has a tendency to remain intact and to become "eternal." As F. Braudel notes, "Thus history moves to strengthen borders, which are transformed into natural features of the locality, inalienably belonging to the landscape, and do not easily give way to being displaced."[27]

The geography of power denotes the complex process of adaptation of Russian bureaucracy to regional conditions, the creation of a particular administrative milieu that influenced both general imperial structures and the methods of rule and specific conditions of the region. The center was interested in an effective and inexpensive bureaucratic apparatus; in those instances when a particular region had little appeal, the center was forced to take supplementary measures to attract officials, thereby creating a regional system of perks and privileges.

A special type of Russian official emerged in the Asiatic borderlands: the conveyor of civilizing values, imperial norms, and imperial techniques that were alien to the borderlands. The official's administrative conduct could become deformed under the influence of the surrounding sociocultural milieu, a phenomenon M. E. Saltykov-Shchedrin noted. It is, however, important to emphasize one other development: the appearance of the specialist-administrator who often served in different regions and conveyed the administrative methods and imperial techniques from one region to another, adapting his experience to local realities. The practice of the regional administration in the Asiatic borderlands required Russian officials to be able to interact with the local elite (however, this could include not only the national elite, but also, for example, influential merchants, as in Siberia in the first half of the nineteenth century), and to be able to negotiate between different groups in the area. This explains the need to draw into the administration local elites, who would temporarily retain their influence, yet still be under the control of the Russian administration. Russian authorities initially limited their presence to supervision (often reducing tax burdens or even postponing tax duties), interfering in the life of the local population only in the case of breaches of security in the region. The main argument for such interference was the need to establish order and to secure the inhabitants from internal strife and external aggression. Another significant factor was the effectiveness and low cost of traditional institutions of self-rule and courts. However, the autocracy severely limited the political independence and the political claims of traditional leaders. Germans, Poles, and Tatars were widely used as a so-called "mobilized diaspora" in the Asiatic borderlands of the empire.

The Russian official transmitted from borderland to borderland not only the St. Petersburg official style, but also the administrative methods and techniques that he had acquired in various regions. Thus, in Siberia and in the Far East many high-ranking officials had undergone bureaucratic training in the Caucasus or in Poland. In imperial practice, the frequent transfer of regional chiefs (and even governors-general) from one region to another was significant, for example, from the Far East to Turkestan (N. I. Grodekov, S. M. Dukhovskoi, D. I. Subbotich). Regional officials and military personnel had expanded career prospects (regional benefits, the possibility to receive medals and promotions for special achievement), which allowed them to occupy prominent posts in the capital hierarchy and thereby to influence both the formation of Russian bureaucratic-administrative culture and the general formulation of government policy.

"Scientific conquest"—physical geography, cartography, statistical descriptions, and ethnography—of new territories and peoples represented an important current in the imperial geography of power. Scientific expeditions and special research programs, organized at the initiative or under the control of the central or local administration, were supposed to ascertain the economic potential of the region (its orography, hydrography, geology, climate, soil, flora, and fauna), observe the course of economic assimilation and the prospects for agricultural and industrial colonization, and work out a strategy of administrative conduct with respect to the indigenous peoples, taking into account their socio-cultural particularities.

To a significant extent, the nineteenth century was the century of geographers and geography, which penetrated many areas of learning and political practice. At the International Geographical Congress in Berne in 1890, the builder of the Transcaspian Railroad M. N. Annenkov compared the geographical events of the nineteenth century with the great geographical discoveries at the turn of the sixteenth century, when the "European subjugation of the world," now nearly complete, was just beginning. His speech advocated the study of the "laws of nature," according to which historical events unfolded: "What great services geographical societies could render all of mankind, if they turned their attention to those countries, once unattainable, but which have now become accessible to us, and to which we could direct emigration and colonization."[28] On the occasion of the opening of the Siberian branch of the Russian Geographic Society in Irkutsk, one of N. N. Murav'ev-Amurskii's colleagues recalled that "the opening of the Siberian branch of the Imperial Geographic Society had proved once again how it was meant to be not only a geographical society, but more precisely a Russian society, not simply a learned society, but a learned patriotic society."[29] According to one of N. N. Murav'ev-Amurskii's associates, everything, including science, ought to be subordinate to the interests of the empire; "We don't need beetles and cuckoos, if only scholars were to show us where we can find iron in Amur, where there is coal, where there are forests suitable for shipbuilding, where there is rich earth for agriculture, where plants grow best, in what parts of the Amur one can establish the best agricultural system."[30]

The Geographic Society brought together the most diverse people involved in studying the new lands and peoples of the east. These were not only professional scholars, but also officers, officials, priests, and even political exiles. Their research interest concentrated on the strategically important internal regions and the contiguous territories of other states, which might fall within the zone of imperial interests. Thus purely scientific studies became intertwined with military interests.[31] The military departments of the empire and the Imperial Russian Geographic Society were clearly linked.

Russian travelers from among the officers of the general staff simultaneously pursued scientific goals and purely reconnaissance aims (P. P. Semenov-Tian-Shanskii, M. I. Veniukov, A. I. Maksheev, N. M. Przheval-skii) and played an important role in the formation of a new political worldview, as did the "eastern" specialists (V. S. Solov'ev, E. E. Ukhtom-skii). This can be most clearly seen at the turn of the twentieth century in Far Eastern policy. The ideological foundation for this policy included new geopolitical motives, alongside traditional assertions about the spontaneous movement of Russians to the east ("to the sea and ocean"), the gathering of the lands, or the fulfillment of the Orthodox Christian mission. Ideologues of Russian imperialism debated the theories of natural borders, the maritime or continental character of the Russian empire, colonial policy, the desire to bring European civilization to the Asians, and the prophecy of the "yellow peril" or the coming Mongol yoke. Even as they demonstratively accented the difference of Russian Asiatic policy from the colonial policy of other world powers, Russian imperial ideologues tried to imitate their rivals' ideological and administrative experience. A fruitful direction for understanding imperial discourse is to observe the evolution of the imperial lexicon with the emergence of new imperial concepts and terminology and the borrowing of foreign colonial and administrative ideas. It is important to understand who accomplished this intervention of new terms and ideas into the political practice of the empire and how this was done.

A region is not only a historical-geographic or politico-administrative reality, but also a mental construct with dynamic borders that are difficult to define. In this connection, what is critical is the process of the genesis of a new mental-geographic spatial form, its isolation as a special subject of public geopolitical consciousness and it segmentation in government policy. The formation of a new region was accompanied by its introduction into the hierarchy of politically marked imperial "questions" (Polish, Caucasian, Finnish, Baltic, Siberian, Far Eastern, etc.).

The territory of power needs its own markers, which include ideologically and politically colored toponymies and symbolic figures of regional historic actors. The building of the imperial administrative structures proceeded in parallel with the process of verbally mastering the new territories and interpreting them in the customary imperial terminology and imagery. Thus, in the toponymy of the Russian Far East one could read a geopolitical meaning, a certain nostalgia for the unrealized imperial dream of Constantinople and the Black Sea Straits. In his discussion of the unsuccessful Crimean War and the loss of the Black Sea Fleet, V. V. Krestovskii, the secretary of the chief of the Russian naval forces in the Pacific (and later a popular writer), wrote in 1881:

> It will become understandable why in the new designations of these places and waters appeared such significant—if not for the present then for the future—names, such as the Gulf of Peter the Great, the Eastern Bosphorus, the Bay of the Golden Horn, and the port of Vladivostok. Through these names, the prescient mind of the statesman seems to have been marking out plans for the future, showing future generations of Russia that here lies your direct access to the oceans, here is the place for the development of our naval forces—military and commercial— and here in time must follow a radical resolution of the Eastern question."[32]

Vladivostok and Vladikavkaz were seen as Russia's windows to Asia. The names of N. N. Murav'ev-Amurskii, his associates, and their historical predecessors, as well as the heavenly and imperial patrons, furnished names for the new centers of the region's imperial cartography, symbolically securing the new territory for Russia.

It was not only political and economic guidelines coming from the center of the empire that influenced the formulation of administrative tasks, but also the "geographic vision" of the region and transformations of its images in the consciousness of the government and society. Geographic images can be seen as "cultural artifacts, and as such they involuntarily reveal the predispositions and prejudices, the fears and hopes of their authors. In other words, learning how society takes account of, thinks about, and evaluates an unknown place is a productive way to study how society or parts thereof thinks about and evaluates itself."[33]

A region has its own historical spatio-temporal limits and can disintegrate into new regions. This was the case with the regional division of "great" Siberia from the Urals to the Pacific Ocean, and later toward the end of the nineteenth century, when the Far East and the Steppe region appeared on the geo-economical and administrative map of Asiatic Russia. The cutting off of the Far East from Siberia, which started at the turn of the nineteenth century, received a new political impulse in the 1850s and was completed in 1884 with administrative separation in the general-governorship of the Amur region. D. N. Zamiatin concluded that "the construction of the Transiberian railroad and the Chinese Eastern Railroad effectively structured the Far East, and later customs and tariff measures effectively defined this region as an independent geo-economic space."[34] Behind the changes on the administrative map of the empire stood the process of internal organization. With the creation of the general-governorship of the Amur region, not only was the Russian Far East administratively separated from Siberia, but the process of the internal economic consolidation of the region, with its primarily maritime orientation, was also accelerated. Furthermore, the process of creating a Far Eastern identity separate from a Siberian identity had begun (Amurites, Far Easterners). The writer and railway engineer N. M Garin-Mikhailovskii, when traveling through the Far East at the very end of the nineteenth century, was struck by how different Vladivostok looked in comparison with all the other Russian cities he had seen. Its distinctiveness included the proximity to the sea, the city's architecture, and the passers-by in the streets, among whom there were a number of Chinese, Korean, Russian, and foreign sailors standing onboard the decks of battleships and minesweepers. A resident of Vladivostok proudly told him: "This isn't Siberia any more."[35]

Over the course of the nineteenth century, the name "Siberia" gradually disappeared from the administrative map of Russia. In 1822 the Siberian governor-generalship was divided into two (Western and Eastern Siberia); in 1882 the West Siberian governor-generalship was abolished; in 1884 the Far East was separated from Siberia, giving rise to a prolonged border dispute; and in 1887 the East-Siberian governor-generalship was renamed Irkutsk Province. The term "Asiatic Russia" was encountered more and more often. Renowned Russian judicial scholar N. M. Korkunov maintained that "the very word Siberia no longer has any meaning as a definite administrative term."[36]

This gave rise to the fear that Siberia would disappear. It was not by chance that in the 1870s N. M. Iadrintsev, the leading ideologue of Siberian *oblastnichestvo,* did not support the idea of abolishing the Siberian governor-generalship, which he viewed as a threat to the economic, political, and cultural unity of Siberia. Another prominent *oblastnik,* G. N. Potanin, not only shared this view, but even expressed the wish to broaden the governor-general's powers and make him equal to a *namestnik.* The tendency toward the administrative subdivision of Siberia could not but alarm the *oblastniki.* In their fight against the all-encompassing centralization coming from St. Petersburg, they advocated the "centralization of Siberia, which had been split in two . . . by administrative division."[37] The center could not help but recognize the threat coming from prolonged administrative unity of a huge peripheral region of the empire, which was not supposed to challenge the prerogatives of the center.

The Russian imperial project envisioned the gradual absorption of the periphery by the imperial core (above all, through peasant colonization and the development of communication networks). Thomas Barrett notes that the theme of expanding the "frontiers" into the non-Russian borderlands through military actions and administrative organization included the "constructive" aspects of Russian colonization: "the birth of a new social identity, ethnic relations, new landscapes, a regional economy, and material culture."[38] In imperial policy, the prevailing stereotype held that one could only consider those lands truly Russian where the plow of the Russian plowman had passed. Peasant colonization became an important component of imperial policy and peasants the most effective conveyors of imperial policy. As Dominic Lieven noted, "It was difficult for the Russian colonist to answer the question, where exactly does Russia end and the empire begin?"[39] For an Englishman the answer to this question was obvious as soon as he got on a ship and sailed away from Foggy Albion. The difference was not just a product of geographic determinism differentiating a continental empire from the overseas colonies of European powers; it also grew from the consciousness that had historically developed as the "gathering of the Russian lands" turned into an empire. In this vein, P. N. Miliukov noted, "The latest product of Russia's colonizing effort was her first colony—Siberia stands on the border then and now."[40] This process had begun in the seventeenth century, with the goal of making Siberia not just a peripheral region of the empire, but an inseparable part of Russia.

Territorial empires such as the Russian empire did not have distinct internal boundaries within the imperial space, which would set conditions for the extension of ethnic Russian borders. Thus, the founder of the Russian-American Company, the merchant G. I. Shelikhov, was concerned not only about commercial interests, but also about the expansion of Russian territory. He noted in 1794, concerning the relocation of peasants to one of the Kurile islands, "There it was and it is my intention to gradually introduce Rus."[41] After N. N. Murav'ev-Amurskii freed exiles and convicts and sent them to the Amur region in the mid–nineteenth century, he counseled: "Go with God, my children. You are now free. Work the land, and make it a Russian land."[42] It was no accident that later, in the early twentieth century, this was instinctively understood by the exiles of Sakhalin, who declared with pride: "Our unhappy fate has forced us to forget our homeland [*rodina*], our origins, and to relocate to the edge of the earth, amongst impassable forests. God helped us. In a short time we have built houses, cleared the valley for fields and meadows, raised cattle, erected a church, and you yourself now see that here it smells of Rus."[43]

In the early nineteenth century, F. F. Vigel wrote that Siberia would be useful for Russia as an immense land reserve for the quickly growing Russian population, and as it was settled, Siberia would shrink, and Russia would grow.[44] Here we see a cardinal difference between the Russian empire and the Western colonial empires. In his "Survey of the History of Russian Colonization," M. K. Liubavskii determined that the degree of integration of one or another territory that made up the Russian state was a function of the success of Russian colonization, and, in particular, of peasant colonization.[45] A kind of popular justification of imperial expansion sanctioned increasing the amount of arable land so that it could be settled by Russians.[46]

Isolated from their habitual socio-cultural surroundings, settlers found themselves in unknown regions in different natural-climatic conditions and forced to readjust fundamentally their economic pursuits. They came into direct contact with the culture of the East (unusual and attractive) and acutely felt their Russianness, which was stripped of local particularities that were otherwise so fiercely preserved in their former homeland. All this created more favorable conditions than in European Russia, Ukraine, and Belarus for the success of the project of the "great Russian nation," in which ethnic lines did not prevail, but rather the idea of an empire-wide identity.[47]

L. E. Gorizontov sees in this the prospect of "a double expansion" of the Russian empire: the external territorial growth of the empire as a whole, enhanced by the parallel growth of the "imperial core," as it impinges upon the borderlands.[48] The Russian imperial project envisioned the gradual absorption of Siberia, the Far East, and even the Steppe region by the imperial core. This was a long and complicated process, which combined the tendencies of empire-building with nation-making, the determination to unite the nation with dynastic empire. It was supposed to provide the empire with greater stability, to give the Russian imperial structure an important internal impulse, and to guarantee the Russian national future.

Thus the most important role in the building of the Russian empire was to be played not by the military and officials, but by peaceful peasant settlers. This was a conscious political aim. In his political testament of 1895, the chair of the Committee of Ministers, N. Kh. Bunge, pointed to Russian colonization as a way, following the example of the United States and Germany, to erase national differences: "The weakening of the racial differences in the borderlands can only be achieved by attracting the core of the Russian population to the borderlands, but this will only work if the Russian population does not adopt the language and habits of the borderlands but rather brings their own there."[49] It was not by chance that the Committee of the Siberian Railway, where N. Kh. Bunge was vice-chair, paid such attention to the experience of the Germanization of the Polish provinces.

Military science, where much of Russian geopolitics was formulated, highlighted "population policy" as one of the most important imperial tasks. This presumed the active intervention of the state in ethno-demographic processes, the regulation of the flow of migration, and the manipulation of the ethno-confessional composition of the population in the imperial borderlands in order to solve the task of military mobilization.[50] This was connected first and foremost with the settlement of the Russian Orthodox element in regions with a diverse ethnic composition, or, as was the case in the Amur and Maritime regions, in territories threatened by demographic and economic expansion from outside. There was recognizable anxiety concerning the cultural influence on the Russian population from the Chinese, Koreans, Japanese, Mongols, and even Iakuts and

Buriats, who were perceived as rivals with respect to the imperial colonization project. As wars ceased to be dynastic or colonial and became national, the attention of imperial policy-makers and ideologues focused on the geography of the "tribal composition" of the empire. The peoples of the empire were classified according to degrees of trustworthiness, and an attempt was made to supplement the imperial allegiance of ethnic elites with feelings of national duty and Russian patriotism. It was deemed necessary to thin out the population of the national regions by means of the "Russian element," and to minimize the alien national threat from within and outside the empire through preventive measures.

Together with the widespread understanding of the desirability of a "Russian" colonizing element to "make the region Russian," there nonetheless existed a certain tolerance in the Asian borderlands with respect to the non-Russian and non-Orthodox national and confessional population. Local authorities in the region often found themselves in situations where the state aim of spreading the Orthodox faith, an important part of imperial policy, contradicted the goals of the colonization. They also tried to use the American immigration experience and to attract German Mennonites, Finns, Czechs, and Montenegrins to Asiatic Russia. When N. N. Murav'ev-Amurskii defended his proposal to the tsar, he noted, "Slavs understand Russia as their homeland [*kak rodnuiu im zemliu*]; they identify their own advantage with the advantage of the Russian population. They will convey their expertise in the improvement of agriculture, and they will be devoted to the general good of their new fatherland. Slavs emigrate to other countries, but repressed by alien elements, they adapt themselves with difficulty—in Russia it should be the opposite."[51] There were plans to settle about 1,000 Czech colonists along the shore of the Amur from its mouth to the Korean border. However, in this matter of resettling the "Czecho-Slavs," political fears outweighed Slavophile arguments, despite the tsar's approval. The military governor of the Maritime region, P. V. Kazakevich, hastened to remind them that foreign colonists, even in the interior of Russia, created certain difficulties. He warned,

> We are introducing a strong foreign element into a deserted land that only bears the name of Russia. We are giving them by means of special privileges the opportunity not only to put down roots, but also to subordinate to their influence the weak rudiments of a Russian population that has just begun to establish itself. Not to mention the fact that numerous natives will inevitably subordinate themselves to the stronger

nationality, the one that has more privileges and the most means at their disposal.

Kazakevich further noted that the Czechs were Catholic and that the recent Polish events had showed that "despite the tribal unity of the race, Catholicism places a definite obstacle in the way of rapprochement."[52]

Nonetheless, a broad interpretation of Russianness competed successfully with Orthodox missionary work as a culture-forming component of Russian nation-building in Asiatic Russia. The autocracy could not fail to notice how firmly peasant Russian Old Believers and Dukhobors resisted assimilation by the alien ethnic environment, and how they had preserved their Russianness at great distances from Russian cultural centers. The "Russian cause" in Siberia and in the Far East throughout the entire imperial period continued to be tolerant of ethnic and confessional characteristics. The notion of a "yellow" or "Muslim" peril did not appear until the end of the nineteenth century.

Peasant colonization laid the foundation for a kind of geopolitical super-mission, namely, the call to change, in the recommendation of P. P. Semenov-Tian-Shanskii, the ethnographic border between Europe and Asia by pushing it further and further to the east.[53] Finance Minister S. Iu. Witte pointed out that it was precisely Russian settlers who would change the empire's civilizational borders: "For the Russian people, the border post that separates them as a European race from the peoples of Asia has long since been shifted beyond the Baikal—to the steppes of Mongolia. With time, its place will be at the last stop on the Chinese Eastern Railroad."[54] He linked the colonization of Siberia not only with an economic task, but also with a political one. The Russian population of Siberia and the Far East was supposed to become the bulwark in "the inevitable struggle with the yellow race." Witte emphasized that

> otherwise, it will again be necessary to send soldiers from European Russia; the impoverished center will once again have to take upon itself the full weight of the struggle for the peripheral regions and carry on its shoulders the resolution of questions coming to a head in the Far East. And it will be necessary for the peasants of the black soil belt or western provinces to go fight for what are for them alien and incomprehensible interests, lying thousands of versts from their regions.[55]

In addition to cultural activity, economic and communications initiatives were necessary to turn Siberia into Russia. The post, the telegraph, and most importantly, the Siberian Railroad were supposed to pull Siberia toward European Russia and give a powerful impulse to the resettlement movement.[56] General Staff Colonel N. A. Voloshinov wrote in 1899,

> For three hundred years Siberia has been considered subjugated by Russians, but does Russia actually control it? Does Siberia actually belong to the Russian people and the Russian state? Do the 100 million Russians derive benefit from this huge space, or is it controlled by the thousand or so emigrants who have been dumped there and who call themselves Siberians and are prepared to forget that they are Russian . . . [57]

Railway policy was seen as an alternative to the Western oceanic variant of building a colonial empire. When Transportation Minister M. I. Khilkov arrived in Irkutsk in 1895, he tellingly spoke out at a local public meeting about the civilizing mission of the railroad: "The railroad will unite two cultures—the culture of the West and the culture of the East."[58] Prince E. E. Ukhtomskii's *Sankt-Peterburgskie vedomosti* painted a poetic picture of the "iron bridge" between Europe and Asia. If Peter had opened the "window" to Europe, then Nicholas II "had opened the gates of the Great ocean for us," leading us across Manchuria to "a new threshold of international life."[59] In the framework of "one and indivisible Russia," Prime Minister P. A. Stolypin made an appeal to further strengthen the "state power of Great Russia" by means of the rails.[60] A. V. Krivoshein, the ideologue and implementer of Stolypin's resettlement policy, known as the "Minister of Asiatic Russia," staunchly tried to transform Siberia "from an appendage of historical Russia into an organic geographic part of the rising Eurasian, but Russian in culture, Great Russia."[61]

However, in Siberia and in the Far East a new threat (real or imagined) to imperial policy arose. The formation of a sense of territorial separation among the local population, and the recognition of their differences and economic disadvantages in relations between the center and the borderlands, led to the construction of a different Siberian identity, one that competed with the "great Russian nation."

Because Russian government circles recognized significant differences between the conditions of the regions of the Russian empire and the overseas colonial territories of European powers, there was a definite reluctance to use the term colony. Nicholas I himself reflected on the place of Siberia within Russia, and left a handwritten resolution on the matter. "Under no circumstances should the main leadership of Eastern Siberia be removed from its dependence on the highest government organs of the empire.

Consequently, it cannot and must not find itself in that relationship, which a colonial administration normally finds itself with respect to the metropolis." Though he recognized the colonial character of his policy in the Transcaucasus, separated from Russia by mountains and populated by "hostile and unconquered tribes," Nicholas I explained that Eastern Siberia was merely remote from the "inner parts of the state" and populated "by people, who, for the most part, were Russian."[62] In connection with the dissolution in 1865 of the Second Siberian Committee of the Ministry of People's Enlightenment, A. V. Golovnin noted that Siberia, the Caucasus, the Crimea, and the Baltic provinces, unlike Poland and Finland, were constituent parts of the Russian empire.[63]

Obviously, the American syndrome was partly behind this reluctance to view Siberia as a colony. Russian policy makers and intellectuals were convinced that in the future all colonies would separate themselves from the metropolis. European colonial scholarship reiterated this conclusion. In the words of one of the most authoritative researchers, P. Leroy-Beaulieu, "The metropolis must get accustomed . . . to the idea that at some time the colonies will reach maturity and then they will start to demand more and more, and finally, they will want absolute independence."[64] The Polish national factor also played a role. It was transferred to Siberia not just by rumors and sparse official information, but also through direct contact with the numerous Polish exiles who began to appear in the region in the late eighteenth century. In the East, not just the "enemy from without" was feared but also the "enemy from within." As early as the first half of the nineteenth century, government circles began to have misgivings about the loyalty of the Siberians, sensing that Siberia might follow the example of the British North American colonies.

However, the phobia of Siberian separatism had arisen even before autonomist sentiments had been formulated in Siberia and before the appearance of Siberian *oblastnichestvo*.[65] Fed by feelings of growing Siberian patriotism, the *oblastniki* creatively adopted contemporary federalist and colonialist theories and laid the foundations of regionalism not only as an influential social movement, but also as a special subject of study. The political aspect of regionalism manifests itself in a region's recognition of political or socio-economic inequality or superiority, and in the potential for and aspiration to autonomy or even to state separation. The momentum of a regional dynamic can be partly explained by turning to the phases of the national movement suggested by Miroslav Hroch: a sequence of moves from a spontaneously formed regional self-consciousness and local patriotism, to political actualization and theoretical construction of a regional identity by local intellectuals (political figures, public activists, scholars), to the propagation of ideas of administrative and economic autonomy and even state separatism.[66]

While they recognized the importance of the national factor in state-building, the *oblastniki* believed that the territorial factor was more important for Siberia; it was continually active and stood higher than the social factor. G. N. Potanin, one of the ideologues of Siberian *oblastnichestvo*, countered the Marxist position, which supported principles of proletarian internationalism, and spoke about the community of interests of all the workers of Russia, declaring: "As we analyze the relationship of the colony to the metropolis, we cannot help but recognize the existence of special Siberian interests. Let's assume that in the metropolis the class of factory owners is eliminated, and worker artels become the managers of the plants and factories. Does this mean that Siberian claims on Moscow will disappear with the fall of the factory owners?"[67]

The acute divergence of economic interests between the center and the region were evident in issues of colonization, freedom of trade—internally as well as externally (Chinese Eastern Railway, porto-franco of the Far Eastern ports and estuaries of Siberian rivers, the "Cheliabinsk tariff," etc.)—as well as the allocation of budgetary funds for the benefit of the regions. Serious opposition emerged concerning the character of industrial development and the direction of transportation arteries. Siberian society, for example, actively opposed transforming the region into a source of raw materials for the center, and demanded to be liberated from the "yoke of Moscow manufacturers." Dissatisfaction was also provoked when a number of reforms that had been implemented in European Russia (primarily the judicial and zemstvo reforms) were not extended to the Asiatic regions. For many years, Siberia and the Far East remained a place of criminal and political exile. The metropolis was accused of sucking dry not only the periphery's material resources but also its spiritual resources, by centralizing all scholarly activity and the system of higher education. There existed serious differences of opinion on the goals and aims of peasant resettlement ("settlement" or "colonization"). Strictly Siberian or Far Eastern needs were most often put aside as secondary and were sacrificed to the interests of imperial policy.

The psychological and cultural particularities of the Siberians startled and frightened contemporaries. Siberian *oblastniki* created an entire field of study concerning the formation in Siberia of a special cultural-anthropological type ("Sibero-Russian people"), in accord with similar developments in America. It was thus not enough to settle the region with the type of colonists that the Russian state desired; it was also important to strengthen the unity of the empire with cultural ties. Forced beyond the Urals from European Russia because of overcrowded land and poverty, the settler carried with him complicated feelings of sadness for his abandoned home and an open contempt for the ruling order in his lost homeland.

It was feared that Russians who resettled to distant regions would fall under the influence of foreigners and native tribes, lose their customary national traits, distance themselves from their homeland, and lose their sense of allegiance. The writer I. A Goncharov referred to the "Iakutization" of the Russians, a phenomenon confirmed by many local officials.[68] The military governor of the Maritime region, P. V. Kazakevich, pointed out that it was not only the Iakuts who exerted this type of influence, but the Kamchadals as well. Living among the Kamchadals, the Russian settlers in only ten years "had assimilated all their habits and their way of life. The descendants of our first settlers in Gizhig, Okhotsk, and Udsk have almost completely lost their Russian character, and this is nothing compared to what would happen if these people had been of a higher level of civilization."[69] A similar phenomenon could be observed in the Transbaikal region, where Siberians, who mixed with Buriats, to a significant degree lost their original anthropological character. The process of "nativization" of Russians went hand in hand with the process of Russification of the Buriats and created a new ethno-cultural and confessional situation. There, "the ceremonial piousness of the Russian population was replaced by purely pagan superstitions, in part borrowed from indigenous peoples, in part coming to them from the new and unfamiliar way of life."[70]

A special note on the condition of church affairs in Siberia, prepared by the chancellery of the Committee of Ministers, pointed to the need to unify the spiritual life of the Siberian borderlands with that of the central provinces "by strengthening Orthodoxy, Russian nationality and citizenship in these regions." It was Siberian particularities—the religious indifference of old-time Siberian inhabitants and the variegated ethno-confessional composition of the population—that, from the administration's point of view, made this spiritual effort necessary and important. Many contemporaries who visited Siberia in these years wrote in a similar fashion. Impressed by the domestic prosperity of Siberian homes, they were nonetheless struck by the absence of ornately decorated icons and of icon-lamps, and noted that wax candles were merely stuck on wooden planks. The expanse and natural wealth of Siberia was startling—"Look at the country we have arrived in; it is even somewhat strange"—as was the absence of thatched roofs, but so too was the fact that in Siberian villages, despite the prosperity of the inhabitants, the churches were wooden, poor, and many simply wretched.[71] The large number of schismatics (*raskol'niki*) and the influence of Islam and Lamaism were also causes for concern.

Nationalistically inclined authors wrote about the neglect of Russian interests in the borderlands, the absence of the necessary support for the Orthodox Church's missionary activity, and the indulgence of non-Russian minorities, especially on the part of local authorities. These conditions, they thought, would lead the Russian population of Siberia, "being in constant contact with non-Russians, even as friends and relatives, to have no objection at praying to their gods now and again."[72] The chief-procurator of the Holy Synod, S. M. Luk'ianov (biographer and admirer of the philosopher V. S. Solov'ev) called for creating in the Far East that internal structure of life "which would actively give the settler the character of a Russian person." The role of the Orthodox Church would be particularly important for a Russian in this region, where he finds himself in unfamiliar living conditions, yearns for his abandoned homeland, and can fall under the influence of different types of sectarians. In 1909 the Vladivostok Diocesan Council interpreted the situation in the following manner: "The Russian people who have resettled here need the church's influence more than anything. They have been thrown into the remote taiga, where they do not have church services and do not study the word of God; the Russian people easily run wild and become the most crude materialists and most intolerant individualists."[73] This could not but worry the authorities, who were anxious to settle the Russian element in the borderlands.

To halt the process of alienating the settlers from "old" Russia and to establish in a "new" Russia characteristics the authorities considered to be essentially Russian, it was necessary to adopt a purposeful cultural policy. Recognizing that the long-time inhabitants of Siberia, as a whole, had a higher level of intellectual development than the Russian peasants, A. N. Kulomzin called the government's attention to the fact that the absence "of leadership by the church and schools and the influence of exiles did not bode anything good for the development of the Siberian." According to his observations, the Siberian was characterized by the coarsening of moral standards, the predominance of "individual interests over social ones," and a "complete absence of any historical legends, traditions, beliefs, and attachments." The Siberian, affirmed Kulomzin, had forgotten his history, forgotten his homeland and, after having lived a secluded life beyond the Urals for several centuries, had ceased to think of himself as a Russian. However, a love for his new homeland had been awakened in him, and the Siberian reacted scornfully to the fact that "in Russia they speak contemptuously of Siberia." This was a reflection not only of the process of regional identification, but also a kind of Siberian chauvinism, which manifested itself in disdain for new settlers, who were often called *lapotniki* (wearers of bast shoes; i.e., poor peasants), "unwashed" and "uneducated."

As before, people feared that Siberia would follow the example of the colonies of West European countries by seceding and forming an independent state. In his memoirs, Kulomzin writes that he had been visited by a "nightmare," in which "in a more or less distant future, the whole country on the other side of the Enisei will inevitably form a special state separate from Russia."[74] These misgivings often led to groundless searches for Siberian separatism. The Irkutsk governor-general A.D. Goremykin sought and struck out the words "Siberia and Russia" in newspaper articles and replaced them with the words "Siberia and European Russia." Instead of "Siberians" he demanded that one write "natives of Siberia." He even treated political exiles better than Siberians, who he believed were all separatists.[75] Conservative government officials M. N. Katkov and K. P. Pobedonostsev on more than one occasion reminded Alexander III about the danger of autonomist sympathies in Siberia and the intrigues of Poles.

However, Fridtjof Nansen, another commentator on Siberian separatism, was skeptical about the possibility of its realization. On the contrary, he maintained that the Siberians were not the Irish striving for Home Rule. "They will never forget that they are Russian and they will always feel separate from the Asiatic peoples." Nansen also disputed the fear that the Asiatic possessions of the Russian empire were extracting the best talents from the center, thus reducing its own economic and cultural standards. Unlike the Spanish, Portuguese, or British colonies, Nansen believed, Siberia represented "in essence a natural continuation of Russia, and one must view it not as a colony but as a part of the homeland, which in its boundless steppes can provide shelter for many millions of Slavs."[76]

The recognition of Siberia's economic and cultural distinctiveness and the Siberians' irritation at their unjust treatment by the central authorities created in Siberian society an atmosphere of alienation from European Russia and a general dissatisfaction that indeed fed Siberian separatism. But despite considerable evidence of separatist feelings, along with the government's fears and its persistent search for fighters for Siberian independence (or autonomy), Siberians' discontent with their humiliating conditions never grew into a real danger of Russia losing Siberia. Although the Russian empire, and later the USSR, collapsed, Dominic Lieven notes that the new Russia was able to absorb and take to its "maternal bosom" the jewel of its imperial crown—Siberia. For this reason, Russia has remained a great power (unlike Turkey, Austria, or even England and France). Lieven adds, however, that had the Siberians received freedom and the representative regional institutions that would have provided a focus for regional patriotism, they might have elaborated an independent identity that could have led to an independent nation-state, not unlike Australia or Canada.[77] Instead the problem of Siberian regionalism is still alive, and an important factor in the contemporary politics of interrelations between the center and regions of Russia beyond the Urals.

Notes

1. S. I. Kaspe, *Imperiia i modernizatsiia. Obshchaia model' i rossiiskaia spetsifika* (Moscow, 2001).

2. B. E. Nol'de, *Ocherki russkogo gosudarstvennogo prava* (St. Petersburg, 1911), 280–281.

3. S. M. Prutchenko, *Sibirskie okrainy,* vol. 1 (St. Petersburg, 1899), 5–6.

4. M. M. Golubchik, S. P. Evdokimov, et al., "Geografiia. Regional'nye issledovaniia i regional'naia nauka (nekotorye iskhodnye polozheniia)," *Regionologiia,* nos. 3–4 (2000).

5. F. Braudel, *Vremia mira* (Moscow, 1992), 18–49.

6. A. Kappeler, "'Rossiia—mnogonatsional'naia imperiia': nekotorye razmyshleniia vosem' let spustia posle publikatsii knigi," *Ab Imperio* 1 (2000): 21. See also the view of K. Matsuzato on the research possibilities of regionalism and the "geographical approach," *Regions: A Prism to View the Slavic-Eurasian World. Towards a Discipline of "Regionology"* (Sapporo, 2000), ix, x.

7. Sh. Eizenshtadt, *Revoliutsiia i preobrazovanie obshchestv. Sravnitel'noe izuchenie tsivilizatsii* (Moscow, 1999), 135, 147.

8. Ibid., 177.

9. V. V. Ivanovskii, *Voprosy gosudarstvovedeniia, sotsiologii i politiki* (Kazan, 1899), 244.

10. M. Hechter, "Vnutrennii kolonializm," *Etnos i politika* (Moscow, 2000), 210.

11. Cited in: E. N. Pertsik, *K.I. Arsen'ev i ego raboty po raionirovaniiu Rossii* (Moscow, 1960), 99.

12. K. I. Arsen'ev, *Statisticheskie ocherki Rossii* (St. Petersburg, 1848), 26.

13. O. V. Gritsai, G. V. Ioffe, and A. I. Treivish, *Tsentr i periferiia v regional'nom razvitii* (Moscow, 1991), 5.

14. P. Bourdieu, *Sotsiologiia politiki* (Moscow, 1993), 42.

15. D. N. Zamiatin, "Russkie v Tsentral'noi Azii vo vtoroi polovine XIX veka: strategii reprezentatsii i interpretatsii istoriko-geograficheskikh obrazov granits," *Vostok* 1 (2002): 44.

16. V. A. Kolosov, N. C. Mironenko, *Geopolitika i politicheskaia geografiia* (Moscow, 2000), 412–413.

17. The original terms are *inorodcheskoe* and *voenno-narodnoe.*

18. *Sbornik glavneishikh ofitsial'nykh dokumentov po upravleniiu Vostochnoi Sibir'iu,* vol. 1, vyp. 1 (Irkutsk, 1884), 66.

19. Rossiiskii gosudarstvennyi istoricheskii arkhiv [hereafter RGIA], f. 1284, op. 60, 1882 g, d. 47, l. 166.

20. For more information, see A. V. Remnev, "Komitet ministrov i vysshie territorial'nye komitety v 60–80-e gg. XIX v.: (Rossiiskii variant organizatsii regional'nogo upravleniia," *Obshchestvennoe dvizhenie i kultur'naia zhizn' Sibiri (XVIII–XX vv.)* (Omsk, 1996), 55–66.

21. E. Ignat'ev, *Rossiia i okrainy* (St. Petersburg, 1906), 6.

22. I. A. Blinov, *Gubernatory. Istoriko-iuridicheskii ocherk* (St. Petersburg, 1905), 3.

23. A.D. Gradovskii, "Istoricheskii ocherk uchrezhdeniia general-gubernatorstv v Rossii," *Sobranie sochinenii,* vol. 1 (St. Petersburg, 1899), 299–338.

24. D. Ia. Rezun, V. A. Lamin, et al., *Frontir v istorii Sibiri i Severnoi Amerike v XVII–XX vv.: obshchee i osobennoe* (Novosibirsk, 2001).

25. A. I. Gertsen, *Sochineniia v 9-ti tomakh,* vol. 8 (Moscow, 1958), 135.

26. D. N. Zamiatin, *Modelirovanie geograficheskikh obrazov* (Smolensk, 1999), 157–158.

27. F. Braudel, *Chto takoe Frantsiia?* Book 1, *Prostranstvo i istoriia* (Moscow, 1994), 274.

28. M. N. Annenkov, "O znachenii v XIX stoletii geograficheskogo obrazovaniia, kak osnovy emigratsii i kolonizatsii," *Izvestiia Russkogo geograficheskogo obshchestva* 28 (1892): 88.

29. B. Struve, "Vospominaniia o Sibiri," *Russkii vestnik* 6 (1888): 119.

30. "Pis'ma ob Amurskom krae," *Russkii arkhiv* 1 (1895): 390.

31. On the connection between Russian science and imperialism, see D. A. Aleksandrov, "Nauka i imperialism," *Imperii novogo vremeni: Tipologiia i evoliutsiia (XV–XX vv.). Vtorye Peterburgskie Kareevskie chteniia po novostike* (St. Petersburg, 1999); D. Rich, "Imperialism, Reform and Strategy: Russian Military Statistics, 1840–1880," *Slavonic and East European Review* 74, no. 4 (1996); N. Knight, "Science, Empire, and Nationality: Ethnography in the Russian Geographical Society, 1845–1855," in *Imperial Russia. New Histories for the Empire,* ed. Jane Burbank and David L. Ransel (Bloomington: Indiana University Press, 1998); V. A. Esakov, *Ocherki istorii geografii v Rossii. XVIII–nachalo XX v.* (Moscow, 1999).

32. "O polozhenii i nuzhdakh Iuzhno-Ussuriiskogo kraia. Zapiska shtab-rotmistra V. Krestovskogo (byvshego sekretaria glavnogo nachal'nika russkikh morskikh sil Tikhogo okeana)" (St. Petersburg, 1881), 2.

33. M. Bassin, *Visions of Empire: Nationalist Imagination and Geographical Expansion in the Russian Far East, 1840–1865* (Cambridge: Cambridge University Press, 1999), 274.

34. D. N. Zamiatin, *Modelirovanie geograficheskikh obrazov* (Smolensk, 1999), 97.

35. N. Garin, "Cherez Sibir' na Okean," *Russkii razliv* 1 (Moscow, 1996): 418.

36. N. M. Korkunov, *Russkoe gosudarstvennoe pravo*, vol. 2 (St. Petersburg, 1909), 480.

37. *Pis'ma G. N. Potanina*, vol. 1 (Irkutsk, 1987), 49, 145–146.

38. T. M. Barrett, "Linii neopredelennosti: severokavkazskii 'frontir' Rossii," *Amerikanskaia rusistika: Vekhi istoriografii poslednikh let. Imperatorskii period: Antologiia* (Samara, 2000), 168.

39. D. Lieven, "Russkaia, imperskaia i sovetskaia identichnost'," *Evropeiskii opyt i prepodavanie istorii v postsovetskoi Rossii* (Moscow, 1999), 299.

40. P. N. Miliukov, *Ocherki po istorii russkoi kul'tury*, vol. 1 (Moscow, 1993), 488.

41. *Russkie otkrytiia v Tikhom okeane i Severnoi Amerike v XVIII v.* (Moscow, 1948), 351.

42. P. A. Kropotkin, *Zapiski revoliutsionera* (Moscow, 1990), 173.

43. I. P. Miroliubov (Iuvachev), *Vosem' let na Sakhaline* (St. Petersburg, 1901), 214.

44. *Zapiski F. F. Vigelia* , part 2 (Moscow, 1892), 196–197.

45. M. K. Liubavskii, *Obzor istorii russkoi kolonizatsii s drevneishikh vremen i do XX veka* (Moscow, 1996), 539.

46. I. G. Iakovenko, *Rossiiskoe gosudarstvo: natsional'nye interesy, granitsy, perspektivy* (Novosibirsk, 1999), 103.

47. On the project of the "great Russian nation," see A. I. Miller, *"Ukrainskii vopros" v politike vlastei i russkom obshchestvennom mnenii (vtoraia polovina XIX v.)* (St. Petersburg, 2000), 31–41.

48. L. E. Gorizontov, " 'Bol'shaia russkaia natsiia' v imperskoi i regional'noi strategii samoderzhaviia," *Prostranstvo vlasti: istoricheskii opyt Rossii i vyzovy sovremennosti* (Moscow, 2001), 130.

49. N. Kh. Bunge, "Zagrobnye zametki," *Reka vremen (Kniga istorii i kul'tury)*, book 1 (Moscow, 1995), 211.

50. P. Kholkvist, "Rossiiskaia katastrofa (1914–1921 g.) v evropeiskom kontekste: total'naia mobilizatsiia i politika naseleniia," *Rossiia XXI*, 11–12 (1998): 30–42.

51. "Otchet po Vostochnoi Sibiri za 1860 g.," RGIA, f. 1265, op. 10, d. 202, l. 3.

52. P. V. Kazakevich—M. S. Korsakovu (24 iiunia 1864 g.), Rossiiskii gosudarstvennyi istoricheskii arkhiv Dal'nego Vostoka [hereafter RGIA DV], f. 87, op. 1., d. 287, ll. 25–31.

53. P. P. Semenov, "Znachenie Rossii v kolonizatsionnom dvizhenii evropeiskikh narodov," *Izvestiia RGO,* 28, vyp. 4 (1892): 354.

54. RGIA, f. 1622, op. 1, d. 711, l. 41.

55. "Vsepoddanneushii doklad ministra finansov S. Iu. Vitte," RGIA, f. 560, op. 22, d. 267, ll. 8–9.

56. *Moskovskie vedomosti,* April 5, 1891.

57. N. A. Voloshinov, *Sibirskaia zheleznaia doroga* (St. Petersburg, 1890), 17.

58. N. S. Romanov, *Letopis' goroda Irkutska za 1881–1901 gg.* (Irkutsk, 1993), 337.

59. *Sankt-Peterburgskie vedomosti,* January 13, 1904.

60. I. I. Tkhorzhevskii, "Poslednii Peterburg," *Neva* 9 (1991): 190.

61. K. A. Krivoshein, *Aleksandr Vasil'evich Krivoshein. Sud'ba rossiiskogo reformatora* (Moscow, 1993), 131.

62. RGIA, f.1265, op. 1, d. 132, ll. 76–77.

63. RGIA, f. 851, op. 1, d. 11, l. 155.

64. P. Leroy-Beaulieu, *Kolonizatsiia u noveishikh narodov* (St. Petersburg, 1877), 512.

65. A. V. Remnev, "Prizrak separatizma," *Rodina* 5 (Moscow, 2000): 10–17.

66. M. Khrokh, "Orientatsiia v tipologii," *Ab Imperio* 2 (2000): 15.

67. G. N. Potanin, "Vospominaniia," *Literaturnoe nasledstvo Sibiri,* vol. 6 (Novosibirsk, 1983), 211.

68. "I. A. Goncharov—A. A. Kraevskomu (sentiabr' 1854g., g. Iakutsk) Putevye pis'ma I. A. Goncharova," *Literaturnoe nasledstvo,* vols. 22–24 (Moscow, 1935), 423–424.

69. P. V. Kazakevich—M. S. Korsakovu (24 iiunia 1864g.), RGIA DV., f .87, op. 1, d. 287, l. 29. The Third Section received a report on the doubtful political advantage of settling Czechs in the Amur. M. S. Korsakov mentions this in a letter to V. P. Butkov (December 24, 1862), RGIA f. 1265, op. 11, d. 151, l. 40.

70. G. M. Osokin, "Moskoviia na Vostoke," *Russkii razliv* 2 (Moscow, 1996): 145.

71. P. S. Alekseev, "Kak, byvalo, ezzhali. Vospominaniia o proezde zimoiu iz Moskvy v Chitu," *Russkii vestnik* 10 (1899): 606; *Mitrofan Serebrianskii. Dnevnik polkovogo sviashchennika, sluzhashchego na Dal'nem Vostoke* (Moscow, 1996), 32, 37.

72. *Zhivopisnaia Rossiia. Otechestvo nashe v ego zemel'nom, istoricheskom, plemennom, ekonomicheskom i bytovom znachenii,* vol. 12, part 1, *Vostochnaia Sibir'* (St. Petersburg-Moscow, 1895), xi.

73. S. M. Luk'ianov—P. A. Stolypinu (16 ianv. 1910 g.), Arkhiv vneshnei politiki Rossiiskoi imperii, f. Tikhookeanskii stol, op. 487, d. 762, l. 177-b.

74. "A. N. Kulomzin, Perezhitoe," RGIA f. 1642, op. 1, d. 204, l. 207.

75. I. I. Popov, *Zabytye irkutskie stranitsy. Zapiski redaktora* (Irkutsk, 1989), 59; S. G. Svatikov, *Rossiia i Sibir'* (Prague, 1930), 78.

76. F. Nansen, "Strana budushchego," *Dal'nii vostok* 4–5 (1994): 185.

77. D. Lieven, "Rossiia kak imperiia: sravnitel'naia perspektiva," in *Evropeiskii opyt i prepodavanie istorii v postsovetskoi Rossii* (Moscow, 1999), 273.

17 Imperial Political Culture and Modernization in the Second Half of the Nineteenth Century

Sviatoslav Kaspe

Russia between the Poles of Empire and Nation-State: Conceptual Landmarks

The new phase of modernization Russia is experiencing today once again raises the question of modernization's impact on the essential characteristics of Russian civilization, including what may be called Russia's "paradigm of statehood"—that is, the complex of cultural, religious, mental, psychological, and other conditions that determine the structure of an institutional design. Although this paradigm is only partially articulated in social-political theory and practice, it in fact defines both of them, and we can assume that it possesses its own internal logic, coherency, and potential for evolution.

It has become a commonplace in both scholarship and journalism that a choice has not yet been made between the two possible variants for the reorganization of the Russian state paradigm. These alternatives are described in ethno-political terms as the *empire* and *nation-state* paradigms. (The latter term has multiple possibilities, since a nation-state can be based upon ethnic as well as upon a purely civil, constitutional understanding of the word "nation.") The natural attempt to take into account the experience of the past in order to answer this question leads us to consider the events of another period when Russia faced a similar problem. In the second half of the nineteenth century, a first round of systemic modernization, initiated by the Great Reforms, led to significant changes in the ethno-political structure of the Russian empire. These changes in their turn predetermined to a great extent the course and the outcome of the systemic crisis that shook the empire in the early twentieth century. The more precise chronological limits of my study are 1855–1894, the reigns of

Alexander II and Alexander III. These temporal boundaries encompass large-scale transformations of the regime, a crisis (with an ethno-political dimension) initiated by these transformations, measures taken to overcome this crisis, and a temporary stabilization in the mid-1890s.

Although in many ways the reign of Alexander III signified a break with the principles of his predecessor and a turn toward counter-reform, a national-cultural policy continued without interruption throughout this period.[1] The chronological boundaries of my research reflect this continuity. An analysis of this period allows us not only to uncover the presence of an explicitly imperial component in the Russian statehood paradigm, but also to describe the specifics of its operation. My analysis provides a basis for understanding the impact of modernizing processes during the second half of the nineteenth century upon the imperial dimension of the statehood paradigm.

This chapter derives from my larger study of the imperial component of the Russian statehood paradigm and is based upon the conceptual approach I introduced in my article, "Empire: Genesis, Structure, Functions."[2] I attempted to shift from a symptomatic definition of empire that describes it as a collection of certain attributes to a genetic definition that reveals the roots of the imperial phenomenon, its contents, and therefore its possible courses of development. Of course, such a definition can only be an ideal type in the Weberian sense. It does not claim to cover the entire temporal and spatial spectrum of real empires, but nonetheless provides a general conceptual foundation for analysis of the question at hand.

In the course of reconstructing an ideal type of an empire, I isolate the following critical attributes, critical in that they are common to the majority of symptomatic definitions: a considerable territorial scale, ethno-cultural and ethno-political heterogeneity, and the presence of universalistic perspectives in mechanisms of legitimization and in political practices, going as far as claims to the universal significance of the particular empire's existence. This formulation of the question allows me to propose the following working hypothesis:

> Imperial political systems represent a method of resolving conflict-ridden tensions arising from the collision of universalistic, culturally motivated political orientations with the de facto variety and diversity of political cultures represented within a particular political space. This hypothesis allows us to analyze to what extent and by what means particular components of the imperial structure provide for cultural and

political integration of the imperial territory. It thus lays the ground for a structural-functional analysis of imperial systems, as well as for a shift from a symptomatic definition of the empire to a genetic one.[3]

The proposed definition permits us to make an organic connection between two levels of imperial being: the real and the ideal. The indivisibility of imperial mythology and the imperial political system provides an empire with stability, making it a self-sufficient universe. The conditions of this imperial universe are, first, the presence of absolute, universalistic components in the state's system of political legitimization; second, the presence in the political practice of the state of a stable tendency toward further territorial expansion; third, the absence or only limited degree of assimilation of populations of territories newly included in the state, and the preservation of their ethno-cultural features. The basic functions of such a system are exponential growth of accessible and controlled resources; affirmation of imperial pretensions to "cosmic sovereignty";[4] and integration of ethno-culturally heterogeneous imperial territory into a unified social-political organism through the creation of a particular regime of interaction between central and peripheral elites. The most important characteristics of an imperial system are its unboundedness—latent on the plane of actual policy, but very real in the framework of imperial mentality—as well as its universalization of the context of communication in spheres of social interaction crucial to systemic stability, combined with the preservation of local particularities in all other spheres. My work also describes the major evolutionary tendency of imperial systems —a process of equalization of center and periphery (in various senses, from the economic to the ontological) that leads to the destruction of asymmetric social interactions and the disintegration of the empire, in addition to the ordinarily less significant effects of external influences.

Based on this conceptualization, I analyze the circumstances of formation and evolution of the imperial component of Russian statehood until the middle of the nineteenth century. The existence of an imperial component of Russian statehood is unquestionable and has been repeatedly asserted by researchers. But in addition to the thesis of the internal heterogeneity of both Russian political culture and Russia's statehood paradigm, my study suggests the presence of a clearly articulated nation-state component as well. While generally adhering to Ernest Gellner's widely accepted approach to the concept of nationalism, I introduce certain modifications. Whereas Gellner argues that the demands of an industrial economy are the sole basis for the establishment of a rigid connection between state and culture and for the emergence of demands to unify political and cultural societies, I suggest that this connection could appear for other reasons. The reasons for hypertrophy of the state principle in comparison with all other components of a civilizational structure have often been described. They can be labeled the "fortress under siege" complex—in all senses, from the economic and military-political to the cultural and religious. It is the combination of the national component of political culture ("the Russian Land" [*russkaia zemlia*]) with the imperial goal of limitless expansion that gives the latter an additional impetus, providing for the participation of the masses in expansion (peasant colonization), and at the same time extending the significance of this expansion beyond the limits of purely military-political activity and transforming it into an enterprise with global scope and meaning.

I also analyze the causes of increased tensions between the national and imperial principles. Their "peaceful coexistence" became more and more problematic beginning with Peter the Great's reforms. The change in self-representation of the Russian state and its metamorphosis from tsardom to empire did not signify a choice for an imperial orientation; these developments must be understood in the context of radical Westernization of Russian life undertaken by Peter. Although Westernization was in many respects superficial and Russian statehood undoubtedly preserved its particularities, the fact that localized European monarchies that already had been emptied, to a great extent, of their universalistic claims (however strongly they were oriented toward attaining the standard of the "regulated state") were chosen as the model to be emulated could not but have an influence upon Russian political culture, especially upon the ideas of ruling elites, who were especially affected by Western cultural and ideological examples. Thus, during the eighteenth and the first half of the nineteenth centuries, one can observe increasing fluctuations between two vectors, in ethno-national, religious, and regional policy. On the one hand, one can find a significant number of examples of "nation-state" policies that narrowed the scope of local autonomy, rationalized and unified the administrative system, and gradually included ethno-cultural parameters in political considerations. On the other hand, many political actions are more readily understood in the context of an imperial logic that presumed nonintervention in local customs as long as they did not conflict with loyalty to the supreme imperial power. This orientation provided for the preservation of traditional local elites as political subjects.

However, the full picture is even more complex, since within the same region one can find evidence of both vectors. The highest tension between these contradictory principles was reached during the reign of Nicholas I. On the one hand, we find a clear strengthening of nation-state tendencies, expressed in the first attempt to create an official ideology using sacral and quasi-sacral mechanisms, not imperial in nature, as legitimizing mechanisms and in the beginnings of Russification in a number of regions. On the other hand, we can cite such examples as the famous debate between the emperor himself and Iu. F. Samarin about the situation in the Ostsee region, and the "Instruction to the Chief Administration of the Caucasus" (1842), which preserved in full the policy of religious toleration and cooperation with traditional elites and other analogous fully imperial practices.

Before turning to our basic problem—the fates of imperial political culture and imperial systems in conditions of systemic modernization—one more terminological explanation is in order. The concept of "modernization" has too long and too ambiguous a history to be used without concrete definition.

First of all, when writing of modernization, I assign the term quite traditional contents. I am addressing the complex of processes, observable in both the West and in a large part of the rest of the world. Among these processes, as a rule, are the establishment of an industrial mode of production (usually, but not obligatorily, in the form of market capitalism), the transition from direct redistribution of various kinds of resources to their more or less free circulation in a regime of equivalent exchange, the supplanting of ascriptive social estates by individuals, highly specialized and differentiated social structures, the formation of new, usually "national" or "quasi-national" forms of broad-based social identification, the rationalization of consciousness, etc.[5] I believe that the criticism of earlier variants of modernization theory, which was indeed a characteristically cruel, one-sided representation of the predetermined course and results of historical process, should not necessarily lead to a categorical refusal of modernization as a concept and as a model for interpretation. S. N. Eisenshtadt proposed corrections to the model as early as the 1970s, according to which the process of modernization should be not be regarded as an automatically active force in history, drawing all societies with different speeds toward a single goal, but rather as the complex of challenges posed to societies, which respond in significantly and principally different ways. To my knowledge, no convincing objections have been posed to this refinement.

From this perspective, the concept of modernization turns out to be very close to the concept of Westernization. This assimilation can be justified: R. Bendix has convincingly demonstrated that Western European modernization was the organic continuation of the traditions of this civilizational zone.[6] The same reason justifies the opposition of the Western European variant of modernization to all others. Only Western European modernization can be regarded as truly organic and endogenous, since in all other civilizations, regions, and countries, modernization began as a result of a direct instruction [*diktat*] from the West or as the consequence of expanded interaction with the West (begun at the initiative of the West), or, finally, as a way to attain a sufficient degree of competitiveness with the West. Therefore, any modernization, apart from that of the West itself, inescapably involves "catching up." First, chronologically, it will come later than that of the West; second, it will, as a rule, be undertaken in search of an adequate response to the challenges presented by the already existing modernization of the West. For this reason, "modernization . . . has to be seen as one specific type of civilization which has originated in Europe and which has spread, in its economic, political, and ideological aspects, all over the world, encompassing . . . almost all of it."[7] Moreover, societies caught up in this process will necessarily acquire certain fundamental characteristics, but will also inescapably preserve their own specificity, just as the societies of the West have kept their own multiplicity of differences internal to their civilization.[8]

Russian Ethnic Policy during Systemic Modernization in the Second Half of the Nineteenth Century

Russia's defeat in the Crimean War demonstrated that the policy of limited modernization, followed more harshly during the reign of Nicholas I than in the beginning of the century, could no longer be justified. Once again, the need to reestablish the military-political status of a great power became the stimulus for a new round of modernization initiatives. However, both the motives of the Great Reforms and their features differed substantially from previous large-scale efforts to modernize.

As before, the reforms were begun at the initiative of the supreme power; this was indeed "modernization from above." However, public opinion also played a significant role in this initiative. (We are referring to the numerous letters and pamphlets that circulated in educated society during the first years of Alexander II's rule.) Disregarding public opinion was no longer possible, particularly since reformist aspirations had seized the highest stratum of the Russian elite. In this regard, it is sufficient to recall the Grand Princess Elena Pavlovna and her circle, or P. A. Valuev, later minister of internal affairs, known as the author of the memorandum, "Thoughts of a Russian in the Second Half of 1855." On the one hand, this public attitude meant that the government could rely upon a substantial "modernization reserve"; on the other, the mood of these groups was to a great extent beyond the government's control. European-educated and, most important, European-thinking intellectuals, bureaucrats, and military officers were significantly liberated from Russian tradition. Because the implementation of policy, for the most part, fell to these elites, their position could substantially alter the administration's course of action.

Moreover, by this time the sphere of Western-oriented mentality had expanded beyond the nobility. The role of the intelligentsia was becoming more pronounced not only in the imperial center, but also in a number of peripheral regions. This development further weakened the natural coalition (already undermined during Nicholas I's reign) of the central government with modernizing elements of society, as initiative passed into the hands of the latter. The coalition acquired a conditional character and could continue to exist only in so far as the course, character, and pace of the reforms matched the heightened expectations of society. The tensions of this situation were increased by a widening of the gap between the state and the emerging structures of emancipated civil society, and finally by the transformation of their relations into a phase of open opposition.

The impact of Westernization across a wide spectrum of social strata, on the one hand, and the quite deep penetration of corresponding values into their mentalities, on the other, led to the adoption of a new vision of Russian modernization, uncharacteristic of previous stages. Pragmatic considerations still constituted the basis of modernization. However, the attempt to bring all aspects of the Russian state and society into compliance with the "demands of modernity" (i.e., Western standards) was significantly motivated by a choice of values that reflected these standards. An indicator of the gravity of this tendency was that even the "Palladium of Russia"—the autocratic order itself—became an object of discussion.

Evidently, it was precisely the presence of explicitly normative motives that ensured the systemic quality of modernization in the middle of the nineteenth century and led to the cumulative effect that distinguishes systemic modernization—a process of fundamental transformation of the whole social fabric—from a partial and controlled implementation of certain of its elements. The Great Reforms intruded so deeply into traditional Russian systemic identity and its paradigm of statehood, because they were brought about not so much by an institutional logic (which sooner or later changes mentality and political culture) but rather by mental changes that occurred primarily among intellectual and bureaucratic elites and did not permit the survival of the old regime and its institutional and normative structure. The criterion of primacy of one of two impulses—these can be labeled "structural" and "cultural"—was used by A. N. Medushevskii in his typology of Russian modernization efforts:

> Russian history provides us with two alternatives for reforms directed toward the modernization of social relations. The first of these consists of an accelerated process of catching up, implemented exclusively through administrative regulation aimed at the rapid attainment of strategic goals. . . . The alternative mode of modernization is represented by the reforms of the 1860s, which relied on the support of wider circles of society and on their recognition of the necessity for reform. The major distinguishing quality of the latter type of modernization is that it legally proclaims a fundamental social transformation, which facilitates drawing all strata of the society into the reform process. The reforms opened up possibilities for the participation of society in transformations aimed at creating a civil society and a legal state. The abolition of serfdom, the introduction of zemstvo self-government, democratic reforms of the judicial system, education, and the press, served as a real foundation for the gradual rationalization and Europeanization of social relations, and for liberation from traditional institutions.[9]

Naturally, transformations of such magnitude, whose consequences far exceeded their limits as initially conceived, could not but affect the ethno-political sphere—one of the most critical from the perspective of imperial stability. In this sphere, a logic similar to that of the reforms in general can be observed: changes in political culture preceded institutional changes and defined their character. The accelerating erosion of traditional imperial ethno-political ideas, principles, and orientations, accompanied by their replacement with fundamentally new stereotypes, led to a radical shift in governmental policy and to a change in the entire ethno-political situation on the imperial space.

Ethno-political processes in the second half of the nineteenth century can be clearly divided into two stages that do not coincide with either the periodization of the Great Reforms or the traditional perception of Alexander II's reign as reformist and Alexander III's as reactionary. The year 1863 appears to have been the real divide. As is well known, the fundamental substance of the first years of Alexander II's reign (before the real transformation) was a general liberalization of the regime, liquidating the most odious aspects of the Nicholaevan epoch. The enthusiasm about forthcoming changes, so widespread in Russia at the time, "was initiated simply by loosening the leash that had constrained the press and all displays of civil society: there were as yet no real signs of transformation itself."[10] This liberalization also touched upon national (*natsional'nyi*) policy, even though it is impossible to find any indications of a well-founded reform strategy in this area. Reformist efforts were concentrated in other directions where it seemed necessary and sufficient to bring the situation into correspondence with elementary liberal norms. Apparently, it was no accident that the changes of 1855 to 1863 affected almost exclusively those peoples and zones that could be regarded, from the perspective of modernizing ideals, as the most advanced—that is, the most subject to Western influence. Among the reforms of this first stage were the 1859 extension of the right of settlement on Russian territory to certain categories of the Jewish population (determined by the modernizing criteria of wealth and education); the granting of a new degree of Finnish autonomy (including the introduction of the Finnish mark in 1860); and, finally, the experiments in Poland, the consequences of which finally forced the regime to abandon such policies and redefine its ethno-political line.

It would be difficult to interpret the national policy of 1855–1863 as a partial rehabilitation of imperial methods, for the break with them under Nicholas I had been quite serious, even if forced. Nicholas's policy of coercive maintenance of stability was appropriate to the objective conditions in which the empire found itself at that time. The politicization of ethnicity triggered by modernization led to the inclusion of ethno-cultural factors in imperial policy as well as to their strict control. Stabilizing mechanisms that had more or less effectively constrained the politicization of ethnicity were relaxed spontaneously; this led to an explosive process and to the failure of attempts to channel this politicization in any predictable way. The strategy of Count Wielopolski, formulated in 1858, consisted of restoring Polish autonomy within the empire on the basis of the 1815 constitution, combined with a concurrent moderate democratization of the internal institutions of state administration. However, even the middle class upon which Wielepolski had planned to rely (as the group most tied to the empire by economic interests and therefore the least inclined toward political radicalism) was so much in the grip of nationalist sentiment that it could not be satisfied with a middle-of-the-road program. Granting even quite broad political autonomy could not stop the nationalist struggle, but rather was perceived as a substitute for complete independence, the attainment of which had become a priceless ideal.

The immediate consequence of the suppression of the rebellion of 1863 was the effort "to resolve this question once and for all by means of repression and forced integration"[11]—this time both ethno-culturally and institutionally. The direction of this policy is clearly illustrated by such measures as the elimination of the name "Poland" itself from official use and its replacement with the "By-Vistula Territory," personnel purges in local administrations and the substitution of even loyal ethnic Poles with Russians, drastic and compulsory reduction of the sphere of usage of the Polish language and its complete elimination from administrative, judicial, and educational institutions. The policy of collaboration with local elites was changed to its direct opposite, which resulted in intensified economic and legal pressure on large Polish landowners. Both the peasant reform of 1864 in this region and subsequent governmental policy concerning this issue were directed explicitly against landowners, as demands of ethno-cultural (or rather already national) solidarity prevailed over estate-based solidarity, which had been traditional in imperial policy. Moreover, estate-related considerations lost their importance not only with respect to Poles, but also to Russians. Russian colonization of the Vistula and western regions, instigated directly by the government, could be conducted by either landlords or peasants. As L. E. Gorizontov persuasively demonstrated, both governmental circles and public opinion considered these two options from the point of view of their efficacy as instruments for Russification of the region and for "weakening the Polish element," not with respect to the interests of a certain social group.[12] The ultimate goals of colonization and transformation of land ownership were perceived as exclusively political and were never discussed.

The Polish events of 1863 and governmental policy in the years that followed affected more than just the situation in the region, where all expressions of Polish political separatism were blocked for decades (therefore giving grounds for new indignation). The Polish question for the first time forced both governmental circles and public forces to pay extremely serious attention to the ethno-political consequences of the processes unfolding in Russia. The deep connection between democracy and nationalism as elements of a unified phenomenon of statehood in the industrial era has been discussed above. Even such moderate democratization as that of the Great Reforms inevitably lent urgency to deciding on the national versus imperial nature of a renewed Russian state. What emerged was not so much a distinctly articulated official position on this issue, but rather partially realized changes in political culture. Though certain manifestations of nationalism had appeared earlier in Russian history, Russian nationalism per se took shape precisely in the early 1860s under the direct influence of Polish events.

Two features of this phenomenon are worth highlighting. On the one hand, this nationalism was not an internally unified phenomenon. Andreas Kappeler has classified its varieties as radical-democratic (idealization of the Russian peasantry, characteristic of the populists [*narodniki*]); liberal (indifferent to the specific interests of the population at the periphery of the empire in its battle for further democratization); extremist (associated with the name of M. N. Katkov); and, finally, Pan-Slavic (the latter movement, however, with its deep roots in the imperial tradition, hardly qualifies unambiguously as a nationalism).[13] On the other hand, despite its internal heterogeneity, Russian nationalism "had a strong consolidating impact on polarized Russian public opinion, which decisively spoke out against Polish aspirations,"[14] with only rare exceptions, for example, Alexander Herzen.

Nationalism thus facilitated the resolution of one of the most acute problems arising from the course of modernization—the problem of providing a sufficiently wide social consensus between elites and other strata, as well as among elites. In P. N. Miliukov's analysis:

> The part of the Russian intelligentsia that preached nationalism . . .
> entered into a coalition with the Russian government on the basis of
> nationalist ideals. We have seen that this government was initially favorably predisposed to the national cultures of newly annexed nationalities . . . However, largely influenced by the nationalist part of the
> intelligentsia, this attitude gradually changed.[15]

Miliukov considered that it was precisely intellectuals who were responsible for the acceptance of a nationalist policy, thus anticipating the constructions of Gellner[16] and Hroch.[17] The desired consensus was reached to some extent. In the words of another observer, "In the implementation of its nationalist policy, which consisted of suppressing all aspects of national life among the non-sovereign nationalities, the imperial government was not alone. To a great extent it enjoyed public support from the dominant Great Russian nationality, whose national representative it was and intended to remain in the future."[18]

The government failed to eliminate intelligentsia opposition in its entirety. However, it succeeded at least in splitting the intelligentsia and in constructing a coalition with parts of it. "The year of the second Polish uprising, 1863, was the chronological watershed on which the major political movements in Russia—nationalism, liberalism, and socialism—finally split and went each its own way."[19] The consolidating role of nationalism allowed the government to "use nationalism as an instrument to stabilize the ruling regime,"[20] or to be more precise, the entire social-political organism, whose entrance onto the stage of systemic modernization had severely sharpened many old social contradictions and had given birth to new ones. Political integration that unites society around some super-group social project is one of the most important conditions for the success of modernization. "In the circumstances of increasing differentiation of society, it provides a minimal level of mass support for industrial development, and reconciles traditional groups and classes to it."[21]

In Western Europe, it was nationalism that played the role of an integrating factor; Russia followed the same example during its course of Westernization. The notion of a strong connection between the Great Reforms and the growth of nationalistic tendencies is rarely found in contemporary scholarship. Nationalism is usually considered either in the context of political reaction inconsistent with liberal-democratic reforms, or as a situational policy without an objective foundation. Yet even as the nineteenth century was drawing to a close A. D. Gradovskii treated Russian nationalism (as such, not only its extreme forms) precisely as a logical consequence of liberal-democratic modernization: "It is not hard to see that as soon as Russia made the first steps toward equalizing estates, toward developing personal and public freedom, the idea of nationality as a basis and standard for politics enjoyed substantial success."[22] Gradovskii reasoned that "because of these 'cosmopolitan' reforms, which freed the masses of the Russian population, and provided the best support for the security of the individual, for more free thought, and for more space for self-expression—because of all these, the development of Russia in a *national* sense became possible."[23]

A direct orientation toward Western European models can be traced even in the activity of those representatives of the regime who normally are associated exclusively with the defense of the autocracy and not with the Great Reforms. For instance, D. A. Tolstoi in 1868 formulated and justified the autocracy's educational policy in Poland in the following way:

> The Sovereign Emperor, who is so generously spreading the means of education in this region, is fully justified in his hope that this will serve not to alienate it, but to bring it closer to other parts of Empire. The introduction and intensification of the teaching of Russian is designed with this goal . . . This measure is by no means new; you can see it in all European states where national consciousness is strong, where the numerousness of the pre-eminent tribe naturally attracts other peoples to it, and where therefore the state language becomes the school language.[24]

Ethno-cultural unification was perceived as an essential element of modernization, and not just as a means of counteracting it. Moreover, Tolstoi used this approach not only in Poland but everywhere: "In the local educational institutions Russians sit next to Moldavians, Bulgarians, Greeks, and Jews. They all are united by the Russian school, and the unifying power of civilization is the most solid one."[25]

Nevertheless, the government's adoption of a nationalist course was not unambiguous and in any case did not achieve a solid union of the government and nationalist intellectuals. As Kappeler correctly noted, by virtue of its European origins any national movement (including the Russian one) "naturally had to connect purely national aspirations with social and political demands and thus to define its anti-state direction, because the autocratic state impeded essential transformations."[26] "Impeded" here of course assumes the opposition's point of view. The objective facts of the government's reformist activity were perceived by public opinion, with its typical impatience, as absolutely insufficient.

N. I. Turgenev, who devoted a special work to ethno-political problems in Russia, offers an example of the unification of democratic and nationalist premises during the reform period. According to Turgenev's book, published in Paris in 1866, "the weakness of the Russian element—civil, moral, religious weakness—is a major, essential reason for the calamitous position of the Western region."[27] His proposal for solving this problem was completely democratic—replacement of estate inequality by national equality. It is revealing that for Turgenev the empire's traditional preservation of a decisive position for peripheral elites had completely lost any basis. He saw this policy as completely inappropriate to a modernized system of values, and did not even consider the question of its functionality. "Put the Russian on the same level with the Pole who has dominated him thus far; make him abide by the same law that the Pole was abiding by before"— he is apparently talking about the necessity of developing the foundations for representative democracy—and "the question of the dominance of the Russian element in the Western region will be solved by itself, since then seven will stand with equal rights versus one."[28] Moreover, Turgenev considered it essential to carry out an extremely explicit program of building a democratic national state (national precisely because of its democratic nature) on the entire territory of the empire.

> All this roughness, all this odd inappropriateness that we now see in the state life of the Russian people and in its relationship to other nations will then disappear. The latter, of course, will not disappear—let them live and prosper—however, the Russian element then will be so powerful and influential that the proximity with alien elements will only be useful, and in any case harmless, for the common work of the land. Foreign and non-Russian [*inostrannaia i inorodnaia*] speech will not lapse into silence. However, when in the press and in zemstvo meetings Russian speech rings out with its full rights, then drowning out all others, it will reach all corners of the state and persuade all its inhabitants of the undervalued benefit of state unity, unity in greatness, in well-being, unity in conditions of common prosperity.[29]

The same evolutionary course was considered optimal by many representatives of the liberal bureaucracy. Thus, P. A. Valuev wrote in his diary:

> In order to keep Poland from ever being independent, it is sufficient that Russia continues to live. However, in order for Poland to irrevocably join Russia and become closely tied to it, it is necessary to grant Russian people political life. People whose political rights are limited to the right to pay taxes, the right to become an army recruit, and the right to shout "hurrah!" do not yet have the strength to assimilate [others].[30]

Valuev fully acknowledged that regional unevenness in the course of modernization, especially in the civic-political sphere, presented a major obstacle to the implementation of the nation-state program. He observed, "We constantly forget that besides the complication of the Polish question arising from differences in religious confessions, it is made more difficult by the differences in degrees of public life and civilization."[31]

But this realization was not adequately reflected in actual politics, since the inescapable question of revising the autocratic character of the Russian state structure was absolutely unacceptable. The administration, whose imperative was the maximum preservation of stability and maximum retention of control over the course of transition, "was watchful and suspicious of all trends within the Russian national movement that called into question traditional legitimacy and the autocracy's monopoly on power."[32] This position spread to nationalists loyal to the autocracy simply because a consistent implementation of their proposals would have in any case led to an excessively sharp break from tradition. A similar view was expressed in the negative reaction of Nicholas I to the suggestions of Iu. F. Samarin concerning the Ostsee region. These suggestions were repeated by Samarin in even more resolute form in the 1860s in a series of works published for the most part abroad under the general title of "The Borderlands of Russia."[33] They encountered the same negative response from Alexander II. That is why "none of the trends of the national Russian movement in Russia became part of a durable coalition with the state, which in principle clung to pre-national estate-dynastic imperial patriotism."[34]

On the other hand, despite a refusal to adopt an unambiguously nationalist program, "nationalist currents penetrated military and upper bureaucratic circles and exercised an influence on politics."[35] Thus, the administration's policy with respect to the Baltic provinces was corrected to a certain extent. The objective conditions for this again were created by the reforms:

> During the period after the emancipation of the peasants and other Great Reforms, the scale of voluntary, spontaneous Russification grew substantially. Railroad construction, economic expansion, and modernization connected the periphery to the Russian center more closely. Development of industry and the domestic market, improvement of communications, and the expansion of prospects for professional growth and social mobility created new advantages not only for Russians, but also for representatives of other peoples.[36]

These developments, produced by the demands of an industrial society in formation, raised the possibility of a closer integration of the Baltic region into Russia. "Supporters of cultural Russification suggested that for the peripheral nations integration into the political and administrative structure of the empire was insufficient. Russia, from their point of view, could become a modern national state only if its peripheral minorities accepted the language, culture, and religious values of the Russian people,"[37] and they seemed to show their readiness for this course. Apparently, this assessment of the situation explains the translation of official correspondence in the Baltic provinces into Russian undertaken during the reign of Alexander II (1867), and also the reform of local city self-government (1877) that eliminated its former domination by Baltic Germans.

After 1863 there was an explicit transition toward the policy of cultural unification and Russification in other areas, but this was not accompanied by any official confirmation of a change of ethno-political course. The government was extremely hostile to the Ukrainian, Belorussian, and Lithuanian national movements, and with a series of administrative repressions slowed their politicization. Both the evident connection between these movements and Polish national-radicalism, and their encouragement by Austria—especially the Ukrainian movement, including the move of organizational and propaganda centers into the region—strengthened the perception of their leaders' cultural and educational activities as a political challenge, one that logically would lead, in the words of N. V. Mezentsov, the future chief of gendarmes and the head of the Third Department, to the "real political separation of Malorossiia."[38] It is revealing that the initiative concerning Russification of Ukraine came from P. A. Valuev, fully in accord with his views on the future of Russia as a national state. At the same time, the very existence of distinct non-Russian ethnic identities among representatives of these nations was denied, often in outright contradiction with appearances. In the words of Kappeler, "Belorussians, Ukrainians, and even Lithuanians were seen as 'Western Russians,' as 'Malorossians,' and thus as a constituent part of the Russian nation that needed to be 'protected' from the Poles."[39] It is important to note that such a response, as paradoxical as this may seem, can be considered adequate to the situation, since in circumstances of industrial modernization any affirmation of the ethno-cultural specificity of a group, even one that does not draw political conclusions, will lead to such conclusions sooner or later. Affirmations of ethno-cultural distinctiveness were easily transformed into demands for national independence through the united efforts of intellectual and other elites at this time. "Between the expression of one's distinctiveness and the demand for limited autonomy a strong connection arises, which cannot be destroyed by any historical circumstances."[40] Preventing events from developing according to this scenario indeed required firm administrative control over supporters of national-cultural enlightenment.

This same pattern—the reevaluation of earlier stereotypes of interaction between the central government and peripheral peoples in order to justify changes in state policy—can also be observed in the Caucasus. Describing certain elements of imperial political culture within the genre of a case study, S. V. Lur'e demonstrated how the de facto complete dominance of regional local elites (above all, Armenians) that had been established through the implementation of imperial standards—no integrative-assimilation measures could be used against Christian nations who had equal rights with Russians to their Byzantine heritage and were more than loyal toward Russian power—began to be more and more negatively perceived.

> A completely closed situation was developing for the Russians: following the general rules of Russian indigenous and colonization policy in the region led to results that were opposite to those expected. Even where there was every external indication of homogeneity—Christian religion, good knowledge of Russian, willing participation in state affairs and military operations for the good of Russia between the population in the region and the population of metropole—in reality it turned out that the distance between peoples did not decrease.[41]

Arrangements that in the context of imperial political culture did not constitute a problem, to the extent that local elites satisfied absolutely all requirements of imperial solidarity, looked unnatural from the point of view of nation-state stereotypes. Substantively different methods of defining imperial-state or nation-state interests gave birth to a conflict, the resolution of which, however, encountered significant obstacles connected with the specifics of the military situation in the region and with the context of great power rivalry.

Nevertheless, some steps were undertaken. The elimination of the autonomous status of the Abkhazian and Megrel princedoms (1864 and 1867 respectively) as well as the extension of judicial and urban reforms into the Caucasus were supposed to advance firmer institutional integration of the region. Forced expansion of the sphere of Russian language usage, especially in educational institutions, expressed a policy, not on the agenda earlier, of cultural unification of the region with the imperial core. Describing the alternatives that appeared in the process of defining state educational policy in the Caucasus, L. S. Gatagova demonstrated how, by 1867, "in the battle between regionalists and centralists the latter won, because they managed to persuade everybody of the desirability of a rapid unification of the public education system in the regions with the system in the central provinces of the empire." This choice, according to Gatagova, was driven by the "desire to turn the Caucasus into a 'natural extension of the Russian territory.' "[42]

D. A. Tolstoi was the inspiration behind this educational policy, and not only in the Caucasus. He wrote to the emperor in 1867 as part of his report on the activity of his ministry: "The goal of the education of the natives is to bring native [*inorodcheskii*] tribes closer to the ruling Russian population and to merge them gradually into Russian civilization."[43] In general, the shift of the autocracy toward a nation-state policy in the Caucasus is associated with the name of P. A. Valuev, who stated as early as 1865 the necessity of blocking "the aspirations of both foreign [Turkish] and to some degree our [Russian] Armenians for the restoration of their national autonomy."[44] In Armenia, this program was on the whole successfully fulfilled, all the more so since the politicization of the Armenian national movement for obvious reasons had a primarily anti-Ottoman tendency. As for Georgia, there an increase in ethno-linguistic pressure led to the implementation of the standard scenario—the gradual transition of romantic patriotism into a political phase, which Kappeler dates to the 1860s.

Serious changes also took place in the relations of the administration to the Muslim peoples of Russia. Muslims in the Caucasus retained a substantial number of their traditional—primarily religious—institutions, including special mountain courts that functioned according to local customary law. Again, this policy is explained by the instability of the military political situation and also by the impossibility of a transition to forceful methods of integration right after the end of the long war in the Caucasus. Nevertheless, despite imperial tradition the Muslim nobility was not automatically equalized in rights with the Russian nobility; integration into the nobility was attained only on an individual basis.[45] As for the Muslims of the Volga region, in this area the narrowing of institutional as well as cultural autonomy was primarily a reaction to the emergence—especially among Tatars—of a movement for restoration of their historical identity, expressed most visibly in the mass exit of baptized Tatars from the Orthodox church.[46] Responses to the Muslim revival movement included not only the renewal of Orthodox missionary activity (associated primarily with the Brotherhood of St. Gurii, founded in Kazan in 1867), but also an intensification of both institutional initiatives, such as the liquidation of Tatar self-government in Kazan and the elimination of the special status of the Bashkirs, including the extension of obligatory military service to them, and cultural repression, in the form of the abolition of Tatar language study in Kazan's gymnasia.

The choice of an ethno-political strategy to be applied to Kazakh and especially Central Asian Muslims turned out to be complex. As O. I. Zhigalina[47] has demonstrated, Russian domestic policy in this region was formed under the strong influence of strategic military considerations connected to Russian-British rivalry. As in the Caucasus, this circumstance set limits upon the intensity of intrusion into the traditional order. Policy was further constrained by ongoing expansion (from 1864 until the end of nineteenth century), since subsequent successes in this endeavor depended, to a large extent, upon the degree of acceptability of concrete forms of Russian rule to the local population. If in Kazakhstan the 1860s were marked by the transition to relatively decisive institutional integration (which led, among other things, to the Kazakh uprising of 1869), the policy in Central Asia was much more careful, associated primarily with the name of K. P. von Kaufman, the governor of Turkestan from 1867.

The literature suggests various assessments of Kaufman's course toward "firm and consistent ignoring of Islam" and its institutions (including the specific local ethno-cultural complex formed by Islam), a strategy that did not make provisions for any harsh unification measures. The preservation of a certain degree of autonomy for lower levels of local self-government (right up to the independent election of *aul* leaders), the free issuing of Russian passports to the population, the absence at first of intervention (except for the abolition of slavery) into traditional forms of social-economic relationships were described as the "bases for a synthesis of local traditional and Russian principles in the sphere of state-building and economic life,"[48] and thus as essentially imperial methods of governing peripheral regions and of solving problems of ethno-cultural heterogeneity. Daniel Brower takes an analogous position, placing Kaufman's policy in the context of traditional Russian imperialism. However, Brower's explanation for the motives behind Kaufman's policy corrects the perception of the latter as unambiguously traditional. Brower connects the resurgence of imperial methods with the expansion of scientific (mostly ethnographic) interest in ethnic diversity and, as a consequence, its reception as a positive value.

> Kaufman had put in place a policy that was a direct descendant of the Catherinian legacy of colonial rule . . . Kaufman's project remained firmly embedded in local practices, and imperial visions of the future.

Paternalistic policies, backed by modern science, sought to combat the vestiges of backwardness and foster constructive cultural, economic, and political ideals and behavior.[49]

Thus the use of imperial methods by Kaufman can be interpreted as a particular side effect of modernizing processes in the sphere of mentality.

One can nonetheless raise serious doubts about the grounds on which Kaufman's policy has been classified as belonging to the imperial tradition. Such facts as the gradual unification of the tax system as well as other structural transformations, and in addition the refusal to integrate local elites into the Russian nobility, allowed Kappeler to conclude that "neither nomadic nor settled Central Asians were considered full citizens of Russia. . . . Thus, Central Asians remained colonial peoples, segregated from Russians, and their leadership, too, was not socially integrated into imperial structures."[50] This occurred despite the fact that, according to the imperial paradigm, the only pretext for any kind of segregation was the criterion of political loyalty, and not ethno-cultural considerations. Based on documentary evidence, V. S. Diakin has suggested that the preservation in Central Asia of local ways of life was motivated situationally, not according to principle, and was considered to be a temporary measure. According to Brower, Kaufman simply considered these methods to be more effective than harsh opposition to Islamic traditions. "He suggested that . . . Islam would collapse 'from patent and rigorous disdain.'"[51]

Doubts about the ultimate assimilationist intention of Kaufman's policy are connected primarily with his explicitly stated and consistently followed principle of religious toleration. However, the absence of any kind of open Orthodox propaganda or missionary activity in Central Asia, as S. V. Lur'e has shown, was quite fully compensated for by the use of secular methods of assimilation, above all, by means of the educational system, including material incentives to local dwellers whose children went to Russian schools. "The dissemination of the Orthodox faith was replaced . . . by Russified educational activities, as if these substituted for Christian civilization."[52] In the governor-general's own formulation: "We must introduce Russian Christian civilization to the Turkestan region, but not try to offer the Orthodox religion to the indigenous population."[53] The obvious contradiction bears witness to the displacement of imperial sacral legitimation of Russian dominion by nation-state legitimation. The notion of a special Russian mission was preserved, but its universalistic character was being emasculated and replaced by civilizationism, based on the per-

474   *Sviatoslav Kaspe*

ception, inherent to nationalism, of a particular culture as unquestionably supreme.

Similar difficulties arise when one attempts an unambiguous interpretation of such a fundamental turn in Russian native policy as the elaboration and implementation of N. I. Il'minskii's pedagogical system. The essence of this system was the introduction of intensive Orthodox education of non-Russians—regardless of their current religious confession—by means of missionary schools, where teaching was conducted in native languages. In particular, the policy required organizing translations of the Bible and other religious texts, which earlier in Russia had only happened sporadically, into these languages, as well as the virtually unprecedented practice of celebrating religious services in the national languages. Il'minskii's system assumed the parallel study of Russian language and a gradual transition to teaching in it. Such wide-ranging rehabilitation of the languages of non-Russian peoples and their de facto co-equality with Russian (at least in one aspect) met with a number of objections from the supporters of cultural homogeneity. These objections were relatively far-sighted, since the long-term effect of the use of Il'minskii's system "turned out to be that with the creation of a written language, the development of schools in the native language, and the formation of a narrow layer of their own intelligentsia . . . the ground was laid for the development of national movements. . . . [T]he methods of missionary activity among Tatars to a significant extent contributed to the creation of the Islamic reform movement."[54]

However, the rise of national cultures and particularly the politicization of the national factor were by no means among Il'minskii's goals; his ideas were not connected with imperial stereotypes. On the contrary, this educational strategy sought to gradually, smoothly, and, it was believed, effectively draw non-Russians (*inorodtsy*) into the orbit of Russian culture. The system reflected that same reassessment of values that can be seen in Kaufman's policies. The religious factor is only of secondary importance, and Christianization is understood not so much as an end in itself, but as a means to Russification. In the end, official circles accepted Il'minskii's system as corresponding fully to the autocracy's general ethno-political policy. This attitude was expressed, for example, in the "Rules on Methods for Educating the Peoples Inhabiting Russia" (1870). The interpretation of the Il'minskii system as a specific and even refined means to implement a nation-state program is supported by D. A. Tolstoi's evaluation—"the ultimate goal of the education of all non-Russians . . . must be their Russification and merging with the Russian people"[55]—and K. P. Pobedonost-sev's opinion that Il'minskii's pedagogy "is the only possible method for the education and, ultimately, Russification of non-Russians."[56]

Thus the systemic modernization initiated by the Great Reforms led to substantial changes in the content of Russian political culture and to a practically universal transition (depending on local specifics, in more or less harsh forms) toward institutional and cultural unification. The only region where practically no such tendencies were found remained Finland, which traditionally possessed a broader autonomy within the empire and at the same time, unlike Poland, did not openly—and especially not violently—revolt against Russian rule. I. N. Novikova, who shares the opinion of L. Kruzius-Arenberg, connects the regime's rejection of the compulsory Russification of Finland with its desire to preserve untouched the "European façade of Russia."[57] Most likely, other factors played a role as well. The Polish part of this "façade" was subjected to considerable reconstruction without any consideration of the position of the West. Evidently, the very requirements of intensive state-driven modernization did not allow, under ordinary circumstances, the extension of the Russification policy to a region that was substantially ahead in the modernization process compared with strictly Russian territories and was also culturally connected with the West through its active Swedish minority. Even in the middle of the nineteenth century Finland was, in all probability, still privately considered as a kind of model, from the perspective of modernizers and their values.

Only a reevaluation of these values opened the way for the aspirations of those "forces that, calling for the preservation of a 'united and indivisible empire,' protested any display of Finnish separatism."[58] Such aspirations for a united empire, as L. V. Suni has shown, were already spreading in this period, but at this time they were more of a defensive nature—expressed in attempts to block further extension of Finnish autonomy—rather than an aggressive policy. Meanwhile, the cause of Finnish autonomy took on new dimensions under the pressure of the already formed and to a great extent politicized national movement, as evinced by the approval of the Sejm's charter in 1869, and the granting in 1878 of permission to the Grand Duchy to have its own army not intended for use outside its boundaries. However, the planned expansion of the Sejm's powers extending to the creation of an administration accountable to it and including the right of legislative initiative did not occur. "The rejection of a new form of government in essence created the necessary basis for a fuller incorporation of Finland into the empire in the future."[59]

The reassessment of imperial traditions brought about by the modernization and rationalization of Russian political culture also led to changes in the system of administrative organs. An element of the system directly connected to the political technology of empire was the institution of *namestniki*, or governors-general, created by the provincial reform of 1775. The legal nature of the power of governor-generals was not clearly defined. In particular, the question of whether the governor-general belonged to the system of administration or only to the system of supervision was not definitively resolved. In practice, "the enormous power of the governor-general was based mainly on the personal trust of the monarch and was almost unchecked."[60] The capacity of the central bureaucratic apparatus to influence the situation in the districts led by *namestniki* and governors-general was minimal, which gave these leaders quasi-political power. Such specialized territorial-administrative units were created above all in the periphery, but also in the capitals or particularly remote territories, that is, in regions where the maintenance of stability required a firm consolidation of authority and of its capacity for action.

The creation of distinctive peripheral governmental institutions is highly characteristic of empires. The situation of the borderlands is substantially different for empires when compared to that of localized states, even if empires, which potentially and ideally comprise all observable *oikumena,* typically do not have a clear border as such. "The state clearly defines its territory and its competence over this territory, as well as outside of it (in international affairs). An empire does not have such clear borders."[61] Accordingly, the mechanisms of government and control used by empires and localized states in the border zone are functionally different. The Roman *limes* or the *marks* of Charlemagne's empire were prototypes of imperial border structures. Besides their tasks of natural defense, they served other, not so obvious, functions, one of which is described by M.V. Il'in:

> Conflict between the unstoppable drive of an open system toward expansion and the instinct of self-preservation presents an extremely serious challenge. The typical answer suggests setting limits for your own expansion that would achieve a balance and even a certain accumulation of resources for the creation of an effective reserve. The solution takes place in the form of a special structure—the frontier zone or *limes.*

Although systems of outposts and fortifications are formally created for protection against the raids of external barbarians, the emergence of a border zone, often relatively wide, whose function consists of extinguishing the system's own expansionist aspirations, becomes more important.[62]

In general, the institution of governors-general patently shows that in the Russian empire there were "no clear distinctions between the spheres of colonial administration and external policy, nor between colonial administration and internal policy."[63] The extraordinary breadth of the authority wielded by governors-generals and their deputies was to a great extent essential, especially in the periphery: "Personal power acted as a substitute for a concentrated administrative presence, which was lacking on the periphery."[64]

But nation-state formation, with its tendency toward rationalization, came to be at odds with the preservation of the governor-generalship, an institution that did not fit into a regular hierarchical structure. A complete abolition of the institution did not occur, because the very size of the empire, combined with underdeveloped communications as well as tensions in internal politics, did not permit a complete renunciation of strong regional authority. Nonetheless, between 1856 and 1881 eight governor-general districts were eliminated, primarily not among those in the periphery. Other steps in this direction included the central administration's attempts to increase control over the activity of the governor-general of Turkestan (not very successful) and, in a certain sense, the liquidation of the Kingdom of Poland and the post of its deputy (the governor-general who replaced him had less authority). After 1879 and in connection with the growth of the revolutionary movement, governors-general were restored in St. Petersburg, Khar'kov, and Odessa. However, their powers were limited to police functions. Organs of local civil authority remained under the direct supervision of central organs, and the semi-independent role of governors-general as direct representatives of the autocrat was never restored. It is highly significant that "P. A. Valuev, while Minister of Internal Affairs, took an explicitly anti-governor-general position,"[65] and consistently supported a nation-state approach for solving current problems.

The gradual abandonment of external expansion, which had been one of the most stable constants of Russian policy, is yet another confirmation of the erosion of the imperial component of Russian state modernization. If peaceful expansion (in Siberia and the Far East) for all practical purposes ceased because natural boundaries had been reached, then military expansion, which often had not required any special explanation, now, in the absence of an explicit rational justification, began to be perceived as meaningless.

The irrational character of imperial expansion and the dispute over its necessity are thrown in to relief when one looks at the situation in Central Asia. As we know, the increasing military-political pressure on Russia's southern neighbors (the Emirate of Bukhara, the khanates of Khiva and Kokand, and also the virtually independent Turkmen tribes) in the second half of the nineteenth century was connected above all with the fact that "certain generals on the periphery managed to take initiative into their own hands. . . . Guided in part by a craving for personal fame, they sometimes carried out military operations on their own,"[66] operations that the central government, informed post-factum, could not prevent. The milieu of liberal bureaucrats such as D. A. Miliutin and A. M. Gorchakov (respectively heads of the ministry of the army and ministry of foreign affairs, i.e., of institutions that should have had exclusive authority over the question of further expansion of state borders) produced a document expressing the limits of future Russian policy in Central Asia. This document stated unambiguously that "further expansion of our possessions [*vladeniia*] in Central Asia does not comply with the interests of Russia and leads only to the reduction and weakening of its forces. We must establish a fixed, permanent border on newly attained lands and give it the meaning of a real state boundary."[67] Nevertheless, despite the emperor's approval of this concept in 1864 and despite the distribution of corresponding instructions to local authorities, in 1865, without any sanction from the central administration, the military governor of Turkestan, M. G. Cherniaev, captured Tashkent. (In full accordance with imperial tradition, the victor guaranteed its inhabitants inviolability of their beliefs and customs.) This destabilizing action further aggravated the situation and made inevitable both more conquests and the use of imperial political technologies to secure their results.

The most typical example of this development was the formal preservation of the state sovereignty of the Emirate of Bukhara and the Khanate of Khiva, both of which were actually under complete Russian control and played the role of buffer states. Direct analogies to this can be found, for example, in Roman political practice. In this instance P. A. Valuev again reacted extremely negatively to the reanimation of imperial traditions, and made the following well-known entry in his diary: "Tashkent is captured by General Cherniaev. Nobody knows why and for what. . . . The ministries of finance and of the army are puzzled. There is something erotic in everything that happens on the remote periphery of our empire."[68] This graphic description can be understood as a testimony to the spontaneous nature of imperial expansion and the absence of a rational explanation.

Russian policy concerning the Eastern question was especially contradictory, precisely because of the collision of substantially differing political programs. "There is no other aspect of Russian policy in the nineteenth century that so clearly displays hesitations, illogicality, and contradictions, as the geopolitical vector leading from Moscow to the south through the Balkans, Constantinople, Palestine, and Ethiopia."[69] S. V. Lur'e has explored this subject in the context of the problem of the imperial character of Russian statehood. She describes in detail how this "ideal geostrategic line" became the "pivot for the confrontation of two ideologies —'Byzantinism' and Pan-Slavism, i.e., the arena of collision between the central principle of Russian empire—the religious principle—and the national one."[70] More precisely, three main positions on the Eastern question can be identified in the second half of the nineteenth century. A comparison of these approaches provides a clear view of the growing internal contradictions in Russian political culture of that period. Opinions about the goals and character of the Russian-Turkish war of 1877–1879 expressed in public and governmental circles can be classified as follows:

(1) Imperial tradition unquestionably defined the capture of Constantinople and the re-establishment of the Orthodox Empire as the main imperative of both the war itself and Russian policy in the region in general. It is interesting that this is exactly how the war was perceived by the masses, the bearers of more archaic layers of political culture and those least touched by Westernization. However, even prominent representatives of the political ideology of "Byzantinism," such as K. N. Leontiev, realized that implementation of this program would paradoxically cast doubt on Russian (*rossiiskii*) identity, because it would move the newly attained sacral-political center outside the limits of the hearth of Russian civilization. The restoration of the Second Rome would inevitably remove the grounds for the existence of the Third Rome.

(2) The nation-state concept in its pure form was expressed by those statesmen who, thinking in categories of state interest rationally understood, did not see any sense in expansion as such. This position was shared, for example, by A. N. Kuropatkin, who served in Turkestan before the war

and personally could have encountered the complications of uncontrolled expansion, and was clearly expressed by R. Streltsov, as cited by S. V. Lur'e: "As attractive as the idea of conquest and annexation of this city veiled in romance appears, it is necessary to remember that any acquisition is only valuable in so far as the sum of unavoidable sacrifices does not exceed the sum of the benefits it brings."[71] These words express a renunciation of the imperial perspective on expansion as a value-rational activity—justified by a belief in its absolute value—in favor of expansion considered as an instrumental-rational strategy of maximization of profits and minimalization of costs, an approach which is followed, as a rule, by local (national) states.

(3) Pan-Slavic ideology occupied an intermediate position between these two poles. It envisioned an intensification of Russian expansion in the direction of the Balkans, Constantinople, and the Near East, but saw this program as inspired not so much by religious-mystical considerations as by pragmatic ones. Among N. Ia. Danilevskii's arguments in favor of the seizure of Constantinople, its "gigantic moral influence" occupies last place, yielding not only to strategic military benefits, but also to "an economy of financial resources."[72] The "Pan-Slavic Federation, with Russia at its head, and its capital in Tsargrad,"[73] as conceived by Danilevskii, did not rely upon an imperial ideal, but was seen as a rational method of guaranteeing the interests of the Slavic cultural-historic type. Slavdom in the framework of this concept was understood as a hypertrophied nation, that is, a community in which both political and cultural identities were blended, even if the degree of commonality of the latter was greatly exaggerated by Danilevskii. E. Tassin describes a fluctuation between two types of temporal orientation occurring during the nation-building stage: one directed into the past and appropriating it, and the other, addressed to the future and forming it by means of selective choices in the present. "In the second case, nationality is the sign not of an existing community but of a theoretically possible one, not of an organically formed group but of a group that is emerging selectively and conventionally."[74] In addition, there may be substantial variations among definitions of the boundaries of this emerging group. For example, Danilevskii and like-minded thinkers essentially proposed an alternative project for the Russian nation-state, assuming its formation not within the actual, but rather within the potential limits of the historic empire. "Danilevskii, breaking with Christian tradition, deprives the state and society of a status 'exceeding the limits of the earthly.' In other words, he performs an act of desacralization, of seculari-

zation of the state, political-legal culture, and society."[75] Despite the extremely negative position of Danilevskii and all thinkers of this circle toward Western civilization, there is clearly a genetic link between this attitude and the mentality of modernization and Westernization.

The clash of all these points of view did not lead to a satisfactory resolution. Neither Alexander II, nor the most rationally thinking ministers such as A. M. Gorchakov, were sure about the necessity of war; they tried in various ways to delay, if not avoid it. The war nevertheless began under the strong pressure of public and mass opinion; "the government was obliged by the people to officially declare war."[76] It was typical that General M. G. Cherniaev, who already in Central Asia had recommended himself as a devoted follower of imperial politics, became one of the leaders of the volunteer movement. The war was carried on almost to the point of achieving its final goal. However, in a decisive moment, nation-state logic again overpowered imperial logic. The decision not to occupy Istanbul in 1878 was evidently not only motivated by the possible intervention of England—military success was nonetheless guaranteed—but also signified a refusal to implement the imperial program, even at the price of a radical reduction of the benefits that Russia could have potentially gotten out of this war. Discussions about the meaning and aims of Russian policy on the Eastern question continued up to World War I, still confined within the same circle of possible alternatives.

Thus, despite the retention in political culture of imperial ideas about the absolute value of external expansion, in this sphere the rational point of view generally prevailed, and expansion, if not brought to an end, was at least significantly slowed down. This conclusion is supported by the research of R. Taagepera. In his diagram, the growth of Russian territory subjected to a logarithmic approximation becomes a smooth curve with only two pronounced fluctuations. The first falls in the middle of the sixteenth century and represents a sharp increase in the rate of territorial growth; this coincided with a period in which the imperial component prevailed in the Russian statehood paradigm. The second occurs in the 1860s and 1870s and indicates a no less sharp decrease in the rate of growth (which until then had been practically continuous) until the curve becomes a horizontal line.[77] This falling off is quite probably connected with the large-scale modernization of Russian political culture at that time and accordingly with a reconsideration of external policy goals.

The nation-state aspect of Alexander II's policy usually remains in the background; it does not fit very well with the image of the Tsar-Liberator.

The following reign is invariably described as a time of the autocracy's resolute transition to a consistently nationalist course. The conversion of nationalism into a semi-official governmental ideology during Alexander III's reign is beyond doubt. However, this change was quantitative, not qualitative. All the basic elements of a nationalist ethno-political course emerged back in the 1860s and 1870s. Nevertheless, the ethno-political situation in the time of Alexander III had, in certain respects, an essentially new character, and thus bore within itself a powerful potential for conflict.

The problems facing the autocracy after March 1, 1881, in many respects were typologically similar to the problems of the first years of Nicholas's reign. The increasing threat of a revolutionary outburst was undoubtedly a consequence of modernization processes getting out of control. The responses to this challenge, as before, were administrative repression and rejection of political modernization. Both policies were justified ideologically by setting Russian tradition against foreign sedition. One of the instruments of this struggle was the actively exploited external appearance and image of Alexander III as a "Russian tsar." However, if, as shown above, during Nicholas I's reign political reaction had meant the conservation of imperial orientations in a struggle against an amalgam of democratic and nationalistic ideas, in the 1880s such a turn was already fundamentally impossible. It would have opened the way to national movements among the peoples of the empire, who were by this time already significantly politicized. Also, by this time modernization had affected the mentalities of governing elites so much that the goal of strengthening statehood was inevitably understood as the goal of strengthening national statehood. This view of the nature of the state was dominant practically everywhere. Thus, both subjective and objective reasons forced the government of Alexander III—which largely regarded modernization as such as a negative phenomenon and had made attempts to slow it down with a whole range of counter-reforms—to follow a modernizing policy in the ethno-political sphere. This development was inexorably turning the Russian empire into a nation-state.

The facts of increased administrative, police, and political pressure on non-Russian peoples during the reign of Alexander III are well known and have been frequently described by scholars. Studies of the ethno-political processes of the time produced by both Russian[78] and foreign[79] authors paint identical pictures of the triumph of a nationalist course, one that did not omit a single ethno-cultural community, whether compactly settled or dispersed, from its purview. The mere existence of multiculturalism began to be perceived as an anomaly that ought to be eliminated. This was, for example, the political position of A. E. Alektorov, a prominent figure in education in the 1870s and 1880s, who had done a great deal to spread the pedagogical system of N. I. Il'minskii and later became engaged in the nationalist movement. Alektorov's work, published in the early twentieth century,[80] contained a list of claims on behalf of the Russian nation directed at all the more or less significant ethnic groups in Russia, clearly demonstrating the depth and radicalism of the changes that had taken place in public consciousness (and unconsciousness as well).

The building of a nation-state was being forced forward. Administrative nationalism was spreading, both in breadth—new attitudes were being implanted everywhere, including such regions as Finland, which had not been subjected to Russification earlier—as well as in depth. "The Russian government had finally decided to move beyond administrative Russification and decisively took up cultural Russification."[81] This analysis of the situation in the Baltic area could be applied to most of the other territories of the empire.

It is possible, however, to agree with Kappeler's objection to the one-dimensional interpretation of the administration's national policy as a Russifying one. Indeed, "the policy with regard to many peoples was not at all directed toward their integration, but rather toward their segregation and discrimination."[82] Such policies concerned peoples that preserved nomadic or hunting and gathering ways of life and, with some reservations, Jews and Muslims of Central Asia. However, in this case, integration and segregation were two sides of the same coin. The building of a monolithic political and cultural community requires lopping off groups whose participation in this process is considered inadmissible for one reason or another. The dissemination of civilizational characteristics to the peoples of Russia and the colossal differences in the degree to which they were included in modernization processes—differences associated with the imperial nature of Russian statehood—predetermined the choice, in a number of cases, of segregating, rather than integrating, political technologies.

Certain elements of imperial tradition were preserved even during this period. However, it is clear that these were relocated to the peripheral zones of political culture, where they either acquired a purely ritual character, or if included in a new context, radically changed their meaning. Thus, pro-governmental propaganda periodically exploited the notions of the providential and sacral character of Russian statehood and, accordingly, the tsar's power. As M. N. Katkov wrote: "The Russian Tsar is granted a special distinction from other world rulers. He is not only the sovereign of his country and the leader of his people. He is appointed by God to be the guardian and protector of the Orthodox Church. The Russian Tsar is not only the heir of his ancestors, but also a successor to the Caesars."[83] However, this reference to the tsar's universal mission (which by its nature is superior to any ethnically specific substratum) served only as an affirmation of national exclusivity. The tsar's universal mission was used as an additional argument in favor of preserving the integrity of the autocratic regime; it did not demand any specific actions toward realizing a global imperial program.

Analogous attempts to reanimate imperial political technologies can also be seen in administrative practices concerning non-Russian peoples. A. I. Termen, who served as a middle-level official in the Turkestan governor-general's office in the 1880s and 1890s, argued against incautious Russification. He based his argument on the notion that "only a person educated in Russia or in Russian educational institutions and working in a Russian environment can be subject to Russian law. The native, even if he knows Russia by name, should be governed by the laws under which his mentality, character, views, and habits were formed. And before changing his laws, one should change his way of life."[84] However, the need for integration, including cultural integration, was never doubted, and it was justified in a consistently modernizing spirit:

> An administrator is a representative of the government, and as such should lead the population entrusted to him on the road of progress. And therefore an administrator is above all an educator in the highest sense of the word . . . He must call to life and action all potential forces, using for this all the information from science and the superior culture, which he represents to the non-Russians [*inorodtsy*]. The end goal of such an administrator-educator is to rework from the material assigned to him an entity, reliably joined to the root element of imperial culture.[85]

Termen considered education to be the one of the most important means of this smooth but steady integration and as an optimal method for correcting traditional cultural stereotypes: "If . . . an official leader [*nachal'nik*] trusted by the people had the opportunity to educate children, then after the first few children, hundreds and thousands of children would be brought to him, and the people would naturally proceed along the path toward merging with the root [*korennyi,* Russian] population."[86]

Imperial technologies, therefore, were perceived only as a means, completely subordinated in the sphere of ends to modernizing, nation-state stereotypes. However, even such an approach was met with suspicion because it appeared too moderate. Termen provides many examples of the negative attitudes of his superiors toward his attempts, for example, to use the norms of *sharia* to resolve disputes among local residents. His work appeared in the form of a polemic against what had become, by the time his book was published, a well-established point of view.

It is important, however, to note that the period of counter-reform did not involve a rejection of modernization as such, but only stricter control over its course. "Segmented" modernization, "associated with administrative systematization, state unification, and social construction as far back as the reigns of Peter I and Catherine II,"[87] aimed primarily at solving military-political and later, in connection with the start of industrial era, economic problems. Even the harsh obstruction of modernization processes in the sphere of politics and ideology was only partial, since all major ethno-political initiatives in this period originated from imperatives of modernization. However, this kind of policy led to further contradictions within Russian political culture. Tensions that had been accumulating in its political space for decades threatened to explode.

The self-perpetuating introduction into Russian political culture of elements alien to it produced an array of negative secondary effects. B. Badie analyzed these in his study, *The Imported State: The Westernization of the Political Order*: "In those areas where the imported structure proved to be universally applicable, it led to the production of particularism; where it was aimed at the construction of a monolithic political order, the discreteness of social spaces only increased; where legal-rational concepts took root, the authorities began to act in a neo-patrimonial way."[88] Modernization, especially in its catching-up form, is constantly threatened by a conflict between traditional and innovative elements, a conflict that usually wreaks havoc at all levels of social life, from the ideological and ethical to the group and the individual. This conflict can cause a breakdown of modernization, incurring a spontaneous massive restoration of traditional structures and orientations. When the pace of change is moderate, a synchronization of changes in various spheres of social life lowers the risk of such a breakdown, while differences in the pace of change in, for example, economic and cultural or social and political modernization—other combinations are possible—increase the risk of extreme reactions.

In the Russian case, a dangerous situation was created by a rupture of the objectively existing, as noted above, connection between nationalism and democracy that arises during the course of modernization under specific socio-cultural conditions of successful industrial development. This circumstance can be seen outside the context of modernization theory: "A non-conservative interpretation of nationality [*narodnost'*], the old dogma of official ideology, came into conflict with the deep and consistently anti-democratic character of this ideology."[89] This contradiction was even more pronounced because the whole nationalist ideology had been built upon a perception of the people—the *Russian* (*russkii*) people—as an unconditionally superior value, but not, paradoxically, as a source of power. The natural development observed by M. Walzer in Eastern Europe a century later had already been set in motion. On the one hand, peoples began to perceive themselves each separately as a *demos*, i.e., as self-sufficient political societies. On the other hand, in multicultural societies the existence even in rudimentary form of democratic institutions or merely democratic ideas leads inexorably, according to Walzer's thesis, to the recognition of the existence of *several demoses*. And this in turn produces certain political results: "The multinational character of these societies was formed by proto-democratic and even anti-democratic regimes. However, since they used the notion of the 'people' in their political terminology, they had to include traditional communities in their organizational structures, thus sanctioning the reproduction of their languages, historical memories, customs, ways of life, and habits."[90] Thus imperial policies enhanced nationalistic politics. "Russian institutions were constantly transmitting their nationalist rhetoric to subordinate peoples, which was no less important for the awakening of local nationalisms than acts of overt repression."[91]

The course chosen by the government thus led, on the one hand, to the growth of radical democratic movements inside the Russian nation itself as it transformed itself into a political community. (In conditions of harsh opposition, these radical movements entered an extremist phase that went as far as rejecting democratic principles in favor of class values.) On the other hand, the government's policy provoked the further politicization of the national movements of non-Russian peoples who were subject to increasingly severe unification and Russification. An alliance of both kinds of movements based on resistance to their common enemy was completely organic to this process and indeed eventually took shape. Both kinds of movements fulfilled the "gaps of sociability" emerging from conditions of "catch-up modernization," as described by Badie.

The imported state suffers from a deficit of civic culture, connected with its insecure legitimacy and low efficacy. These factors increase the significance in the non-Western world of the problem of "empty social spaces" that official policy is not able to mobilize or control, and in which are formed other forces, that substitute themselves for the state, and demand the individual's loyalty for themselves.[92]

This problem was amplified by the imperial past of Russia. As Ernest Gellner noted,

The majority of cultures or of potentially national groups step into the era of nationalism without even attempting to gain anything from it for themselves. Groups that by the logic of "precedence" could have attempted to become nations, and that could have defined themselves based on criteria that in fact defined real and effective nations in other places, are innumerable. Nonetheless, the majority of them passively submitted to their destiny—to be the witnesses of how their culture . . . slowly disappears, dissolves into the broader culture of one of the national states.[93]

The risk of transformation of nationalism from the sphere of the potentially possible into the arena of political reality increases substantially in the case of a multicultural state. This is a consequence of a cumulative effect, when the example of one people leads to analogous actions by others. It increases even more in the case of an extremely heterogeneous empire on whose territory dozens of potential nationalisms are represented and where the state's own shift to a nationalist policy can be perceived as a rejection of an imperial tradition that had amalgamated the conglomerate of diverse societies in the past.

Nevertheless, for a fairly long time the nationalist policy chosen by Alexander II and amplified by the conservative-repressive course of Alexander III produced results and ensured the preservation of relative ethno-political stability throughout the entire imperial territory. "Peace and order reigned in the Russian empire; there was not a single major uprising of the non-Russian population in the period between 1864 and 1905. Administrative unification and centralization of Russia also progressed."[94] But this situation could only last as long as mechanisms of severe social control were applied in full force; the duration of the period of accumulation of latent contradictions is proportional to the intensity of their subsequent open manifestation. The objective process of the emergence of industrial society should have cast a doubt upon the possibility of preserving these mechanisms. The deficit of political will essential to sustain these mechanisms, a deficit clearly present in the next reign, was yet to play its role. In the next century, the weakening of the system of harsh social control led to a large-scale social crisis, a revolutionary explosion, and the breakdown of modernization.

It is characteristic that no substantially new paradigms concerning the organization of Russian geopolitical space emerged during the course of this explosion; more precisely, some were proposed but turned out to be unviable. In the absence of alternatives, the restoration of Russian statehood in its Soviet form necessarily led to the revitalization of imperial mechanisms and arrangements. At the same time, a new stage of modernization was begun, but in conditions of qualitatively harsher social control, which ensured at a horrendous cost the completion of its industrial phase—increasingly considered the major content of the Soviet period in Russian history. The imperial component of Russian political culture thus demonstrated its capacity for re-actualization, which makes all the more important the problem of finding an ethno-political foundation for modernization—a problem that first emerged full-blown in the second half of the nineteenth century and then was met with only a temporary, palliative solution.

Translated by Jane Burbank

Notes

1. As L. S. Gatagova correctly notes, "the question of the degree to which Russia fits the imperial type of state . . . should be preceded by another, as yet unanswered question about the chronological boundaries (if only approximate) of the imperial period of Russian statehood." L. S. Gatagova, "Imperiia: identifikatsiia problemy," in G. A. Bordiugov, ed., *Istoricheskie issledovaniia v Rossii: Tendentsii poslednikh let* (Moscow: AIRO-XX, 1996), 339.

2. See S. I. Kaspe, *Imperiia i modernizatsiia: Obshchaia model' i rossiiskaia spetsifika* (Moscow: Rosspen, 2001) and S. I. Kaspe, "Imperii: genezis, struktura, funktsii," *Polis* 5 (1997): 5.

3. Kaspe, "Imperii," 35.

4. M. Duverger, "Le concept d'empire," *Le concept d'empire* (Paris: PUF, 1980), 8.

5. See, for example, S. N. Eisenstadt, *Tradition, Change and Modernity* (New York: John Wiley & Sons, 1973).

6. R. Bendix, "Tradition and Modernity Reconsidered," *Comparative Studies in Society and History* 3 (1967): 313–344.

7. S. N. Eisenstadt, "Introduction: Historical Traditions, Modernization and De-

velopment," in S. N. Eisenstadt, ed., *Patterns of Modernity,* vol. 1, *The West* (New York: New York University Press, 1987), 5.

8. See my extended discussion of modernization in S. N. Kaspe, "Imperskaia politicheskaia kul'tura v usloviakh modernizatsii," *Politiia* 3(1998); Kaspe, *Imperiia i modernizatsiia,* esp. 70–85.

9. A. N. Medushevskii, "Formirovanie grazhdanskogo obshchestva: reformy i kontrreformy v Rossii," in *Reformy i reformatory v istorii Rossii* (Moscow: IRI RAN, 1996), 73–74.

10. V. E. Cheshikhin-Vetrinskii, "Obshchestvennoe dvizhenie v tsartsvovanie Aleksandra II," in *Tri veka,* vol. 6 (Moscow: GIS, 1995), 117.

11. A. Kappeler, *Rossiia—mnogonatsional'naia imperiia* (Moscow: Progress-Traditsiia, 1997), 187.

12. L. E. Gorizontov, "Pomeshchik ili muzhik? Russkoe zemlevladenie v strategii resheniia pol'skogo voprosa," in *Imperskii stroi Rossii v regional'nom izmerenii (XIX–nachalo XX v.)* (Moscow: MONF, 1997), 105–114.

13. Kappeler, *Rossiia—mnogonatsional'naia imperiia,* 179.

14. A. Cohen, *Russian Imperialism: Development and Crisis* (Westport: Praeger, 1996), 53.

15. P. N. Miliukov, *Natsional'nyi vopros (Proiskhozhdenie natsional'nosti i natsional'nogo voprosa v Rossii)* (n.p., 1925), 158–159.

16. E. Gellner, *Natsii i natsionalizm* (Moscow: Progress, 1991).

17. M. Hroch, *Social Preconditions of National Revival in Europe. A Comparative Analysis of the Social Composition of Patriotic Groups among the Smaller European Nations* (Cambridge: Cambridge University Press, 1985).

18. M. Slavinskii, "Natsional'naia struktura Rossii i velikorossy," in *Formy natsional'nogo dvizheniia v sovremennykh gosudarstvakh* (St.Petersburg: Obshchestvennaia pol'za, 1910), 293.

19. Miliukov, *Natsional'nyi vopros,* 158–159.

20. Kappeler, *Rossiia—mnogonatsional'naia imperiia,* 179.

21. N. N. Zarubina, *Sotsiokul'turnye faktory khoziaistvennogo razvitiia: M. Veber i sovremennye teorii modernizatsii* (St. Petersburg.: PKhGI, 1998), 137.

22. A. D. Gradovskii, "Proshedshee i nastoiashchee," in his *Sobranie sochinenii,* vol. 6 (Moscow, 1901), 313.

23. A. D. Gradovskii, "Semia plevel," in his *Sobranie sochinenii,* vol. 6 (Moscow, 1901), 313.

24. D. A. Tolstoi, "Rech', proiznesennaia 12 sentiabria 1868 g. pri prieme prepodavatelei Varshavskoi Glavnoi shkoly," in *Rechi i stat'i grafa D. A. Tolstogo* (St. Petersburg, 1876), 13–14.

25. D. A. Tolstoi, "Rech', proiznesennaia pri osmotre Odesskogo uchebnogo okruga v Kishineve, 25 oktiabria 1875 g," in *Rechi i stat'i grafa D. A. Tolstogo* (St. Petersburg, 1876), 44.

26. Kappeler, *Rossiia—mnogonatsional'naia imperiia,* 178.

27. N. I. Turgenev, *O raznoplemennosti naseleniia v russkom gosudarstve* (St. Petersburg: Franck, 1866), 8.

28. Ibid., 9.

29. Ibid., 38.

30. *Dnevnik P. A. Valueva, ministra vnutrennikh del,* vol. 1 (Moscow: AN SSSR, 1961), 340.

31. Ibid.

32. Kappeler, *Rossiia—mnogonatsional'naia imperiia,* 179.

33. Iu. F. Samarin, "Okrainy Rossii," in *Sobranie sochinenii Iu. F. Samarina,* vol. 8 (Moscow, 1890); vol. 9 (Moscow, 1898).

34. Kappeler, *Rossiia—mnogonatsional'naia imperiia,* 180.

35. Ibid., 179.

36. E. C. Thaden, "The Russian Government," in Thaden, ed., *Russification in the Baltic Provinces and Finland, 1855–1914* (Princeton, N.J.: Princeton University Press, 1981), 8–9.

37. Ibid., 9.

38. Cited in S. V. Kuleshov, ed., *Natsional'naia politika Rossii: istoriia i sovremennost'* (Moscow: Russkii mir, 1997), 59.

39. Kappeler, *Rossiia—mnogonatsional'naia imperiia,* 188–189.

40. P. Kende, "Comment gérer le problème des minorités en Europe centrale et orientale?" *Notes et études documentaires* 19–20 (1992): 14.

41. S. V. Lur'e, "Rossiiskaia imperiia kak etnokul'turnyi fenomen i etnopoliticheskaia real'nost' Zakavkaz'ia," in *Metamorfozy traditsionnogo soznaniia* (St. Petersburg: Tip. im. Kotliakova, 1994), 161.

42. L. S. Gatagova, *Pravitel'stvennaia politika i narodnoe obrazovanie na Kavkaze v XIX v.* (Moscow: RITs "Rossiia Molodaia," 1993), 55.

43. Cited in Gatagova, *Pravitel'stvennaia politika,* 49.

44. Cited in Kuleshov, *Natsional'naia politika Rossii: istoriia i sovremennost',* 97.

45. V. S. Diakin, "Natsional'nyi vopros vo vnutrennei politike tsarizma (XIX v.)," *Voprosy istorii* 9 (1995): 135.

46. As Kappeler suggests, "Although the vast majority of Russian Muslims spoke Turkic languages, language was not as important for defining their ethnic identity as were their style of life and religion." *Rossiia—mnogonatsional'naia imperiia,* 173.

47. O. I. Zhigalina, "Dvizhushchie sily rossiiskoi politiki v Srednei Azii v XIX v.," *Tsivilizatsii i kul'tury,* vyp. 3 (Moscow: Institut vostokovedeniia RAN, 1996): 251–265.

48. Kuleshov, *Natsional'naia politika Rossii: istoriia i sovremennost',* 118.

49. Daniel R. Brower, "Islam and Ethnicity: Russian Colonial Policy in Turkestan," in Daniel R. Brower and Edward J. Lazzerini, eds., *Russia's Orient: Imperial Borderlands and Peoples, 1700–1917* (Bloomington: Indiana University Press, 1997), 131.

50. Kappeler, *Rossia—mnogonatsional'naia imperiia,* 147.

51. Diakin, Natsional'nyi vopros, 134.

52. S. V. Lur'e, "Russkie v Srednei Azii i anglichane v Indii: dominanty imperskogo soznaniia i sposoby ikh realizatsii," *Tsivilizatsii i kul'tury,* vyp. 2 (Moscow: Institut vostokovedeniia RAN, 1996): 270.

53. Cited in Lur'e, "Russkie v Srednei Azii," 270.

54. Kappeler, *Rossiia—mnogonatsional'naia imperiia,* 195.

55. Cited in A. Kh. Makhmutova, *Stanovlenie svetskogo obrazovaniia u tatar* (Kazan: Izdatel'stvo Kazanskogo universiteta, 1972), 23.

56. K. P. Pobedonostsev, "Nikolai Ivanovich Il'minskii," in Pobedonostsev, *Sochineniia* (St. Petersburg: Nauka, 1996), 156.

57. I. N. Novikova, "Velikoe kniazhestvo finliandskoe v imperskoi politike Rossii," *Imperskii stroi Rossii v regional'nom izmerenii (XIX–nachalo XX v.)* (Moscow: MONF, 1997), 134.

58. L. V. Suni, *Ocherk obshchestvenno-politicheskogo razvitiia Finlandii. 50–70-e gg. XIX v.* (Leningrad: Nauka, 1979), 85.

59. Ibid., 85.

60. A. V. Remnev, "General-gubernatorskaia vlast' v XIX stoletii. K probleme organizatsii regional'nogo upravleniia Rossiiskoi imperii," in *Imperskii stroi Rossii v regional'nom izmerenii*, 53.

61. A. F. Filippov, "Nabliudatel' imperii (imperiia kak sotsiologicheskoe poniatie i politicheskaia problema)," *Voprosy sotsiologii* 1 (1992): 104.

62. M. V. Il'in, "Geokhronopolitika—soedinenie vremen i prostranstva," *Vestnik Moskovskogo universiteta*, 12th series. *Politicheskie nauki* 2 (1997): 104.

63. S. F. Starr, "Tsarist Government: The Imperial Dimension," in *Soviet Nationality Policies and Practices* (New York: Praeger, 1978), 5.

64. Ibid., 16.

65. Remnev, "General-gubernatorskaia vlast'," 58.

66. Kappeler, *Rossiia—mnogonatsional'naia imperiia*, 144.

67. Cited in: N. S. Kiniapina, M. M. Bliev, V. V. Degoev, *Kavkaz i Sredniaia Aziia vo vneshnei politike Rossii (vtoraia polovina XVII-80-e gody XIX v.)* (Moscow: Izd-vo MGU, 1984), 274.

68. *Dnevnik P. A. Valueva*, 60–61.

69. S. V. Lur'e, "Ideologiia i geopoliticheskoe deistvie. Vektor russkoi kul'turnoi ekspansii: Balkany-Konstaninopol'-Palestina-Efiopiia," *Tsivilizatsii i kul'tury*, vyp. 3 (Moscow: Institut vostokovedeniia RAN, 1996): 153.

70. Ibid., 161.

71. Cited in S. V. Lur'e, "Ideologiia i geopoliticheskoe deistvie," 161.

72. N. Ia. Danilevskii, *Rossiia i Evropa* (Moscow: Kniga, 1991), 382.

73. Ibid., 385.

74. E. Tassin, "Identités Nationales et Citoyenneté Politique," *Esprit* 1 (1994): 98.

75. Iu. S. Pivovarov, "Nikolai Danilevskii—v russkoi kul'ture i v mirovoi nauke," *Mir Rossii* 1 (1992): 198.

76. S. V. Lur'e, "Rossiiskaia gosudarstvennost' i russkaia obshchina," in Lur'e, *Metamorfozy traditsionnogo soznaniia* (St. Petersburg: Tip. im. Kotliakov, 1994), 142.

77. R. Taagepera, "Overview of the Growth of the Russian Empire," in *Russian Colonial Expansion to 1917* (London-New York: Mansell Publishing, 1988), 1–7.

78. V. S. Diakin, "Natsional'nyi vopros," 136–141.

79. Kappeler, *Rossiia—mnogonatsional'naia imperiia*, 187–202.

80. A. E. Alektorov. *Inorodtsy v Rossii. Sovremennye voprosy* (St. Petersburg: Obshchestvo revnitelei russkogo istoricheskogo prosveshcheniia v pamiat' imperatora Aleksandra III, 1906).

81. Thaden, "The Russian Government," 54.

82. Kappeler, *Rossiia—mnogonatsional'naia imperiia*, 203.

83. *Moskovskie Vedomosti*, no. 249, September 8, 1882.

84. A. I. Termen, *Vospominaniia administratora. Opyt issledovaniia printsipov upravleniia inorodtsami* (Petrograd: 1914), 11.

85. Ibid., 1–2.

86. Ibid., 1.

87. Kappeler, *Rossiia—mnogonatsional'naia imperiia*, 204.

88. B. Badie, *L'Etat Importé: L'occidentalisation de l'ordre politique* (Paris: Fayard, 1992), 259.

89. V. A. Tvardovskaia, *Ideologiia poreformennogo samoderzhaviia (M. N. Katkov i ego izdaniia)* (Moscow: Nauka, 1978), 212.

90. M. Walzer, "Le Nouveau Tribalisme," *Esprit* 11 (1992): 45.

91. Starr, "Tsarist Government: The Imperial Dimension," 24.

92. Badie, *L'Etat Importé*, 249.

93. E. Gellner, *Natsii i natsionalizm*, 110–111.

94. Kappeler, *Rossiia—mnogonatsional'naia imperiia*, 207.

18 Federalisms and Pan-movements: Re-imagining Empire

Mark von Hagen

A few years ago I sketched what I hoped might be a new approach to understanding how the Russian empire (and the Soviet Union) functioned and which I labeled federalism, with its accompanying regionalisms and pan-movements, especially Pan-Slavism and Pan-Turkism. I argued that the constantly evolving complex of ideas I associate with federalism represents an alternative to the state-centralist and/or nation-state-oriented historiography that has shaped much of our understanding of modern Russian history (as well as the histories of non-Russian and post-Soviet nations, such as the Ukrainians) and as such opens up new questions about the locations of power and the persistence of multiple arrangements of relationships between the metropolitan capital, first St. Petersburg and then Moscow, and its far-flung empire.[1] In my earlier essay, I acknowledged that these were never the dominant political perspectives of the ruling imperial or Soviet elites, though they often constituted an important part of the ideological repertoire for oppositionist elites of both reformist and revolutionary camps. Not only has the federalist perspective been combated by state centralizers of the Imperial and Soviet periods, but the federalist or Pan-Slavic or Pan-Turkic periods in the histories of most of the nationalist movements of the empire have also been either casually ignored or actively suppressed in the standard accounts.[2]

What I propose for this concluding essay is to revisit some of our conventional intellectual and political history of the Russian empire from this angle, and to chart an alternative reading of the classics and lesser classics with an eye to restoring some of the authors' concerns with the multicultural aspects of the empire and its overly centralized autocratic political order. In this sense, federalism and the pan-movements represent important and evolving layers of reformist thinking that have not been treated in their common contexts or in relation to one another. Each of these visions tries to reconfigure the boundaries of difference and similarity from those of the currently existing imperial structure of rule. It goes without saying that all of these schemes for rearranging political power in the empire were utopian projects, but in most cases their authors appealed to historical precedents to bolster their political re-imaginings of the empire. Indeed, later historians have looked back on the Russian empire's practice of autocracy and acknowledged it as "really federal by nature of its historical process."[3]

These visions had relatively limited opportunities for realization in modern Russian history, but attracted their greatest attention from political activists and publicists in the period of mass politics after the 1905 revolutions. The delegations of non-Russian deputies to the first Duma actively considered the reconstruction of the empire along democratic and federalist lines with ethno-territorial criteria and measures of cultural autonomy. The only national (all-Russian) party to embrace these ideals with any enthusiasm was the Socialist-Revolutionary Party, which partly explains the success of the SRs in the empire's peripheries in the elections to the Constituent Assembly of fall 1917. SRs did well especially in Ukraine, where their Ukrainian branch won the overwhelming majority of votes, and Siberia.[4] Both Siberia and Ukraine were homes to important traditions of regionalist thinking and, to some extent, regionalist historiography.

The Kadets favored their own model of federalism, but it was distinct from the ethno-territorial model favored by many non-Russian intellectuals and political figures; instead, it was based on a sharing of power with regions that were reconfigured along more "rational" economic and administrative lines. These Kadet ideas also became important during 1917, when the Juridical Commission chaired by Boris Nol'de adjudicated demands for renegotiating the division of power between revolutionary Petrograd and the rest of the Russian state, and when Kadets in the Provisional Government asked for new maps of the realm that reflected "modern" or "rational" territorial divisions.[5]

Following the collapse of the Provisional Government, both the Bolsheviks and their diverse political rivals in the White camp had to respond in one way or another to various currents of federalist and autonomist thought. Siberians and Ukrainians, among them Grigorii Potanin in Siberia and Volodymyr Vynnychenko and Pavel/Pavlo Skoropads'kyi in Ukraine,[6] once again were among the most persistent advocates of a new set of relationships among regions and nations in a democratic Russia.

Short-lived experiments at federation in Transcaucasia lived on in new forms in Soviet ideas of organizing this region along federal lines. The formation of the Soviet Union itself in 1922 was a response to and a new type of federalism.[7] Even in the emigration, Eurasianism at least was conceived as a response to the recent "federalist" history of the Civil War in the Russian empire and a plea for a return to a more authoritarian, more centralized Russian state, even if the Eurasianists were now ready to acknowledge the multiethnic diversity of the Eurasia of their imaginations.[8] Federalist currents would become more evident in their confrontation with Stalinist centralizing at the end of the 1920s, and once again when Stalin's order was partially dismantled after his death and as part of Khrushchev's campaign to establish his own authority via the republican party hierarchs. Finally, Gorbachev's suggestion of a renegotiated relationship between Moscow and the republics and a referendum on the fate of the existing union were part of the ultimate repudiation of Stalin's legacy in the national question; those tentative plans were overtaken by events when the USSR came to an end altogether and was succeeded by a "commonwealth of independent states." This new reworking of federal ideas has not yet been noted for its achievements.[9]

Many scholars have pointed out that the fate of "nation" as a political symbol and of "nation-state" as a political system has been different in Eastern Europe and the post-Soviet lands more generally from the ideal-type of nation-state posited in Western Europe and North America. Those scholars have distinguished territorial from ethnic or, in more crude versions, civic from blood nationalisms. Neither of these formulations helps much to describe the relationship between empire and nation, although I agree that the nation and nation-state do not fit the same way east of Germany as they do west of that central European state. I propose that one way of getting at those differences is by evaluating the character of federalist thought in the region and the inter-relationships of the regional nationalisms and state forms with the pan-movements, federalisms, and regionalisms that evolved in parallel and in some cases in dynamic engagement with one another.

By way of caution, I realize that combining these ethno-territorial understandings of federalism with—for example—the Kadets' more territorial-administrative understandings, let alone to confuse the issue further with the pan-movements, risks losing any hold on a stable definition for the umbrella term of federalism that is at the heart of this discussion. Even in American usage (or perhaps especially in American usage), however, where such traditions were at the heart of the American political experiment, federalism has been described as a "Janus word" by William Safire of *The New York Times*, one of "those confusing terms that mean both one thing and its opposite."[10] This contested character of federalism, meaning on the one hand a diffusion of power to the states (in the definition of Thomas Jefferson and James Madison) and a strong central government on the other (as understood by George Washington, John Adams, and Alexander Hamilton), is no less true for political thought in the Russian empire. This brief survey of aspects of federalist thought, if it succeeds, will capture the sometimes contradictory character of that evolution.

The Decembrists and the Early History of Federalist Thought

The relationships between and among the various currents of federalist thinking are difficult to navigate. Let me try to set out a scheme for approaching those relationships.[11] One possible source for Russian federalist thinking is the idealization of Novgorod and Pskov championed by Aleksandr Radishchev in his project of recovering a pre- or anti-autocratic political tradition of liberties before Muscovy. Radishchev's vision of a more democratic constitutional order was nonetheless revolutionary, and the cult of Novgorod was resisted by imperial authorities, most notably Empress Catherine the Great.[12] But very soon Emperor Alexander I's own gestures at constitutionalism, namely, the preservation of Finnish liberties after the end of the war with Sweden in 1809 and a new status for Poland after 1815[13] (under the influence of the Emperor's friendship with the Polish statesman Adam Czartoryski) seemed to sanction reformist schemes. Alexander's state secretary, Mikhail Speranskii, proposed an administrative reorganization of the empire along rationalist lines but also began to devise other measures, suggesting that the multi-ethnic diversity of the empire's population demanded a more differentiated set of policies.[14] The most thorough-going official, though secret, project for a Russian constitution was that of Nikolai N. Novosil'tsev (a member of the Unofficial Committee under Alexander I) in 1819, a project that Marc Raeff singled out as "one of the few instances in Russian administrative history of a proposal along genuinely federal lines.[15]

Both Radishchev's influence and the short-lived imperial flirtation with constitutional reforms help explain the appearance of Russia's federalist projects. The Decembrist Nikita Murav'ev, in his "Project for a Constitution," called for a Slavic Russian constitutional monarchy, where autonomous states (*derzhavy*) would be organized along the geographic principle, but would respect the distinctive historical traditions of Ukraine and the Baltic provinces as well. He appealed to the traditions of Novgorod, Pskov, the Boyar Duma, and the 1730 constitutional plan of the Panin brothers. Murav'ev saw his federal structure as a means to prevent the chronic oppression of smaller nations by their more powerful neighbors; the offer of some guarantees of liberties would forestall the eventual separatism of the nations in the west. The example of the United States was influential in Murav'ev's division of the empire into 13 states, each with its capital city.[16] Poland was to remain in the federation, but with considerably more independence than the other states. Federalism as an alternative to monarchist centralism emerged in response to the official ideology of early nineteenth-century autocracy, that is, before Uvarov's formulation of autocracy, Orthodoxy, and nationality. And it is very likely that "official" hostility to federalism remained rooted in the fear of the Decembrist movement's oppositional challenge to the very principles of autocratic rule.

Murav'ev was a principal spokesman for the Northern Society, with its headquarters in St. Petersburg. But another part of the Decembrist tradition, that of the Southern Society, had a very different attitude toward federalism, one that opposed federalism to preferred unitary, strong, central, and republican government. The very different model of imperial reconfiguration that emerged was the program of Pavel Pestel, who already in the 1820s, in his *Russkaia pravda*, wrote of a Russia "one and indivisible" but without autocracy, and proposed Russification to achieve the rational administrative state that he thought appropriate to Russia's future development.[17] Pestel emerged as the first "unofficial" critic of federalism from a democratic-republican position. He opposed Murav'ev's variant of federalism, with its power-sharing between center and regions, because of the empire's ethnographic diversity; federation would strengthen distinctiveness and thereby endanger Russia's great power standing. Pestel pointed to the appanage period of Russian history as evidence of the dangers of centripetal forces.

The Turn to Culture and the Invention of Slavdom

But even Pestel could agree with fellow Decembrists that autocracy was neither beneficial, as court historian and conservative Nikolai Karamzin argued, nor an organic part of Russian tradition. The Decembrists viewed autocracy as an aberration from Russia's true path, one forced on it by the victory of Tatar political principles. With the crushing of the Decembrist uprising and Alexander's turn away from constitutionalism, much of the innovative re-imagining of the Russian empire was diverted to more cultural or civilizational agendas that centered on defining the "genuine" character of Russians and Slavs more broadly. Under Nicholas I, this turn to national distinctiveness is reflected both in the "trinity" of Enlightenment Minister Uvarov and the worldviews of the early Slavophiles.[18] In part a response to the Napoleonic invasion of Russia and Eastern Europe and a defense of distinctive national traditions, Pan-Slavic federalist or confederationist utopias also emerged among Poles, Czechs, and South Slavs, and their civilizational vantage points were shared by the Ukrainian Society of Cyril and Methodius.[19] Developing along another axis to the Decembrists' projects, sometimes parallel but often overlapping with them, were various Pan-Slavic schemes for restoring more egalitarian relations among Slavic nations, also with the aim of countering the Muscovite tradition with more democratic historical models and viewing the Muscovite tradition as "alien" to Russians. The disciplines of linguistics and ethnography, with the support of the imperial government, began to gather folkloric evidence to bolster claims of uniqueness and cultural virtue.[20]

Schemes for Slavic federation were shared by conservatives and oppositionists, who understood federation variously depending on their starting points. Aleksandr Herzen criticized state centralization and autocracy as a violation of Slavic nature, which for him was captured by the ideals of the peasant commune and self-rule and identified with the Novgorod and Kiev counter-models. Herzen supported freedom for Poland. The conservative Russian historian Mikhail Pogodin promoted a Russian-led Slavic League; in his championing of the autocracy, Pogodin's views were close to those of Ivan Aksakov, among the conservative Pan-Slavists of the Slavophiles. In contrast, Prince Adam Czartoryski at one point championed a Pan-Slavic federation under the Russian tsar, with Warsaw taking its place of honor alongside Moscow and Petersburg.[21] And the great messianic poet Adam Mickiewicz had ties to the Russian Decembrist Kondratii Ryleev and the Society of United Slavs, a branch of the Decembrists that formed in 1823 in Poltava and eventually joined the Southern Society. The Society of United Slavs championed a democratic, republican federation of Slavic peoples, strangely including Hungary, Moldavia, and Wallachia.

The revolutions of 1848 in Eastern Europe, the "springtime of nations," gave added impetus to historians and intellectuals in the Russian empire and ideas of Pan-Slavic federation. Prague was the site of a Slavic Congress in 1848, which produced a manifesto, one of whose authors was the Russian anarchist Mikhail Bakunin. Bakunin as early as 1846 had called for a Polish and Russian union to wage revolution against the despotism of Nicholas I in the name of liberation of all Slavs. For Bakunin, the essence of Slavdom was equality, freedom, and brotherly love, an East European re-edition of the French Revolution's ideals.[22]

The same "civilizational" methodology that lies at the core of much of the Pan-Slavic federalist thinking about distinctive nations within the Russian empire, or Eastern Europe more broadly speaking, was transformed later in the nineteenth century into something closer to Russian, Ukrainian, and other nationalisms and was also at the base of most of the pan-movements, for example, Pan-Turkism, Zionism, and others. Because the Russian empire was at the crossroads of so many earlier "great civilizations," its intellectuals were attracted by ideologies that questioned the imperial division of power in the name of emergent nations (the Ukrainian movement appealed to co-ethnics in at least two empires, as did Zionism and Pan-Germanism). Clearly these movements are not equivalent, but their challenge to the existing arrangement of peoples and political units did share many similar tropes.

A New Synthesis: The Case for Regional Autonomy in Historians' Accounts

By the second quarter of the nineteenth century, federalism began to develop another foundation in historians' challenges to the imperial myth that had been so effectively elaborated by Karamzin and his followers. In many instances, these explicit historical critiques of autocracy, serfdom, and centralism emerged not in the capitals of the empire, but in the "provinces," or the outlying regions, particularly in Ukraine, Siberia, and along the Volga. In all cases, the historians were confident that they had discovered the truly Russian or Slavic essence that had been suppressed and deformed by centuries of Muscovite despotism.[23] The Ukrainian case is characteristic of the ironies of imperial cultural and educational policies. In the Habsburg lands, Lemberg University was an incubator of autonomist thinking. To combat these trends and Polish influence more generally, especially after the 1830 uprising, the Russian ministry of enlightenment founded a new university in Kiev in 1833. A decade and a half later, Kiev University itself was the birthplace for the Cyril and Methodius Society, which took up the mantle of Slavic federation to address the pernicious influences of Russification on Ukrainian culture.

The major intellectual inspiration for the Society's manifesto came from Nikolai/Mykola Kostomarov[24] and the poet Taras Shevchenko; in that document we can see the traces of both the Decembrists' constitutional reformist thinking and the more recent concern with cultural, ethnographic identities. In their manifesto of 1846–1847, the Society advocated a program of emancipation, education, and the convening of an all-Slavic *sejm* (parliament, based on Polish models) in Kiev.[25] In deference to the 1823 program of the United Slavs branch of the Decembrist movement, they also envisioned a Slavic federation of free republics with fourteen district divisions. The Society was forcibly disbanded by tsarist authorities, with Shevchenko sentenced to hard labor and military service and Kostomarov banished to exile in Saratov. There Kostomarov continued his historical research; he moved from his earlier messianic views[26] to more moderate ones, but throughout remained influenced by democratic, republican, and populist ideals. In the civilizational vein referred to above, Kostomarov contrasted what he referred to as two "Russian peoples," the Great Russian, centered in Vladimir and later in Moscow, and the South Russian, centered in Kiev and later Vladimir-in-Volynia.[27] These contrasts are cast in the guise of national characters that take on almost racialist tones, with the South Russians described as genuinely spiritual, tolerant lovers of personal liberty, whereas the Great Russians are xenophobic, intolerant, materialist, and tied to the repartitional commune. Even after he claimed that he had abandoned his federalist leanings,[28] Kostomarov continued to highlight the lost traditions of republicanism in Poland, Novgorod, and the "south Russian" Dnepr Cossack state, or Ukraine, in his works on the uprisings of Stenka Razin and Bohdan Khmelnyts'kyi. He contrasted the Cyril and Methodius Society's Pan-Slavic federation with what he referred to as the Pan-Russianism of the Slavophiles, which, in his understanding, differed little from Russian imperialism and the domination of other Slavic nations.

Platon Pavlov, a colleague of Kostomarov's in Kiev,[29] shared his idealization of the Novgorod and Cossack republics, as well as his critical stance toward the Muscovite centralizing state. For him the cause of Russia's woes could be traced to the Romanov dynasty who, together with the freedom of the boyars and servitors, had also destroyed the federative character of the appanage period. Pavlov is partly responsible for the career advancement of the next historian under consideration, Afanasii Shchapov. A Siberian by origin, Shchapov studied in Irkutsk and Kazan, where he wrote his dissertation on the schismatics (*raskol'niki*). Pavlov facilitated Shchapov's appointment to the chair of Russian history at Kazan University, where he quickly became known for his oppositionist views and was arrested, and his young career came to a premature end. Shchapov's views were also federalist; however, he envisioned a federalist division based not on nations or ethnic ties but rather on geographic unities. His federalism of territorial autonomy came closer to that of the anarchists Proudhon and Bakunin. Shchapov saw the regions being ruled by zemstvos at various levels, with a *zemskii sobor* as the crowning edifice of a democratic structure. He developed Pavlov's and Kostomarov's opposition of Novgorod to Muscovy further, by emphasizing that relations between Novgorod and its colonies were much more mutually beneficial than those of Muscovy with its conquered lands. And he reinterpreted the Time of Troubles as, in part, a rebellion of non-Russian peoples (Tatars, Chuvash, etc.) against the Muscovite state. Over time, he insisted, the regional movements for autonomy against Muscovy became entangled with nationalist movements. Finally, Shchapov saw the Russian north as a last outpost of federalist traditions and came to view the Russian Church schism—and the Old Believers themselves—as the origins of all later Russian revolutionary ideas.[30]

Siberian Regionalism and Ukrainian Federalist Theory

The legacy of Kostomarov and Shchapov was crucial for the emergence of Siberian regionalism, *oblastnichestvo,* in the 1860s. The most influential members of the Siberian circles, Nikolai Iadrintsev, Grigorii Potanin, and Serafim Shashkov came together in St. Petersburg, where the two regionalist historians had ended up due to the circumstances of their oppositional activities in Kiev and Kazan.[31] Shashkov became an ethnographer of Siberian native populations; Iadrintsev and Potanin were publicists and journalists. Iadrintsev left behind the most sustained political statement of the regionalists in his 1882 critique of Russian imperialism, *Sibir' kak koloniia* (Siberia as a Colony). From Kostomarov he took the formulation of Russian colonization as having had a more democratic character before the onset of Muscovite absolutism and centralization. Iadrintsev, Potanin, and Shashkov all stressed the regional peculiarities of Siberia and, following Kostomarov, contrasted Siberian and Russian interests. Their reform program was designed to lessen the dependence of Siberia on St. Petersburg and to establish something close to dominion status for the region. Their platform included a demand for the founding of a Siberian university, the extension of the zemstvo to Siberia, and the call for a Siberian press.

Despite the era of relative freedom that had been launched under Alexander II as *glasnost'*, when in 1865 students in Omsk spread regionalist proclamations, the authorities reacted harshly with a trial and the arrests of 1,700 for separatism and treason. During the questioning and searches, incriminating materials were found related to Iadrintsev and Potanin, both of whom were caught up in the wave of arrests.[32] After their release the two returned to their political activities, Potanin playing a highly visible role after 1917 in the Siberian regional movement.[33] It is very likely that the writings of the Siberian regionalists introduced the concept of colony (in this case for Siberia) as part of a critique of imperial rule.[34]

The other pole of the Russian empire where federalist and regionalist thinking survived was Ukraine.[35] Here the most influential voice belonged to the historian Myhailo Drahomanov. Drahomanov, the descendant of Poltava Cossack petty nobility, began his career as a lecturer on Roman history at Kiev University. After he critically reviewed a school primer, he was accused of separatism and placed under police surveillance. He turned to collecting Ukrainian folklore, which was not banned by the 1863 circular of Interior Minister Petr Valuev. In 1870–1873 Kiev University permitted Drahomanov an extensive European research trip. Under the influence of his travels in Europe and his acquaintance with contemporary European minority national movements, particularly the Lusatian Slavs and Galician Ukrainians, he began writing critical articles for liberal journals about Russian policy toward non-Russian peoples. After more accusations of separatism, Drahomanov left Kiev for Galicia and was subsequently dismissed from his post at the university. In 1875 the tsar announced the creation of a special commission to investigate Ukrainian separatism, the result of which was the further prohibition of printing and cultural life in the Ukrainian language. From Galicia Drahomanov went to Vienna, but the Austrian authorities also soon launched a campaign against the Ukrainian socialist movement, so he left once again, this time for Switzerland, where he found a lively community of political émigrés from the Russian empire, as well as the target for much of his polemical writings on the Russian revolutionary movement.[36]

Drahomanov's ideas blended many aspects of the thought of his predecessors, from the Decembrists and the Cyril and Methodius Society to the historians and folklorists of the Slavophile and Pan-Slavic orientations.[37] He believed firmly that Ukrainians had to ally with the all-Russian progressive movement, but his intimate acquaintance with the Russian revolutionary emigration led him to conclude that they, for all their oppositionist fervor, were no less centralist and intolerant of national difference than the regime against which they railed. He found especially alarming Bakunin's anarchism and Petr Tkachev's centralism and advocacy of terror.[38]

Drahomanov also responded to the transformation of Russian Pan-Slavism into reactionary Pan-Russianism in the 1870s and 1880s, though he too advocated the liberation of Slavs from Turkish and German rule. He saw himself as part of a movement to reclaim the legacy of Pan-Slavism from the tsars and insisted that the idea was born among the nationalities who had lost their status as sovereign states; he traced the connections of Ukrainians with their counterparts in the Serbian, Polish, Czech, and other branches of Pan-Slavism. And he studied the pan-movements of contemporary Europe, particularly the Latin Alliance that was the organ of the Provençal movement to recover Languedoc, between France and Spain. The Latin Alliance had started with a demand for cultural autonomy, and then administrative and political autonomy. This was proof for Drahomanov that federalism was the ideal solution to the problems of modern national minorities.[39]

In contrast to what he considered the extreme positions of the Russian revolutionary movement, Drahomanov proposed a constitutional federation that respected the rights of ethnic groups as well as the rights of individuals, in the spirit of Nikolai Mikhailovskii, and that was grounded in the zemstvo movement. He envisioned the creation of a semi-sovereign state form made up of all Ukrainian-settled lands in the framework of a Slavic union. With the revival during the Russo-Turkish War of the discussion of a *zemskii sobor,* a sort of estates-general of the Russian empire, Drahomanov submitted a plan for a thorough-going administrative reform of the empire toward autonomy for its constituent peoples. Despite the imperial administration's policy of replacing historic and ethnographic regions with more rational administrative divisions, those earlier regions had survived and could serve as the basis for a new federal rebuilding of Russia, building from the smallest units to the largest. Through his more positive orientation to the state, Drahomanov was careful to distinguish his local-based federalism from that of the anarchists Proudhon

and Bakunin. Drahomanov's reform projects were grounded in his interpretation of Ukraine's history under Russian rule, an interpretation that
drew heavily on Kostomarov, despite Drahomanov's criticism of Kostomarov's excessively populist prejudices.[40]

Later in the 1880s Drahomanov outlined a project for a Slavic Union
based on his studies of the Swiss and American constitutions. His project
envisioned dividing the Russian empire into 20 regions, 14 of which overlapped with the original Decembrist plan of Murav'ev.[41] Not everywhere
was the ethnographic principle recognized as the most desirable solution
for a region's population; for example, the Caucasian peoples were so thoroughly intermixed that they ought to coexist in a multi-national region.
The new state would have a bicameral legislature: a State Duma with deputies elected according to proportional representation, and a Union Duma
to represent more equitably the regions and nationalities. A State Assembly
(*Gosudarstvennyi sobor*) would form the crowning edifice of the structure.
Political freedom would be the means for the return of the Ukrainian nation to the family of civilized peoples.[42]

To return to one of the hypotheses that I proposed at the start of this
essay, namely, the ill fit of the nation-state model in the half of Europe
under Habsburg, Ottoman, and Russian rule, Drahomanov came to reject
the experience of France in nation-building because of the National Convention's repression of the Provençals, Bretons, Basques, Corsicans, and
Alsatians. He understood the French Revolution as the first "modern example of the policy of denationalization by the systematic pressure of the
State machinery."[43] Drahomanov took a great interest in the policies of the
Austro-Hungarian and Ottoman empires, in particular the situations of
Jews, Poles, and other Slavs. His program for Austria-Hungary was similar to that for Russia—federalization and democratization. For the Ottoman Empire, however, his Pan-Slav sympathies led him to advocate not
federalization, but the destruction of that empire and the liberation of the
Slavs under a democratic federation. Drahomanov's influence was particularly strong in Austria-Hungary among members of the Radical Party,
organized in 1890, and among Galician Ukrainophiles who formed the
Ukrainian National Democratic Party in 1899. In the Russian empire, his
ideas were closest to the principles of the Democratic Radical Party, later
the Socialist Federalist Party, and the Ukrainian Socialist Revolutionaries.

As this brief and far from complete survey suggests,[44] the parallel, at
times overlapping, currents of federalist and autonomist thought, on the
one hand, and Pan-Slavic thought on the other, made for a vital tradition

of re-imagining the Russian empire along lines other than those of Muscovite or Petrine centralism, as most critics understood it. Their origins were diverse, but there was more borrowing and adaptation than has been allowed by even the historians of federalist thought, such as von Rauch. Finally, these authors' projects were not only interesting proposals for contemporary reform of the empire, but also suggestive vantage points for historians looking back on the diversity of imperial policies and their consequences.[45] Ideas that emerged and evolved over the nineteenth century provided most of the material for the further elaboration of imperial reform after the onset of mass politics in Russia after 1905, when, in the context of legal, political discussions and a vigorous regional and national press, federalist, autonomist, regionalist, Pan-Slavic, and other pan-movements took on a new dynamic.

Notes

1. "Writing the History of Russia as Empire: The Perspective of Federalism," co-edited with Catherine Evtuhov, Boris Gasparov, Alexander Ospovat, *Kazan, Moscow, St. Petersburg: Multiple Faces of the Russian Empire* (Moscow: ITS-Garant, 1997); translated into Russian as "Istoriia Rossii kak istoriia imperii: perspektivy federalistskogo podkhoda," in P. Vert, P. S. Kabytov, A. I. Miller, eds., *Rossiiskaia imperiia v zarubezhnoi istoriografii: Raboty poslednikh let: antologiia* (Moscow: Novoe izdatel'stvo, 2005).

2. I treat these issues with regard to Ukraine in "Does Ukraine Have a History?" *Slavic Review* 54, no. 3 (Fall 1995): 658–673.

3. See Leonid Strakhovsky, "Constitutional Aspects of the Imperial Russian Government's Policy toward National Minorities," *Journal of Modern History*, 13, no. 4 (December 1941): 468–469. Strakhovsky argued that "it was not until the constitutional period of the Russia Empire, following the Revolution of 1905, that the federal characteristics disappear from the statute books." Strakhovsky refers to the Fundamental Law of 1906, where the Russian state is declared one and indivisible for the first time.

4. See Oliver Radkey, *The Elections to the Constituent Assembly of 1917* (Cambridge, Mass.: Harvard University Press, 1950).

5. For Nol'de's own survey of the constitutional order of the Old Regime, see his *La Formation de l'empire russe: Etudes, Notes et Documents*, vol. 1 (Paris: Institute d'études slav, 1952) ; and the important review of this work by Yale historian George Vernadsky in *American Historical Review* vol. 58, no. 2 (January 1953): 377–378.

6. See Anna Procyk, *Russian Nationalism and Ukraine: The Nationality Policy of the Volunteer Army during the Civil War* (Toronto: Canadian Institute of Ukrainian Studies Press, 1995).

7. See the recent reevaluation of the place of federalism and autonomist ideas leading up to the 1922 Soviet constitution, in Jeremy Smith, *The Bolsheviks and the National Question 1917–1923* (London: MacMillan Press, 1999).

8. For the history of the Eurasianist movement, see Nicholas Riasanovsky, "The

Emergence of Eurasianism," *California Slavic Studies* 4 (1967): 39–72; Ilya Vinkovetsky, "Classical Eurasianism and Its Legacy," *Canadian-American Slavic Studies* 34, no. 2 (Summer 2000): 125–140. The best English-language introduction to their writings is N. S. Trubetzkoy, *Legacy of Genghis Khan, and Other Essays on Russia's Identity*, A. Liberman, ed. (Ann Arbor: Michigan Slavic Materials, 1992). It is also important to acknowledge that earlier generations of American and European historians were influenced by the ideas of the interwar émigré Eurasianists, especially George Vernadsky, who taught at Yale University and authored an influential multivolume history of Russia.

9. During Gorbachev's reforms, historians sought to rehabilitate the legacy of federalist thought in the Soviet past. See Albert P. Nenarokov and M. G. Gorshkov, eds., *Nesostoiavshiisia iubilei: pochemu SSSR ne otprazdnoval svoego 70-letiia* (Moscow: Terra, 1992).

10. William Safire, "On Language," *New York Times* (January 30, 2000), 20–21.

11. These preliminary reflections are based on primary sources and interpretive histories of these alternative currents, especially Georg von Rauch's *Russland: Staatliche Einheit und nationale Vielfalt: Foederalistische Kraefte und Ideen in der russischen Geschichte* (Munich: Isar-Verlag, 1953); Wolfgang Faust's *Russlands Goldener Boden: Der sibirische Regionalismus in der zweiten Haelfte des 19. Jahrhunderts* (Cologne: Boehlau Verlag, 1980); S. V. Utechin's *Russian Political Thought: A Concise History* (New York: Praeger, 1963); Andrzej Walicki's *A History of Russian Thought from the Enlightenment to Marxism* (Stanford, Calif.: Stanford University Press, 1979).

12. Catherine forbade the production of a play on the Novgorod theme by Vadim Kniazhnin, *Vadim*. The Vadim motif thereafter, together with Pskov and Novgorod, became identified with opposition to the coercive methods of the Muscovite period; Kondratii Ryleev persuaded Alexander Pushkin to idealize Pskov, and Alexander Bestuzhev-Riumin also devotes a story to this theme.

13. See "Polish Freedoms under the Constitution of 1815," in Basil Dmytryshyn, ed., *Imperial Russia: A Source Book, 1700–1917* (New York: Holt, Rinehart and Winston, 1967), 145–155.

14. See Marc Raeff, *Michael Speranskii, Statesman of Imperial Russia* (The Hague: M. Nijhoff, 1957); and his *Siberia and the Reforms of 1822* (Seattle: University of Washington Press, 1956).

15. "N. N. Novosil'tsev: Constitutional Charter of the Russian Empire (1818–1820)," in Marc Raeff, ed., *Plans for Political Reform in Imperial Russia, 1730–1905* (Englewood Cliffs, N.J.: Prentice-Hall, 1966), 110–120. See George Vernadsky on this project and his insistence on Novosil'tsev's federalist sympathies, *La Charte Constitutionelle de l'Empire russe de l'an 1820* (Paris, 1933). Baron Nol'de, in his critique of Vernadsky, asserts that Alexander I never had any intentions of approving Novosil'tsev's ideas, though it is very likely that Alexander was familiar with contemporary political tracts on federations, including the American example.

16. See "Project for a Constitution by Nikita M. Muraviev: First Draft," in Marc Raeff, ed., *The Decembrist Movement*, (Englewood Cliffs, N.J.: Prentice-Hall, 1966), 103–118. See also P. Gronskij, "L'idée fédérative chez les décabristes," *Le monde slave* (June 1926).

17. Pestel chose to call the Russians Slavs, but acknowledged that the Slavs spoke five dialects reflecting diverse national traditions: Russians, Little Russians, White Rus-

sians, Ukrainians, and Ruthenians. See "The Russian Law by Pavel Ivanovich Pestel," in Marc Raeff, ed., *The Decembrist Movement*, 124–156.

18. Konstantin Aksakov in particular saw the Russian people's virtues in their ancient freedoms as attested to by their communal life and their openness to neighboring peoples and contrasted this with the artificial empire, which oppressed foreign peoples. Of course, for Aksakov Russian freedom had nothing in common with republican liberty.

19. For the history of Pan-Slavism, see Hans Kohn, *Pan-Slavism, Its History and Ideology* (New York: Vintage Books, 1960); on Russian Pan-Slavism, see Michael Boro Petrovich, *The Emergence of Russian Panslavism, 1856–1870* (New York: Columbia University Press, 1956). The ideas of Czech and Slovak Pan-Slavism were developed by Josef Dobrovský, Ján Kollár, Pavel Josef Safarík, and others; South Slav Pan-Slavism was led by the Serbian folklorist Vuk Karadžić and Croatian, Serb, and Slovene poets. Most of these early thinkers were influenced by the culture of European romanticism.

20. On ethnography's role in articulating national identities, see Nathaniel Knight, "Science, Empire, and Nationality: Ethnography in the Russian Geographic Society, 1845–1855," in Jane Burbank and David Ransel, eds., *Imperial Russia: New Histories for the Empire* (Bloomington: Indiana University Press, 1998); and his "Ethnicity, Nationality, and the Masses: *Narodnost'* and Modernity in Imperial Russia," in David Hoffmann and Yanni Kotsonis, eds., *Russian Modernity* (New York: Macmillan Press, 2000).

21. Federalism was a vibrant political alternative discussed by a variety of Polish intellectuals, who traced its origins to Polish history, particularly the Union of Lublin and the constitution of the Polish-Lithuanian Commonwealth. Karol Libelt proposed a federation of Lithuanians, Ruthenians, Prussians and other peoples in a great Poland from sea to sea. Galician Poles envisioned a federative reorganization of the Habsburg lands, with Galicia as the starting point for a future restoration of Poland. Adam Czartoryski and Zygmunt Krasinski hoped for a Polish-led Slavic federation. In some measure, Adam Mickiewicz launched this tradition with his vision of Polish messianism and Poland's role in liberating other suffering nations of the world. See Peter Brock, "Polish Nationalism," in Peter F. Sugar and Ivo John Lederer, eds., *Nationalism in Eastern Europe* (Seattle & London: University of Washington Press, 1994; original 1969), 310–372. See also the documentary collection, edited by Manfred Kridl, Wladyslaw Malinowski, and Józef Wittlin, *"For Your Freedom and Ours": Polish Progressive Spirit Through the Centuries* (New York: F. Ungar, 1943).

22. "Appeal to the Slavs" (1848), in Sam Dolgoff, ed., *Bakunin on Anarchy* (New York: Alfred A. Knopf, Inc., 1971), 62–68.

23. Good brief surveys of the writings of the historians discussed below can be found in N. L. Rubinshtein, *Russkaia istoriografiia* (Moscow, 1941). See a fascinating Soviet study of federalist thought, in fact a scholarly denunciation, by M. A. Rubach, "Federalisticheskie teorii v istorii Rossii," in M. N. Pokrovskii, ed., *Russkaia istoricheskaia literatura v klassovom osveshchenii*, vol. 2 (Moscow, 1930), 3–120.

24. Kostomarov was educated at Kharkov University and received his first teaching position as an adjunct professor at Kiev University. After his arrest in 1847 and exile to Saratov, he moved in 1859 to St. Petersburg, where he was appointed professor of history.

25. "Statute and Rules of the Cyril-Methodius Society," and "Appeals of the Society," in Basil Dmytryshyn, ed., *Imperial Russia: A Source Book, 1700–1917*, 192–195.

26. See his "The Books of the Genesis of the Ukrainian People," (1846), in Ralph Lindheim and George S. N. Luckyj, eds., *Towards an Intellectual History of Ukraine: An Anthology of Ukrainian Thought from 1710–1995* (Toronto: University of Toronto Press, 1996), 94–100.

27. See his "Two Russian Nationalities" (1860–1861), in *Towards an Intellectual History*, 122–134.

28. In an 1863 letter to Ivan Aksakov.

29. In fact, Pavlov was appointed to the chair in Russian history at Kiev University that Kostomarov was forced to give up upon his arrest; in 1859, Pavlov also moved to St. Petersburg, when he was appointed to the Archeographic Commission. His radical ideas ended in his arrest and internal exile for a particularly incendiary historical speech in 1862.

30. This idea was taken up by Nikolai Chernyshevskii under Shchapov's influence. Through Chernyshevskii's mediation, the Old Believers came to be the center of much oppositionist attention in the second half of the nineteenth century.

31. Shashkov took a room in Shchapov's house and moved with him from Kazan. For more on the university years of the Siberian regionalists, see Faust, *Russlands Goldener Boden,* esp. chapter 3. Another member of their circle in St. Petersburg was Chokan Velikhanov, who played an important role in the formulation of Kazakh political thought.

32. See Faust, 186–225.

33. For more on Siberian regionalism in this later period, see Paul S. Dotsenko, *The Struggle for Democracy in Siberia* (Palo Alto, Calif.: Hoover Institution Press, 1983). Dotsenko, a Siberian Socialist-Revolutionary, attributed the success of his party in Siberia to their having adopted many articles of the regionalists' platform.

34. According to Faust, the usage might have been inspired by an 1862 proposal of Governor-General Murav'ev to colonize the Amur River valley with Russian settlers. Murav'ev served as governor-general of East Siberia from 1848 to 1861.

35. Elsewhere in the empire there is some evidence of federalist thinking, but very little is known about most of the individuals and groups involved or about their interrelationships. For example, among the newspapers that began to appear in emigration in Geneva during the 1880s was *Der Baltische Foederalist,* which appears to have had as its aim the winning over of Russian socialists to a greater receptivity to national liberation movements.

36. In 1889 he accepted an invitation to teach history in Bulgaria at the University of Sofia, and he withdrew from politics. See Volodymyr Doroshenko, "The Life of Mykhaylo Drahomanov," in Ivan L. Rudnytsky, ed., *Mykhaylo Drahomanov: A Symposium and Selected Writings* (New York: Ukrainian Academy of Arts and Sciences in the U.S., 1951), 6–22.

37. One of the most important historians of Ukrainian thought, Ivan L. Rudnytsky, characterizes his thought as "syncretic. It combines democratic and socialist, patriotic and cosmopolitan, Slavophile and occidentalist elements." See his "Drahomanov as a Political Theorist," in Rudnytsky, ed., *Mykhaylo Drahomanov,* 70–130.

38. "The Centralization of the Revolutionary Struggle in Russia," in *Drahomanov: A Symposium,* 181–192.

39. He also followed the fates of Bretons, Welsh, Irish, Flemish, and even the Dutch and the Danes in earlier periods. See his "Pan-Slav Federalism" (1878), in *Drahomanov: A Symposium,* 175–180.

40. See his essay, "The Lost Epoch: Ukrainians under the Muscovite Tsardom, 1654–1876," in *Drahomanov: A Symposium,* 153–160. See also Dmytro Doroshenko, "Drahomanov and Ukrainian Historiography," in *Drahomanov: A Symposium,* 23–35.

41. Drahomanov pays tribute not only to the Decembrists' Society of United Slavs, but to the Society of Cyril and Methodius as well.

42. "Free Union; Draft of a Ukrainian Political and Social Program" (1884), in *Drahomanov: A Symposium,* 193–205.

43. Rudnytsky, "Drahomanov as a Political Theorist," citing his *Peculiar Thoughts on the Ukrainian National Cause* (Vienna, 1915), 76–81.

44. I apologize for failing to integrate my readings on Pan-Turkism and Turkic-Muslim projects for reorganizing the imperial space and populations. The classic treatment of these movements is Serge A. Zenkovsky, *Pan-Turkism and Islam in Russia* (Cambridge, Mass.: Harvard University Press, 1960); for more recent treatments, see Adeeb Khalid, *The Politics of Muslim Cultural Reform: Jadidism in Central Asia* (Berkeley and Los Angeles: University of California Press, 1998); and several essays in Daniel R. Brower and Edward Lazzerini, eds., *Russia's Orient: Imperial Borderlands and Peoples, 1700–1917* (Bloomington: Indiana University Press, 2001).

45. One valuable and virtually unknown source for this history is the memoir of a Finnish professor and determined federalist, Karl Tiander. See his *Das Erwachen Osteuropas. Die Nationalitaetenbewegung in Russland und der Weltkrieg* (Wien-Leipzig, 1934).

Contributors

Vladimir Bobrovnikov is a research fellow at the Institute for Oriental Studies in Moscow. He is author of *Custom, Law, and Violence among North Caucasus Muslims* [in Russian].

Jane Burbank is Professor of History and Russian and Slavic Studies at New York University. She is author of *Intelligentsia and Revolution: Russian Views of Bolshevism, 1917–1922* and *Russian Peasants Go to Court: Legal Culture in the Countryside, 1905–1917.*

Elena Campbell is a visiting lecturer in history at Harvard University and an associate of the History Department of the European University at St. Petersburg. She is currently completing a monograph entitled *Toward State Unity: The Muslim Question in Late Imperial Russia.*

Leonid Gorizontov is Professor of Russian History at Russian State University for the Humanities and a research fellow at Institute of Slavic Studies, Russian Academy of Sciences. He is author of *Paradoxes of Imperial Politics: Russians in Poland and Poles in Russia, XIX–early XX centuries* [in Russian] and editor of several collections of essays on the history and culture of eastern Slavs.

Francine Hirsch is Associate Professor of Russian and Soviet History at the University of Wisconsin–Madison. She is author of *Empire of Nations: Ethnographic Knowledge and the Making of the Soviet Union.*

Sviatoslav Kaspe is deputy director and head of the analytical department at Russian Public Policy Center (Moscow). He is author of *Empire and Modernization: A General Model and Russian Specificity* [in Russian].

Irina Novikova is Associate Professor in the School of International Relations at St. Petersburg State University. She is author of *The Finnish Card in German Patience: Germany and the Problem of Finnish Independence during the First World War* [in Russian].

Ekaterina Pravilova is Assistant Professor of Russian History at Princeton University. She is author of *Human Rights and the Rule of Law: Administrative Justice in Russia* [in Russian] and *Finances of Empire: Money and Power in Russia's Imperial Borderlands* [in Russian].

Anatolyi Remnev is Professor at Omsk State University. He is author of *Autocracy and Siberia: Administrative Politics from the 19th through the Early 20th Century* [in Russian] and *Russia's Far East: The Imperial Geography of Power from 19th through the Early 20th Century* [in Russian].

Shane O'Rourke is Lecturer in the history department at the University of York. He is author of *Warriors and Peasants: The Don Cossacks in Late Imperial Russia.*

Nikolai Ssorin-Chaikov is Lecturer in Social Anthropology at the University of Cambridge. He is author of *The Social Life of the State in Subarctic Siberia.*

Charles Steinwedel is Assistant Professor of History at Northeastern Illinois University in Chicago. He is currently completing a monograph on the Russian empire in Bashkiria from 1550–1917.

Willard Sunderland is Associate Professor of History at the University of Cincinnati. He is author of *Taming the Wild Field: Colonization and Empire on the Russian Steppe.*

Nailya Tagirova is the chair of economic history at Samara State Economic University. She is author of *The Volga Market (1861–1914)* [in Russian].

Rustem Tsiunchuk is Professor of History and Russian and East European Studies at Kazan University. He is author of *The Duma Model of Parliamentarianism in the Russian Empire: Ethnic-Religious and Regional Dimensions* [in Russian] and *In the Name of the Proletariat: The Historiography of the History of Bolshevik Strategy in the Duma, 1905–1907* [in Russian].

Aleksei Volvenko is a senior lecturer in Russian history at Taganrog State Teacher Training Institute. He is working on a monograph on

Cossack resistance to the state in the nineteenth and the early twentieth centuries.

Mark von Hagen is Professor and Chair of the Department of History at Arizona State University, where he teaches Russian, Ukrainian, and Eurasian history. Previously, he was Boris Bakhmeteff Professor of Russian and East European Studies at Columbia University. He is author of *Soldiers in the Proletarian Dictatorship: The Red Army and the Soviet Socialist State, 1917–1930* and coeditor of several collections of essays devoted to empire, nationality, and Russian-Ukrainian relations.

Paul Werth is Associate Professor of History at the University of Nevada, Las Vegas. He is author of *At the Margins of Orthodoxy: Mission, Governance, and Confessional Politics in Russia's Volga-Kama Region, 1827–1905.*

Index

Italicized page numbers indicate illustrations.

animism, 170
Annenkov, M. N., 436
anthropology, 143, 145, 219
Antonii (Amfiteatrov), Archbishop, 322, 323
Anuchin, D. G., 431–32
Anzoronov, Muhammad, 256
Arabic script/language, 249, 259, 264n29
Arctic regions, 33, 51
Arkhangel'sk (city and province), 80, 83, 149, 372, 380
Arkhiv Marksa i Engelsa (journal), 275
Armenia/Armenians, 79, 146, 471, 472; Duma elections and, 383, 384, 388, 393; in Soviet Union, 156–57, 158
Arsen'ev, K. I., 71–72, 84, 128, 131, 136, 428
Asia, *xvi*, 43, 73, 77, 86
assimilation, cultural, 169, 170, 173, 174; educational system and, 474; of Muslims, 326; Russian policy concerning, 180
Astrakhan (city and province), 39, 77, 79; Duma elections in, 370, 371, 372, 382; khanate of, 56n11; "remoteness" of, 83
Atabay of Karachay, 257
Atazhukin, Tau-Sultan, 256
Atlas of Materials for Statistics on the Russian Empire, 127
atlases, 38, 46, 47–48, 60n42, 127, 128
Atlasov, Kh. M., 394
Australia, 451
Austria, 299, 369, 451, 470
Austro-Hungarian Empire, 505
autocracy, 13, 15, 207, 444, 467, 495; administration of periphery and, 426; corrupt administrative practices of, 110; Decembrists and, 498–99; decentralization and, 368; empire as state form and, 25; historical critiques of, 500–502; modernization and, 461; multi-confessional elite and, 104; nationalism and, 483; nation-state policy, 472; noble landowners and, 97; "popular," 320; revolutionary overthrow (1917), 204, 404, 405; territorial expansion and, 54, 431, 433; *zemstvo* as limit on, 121n73
Avars, 240, 241, 244, 246, 249; khans, 256; language of, 249; songs and epics, 252–53
Aver'kov, P. B., 352, 353
Azerbaijan: *abreki* in, 247, 258, 259; Azeri language, 248; Duma elections and, 384, 387, 388, 389, 393; in Soviet Union, 148, 149, 154, 156–57, 158

Badie, B., 486, 487–88
Bagin, S., 330
Baku, 376, 380, 382
Bakunin, Mikhail, 500, 504, 505
Balkans, 480, 481
Balkars, 260
Baltic provinces, 43, 296; Baltic question, 320; as constituent part of Russian Empire, 446; Decembrists and, 498; integration into Russia, 469–70; Russian zloty in, 301
banditry. *See abreki/abrechestvo* (bandits/banditry)
baptism, 171–72, 185, 186
Baraev, Arbi, 260
Bardizh, K. L., 392, 393
Bariatinskii, Prince A. I., 254
Barkaul (Evenki shaman), 273–74
Barrett, Thomas, 440
Bashkir language, 95
Bashkiria (Bashkortostan), 6, 95–99, 111–13; cantonal administration of, 102–11, 116n32, 121n71; Orenburg Muslim Spiritual Assembly, 99–102; in Soviet Union (Bashkir ASSR), 157, 160
Bashkirs, 173, 191n28; Congress of Muslims and, 330; Duma elections and, 384, 387, 388, 389; special status of, 472–73
Baskin, G. I., 134–35
Bassin, Mark, 94, 177, 288
Bavaria, 307
Belinskii, V. G., 81
Belorussia/Belorussians, 84, 87, 88, 177, 442; Duma elections and, 387–88; national movement, 460; Orthodoxy and, 193n61; as part of Russian nation, 321; Polish influence over, 85, 182, 296; in Soviet Union, 148, 149, 158
Bendix, R., 460
Bennigsen, Alexandre, 245
Beremzhanov, A. K., 394
Bering, Vitus, 33, 59n35
Bering Sea, 51, 52
Bessarabia, 87, 181, 301, 372, 381
Bethmann-Hollweg, Theobald von, 403
Biernacki, M., 311
Biggs, Michael, 54
Biglov, M. M., 394
bilet (internal passport), 255
billon (Polish coin), 307, 308–10, 314
Black Earth regions, 76, 129

Black Sea region, 50, 438
Bliev, Marx, 244
blood feuds, in Caucasus, 250–51, 254, 255, 257, 261
Boborykin, P. D., 76
Bobrinskii, Count A. V., 179
Bobrovnikov, Vladimir, 9–10, 23
Bobyls, 105
Bogoraz (-Tan), V. G., 281
Bolsheviks, 3, 20; Caucasian *abreki* and, 259; colonization viewed by, 153–54; Don Cossacks and, 9, 224, 226–34; estate principle and, 196; ethnographers and, 144–46; federalism and, 495; Finnish policy and, 413; internationalism of, 150; "principle of nationality" and, 144, 146; Provisional Government and, 411, 412; regionalization debate and, 147; territories of Russian Empire and, 139. *See also* communism; socialism
Bonsdorf, Alexis, 403
borderlands/boundaries, 5, 6, 11, 22, 57n12; in Catherinian era, 52–53; with China, 35, 44, 57n12, 434; colonization of, 49–50; Duma representation and, 19, 390, 392; European strategies of governance in, 196; First World War and, 142; frontier outposts, 35; geographic surveys and, 49; indeterminate, 35, 440–41; level of economic development, 296; limits of imperial expansion and, 477–78; Russian settlement in, 442; standardization and diversity in, 17, 317; *ukrainy* ("frontiers"), 69, 71, 74, 86; Western Borderlands oblast, 129
Borodin, N. A., 391, 393
Borovitinov, Mikhail, 401
Bourdieu, Pierre, 428–29
Boyar Duma, 498
boyars, 84, 501
Braudel, F., 427, 434–35
Britain/British empire, 2, 3, 24, 450; as colonial power, 159; in India, 178; internal colonization in, 189n5; loss of great-power status, 451; Muslim question and, 337; rivalry with Russian Empire, 473; Russo-Turkish War and, 482
Broido, Georgii, 155
Brok, P. F., 312
Bronevskii, S. M., 240
Brounov, P. I., 131

Brower, Daniel, 473, 474
Broxup, Maria Bennigsen, 245
Bruk, G. Ia., 394
Buba, 259
Buddhists, 386, 389
Bukeikhanov, A. N., 393
Bukhara, 116n27, 479
Bulatova, A. G., 254
Bulgarians, 150, 385, 387, 467
Bulota, A., 393
"Bulygin" Statutes on Elections, 369
Bunge, N. Kh., 442
Burbank, Jane, 8
bureaucracy/bureaucrats, 17, 24, 104, 110, 367, 435
Buriat Mongols, 385, 387, 388, 443, 448
"By Vistula Territory," 464
byt (customs, everyday life), 129, 142, 149
Byzantine Empire, heritage of, 471
Byzantinism, 480

Calvinism, 182
Campbell, Elena, 11
Canada, 451
canals, 44
capital cities, 76, 81–82, 107, 134, 135. *See also* Moscow; St. Petersburg
Capital (Marx), 278
capitalism, 1, 21, 155, 275, 278, 459
Carr, E. H., 140
cartography. *See* maps/mapping (cartography)
Caspian Sea, 40, 240, 241
Catherine II ("the Great"), Empress, 34, 96, 486; Bashkiria and, 95, 97, 98, 99, 108, 111, 112; borderland colonization and, 49–50; Caucasian fortifications of, 253; coinage and, 297; cult of Novgorod and, 497, 507n12; Edict of Toleration, 6; European style of court, 97; "interior Russia" and, 68; Islam and, 99, 102, 115n18, 323; mapping and, 126; provincial reforms, 97; Russification of western provinces, 84; territoriality and, 5, 45, 48, 51, 64n76, 196
Catholics, Roman, 118n41, 177; Czech settlers in Asiatic Russia, 444; Duma elections and, 388, 389; "Latinism" in western provinces, 322; Polishness and, 183; State Duma and, 386

Caucasian war (1817–1864), 240, 241, 244, 255, 257, 261

Caucasus, 9–10, 23, 50, 79, 432, 436; *abreki* in historical transformation, 249–53; center-periphery relations and, 471–72; "culture of violence" in, 10, 239, 250–53, 261; Duma elections in, 370, 371, 376–77, 378, 380, 389; exploration of, 40; highlanders' response to state reforms, 253–57; hospitality among highlanders, 252, 254–55, 256; languages of, 246; mapping of, 143; Muslim clergy in, 328; Orientalized view of highlanders, 240–45, *242, 243;* origin/meaning of *abrek* as term, 245–49; "productive forces" in, 155; regionalization and, 132, 148, 149; Russian conquest, 196, 248; Russia's civilizing mission and, 178; Soviet ethnographers in, 145; Soviet regionalization and, 156–57, 160; sporadic revivals of banditry, 257–61; war in northern Caucasus, 129. *See also* Transcaucasia

censuses, Russian and Soviet, 133, 143, 161, 162n17, 386, 387

center-periphery relations, 4, 22, 54, 89, 457; administrative policy and, 432–35; Cossacks and, 224; "double expansion" of empire and, 442; geography of power and, 426, 427–29; Great Reforms and, 469; peasant colonization and, 440; religion and colonialism, 180; in Volga-Kama region, 180

Central Agricultural Region, 130

Central Asia, 40, 86, 432; colonial status of, 170; deportations to, 260; Duma elections in, 370, 371, 378–79, 381; inhabitants as *inorodtsy,* 180; Muslim clerics from, 100; Muslim question and, 324; regionalization and, 132; Russian annexation of, 129, 178, 196, 430, 479; Russian settlement in, 90; Russian-British rivalry and, 473; Russification policy in, 484; Soviet ethnographers in, 145

Central Black Earth Region, 90

Central Industrial Region, 90, 129

Chaianov, A. V., 131

Chakste, Ia., 393

Chebotarev, Kh. A., 126, 127, 135

Chechnya/Chechens, 3, 241, 246; *abreki,* 248; Chechens deported by Soviets, 260; Duma elections and, 384, 387, 388; military leaders, 249, 250; revivals of banditry,

258–59, 260–61; Russian state reforms and, 253, 255, 256

Cheliabinsk Province, 160

Chelintsev, A. N., 131

Cheremiss (Mari), 78, 147, 171, 172

Cherkaskii, Mamat Girei, 115n26

Cherniaev, General M. G., 479–80, 482

Chernigov Province, 74, 75–76, 89, 375

Chernyshevskii, Nikolai, 509n30

Chertkov, Major-General M. I., 355–56

China, 34, 35, 57n12, 324, 325, 434

Chinese Eastern Railroad, 439, 444, 447

Chinese population, 439, 442

Chingis-Khan, 272, 276

Chizhevski, P. I., 393

Chkheidze, I. S., 393

Chkhenkeli, A. I., 393

Christianity, Orthodox, 6, 19, 75; conversion to, 98, 114n16, 171–72, 181, 185, 186–87; Cossacks and, 9, 220, 222; Holy Rus and, 87; imperial expansion and, 437, 442, 443–44; *inorodtsy* and, 174; nation-state policy and, 474; non-Russian peoples practicing, 383; Russianness and, 181; schismatics *(raskol'niki),* 449, 502; as Slavic cultural world, 170; Tatars and, 322, 324; in Ufa Province, 95; Uniate church incorporated into, 176. *See also* Orthodox Church, Russian

Chud, 78

Chuprov, A. I., 131–32

Chuvash, 78, 174, 502; assimilation of, 180; Duma elections and, 384, 387, 388

Circassians. *See* Adygs (Circassians)

cities: city dumas, 104, 112, 122n74; population of peasant origin, 203, 204; role in territorial expansion of empire, 434

citizenship, 18, 24, 197, 448; democracy and, 26; law and, 204; *soslovie* (estate) system and, 200

civic-mindedness *(grazhdanstvennost'),* 170, 184, 185, 194n74, 381

Civil Code, 199, 200

civil society, 106, 363, 394, 462, 463

civil war, Russian, 9, 146, 149, 394; Caucasian *abreki* and, 257, 259, 261; Cossacks and, 218, 220, 222, 232, 233–35; federalism and, 496; green partisans, 259; regionalization and, 148

civilization, European/Russian, 17, 20,

115n23, 366; cities as regional centers of, 80; eastward expansion of Russian Empire, 437; educational policy and, 472; ethnocultural unification and, 467; modernization and, 455, 460; Muslims considered hostile to, 181, 326; non-Russian peoples of Volga region and, 78; Orthodox missionary work and, 179; peasant settlers as bearers of, 24; Russia's European identification, 178; southern steppe and, 51; state officials in borderlands and, 435; state principle and, 458

class differences, 23; in Caucasian highlands, 250, 251; democracy and, 487; *soslovie* (estate) system and, 197, 198, 212

climate, 72, 425, 436; agriculture and, 74; regionalization and, 7, 127, 131, 134

Cold War, 245

colonialism, 17, 21, 25, 65n81; in Caucasus, 244–45; European and Russian empires compared, 440, 441, 445–46, 450; independence of colonies, 446; internal colonization, 189n5; Russian Empire and, 156, 170, 178, 181; in Siberia, 276, 277; Soviet socialism and, 140, 153–54, 156–57, 159, 160

Commission for the Regionalization of the USSR, 160

Commission for the Study of the Natural Industrial Forces of Russia, 134

Commission for the Study of the Tribal Composition of Russia and the Borderlands (KIPS), 142, 143, 145–46, 148, 154, 161

Committee for the North, 270, 271–72, 275; on clan-based community, 276; indigenous land tenure and, 281; meetings organized by, 283; Resolution on Class Stratification in the Yenisei North, 278; Siberian natives' responses to, 286; *tundra* groups and, 279

Commonwealth of Independent States, 496

commune, repartitional, 275, 501

communism, 20, 140, 155, 159; "primitive communism," 270, 278, 281–82; Soviet Communist Party, 144, 158–59. *See also* socialism

Congress of Muslims, Second and Third (1906), 330

consciousness, national, 53, 55, 459

conservatives, 202, 450

Constantinople, 438, 480, 481

Constituent Assembly, 20, 142, 207, 393; federalism and, 495; Finnish nationalism and, 405, 406, 416

Constitutional-Democratic Party. *See* Kadets (Constitutional-Democratic Party)

Cossack Trading Society, 352, 354

Cossacks: Black Sea, 128; in Caucasus, 253, 257, 382; customary law and, 204; Duma elections and, 370, 376–79, 381, 382, 390, 392, 393; "Free," 50; imperial expansion in east and, 430; in Ukraine, 176, 501, 503

Cossacks, Don, 9, 10, 23, 24, 75; administrative designations and, 128; collective identity of, 218, 219–21, 222–23, 227, 234; Don Cossack Host Territory, 89; Duma elections and, 373; *frontoviki*, 225–27, 228; independent nation of, 226–27; "interior Russia" and, 88; military service to empire, 103, 221–22, 349, 359; nationalism/nationhood of, 230–31, 233–35; relation to Russian people and state, 218, 220–22; revolutions of 1917 and, 223–27; self-governing assemblies of, 350; social organization of, 221, 222–23, 229; Soviet regime and, 228–34, 238n77; *zemstvo* reforms and, 12, 348–63

counties *(provintsii)*, 44

Crimea, 52, 99, 297, 301, 327, 446

Crimean War, 14, 104, 176, 310, 438

crown peasants, 173

culture, 19, 219, 245

custom, law and, 202, 203–204, 215n23; in Caucasus, 250–51, 254, 256, 264n29; Islamic *(adat)*, 328

Cyril and Methodius Society, 499, 501, 504

Cyrillic alphabet, 327

Czartoryski, Adam, 497, 499, 508n21

Czechs, 385, 387, 443–44, 499, 504, 508n19

Dagestan, 240, 241, 245, 248; customary law in, 251; Duma elections in, 370, 376, 382; ethnography in, 242–44, *243;* Iranian Safawi dynasty and, 253; military leaders in, 249, 250; revivals of banditry in, 259, 260–61; Russian state reforms in, 253–56; uprising against Russians (1877), 258

Dal, Vladimir I., 86, 129, 247

Dali-Ali, 258

Danielson-Kalmari, J. R., 402

Danilevskii, N. Ia., 481–82

Daniyal-Bek, 256
Danube campaign, 310
Darghi language, 249
Decembrists, 58, 497–99, 501, 504, 505
Dem'ianovich, A. K., 392
democracy/democratization, 21, 25, 209,
  366, 465; empire and, 13, 25–26; February
  revolution (1917) and, 18; in multicultural
  societies, 487; national question and, 413,
  417, 468; nationalism and, 465, 487; peasants and, 210; in Russian Poland, 463–64
demographics, 129, 132, 427, 431, 442
Den' (newspaper), 411
"The Development of Capitalism in Russia"
  (Lenin), 130
Diakin, V. S., 474
Dictionary of the Russian Language (Ozhegov), 248
Dictionary of the Russian Language [Tolkovyi
  slovar' zhivogo velikorusskogo iazyka] (Dal),
  86, 247
difference, 170, 173, 180, 187; ethnic/
  national identity and, 219; seen as or-
  ganic, 173; shifts in marking of, 188
Dimanshtein, Semen, 147
Dimitriev, I. I., 78–79
Dmovski, R., 392, 393
Dobrotvorskii, Petr, 109, 110, 113
Dobrova-Iadrintseva, Lidiia, 276, 278, 288
Dolgurukii, I. M., 75
Don Province, 130, 223, 224; Duma elec-
  tions in, 372; Soviet power in, 227, 230;
  zemstvo in, 348–63
Don River, 38, 43
Dondukov-Korsakov, A. M., 351
Donets Mountain region, 134
Donskaia volna (newspaper), 227, 228, 229
Donskie oblastnye vedomosti (newspa-
  per), 361
Donskoi golos (newspaper), 360–61
Donskoi vestnik (newspaper), 353
Drahomanov, Myhailo, 503–505
Dukhobors, 444
Dukhovskoi, S. M., 324–25, 436
Duma, State, 12–13, 505; "center-regions"
  system and, 367–68; ethno-confessional
  composition, 383–89; formation of na-
  tional political elites and, 389–95; Muslims
  and, 330, 338, 341, 343; national-regional

particularities in legislation, 368–83; politi-
  cal parties in, 390–92
Dzhafarov, L. M., 393
Dzhantiurin, S. S., 394

Eastern Question, 310, 336, 480, 482
economic activity/conditions, 7, 22, 24, 425;
  in conquest stage of expansion, 430; integration of Asiatic Russia and, 444–45;
  Marxist discourse and, 271; regional, 126–
  28; regionalization of, 90; in Siberia and
  Far East, 277, 290n29, 447; silver standard
  and currency, 299, 308; Soviet regionalization and, 148–49, 150, 154; "stage" of development, 17; trade routes, 132
education, 335–36, 472, 474, 500–502
Efremov, I. N., 393
Eisenstadt, S. N., 427, 459
Ekaterinburg (city and province), 149, 160
Elena Pavlovna, Grand Princess, 461
elite, Russian, 39, 46; parliamentarism and,
  394; peasant township courts and, 202; in
  provincial European Russia, 95; public
  opinion among, 460–61; soslovie (estate)
  system and, 203; territoriality and, 45, 53
Elizabeth, Empress, 297
"Empire: Genesis, Structure, Functions"
  (Kaspe), 456
empires, 1, 15; borderlands of, 477; democracy and, 25–26; ethnography and, 161; as
  geopolitical communities, 427; ideal type
  of, 456–57; maritime and terrestrial, 440–
  41; monarchy and, 25; nation-state as alternative paradigm, 455; rise and fall of, 295
Enckell, Karl, 401, 416–17
Encyclopedic Dictionary (Brokhaus-Efron),
  131
Engels, Friedrich, 145
Eremeev, Court Councillor Sergei, 352
Erich, Rafael, 405–406
Eshevskii, S., 178
estate categories, 105, 121n68, 196
Estonia/Estonians, 174, 182, 298; Duma elections and, 383, 384, 388, 390–91, 392; Orthodoxy and, 194n84
Estonian language, 181
ethnicity, 4, 17, 21, 321; boundaries and,
  22; collective identity and, 219; constitution of Russian Federation and, 26; "inte-

rior Russia" and, 85; nation-states and, 2; *soslovie* (estate) system and, 197, 199; State Duma representation and, 383–89
ethnography/ethnographers, 3, 7, 473–74; Caucasian highlanders and, 239, 242–45; on Great Russian provinces, 87; Imperial Russian Geographical Society, 141; "interior Russia" and, 70; peasant township law and, 202; Provisional Government and, 142, 143; "scientific conquest" and, 436; in Siberia, 10, 268; state mandate for development and, 20. *See also* Soviet ethnography
Etymological Lexicon of the Ossetian Language (Abaev), 246
Eurasia, 1, 17
Eurasianism, 496, 507n8
Europe, boundary with Asia, 43, 73, 77
Europe, Eastern, 219, 288, 487, 496, 500
Europe, Western, 25, 174, 213n7; influence on Bolsheviks, 156; modernization in, 460; Muslim question and, 337; nation-state as ideal type for, 496; Polish economy and, 316; revolutionary era in, 196; role of nationalism in, 466; Russian ethnographers and, 144; Russian imperial borderlands and, 296; Russia's identification with, 38, 43, 61n53, 178, 326; *soslovie* (estate) system and, 198
Evenki, 268–70, *269*, 277; response to Soviet organizers, 283–86; Sovietization meetings and, 273–75
Evenki Autonomous District, 268
exiles, political, 437, 441, 446

Factory and Plant Industry and Trade in Russia, 132
The Family Chronicle (S. Aksakov), 97
Far East, 14, 170, 371, 429, 436; differentiation from Siberia, 439; exiles in, 447; imperial terminology and imagery of, 438–39; integration/absorption into Russia, 442; limit of imperial expansion in, 478–79; Russian settlement in, 444
February Revolution (1917), 141, 142, 208; Cossacks and, 223, 226; German war policy and, 414; Muslim Duma deputies and, 394; Russian-Finnish relations and, 398, 400, 402, 403, 404, 417
federalism, 19, 26, 68, 366, 394; in American

usage, 496–97; Decembrists and, 497–98; evolving complex of ideas associated with, 494; historical critiques of autocracy and, 500–502; national minorities and, 504; regional administration in Asiatic Russia and, 433; Siberia and, 446; Soviet Union and, 21
feminists, 207
feudalism, 244
financial systems, 295–98
Finland, 20, 82, 386n, 463; class conflict in, 415–16, 420n47; currency crisis in Russia and, 410; currency of, 19, 316; in First World War (Jäger Battalion), 400, 401, 409, 415, 418n13; Germanophile sentiments in, 403, 415; as model of modernization, 476–77; moves toward independence, 404–10; Provisional Government and, 13, 400–17; revolutionary situation in Russia and, 412–13; in Russian Empire, 130, 132, 296, 398–400; Russification policy and, 84, 484; Swedish-Russian war in, 317n4, 497
Finnic (Finno-Ugric) peoples, 82, 174; animism and, 170; assimilated by Tatars, 339; Christianization of, 327; as *inorodtsy,* 180
Finnish language, 399
Finnish question, 337, 343, 401
Finns, 174, 335, 346n62, 385, 443
folk culture, 78, 143, 172, 503
folklorists, 504
France, 71, 504; Algeria and, 178, 196; as empire, 1, 2, 3, 15, 24; loss of great-power status, 451; Muslim question and, 337; national minorities of, 505
Free Economic Society, 48, 203
Freeze, Gregory, 121n68, 171
French Revolution, 15, 25, 402, 500, 505
Fridtjof of Nansen, 450
Frierson, Cathy, 202
Furman, R. F., 303–304

Gaidarov, I. I., 393
Gamzatov, Rasul, 249
Garavodzhev, Salambek, 258
Gardanov, V. K., 245
Garin-Mikhailovskii, N. M., 439
Garusevich, Ia., 392
Gasprinskii, Ismail Bey, 329
Gatagova, L. S., 471–72

Habsburg Empire, 3, 500, 505, 508n21
Hajji-Ali, 240
Hajji-Murad, 241, 256
Hamilton, Alexander, 497
Hamzatkhan, 258
Hechter, Michael, 428
Hermanson, Robert, 405
Herzen, Alexander, 76–77, 83, 434, 465, 499
Hirsch, Francine, 7, 16, 24, 282
history, Marxian theory of, 156
Hjelt, Edvard, 402, 403
Holquist, Peter, 219–20
Hroch, Miroslav, 446, 465
Hülsen, Gen. Ernst von, 414
human rights, 26
Hungary, 300, 499
Husein, *Akhun* (Mufti) Mukhametzhan, 99, 100, 115n26, 118–19n45

Iadrintsev, N. M., 440, 502
Iakobii, Gen. Ivan Varfolomeevich, 97, 98, 114n9
Ianovich, D. T., 280, 281
Iaroslavl Province, 71, 72, 81, 82, 375, 381
identity: collective, 218–19; ethnic, 219, 235n7, 491n46; national, 36; of *novokresh-chenye* ("new converts"), 172; provincial, 48; regional, 88, 447; in regions of Asiatic Russia, 439; religion and cultural identity, 188; Russian, 442, 480; Siberian, 445, 451; standardization of, 173
Idman, Karl Gustav, 401, 406
Igel'strom, Baron Osip, 97, 98, 100, 114n9; cantonal administration and, 102–103; Kazakh hordes and, 115n26, 116n27; Khanate of Crimea and, 99
Il'in, M. V., 477–78
Il'men, Lake, 83
Il'minskii, Nikolai, 182, 183–84, 332; missionary activity and, 327; on Muslims and national idea, 329; pedagogical system of, 475–76, 484; on Tatar apostasy movement, 323
Imperial Free Economic Society (IVEO), 126, 127, 132
Imperial Russian Geographical Society (IRGO), 127, 132, 141
imperialism, 54, 147, 150, 159, 177–78

The Imported State: The Westernization of the Political Order (Badie), 486
Imshenetski, Ia. K., 393
India, 178
industry, 131, 132, 135; as element of modernization, 459; financial-industrial elites, 367; formation of Soviet Union and, 140; in imperial borderlands, 296; in Soviet Union, 149, 154
Ingushetiia, 246, 250, 255, 258; *abreki* in, 260; Ingush deported by Soviets, 260
inogorodnie (non-Cossack peasants), 223, 228, 229, 349, 353
inorodtsy ("those of other origin"), 8, 181; baptized, 174; Bashkirs as, 105, 156; civic equality for, 367; colonialism and, 178; Duma elections and, 370–71, 382; education policy toward, 475, 485; expanded use of term, 169, 321; generic otherness of, 174; native Siberians as, 172; organic difference and, 173; Orthodoxy and, 182; peoples of "Asiatic Russia" as, 143; Russification of, 175, 183; as shorthand for non-Russians, 173; unbaptized, 173
inovertsy ("those of other belief"), 8, 171, 173
Inspector General (Gogol), 85
intellectuals/intelligentsia: Cossack, 355; federalism and, 15; modernization and, 203, 461; nationalism and, 465; pan-ethnic nationalisms and, 500; Polish insurrection (1863) and, 466; Tatar-Muslim, 328, 329; township court system and, 204; *zemstvo* and, 210, 358, 362
Interiano, Giorgio, 240
internationalism, 140, 150
Iosef, Khan, 221
Iran. *See* Persia (Iran)/Persians
Irkutsk (city and province), 436, 439, 445, 502; Duma elections in, 377, 380; governor-general of, 450
Iskander, Fazil, 249
Islam, 11–12, 335; baptized Tatars and, 194–95n87, 322–24; Catherine II's policy toward, 99; Caucasian *abreki* and, 259; cultural institutions of, 338; as cultural world, 170, 181; as influence in Siberia, 449; modernization of, 328; prayers, 101, 118n43; religious law *(shari'a),* 254, 327, 486; Rus-

sian officials' views of, 324–26, 473, 474; strength in Volga region, 332; Tatar culture and, 340. *See also* Muslims

Italy, 176

Ittifak al-Muslimin (Union of Muslims), 330, 383

Iurine, T., 393

Ivan III, Grand Prince, 73

Ivan IV ("the Terrible"), Tsar, 221

Ivan V, Grand Prince, 297

Ivanovskii, V. V., 428

Izhorts, 385, 387

Iznoskov, I. A., 323

Jadidism, 328–29, 330

Japan/Japanese, 258, 442

Jaronski, L. V., 392

Jefferson, Thomas, 497

Jersild, Austin, 178

Jewish question, 12, 320, 337, 338, 343

Jews, 118n41, 150, 177, 467, 505; Duma elections and, 383, 384, 386, 387, 388, 389; as *inorodtsy*, 174, 180; kahal institution, 176; Karaim, 385, 388; removal of quotas on, 207; right of settlement on Russian territory, 463; Russification and, 175, 484

Journey across Three Seas (Nikitin), 240

Jurashkevski, R., 393

Kabarda/Kabardians, 245, 251, 256, 258, 259, 260

Kabarda Temporary Court, 254, 255

Kabardian language, 241, 246, 249

kachak (robber/outlaw), 247

kachak-'Omar, 259

Kadets (Constitutional-Democratic Party), 196, 224, 229, 383; federalism and, 495, 496; Finnish policy and, 400, 411; Jadidism and, 330; State Duma elections and, 383, 391

Kaledin, General A. M., 224, 226, 227, 228, 230, 232

Kalinin, M. I., 157

Kalinin Commission, 156, 157

Kalmyks, 147, 236n14; Duma elections and, 371, 385, 387, 388; impressions of "interior Russia" and, 73, 79

Kaluga (town and province), 69, 71, 72, 74

Kama River, 133

Kamchadals, 448

Kamchatka, 41, 51, 59n35

Kamyshanskii, P. K., 335

Kankrin, Egor, 301, 304, 305–306, 307

Kappeler, Andreas, 172, 399, 427, 465, 472; on Central Asians, 474; on nationalism and autocracy, 467; on Polish nationalism as menace, 470; on Russification, 484

Karachay (land and people), 259, 260

Karaev, Kara, 259

Karaim, 385, 388

Karamzin, Nikolai, 82, 498–99, 500

Karaulov, M. A., 393

Karelia, 82

Karskii, Evfimii, 143

Kaspe, Sviatoslav, 14, 24, 176

Katkov, M. N., 450, 465, 485

Kaufman, General K. P. von, 326, 473–74

Kazakevich, P. V., 443–44, 448

Kazakhs (Kirghiz), 79, 100, 115n26; administrative reforms and, 102; "civilized" by imperial regime, 115n24; Duma elections and, 371, 384, 387, 388, 389, 393–94; in Soviet Union, *151, 152,* 154, 156, 164n65; uprising (1869) of, 473

Kazakhstan, 260, 370, 371, 379, 381, 430

Kazan (city and province), 76, 78, 81, 89, 502; Central Baptized-Tatar School, 327; corrupt administration in, 109; dual European-Asian character, 77; Duma elections in, 373, 380, 381, 394; khanate of, 56n11; Muslim nobles from, 98; Muslim question in, 333, 337; Orthodox clergy of, 322, 332; as Orthodox missionary center, 87, 183, 189n10, 323, 327, 472; as regional "capital," 127; Tatar apostasy movement in, 323–24; territorial administration of, 34; Theological Academy, 337

Kazem-Bek, A. K., 322

Kazharov, Valerii, 251, 255

Kenez, Peter, 220

Keppen, Petr, 82, 174

Kerenskii, Aleksandr, 407, 408–409

Ketola, Eino, 413, 421n73

Khanty, 280

Khar'kov (city and province), 74, 75, 81, 89, 380, 381; Duma elections in, 375; governor-generalship of, 478

Kharlamov, V. A., 392, 393

Kharuzin, A., 333, 335, 346n62

Khasanov, K. G., 394

Khas-Mamedov, Kh. G., 393
Khilkov, M. I., 445
Khiva, khanate of, 479
Khmelnyts'kyi, Bohdan, 501
Khochbar, 252–53
Khodarkovsky, Michael, 190n15
Khoiskii, F. L., 393
Khrushchev, Nikita, 496
Khvostov, A. N., 341
Kiev (city and province), 68, 80, 499; Duma elections in, 380, 382; "interior Russia" and, 71, 74; Monastery of the Caves, 87; as "mother of Russia cities," 87; roads and, 81; university in, 501, 503, 508n24
Kirghiz. *See* Kazakhs
Kirgiz ASSR, 150
Kirilov, Ivan, 38, 39, 42, 60n42, 125
Kiselev, Count, 102, 194n74
Kishinev, 380
Klembovskii, V. N., 411–12
Kliuchevskii, V. O., 73
Knight, Nathaniel, 174
knowledge, governance and, 21, 47, 205; Bolsheviks and, 139; regionalization and, 125; scientific expeditions and, 51; territorial, 35–36, 37, 40, 48, 54
Koialovich, M. O., 72–73, 86
Kokand, khanate of, 479
Kokovtsev Commission, 89
Kolchak, Admiral A. V., 231
Kolo, Polish, 389–92, 393
Komi (Voguls), 78, 385, 387
Kondrat'ev, N. D., 131
Koreans, 439, 442
Korkunov, N. M., 440
Kornilov, General L. G., coup of, 224, 413
Korzhinskii, S. I., 131
Kostomarov, Nikolai/Mykola, 501, 502, 505, 508n24
Kostroma Province, 89, 373
Kotoshikhin, Grigorii, 56n10
Kovalevskii, M. E., 109, 123n99
Kovno Province, 373, 382
Krasilnikov, M. P., 135
Krasnodar region, 246, 260
Krasnokutskii, N. A., 357, 360, 361, 362
Krasnov, General P. N., 230, 231, 232
Kreitsberg, Ia., 393
Krestovskii, V. V., 438
Krivoshein, A. V., 445

Krizhanich, Iurii, 35, 49
Krug (Cossack general assembly), 221, 224–25
Kruzius-Arenberg, L., 476
Kryzhanovskii, Nikolai, 107–10, 112, 113, 122n85, 324
Kryzhanovskii, S. E., 369
Kubachi language, 249
Kuchera, Sergey, 251–52
Kuliabko-Koretskii, N. G., 131
Kulomzin, A. N., 449–50
Kurds, 146
Kureiski, Semen, 283
Kurile Islands, 40, 441
Kuropatkin, A. N., 480–81
Kursk (city and province), 71, 72; Duma elections in, 373, 381; "interior Russia" and, 75; Korenaia fair, 79–80; steppe of, 74; Zvegintsov Commission and, 88
Kutuzov, M. I., 68
Kuusinen, Otto, 407

Ladoga, Lake, 83
Lake Territory *(Priozernyi krai)*, 83
Lamaism, 449
land allotments *(uchastki)*, 50
Land Commandant *(zemskii nachal'nik)*, 201, 207, 210
Land Credit Society (Poland), 304, 313
landowners, 44, 47, 97; Bashkir, 107–108, 121n72, 123n86, 191n28; Duma elections and, 368; Polish, 464; preservation of privilege, 367; "Stolypin" reforms and, 214n11; *zemstvo* and, 361
languages, 19, 26; "alien questions" and, 338; census data and, 162n17; Cyrillic alphabet and missionary activity, 327; diversity in Russian Empire, 169; education policy and, 475; ethnic identity and, 219; ethnographers and, 143, 145; imperial space and, 42, 43, 428; legal status of, 368; *narodnost'* (nationhood) and, 172; *opisaniia* (geographic descriptions) and, 41; Slavic, 507–508n17; Soviet regionalization and, 161; as vehicle of Russification, 183. *See also specific languages*
Lappo, Dmitri, 276–77, 278–80, 282, 288, 290n29
lashmany, 173
Latin Alliance, 504

"Latinism," 322

Latvia/Latvians, 75, 87, 182; Duma elections and, 383, 384, 387, 388; Orthodoxy and, 194n84

Latvian language, 181

law, 8–9, 350, 425–26; civil, 20; "common law" of Siberian natives, 276, 282, 287, 290n29; criminal, 101; customary law in Caucasus, 250–51, 254, 256, 264n29; Great Reforms and, 175; Islamic religious law *(Shari'a)*, 254, 327, 486; peasant township courts, 200–207, 216n39; Provisional Government and, 207; Russian imperial law in Caucasus, 254; Russification and, 176, 485; *soslovie* (estate) system and, 199–200; Soviet, 154; State Duma legislation, 368; township *zemstvo* and, 209

Lednitski, A., 392

LeDonne, John, 115n23

legitimization, political, 456, 457

Leibniz, Gottfried Wilhelm, 36

Leino, Eino, 402

Lenin, V. I., 130, 147, 164n65, 413, 420n72

Leninism, 220

Leonas, P., 393

Leontiev, K. N., 480

Leontovich, F. I., 245

Leroy-Beaulieu, P., 446

"Letters of a Russian Officer" (Glinka), 68

Levin, Sh. Kh., 394

Lezghis/Lezgins, 243–44, 258, 384, 387

Liadov, V., 83, 89

liberalization, 176, 463

liberals/liberalism, 9, 13, 15; extension of citizenship and, 24; in Finland, 415; imperial thinking and, 18; legal codes and, 20; Muslim, 338–39; peasant tradition and, 202; Polish insurrection (1863) and, 466; in Provisional Government, 207; Russian-Finnish relations and, 400; *soslovie* (estate) system and, 198; township courts and, 211

Lieven, Dominic, 440, 451

linguistics, 143, 499

L'Isle, Joseph-Nicolas de, 41, 60n42

Lithuania/Lithuanians, 84, 141, 177; Duma elections and, 384, 387, 388, 390, 392; law code, 176; national movement, 460; Protestantism in, 183; Russian coinage in, 297, 298, 299

Little Russia, 74, 75, 80; border with Great Russia, 76; Polish and Western coinage in, 296; Russification policy and, 84. *See also* Ukraine

"Little Russians," 43, 74–75

Litvak, B. G., 348

Liubavskii, M. K., 441

Lodz, 375, 380

Lomonosov, Mikhail, 60n42, 126, 127, 135

Longworth, John, 251

Loris-Melikov, Count M. T., 109

Lower Country, 79

Lubowidzki, Jósef, 303

Ludendorff, Gen. Erich, 415

Luk'ianov, S. M., 332, 449

Lulie, L., 251

Luntinen, Pentii, 412

Lur'e, S. V., 471, 474, 480, 481

Lutherans/Lutheranism, 118n41, 181, 382, 386, 388, 389

Madison, James, 497

Main Committee for the Review of Cossack Law, 351

Maksheev, A. I., 437

Maksimov, Admiral A. S., 402, 418n13

Maksimov, S. V., 70–71, 80, 84

Maksudov, S. N., 338, 343, 394

Malov, Evfimii, 184, 187, 188

Mamakaev, M. A., 248

Manchuria, 430, 445

Manner, Kullervo, 407

manorial peasants, 173

Map of the Industries of European Russia, 127

maps/mapping (cartography), *xiv–xviii*, 5, 16; of borders, 44; European knowledge of Russia and, 42; explorers and, 52; history and, 60n42; of peoples, 33; in period of high territoriality, 46, 48; Peter the Great and, 37–38; in Petrine period, 38–40; regional, 126; of Siberia and Far East, 35, 436, 438

Maps of Products of the Russians, 126

Mari (Cheremiss), 78, 147, 171, 172

mark (Finnish currency), 19, 316, 410, 463

Markov, Vladimir A., 401

Marx, Karl, 145, 275, 278

Marxism, 161, 447; Caucasian highlanders and, 244; Marxism-Leninism, 145; *soslovie* (estate) system and, 198; Soviet ethnography and, 271, 273, 276, 278, 283, 287–88

Mashanov, M. A., 337
Maslakovets, Major-General N. A., 360, 361
Materials for Geography and Statistics Compiled by Officers of the General Staff, 127
McNeal, Robert, 220
Medushevskii, A. N., 462
Megrel princedom, 471
Mendeleev, D. I., 90, 131, 132, 136
merchants, 23, 81, 356, 362; Cossack, 354, 357; as estate, 197; in Siberia, 435; township courts and, 206
Meshcheriaks, 103, 120n60
Mezentsov, N. V., 470
Mickiewicz, Adam, 499, 508n21
Mikhail Pavlovich, Grand Prince, 119n47
Mikhailov, Spiridon, 174
Mikhailovskii, Nikolai, 504
Mikoian, Anastas, 159
military conscription, 101, 102, 103, 104, 120n60, 472–73
Military-Statistical Survey of the Russian Empire, 127
Miliukov, P. N., 440, 465
Miliutin, D. A., 350, 351, 355, 357, 360, 479
mining, 38
Ministry of Finances, 130, 136; conversion to Orthodoxy and, 186; currencies in use and, 298, 300, 302, 305, 310, 316; Department of Trade and Manufacturing, 132; Muslim question and, 325; paper rubles in Poland, 311, 312, 313–14; Polish treasury and, 315, 316
Ministry of Foreign Affairs, 336–37
Ministry of Internal Affairs, 101, 105, 106, 322, 324; Central Statistical Committee, 129; Don Cossacks and, 355, 357; mapping/surveying and, 128; Muslim question and, 326, 331, 332–33, 339, 340–41, 342; Postal Department, 127; Russian electoral system and, 369; State Duma elections and, 371
Ministry of State Property, 130
Ministry of Trade and Industry, 133, 136
minorities, national, 26, 180, 410, 414, 504
Mironov, Filipp, 231
missionaries, 24, 169–70, 178–79, 180, 185; Jadidism and, 328–29; methods used by, 187; Muslim question and, 326–27, 331–32; Tatar "apostasy" movement and, 322, 323

modernization, 14, 24, 85, 426; Bolsheviks and, 146; breakdown of, 486, 489; as "catching up" with the West, 460, 486, 487–88; "center-regions" system and, 367–68, 428; Crimean War and, 176, 460; defined, 459–60; industrial reorganization, 131; Muslim question and, 328, 343; regionalization and, 129; revolution and, 483; Russification policy and, 476; "segmented," 486; of social relations, 462; in Soviet Union, 161n3
Mogil'ev Province, 85, 88
Moldavia (Moldova)/Moldavians, 384, 387, 467, 499
monarchy, 25
Monastery of the Caves (Kiev), 87
Mongols, 437, 442; Buriat, 385, 387, 388, 443, 448; Oirat, 276
Montenegrins, 443
Mordvins/Mordvinians, 78, 384, 387, 388
Morgan, Lewis Henry, 275, 289–90n17
Moscow, 4, 22, 77; as capital city, 76, 81, 127, 494; economic activity around, 133; "interior Russia" and, 67, 68–71, 76–77, 79; rival cities of, 80
Moscow Industrial Region, 130
Moscow Province, 72, 126, 127; Duma elections in, 373; township courts in, 204, 216n39
Müller, Gerhard Friedrich, 40, 41, 60n42
Murav'ev, Nikita, 497–98, 505, 509n34
Murav'ev-Amurskii, N. N., 436–37, 438, 441, 443
Muscovite period, 9, 33, 38; ethnicity and faith coupled, 181; exploration during, 40; "interior Russia" in, 67
Muscovy, 22, 53, 497; centralizing state of, 501, 506; expansion of, 114n15; Muslim nobles in service of, 98; territoriality and, 34–36, 56n10; Volga-Kama peoples and, 171
Muslim question, 11–12, 13, 320, 321–22, 326–28, 341–43; apostasy of baptized Tatars and, 322–24; Jadidism and, 328–29, 330; Orthodox missionaries and, 322–24, 331–35, 337–38, 342, 343; Pan-Islamism and, 334, 337, 339; revolutionary situation in Russia and, 330–31; Russian government conferences on, 332–37, 339–41; Russian territorial expansion and, 324–25

Muslims, 6, 12, 22–23; baptized Tatars as, 188, 194–95n87; Bashkir, 98–102; Catherine II and, 323; of Caucasus, 240, 258, 472; Christianization of, 342; conversion to Orthodoxy, 185; of Dagestan, 241; "fanatical," 178; "formal" loyalty to empire, 335, 346n62; heterogeneity of, 333; incorporated into tsarist administration, 100; international connections of, 336–37; Orenburg Muslim Spiritual Assembly (OMSA), 99–102, 116n29, 117nn34,35; Orthodox missionaries and, 180; Russification policy and, 193n59, 484; in State Duma, 386, 388–89, 392, 394. *See also* Islam
My Past and Thoughts (Herzen), 83

Nadezhdin, N. I., 87
Nadir-shah, 244
Nakaz (Catherine II), 61n53
Nakaznyi Ataman, 349, 350, 351, 352, 354, 355; for Civil Affairs, 360; taxation and, 359
Nakh language, 246
namestnichestvo, 48, 96, 97, 430
Napoleon I, emperor of France, 1, 5, 15, 68, 84, 120n60
Napoleonic Wars, 222
Narkomnats (People's Commissariat of Nationalities), 18, 144, 145, 146–48, 150, 156; dispute with Gosplan, 153–55; dissolution of, 161; on "weak" and "strong" nationalities, 158
narod (people, nation), 198, 204
narodnost' (nationality), 172, 178, 487
narodnosti (nationalities), 157, 381
narodtsy (little peoples), 78
nation-states, 1, 2, 427; democratization and, 468; empire as conflicting state principle, 14, 15; governor-generalship and, 478; as ideal-type, 496; imperial policy in Caucasus and, 472; imperial-state in contrast to, 471; modernization of Russia and, 455, 458–59
nationalism, 55, 465–66; "alien questions" and, 331; Bolsheviks and, 140, 144; civic versus ethnic, 496; Cossack, 220, 231; democratization and, 13, 14; ethnicity and, 219; industrial economy and, 457–58; modernization and, 466; non-Russian, 18, 320, 346n62; pan-ethnic, 500, 504; Polish insur-

rection (1863) and, 464, 465; "religious" versus "ethnic," 334; Romantic, 1, 2; Soviet Union and, 20–21, 159, 417
nationality, 7, 21, 22, 170, 466; "backward" peoples and, 155–56; "ethnographic principle" and, 140; ethnography in First World War and, 143; Great Reforms and, 176; Muslim question and, 323, 326, 333; Pan-Slavism and, 481; principle of, 141–46; Protestantism and, 183; religious confession and, 323; in Siberia, 448; *soslovie* (estate) system and, 197; Soviet regionalization and, 150; State Duma representation and, 384–85; territoriality and, 54
Nedelia (newspaper), 109
Nekrasov, Nikolai V., 416–17
Nentsy, 280
Nepenin, Adm. Andrian, 401
New Economic Policy (NEP), 148, 159
New Land *(Novaia Zemlia)*, 33
New Russia, 50, 51, 52, 74
New Serbia, 50
Nicholas I, Emperor, 69, 101, 169, 483; Bashkiria and, 95, 113; modernization and, 460, 461, 469; Muslims and, 102; Orthodox missionary work and, 182, 188; Russian zloty and, 301, 305, 306, 307; Russification policy and, 175, 176, 459; on Siberia, 445–46; Slavophiles and, 499
Nicholas II, Emperor, 320, 399, 445
Niepokojczycki, W., 311, 312
Nikitenko, Aleksandr Vasil'evich, 82–83
Nikitin, Afanasii, 240
Nizhnii Novgorod (city and province), 72, 76, 78, 89; Duma elections in, 373, 380, 381; fair of, 79, 82
nobles, 6, 17, 23; Cossack, 12, 357; as estate, 197; landownership and, 97; Muslim, 98, 108, 114n16; Polish, 22, 177; *soslovie* (estate) system and, 212; township courts and, 206
Nol'de, Baron B. E., 3–4, 21, 425–26, 495, 507n15
nomads, 50, 140, 144; of Central Asia, 474; on Russian-Chinese border, 434; in Siberia, 268, 279, 286, 321
"The Non-Capitalist Development of the Peoples of the North" (Sergeev), 288
North America, 33, 51, 52, 430

Novgorod (city and province), 74, 80, 89, 497, 498, 499; Duma elections in, 373; "interior Russia" and, 71; lost republican tradition of, 501; as rival of Moscow, 80–81

Novikova, Irina, 13, 18, 476

Novoe vremia (newspaper), 330, 411

novokreshchenye ("new converts"), 171–72, 174, 185, 186–87

Novosil'tsev, Nikolai, 302, 497, 507n15

Nurminskii, Sergei, 174

oblastnichestvo movement, 429, 440, 446–48, 502

oblasts (districts/regions), 129, 132, 429; Don region as, 348, 349, 356; in Soviet Union, 147, 149, 150, 156–57, 158, 160, 161, 164n48

Obninskii, V. R., 389–90

obrusenie. See Russification *(obrusenie)*

October Revolution (1917), 144, 159; Cossacks and, 226–27, 228, 393; Finland and, 398, 421n73

Odessa, 77, 81, 375, 380, 478

officials, state, 19, 169; in Asiatic borderlands, 432, 435–36; in Bashkiria, 97, 108; modernization and, 176

Ogarev, N. P., 128

Oka River, 133

okrugi (districts, settlements), 50, 51, 127, 370

Old Believers, 50, 382, 502, 509n30; Duma elections and, 388, 389; Russianness and, 444; in State Duma, 386

Ol'denburg, Sergei F., 142

Olonets (town and province), 80, 82, 371, 373, 380

Omsk, 90

Onega, Lake, 83

opisaniia (geographic descriptions), 35, 41, 46, 52

Orel (city and province), 69, 71, 72, 74; Duma elections in, 374, 380, 381; Zvegintsov Commission and, 88

Orenburg Muslim Spiritual Assembly (OMSA), 99–102, 116n29, 117nn34,35; Muslim clerics and law, 119n50, 119–20n52; property law and, 118n40; "Tatar-Muslim question" and, 336

Orenburg Province, 47, 51, 77, 89; as beachhead for imperial expansion, 430; as "borderland," 83; Duma elections in, 374, 382; Europe-Asia boundary in, 94; incorporation into European Russia, 104; town of Orenburg, 96; Turkic speakers in, 95

Orenburg Province, governor-general of, 97, 103, 111, 112, 114nn11,12, 324; corrupt administration and, 107; Pugachev uprising and, 96

Orientalism, 240–45, 346n62

O'Rourke, Shane, 9

Orthodox Church, Russian, 11–12, 101; Duma elections and, 389, 390; Kazan and, 77; missionary work, 178–80; Muslim question and, 322–24, 326; in Siberia, 449; State Duma and, 386; tsar's relation to, 485. *See also* Christianity, Orthodox

Osharov, M. I., 268

Osman-Turks, 146

Ossetia/Ossetians, 250, 259, 260

Ossetian language, 246

Ostroumov, A. A., 334

Ostroumov, N. P., 328, 329, 337–38

Ottoman Empire, 3, 25; currency of, 301; "Eastern Question" and, 336; influence with Kazakhs, 116n27; nation-state model and, 505; Russia's borders with, 52; Russia's "Tatar-Muslim question" and, 329; territory conquered by Russia, 50; wars with Russia, 100, 116n27, 359; Young Turk revolution, 333. *See also* Turkey

Ozhegov, S. I., 248

Ozolin, K., 393

Paasikvi, Juho Kusti, 402

Paasivirta, J., 415

Palen, Duke M. I., 302

Pan-Germanism, 500

Pan-Islamism, 325, 331, 333, 334, 337, 339

Pan-Slavism, 465, 480, 481–82, 506; federalism and, 494; folklorists and, 504; invention of Slavdom, 498–500

Pan-Turkism, 12, 330, 334, 335, 339; "civilizational" methodology and, 500; federalism and, 494

Panin, N. I., 498

Panin, P. I., 498

Pantiukhov, I., 243

Papadzhanov, M. I., 393

Parchevski, A., 392

Paris Peace Settlements, 140

parliamentarism, 366, 367, 394–95
parties, political, 383, 390–91; Finnish, 398, 401, 405; Russian, 411; Ukrainian, 505
Paskevich, I. F., 304–305, 310, 311
Passek, V. V., 71, 74, 76, 77, 80, 84
Paul I, Emperor, 118n45
Pauluchchi, Marquis F. O., 302
Pavlov, P. I., 352, 353–54
Pavlov, Platon, 501–502, 509n29
Peasant Icons (Frierson), 202
peasants, 6, 10, 22–24; baptism into Orthodox Church and, 172; Bashkir, 105–106, 157; Bolsheviks and, 140; categories of, 173; in Cossack territory, 223, 349, 353, 356, 360, 362; Duma elections and, 368, 395; emancipation of, 469; as estate, 197, 198, 199–200; Great Reforms and, 175; idealization of, 465; imperial mode of thinking and, 211; as judges of imperial law, 8; of Kursk Province, 75; nationality concept and, 144; Polish, 177; resettlement in borderlands, 90; Russian peasant commune, 275, 501; as settler-colonizers, 440, 441, 442, 444, 447; Siberian natives compared to, 276; state peasants, 50, 171, 173, 176; township courts and, 200–207, 211; of Volga region, 78, 79; *zemstvo* and, 208, 209–11
Pecherin, V. S., 87
Penza Province, 79, 88, 119n50, 374
Perm (city and province), 80, 83, 94, 374; Bishop of, 179, 184; in Soviet Union, 160
Persia (Iran)/Persians, 36, 79, 244, 246; Caucasian highlanders and, 253; language of, 246
Pestel, Pavel Ivanovich, 15, 68, 498
Peter Alekseevich, Grand Prince, 297
Peter I ("the Great"), Emperor, 5, 33, 53, 486; Cossacks and, 221, 224; Kamchatka expedition and, 59n35; Table of Ranks and, 114n13; territorial consciousness and, 34, 36, 37–38, 49, 54, 60n40; Westernization of Russia and, 458
Petrazhycki, L., 392
Petrograd, 142, 209, 403, 406, 412, 495; political crisis in, 411; revolutionary situation in, 404. *See also* St. Petersburg
Petrova, Tatiana, 284–85
Petrozavodsk, 82–83

Philological Society, Linguistic Department, 142
Pipes, Richard, 4
Plehve, V. K., 89–90
Plekhanov, G. V., 358–59
Pleshcheev, S. I., 62n55, 126
Pobedonostsev, Konstantin, 323–24, 329, 450, 476
Podkamennaia Tunguska basin, 268, 269, 270, 273, 274–75; changes in Soviet policy, 287; Soviet meetings organized in, 283–84
Pogodin, Mikhail, 499
Pokrovsky, N. I., 245
Poland/Polish lands, 6, 22, 34, 181, 436, 476; administration of, 478; Alexander I and, 497; Catholic Church in, 177; currency denominations in, 11, 12, 19, 315–17; Duma elections in, 387, 390; federalism and, 498; Germanization in, 442; independence (1918), 406–407; mountain regions of, 134; Orthodox population of, 371, 376; Pan-Slavic ideas and, 499, 500, 501, 504, 508n21; partition of, 299; Poland-Lithuania, 35, 84–85, 176, 177, 296, 508n21; political parties in, 383, 390, 391, 392–93; in Russian Empire (Congress Kingdom), 85, 130, 132, 175, 296; Russia's borders with, 52; Russification in, 464; Smolensk Province and, 84; State Duma and, 367, 370, 371, 375–76, 381; zloty and ruble in, 298–315
Poles, 24, 468, 505; Duma elections and, 384, 387, 388; exiles in Siberia, 446, 450; Pan-Slavism and, 499; in Russian imperial service, 435; Russification and, 175
Polish insurrection (1830), 303, 317, 500–501
Polish insurrection (1863), 11, 14, 18, 194n82; counter-reform in Russian Empire and, 177, 463–65; as influence on other nations, 470; monetary reform in Russia and, 315; Russification policy and, 182
Polish language, 304, 464
Polish question, 12, 337, 338, 343, 464–65; democratization and, 468; First World War and, 340
Politburo, Soviet, 159
Polozov, B. N., 247–48, 258
Poltava (city and province), 74, 75, 89

Popov, General P. Kh., 230
populations, 49, 129; center of population distribution, 90; demarcation of, 8; diversified, 15, 16, 169; imperial law and, 8; nomadic, 103; non-Russian and non-Orthodox, 78, 82, 99, 112, 144; regional representation in State Duma, 372–79; Russian settlers in Asiatic borderlands, 442–43; urban and rural, 132
populism/populists, 202, 204, 211, 465, 501, 505
post-colonial studies, 1
Potanin, G. N., 73, 76, 77, 440, 495
Potanin, Grigorii, 502–503
Potapov, Major-General (Ataman) A. L., 352, 353, 354, 355, 357
Potemkin, Grigorii, 64n76, 68, 97
Potto, General A. V., 241
power, geography of (geopolitics), 14, 16, 316–17, 426; centralization of power, 427–29; historical dynamics, 429–31; "scientific conquest" and, 436–37
Pravilova, Ekaterina, 11
property, 24, 118n40; Caucasian "culture of violence" and, 239, 240; Cossacks and, 349, 355, 356; soslovie (estate) system and, 199; Soviet law and, 154; township courts and, 205
Protestantism, 182–83, 386, 389
Protopopov, Dmitrii, 411
Proudhon, Pierre-Joseph, 502, 504
provinces (gubernii), 4, 44, 163n33, 430; black-earth, 88; "borderland," 83; capital cities, 81–83; Catherinian reform and, 47–48, 48–49; of Great Russia, 87; regionalization and, 125, 127, 129–30, 134–35
Provisional Government, 13, 20, 142, 143; Cossacks and, 224, 226, 393; currency crisis and, 410; dismantling of old regime, 207, 208; ethno-territorial federalism and, 495; fall of, 417, 495; Finnish question and, 398, 400–17; First World War and, 400, 415; Juridical Council, 3; March (1917) Manifesto, 401, 403–404, 405; soslovie (estate) system and, 196; township courts and, 207, 211
Provisional Statue of Administration over Native Peoples and Tribes of the Northern Borderlands, 270, 279, 280, 282

Prussia, 297, 298, 299, 303
Prutchenko, S. M., 426
Przhevalskii, N. M., 437
Pskov, 497, 498, 507n12
Pugachev uprising, 96, 111
Pushkin, Alexander, 69, 73, 81, 256–57, 507n12
Pypin, A. N., 78

Qaytag, Utsmiyat of, 240, 241
questionnaires, 48, 49
"questions," national/alien, 4, 12, 320, 321, 343, 438

Radishchev, A. N., 126, 497
Raeff, Marc, 4, 173, 497
railroads, 80, 81, 469; Chinese Eastern Railroad, 439, 444, 447; regionalization and, 129, 132, 133–34; tariffs and, 88, 89; Transcaspian Railroad, 436; Transiberian Railroad, 439, 442, 445
raionirovanie (regionalization), 7, 125, 128
Ramiev, M. M., 394
Ramishvili, I. I., 393
rapprochement (sblizhenie/sliianie) policy, 175, 321, 324, 327; Muslim question and, 335, 337, 341, 342; religion and, 444
Rauch, Georg von, 506
Razin, Stenka, 501
Rech' (Kadet newspaper), 411
Red Army, 139, 260
Red Guards, 230
"Red Sejm," 407
Region and Country (V. P. Semenov), 134
regionalism, 366, 471, 494, 506
regionalization, 133–35, 156; history of, 125–29; main trends in, 131; in Soviet Union, 140, 146–50, 151, 152, 153–56
regions, 4, 45, 46–47, 126–28, 368–83
Regulation on the Rural Estate, 199
Reitern, M. Kh., 313
religion (confessional group), 4, 21, 42, 169; cultural identity and, 188; ethnic identity and, 219; ethnography and, 143; imperial administration and, 8; nationality and, 323; religious toleration policy, 474; Russification and, 169–70; soslovie (estate) system and, 197, 198; State Duma representation and, 386

Remezov, Nikolai, 110–11, 113, 123–24n99
Remezov, Semen, 35
Remnev, Anatolyi, 14, 24
resources, 16, 21, 35, 39, 48
revolutions (1848), 310, 500
revolutions (1905–1906), 12, 257, 258,
506n3; Duma and, 495; state-building
principle and, 366; "Tatar-Muslim question" and, 330, 331
revolutions (1917), 18, 141, 144; Caucasian
highlanders and, 255, 261; Cossacks and,
218, 222. *See also* February Revolution
(1917); October Revolution (1917)
Riazan (town and province), 69, 71, 72, 74,
374; as provincial capital, 70; Zvegintsov
Commission and, 88
Riga, city of, 77, 373, 380, 382
Rikhter, Dmitrii, 148
rivers, 41, 71–72, 74
roads, 38, 44; capital cities and, 81, 82; Moscow as radiating center and, 69; regionalization and, 133; in settlement districts, 51
Romanov dynasty, 3, 25, 196, 320, 501
Romanticism, 70, 80, 508n19; organic differ-
ence and, 173; Orientalist view of Cauca-
sian highlanders, 242
Rossiia (newspaper), 331
Rostov, 227
Rozenbaum, S. Ia., 394
Rubakin, N. A., 198, 213n7
ruble (Russian currency), 11, 12, 19, 296; in
Lithuania, 298; as paper banknotes, 310–
15; in Poland, 299, 304, 306; zloty and
transition toward, 307–10
Rudenko, Sergei, 143
"Rules on Methods for Educating the Peoples
Inhabiting Russia" (Il'minskii), 475
Rumania, 176
Rumanian language, 181
Runovsky, Colonel A. I., 241, 246–47
Rus, ancient, 42, 74, 84
*Russia: A Full Geographical Description of
Our Homeland* (Semenov and Semenov),
130–31
Russia, Asian/Asiatic, 43, 60n46; administra-
tive policy in, 432–35; disappearance of
"Siberia" and, 439–40; indigenous peoples
of, 143; map, *xvi;* regions of, 130, 439–40
"Russia, central," 5, 67

Russia, European, 6, 43, 60n46, 90, 428, 441;
Bashkiria's incorporation into, 103, 106–
107, 111; Duma elections in, 369, 371, 372–
75, 380, 381; economic zones of, 133; "inte-
rior Russia" and, 71–72, 73, 87; regions of,
130, 132, 133; territorial expansion in, 68;
Urals as eastern boundary, 94
"Russia, interior," 5, 67; definitions of,
67–73; East and Southeast regions, 76–
80; North and Northeast regions, 80–83;
South and Southwest regions, 73–76; Western region, 84–87
"Russia, native," 5, 67, 69, 86
*Russia in Numbers: Country. People. Estates.
Classes* (Rubakin), 198, 212, 213n6
Russian-American Company, 441
Russian Anthropological Society, 142
Russian Empire: Bolsheviks and territory of,
139, 148; boundaries of, 5, 6, 22, 52–53, 85;
capital cities, 4; "center and regions" system, 366–68, 394; comparison with other
empires, 3, 17, 21, 24–25; conquest and
governance of Caucasus, 9–10; as diverse
polity, 169; diversity of, 425; émigrés from,
503; end of tsarist regime, 451; European
identification of, 38, 43, 46, 61n53, 326,
366; expansion of, 14, 16, 479–82; federalism and, 494, 505; financial system of, 295–
98; Fundamental Laws of, 368; historical
persistence of, 2–3; as hybrid state form,
19, 170; indeterminate core of, 5–6, 67;
"interior Russia" and, 85; mapping/survey-
ing of, 126, 127; maps, *xiv–xviii;* Muslim
world and, 325; nation-state concept and,
478, 480–81, 483; Orthodox missionary
work and, 187–88; Pan-Slavic ideology
and, 480, 481–82; regional policy in Asiatic borderlands, 431–36; regionalization
in, 125, 135–36; religious and national principles in collision, 480; rights of subjects
in, 200; rivalry with British Empire, 473;
Siberia as jewel in crown of, 3, 451; state
institutions, 12, 101; Urals as continental
boundary, 94; vastness of geographical
space, 429; western provinces, 181, 299,
302; Westernizing currents in, 34; as
world's largest state, 46, 62n55
Russian Federation, 3, 26, 260, 399
Russian Geographic Society, 436–37

proach, 278–82; on social organization of Siberian natives, 275; technologies of vision in Siberia, 273–75. *See also* ethnography/ethnographers

Soviet Union, 15, 24, 489; archives of, 4; Caucasian highlanders and, 239, 244–45, 254, 258, 259–60, 261; collapse (1989–1991), 2–3, 20, 260, 417, 451, 496; collectivization in, 271, 283, 287; Cossack identity and, 220; ethnographic projects of, 18, 244–45; federalism and, 20–21, 26, 494; formation of, 139, 158, 161, 496; group-based rights and penalties in, 196; map (1930 borders), *xviii;* nationality policy, 140–41, 158; "pacification" of Caucasus, 239; political unification of, 159–60; Provincial Statistical Committee, 135; reemergence of imperial form of state, 14, 18; regionalization debate, 7, 146–50, *151, 152,* 153–56, 160; Russian Soviet Federated Socialist Republic (RSFSR), 147, 148, 149, 155, 158; Siberian aborigines and, 269–70, *269*

Sovnarkom (Council of People's Commissars), 144

space, imperial, 7, 11, 16; boundaries of, 44; economics and, 90; geography of power and, 14, 426, 429; open-ended view of, 22; regionalization and, 134; Russian nation and, 42–43, 46; Siberia as enduring part of, 3; territoriality and, 5. *See also* territory

Speranskii, Mikhail, 272, 276, 299, 497

Ssorin-Chaikov, Nikolai, 10

Stakhovich, Mikhail A., 401, 411, 412

Stalin, Joseph, 158, 255, 496

Stalinism, 282–83, 496

Startsev, Vitalii, 412

Starynkevich, S. A., 310, 314–15

state peasants, 171, 173, 176

state principle *(gosudarstvennost'),* 366

Statistical Outline of Russia (Arsen'ev), 128

statistics, 197–98

Statute of Alien Administration (1822), 276, 290n29

Stavropol Province, 83, 260, 370, 371, 372, 382

Stecki, Ia., 392

Steinwedel, Charles, 6

steppe, 24, 57n12; absorption into Russia, 442; diplomacy on, 100; Don Cossacks and, 218; environmental divide with for-

est, 85; Muslim clergy in, 328; nomads of, 140; settlement of southern steppe, 50–51, 64n76

Steppe Code of the Oirat Mongols, 276, 290n29

Steven, Kh., 250

Stödten, Helmuth Lucius von, 403

Stolberg, Karl, 406, 416

Stolypin, P. A., 332, 445

Streltsov, R., 481

Subbotich, D. I., 436

Sukhozanet, N. O., 350

Suleimanov, Abdulvakhit, 119n47

Sunderland, Willard, 5

Suni, L. V., 476

Sura River, 78

"Survey of the History of Russian Colonization" (Liubavskii), 441

Survey of the Physical Conditions of Russia (Arsen'ev), 128

Suslov, Innokentii, 268, 269–70, 271, 275, 288; on clan organization of Siberian natives, 279–80, 285–86; ethnographic socialist realism and, 278; report on Evenki "circle dance," 273–74, 277; Russian fur hunters in Evenki territory and, 285; on Sovietization of Tungus, 283

Sviatopolk-Mirskii, Major-General, 362

Sweden/Swedes, 35, 174, 476; currencies minted by, 298, 317n4; Duma elections and, 385, 387; Finnish separatists and, 400, 403; rule over Finland, 417n1; Swedes as citizens of Finland, 417n; war with Russia, 36, 398, 497

Switzerland, 15, 503, 505

Taagepera, R., 482

Table of Ranks, 17, 97, 114n13, 349

Tagirova, Nailya, 6

Tambov (city and province), 69, 71, 72, 90; agriculture in, 73–74; cultural transition in, 75; Duma elections in, 374; Zvegintsov Commission and, 88

Tanfil'eva, G. I., 131

Tanyshpaev, M. M., 393–94

Tashkent, 370, 380, 479–80

Taskin, S. A., 393

Tassin, E., 481

Tatar language, 117n34, 182

Tatars, 79, 150; apostasy of baptized Tatars,

322–24, 334, 472; Catherine II and, 98; conversion to Orthodoxy, 187; Crimean, 50, 221; Duma elections and, 384, 387, 388, 389; Jadidism and, 328–29; Muscovy and, 502; origin of Russian autocracy and, 499; Orthodoxy and, 194–95n87; place names in Russia and, 78; religious status of, 188; in Russian imperial service, 24, 435; Russification of, 183; "Tatar-Muslim question," 322, 329, 334, 339–40

Tatishchev, Vasilii, 37, 39–40; on boundary of Europe and Asia, 43, 55, 94; on European maps of Russia, 42; geographical expeditions and, 125

taxation, 35, 119n48, 207, 296; in Asiatic borderlands, 435; in Bashkiria, 102, 103; Don Cossacks and, 349, 354, 356–59, 361, 363; estate-based, 208, 214n17; in Finland, 418n2; religious conversion and, 185; in Siberia, 272; soul tax, 171; State Duma and, 368

Taymiev (Taymazoghly), Bey-Bulat, 241, 257

Tennisson (Tynisson), Ia., 393

Teptiars, 105, 173

Tercüman (newspaper), 329

Terlecki, Władysław, 303

Termen, A. I., 485–86

territorial administration, units of, 7, 34, 86, 103, 120n57, 128; Duma elections and, 370, 371; in Soviet Union, 157, 163n33

territory, 3, 7, 17, 22, 53–55, 425; European style of governance and, 196; high territoriality (late 18th century), 5, 45–53; imperial expansion and, 14, 16; of "interior Russia," 68; measured against social factor, 447; in Muscovite period, 34–36, 38, 41, 44; Petrine transition and, 36–45; regional surveys of, 128–29; voyages of exploration and, 33. *See also* geography; space, imperial

Tevkelev, K.-M. B.-G., 392

Third Department, 357, 470

Third Rome, 480

Tiflis (Tbilisi), 79, 377, 380, 382

Timashev, A. E., 355, 357

Time of Troubles, 76, 84, 502

Tkachev, Petr, 504

Tokoi, Oskari, 402, 407

Tolkovyi slovar' zhivogo velikorusskogo iazyka (Dal), 86

Tolstoi, A. K., 80

Tolstoi, D. A., 175, 186, 467, 472, 475–76

Ton, Konstantin, 94, 113n3

Topchibachev, A.-M.A., 393

topography, 47

Tornau, F., 241

towns, 34, 35, 39, 41, 70

The Township Zemstvo (magazine), 209, 210

townspeople, 197

trade routes, 132

Trainin, Il'ia, 144, 153

Transcaucasia, 144, 158, 193n59; *abreki* in, 259, 260; bandits in, 247; colonial status of, 170, 446; Duma representatives from, 393; federalism in, 496; Muslim clergy in, 327; Russian coinage in, 298. *See also* Caucasus

Travel Notes (Passek), 72, 74, 76

tribes, 23, 159, 171

tribute, payment of, 171, 272, 274

tsars (emperors), 36, 368; authority in Finland, 405, 406; Muslims and, 101, 102; nationalism and, 320; Orthodox Church and, 485; representations on coinage, 300–301; territoriality and, 33–34

Tsereteli, I. G., 393

Tsiunchuk, Rustem, 12–13

Tuchkov, P. A., 85

Tugarinov, A. Ia., 280

Tula (town and province), 69, 88, 375, 381

Tungusic peoples, 276, 277, 280, 288

Turgenev, N. I., 467–68

Turkestan, 143, 149, 154, 436, 480; governor-general of, 485; Muslim clergy in, 328; Muslim question and, 324–25; Orthodox missionary activity in, 338, 474; "productive forces" in, 155; regionalization of, 156; Russian governor of, 473, 478

Turkey, 331, 334, 335, 394, 451. *See also* Ottoman Empire

Turkic languages, 246, 248, 249, 252, 272, 491n46

Turkic peoples, 174, 327, 335

Turkmen, 156, 164n65, 385, 387, 388

Turks/Turkish culture, 36, 170, 329

Tutashkhia, Data, 248

Tver (town and province), 69, 70, 71, 82, 374

Udmurts, 172, 384, 387, 388

uezdy (districts, counties), 44, 48–49, 96, 163n33; in Bashkiria, 111; frontier military, 34; *zemstvo* and, 208